TQM

Management • Process Design • Marketing • Accounting • Statistics • New Product Management • Organizational Behavior • Informational Systems • Quality Control •

Total Quality Management:
A Cross Functional
Perspective

Total Quality Management: A Cross Functional Perspective

♦ ♦ ♦

Ashok Rao

Lawrence P. Carr

Ismael Dambolena

Robert J. Kopp

John Martin

Farshad Rafii

Phyllis Fineman Schlesinger

John Wiley & Sons

New York • Chichester • Brisbane • Toronto • Singapore

ACQUISITIONS EDITOR	Beth Lang Golub
SUPPLEMENTAL EDITOR	Andrea Bryant
EDITOR	Marian Provenzano
MARKETING MANAGER	Leslie Hines
PRODUCTION MANAGER	Linda Muriello
PRODUCTION EDITOR	Edward Winkleman
DESIGN DIRECTOR	Karin Kincheloe
TEXT DESIGNER	Levavi/Levavi
COVER DESIGNER	Carolyn Joseph
COVER PHOTO	©Bob Torres/Tony Stone Worldwide LTD.
MANUFACTURING COORDINATOR	Dorothy Sinclair
PRODUCTION ASSISTANT	Melanie Henick
ILLUSTRATION DIRECTOR	Ishaya Monokoff

This book was set in 10/12 ITC Garamond Light by Carlisle Communications and printed and bound by Donnelley/Crawfordsville. The cover was printed by Phoenix Color.

Library of Congress Cataloging-in-Publication Data

Total quality management : a cross functional perspective / by Ashok
    Rao . . . [et al.].
        p.   cm.
    Includes bibliographical references.
    ISBN 0-471-10804-9 (cloth : alk. paper)
    1. Total quality management.   I. Rao, Ashok.
HD62.15.T67926   1996
658.5'62—dc20   95-46097
                                                                 CIP

Printed in the United States of America

10 9 8 7 6 5 4 3 2 1

To
Our Families for Their Support
and
Our Parents Who Made It Possible

Preface

◆ ◆ ◆

The overarching purpose of a company about to embark on a Total Quality Management (TQM) program is to be more competitive. In order to be competitive, the company needs to be more productive relative to the competition. It also needs to supply goods and/or services that are attractive to the consumer. To support this drive for higher productivity and attention to the market, TQM practitioners have created a mix of tools and practices. The concepts undergirding these tools are:

- *Customer focus:* the notion that all work is performed for a "customer" and it is the customer who determines its value. Customer in this context is defined in a broad sense. In some cases, it is a person who pays for the goods and services. It may also be the next person in the chain of operations that culminates with a customer external to the organization. Consulting organizations prefer to think of their "customers" as clients since the service they deliver would have benefits only if the client actively participated. Doctors work with patients, schools work with students, and so on. In all these cases, the person receiving the service fits into the broad definition of customer.
- *Total participation:* the idea that work has an additional dimension. In traditional organizations, the worker expects to be told what to do and how satisfactory performance will be measured. Others—managers, supervisors, trainers, engineers—tell him what has to be done and how to do it. The concept of total participation implies that the person closest to the task is most qualified to suggest improved ways of doing the job. So, part of a worker's responsibility is to suggest ways to make improvements aimed at enhancing productivity and value to the customer.
- *Continual improvement:* the notion that the performance standard to reach is perfection. Phillip Crosby states this as zero defects. The Japanese characterize it as "picking the last grain of rice." This theme also assumes the existence of a methodology to make incremental improvements and breakthroughs. Once the improvements have been devised, they are made part of the daily work process and a mechanism for monitoring is provided to stabilize the improvement.

- *Wide range of applicability:* The argument that these concepts can be applied at several levels. They can be applied to individuals, small organizations, or large organizations; any type of organization—manufacturing, banks, hospitals, education, or government; and a variety of processes ranging from accounts payable to monitoring a patients's progress and developing new products.

These concepts surface time and again throughout this book. Each author brings a functional and general management perspective. Therefore, the book is designed to appeal to students seeking to specialize in any functional area by offering them a view they can relate to the rest of the organization.

◆ WHY THIS BOOK WAS WRITTEN

Total Quality Management has evolved beyond its roots in statistics and the quality control function. Today, many observers consider it to be a framework for "excellent" management. At its inception, it focused on the shop floor; at present, it encompasses all functions of a company's value chain from Product/Service Design through Purchasing and Production to Distribution and Marketing and After-Sales Service. It also involves all levels of the workforce, both management and labor. The Malcolm Baldrige National Quality Award discussed in Chapter 3 has increasingly emphasized the business aspects of TQM, moving away from a narrow definition of quality as defects in a process or service. The dominant themes are a data-based approach to problem solving, a strong emphasis on organizational and behavioral considerations, a customer-oriented market-sensitive approach to designing and delivering both products and services, and, finally, a desire for continual improvement.

One limitation of most existing books is their failure to specify the "nuts and bolts" of a tool unless dealing with statistics when illustrating the value of that tool and perhaps even showing how it was used in a particular case. For example, many books discuss control charts in great detail, but they do not provide the same level of specifics when offering calculations for the Cost of Quality. This book gives detailed instructions in the text followed by exercises and, when appropriate, team exercises are also indicated. In addition, the book offers a mix of cases to highlight implementation issues. The cases are intended to sensitize students to issues that occur frequently when TQM is introduced.

As the management approach labeled TQM spread throughout the organization, each function contributed to developing tools and methodologies that facilitated integration across the functional boundaries. For example, Marketing and Product Design have to collaborate in converting the Voice of the Customer to Product Design Requirements. They came up with the Quality Function Deployment (QFD) tool. This same tool is useful for converting design requirements to operating requirements and subsequently distribution requirements. Accounting helped operationalize the Cost of Quality concept as a way of communicating the need for continual improvement to several levels of management. The flowcharting tool used by Process Engineering and Information Systems was adapted by Marketing as service maps to highlight the customer interface. These maps convey to the Operations function the activities critical to ensuring customer satisfaction.

These examples and many others underscore the importance of using a multi-functional approach when teaching TQM. Many of the existing texts deal with the topic from the perspective of Quality Control Specialist, an Operations Manager, or an Organizational Behaviorist. Frequently, the perspectives of Marketing, the Product Designer, the Information Systems Specialist, and Accounting are missing. As a result, the student comes away with a narrow view of TQM.

This text has involved people from many different disciplines. Each has taught TQM either as part of their course or the TQM course taught at Babson College or the Harvard Extension. Larry Carr provides the Accounting perspective. Ismael Dambolena outlines the basic statistics used for problem solving and process control; he also describes more sophisticated quantitative techniques such as Taguchi's methods and qualitative techniques involving Structured Brainstorming. Bob Kopp presents the traditional approach to Marketing and explains how it can be linked to Quality Function Deployment. John Martin, who was a Baldrige Examiner and Judge for the Massachusetts Quality Award, describes the Baldrige Award. Ashok Rao discusses the general TQM framework and provides insight from the Operations Management and Information Systems perspectives. Farshad Rafii addresses the Product Development process. Phyllis Schlesinger provides an understanding of certain aspects of employee involvement and the management of change from her perspective as an Organizational Behaviorist. In the spirit of TQM, this was a cross-disciplinary group working as a team to create a book.

◆ ORGANIZATION OF THE BOOK

The Chapters Are:

1. Quality as a Strategy
2. What Is TQM?
3. The Baldrige Award
4. Measures of Quality Product and Quality Process: The Traditional Approach
5. Measures of Quality Product and Quality Process: The Emerging Cost of Quality Model
6. Continual Improvement: Basic Tools
7. Continual Improvement: Statistical Process Control
8. Continual Improvement: Some Advanced Tools
9. Customer Measurement I: Traditional Multiattribute Methods
10. Customer Measurement II: Quality Function Deployment

Chapter 1 outlines the history of quality in U.S. industry. It presents past and existing theories on the importance of product quality and its relationship to other elements of competitive strategy. Chapter 2 describes the evolution of the TQM movement in Japan. It argues that TQM has grown beyond simply being concerned with product quality to a broader perspective of quality of management. This is further emphasized in Chapter 3, where the Baldrige model describes quality in terms of customer satisfaction and outlines the extensive infrastructure that must be put in place to support employee efforts in meeting that goal.

Chapters 4 and 5 present an accounting tool that can be used to underscore the importance of quality to management. Other tools can also be used, such as benchmarking described in Chapter 15. However in many organizations, management relies heavily on accounting data. For them, an accounting-based measure is the most meaningful. Once they are convinced of the cost of poor quality, they may embark on benchmarking projects as described in Chapter 15, proactive improvement as described in Chapter 8, or reengineering as outlined in Chapter 14.

Chapters 6, 7, and 8 describe many of the basic tools, including those used to educate all employees so that they can improve the processes on which they work daily. Tools for use by management and teams that can reach conclusions based on qualitative data are also presented. Finally, examples of the more exotic statistical tools including Design of Experiments and Taguchi methods are presented. These tools are the fundamental enablers of the quality improvement process.

Chapters 9 and 10 show how the customer's view is brought into the TQM process. Chapter 9 describes some of the commonly used marketing research tools and illustrates how these can be used to define the customer segments and identify gaps in competitive product offerings. Having identified these gaps, Chapter 10 outlines a powerful TQM approach for establishing customer requirements in depth and creating the product. This approach, termed Quality Function Deployment, enables a cross-functional to product definition that involves engineers and marketeers.

Chapters 11 and 12 describe a methodology for changing the existing culture of the organization to a TQM culture, which embraces the four principles described earlier in the preface. Chapter 11 offers methodologies for initiating and executing change and for stabilizing the gains after the change has been made. Chapter 12 describes ways to deploy the TQM message throughout the organization.

Chapter 13 deals with new product introduction. Once marketing and engineering have defined the new product's characteristics as described in Chapter 10, the concept has to be brought to market. Traditional project management techniques relied on passing the design to development, who handed it off to manufacturing, and so on. At each hand-off, there was high likelihood of miscommunication. New organizational designs have been created to improve the communications between departments and, as a result, the quality of the final product.

Chapters 14 and 15 deal with approaches to achieving breakthrough improvements. The first part of Chapter 14 describes a methodology for reengineering, and Chapter 15 focuses on benchmarking. Reengineering and benchmarking will frequently work together in order to maximize the potential benefits. The search for these breakthrough improvements is motivated by Cost of Quality studies as described in Chapter 15 or new information systems that provide operational measures as discussed in the second part of Chapter 14.

The flowchart here provides a picture of the overall flow linking Chapters 1 through 15. Chapter 16 describes how TQM has worked in practice. It illustrates some cases where TQM implementation has failed and also describes successes. The experiences of Xerox, one of the early winners of the Malcolm Baldrige National Quality Award, are explained in some detail. This chapter reiterates the notion that TQM needs to be viewed as a never-ending journey and suggests improvements that companies can continue to make even after winning prestigious quality awards such as the Baldrige.

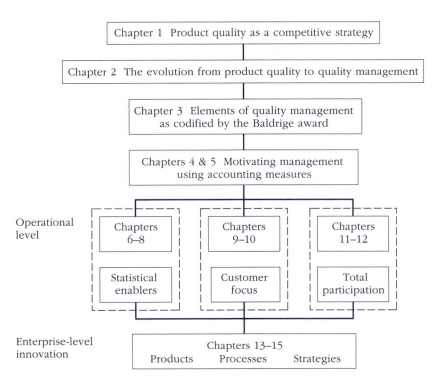

◆ FEATURES AND PEDAGOGY

This book has several features that allow the instructor to use a mix of pedagogical styles—lecture, case discussions, and participative hands-on exercises:

- Most chapters provide a practical background by offering an introductory vignette.
- In most chapters, several cases and minicases are presented to reinforce the concepts explained in the text.
- Hands-on exercises permit students to gain experience with TQM tools and understand how they may apply them in practice.
- The material is cross-functional, which allows a team-teaching approach.
- Key terms have been included at the end of each chapter.
- Tools and techniques have been described in detail so the book can be used as a how-to text.

The following generic outline is based on the last time the editor taught a TQM course. Prerequisites were courses covering Operations Management and Statistics:

TOPIC	CHAPTERS	WEEKS
Introduction to TQM	1, 2	1 and 2
Cost of Quality	4, 5	3
Statistical tools	6–8	4 and 5
Customer focus	9, 10	6 and 7
Initiating change and employee practices	11, 12	8 and 9
Advanced topics (reengineering and benchmarking)	14, 15	10 and 11
TQM in practice (includes project and outside speakers)	3, 16	12–14

◆ NOTE TO STUDENTS

It has been our experience that students tend to approach this subject from one of three perspectives: TQM is a fad, TQM is a set of tools, or TQM is common-sense. Each of these perspectives has some basis.

The fad argument is based on the attitude of some management who introduce TQM without understanding the efforts required on their part to make it work. They do not comprehend a basic tenet articulated by all TQM gurus (see Chapter 2) that TQM requires constant commitment. This book is full of examples of many companies who have successfully introduced TQM and continue to work at it. Toyota claims to have been at it for more than forty years; Motorola and Xerox have been on the TQM journey for more than fifteen years.

TQM does consist of a set of tools. These tools help the organization to focus on the customer and continually improve. A key characteristic of these tools is that they are simple to understand and use. Today, we often hear of companies empowering their employees. The intent of TQM is also to enable employees by providing simple tools that encourage team-work and cross-functional cooperation.

TQM is commonsense management. As Will Rogers is reputed to have said, "The only trouble with common sense is it's not so common." Many professional organizations dismiss a customer focus, claiming to know better than the customer what the customer wants. Many managers are reluctant to surrender control and empower their employees, feeling that they know what has to be done and employees must be told what to do. Many managers also subscribe to the philosophy, "If it ain't broke, don't fix it." This is directly opposed to the concept of continual improvement.

We hope that when you finish reading this book, you will understand the underlying philosophy of TQM. In our experience, companies that have been successful over a long period of time have ingrained these principles in their employees, even when not calling it TQM. If you read the principles of business outlined by Henry Ford (Ford Motor Company) or Sam Walton (Wal-Mart), they reiterate the basic TQM principles:

- *A value-added ethic*—continually strive to provide the best value to others.
- *An external focus*—listen to the customer and study the competition.
- *Cooperation*—be willing to work with other functions and in teams and respect the people with whom you work.

◆ ACKNOWLEDGMENTS

We would like to acknowledge the many people who contributed to our understanding of Total Quality Management such as it has been outlined in this book. This includes experts like Deming and Shiba; company presidents, especially Kearns at Xerox, who provided some of the funding that allowed us to start our investigation of the field; the Center for Quality of Management for generously sharing materials; and the many colleagues and students who helped by guiding our focus and providing feedback on many of the exercises and discussions in this book. We would especially like to thank President Bill Glavin of Babson College who introduced TQM at that institution and has encouraged our efforts from the beginning. Special thanks are also due to our editors at Wiley, Beth Golub and Marian Provenzano, for their encouragement, patience, and skill at gently keeping us on schedule.

Finally, we appreciate the comprehensive feedback and suggestions from our reviewers, who responded in a timely fashion and helped make this book much better: Janelle Heineke, Boston University; George Heinrich, Wichita State University; Chandra Das, University of Northern Iowa; Sanford Temkin, Rider University; Erwin Saniga, University of Delaware; Nael Aly, California State University–Stanislaus; Kalyan Singhal, University of Baltimore; Eugene Kartchner,

Utah State University; Jay Vorzandeh, California State University–San Bernadino; Glen Milligan, Ohio State University; Alan Raedels, Portland State University; Jane Humble, Arizona State University; Susan Tong Foo, Marquette University; Jen Tang, Purdue University; Lawrence Robinson, Cornell University; Mostafa El Agizy, California State Polytechnic University; and Larry Arnold, Tulane University.

Ashok Rao

Contents

◆ ◆ ◆

Quality as a Strategy

❖ ❖ ❖

*I*n the early 1980s Motorola was losing market share to the Japanese competition in their core product lines—semiconductors, cellular phones, and pagers. Following visits to Japan, Motorola executives realized that the competition was producing better quality product at a lower cost. While Motorola was satisfied with an acceptable quality level, the Japanese were pushing for perfection. The conventional thinking was that the higher quality could only be achieved at a higher cost. The Japanese were proving this theory wrong. Bob Galvin, the chairman of Motorola, was determined to match and beat the Japanese, and so, in 1983 he initiated a Total Quality Management program. By 1987 the concepts Motorola learned from the Japanese and the Quality gurus like W. Edwards Deming, Joseph Juran, and others were adapted to their culture and labeled the Six-Sigma program. The result was a drop in defect rates from 6 per thousand in 1986 to 40 per million by the end of 1991. But Motorola did not stop at applying their TQM techniques to manufacturing. The same approach helped the corporate finance department close its books in four days instead of twelve and, service centers have cut their repair time from twelve days to seven. As a direct result of the program, new products are also brought to market quicker. In 1988 Motorola won the Malcolm Baldrige National Quality Award. In addition to the recognition, the results have also been spectacular. Motorola has regained market share and at the same time increased its profits.

*I*n 1981, Marshall McDonald, the chairman of Florida Power and Light (FP&L), recognized that the utility faced a crisis. Costs were rising faster than regulators permitted rate increases. In addition, FP&L compared poorly to utilities in the other states. McDonald determined to transform it into the best managed utility in the United States. At the same time, Kansai Electric in Japan was performing impressively. The average FP&L nuclear reactor shut down five to seven times a year with false warning signals, whereas Kansai had no shutdown for the entire year; FP&L customers averaged 85 minutes of outage per year, but customers of Kansai averaged only 7 minutes per year. In 1984 Kansai had won the Deming Prize for Quality. This highly regarded prize, named after TQM guru W. Edwards Deming (see Chapter 2), is awarded only to the exemplary practitioners of TQM in

Japan. McDonald charged the president, John Hudiburg, with introducing the TQM concepts employed at Kansai to FP&L. Between 1986 and 1989 customer complaints declined 60 percent, lost-time injuries fell almost 70 percent, and the reliability had improved 30 percent. In 1989 FP&L won the Deming Prize for Quality—the only American company to have done so. In 1994 a Deming Prize review committee commended FP&L for the progress made over the five years. The Turkey Point nuclear plant, which had been rated one of the worst by the Nuclear Regulatory Commission, was rated among the best by 1993. In constant dollars, the cost of energy supplied by FP&L today is lower than at any time since 1980.

◆ THE GLOBAL BATTLEGROUND

Motorola embarked on its TQM initiative in response to competition from across the globe. FP&L adopted the TQM practices when it recognized that their customers got lower levels of service than utilities in other states provided their customers. Increases in world oil prices had forced them to raise their prices. But customer dissatisfaction was rising fast, and the state's Public Service Commission was pressing them to improve.

Other companies were faced with their own crises in the early 1980s. In many cases these crises were brought on by changes in the global business environment. For FP&L it was a global increase in prices, whereas for Motorola it was a global increase in competition.

Economists consider the trade deficit to be an indicator of manufacturing competitiveness. By 1986 the overall trade deficit for the United States was $170 billion (see Exhibit 1.1). Among those that had lost more than 50 percent of their share of the world market since 1960 were manufacturers of automobiles, computer chips, machine tools, televisions, and microwave ovens.

Dertouzos, Lester, and Solow (1989), as leaders of the MIT Commission on Industrial Productivity, studied eight major industries—automobiles, chemicals, commercial aircraft, consumer electronics, machine tools, semiconductors and computers and copiers, steel, and textiles. Of these, by 1987 only two (commercial aircraft and chemicals) had a positive trade balance. Exhibit 1.2 shows the trade deficits in 1987, comparing them to trade deficits ten years earlier.

The automobile industry is the largest industry in the United States. In 1970 more than 70 percent of all cars in the world were made in the United States. By 1987 both Europeans and Japanese built more cars, with the United States now third in automobile production. Consumer electronics—radios, televisions, and video recorders—are now dominated by the Japanese. The machine tool industry was also being taken away by the Japanese at the low end and the Germans at the high end. Japanese competition also threatened the semiconductor and copier industries. Xerox has successfully regained some of the market share it lost but only because it copied the TQM practices of the Japanese. Steelmaking capacity in the United States dropped to third place behind the Soviet Union and Japan. Today textiles are dom-

**Exhibit
1.1**

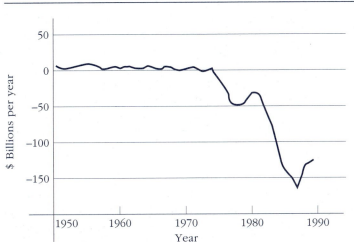

**Exhibit
1.2**

Trade Balances 1977 and 1987

INDUSTRY	TRADE BALANCE IN 1987 DOLLARS (BILLIONS)	
	1977	1987
Automobiles	(12)	(58)
Chemicals	6	10
Commercial aircraft	6	15
Consumer electronics	(4)	(10)
Machine tools	—	(1.5)
Semiconductors, computers, copiers	2	(15)
Steel	(5)	(8)
Textiles	(5)	(24)

SOURCE: U.S. Department of Commerce, International Trade
Administration, Office of Trade Information and Analysis.

inated by Italy, Hong Kong, and Germany. The United States still dominates the commercial aircraft industry, but competition is increasing with the formation of Airbus Industrie by the British, French, and German governments. The U.S. chemical industry is also a success story. Competition is primarily from the large chemical companies in Germany (Bayer, BASF, and Hoechst) and England (ICI). Each is 30 to 50 percent larger than the largest U.S. company (Du Pont).

Although Japan has been a very effective competitor, other countries have also been successful competitors. Germany, for example, is a strong competitor in machine tools, textiles, and chemicals. England, Italy, France, and others each have industries in which they excel. As these foreign companies improve their earnings, they accumulate funds that they naturally invest. A prime target has been American firms, real estate, and farmland.

In 1988 the British invested almost $200 billion in the United States. The Japanese were second, with slightly more than $100 billion. Some of the Japanese purchases have been eye-catching. Mitsubishi bought Rockefeller Center and Radio City Music Hall; Sony Corporation purchased Columbia Pictures; Bridgestone bought Firestone Tires. Other purchases can put U.S. industry at a permanent disadvantage:

- Foreign companies own almost 25 percent of the American chemical industry. As a result, American companies no longer find it profitable to make commodity chemicals. So, they are redirecting their efforts to specialty chemicals.
- Almost all of the research and development is performed by manufacturing companies. When these companies are purchased by foreign interests, the innovations will be more quickly available in their countries, enabling their industries to build a technological lead over the United States.
- If better technology is available abroad, the Department of Defense may be forced to depend on other countries for armaments and materiel. This could compromise national security.

In their conclusions, the MIT Commission focused on two outdated strategies that contributed to the plight of American industry in the 1980s:

- Mass-production systems designed for large volumes of standard products, which encouraged maintaining a distance from suppliers and customers.
- Parochialism, which led to manufacturers concentrating on the large domestic market while ignoring foreign markets and foreign competitors.

Other studies have confirmed that these strategies are no longer effective. Over the years foreign markets have grown, and more companies have risen to satisfy that demand. As consumers are offered more choices, they become more discriminating. The sophisticated consumer is no longer satisfied with the standard product delivered by mass-production systems and created to satisfy the tastes of Americans.

◆ THE PIMS STUDY

One of the more comprehensive studies documenting the impact of product quality was conducted by the Strategic Planning Institute (SPI). SPI analyzed data from 3000 business units collected over a two- to twelve-year period. The data consisted of

- The market conditions describing the size of the market, the rate of growth, inflation, and the distribution channels.
- The competitive position measured by market share and, relative to the competition, the quality, prices and costs, and degree of vertical integration.
- The financial and operating performance.

Then they analyzed the data to uncover the strategic actions that affected performance. They found that "In the long run, the most important single factor affecting a business unit's performance is the quality of its products and services relative to those of its competitors."

One reason why is that customers are willing to pay premium prices for superior quality. The 1989 ASQC/Gallup survey asked executives how much more they felt the average consumer would pay for a higher quality product. Answers ranged from a $20 premium for a $30 pair of shoes to almost $2700 for a $12,000 car. At all price levels the premium was at least 20 percent. The following incident supports their view:

> In the mid-eighties a person known to one of the authors wanted to buy a new car. Consumer Reports and other media were consistently reporting that GM quality was not as good as Toyota. So, she shopped for a Toyota and finally decided to buy a Corolla. At the time, the Corolla was being made in the New United Motor Manufacturing Inc. (NUMMI) in Fremont, California, as a joint venture involving GM and Toyota. The author encouraged her to look at the Nova which was made in the same plant. She saw it had the same design and it was $600 cheaper!
> But Toyota had the quality reputation. She bought the Toyota.

Another reason is that superior quality results in an increased market share. This may result in economies of scale that can drive down costs. Using a cost-cutting approach that sacrifices quality does not help. As an example, consider what happened to Schlitz in the early 1970s. In an effort to improve the bottom line, Schlitz reduced material costs, relying on lower quality hops, and shortened the brewing cycle by 50 percent. In the short term, the results were spectacular and significantly better than the industry leader Anheuser-Busch. But by 1980 Schlitz had dropped from being the second largest beer producer to the seventh. Even with a new formula Schlitz was unable to regain its former market share.

Significantly, the data also show that companies with the same market share but with superior quality products have costs that are not much different from those of their competitors (Exhibit 1.3). This may be because the costs of rework, scrap, and handling customer complaints and failures in the field are much lower. Lifeline Systems Inc. in Watertown, Massachusetts, improved its product quality, enabling it to eliminate its entire field service department.

Exhibit
1.3

Effect of Share and Quality on Costs

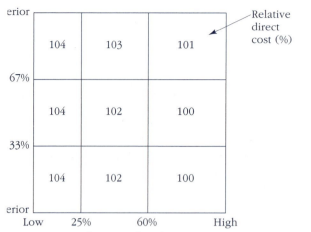

Relative direct cost (%)

erior	104	103	101
67%	104	102	100
33%	104	102	100
erior	Low 25% 60% High

Relative market share

Reprinted with the permission of The Free Press, a Division of Simon and Schuster Inc. from THE PIMS PRINCIPLES Linking Strategy to Performance by Robert D. Buzzell and Bradley T. Gale. Copyright© 1987 by The Free Press.

◆ THE HISTORY OF QUALITY IN THE UNITED STATES

With such strong evidence of the competitive advantage of good quality, why did American management choose to emphasize alternative competitive strategies? The answer lies in the outdated systems mentioned in the MIT study and how they evolved.

At the turn of the century, the workplace was significantly affected by the works of Frederick W. Taylor, generally regarded as the Father of Scientific Management. The workforce at the time consisted mostly of new immigrants and displaced farm workers who had no understanding of the machinery they were expected to operate. Taylor suggested that the work be designed by engineers who would standardize tools and procedures. The worker was not expected to think but merely perform the work assigned. The quality of the work was the responsibility of the inspector. Large tasks were sliced up into smaller tasks, and each was assigned to a person. The result was a high degree of task specialization. Workers performed to meet the standards set by engineers, and managers and inspectors ensured the workers met the standards. Naturally, inspectors and workers often viewed each other as adversaries.

Task specialization also led to the introduction of the assembly line. It had made possible volume production of standard and interchangeable parts. As volume increased, the tasks would be sliced into still smaller units. The costs for material handlers to move materials from one operator to the next began to get inordinately high. Henry Ford decided to automate the material-handling task by introducing the assembly line. His adaptation of Taylor's ideas to the production floor enabled him to reduce the cost of a Model T Ford from $850 in 1908 to $290. In terms of 1990 dollars, he reduced the cost from $12,000 to $2,100.

As products became more complex, inspectors were called on to do more than simply conduct a visual check of the parts. Checking dimensions required increasingly more sophisticated measuring tools. These tools had to be calibrated on an ongoing basis. The work for the quality inspectors was growing at an exponential rate.

In the 1920s inspection activities were formally recognized as a quality control function. Quality control was responsible for developing tools to check product dimensions and characteristics, detecting errors, and having the necessary rework be performed. It was assumed that the only way to ensure good quality was to inspect all of the items being produced.

It was at this time that Bell Labs hired Walter Shewhart as a quality control inspector for telephones. At the time the Hawthorne Plant had 40,000 employees, of which 5200 formed the quality control department. Shewhart studied the chronic variation of production. He suggested using statistics as a way of reducing the amount of inspection, and found that indeed this approach significantly reduced the amount of inspection that had to be done. Instead of checking the entire lot, only a sample drawn from the lot would have to be checked. This might mean some defectives could get shipped. Shewhart argued that if the number of defects was small, the savings in inspection costs would make it worthwhile.

Mathematical statistics made it possible to infer with a high level of certainty a range within which the true defect rate would fall. So, it was possible for the quality control inspector to make statements such as, "I am 95 percent certain this production lot has only 5 percent defects." If management would be satisfied with this level of defect rates, the inspection costs could be reduced substantially. This acceptable average defect rate was called the **Average Outgoing Quality Level (AOQL).** Reducing the AOQL could be achieved by inspecting larger samples. This meant more inspection would be performed, which in turn would raise the producer's costs. Raising the AOQL meant that more defective items were passed on to the customer, thereby raising the consumer's costs and resulting in dissatisfied customers. This tradeoff is captured by the Cost-of-Quality model discussed in Chapter 2 and described in more detail in Chapters 4 and 5. Management selected an AOQL to balance the costs to the producer and to the consumer.

Shewhart also recognized the importance of process control. He is reputed to have created the first **control chart** (an in-depth explanation of control charts is provided in Chapter 7). The control chart is used to monitor the performance of the process by periodically sampling critical aspects of the process, most commonly the output. Today TQM organizations agree that focusing on the process and ensuring it is in control is an effective approach to producing quality parts; the control chart is considered one of the seven basic statistical tools (see Chapters 6 and 7).

During World War II, the Defense Department needed to make sure arms and ammunition delivered to the front lines had a high level of quality. Since the statistical methods developed by Shewhart had not been widely disseminated through industry, the Defense Department was relying on the traditional approach of 100 percent inspection. As a result, the inspection process became a major bottleneck in the production of war materials.

Shewhart was convinced that the sampling techniques he had developed could have wider applicability. He proposed that the Department train all of the contractors in process control techniques and train the inspectors in acceptance sampling. After the Department decided that the latter approach was more expedient, 8000 people were trained in statistical methods for acceptance sampling by the end of the war. The number of inspectors required fell from 42 to 12 per million dollars of accepted material.

After the war, the initiative for improving quality remained with the Defense Department. Defense contractors learned of the statistical sampling methods and applied it to their processes, and some even applied the concepts of process control. Although they reported spectacular gains, these statistical methods were not readily accepted.

Perhaps part of the reason was that nondefense businesses were supplying customers in a booming American economy. In 1945 this economy made up 80 percent of the world market, and it retained a dominant share for the next 20 years. Business capacity was less than the demand. Thus, business could build standard products, supply them to the domestic market, and make good profits.

Foreign markets were small, and so were the foreign competitors. American industrialists surveying the world economy saw no significant competition. It appeared obvious that American manufacturers were more efficient than those of any other country. John Kenneth Galbraith, writing *The Affluent Society,* pronounced the manufacturing problem was solved.

The Defense Department continued to demand better quality. In 1961 it demanded and received from the Martin Corporation a Pershing missile with zero defects. Philip Crosby, another of the TQM gurus (see Chapter 2 for a detailed discussion of his philosophy), was in charge of the quality control activities for the Pershing. He proposed a broader approach to achieving zero defects, one that included behavioral changes in the organization in addition to using statistical methods. Despite his success with the Pershing, his ideas met with resistance from other industries.

Meanwhile, the Defense Department, recognizing that it could get top quality at delivery, pushed contractors to provide better quality over the life of the product. Just as quality assurance checks a product after it is made, so this new emphasis on reliability checked a product after it was put into service. Quality professionals concentrated on measuring quality after the product was made. As this thinking made its way into consumer goods, companies began to provide warranties and after-sale service and parts. The parts and service business proved to be very lucrative. As a result, the concept of improving quality by focusing on process control and process improvement while making the product was pushed deeper into the background.

As competition started to increase, American managers complained that "the playing field was not level." They felt that the United States did not hold foreign competitors to the same standards. Many claimed the foreign competition was "**dumping**" products—selling them in the U.S. market for less than it cost to make it. They ascribed the lower prices to lower labor costs, suggesting the unions were to blame. The U.S. dominance in one industry after another eroded. First, it was the shoe industry, then textiles, and finally steel. By 1980 the competition was taking market share from the automobile and electronic component industries. Several companies conducted studies to prove the competition was "dumping" and to evaluate the impact of lower labor costs. Many of these studies concluded that the competitors truly were more efficient manufacturers and that this was largely a result of their obsession with quality.

One of the studies that struck home was conducted by Hewlett-Packard. In 1980 it tested 300,000 RAM chips from three Japanese manufacturers and three American manufacturers. The Japanese chips had a zero failure rate during incoming inspection, whereas the American chips ranged between 0.11 and 0.19 percent. After 1000 hours of use, the Japanese chips failed between 0.01 and 0.019 percent. The American chips failed between 0.059 and 0.267 percent.

Along with the Hewlett-Packard study, other studies confirmed the dominance of Japanese manufacturers in quality. It was also an eye-opener to realize these improvements had not increased costs. Toyota talked with 53 of its North American suppliers in 1990 and told them that if they wanted more business they would have to improve their quality and at the same time reduce costs. Although these suppliers had a defect rate of only 1 per thousand, their Japanese counterparts had defect rates of 10 per million.

◆ A NEW THEORY OF QUALITY

It was becoming apparent that the manufacturing infrastructure had a significant impact on the corporate strategy. Management could no longer use the same approach in every market in which it wanted to compete. Skinner (1969) argued for defining a **manufacturing policy** that could support the corporate strategy. Such a policy would require management to understand the many aspects of the production system, such as types of processes, the impact of plant location and facility layouts, planning and control systems, and ways of motivating and organizing the workforce.

The first step toward defining a manufacturing policy is to establish a viable competitive edge that differentiates the company's products. Most managers can think of several specific elements, such as lowest cost, best quality, many models, readily available goods, ability to adapt to technological change, and reliable product. These elements can be categorized along four dimensions:

- Cost or efficiency of process that would result in low-cost product.
- Quality implying the product would have greater functionality than the competitors, consistently meet the designed specifications, and perform well in the field.
- **Dependability** of delivery so commitments to customers would be met with a high degree of reliability.
- **Flexibility** so new models could be created quickly in response to customer needs and technological changes.

In 1969, Skinner postulated a **tradeoff model.** He argued that a company would have to trade off performance in one area to excel in another. For example, with respect to quality he posed the tradeoff as "high reliability and quality or low costs"; in other words, improvement in one area would result in a degradation of performance in other areas. This model prevailed for years. Shorter lead times could be obtained by building inventory, which meant increased costs; increased flexibility required more capacity and general-purpose machines which would also increase cost, and so on.

In 1980 the Japanese proved that the tradeoff model was flawed. In comparing Japanese and American automobiles, it was clear that the Japanese had lower costs (one study showed a car from Japan cost $2000 less landed in California than the comparable American car), better quality (see *Consumer Reports* assessments over several years), and better flexibility (time to market for a new model was three years compared to the U.S. norm of five to seven years). American industry, relying on the tradeoff model, assumed that an improvement on any one of these dimensions had to be accompanied by a deterioration on another. The tradeoff model could not explain the ability of the Japanese to improve their performance on multiple dimensions.

During the 1980s, researchers of manufacturing policy wondered whether such improvement could be obtained by working simultaneously on all fronts or whether there was a hierarchy. In other words, in order for a company to improve in any one dimension, did it have to improve in other dimensions as well?

One fact seemed evident: improved quality practices could result in lower costs, but practices aimed at lowering costs did not usually improve quality. The experience of Schlitz Brewing described earlier was an example of lower costs achieved at the expense of quality. There appeared to be a hierarchical relationship between cost and quality. Perhaps, they theorized, there was a hierarchical relationship between the four dimensions.

Nakane (1986) proposed a **cumulative model,** which suggested that quality was at the base of all improvements (Exhibit 1.4a). Once quality had reached a critical level, then dependability could be improved. Next, the company could improve cost efficiency and finally speed or flexibility. Each dimension of improvement was a slab of a building block. If the company emphasized cost reduction, that slab would grow too large for the slabs below it (quality and dependability) to support it. So, in the long term, the cost reductions could not be maintained. Conversely, if the foundations were broadly built, management could focus attention on the next layer, improving it before having to further improve the foundations.

This pattern was followed by some of the more formidable Japanese competitors. After World War II these companies, urged on by General Douglas MacArthur, initiated quality programs. Known across the world for their shoddy consumer goods, the Japanese were not a significant competitive threat. As their quality improved, they moved up the pyramid to dependability and then cost efficiency with Just-In-Time systems. Improvements in each of these dimensions are so closely synchronized that the systems are often termed Just-In-Time/Total Quality Control. More recently, these companies have built a competitive edge in flexibility by bringing more new products to market sooner than their competitors.

Ferdows and De Meyer (1990) have proposed a **sand cone model** (Exhibit 1.4b). They also argue that quality is the basis of any subsequent improvement. Once a base of quality is constructed, management can build the sand cone

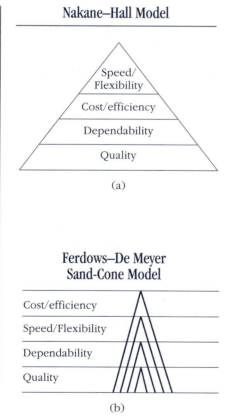

Exhibit
1.4

Nakane–Hall Model

Speed/
Flexibility

Cost/efficiency

Dependability

Quality

(a)

Ferdows–De Meyer
Sand-Cone Model

Cost/efficiency

Speed/Flexibility

Dependability

Quality

(b)

higher by focusing on dependability. But while improving dependability they have to continue to improve quality. The company should next focus on speed. Again, while improving speed, more sand has to be poured on the cone to improve both quality and dependability. Improving cost efficiency is the last to be improved and would require continuing improvements on each of the other three dimensions.

Put another way, to get a 10 percent improvement in costs, management should get a larger (15 percent) improvement in speed and a still larger improvement (20 percent) in dependability, with the largest improvement (30 percent) in quality. But this would only be so if the company was already pushing its performance on each of these characteristics to the limit. If there were obvious inefficiencies such as poor factory layouts or being locked into unfavorable contracts, then cost could be improved without concurrent improvements in other areas.

The two models are similar, but what is especially interesting is that both postulate that quality is fundamental to any improvement that can be expected to be long-lasting. And without quality having achieved a critical level, improvements on any of the other dimensions would not be sustainable.

It is instructive to look at the activities Ferdows and De Meyer considered to be part of an overall quality program:

- More planning responsibility for workers
- Zero defects
- Value analysis/product redesign
- Group technology
- Narrowed product lines/standardization
- Vendor quality
- Reconditioned physical plants
- Flexible manufacturing systems
- Process Statistical Quality Control
- Quality Circles

The primary focus of all these activities is the shop floor where the purpose is to make products that conform to a product design. But TQM represents a much broader group of strategies. These are more completely identified by other research, notably that completed by the MIT Commission on Industrial Productivity (1989).

◆ THE MIT COMMISSION FINDINGS

The MIT study completed in 1987 was one of the more influential in directing American management to the causes underlying declining competitiveness. The study found significant weaknesses in areas of research and product development, production, and cooperation within the organization, with suppliers and with customers.

Research and Product Development was lacking in two areas: **Design for Manufacturability** and **Project Management.** The Design for Manufacturability approach recognizes that products designed for ease of manufacture lead to fewer **internal failures** (defects occurring during the manufacturing process). American engineers did not consider in their design what could be done to make the product easier to manufacture or service. And the internal failure rate is strongly correlated with **external failure** rates (defects occurring once the product reaches the hands of the customer). A study of internal and external failure rates by Garvin (1988) supports this relationship. Project management refers to the systems, the organization structure, and the policies used to develop new products and new processes. In this area too, the MIT Commission study noted that Japanese engineers were more effective. They spent 50 percent less engineering time than their American counterparts in bringing a car from concept to market. One crucial difference was the assignment of a strong project manager at the design stage. This person would insist on clearly defined objectives and roles at the start of the project. In order to accelerate the time to market, the Japanese scheduled many of the development activities to take place simultaneously. This increased the requirements for communication between functional groups. It was the responsibility of the project manager to facilitate the flow of information.

Production placed less emphasis on process improvements than did the Japanese and the Germans. The Japanese allocated a larger percentage of the research and development efforts to improving the process technology than the Americans. They also organized their process improvement specialists so that they would be closer to where the improvements would take place. Typically, American companies would locate the technical experts in the process at the corporate office. Whenever a problem arose at a plant, it would request help from the corporate group. A technical expert would be sent to the plant when that person became available. Typically, the Japanese located their technical specialists at each plant. When a process problem occurred, the technical specialist was immediately available. The Japanese also encouraged their workers to tinker with the process to improve its efficiency. In contrast, the Americans, discouraged such tinkering unless the process was not functioning well. In Germany, the users were encouraged to work with the suppliers of machine tools and help in their development. The lack of interest in the production process led to American industry being less inclined to experiment with technically sophisticated equipment. As a result, the technological expertise and the infrastructure needed to support the machine tool industry are far better developed in countries like Japan and Germany.

The overseas competitors also worked more consistently at altering the processes designed to improve product quality and reliability. The Japanese closely monitor the performance of products in the hands of the customer. The product is redesigned to make it more usable, and the process is redesigned to ensure conformance to customer needs. British Steel has salesmen work with production engineers, describing what the customers want and what the competition is doing to satisfy them. Contrast that to most American companies where marketing and manufacturing coexist with difficulty.

Cooperation with business allies, specifically with labor, with suppliers, and with customers, was weak. In the United States the relationship between labor and management has traditionally been hostile. Labor practices (discussed in detail in Chapters 11 and 12) such as **cross-training** and **participative management,** which have been employed successfully in other countries, have had trouble making headway in the United States. But, the Commission noted, these practices were beginning to spread. In dealings with suppliers American management takes an adversarial approach. Other countries such as Japan, Germany, and Italy have a more cooperative relationship. They share information about the market, consumer needs, and methods for cutting costs and maintaining quality. When Honda opened its facilities in Marysville, Ohio, it arranged a cooperative relationship with suppliers such as Inland Steel. Honda worked with Inland to improve Inland's product quality, and Inland suggested ways for Honda to improve the stamping process. Such close relationships result in improved quality as well as lower costs. These companies also maintain stronger links with their customers. This approach has profound implications for new product development, for most innovations originate from the users (von Hippel, 1988). Companies get ideas for enhancing existing products by seeing how the customer uses the product and by incorporating the changes customers suggest. Mansfield (1988) collected data showing that one-third of Japanese R&D projects resulted from users' suggestions. For American companies the figure was only one-sixth.

◆ THE NEW MANAGEMENT APPROACH

The United States' reduced ability to compete and the subsequent studies (some of which are described above) indicated that management needed to take a different approach. Teams of American managers went to Japan to see for themselves what was at the basis for Japanese success. They found that the Japanese attributed much of their success to two Americans—Deming and Juran—who had shown the Japanese how to improve product quality. Now Deming and Juran were asked to teach their fellow Americans.

The philosophy they preached was called Total Quality Management (TQM) by the Japanese and is described in detail in Chapter 2. Some of the more significant factors are themes you will see throughout this book:

- **Productivity** used to mean product shipped on time and workforce fully utilized. With a workforce having people specializing in certain tasks, the focus was on process engineers designing assembly lines that were balanced and on production planners making sure each workstation had enough work. The TQM approach is to ship good product on time. If the product does not meet quality standards, it will not be shipped, even though the delivery targets for the month will not be met. And if workers are idle, they are encouraged to perform other tasks rather than make parts that will be inventoried because there is no demand for it as yet. The tasks may be housecleaning or participating on a process improvement team or learning new skills.

- **Innovation** used to mean engineers would sit in their lab creating new designs that were transferred to manufacturing, which had to design processes to make it. Manufacturing in turn would deliver the product to marketing which had to come up with ways to sell it. Innovation for a TQM organization starts with the customer. Engineers are encouraged to meet the customer to see how the product would be used and to harvest their suggestions. Cross-functional teams are formed to specify the quality characteristics of the product or service that will best meet the customer's needs. Since customers' needs change over time, bringing ideas more quickly to the market is crucial. The time from concept to market for new automobiles used to be five to seven years. Recently, Ford took the Mustang from concept to market in just 38 months.

- **Problem solving** in the old approach required management to detect the problem, affix the blame, punish the culprits, and fix the problem. The rewards were for solving the problem quickly and not necessarily in the most effective manner. This approach gave rise to a trial-and-error approach to problem solving. In order to reduce the occurrence of problems, management would introduce increasingly sophisticated control systems. That, in turn, created an adversarial environment as workers would try to outfox the control systems. With TQM, problem solving is everyone's job. When a worker identifies a problem, he or she is encouraged to solve it or form a team with the necessary skills. Workers are also trained to collect data and analyze them. Management's role is to coach and provide resources to fix the problem. The emphasis is on process. The underlying assumption is that a consistently applied good process will provide consistently good results.

- **Customer satisfaction** in traditional environments means that the specifications and standards for a task are prescribed. The worker does the job and is rewarded for meeting the standards. In a TQM environment the job is not done until the customer is satisfied. The onus is on the worker to find the needs of "the customer." The worker on the line is trained to think of "the customer" as the next person on the line. The job is done only after the customer inspects the items delivered and pronounces them satisfactory.

- **Change** in the old approach was often a reaction to a crisis. Management would deploy new methods and reorganize in order to achieve the big breakthrough needed to maintain profits. Change was massive and frequently driven from the top. With TQM all employees are encouraged to initiate change and learn to do what they are doing better. Key processes are benchmarked to identify performance gaps. There is a constant push to close the gap. If the gap is small, the focus is on incremental improvements. In the case of large gaps, a breakthrough project is defined. Employees are encouraged to take a proactive approach to problems.

◆ TQM AND THE CORPORATE STRATEGY

Walter Kiechel of *Fortune* magazine (Reimann, 1992) notes that the problem for strategic planners is that many of their plans were never implemented. But he notes that TQM with its focus on implementation has resulted in significant changes to the organization. Kiernan (1993) developed a model of the Strategic Architecture in which he incorporated TQM as a way of executing strategy. The strategy itself is based on an analysis of the market and the customer's needs, and the sources of competitive advantage. After a generic strategy is synthesized and honed for execution, he suggests several core elements to enable execution. Aspects of TQM that are included are:

- Empowerment/Diffused Leadership
- Organizational Learning
- Innovation /Experimentation

Empowerment recognizes that all of the firm's employees need to work together to meet the challenges faced by the company in what Kiernan terms the posthierarchical organization. As an example, he describes empowerment at a Brazilian machinery manufacturer, Semco. The organization had 11 layers of management which has been reduced to only three. Workers are organized in self-managed teams. They are responsible for making most personnel decisions even including salaries, and they also set work schedules. To do this effectively, they are given financial and performance data, and they are trained to interpret it. The example is similar to happenings in many other companies—fewer layers of management and more information to the workers.

Organizational learning reflects the ability of the organization to learn new concepts and adapt them effectively to their unique business environment. It is fostered by encouraging teamwork, communication across functions, and a willingness to communicate with business allies to improve performance. Kiernan describes three approaches to facilitate learning:

- **Benchmarking** to look outside the organization and find who (not necessarily a competitor) is achieving better performance of a process.
- Customer **feedback,** particularly from the people in closest contact with the customer such as salespeople and field service technicians.
- Temporary job assignments between departments and also with business partners such as suppliers and customers.

The emphasis is on encouraging people to work in teams, learn from each other, and understand what needs to be done to introduce the change and make it part of the daily practice.

Innovation/Experimentation is an attitude organizations fuel through an inspiring vision and support of practices that celebrate experimentation and through toleration of failures that can result. The successful innovators bring products/services to market quickly so that they can be tested quickly. The feedback is incorporated in the next design. 3M promotes a company policy requiring that at least 30 percent of its products be less than five years old. Sony and Mitsubishi set **sunset dates** when the product is introduced; this is when the product will be replaced by another product. By formally placing a stake in the ground, they encourage work to start immediately on replacement products. These products are categorized as improvement of the old version, a spinoff, and something totally new. Potentially, when the product is removed from the market, three new products may be introduced. Panasonic replaces products with new models on a 90-day cycle, and as a result, there has been a greater range of choices. Goldman, Nagel, and Preiss (1994) refer to a new level of **segmentation,** with companies targeting "**niches** within niches." Bicycling shoes used to cater to a niche within customers for sneakers. Today they have specialized for racing, riding, off-road, and track and are matched to pedal-and-shoe locking "systems."

◆ DOES TQM WORK?

There is plenty of anecdotal evidence to indicate that TQM can improve performance. David Kearns as chairman of Xerox Corporation initiated TQM when his company began losing market share to the Japanese. After six years, manufacturing costs were down, defective parts decreased from 8 percent to 0.3 percent, and Dataquest reported customers rated them No. 1 in product reliability and service. More importantly, Xerox regained market share from the Japanese without the help of any tariff or trade protection from the federal government. 3M at its St. Paul, Minnesota, plant over a two-year period cut waste in production by 64 percent, reduced customer complaints by 90 percent, and raised production by 57 percent. Profits skyrocketed.

Several surveys have also been done on TQM. One, conducted by the General Accounting Office (GAO), surveyed 20 of 23 companies that had received site visits to evaluate their application for the Baldrige National Quality award. The GAO examined company performance in terms of

- Employee relations
- Operating procedures
- Customer satisfaction
- Financial performance

Employee relations is a key indicator of workforce participation. The study focused on employee satisfaction, attendance, turnover, safety and health, and number of suggestions made to improve quality. The average rate improved on all measures. Not all companies, however, always reported an improvement. For example, one company found employee satisfaction had declined, but it attributed this finding to concern about a merger.

Operating procedures were measured along eight dimensions ranging from errors to cost savings to timeliness of delivery. Only two companies reported a decline in one of the dimensions. One of the negatives was a company reporting a 0.1 percent decline from a high percentage of 97 in on-time delivery. Another was a company reporting declining inventory turnover because of a weak industry demand; however, its turnover was better than the industry average.

Customer satisfaction was measured using overall customer satisfaction indicators as well as customer complaints and customer retention. Overall customer satisfaction did not decline for any company. One company did receive more customer complaints, but that was a result of implementing a new complaint-handling system. Customer retention also generally improved, with only two companies noting a slight decline. Four companies experienced no change, but they already had a high retention rate of 90 to 100 percent.

Financial performance was measured in terms of market share, sales per employee, return on assets, and return on sales. The annual average increase in market share was 13.7 percent. Two companies suffered a decline but had since recovered the lost market share. Sales per employee improved in all reporting companies by an annual average of 8.6 percent. Two companies, both of which were in intensely competitive industries, experienced a decline in return on assets and return on sales. The average annual increase was 1.3 percent in return on assets and 0.4 percent in return on sales.

The GAO report concluded that "total quality management is useful for small companies (not larger than 500 employees) as well as large (more than 500 employees) and for companies that sell services as well as for companies that produce and sell manufactured products."

Another report (Hiam, 1993) was commissioned by the Conference Board in 1993. This report reviewed 20 studies whose results were published between 1989 and 1992. The author concluded that, while TQM can work, some approaches for introducing TQM are better than others. In addition to the GAO study reviewed above, two studies were not industry specific and represented different viewpoints:

- Booz, Allen, and Hamilton studied approximately 30 service companies. They were studying the possibility that TQM is more applicable to manufacturing companies and that the response from service companies would be different.
- Sirota and Alper studied all of the employees at 30 companies. Theirs was the only one to include workers as well as managers.

The Booz, Allen, and Hamilton study of service companies listed seven common problems:

- Lack of leadership from the top
- Lack of an overall direction to guide the incremental improvements
- Use of a generic model rather than adapting the model to the company culture
- Quality metrics that were not focused on the customer
- Training with a narrow focus

- Lack of support for implementing the quality process after people have been trained
- Assigning quality to a separate department rather than making it part of the daily work

Interestingly, these problems could just as easily apply to manufacturing companies. The research concluded that if these problems were avoided, "TQM can be the right management approach for changing behavior and performance."

Sirota and Alper's study of employees at 30 companies identified 12 elements of corporate culture that had to be addressed if a TQM program were to reach goals of quality and customer satisfaction. They concluded that TQM programs that did not affect a change in the corporate culture but used a "tools and techniques" approach did not maintain a sustainable improvement. Responses to questions were compiled by category—management, exempt, or nonexempt.

Two questions, in particular, were considered to be key indicators because of the responses generated. One question was: Do you agree with the statement: "Prevention is truly emphasized in Company X; that is, we act to prevent quality problems from occurring rather than 'fire fighting'"? This question received the most negative responses. Forty-eight percent of the managers and 38 percent of the nonexempt employees disagreed. The other key question asked if employees feel top management is highly committed to quality. Only 42 percent of managers felt this was so, but 57 percent of the hourly employees agreed. Exempt employees were the most skeptical, with only 27 percent agreeing. The study concluded that "Most of the companies we work with are not making the types of cultural changes necessary to have a significant impact on their quality, customer service and performance."

The most comprehensive study was conducted by Ernst and Young and the American Quality Foundation; these results are described in more depth in Chapter 2. The study categorized companies by performance level, and then, based on a company's existing performance level, specific practices were prescribed as being more or less useful to a company.

Overall, these studies conclude that TQM has positive benefits. In no case did it appear that the introduction of TQM had caused harm. Most companies felt it worked, but some companies thought the results were only "so-so." In these cases, the cause could usually be traced to a lack of top management commitment to carry through a change in the corporate culture.

Although TQM is not specifically oriented toward raising the stock price, it could be argued that better financial performance in terms of profits and market share should be appreciated by the financial community. Heller (1994) conducted a study comparing the stock market performance of 150 companies initiating TQM and the Standard and Poors 500. He concluded that the group of TQM companies performed significantly better than the S&P 500. Between January 1993 and March 1994, the S&P 500 gained 4.6 percent, while the TQM companies gained 10.1 percent.

Recently, some studies have appeared to indicate a resurgence in American competitiveness. Two recent studies confirm these results. The *Wall Street Journal* of September 1994, based on research conducted by the Alexis de Tocqueville

Institution in Virginia, charted the share of profits in world markets of U.S., Japanese, and European companies. The chart showed that U.S. companies garnered more than 50 percent of the profits in world markets for industries ranging from electronic components to aerospace and data processing. But the United States still lagged in industries such as steel and machinery/engineering. Another study was the World Competitiveness Report compiled by the International Institute for Management Development. The study considers a wide range of elements, including the infrastructure, to assess competitiveness. In 1994 the study placed the United States first, ahead of Japan and Germany. Although this improvement cannot be directly related to TQM, it is indicative that a country whose companies have been focusing on TQM for so many years is demonstrating improvement with tangible measures.

◆ OVERVIEW OF THE BOOK

Quality has been a key element of competitiveness. Repeatedly, studies have shown the central role quality plays in improving market share and raising profitability. Today researchers of manufacturing policy describe quality as the foundation that must be laid before a company can compete successfully on cost, dependability, or flexibility. A TQM program is aimed at improving all of these elements, and the results can be striking. However, it requires a sustained level of commitment from top management. In addition to using "fact-based" tools and techniques, it requires a change in the corporate culture. The message is that TQM crosses many different functions and draws on techniques from several disciplines.

This book describes the tools and practices that are part and parcel of a TQM program. Undergirding these tools and practices are four concepts that will appear frequently in the book:

- **Customer focus**—the value of the work done is determined by the customer.
- **Continual improvement**—the quality of work can always be improved, and this can be done gradually or through breakthroughs.
- **Total participation**—the person closest to the task is the most qualified to suggest improved ways of working. That person should be encouraged to make and implement those suggestions as part of his or her daily work.
- A wide range of applicability—the concepts of TQM can be applied to service companies and manufacturing companies and can be used by large and small operations. Throughout this work you will see examples of applications in a wide variety of settings.

This chapter has focused on the importance of product quality as an essential element of the corporate strategy. Chapters 2 and 3 describe the broadening of the meaning of TQM to include service quality and finally to imply quality in management.

◆ Key Terms

Average Outgoing
   Quality Level (AOQL)
Control Chart
Dumping
Manufacturing policy
Dependability
Flexibility
Tradeoff model
Cumulative model
Sand cone model
Design for
   Manufacturability

Project Management
Internal failures
External failures
Cross-training
Participative manage-
   ment
Productivity
Innovation
Problem solving
Customer satisfaction
Change
Empowerment

Organizational learning
Benchmarking
Feedback
Sunset dates
Segmentation
Niches
Customer focus
Continual Improvement
Total participation

◆ Assignments

1. Find five companies that have won the Malcolm Baldrige National Quality Award. Compare their average performance for the five years before they won to the years after they won. *Note:* You will need to find companies like Xerox which won the Baldrige as a company. It would be difficult to obtain performance figures for divisions of large companies such as Cadillac.
2. Use the seven common problems identified by the Booz, Allen, and Hamilton study to create five questions you would ask the managers and workers at a company to assess if they had discarded the old approach to management in favor of the new TQM approach.
3. For the following industries look up a recent *Consumers Report Guide,* note the top performer (*Note:* this may not necessarily be identified as the Best Buy), and record the difference in price between their product and the average price of the competitors:
   - Large-screen televisions (31″ to 35″)
   - Small microwave ovens
   - Dishwashers
   - Electric toothbrushes
   - Lawn tractors (with gear drive)

Case Study

Provisions Inc.—The Cooked Meat Division

Provisions Inc. was a major supplier of beef, pork, and cooked meats to much of Canada. Founded in 1854 as a hog processing company with headquarters in Toronto, it gradually diversified into beef processing and cooked meat operations. Cooked meats consisted of hot dogs and a large variety of sausages such as bologna, salami, and liverwurst. In recent years, new variations had been added such as bologna with macaroni and cheese or with pickles and pimento. By 1985 Provisions Inc. had a 32 percent market share. It supplied stores ranging from supermarkets to small stores known as "Mom-and-Pop" stores. Its product could be found in stores in New Brunswick and Prince Edward Island through Vancouver in British Columbia.

Corporate headquarters for Provisions Inc. remained in Toronto. The three major divisions were known as the Beef, Pork, and Cooked Meats Divisions. Each Division had a national director who reported to the chief operating officer of the company. The director of the Cooked Meats Division was responsible for the production of cooked meats in four plants. These plants were located in Edmonton, Winnipeg, Toronto, and Montreal. Each plant had a Cooked Meat manager who reported to the director of Cooked Meats. Each manager was responsible for distributing product in a specific region. For example, Montreal's Cooked Meat manager was responsible for supplying Quebec and the Maritime Provinces.

Product was shipped to stores using a combination of rail and truck. When a particular plant did not manufacture enough to supply

an area, the cooked meats would be shipped from other plants. In fact, this was a common occurrence for the shipments to the Maritime Provinces. The capacity of the Montreal plant was barely sufficient to fill the needs of the markets around Quebec. So, the product would be brought in by railcar from Toronto and occasionally from Winnipeg. At Montreal, these railcars would be unloaded and then were reassembled for shipment to the Maritimes. Upon arrival, they were unloaded and taken to a warehouse where they were assembled for trucks to carry to their final destination. Whereas most of Quebec received their cooked meats the day after they were prepared, grocery stores in the Maritimes would receive their shipments three to seven days after preparation.

Cooked meats typically had a shelf life of 10 to 14 days. Beyond that period, decay-causing bacteria could affect the taste of the food. With so many days being taken simply transporting the product, much of the product was sitting on the shelves beyond the recommended shelf life. Provisions Inc. had a policy for reimbursing the grocer for food that sat on the shelves beyond the recommended shelf life. But since grocers knew the product was not unhealthy, they continued to sell it until a Provisions Inc. salesperson arrived and provided fresh product in exchange. As a result, much of the product was sold close to or beyond the recommended shelf life.

To the new Cooked Meat director, this was clearly undesirable, and so he changed the distribution system. Now the product would be shipped directly from Toronto to the

Provisions Inc.—The Cooked Meat Division (Continued)

Maritimes without stopping for unloading and reassembling in Montreal. By adding more truck routes, he was able to ensure that the product reached the grocer two to three days after manufacture.

He expected these changes to be accepted with great enthusiasm. Customers got fresher product, and Provisions Inc. exchanged far fewer products for expired shelf life. Instead, he received a flood of complaints from consumers complaining of the lack of flavor in the "new" cooked meats and sales dropped significantly. What had gone wrong? What should he do next? Distribution to the northern areas of British Columbia was also taking several days. Based on what had happened to his initiatives in the Maritimes, he wondered what he should do there.

CASE QUESTIONS:

1. What should the Cooked Meat director have done differently before introducing the new system for distribution?
2. What should he do now?

◆ Bibliography

Barclay, C. A. "Quality Strategy and TQM Policies: Empirical Evidence." *Management International Review* 33 (First Quarter 1993): 87–98.

Buzzell, R. D. and B. T. Gale. *The PIMS Principles: Linking Strategy to Performance.* New York: Free Press, 1987.

Dertouzos, M. L., R. K. Lester, and R. M. Solow. *Made in America : Regaining the Productive Edge.* Cambridge Mass.: MIT, 1989.

Ferdows, K., and A. De Meyer. "Lasting Improvements in Manufacturing Performance: In Search of a New Theory." *Journal of Operations Management* 9, No. 2 (April 1990): 168–194.

Garvin, D. A. *Managing Quality: The Strategic and Competitive Edge.* New York: Free Press, 1988.

Godfrey, A. B., and P. J. Kolesar. "Role of Quality in Achieving World Class Competitiveness." In M. K. Starr. *Global Competitiveness.* New York: W. W. Norton, 1988.

Goldman, S. L., R. N. Nagel, and K. Preiss. *Agile Competitors and Virtual Organizations: Strategies for Enriching the Customer.* New York: Van Nostrand Reinhold, 1994.

Heller, T. "The Superior Stock Market Performance of a TQM Portfolio." *Journal of the Center for Quality Management* (Winter 1994): 23–32.

Hiam, A. "Does Quality Work? A Review of Relevant Studies." Report No. 1043. New York: The Conference Board, 1993.

Kiernan, M. J. "The New Strategic Architecture: Learning to Compete in the Twenty-first Century." *Academy of Management Executive* 7, No. 1 (1993).

Management Practices: U.S. Companies Improve Performance Through Quality Efforts. U.S. General Accounting Office. May 1991.

Mansfield, E. "Industrial Innovation in Japan and the United States," *Science* 241 (1988): 1771.

Nakane, J. "Manufacturing Futures Survey in Japan, A Comparative Survey 1983–1986." Tokyo: Systems Science Institute, Waseda University, May 1986.

Quality: Executive Priority or Afterthought? Survey conducted by the Gallup Organization for the American Society for Quality Control. October 1989.

Reimann, B. C. "The 1992 Strategic Management Conference: The New Agenda for Corporate Leadership." *Planning Review* (July/August 1992): 38–46.

Skinner, W. "Manufacturing—Missing Link in Corporate Strategy." *Harvard Business Review* 46, No. 3 (May–June 1969): 136.

Therrien, L. "Spreading the Message," *Business Week,* January 15 1992. New York: McGraw-Hill, p. 60.

von Hippel, E. *The Sources of Innovation,* New York: Oxford University Press, 1988.

Chapter 2

What Is TQM?

◆ ◆ ◆

*I*n 1984 Domino's Pizza Distribution Corporation devised an "Olympic" competition to make employees more aware of the importance of quality. Among the events scheduled were doughmaking, driving, and delivery. This corporation's operations were spread across three regions, and each commissary in a region would hold quarterfinals. The winners would compete in the semifinals at regional headquarters. The finals were held in Ann Arbor where many of the judges were the customers. After the game, the winners met for three days with management to suggest what could be done to improve the company. One suggestion was a series of safety seminars for drivers to help them comply with Department of Transportation regulations. The relationship of safety seminars to quality of pizza is not immediately obvious: is this an example of Total Quality Management?

*S*teinway is known for the quality of its pianos. In 1980 the company, using craftsmen, made a small volume of pianos (only 6900); in comparison, Yamaha built 250,000 pianos the same year. Steinway relied on skilled labor and the finest materials. Its Research and Development Department continuously experimented with new materials, with the product design, and with construction methods. A Steinway grand was estimated to have 12,000 parts. While each operator was responsible for his or her work, inspectors would check their output. The president of Steinway recognized the paramount nature of quality and he also thought it was important that workers felt there were no barriers to management. He would personally tour the factory to seek suggestions for improvement. One suggestion involved installing a new router in a department. Does Steinway represent a good example of a company practicing TQM?

◆ **INTRODUCTION**

This chapter reviews four approaches to defining Total Quality Management. Each of these approaches will further our understanding of the phrase. Several of the concepts introduced in this chapter are discussed in greater detail in later chapters. Finally, the summary section develops the philosophy used through this book.

The first approach attempts to grasp the exact meaning of quality. Presumably, if we have a common definition of quality, the phrase TQM can be universally understood. The second approach examines some of the practices used by companies practicing TQM. The Criteria for the Baldrige award offer a concise framework for listing the practices. In this connection, the International Quality Study is arguably the most extensive study of quality practices. The third approach describes the TQM philosophies of the leading sages—Deming, Juran, Crosby, Feigenbaum, Ishikawa, and Taguchi. The fourth approach traces the evolution of TQM in Japan based on work done by a leading Japanese quality consultant, Shoji Shiba.

◆ THE FIRST APPROACH: DEFINING QUALITY?

Since TQM deals with quality, it seems evident that a first step toward understanding the meaning of the phrase would require an understanding of the word "quality." This word is frequently used to describe goods or services, but it also means different things to different people. Garvin (1988) was the first to categorize the numerous definitions of quality existing in the literature in an effort to create a common understanding. In his book he lists five approaches to defining quality: the transcendent; product-based; user-based; manufacturing-based; and value-based.

The Transcendent Approach

This **transcendent approach** is typified by Barbara Tuchman's (1980) definition: "a condition of excellence implying fine quality as distinct from poor quality. . . . Quality is achieving or reaching for the highest standard as against being satisfied with the sloppy or the fraudulent." Examples of fine quality that meet this definition are most obviously present in the arts and literature. Beethoven's symphonies, Da Vinci's "Mona Lisa," Michelangelo's "David," and Dickens's *David Copperfield* are all examples of "achieving or reaching for the highest standard." However, these items may not represent quality to everyone, and this lack of objectivity creates a problem for the worker in a business environment who is striving for quality. When a factory worker produces an item, this definition does not allow that person to state definitively that the item is of high quality. The other four approaches to defining quality are based more on objective measures.

The Product-based Approach

The **product-based approach** identifies specific features or attributes that can be measured to indicate higher quality. Leather upholstery for car seats is considered higher quality than vinyl, the lack of blemishes in gems viewed using a 10X magnifying glass indicates a higher quality.

This approach provides objective measures of quality. Its disadvantage is that it assumes that the absence or presence of an attribute implies higher quality. Since leather is more highly regarded than vinyl, the presence of leather upholstery in a car with no regard to the color or finish of the leather would imply higher quality.

The User-based Approach

The user determines the quality of the goods. The product or service that best satisfies the user is the higher quality product. Juran refers to the **user-based** approach as **"fitness for use."** It implies learning how the user plans to use the product and making the product to fit that need. The designers at Ford found that when drivers placed grocery bags in the large trunks of the Taurus these bags would fall during the drive home, causing the contents to spill out and roll around the trunk. Upon getting home, the driver would have to refill the bags before taking them into the house. As a result, the Ford designers provided a net to hold the bags upright and prevent spillage.

The user-based definition equates customer satisfaction with quality. Customer satisfaction reflects the attitudes of the consumer. An organization adopting this view of quality needs to accurately identify the target market, ferret out its needs, and then design, construct, and deliver the appropriate product. For success, all of the functions contributing to the value of the product have to be involved. The benefits expected are increased market share. However, customer satisfaction may not be achieved for reasons that have nothing to do with the quality of the product. For example, the customer may not understand or appreciate the benefits of a new product right away but may do so if given time. And until the customer says the product is good, it will not be considered good quality. Companies using this approach develop products after the customer has articulated the need. Here Deming uses the analogy of driving a car while looking in the rearview mirror.

The Manufacturing-based Approach

Crosby described the **manufacturing-based approach as "conformance to requirements."** Engineering specifies the product characteristics, and the more closely manufacturing can conform to those requirements, the better the quality of the product. If a process results in a product that has a precision of $+/-$ half-an-inch, it is considered worse than the process that makes a product with a precision of $+/-$ one-tenth of an inch. The importance of this approach to quality was brought home to Ford when it compared the parts it used to make transmissions to those made by Mazda. When the Ford parts were tested, all were found to be within the tolerance limits. But the Ford transmissions were having problems. When the inspectors tested the Mazda parts, they thought their instruments were broken. The Mazda parts were so precise that the instruments showed no deviation. Mazda transmissions were also not having any problems.

This definition has the advantages of providing objectively measurable quality standards and of reducing the costs of quality. Signetics Corporation (Lovelock

1991) reported that its reduction of defectives from 7000 ppm to 150 ppm saved the company $20 million by reducing costs such as rework, scrap, inspection, and returns from the customer. The disadvantage of this measure is its lack of concern for the customer's preferences. Its implicit assumption is that customer satisfaction is directly related to the precision of meeting the target specifications of a product or service.

Value-based Approach

This definition of quality introduces the element of price. Broh (1982) provides one expression of this approach: "Quality is the degree of excellence at an acceptable price and the control of variability at an acceptable cost." The **value-based approach** assumes that consumers' purchase decisions are based on a model similar to one proposed by well-known marketing consultant, Gale.[2] (Exhibit 2.1). In this definition one attribute of value is quality. The purchase decision involves trading off the quality against the price. Because many of the attributes of quality are subjective assessments, the approach is not effective in introducing objective criteria.

Unfortunately, most of these definitions are subjective. Although the manufacturing and product-based approaches are the most objective, both fail to account sufficiently for customer preferences. The user-based approach relies solely on the consumer's input, but methods for obtaining this input are unreliable and unable to predict changes in preferences.

In practice, a company adopts a mix of these approaches. Since the manufacturing- and product-based approaches are objective, it is relatively straightforward to measure competitive quality on these yardsticks. When a company tries to assess the competition as perceived by the user, the company will usually establish objective criteria based on responses to customer surveys. Chapter 9 describes some of the ways marketeers have devised to identify key characteristics from customer data. The analysis informs a company of the degree to which its product is differentiated from the competition in quantitative terms.

In order to link the user's criteria to the engineer's design, Garvin (1988) argued for an understanding of the elements of quality as perceived by the user. If a product or service was rated better than the competition on one or more of these dimensions, it would be considered a higher quality. The criterion Garvin used for

Exhibit 2.1 | **Gales Model of the Purchase Decision**

Value — Quality — Product / Service; Price

defining the eight dimensions was that the ranking could be high on one dimension and still be low on the other; that is, the company could choose to make tradeoffs between these elements. He defined the eight dimensions of quality as

- Performance
- Features
- Reliability
- Conformance
- Durability
- Serviceability
- Aesthetics
- Perceived quality

Performance refers to the primary operating characteristics of the product or service; they are usually measurable. For a house these characteristics would include the number of rooms, the size of the lot, the number of bathrooms, and so on. For a service they could be the number of rings before the phone is answered or the promptness of filling a customer's food order.

Features are additional characteristics that enhance the product/services appeal to the user. Examples are the light on the handset of the Princess telephone to enable users to see the numbers in the dark, deleaded ink for newspapers, and glare-reducing coatings on light bulbs.

Reliability of a product is the likelihood that a product will not fail within a specific time period. This is a key element for users who need the product to work without fail. An example is the elderly lady who needs to be sure her car will work when she needs it. Although Garvin states that reliability is "more relevant to durable goods," there are many examples of reliability as a key element of a service. People buy services that guarantee mail delivery. They complain loudly if electric power is subject to frequent blackouts and brownouts.

Conformance is the precision with which the product or service meets the specified standards. The traditional American approach to conformance was to meet requirements within prespecified tolerance limits. Quality was considered high if 95 percent or more of the products were within the tolerance limits. Upon studying the Japanese, a second approach to conformance became apparent. (This thinking is embodied in Taguchi's approach, which is detailed in Chapter 8.) The idea behind this approach is the greater the deviation from the intended value, the less satisfied the customer. So, the process that has more parts meeting the target requirement is better than one that does not, even if all the parts of the latter are within tolerance limits. Motorola changed its definition of quality to mean conformance. This change (which is conceptually similar to Taguchi's) is reflected in the six-sigma approach discussed in more detail in Chapter 8.

Durability measures the length of a product's life. For some products such as light bulbs, it measures how many hours the bulb will burn before it needs to be replaced. Car mufflers are another example; once the muffler develops a hole, it is discarded. When the product can be repaired, estimating durability is more complicated. The item will be used until it is no longer economical to operate it. This happens when the repair rate and the associated costs increase significantly.

Serviceability is the speed with which the product can be put into service when it breaks down, as well as the competence and behavior of the serviceperson. The speed of service can be measured by response time and mean time to repair (MTTR). Measuring the behavior of a serviceperson is more difficult. Often it is accomplished by surveying the customer after the service has been completed. Another measure of serviceability is to assess the number of return calls, and, if the service continues to be unsatisfactory, the process for handling the complaints.

Aesthetics is the subjective dimension indicating the kind of response a user has to a product. It represents the individual's personal preference—the ways an individual responds to the look, feel, sound, taste, and smell. A person judging a wine to look, taste, and smell better than another would say it is of higher quality. Similarly, better sounding stereo speakers would be considered higher quality, as would suits whose material and style are perceived to be "better."

Perceived quality is also a subjective dimension: it is the quality attributed to a good or service based on indirect measures. An example is the saying, "You know a good workman by his tools." Well-maintained tools and an immaculate workplace may indicate a good workman, but it may not be a definitive clue. Some fliers infer the quality of an airline by the cleanliness of the flip-down tray. Others infer quality by the brand name. IBM has a quality image, so, when IBM first started to make personal computers to compete with Apple, its machines were perceived to have high quality.

The eight dimensions enumerated by Garvin were not directly applicable to service. A study done by Berry, Zeithaml, and Parasuraman (1990) identified five principal dimensions. In order of relative importance they are:

- Reliability
- Responsiveness
- Assurance
- Empathy
- Tangibles

Reliability of service is the ability to perform a service reliably and dependably; it means the customer's expectations are met consistently. Garvin would define this dimension as conformance. When customers go to a McDonalds, they have a set of expectations; namely, that orders will be filled quickly once placed, that the surroundings will be clean, and that the order takers will be courteous. Reliability is a measure of McDonald's ability to meet these expectations consistently.

Responsiveness is the willingness to help customers and provide prompt service. With regard to dealing with a long checkout line at a supermarket, responsiveness would be a willingness to add an additional checkout counter. After checking into a hotel room and finding the television did not work, responsiveness would be the speed with which the repairs were completed.

Assurance is the ability to communicate to the customer a level of competence and to provide the service with the necessary courtesy. Communicating a level of competence often fits Garvin's perceived value dimension. Professionals such as doctors and lawyers display their earned degrees prominently on office walls; and they have well-appointed offices in reputable locations.

Empathy is the approachability and the ability to communicate with and understand the customer's needs. At Disneyworld the guides are trained to respond to visitors' questions with a friendly smile.

Tangibles is the appearance of the physical facilities, equipment, personnel, and communication materials. Thus, International Business Machines (IBM) requires its service technicians to dress professionally, and McDonalds has been known to shovel the sidewalks of neighboring stores to improve the appearance of the area.

Performance on these dimensions is usually measured by surveying the customer. The performance-based theory states: As performance improves, customer satisfaction increases. When a service is experienced often, it is easier for the customer to measure improvement in performance. Examples of such services are fast-food, haircuts, or cashing a check at a bank. When services are experienced occasionally, the customer develops a set of expectations based on information obtained from a variety of sources such as friends and acquaintances, readings, and competitive advertisements. These services would include visiting the doctor, going on a cruise, or eating at a gourmet restaurant. In these cases, the customer is satisfied if the perceived service exceeds the expectations.

◆ THE SECOND APPROACH: TQM PRACTICES

Logically, Total Quality Management should be the set of practices that enable an organization to deliver quality products or services. As a starting point, the International Organization for Standardization (ISO) has defined a set of standards, and if a company conforms to these standards, it is considered to have the basis for ensuring quality output. There are other awards earned by companies that have developed these procedures to exceptional levels. One framework that is popular in the United States is the Malcolm Baldrige National Quality award. These two awards are described briefly below. For a comparison of the the two standards, see Chapter 3.

ISO Standards

In 1987 the European Committee for Standardization (ECS) adopted the **ISO 9000 standards**. ISO, an acronym for the International Organization for Standardization, is a truly international organization, being made up of representatives from the standards boards of 91 countries including the United States.

The ECS acknowledged a need for a common standard for quality in order to facilitate the flow of goods between the 12 member countries. In the past, each country had maintained several technical standards, which hindered this free flow. Sometimes this was done to protect the national industry from foreign competition. Requiring each country to consolidate its standards into a single national standard would still require companies wishing to do business in the European Commission (EC) to negotiate 12 sets of standards.

By adopting the ISO 9000 standards, the ECS has tried to eliminate technical trade barriers. In order to encourage companies to get registered, the ECS publishes a Registry of companies that are ISO compliant. This method gives registered companies a competitive edge since potential customers are likely to select companies from this register. This strategy has proved to be very effective. Within the first two years of the adoption of ISO 9000 standards, more than 10,000 British companies were registered. In addition, a number of other organizations have adopted these standards. A notable example is the Department of Defense (DOD), which uses ISO standards in place of MIL-Q-9858A. An additional benefit to a company once it is registered is that it has to undergo far fewer audits. Many customers such as AT&T and Ford perform their own quality audits of suppliers, which require both the buying and the supplying company to commit resources and time. If the supplying company is ISO registered, there is less need for the buying company to perform its own audits.

Presently, the standards consist of three levels (see Exhibit 2.2):

- ISO 9003. Companies registered at this level have satisfied the quality requirements for inspection and testing. Auditors check to ensure documents are adequate and well-controlled. They check the test equipment and make certain it is calibrated on a regular schedule.
- ISO 9002. This level of registration states that a company has satisfied the ISO 9003 requirements and in addition has deployed these practices through the production organization. Auditors check for items such as evidence of Statistical Quality Control through the process, and efforts are made to monitor and improve supplier quality.
- ISO 9001. This level implies that quality practices have been spread through design control and through after-sales servicing. It is the most comprehensive of the three levels of registration. As one of its checks, the auditors pick up a packet with an existing shop order and make sure it includes the latest revisions issued by Engineering.

The standards were constructed as a generic basic set of requirements for any Total Quality Management System. The standards are intended to apply to any industry in any of the 91 countries represented on the ISO. ISO 9001/2/3 are intended for use for external quality assurance purposes in contractual situations between two parties. They reflect the interests of the buyer. Since buyers have some additional needs peculiar to their industry, supplements may be added. For example, the Chemical Industry Association provides guidelines for its industry.

Exhibit 2.2

ISO 9000: Elements of the Standards

Topic	Contractual		
	ISO 9001 CLAUSE	ISO 9002 CLAUSE	ISO 9003 CLAUSE
Management responsibility	4.1	4.1 *	4.1 **
Quality system principles	4.2	4.2	4.2 *
Auditing the quality system (internal)	4.17	4.16 *	—
Economics—quality-related costs	—	—	—
Quality in marketing (contract review)	4.3	4.3	—
Quality in spec. and design (design control)	4.4	—	—
Quality in procurement (purchasing)	4.6	4.5	—
Quality in production (process control)	4.9	4.8	—
Control of production	4.9	4.8	—
Material control and traceability	4.8	4.7	4.4 *
Control of verification status (inspection and test)	4.12	4.11	4.7 *
Product verification (inspect and test)	4.10	4.9	4.5 *
Control of measuring and test equipment	4.11	4.10	4.6 *
Nonconformity (control of nonconformity)	4.13	4.12	4.8 *
Corrective action	4.14	4.13	—
Handling and post-production functions	4.15	4.14	4.9 *
After-sales servicing	4.19	—	—
Quality documentation and records	4.5	4.4	4.3 *
Quality records	4.16	4.15	4.10 *
Personnel (training)	4.18	4.17 *	4.11 *
Product safety and liability	—	—	—
Use of statistical methods	4.20	4.18	4.12 *
Purchaser supplied product	4.7	4.6	—

* Less demanding than ISO 9001.
** Less demanding than ISO 9002.

Becoming ISO-registered does not imply that the company has a world-class quality system in place. In order to realize the full benefits of lower costs and productivity improvements, the quality system would have to be developed beyond the requirements laid down by ISO 9000. These standards merely serve to document the status quo.

The Malcolm Baldrige National Quality Award (MBNQA)

The MBNQA was established by the federal government to promote the diffusion of TQM practices. Chapter 3 describes in detail the relationships among the seven groups of criteria, which are described briefly below:

- Senior Executive Leadership: How the senior executive promotes quality values within the company and to the public.
- Information and Analysis: The management of quality data, how benchmarks are derived, the analysis of the data, and the accessibility of data to people in the company.
- Strategic Quality Planning: The process used for setting quality goals and plans and its effectiveness.
- Human Resource Development and Management: Programs designed to involve employees, to provide education in quality, to recognize employee efforts in meeting quality goals, and to ensure employee well-being and morale.
- Management of Process Quality: The use of Statistical Process Control and Continuous Improvement methods, efforts to ensure supplier quality, and documentation of processes to facilitate assessment of quality and support service quality.
- Quality and Operational Results: Results of quality at the supplier, in the process, the product or service, and the support services.
- Customer Focus and Satisfaction: Efforts made to establish the customer's requirements, to communicate these requirements through the organization, the extent of commitment to satisfying the customer, and the results.

These seven categories cover a large number of tools, techniques, management practices, and policies; many of these are described in later chapters. As a way of beginning to understand specifically what these categories contain, the rest of this section describes the results of the International Quality Study(SM).

The International Quality Study (SM)

In 1989 the American Quality Foundation and Ernst and Young initiated a massive study of 580 organizations in four industries on three continents. Their objective was to identify the several management practices that result in quality improvement. The study measured company performance on three criteria:

- Profitability using Return on Asset (ROA) figures.
- Value Added per Employee where value added was defined as the difference between revenue received and expenditures on purchased materials, components, and energy.
- Quality measured as an index averaging quality relative to the competitors of three items: the basic product or service, ancillary services, and the overall reputation.

Over 900 specific management practices were studied to determine those practices that gave a company a competitive advantage. The categories they used do not map directly to the Baldrige framework, but they do overlap:

1. Business Organization consisting of Management Systems, Human Resource Management, and Administrative Support Departments. The focus was on the spread of education, the use of quality tools, and the evaluation and reward systems. These questions map to the Human Resource and Information and Analysis sections of the Baldrige.
2. Product/Service Development consisting of identification of new products/services, their development, methods to speed up introduction, and the application of technology. These questions mapped to the Customer Focus and the Management of Process Quality sections of the Baldrige.
3. Delivery Process and Customer Satisfaction consisting of supplier management, process management, quality assurance function, and customer interface. The focus here was on methods for improvements that were in place at each of the three segments of the production chain: the supplier, the process, and the customer. These questions mapped to Customer Focus, Quality and Operational Results, Management of Process Quality, and the Information and Analysis sections of the Baldrige.
4. Quality and Strategic Positioning dealing with the planning process, the resolution of several strategic choices, the overall quality strategy, and the quality position. This group of questions attempted to determine the goals set by the company to achieve quality and the results as indicated by end-users. The corresponding sections of the Baldrige are Quality and Operational Results, Leadership, Information and Analysis, and Strategic Quality Planning.
5. Culture looking at specific cultural characteristics including those related to education and quality. These corresponded to the Leadership and Human Resource sections of the Baldrige.

The study found that certain practices would benefit all companies:

1. Process improvement methods impacted all three dimensions of performance but had the most significant effect on productivity. These methods included cycle time analysis, process value analysis, and process simplification.

While most organizations used these techniques only "occasionally," the best performers used them "always or almost always."

2. Deploying the strategic plan inside and outside the organization was beneficial. The most benefit was achieved by having middle management and customers understand the plan. Positive impacts were seen on all three performance dimensions. Increasing suppliers' understandings also showed benefits.

3. Supplier certification programs showed a positive impact on performance, especially in quality and productivity. These practices were more prevalent in manufacturing but relatively rare in the service industries.

The study found that the remaining practices were beneficial only to some companies. The effectiveness of the practices depended on their current performance level. For example, if the organization was a low performer (based on the three performance criteria mentioned earlier), they needed to focus on a few basic TQM practices. Higher performers used these practices and added others. As a result, the best performing companies used a large variety of TQM practices.

1. Quality teams were a useful practice for low-performing companies. Department-level teams and cross-functional teams were particularly useful in improving performance. For medium-level performers, department-level teams and problem-solving training were useful. For high-level performers, only problem-solving training was useful. Broad participation in department-level teams actually showed a negative impact.

2. Training in quality and interacting with customers were important primarily for the lower performing organizations. But once people have been trained, the organization only needs to maintain the skills. So, building skills in these areas for medium- and high-level performers was less relevant.

3. Meetings to discuss quality were generally not beneficial for low-performing organizations. They were useful for medium performers at all levels of the organization. High-performing organizations benefited from quality-related meetings held at the nonmanagement employee level.

4. Developing quality-related criteria for assessment was useful when done at nonmanagement levels for low performers, middle management levels for medium performers, and senior and middle management for high performers. Apparently, until measures have been developed for the nonmanagement level, it is difficult to create meaningful measures at higher levels.

5. Identifying new products and services is a key task for most companies. Low-performing companies can get their new ideas directly from customers based on customer requests, focus groups, and visiting customers. Medium performers would expand their sources for new ideas to include informal market research techniques (surveys and personal contacts, for example) and suggestions from suppliers. The high performers needed to formalize market research using these techniques to anticipate new opportunities.

6. With regard to translating customer requirements into product or service specifications, the differences in practices are dramatic. Low performers benefit from using cross-functional teams that include the customer. Medium performers benefit from relying only on their development department. High performers prosper by using cross-functional teams but without the customer.

7. Measuring the improvements resulting from advances in technology and process is most beneficial to medium performers. The need for improvement is so obvious in low performers that there is little need to measure it. Medium performers need to measure it so that they can apply the continuous improvement techniques (also known as *kaizen*). For high performers, measuring the effect usually showed negative results, perhaps because the high performers had already improved processes substantially and needed to focus on making "breakthrough" improvements.

8. Benchmarking was found to have the most benefit for high-performing organizations. For low performers it had a negative impact. This could be because world-class practices may not be suitable for a low-performing company. The study recommends that low performers benchmark medium performers and focus on improving their core practices.

The study highlights some of the more commonly used techniques in use—process improvement methods, deployment of the corporate plan, supplier certification, quality teams, training, quality meetings, performance assessment and rewards, new product development, measurements, and benchmarking. This approach to defining TQM would conclude that TQM is a set of tools and techniques used to ensure quality products and services.

◆ THE THIRD APPROACH: THE PHILOSOPHIES OF THE LEADING SAGES

The initial success of the quality movement in Japan has been attributed to two sages: W. Edwards Deming and Joseph Juran. Later on, leading thinkers among the Japanese helped to make the quality movement what it is today. Notable among these were Ishikawa and Taguchi. In the United States, Philip Crosby and Armand Feigenbaum are most closely involved with the early years of initiating TQM.

Deming

Deming was the first American to introduce quality principles to the Japanese on a large scale. Deming met Shewhart in 1927, and it was from him that Deming learned the basic concepts of Statistical Quality Control as Shewhart developed it for Bell Labs. Deming later used some of these methods in the Census Bureau. When he was sent to Japan, he was already a well-known and respected statistician. In Japan he found a poor country that was willing to listen to his message about quality, and he was more than willing to help them. Knowing the country was poor, he refused payment for his lectures. The Japanese Union of Scientists and Engineers (JUSE) that sponsored Deming's seminars used the moneys from the registration fees to establish the Deming Prize. Today it is the most coveted quality award in Japan.

Over the years Deming condensed his philosophy into 14 points which became action items for top management to adopt. He also outlined the seven deadly diseases that prevent the successful introduction of TQM. The14 points have changed over the years; as a result, there are some inconsistencies between lists seen in the literature. The following seem to capture the essence of Deming's thinking:

1. Create constancy of purpose toward improvement of product and service.
2. Learn the new philosophy.
3. Cease dependence on inspection of the product to achieve quality. But require statistical evidence of process control along with incoming critical parts.
4. Buy materials only if the supplier has a quality process. End the practice of awarding business on the basis of the price tag alone.
5. Use statistical methods to find troublespots and constantly improve the system.
6. Institute modern aids to training on the job.
7. Institute modern methods of supervision.
8. Drive out fear.
9. Break down barriers between departments.
10. Eliminate numerical goals.
11. Review work standards to account for quality.
12. Remove barriers that rob people of their pride of workmanship.
13. Institute a vigorous program for training people in new skills.
14. Create a structure in top management that will push the above 13 points everyday.

Basically, Deming's 14 points can be regarded in terms of three broad philosophical categories:

- Constancy of purpose
- Continual improvement
- Cooperation between functions

Constancy of purpose is the first point and is reiterated in the last point. Deming strongly believed that the rest of the organization could not be expected to subscribe to the improvement program if management kept changing its approach. For example, he wanted companies to build a long-term relationship with suppliers. But suppliers would only accept this if they saw through practice and experience that policies would not change as the purchasing manager changed. As the Japanese built this kind of relationship with their suppliers, they developed a close-knit organization called a **keiretsu**. Being committed to these suppliers develops a cooperative relationship. Often these suppliers will help the buying company to reduce costs by suggesting different parts or alternative designs. In contrast, after General Motors (GM) had decided to adopt these same practices with their suppliers, they hired purchasing executive Jose Ignacio Lopez de Arrioutua. He was put in charge of GM's purchasing operations with the mandate to cut costs. Lopez excelled at the traditional approach of purchasing parts and materials based on price. He canceled existing contracts and demanded price cuts of at least 10 percent. As a result, the relationship between suppliers and GM became more adversarial. This lack of constancy also prevailed in the relationship with the employees. When GM elicited major concessions from the unionized workforce, the workers expected management to follow suit. Instead, GM gave its managers a huge bonus. Predictably, the workers felt that top management was not committed to the TQM program.

The second major theme running through the 14 points is continual improvement. Several of the points address this issue. When he says managers should learn the new philosophy, he means they should learn to continually improve and not accept the existing error rates. He proposes to determine existing causes using statistical methods. But instead of assigning this job to a group of technicians, he believes in mass education to involve everyone in the improvement process.

Education would enable workers to monitor their work and, when defects were found, to determine the causes. Deming characterized these causes as "common" and "special." The **common causes** were evident in many operations throughout the factory. They were a result of poor product design, machines not capable of performing the work assigned, uncomfortable working conditions, and so on. These causes could be best fixed by management. **Special causes** were specific to a situation. Examples were lack of training for the task, malfunctioning equipment, poor incoming materials, or a mistake by the worker. Typically, special causes were within the control of the worker or department and could be corrected without management assistance. Deming proposed to use process control charts to discriminate between the two types of causes. (A more complete description of how the process is applied is presented in Chapter 7.)

A third major theme is the notion of cross-functional collaboration; items 8 and 9 were directed to these. The first step is to ensure that each person knows what job they are required to do. In one company the manager and subordinate meet to construct a list of tasks, and then each independently weights the importance of each task. By comparing the two lists, each worker gains a better sense of what needs to be done. The result is to drive out fear.

Working across functional lines is also a key teaching tool. For example, one school had the American and its college flags flying on adjacent flagpoles. When a staff member noted that the college flag was flying higher than the U.S. flag (a violation of federal regulations), he contacted the department responsible for the U.S. flag, assuming the error would be corrected. But a week later there had been no change. Upon contacting the department, he found that no action had been taken because the college flagpole was controlled by a different department!!

In his later years Deming proposed an additional theme, **profound knowledge**—that is, an "appreciation for a system, the theory of variations, theory of knowledge, psychology." He argued that each of the four elements had to be learned for a complete knowledge. By *system,* Deming meant the agglomeration of functions that worked together to further the aims of the organization. The study of *variation* refers to an understanding of statistical theory, by which he meant understanding the difference between common and special causes and knowing how to distinguish between them. By *theory of knowledge,* he meant that people need to understand the theory before something can be copied. Accordingly, Deming would insist that managers learn what makes quality programs work before they initiated them in their organizations. Without this level of understanding, he felt the results could be chaos. Finally, he felt managers should learn *psychology* to understand the basic motivations of people. This would give them the tools needed to motivate employees and enable them to enjoy their work.

Juran

Juran is regarded as one of the prime architects of the quality revolution in Japan. After graduating as an engineer, in 1924 he joined the Western Electric Hawthorne Works where he was assigned to the inspection function. In 1951 he published the *Quality Control Handbook,* which later became a seminal work in the area. He arrived in Japan four years after Deming. He founded the Juran Institute in 1979.

Juran expressed his approach to quality in the form of the **Quality Trilogy**. Managing for quality, he stated, involved three basic processes:

- Quality planning
- Quality control
- Quality improvement

By *quality planning* Juran meant first identifying the customer, who is defined as anyone impacted by the process; this included external and internal customers. After determining the customer's needs, it was necessary to develop the goods and services to meet those needs and establish quality goals that included the minimum possible cost. Then came the process design, which should be proven capable of making the product under actual operating conditions. Finally, the process should be transferred to the operators by including all those involved with the plan and training them appropriately.

Quality control was directed at the critical elements that needed to be controlled. These elements had to be identified, and measures and the methods of measurements had to be defined. Standards of performance had to be established. As actual performance was measured and compared to the standard, action would be taken on the difference. Juran advocated quality control be delegated to the lowest possible level, and that if possible, it should be done by the workers responsible for performing the task. This meant widespread training in data collection and problem-solving techniques.

Quality improvement followed by proving the need for improvement and establishing specific improvement projects. The appropriate team had to be organized to guide the project, discover the causes, and provide remedies that work under operating conditions. Finally, mechanisms to control the new process and hold the gains had to be developed.

The relationship among the three processes is shown in the Quality Trilogy (Exhibit 2.3). At the beginning is Quality Planning. When the product and the process design are completed, the operators become responsible. The errors made during the initial planning result in a higher cost which Juran labeled **chronic waste.** At the beginning, the process stays within control limits. Occasionally, a spike, akin to Deming's special causes, occurs and is addressed and brought under control. At some point management recognizes the cost of the chronic waste as being excessive. A quality improvement project is initiated and succeeds in reducing the chronic waste. A new quality control zone is then established.

Juran (Juran, and Gryna, 1993) also created the concept of Cost of Quality (discussed in more detail in Chapters 4 and 5). Since management was best able to

Exhibit
2.3

The Quality Trilogy

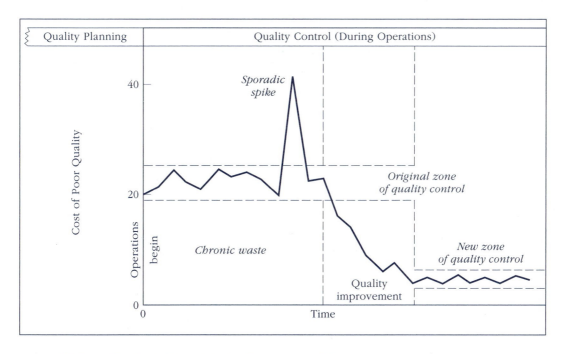

SOURCE: J.M. Juran, "The Quality Trilogy." *Quality Progress.* August 1986.

understand the impact of policies when expressed as dollars, he felt that a cost measure would be an effective form of communication. The graph in Exhibit 2.4 shows that costs of conformance (appraisal and prevention) increase as the defect rate declines. However, the costs of nonconformance (internal and external failures) decrease. The tradeoff leads to an optimal conformance level. Juran argued that most companies had costs of nonconformance as high as 50 to 80 percent of total quality costs. This implied that they operated at a quality level below the optimal.

The implication of this approach was that zero defects was not a practical goal, for at a certain level of quality, the costs of conformance would exceed those of nonconformance. Since further improvements in quality would not be justified, the emphasis should then be on maintenance of quality levels. Juran (1993) has argued in recent years that improvements in technology have now made zero defects a realizable goal.

In Juran's view, Total Quality Management involves several steps:

1. A quality planning council consisting of senior managers establish policies, set quality goals, provide the resources to carry out the plans, and change the performance review system to include attainment of the quality goals.

**Exhibit
2.4**

Juran's Cost of Quality Curves

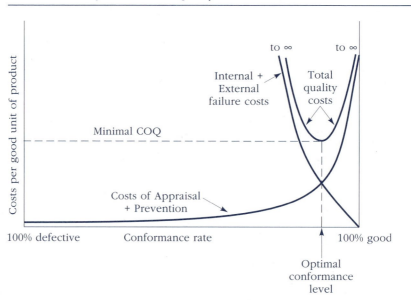

2. The goals should not be based on historical performance. Instead, external customer goals should be based on benchmarks. Internal customer goals should be aimed at getting rid of waste.
3. The organization infrastructure may need to be altered to meet the organization's quality goals. For example, Analog Devices Inc. long used financial measures to evaluate performance. To support the quality goals, they devised an additional system of measures including on-time delivery and defect rate.
4. Resources need to be made available to carry out the plans. In this regard, one obvious area is training. Training costs can be substantial. One company traditionally provided a training budget for each department. When the training budget was not spent by the end of the year, managers would use it to make their performance against budget look favorable. Once the company decided to embark on a TQM program, it included as a measure of quality the percentage of training budget spent by the department manager.

Crosby

Crosby originally intended to follow his father's profession, podiatry, but he soon abandoned these studies and began working as a reliability engineer for the Crosley Corporation and later joined the Martin Marietta Corporation. He became involved with the Pershing missile project which achieved an exceptionally high level of quality. In 1965 he joined ITT as a corporate vice president of quality, the first one in the United States. In 1979 he launched a consulting practice focused on quality.

Crosby described quality as "free" and argued that zero defects was a desirable and achievable goal. He defined quality as conformance to requirements. Accordingly, a Pinto meeting the requirements for a Pinto was a quality product just as much as was a Cadillac conforming to Cadillac requirements. Recognizing that improving quality by increasing the level of inspection would raise costs, he insisted that the way to achieve zero defects was to improve prevention techniques.

Exhibit 2.5 shows the relationship between the cost of conformance and quality. Conformance costs include appraisal and prevention costs. The traditional view, as expressed by Juran, is that the cost of appraisal must increase if quality is to increase. Crosby's contribution was that, by improving prevention approaches, the cost would decline since the entire quality-appraisal tradeoff curve would move in the direction shown.

He articulated his view of quality as the **four absolutes of quality management:**

1. Quality means conformance to requirements. Requirements needed to be clearly specified so that everyone knew what was expected of them.
2. Quality comes from prevention. And prevention was a result of training, discipline, example, leadership, and more.
3. Quality performance standard is zero defects. Errors should not be tolerated.
4. Quality measurement is the price of nonconformance.

Exhibit
2.5

Crosby's Interpretation of Conformance Costs

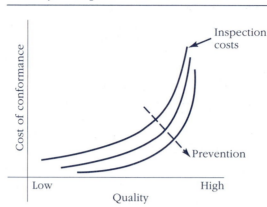

In order to improve quality, Crosby proposed a 14-point program:

1. Demonstrate management commitment by being convinced that quality improvement is needed and subscribing to a written quality policy. This policy should specify clearly that each person is expected to perform exactly as specified or cause the specifications to be changed to match the needs of the company or the customer.
2. Form quality improvement teams. These should be cross-functional and include department heads to oversee the quality improvement process. The team of department heads should be responsible for promoting quality through the entire company.
3. Establish measurements for quality in all activities. Although many of these measures could be error rates, he also included some others. As examples, he suggested that accounting could use the percentage of late reports; plant engineering could use time lost because of equipment failures.
4. Evaluate the cost of quality and use it to identify where quality improvements could be profitably made.
5. Raise the awareness of quality through the organization. Get employees involved by making them aware of costs.
6. Take corrective action to improve quality in areas identified in the previous steps.
7. Plan for zero defects. Using members of the quality improvement team, plan a zero defects program that fits the company and its culture.
8. Train all employees to carry out their part of the quality improvement program.
9. Hold a Zero Defects Day to signal to all employees that the company has established a new performance standard.

10. Encourage people to set goals for themselves and their groups. These goals should be specific and measurable, and progress should be measured against them.

11. Remove obstacles that prevent employees from achieving these goals by encouraging them to report these obstacles to management.

12. Provide recognition for those who participate. This should be public and nonfinancial.

13. Establish quality councils consisting of team chairpersons and quality professionals. They should meet regularly, share experiences, and generate ideas.

14. Do it all over again to stress that quality improvement is a continuous process.

In addition to using the Cost-of-Quality concept as a way to motivate management, Crosby developed a **management maturity grid** (Exhibit 2.6) in which he listed five stages ranging from uncertainty to certainty. In the first stage, management fails to see quality as a tool; problems are handled by "firefighting" and are rarely resolved; there are no organized quality improvement activities. By the last stage, the company is convinced that quality is essential to the company's success; problems are generally prevented; and quality improvement activities are regular and continuing.

A theme that is more evident in Crosby's writings than in those of the others is the scope of quality. It is not related solely to the product or service the company delivers. Moreover, it is not simply defects. For any process to be performed in a quality fashion it should conform to specifications. Measures could be developed for each process. TQM would encompass all processes in the company.

Feigenbaum

Armand Feigenbaum joined General Electric in Schenectady, New York, in 1944. While working on the jet engines he found that statistical techniques helped him improve their performance, and, as a result, GE put him in charge of its quality programs. Later, at MIT he developed the concept of Total Quality Control. In 1968 he founded his own consulting company, General Systems. Throughout his career he promoted the concept of Total Quality Control.

Feigenbaum defines total quality as an excellence-driven rather than a defect-driven concept. In his view quality is defined by the customer, and in this regard he is similar to Juran. He also feels that the quality philosophy extends beyond the factory floor to include all of the functions in an organization. This is similar to Crosby's view of a broader scope for TQM. In order to persuade management to adopt a quality strategy, he also used the Cost-of-Quality approach. Brocka and Brocka (1992) assembled Feigenbaum's prescription as 19 steps to quality improvement.

These steps emphasize an integrated systemic approach to improving quality that is driven by top management. This approach requires that management have

Exhibit

2.6

Crosby's Five Stages of Quality Maturity

QUALITY MANAGEMENT MATURITY GRID

RATER _____

MEASUREMENT CATEGORIES	STAGE 1: UNCERTAINTY	STAGE II: AWAKENING
Management understanding and attitude	No comprehension of quality as a management tool. Tend to blame quality department for "quality problems."	Recognizing that quality management may be of value but not willing to provide money or time to make it all happen.
Quality organization status	Quality is hidden in manufacturing or engineering departments. Inspection probably not part of organization. Emphasis on appraisal and sorting.	A stronger quality leader is appointed but main emphasis is still on appraisal and moving the product. Still part of manufacturing or other.
Problem handling	Problems are fought as they occur; no resolution; inadequate definition; lots of yelling and accusations.	Teams are set up to attack major problems. Long-range solutions are not solicited.
Cost of quality as % of sales	Reported: unknown Actual: 20%	Reported: 3% Actual: 18%
Quality Improvement actions	No organized activities. No understanding of such activities.	Trying obvious "motivational" short-range efforts.
Summation of company quality posture	"We don't know why we have problems with quality."	"Is it absolutely necessary to always have problems with quality?"

Source: Crosby, P.B., *Quality Is Free*, Copyright 1980, New American Library, reproduced with permission of McGraw-Hill, Inc.

Exhibit 2.6 Cont.

UNIT _____

STAGE III: ENLIGHTENMENT	STAGE IV: WISDOM	STAGE V: CERTAINTY
While going through quality improvement program learn more about quality management; becoming supportive and helpful.	Participating. Understand absolutes of quality management. Recognize their personal role in continuing emphasis.	Consider quality management as essential part of company system.
Quality department reports to top management, all appraisal is incorporated and manager has role in management of company.	Quality manager is an officer of company; effective status reporting and preventive action. Involved with consumer affairs and special assignments.	Quality manager on board of directors. Prevention is main concern. Quality is a thought leader.
Corrective action communication established. Problems are faced openly and resolved in an orderly way.	Problems are identified early in their development. All functions are open to suggestion and improvement.	Except in the most unusual cases, problems are prevented.
Reported: 8% Actual: 12%	Reported: 6.5% Actual 8%	Reported: 2.5% Actual: 2.5%
Implementation of the 14-step program with thorough understanding and establishment of each step.	Continuing the 14-step program and starting Make Certain.	Quality Improvement is a normal and continued activity.
"Through management commitment and quality improvement we are identifying and resolving our problems."	"Defect prevention is a routine part of our operation."	"We know why we do not have problems with quality."

an understanding of what quality means and the benefits to be obtained as it relates to the company's profitability. As leaders, management had to demonstrate that quality was everybody's job. Feigenbaum believed that the jobs of the quality inspectors should be redefined and that they should act as internal consultants promoting new methods and techniques. The organization's focus should be on improving quality as defined by the customer. These improvements would be achieved primarily through statistical methods; through the control of processes starting with product design; and through installation and field service. Automation would be used to improve quality only after all other methods had been tried.

Feigenbaum's ideas include elements of the ideas described by Deming, Juran, and Crosby. He advocates constructing a total system managing the entire value-chain connecting supplier to customer; he argues that many of the nonvalue-adding activities in a company exist to correct product defects; he urges the involvement of all employees; and, more importantly he argues that quality be part of the employee culture as an ethic that supports the constant improvement of performance. However, more than any of the others Feigenbaum adopts a user-based approach to quality. "If you want to find out about your quality, go out and ask your customer." He has developed several quantitative methods for improving product quality and prefers these methods to the more traditional approaches of automating to improve quality. However, it is significant that few of his methods are intended to determine the customers' needs. Product improvements are based on experience obtained by using the product in the field. Unlike Deming who advocated fewer suppliers, Feigenbaum concentrates on monitoring the supplier's quality. As one supplier improves its quality, he encourages others to meet the new standards.

Whereas the others argued that their approaches be used for any process in the organization, Feigenbaum focuses on quality of the product or service created by the organization. Like the other gurus, he feels that top management should be the driver, but unlike others, he explicitly defined a role for the quality control staff as facilitators. The methods he developed were based primarily on statistics. And while he advocated a customer focus and the total participation of employees, he did not develop specific approaches to achieving these goals.

Ishikawa

Kaoru Ishikawa graduated from the University of Tokyo in 1939 with a degree in applied chemistry. His father was Ichiro Ishikawa, the president of both the powerful Keidanren (an industry group) and JUSE, and in this capacity he gave his son access to the top Japanese industrialists and engineers. From the beginning Kaoru Ishikawa advocated the use of statistical methods. His life was totally committed to the promotion of Total Quality through Japan.

Ishikawa believed that all divisions and all employees in the organization should be involved in studying and promoting quality control by learning seven statistical tools. He created one of these tools, the cause-and-effect diagram, which is also known as the Ishikawa diagram. Ishikawa's second concept was that of the customer as primary in defining quality. He defined the customer as the next person in the line, the person who gets your work, or anybody who relies on you. In other words, the customer was not only the person who paid for the final product, but also included co-workers. Ishikawa's third concept was the **Quality Control Circles,** which involved putting workers into teams to solve quality problems. Using the seven tools Ishikawa outlined for analysis and problem solving, they would then implement their solutions with the support of management.

Ishikawa's quality philosophy can be summarized as a reliance on the education of the workforce. Educated workers could solve problems with products and processes and work to improve them. Management's role was to act as coach—listening to facts presented by the workers and helping them to apply the problem-solving tools. With a workforce trained in his approach, quality control would not be needed as a separate department since making quality products would be part of each worker's job.

Ishikawa understood the value of using teamwork in solving these problems. Quality Control Circles were composed of workers who understood the problem and who could implement the solution. Whenever a problem or an opportunity for improvement arose, the workers voluntarily formed the circles. These circles would then determine whether the solution achieved the targets, and if it did, they would standardize the activities, making it part of their "daily work." The process used by the circles was a standard process taught all Japanese companies through JUSE. It operationalized a process for continuous improvement called the P-D-C-A cycle that Deming introduced to Japan.

Ishikawa also had a strong bias for the user-based approach to quality—"Marketing is the entrance and exit of quality." He developed a system to convey these customer requirements to the entire company. Conceptualizing the next person in line as an internal customer was a key to this system. The person closest to the customer knew the customer's needs the best. As an internal customer, this person's needs were known to the supplying workers. These workers would transmit their needs to their suppliers and so on up the line. In this way, each worker knew what had to be done in order to meet the needs of the final customer.

Ishikawa's genius was in creating methods that could be taught to large numbers of people and organizational approaches that could be used to mobilize them. He took the concepts proposed by people like Deming and Juran and brought them to the level of the common worker.

Taguchi

Genichi Taguchi formerly an employee of Nippon Telephone and Telegraph, has had significant influence on the quality movement in Japan. His prime focus was in making statistics practical. For this endeavor he won the Deming Prize in 1960, and since then he has won the prize again on three separate occasions. His ideas are promoted in the United States through the American Supplier Institute.

Taguchi viewed quality as an issue for the entire company and focused on the use of statistical methods to improve quality, particularly in the area of product design. Two of his concepts are particularly significant:

- The loss function
- Design characteristics and "noise"

The loss function is described briefly here and discussed in more detail in Chapter 8. Like Crosby, Taguchi viewed quality as conformance to requirements. The **loss function** (Exhibit 2.7) attempts to provide a formal process for computing the cost of deviation from the target value. The cost measured in this case is a social cost. If a part is made and it meets the target dimensions exactly, the cost is very low. This is because people buying the product will be happy that the product is precisely as specified. However, if the dimension of a part deviates from the target, some people become unhappy. As the deviation increases, more people become unhappy and the social cost increases; Taguchi terms this social cost the loss. In his approach, by which the costs of deviating from the target can be evaluated; the loss due to product performance is defined as proportional to the square of the deviation from the target value. The costs can then be accumulated and communicated to management.

Taguchi's second contribution relates to the design of products. He postulated two causes for variations in products: design characteristics and "noise." On-line activities such as statistical control charts to check for defects control only some of this noise. The more significant causes of noise are "outer noise" and "inner noise." **Outer noise** is the result of variations in the operating environment and human errors and these are generally factors that cannot be controlled. **Inner**

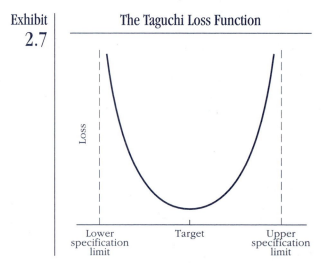

Exhibit 2.7 | The Taguchi Loss Function

noise is variation due to controllable factors such as deterioration. Both kinds of noise are more significantly impacted by off-line activities:

- System design
- Parameter design
- Tolerance design

System design involves designing a product to satisfy the customer's requirements. Besides functionality, Taguchi suggested additional criteria—robustness to changes in operating conditions, minimal functional variation due to use such as wear, and maximum value for the price. He used Quality Function Deployment (discussed in Chapter 10) to establish the customer's requirements and convert them to design characteristics.

Parameter design involves identifying key process variables that affect variation and then establishing levels for these parameters that will minimize the variation. Taguchi used statistical experimental designs to identify these parameters. The designs he created were new and enabled parameters to be identified with greater efficiency.

Tolerance design identifies the components that contribute most to variations in the final product and then sets appropriate tolerances for these components. The object is to identify the most significant components and tighten tolerances only for those instead of all components.

Taguchi's primary methodology is design of experiments. Unlike Ishikawa's seven basic tools, Taguchi's approach is very complex, but it has proved very powerful for evaluating new product designs and new processes.

Taguchi's approach to quality focuses on conformance, and in this regard his philosophy is similar to Crosby's. However, whereas Crosby used a managerial approach, Taguchi used a statistical approach. Crosby's approach can be characterized as qualitative; in contrast, Taguchi was quantitative. Typical of the difference in approaches is the definition of costs related to quality. Crosby used the Cost-of-Quality concept in which the cost categories are defined by the organization. Crosby provides general guidelines, but the allocation of costs is unique to each organization. On the other hand, Taguchi specified a loss function with a defined relationship to deviation from target. The loss function is a standard approach for all organizations.

Summarizing the Philosophies

Although Deming, Juran, and Crosby are the most well-known TQM gurus in the United States, it could be argued that Feigenbaum, Ishikawa, and Taguchi have been as influential as they in defining the scope of TQM. In broad terms, they all agree with each other. TQM seeks to improve productivity, and it does so by focusing on satisfying the customer and by involving employees in this process. TQM has the practical goal of improving the bottom line and at the same time raising employee morale.

In recent years, many of these thinkers have begun to view TQM as a philosophy of work. Feigenbaum calls it an ethic for workers. Crosby suggests that managers need a "full understanding," and Juran wants all employees to internalize the desire for continuous improvement. Deming is perhaps the closest to stating it is a philosophy when he equates TQM with "profound knowledge." Clearly, over the years TQM has evolved beyond being a set of tools that ensure a product of good quality.

◆ THE FOURTH APPROACH: EVOLUTION OF QUALITY THINKING IN JAPAN

Before the war the Japanese ensured quality primarily through inspection. The early efforts to develop quality standards were generally theoretical and had little impact on practice. However, while many consumer products were considered shoddy, products made to support the war effort were of extremely high quality. But these were not the result of a systematic effort to obtain good quality; instead they reflected the skills of the craftsmen involved.

The current approach to quality started after World War II. Shiba, Graham, and Walden (1992) chronicle its evolution as a sequence of four steps:

- Fitness to standard
- Fitness to use
- Fitness of cost
- Fitness to latent requirement

Fitness to standard is the concept of conformance and its objective is to build a product that meets the specifications set by the designer. The impetus for this effort came from Douglas MacArthur at the end of World War II, when he asked for reliable radios to transmit propaganda programs through Japan. But the Japanese manufacturers could not provide them. Radios relied on vacuum tubes, and Japanese vacuum tube manufacturers had a 90 percent failure rate. So, he brought two engineers from Bell Laboratories in New Jersey (Homer Sarasohn and Charles Protzman) to teach the Japanese to build quality products. They began by teaching the Japanese the basics of Statistical Quality Control. These were the ideas developed by Walter Shewhart at Bell Labs.

MacArthur required the leading industrialists to attend the seminars. For this audience, it was important to establish the business reasons for needing quality control. Accordingly, the seminars started with the question "Why is your company in business?" Then, the discussion moved into the importance of having a company philosophy that expected more than just profits. The philosophy of the Newport News Shipyard was used as an example:

> We shall build good ships here
> At a profit if we can

> At a loss if we must
> But, always good ships

Sarasohn and Protzman hammered home the message over and over again throughout the seminar: A critical reason for a company to exist was to make quality products; profits were secondary. If sufficient attention was paid to quality, they argued, the profits would follow.

At the beginning the factories were run by Americans, and over time the plan was to turn these over to the Japanese managers. Sarasohn and Protzman believed that the Japanese managers and technical people should be trained in quality control before they would be qualified to take over. They were instrumental in bringing Deming to Japan to teach and promote the tools of quality control. He gave his first lecture to 230 Japanese engineers and technicians in July 1950.

The purpose at this stage was to define clearly the product specifications and specify the steps needed to make the product. Then managers would train the workers and have inspectors check the work to ensure it had been done properly. These were the steps of the Shewhart cycle, which is also called the **P D C A cycle** for Plan-Do-Check-Act. In the Plan stage, the process and standards were established; in the Do stage, the process was executed and the product made; then, the work was Checked; and if there was a deviation from standard, Action had to be taken to correct the process.

This approach greatly improved the quality of the finished product. But three major issues surfaced. First, when inspectors removed defective products, workers felt the inspectors had passed judgment on their capabilities. Thus, the workers began to view inspectors as adversaries. If, at the same time, managers were being pressured to produce, the pressure would be passed on to the worker. As workers wanted to satisfy their manager with increased production, they would try to influence the inspectors. As a result, defective products were sometimes allowed to pass. Second, inspectors were not available to check products after each operation. Instead, they would perform their tests after a series of operations were completed. Thus, when faults were found it was difficult to determine which worker or which operation created the defect. The approach encouraged workers to hide their errors rather than suggest changes to improve the process. Finally, the approach neglected the customer's needs. Each worker completed his or her task according to specifications, using the process designed by the engineers. Whether the product met the needs of the customer was not their concern.

Fitness to use is understanding the needs of the customer. Juran popularized this term, which he defined as having five dimensions:

- Quality of design
- Quality of conformance
- Availability
- Safety
- Field use

Quality of conformance is the same as the fitness to standard concept. The remaining parameters are based on the user's perceptions. Quality of design is a measure of craftsmanship, and it sets apart a Steinway or a Rolls Royce from the competition. Availability and safety are also clearly user-based criteria. Field use is a key parameter. It ensures that the product can be used as needed by the customer. Thus, a high-performance car like a Porsche would probably not meet the needs of a retired couple who use the car primarily for short trips to the supermarket. The introduction of airbags by the automobile companies is an example of fitness for use by satisfying the safety dimension.

This approach continued to rely on inspecting the quality in the product. When the customer demanded tighter tolerances, the inspector would simply discard more product as defective, resulting in higher costs. This led to the thinking that quality could only be improved by more inspection.

At this point, Juran introduced the concept of the Cost of Quality (COQ). In addition to inspection costs, Juran posited costs of prevention, and internal and external failures. Juran maintained that the internal and external failure costs were significantly higher than the costs of appraisal and prevention. The COQ estimates would show that focusing on inspection and prevention would improve quality, thus reducing failure costs and overall costs. This thinking led to the next stage.

Fitness of cost was aimed at obtaining high quality and low cost. In order to achieve this dimension, the product and process would have to be designed so as not to have any rejects. The approach to achieving fitness of cost would be to design the product so that it could be easily manufactured. The process would be structured in such a way that it would allow the product to be made within specified tolerances. Finally, the product should be tested frequently as it proceeds through the process. This "build a little, test a little" concept would be costly to implement if an inspector were required at each stage. In addition, the experience through the earlier stages had shown the adversarial tensions that this approach created between inspector and worker.

Ishikawa suggested that each worker be regarded as a customer to the preceding worker. As noted earlier, he called each worker an internal customer. Essentially, each worker performed a task that the next person in line would check. If a defect was discovered, the cause could be traced and fixed more readily.

This notion also expanded the scope of the job to include inspection of work done at the previous station. Furthermore, since workers now received rapid feedback on work performed, they could continuously improve the process. In order to achieve this improvement, workers needed to learn some simple analytical tools. The seven statistical tools were now taught to all workers.

Finally, this stage also saw a broadening in the definition of quality. In addition to viewing quality in terms of the proportion of defects, the definition expanded to include other elements. Shiba notes that Toto Limited in Japan lists five dimensions for quality improvement:

- Q Quality
- C Cost
- D Delivery
- S Safety
- M Morale

The Toyota Motor Company in Lexington, Kentucky, lists four dimensions:

- Safety
- Morale
- Quality
- Productivity

It is important to note that each of these dimensions was related to improving the practices on the shop floor. While conditions improved for the average Japanese worker, the companies found that they were increasingly susceptible to competition from developing countries. This was due partly to the less critical nature of the human issues of safety and morale in those countries. In searching for a natural advantage, they looked at their closeness to the customer. This led to the next concept.

Fitness to latent requirement is aimed at determining the customer's needs before the customer becomes aware of them. An example involves the 1984 Toyota Camry LE. Drivers getting into their car at night have trouble finding the key to the door and the ignition. So, when the door handle of the car is pulled, a light shines around the keyhole. Once the driver opens the door and gets in, a light shines on the ignition switch.

Kano, a noted Japanese TQM consultant, created the concept of latent requirements and explained the concept using the **Kano diagram** (Exhibit 2.8). The horizontal axis indicates the level of functionality of a specific product characteristic. Some characteristics are categorized as "must-be." These are characteristics the user expects to find. For example, a student entering a classroom expects the seats and desks to be clean and the room temperature to be within a comfortable range. When these conditions do not exist, the student will be very dissatisfied; but if they do exist, the characteristics are taken for granted. The one-dimensional characteristics are directly related to customer satisfaction. An example may be the lighting in the classroom or the amount of desk space available for writing. As the brightness of the lights increase, satisfaction increases. The "attractive" characteristics are the latent requirements. If these are not present, the customer is not aware that they are missing. Their absence does not detract from the level of customer satisfaction. However, if they are present satisfaction increases dramatically. An example for a classroom might be chairs on rollers.

Products of quality-sensitive American companies exhibit each of the different quality concepts. Consider the evolution of the telephone at AT&T: The original rotary phone reflected quality to standard. Each phone was made with the same

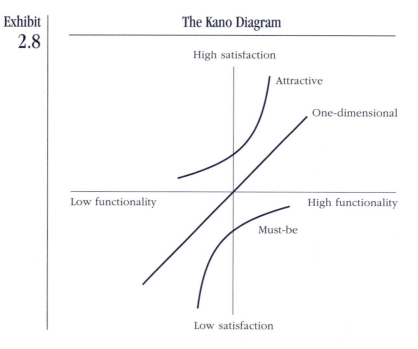

Exhibit

2.8

The Kano Diagram

High satisfaction

Attractive

One-dimensional

Low functionality

High functionality

Must-be

Low satisfaction

black shell. The mechanics of the phone were thoroughly tested against the standards. Standard practices for each manufacturing task and for each level of inspection were thoroughly documented.

AT&T recognized that when in use the phone handle often got knocked off its cradle and got damaged. So, they made the handle stronger. Tests would check samples of handsets to see whether they could withstand being dropped several times from a height of 50 feet. Another finding was the number of wrong phone numbers dialed. They found that the dialers would put their fingers in the wrong holes. To improve the accuracy of the dialing, white dots were centered in the holes.

As cost became an issue, the design was changed to reduce costs while maintaining quality. Instead of two brass bells, one brass bell provided an adequate ring. Various materials were tried to replace the expensive metal bottom. Finally, the electromechanical technology was replaced by electronics.

In order to uncover latent requirements, they studied how the phone was used. For people who use the phone in a dark room, they provided lit dials to enable dialing numbers in the dark. People often write memos for others, so one of the phones designed had a cork bulletin board attached.

The previous sections indicate that as TQM evolved, its scope broadened. At the beginning stages, TQM related to improving the quality of the product or service offered by the company. The definition of quality was elusive, but the two approaches that gained widespread acceptance are:

1. Manufacturing-based emphasizing conformance to standards
2. User-based stating the customer is the ultimate judge of quality

In order to implement both approaches, a company needed to decipher the customer's needs and convert these to the standards. Then as customer's needs changed, the company would respond with changes to standards. The key to being responsive was (and still is) to have a customer focus and a set of tools and management practices that enable continual improvement of the product.

Years of experience have shown that to implement a conformance-based approach, it is necessary to have total participation of all employees in the company. By educating them in problem-solving tools, they can be empowered to respond to customer and process issues. So, the foundation on which a successful TQM effort rests includes

- Customer focus
- Total participation
- Continual improvement

Consider the two vignettes at the beginning of this chapter. Domino's was a company that emphasized all three areas. All employees were encouraged to participate in the "Olympics." With customers as judges, employees gained a fuller understanding of the customer's needs. Finally, the winners suggested improvements to management which were implemented. In contrast, Steinway represents a traditional approach to management. Workers focused on their task, and when asked for improvements, their suggestions seemed to be within the narrow boundaries of their tasks. Management had no systematic process in place for encouraging suggestions. In addition, while the workers performed their individual tasks well, they did not have direct communication with the customer. Their job was to make the product to meet the standards and satisfy the inspectors. Thus, while they produced pianos of extremely high quality, Steinway would not be a good example of a TQM organization.

The previous section described the evolution of TQM in Japan. When American companies began to introduce TQM to their organizations, they observed additional opportunities. Indirect staff had long been a growing expense. The information they created and processed resulted in a "hidden factory" that sometimes employed more people than the real factory. It seemed a natural step to apply the tools that worked so well on the shop floor to the office environment. TQM was applied to functions as diverse as accounting and plant maintenance. Each function would define its processes and the "customer." Then those involved with the process could work to improve the process effectiveness much as workers did in a production environment.

At the same time, management continued to focus on defining the customer's needs. They soon came to realize that customers also valued factors such as variety of product, cost, or on-time delivery. The definition of quality was broadened to include these. A similar expansion of scope had occurred earlier in Japan during the fitness for cost stage. Then the definition of quality had been made broader to improve the environment for the workers on the shop floor. Now, it was expanded to better serve the customer's needs.

Next management realized that the TQM tools used to involve employees in making defect-free products could be employed to gain their support of companywide strategic goals. The Japanese had already formalized a process, termed **Hoshin-kanri**, for the vertical deployment of the company strategy. Several companies studied this methodology and adapted it to their companies.

As companies continued to emphasize TQM practices, employees began to internalize an ethic of continual improvement. Such employees could be expected to search out nonvalue-added activities and suggest ways to eliminate them. They would also be interested in learning and supporting the company's strategic goals. These attitudes form the basis of a learning organization, one that would find it easier to change.

Over time TQM becomes a way of life and part of the company culture. Gradually, the emphasis of TQM shifts from managing quality to ensuring quality management. Today the more progressive companies use TQM as a management philosophy. Peter Drucker has coined the phrase "Zero Defect Management" to mean excellence in management. For these companies TQM and Zero Defect Management are synonymous.

◆ Summary

This chapter develops a definition of Total Quality Management that is used throughout the book. It also introduces several topics:

1. Dimensions of Quality—a framework for defining quality of products and services
2. Cost of Quality and its elements
3. Quality of conformance
4. User-based quality
5. The evolution of the quality philosophy in Japan

The objective of Total Quality Management practices is to improve the performance of an organization. In doing so, it relies on tools that can be placed in three broad categories: Continual Improvement (many of these are statistical tools), Customer Focus, and Total Participation. There has also been increasing recognition among businesses that such tools have a broader range of application.

Recently, more companies are beginning to apply it to improve management practices in addition to products and services.

TQM also represents a philosophy. The leading thinkers in the field generally agree that the three dominant themes mirror the categories of tools. They urge each employee to adopt a way of life that includes continual improvement, customer focus (where the customer is defined as any person affected by what you do), and total participation (which requires respecting others). IBM's philosophy articulated by Tom Watson, Sr., captures the essence:

> Three things we believe in:
> Respect for the individual,
> Striving for excellence
> Service to the customers.

◆ Key Terms

Transcendent approach
Product-based approach
User-based approach
Fitness for use
Manufacturing-based approach
Conformance to requirements
Value-based approach
Reliability of a product
Conformance
Durability
Serviceability
Aesthetics
Perceived quality
Reliability of service

Responsiveness
Assurance
Empathy
Tangibles
ISO 9000 standards
Keiretsu
Common causes
Special causes
Profound knowledge
Quality Trilogy
Chronic waste
Four absolutes of quality management
Management maturity grid
Quality Control Circle

Loss function
Outer noise
Inner noise
System design
Parameter design
Tolerance design
Fitness to standard
P D C A cycle
Fitness to use
Fitness of cost
Fitness to latent requirement
Kano diagram
Hoshin-kanri

◆ Assignments

1. Imagine you are a member of a large extended family. Every year this family gets together for a "fun" cookout. Typically, about 50 people come to this gathering, which is held in a large field adjoining cousins Ralph and Ruth's house.

Each family brings desserts, drinks, potato chips, and so on. One person is responsible for cooking the hamburgers. Ralph and Ruth usually cook these on a large grill rented for the occasion. This year Ralph and Ruth proposed you be the cook. They noted you had talked incessantly about the importance of quality. So, as the family expert, they argued you would cook a quality hamburger.

You took the assignment seriously. The plan is to buy the meat, buns, and fixings the day before. The meat will be made into patties and refrigerated. On the day of the cookout, you will put the fixings out on a large table for each person to add to their hamburger. You intend to cook the hamburgers and toast the buns. Describe the characteristics of your quality hamburger:

Patty

    Meat   _____

    Size   _____

    Doneness   _____

    Other   _____

Bun

    Type   _____

    Size   _____

    Doneness   _____

    Other   _____

    Other considerations

    _____

    _____

    _____

    _____

    _____

2. Look up the report for a product in *Consumer Reports*. Use the report comparing it to the competition to answer the following:
   a. Which of the eight quality dimensions listed by Garvin are used to evaluate the product?
   b. How does the "best buy" product compare with the competition on each dimension?

3. For each of the following services, write one item you would look for or a question you would want answered in order to determine quality along the five service quality dimensions:
   a. Dentist
   b. Hotel
   c. School

4. The TQM philosophy aims at building an organization that stresses Continual Improvement, Customer Focus, and Total Participation. How do each of Deming's 14 points support these dimensions?

5. Categorize the following product improvements as fitness to standard, fitness for use, fitness to cost, or fitness to latent requirements:
   a. Headrests in the front seats of cars
   b. Rearview mirrors that darken when reflecting headlights of following cars
   c. Rear lights that turn on when reversing
   d. Plastic bumpers in place of metal bumpers
   e. Change-holder
   f. Seat belts
   g. Automatic braking systems

◆ Bibliography

Aune, A. and A. Rao; "ISO 9000 Standards, A Baseline for Excellence", *Target,* Sept. Oct. 1992, pp. 23–29.

Berry, L .L, V. A. Zeithaml, and A. Parasuraman. "Five Imperatives for Improving Service Quality" *Sloan Management Review,* (Summer 1990): 29–38.

Brocka, B., and M. S. Brocka. *Quality Management: Implementing the Best Ideas of the Masters,* Homewood, Ill.: Business-One. Irwin, 1992.

Broh, R. A. *Managing Quality for Higher Profits,* New York: McGraw-Hill, 1982.

Crosby, P. B. *Quality Is Free,* New York: New American Library, 1980.

Deming, W. E. "Improvement of Quality and Productivity Through Action by Management," *National Productivity Review,* (Winter 1981–1982): 12–22.

Dobyns, L., and C. Crawford-Mason. *Quality or Else.* Boston: Houghton-Mifflin, 1991.

Feigenbaum, A. V. *Total Quality Control.* 3d ed. New York: McGraw-Hill, 1991.

Fitzsimmons, J. A., and M. J. Fitzsimmons. *Service Management for Competitive Advantage.* New York: McGraw-Hill, 1994.

Garvin, D. A. *Managing Quality: The Strategic and Competitive Edge.* New York: Free Press, 1988.

Gitlow, H. S. and S. J. Gitlow. *The Deming Guide to Quality and Competitive Position.* Englewood Cliffs, N.J.: Prentice-Hall, 1987.

Hopper, K. "Quality, Japan and the US: the First Chapter." *Quality Progress* (September 1985): 61–69.

The International Quality Study: Best Practices Report. Cleveland, Ohio: Ernst and Young and the American Quality Foundation, 1992.

Ishikawa, K. *What Is Total Quality Control? The Japanese Way. Trans.* David Lu. *London: Prentice-Hall International, 1985.*

Juran, J. M. "The Quality Trilogy." *Quality Progress* (August 1986): 19–24.

Juran, J. M, and F. M. Gryna. *Quality Planning and Analysis* 3rd ed. New York: McGraw-Hill, 1993.

Lovelock C. H. *Services Marketing.* 2nd ed. Englewood Cliffs, N.J.: Prentice-Hall, 1991.

Mahoney, F. X., and C. G.Thor. *The TQM Trilogy.* New York: AMACOM, 1994.

Shiba, S., A. Graham, and D. Walden. *A New American TQM: Four Practical revolutions in Management,* Cambridge, Mass.: Center for Quality Management, 1993.

Tuchman, B. W., "Decline of Quality." *New York Times Magazine,* November 2, 1980 p. 38.

The Baldrige Award

◆ ◆ ◆

John Fooks, Vice President, Westinghouse, Electric Corporation

"*W*inning the award accelerated what we were doing in the organization and contributed in a powerful way. We are no longer 'perfect,' like we used to be. We are better than we were and getting even better. We found the Baldrige Award a very powerful reinforcement of the approach we started in the early 1980s."

John West, Manager of Corporate Quality Improvement, Federal Express Corporation

"*F*or us, the Malcolm Baldrige Award was a great scavenger hunt—finding the right information. We went into it for self-improvement. Fred Smith, our CEO, didn't allow us to send it in until four or five days before the deadline. It started a lot of self-analysis, but the self-improvement is just beginning."

Wayland Hicks, Executive Vice President, Xerox Corporation

"*W*hy did it take so long for American organizations to wake up to the power of teams? We're very individualistic. We almost roll out of the womb in this country thinking about personal achievement and success. Even though quality teams were successful in Japan, the U.S. was not ready for them. For us, it took a crisis of great proportions. If it weren't for the crisis, we still might not have equality teams. Xerox also pays much more attention to customer complaints. They used to be handled in a laissez-faire manner. Now the complaints go into a tracking system, and if they are not fixed they go to the next level, right up to the CEO."

Rosetta Riley, Director, Customer Satisfaction, Cadillac Motor Car Division

"Our reason for applying had nothing to do with winning. We looked at the guidelines and decided that this was exactly what we needed. You are on this quality improvement journey and you're never quite sure where you are. The Malcolm Baldrige Award assessment process told us that our processes were right and there is a light at the end of the tunnel. The winners understand the approaches to quality of "quality gurus" such as Deming or Juran. But, for the most part, they do not subscribe to one particular philosophy. They choose the most useful parts of each approach. We use every single one of them. We tried Juran, Ishikawa, Crosby, and Deming. None of them alone worked for us. Our success came when we turned to our people."*

◆ INTRODUCTION

During the 1980s, U.S. corporations found themselves consistently lagging behind Japanese competitors. Japan's success can be largely attributed to its Quality Movement, and this success forced U.S. industries and Congress to face reality: American companies had to adapt product and service "quality" to remain competitive in the United States and world markets. In addition, this action would help improve the American "quality" and standard of living. Today, the Malcolm Baldrige National Quality Award and related state awards function as a major component of the successful response to the quality challenge faced by U.S. organizations.

Several professional associations, such as the American Society for Quality Control (ASQC), and consulting companies, such as Philip Crosby Associates and ODI, developed Total Quality Management expertise which they, in turn, conveyed to corporations. Similarly, many U.S. companies, such as Motorola, Xerox, and AT&T, developed Total Quality Management practices of their own. Yet, a greater impetus was needed if any notable national progress was to be made.

◆ OVERVIEW OF HISTORY, PURPOSE, AND OPERATIONS

Legislation

The Malcolm Baldrige National Quality Award was established by the Malcolm Baldrige National Quality Improvement Act of 1987 (Public Law 100-107, signed by President Reagan on August 20, 1987). It is designed to annually recognize U.S. organizations that excel in quality management and succeed in related perfor-

---

*The four quotes are all taken from "Lessons From the Malcolm Baldrige Award: Implications for Management Practice, Reasearch, and Education," SEI Center for Advanced Studies in Management, The Wharton School, February 8, 1991.

mance criteria, such as profitability and market share. Privately or publicly owned businesses in the United States are eligible to apply for the Award. Interestingly, the Deming Prize, the Baldrige Award's Japanese equivalent, was established in 1950, which demonstrates just how slow the United States was to recognize the need for change.

Award Purpose

Faced with an erosion of American competitiveness and lack of attention to quality, the Award constitutes the federal government's response to the need of United States industries to make substantial improvements in global competitiveness. The stated, immediate purposes of the Award are to promote:

- Awareness of quality as an increasingly important element in competitiveness
- Understanding of the requirements for performance excellence
- Sharing of information on successful performance strategies and the benefits derived from implementation of these strategies

Roles and Responsibility

The Award functions as a joint public-private initiative. There are several organizations that perform integrated roles. Funding is provided mainly through the Foundation for the Malcolm Baldrige National Quality Award, whose primary aim is to raise sufficient funds to permanently endow the Award Program. Trustees are leaders from U.S. corporations. Yet, probably the greatest contributions are made through the extensive voluntary efforts of corporations and individuals.

The Department of Commerce has responsibility for the Award. The National Institute of Standards (NIST), an agency of the Department's Technology Administration, manages the Award Program. This role includes the development of technical facets such as the Criteria and ensurance of all processes and activities. The ASQC assists in administering the Award Program under contract to NIST. This role includes managing of applicants, handling scoring information, and coordinating feedback reporting.

The Board of Overseers advises the Department of Commerce about the Award and is responsible for evaluating every aspect of the program and how it serves the national interest. The Board is appointed by the Secretary of Commerce and includes distinguished leaders from throughout the United States. Recommendations of the Board are made to the Secretary of Commerce and then to the Director of NIST.

The **Board of Examiners** evaluates Award applications, prepares feedback reports, and makes Award recommendations to the Director of NIST. Its members are Examiners, Senior Examiners, and Judges, all of whom are appointed annually by NIST through a competitive application process. Board members are expected to contribute significantly to building awareness of the importance of quality and to engage in activities that disseminate information.

Applications for the Award

Privately or publicly owned businesses located in the United States may apply for Awards. However, there are several restrictions concerning subsidiaries and overseas operations that limit the definition of a U.S. business. The eligibility of organizations is now limited to three categories of "for-profits": manufacturing companies, service companies, and small businesses (no more than 500 full-time employees). Award guidelines for education and health care are presently being established with a "pilot" test run of a Baldrige evaluation conducted in 1994 and a pilot of the application process for 1995.

Up to two awards can be given in each category each year. Award recipients may publicize and advertise their Awards, but they must follow certain guidelines in order to do so. Recipients are expected to share information about their successful quality programs with other U.S. organizations. The dissemination of information constitutes one of the Award's most successful outcomes.

All applicants are provided with a package that includes application forms, instructions, and details on the Award Criteria. The Award process starts with submission of the Eligibility Determination Form. Given eligibility, the candidate must then compile a written submission of no more than 75 pages according to the Award guidelines. Next, a multistage process occurs in which both Examiners and Judges participate. At this time, Examiners score the written submissions, reach group consensus for final scores, and conduct site visits. All applicants receive feedback reports, but considerable efforts are made to ensure the confidentiality of any applicant information obtained during the Award process.

The Award Criteria

The structure of the Examination Criteria is represented by the seven categories detailed in Exhibit 3.1 and summarized below.

- Leadership refers to the success of senior executives in creating, deploying, and maintaining a quality culture and related systems.
- Information and Analysis addresses the scope, validity, management, and use of data and information in quality planning to drive quality excellence.
- Strategic Quality Planning is the vehicle for integration of quality requirements into all business activities.
- Human Resource Development and Management refers to the efforts designed to realize the full potential of the workforce to meet quality achievements.
- Process Management is the design and operation of all work units and their relationships in order to achieve ever higher quality-related performance criteria.
- Quality and Operational Results are the quality levels and improvement trends in operational performance, including that of suppliers, that reflect the outcomes of the quality program.
- Customer Focus and Satisfaction refers to the effectiveness of the quality program to determine and effectively meet customer requirements.

| Exhibit 3.1 | Malcolm Baldrige Examination Categories: Names and Descriptions |

1. Leadership (90 points)

Senior executives' personal involvement in (a) creating and sustaining clear and visible customer-focused quality values, (b) integrating the quality values into the management system, and (c) reflected in how public responsibilities are addressed.

2. Information and Analysis (75 points)

(a) The scope, validity, analysis, management, and use of data and information to drive quality excellence and improve competitive performance, and (b) adequacy of the data, information, and analysis system to support improvement of customer focus, products, services, and internal operations.

3. Strategic Quality Planning (55 points)

(a) The process, (b) how all key quality requirements are integrated into overall business planning, (c) the short- and longer-term plans, and (d) how quality and performance requirements are deployed to all work units.

4. Human Resource Development and Management (140 points)

(a) The key elements of how full potential of the workforce is developed and realized to pursue the company's quality and performance objectives, and (b) the efforts to build and maintain an environment for quality excellence conducive to full participation and personal and organizational growth.

5. Process Management (140 points)

Systematic processes used to pursue ever-higher quality and company performance. The key elements of process management, including design, management of process quality for all work units and suppliers, systematic quality improvement, and quality assessment.

6. Quality and Operational Results (250 points)

(a) Quality levels and improvement trends in quality, operational performance, and supplier quality, and (b) current quality and performance levels relative to those of competitors.

7. Customer Focus and Satisfaction (250 points)

(a) Customer relationships, (b) knowledge of customer requirements and the key quality factors that determine marketplace competitiveness, (c) methods to determine customer satisfaction, current trends and levels of satisfaction, and (d) these results relative to competitors.

SOURCE: 1995 Malcolm Baldrige National Quality Award Criteria.

As the basis for bestowing recognition upon and furnishing feedback to the applicants, the Malcolm Baldrige National Quality Award guidelines and Criteria serve three purposes that reflect the more specific intent of the Award Program:

- To help elevate quality standards and expectations
- To facilitate communication and sharing among and within organizations of all types based on a common understanding of key quality requirements
- To serve as a working tool for planning, training, assessing, and other uses

Strict Award Criteria and a rigorous evaluation process ensure that, in order for a company to win the Award, it must demonstrate (1) a capability to achieve, measure, and continuously improve quality; (2) outstanding quality-related results; and (3) a documented causal relationship between results and process. Every effort is made by the Board of Overseers, NIST, ASQC, and the Board of Examiners to ensure continuous improvement of the Award Criteria and application review process.

Positioning the Award Criteria

The rationale for using the Award Criteria to judge the quality progress of an organization is presented by the guidelines in two ways. First, six key characteristics focus on the ability of the guidelines to provide for an objective assessment that captures the fundamentals of quality management, and second, four characteristics show how the Award requirements are linked to business performance.

The six key characteristics summarized in Exhibit 3.2 demonstrate three provisions of the Award Criteria: lack of prescriptiveness, comprehensiveness, and the actionability of connection to results. Considerable attention is paid to eliminating any prescriptiveness when training Examiners, conducting applicant evaluations, managing the Award application review process, and providing applicant feedback. Consequently, the Criteria and guidelines provide a way to assess progress in quality management without dictating the best means to achieve that progress. This provision is of great significance, given that many options available for implementation are surrounded with controversy about effectiveness.

The Award Criteria purport to be comprehensive. That is to say, it captures all those aspects essential for representing progress in quality management. Therefore, an applicant can be confident that the actions they have taken that are critical to their success will not be "missed" or considered irrelevant when an Award assessment is made. In order to achieve this comprehensiveness, many criticisms of the Baldrige Award Criteria that have identified areas of "deficiency" have been addressed and incorporated, and each year these changes have increased the comprehensiveness of the Criteria.

Such characteristics as "linking actions to results," "continuous learning," "its diagnostic nature," and "alignment" reflect the need to show that the criteria are purposeful or causal in nature. That is, the Award Criteria attempt to prove that well-specified systems, which incorporate the designated values and criteria, do

Exhibit

3.2

Key Characteristics of the Award Criteria

CHARACTERISTIC	DESCRIPTION
Directed toward business results	The values are directed toward company performance, and results are a composite of seven key performance areas.
Nonprescriptive	There is an integrated set of evaluation requirements incorporating the 10 core values, yet no specifications about how to implement the core values in a particular company.
Part of a diagnostic system	The Criteria and scoring system are a two-part diagnostic system. The Criteria focus on requirements, while the scoring system focuses on factors to use in assessing strengths and areas for improvement.
Comprehensive	The Criteria cover all operations, processes, and work units of the company, internal and external.
Interrelated learning cycles	There is linkage and dynamic relationships and feedback among the framework elements. Learning and resultant action take place via feedback among the process and results elements. The learning cycle has four stages: planning, execution, progress assessment, and revision.
Emphasizes alignment	Requires improvement cycles at all levels and in all parts of the company. To ensure that improvement cycles carried out in different parts of the organization support one another, overall aims must be consistent or aligned.

SOURCE: 1995 Malcolm Baldrige National Quality Award Criteria.

achieve planned outcomes. In its early format, the Award did not maintain strong requirements for linking quality actions, such as empowerment, to drive financial performance. This lack was considered a weakness of the Award Criteria. Now, refinement of the Criteria and the education of both Examiners and companies have made the Criteria more "actionable," and this refinement includes having made specific links to corporate issues.

With respect to **corporate goal links,** the Award was founded in order to improve the performance of U.S. businesses. Believing in a direct link existing between a quality organization's conditions and financial attainment is a difficult "leap of faith" for many businesspeople, especially given the perceived risk and personal effort involved in making the paradigm shift. The major task of the Award Criteria, then, is to emphasize the link between "quality" and the performance requirements of a business.

The ultimate evidence of a fruitful connection is best demonstrated by related outcomes, but the Award Criteria have been evaluated and improved to better represent and underscore the business performance connection. The main links referred to in the Award guidelines are summarized in Exhibit 3.3. The Criteria link the focus on two kinds of achievements: development and financial performance. Development refers to the process by which companies consistently strive to select the "right things" to do and do them better. Financial performance refers to simultaneous success in market performance and resource management that lead to profitability.

This quality performance link is a significant issue for Examiners. "Quality" is the essential intervening vehicle for both short- and long-term corporate success. Therefore, it is necessary for an applicant to establish that this link does exist. That is, a company must prove that its quality efforts have led directly to resource efficiency and market (customer) gains such as market share. Proving that a link exists is not always an easy task, especially owing to the confounding effect of changes in external conditions. Thus, an applicant who uses aggregated data for analysis that demonstrates cause-effects and who employs more relative measures (e.g., benchmark comparisons and market share) can provide a more compelling case to the Examiners.

Exhibit 3.3	Key Business Issues and the Award Criteria	
---	---	
KEY BUSINESS ISSUE	CRITERIA LINK
Incremental and breakthrough improvement	Use of nonprescriptive, results-oriented Criteria and key indicators focus attention on what must be improved. This approach helps to ensure that all improvements contribute to the organization's overall objectives.
Business strategy and decisions	The focus on delivering exceptional value through superior offerings and lower costs of operation, connecting to financial performance.
Financial performance	This is addressed by emphasis on (1) quality factors and management actions that lead to better market performance, market share gain, and customer retention; (2) improved productivity, asset utilization, and lower overall operating costs; and (3) support for business strategy development and business decisions.
Innovation and creativity	Many mechanisms encourage this, including the focus on future customer requirements, development of people, value adding for process steps, time cycle reduction, and cycles of learning.

SOURCE: 1995 Malcolm Baldrige National Quality Award Criteria.

◆ THE EVALUATION SYSTEM FOR APPLICANTS

The evaluation is the essential means by which the Baldrige Award accomplishes its purpose. The Baldrige guidelines specify that the Award Criteria promote dual results-oriented goals:

> To promote key requirements for delivering ever-improving value to customers while simultaneously maximizing the overall productivity and effectiveness of the delivering organization.

This statement implies that through customer focus the organization will achieve financial goals and that progressing according to the Baldrige Criteria is a means to achieving this end. At issue, then, is proof of a direct connection between progress according to the Award Criteria and business success. This issue is further developed in a later section.

In order for an organization to understand the key requirements for progress, the Baldrige guidelines include Criteria that are built on a set of **core values and concepts** that, when taken together, address and integrate the overall customer and company performance requirements. These values constitute the essential conceptual guidelines for the framework of categories and related criteria that depict the characteristics one might expect to see in a financially successful Total Quality Management organization.

Although the category framework and criteria represent the indicators of progress, a scoring system is used to show an organization's progress at any given time. The system scores each criterion according to the quality-related approaches (or methods) used, their deployment, and the results achieved. To accommodate situational differences such as organization size or type of industry, Examiners and Judges consider each applicant's business factors and account for these factors when scoring.

The following section examines each of the four elements used for conducting evaluations. First, it explores the core values and concept guidelines. Then, it looks at the categories that provide the Criteria and investigates the scoring system. Finally, it considers the use of business factors when scoring to accommodate differences in organizational settings.

Values and Concepts

Fundamental to the Baldrige guidelines are the core values and concepts summarized in Exhibit 3.4. These core values and concepts represent the conditions considered necessary to the effective Total Quality Management organization. In other words, they are the key assumptions underlying the Award and are expected to pervade conditions of the successful applicant.

All the core values and concepts are interrelated. Some represent specific "people" orientations, such as for customer focus and leadership. Other core values

Exhibit

3.4

Core Values and Concepts for the Baldrige Award

CORE VALUES AND CONCEPTS	DESCRIPTION
Customer-driven quality	Systems address product and service attributes that (1) contribute value to the customer, leading to satisfaction, and (2) enhance and differentiate from competitive offerings.
Leadership	Personal involvement and role models for development and deployment of (1) customer orientation, (2) value and expectations, and (3) strategies, systems, and methods to achieve excellence.
Continuous improvement	All parts of the business have well-defined and executed approaches to provide better quality in a responsible and efficient manner.
Full participation	A fully committed, well-trained, and involved workforce with appropriate reinforcement.
Fast response	A focus on the design and management of processes and activities to reduce cycle time and to ensure rapid response.
Design quality and prevention	The achievement of problem prevention through building quality into products and services, and into the processes through which they are produced.
Long-range outlook	Future orientation with long-term commitments to all constituents (e.g., customers, shareholders, employees, and suppliers).
Management by fact	Development of reliable information, data, and analysis to support quality assessment and quality improvement.
Partnership development	Building alliances with those internal and external to the business related to quality development and delivery.
Public responsibility	Corporate citizenship and obligations to the public, environment, and other institutions consistent with improvement of conditions.

SOURCE: 1995 Malcolm Baldrige National Quality Award Criteria.

and concepts represent approaches or practices, such as partnering and continuous improvement. Because Baldrige avoids prescriptiveness, the Award does not specify how an organization can achieve leadership and customer focus excellence. However, some critics have observed that the highly specific stated values and the causality implied by the criteria framework are, in fact, prescriptive.

Criteria Framework

The seven categories shown in Exhibit 3.1 embody the core values and concepts. These categories are designed to address all components of an integrated, prevention-based quality system built around continuous improvement. The categories are presented in the Award Criteria guidelines using the simple causal-type framework shown in Exhibit 3.5.

The framework has four main elements. The ***Driver*** refers to the leadership of the senior executives who create the values, goals, and systems and guide the sustained pursuit of quality and performance objectives. The ***Systems*** are the set of well-defined and well-designed processes, such as strategic planning, employed to meet the company's customer and performance requirements. The ***Measures of Progress*** are the results-oriented basis for channeling actions to deliver ever-improving customer value and company performance. Finally, the ***Goal,*** or basic aim of the system, is to deliver ever-improving value to customers in order to achieve strategic objectives, such as customer retention.

Exhibit 3.5

Baldrige Award Criteria Framework Dynamic Relationships

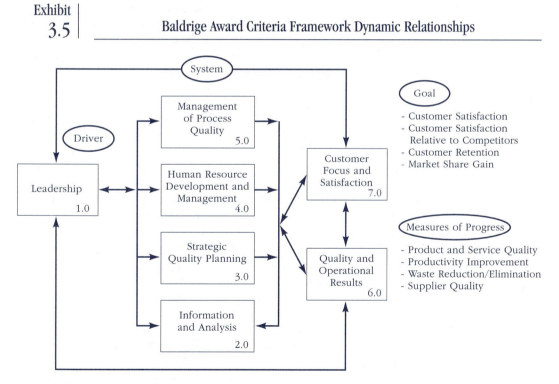

SOURCE: 1995 Malcolm Baldrige National Quality Award Criteria.

Each category consists of Examination Items that exemplify the essential nature of the category and the criteria. For instance, each Item contains between 1 and 4 "Areas to Address." Some of these Areas have extensive explanations that help the applicants, Examiners, and Judges ascertain the kind of information that should be included in an application. In addition, each Item indicates the amount of information an applicant should provide. In order to remove redundancy and simplify the Criteria, there has been a reduction in Items during the Award history. For example, in 1995 there were only 24 **Examination Items** distributed among the seven categories compared to 33 in 1990.

Scoring Guidelines

The most apparent aspect of the scoring system is the weighting of points among the seven categories shown in Exhibit 3.1. The total is 1000 points, with 50 percent allocated to the outcome categories of Business Results, and Customer Focus and Satisfaction. The scoring is applied to the Items that make up each category but not to the individual **Areas to Address** that represent each Item.

The scoring of Items is based on three evaluation dimensions: (1) Approach (2) Deployment, and (3) Results. All Items require applications to furnish information relating to one or more of these dimensions. **Scoring guidelines** are available that relate score levels to conditions for the three dimensions; these are shown in Exhibit 3.6.

The notion of "successful quality strategies" for Baldrige refers to the approach and deployment. Conceptually, the approach must be in place before deployment is possible. Most of the first five categories emphasize approaches and deployment, while results are captured mainly by Items 6.1 to 6.3, 7.4, and 7.5.

Methods for the approach are expected to display characteristics such as prevention-based and quantitative, and must show continual improvement and integration. The approaches should be deployed to all products and services, transactions with external parties (customers, suppliers, and the public), and internal processes, facilities, and employees. The results derived from the approaches must be sustained and demonstrate evidence of outcomes and effects for many features such as quality levels, contributions to quality improvement, rate of quality improvement, impact on the business, and a direct connection to quality processes. The results must also be benchmarked where possible.

The 50 percent score level is considered an "anchor point" as shown in Exhibit 3.6. According to the Baldrige guidelines, here the approach has a sound and systematic prevention basis that includes evaluation and improvement cycles with some evidence of integration. Deployment means that the approach covers most major areas of the business and some support areas. Results would show positive trends in most major areas and some evidence that the results are caused by the approach.

NIST gives notable consideration to **scoring calibration.** This starts at the annual Examiner training and continues for all states in the Award applicant review process. Exercises during training enable Examiners to understand the factors that affect scoring in both negative movements because of expecting too much evidence from a short document and positive movements from accepting very vague statements as evidence.

Exhibit
3.6

Scoring Guidlines

SCORE	APPROACH/DEPLOYMENT	RESULTS
0%	• No systematic approach evident; anecdotal information.	• No results or poor results in areas reported.
10% to 30%	• Beginning of a systematic approach to the primary purposes of the Item. • Early stages of a transition from reacting to problems to a general improvement orientation. • Major gaps exist in deployment that would inhibit progress in achieving the primary purposes of the Item.	• Early stages of developing trends; some improvements *and/or* early good performance levels in a few areas. • Results not reported for many to most areas of importance to the applicant's key business requirements.
40% to 60%	• A sound, systematic approach, responsive to the primary purposes of the Item. • A fact-based improvement process in place in key areas; more emphasis is placed on improvement than on reaction to major problems. • No major gaps in deployment, though some areas or work units may be in very early stages of deployment.	• Improvement trends *and/or* good performance levels reported for many to most areas of importance to the applicant's key business requirements. • No pattern of adverse trends *and/or* poor performance levels in areas of importance to the applicant's key business requirements. • Some trends *and/or* current performance levels—evaluated against relevant comparisons *and/or* benchmarks—show areas of strength *and/or* good to very good relative performance levels.
70% to 90%	• A sound, systematic approach, responsive to the overall purposes of the Item. • A fact-based improvement process is a key management tool; clear evidence of refinement and improved integration as a result of improvement cycles and analysis. • Approach is well-deployed, with no major gaps; deployment may vary in some areas or work units.	• Current performance is good to excellent in most areas of importance to the applicant's key business requirements. • Most improvement trends *and/or* performance levels are sustained. • Many to most trends *and/or* current performance levels—evaluated against relevant comparisons and/or benchmarks—show areas of leadership and very good relative performance levels.
100%	• A sound, systematic approach, fully responsive to all the requirements of the Item. • A very strong, fact-based improvement process is a key management tool; strong refinement and integration—backed by excellent analysis. • Approach is fully deployed without any significant weaknesses or gaps in any areas or work units.	• Current performance is excellent in most areas of importance to the applicant's key business requirements. • Excellent improvement trends *and/or* sustained excellent performance levels in most areas. • Strong evidence of industry and benchmark leadership demonstrated in many areas.

SOURCE: 1995 Malcolm Baldrige National Quality Award Criteria.

Other than training, the procedures used to ensure valid scoring are quite extensive. They include placing both experienced and new Examiners in teams, the checking of Examiner scores by Senior Examiners and those writing feedback reports, and the analysis of all scoring and also monitoring of consensus and site activities by NIST staff.

Business Factors

The Award Criteria are designed to permit evaluation of any quality system for manufacturing and service companies of any size, type of business, or scope of market. The 24 Items and 54 Areas to Address have been selected because of their importance to virtually all businesses. Yet, the importance of the Items and Areas to Address may not be equally applicable to all businesses, even to those of comparable size in the same industry. Specific business factors that may bear on the evaluation are considered at every stage of the evaluation.

An important step, then, when evaluating an applicant is to examine and understand unique business factors. Exhibit 3.7 shows an example for a typical small-business applicant. This step is required of Examiners not only before evaluating the written application, but also before reaching consensus and making the site visits. Moreover, the Judges pay particular attention to these factors at all points of the application review process.

◆ THE BOARD OF EXAMINERS

Appointment and Training

In 1995 the Board of Examiners consisted of 211 Examiners, 50 Senior Examiners, and 9 Judges. Examiners apply to NIST as individuals each year to become board

Exhibit 3.7	Business Factors for a Small-Business Applicant: A Restaurant Chain.

1. Only seven sites employing about 70 people, including part time.
2. Sites in three widely dispersed cities.
3. A large proportion of employees are probably lower skilled.
4. A critical role of suppliers for quality.
5. The nature of suppliers makes quality specifications difficult to quantify and implement.
6. A unique product in a highly competitive industry.
7. Demand fluctuations in the retail business makes supply management difficult.
8. Types of supplies that are used in several other comparable situations (e.g., manufacturers and retail outlets).

SOURCE: Author.

members, whereas Judges are appointed for a three-year term. Appointments are on a competitive basis, and the criteria for selection used by NIST include the highest standards of qualification and peer recognition that reflect breadth, length, and diversity of experience; communication skills; leadership, achievements, and external representation; degree of specialization; broad knowledge of quality management; and education and training. Given the Award Criteria coverage, Examiners must be expert in a wide range of areas.

Board members must be prepared to spend at least 10 days a year performing related duties. The members' responsibilies are defined by NIST as follows:

- **Examiners**—review, comment on, and score written applications, prepare feedback reports, and participate in consensus evaluations and site visits.
- **Senior Examiners**— same as for Examiners except they may lead consensus evaluations and site visits.
- **Judges**—review the comments and scores of Examiners, select applicants for consensus reviews and site visits, review site visit reports, and recommend Award recipients to NIST.

The Board of Examiners must attend an annual three-day preparation program that informs members about Award Criteria, the scoring system, the examination process, and the code of Ethical Standards. Attendance is mandatory regardless of attendance at other Baldrige Examiner training programs. Prior to attending these preparation sessions, members must do background work, such as preparing cases and familiarizing themselves with all aspects of the Award process by reading related materials. Board members must be carefully trained in scoring to ensure valid Examiner calibration. Training focuses on three main issues: (1) establishing "levels" or standard scores that promote inner-examiner reliability for the year's evaluation, (2) maintaining the uniformity of levels or standards from year to year, and (3) preventing "errors" from being made in making scoring assessments.

Examiners are encouraged to engage in personal development activities, network, and contribute to knowledge dissemination. These include programs conducted by the Award to encourage understanding and adoption of quality management practices such as the annual Quests for Excellence Conference and the Regional Conference Series.

Establishing Standards and Consistency

Scoring, site visit, and application feedback "standards" are based on the Baldrige training and Examiner team experience. Results from Examiner evaluations demonstrate a high level of **internal consistency.** In other words, little notable variation occurs among Examiners for a particular evaluation. Still further, there are few discrepancies when Examiners reach consensus and when they discuss cases of score variations.

It is difficult to maintain the consistency of standards from year to year. Throughout the Award's seven-year history, the distribution of scores has tended to decline, as shown in Exhibit 3.8. Given that, historically, application quality has improved each year, it seems that "grade deflation" would have and has occurred. This phenomenon may have occurred because Examiners have generally become more experienced and skillful over the years or because developments made in the Baldrige training program have caused deflation in the calibration level.

Examiners face the following problems when scoring; consequently, these problems have been made a focus of training:

- Distinguishing between anecdotes and illustration
- Overreacting to an individual data point on a trend line
- Setting the requirement for 50 percent too high, expecting that it represents notable results for all areas
- Giving inadequate consideration to key business factors when examining application material
- Seeing opportunities for improvements as weaknesses
- Expecting respondents to address every issue rather than recognizing the basic intent of the Items and Areas to Address.

In the case of Judges, in addition to attending annual training, they are subject to a code of conduct.

Code of Conduct

Basic to Examiner appointment and training is the issue of conduct. Examiners experience a Code of Ethical Standards and several "ethical" exercises when be-

| Exhibit 3.8 | Distribution of Malcolm Baldrige Award Applicant Scores: 1988 to 1993 |

| | | | SCORE RANGE | | | |
RANGE	1988	1989	1990	1991	1992	1993
0–125	0	0	2.8	0	0	2.0
126–250	0	2.5	7.2	13.2	12.0	8.0
251–400	1.6	20.5	18.6	35.8	30.0	24.0
401–600	47.5	37.5	52.6	34.0	40.0	47.0
601–750	34.4	30.0	19.6	14.2	18.0	19.0
751–875	16.4	10.0	2.1	0	0	0
876–1000	0	0	0	0	0	0

SOURCE: NIST training materials.

ing trained. It is imperative that applicant information in no way be compromised. The codes are in summary applied as follows:

- Board members are assigned only when there is no known conflict of interest. In the unlikely case that an examiner receives and notices an inappropriate application, he or she is required to notify NIST and return the personal material unopened.
- Examiners are not allowed to tell anyone, including fellow Examiners, of any applications they evaluated or of any site visits they conducted.
- All materials must be returned to NIST, and at site visits, all materials must be collected before Examiners leave the site.
- Examiners cannot seek any consulting work from applicants they evaluate.
- Examiners must not accept any gift offered by applicants. This rule restricts any entertainment or personal interaction during site visits.

◆ APPLICANT EVALUATION AND FEEDBACK

The Award has a basic four-stage examination process, and each stage has several activities.

Review

An independent review and scoring evaluation of each application is conducted by at least five members of the Board of Examiners. The Judges then select the top scoring applications for consensus review. Names are never exposed to the Judges. If an application is not selected for the next stage, a feedback report is compiled based on written evaluations from the Examiners.

Consensus Review

These consensus discussions among at least five Examiners, led by a Senior Examiner, are usually conducted by telephone and are monitored by a member of the NIST staff. In 1995 the 29 consensus teams averaged five hours for their calls. **Site visits** are allocated by the Judges to applicants based on consensus reports. Again, applicants not selected to progress to the next stage receive a **Feedback Report** based on the consensus evaluations.

The systematic consensus procedure is well documented and a primary focus of Award training. Although Examiner scores are usually closely aligned, consensus is an assurance procedure designed to reduce any variability in scores owing to differences among Examiners in understanding the Criteria, scoring guidelines, information provided in the application, or acceptance of evidence. In practice, about 75 percent of the Items are discussed, with variations typically attributable to individual outliers.

Participation in a consensus notably impacts the total understanding of each participant. This is very valuable, given the difficulty of fully comprehending a complex situation for a large company from 75 pages of text, statistics, and diagrams. Other benefits include agreements among Examiners for a site visit and improving the comments available for the Feedback Report.

Site Visits

Site visits are led by a Senior Examiner and are conducted by a group of at least six Examiners who are personally monitored by NIST staff. Examiners complete final submission reviews on the sites before they go to the Judges. After a site visit, the applicant receives a Feedback Report based on all evaluations, including the site visit.

The main purpose of the site visit is to clarify uncertain points, verify accuracy, and investigate areas difficult to understand from the application. The procedures to prepare for and conduct a site visit are rigorous, well grounded in experience and the Award's continuous improvement program. All members of the Board of Examiners are annually trained in site visit procedures, including initial planning, off-site planning, on-site management and practices, and reporting.

The team must finish site visit conclusions before leaving the site and include reports for each of the seven categories, with pluses and minuses indicating whether the category was found to be stronger or weaker relative to the consensus evaluations. There is an overall summary of findings for the site visit without a score change, but there should be a team consensus about the direction in which the written application score should move.

Judges' Recommendations

The Judges review all evaluation reports for all site visit applicants and then make the Award recommendations to NIST. Then NIST presents the Judges' recommendations to the Secretary of Commerce for the final Award decision. NIST performs a background check of potential Award winners in order to confirm that they would be role models. This information is not used in the judging process. The Awards are then announced and presented at a ceremony in Washington, D.C., during October or November.

The Feedback Report

Most of those involved with the Baldrige Award consider the Feedback Report to be a key benefit for applying. The report is positioned as a tool for assisting companies to plan their continuous improvement efforts. It is not unusual to hear applicants admit that they applied primarily for the feedback, and those who used it to make sufficient improvements may become winners on a subsequent submission. A notable example is the Granite Rock Company which applied for four consecutive years, finally winning in 1992.

The Feedback Report is typically about 30 pages in length, including several components: introduction and background of the application review process, distribution of numerical scores for all applicants and scoring summary for the applicant, and Item level details of the Applicant's Strengths and Areas for Improvement. An example of the last-named is Exhibit 3.9 which is extracted from the Feedback Report used in the 1993 Examiner preparation training about a fictitious manufacturing company called Varifilm.

NIST gives considerable attention to prepare Examiners to write appropriate reports, validate that the reports are accurate and actionable, and ensure confidentiality. Examples of guidelines from Baldrige Examiner training are:

- Be nonprescriptive—state observations and evaluations.
- Address the most important issues.
- Reflect the score—low scores, basic information and high scores, finer points.
- Comment only on areas contained in the Criteria.
- Be specific—refer to specific materials in the application as appropriate and cross-reference information provided in the wrong section.

Since several Examiners evaluate applications at all stages of the Examination process, the Board of Examiner member who writes the Feedback Report has all the comments to use. At this point, the person writing the Feedback Report also evaluates the comments made by all Examiners. These evaluations, in turn, are provided to the Examiners to help their personal improvement efforts.

After six years of application and continuous improvement, the Feedback Report is a major contribution of the Baldrige Award program. This success is reflected through the success of reporting in the State Award programs, and through the many companies that have adopted the Award Criteria for conducting internal "progress" reviews.

◆ THE AWARD CRITERIA IN PRACTICE

Developing the Core Values

The experience of using the core values and concepts teaches the Award applicant many lessons, the most significant of which is an appreciation of the many ways to build an effective quality organization. One hopes that an applicant will realize the limited value in just "copying." It is not unreasonable to suggest that, in order to develop a competitive "uniqueness," an organization is well advised not just to emulate others in selecting its path. One need only consider the dangers companies face when benchmarking to recognize the

Exhibit

3.9

Sample Feedback Report Comments

The comments given below are based on a feedback report used in the 1993 Baldrige Award Examiner Preparation Course. The comments are about a fictitious manufacturing company named Varifilm and are representative of the specific, actionable feedback your company will receive. The relevant Baldrige Award Criteria Item is given in parentheses.

STRENGTHS

- A risk assessment is conducted biannually at each production facility, and the outcomes are used as input to the planning process. In addition, an environmental scan is performed annually to predict future trends. (Item 1.3—Public Responsibility and Corporate Citizenship)
- The Cycle Time Excellence (CTE) process provides a structured methodology which translates customer requirements into design through the use of cross-functional teams, addressed quality requirements early in the process, and provides for a process control plan. (Item 5.1—Design and Introduction of Quality Products and Services)
- Varifilm provides for easy access through a variety of customer contact approaches. Examples include visits to strategic customers once a quarter, visits to larger customers' plants 2–3 times per week, the 800 line, and an electronic mail system connected directly to major customers. (Item 7.2—Customer Relationship Management)

AREAS FOR IMPROVEMENT

- While a planned benchmarking approach is utilized, how Varifilm determines specific benchmarking needs and priorities is not clearly detailed. (Item 2.2—Competitive Comparisons and Benchmarking)
- A systematic process does not exist for aggregating customer-related data with other key data to set priorities. Varifilm does not define the methods it uses to evaluate and improve its data analysis capabilities. (Item 2.3—Analysis and Uses of Company-Level Data)
- Trend data regarding the effectiveness of quality-related training and the key indicators of effectiveness are not presented. (Item 4.3—Employee Education and Training)
- Varifilm does not explain how it evaluates and improves its overall processes for determining customer satisfaction. How gains and losses of customers and customer dissatisfaction indicators are considered is not clear. (Item 7.4—Customer Satisfaction Determination)

SOURCE: NIST training materials.

validity of this warning: making the decision to replicate another company's methods exactly, thereby acting as a "follower," or to use another company's methods as inspiration for developing one's own innovative techniques, thereby acting as a "leader."

Examiners must remain open-minded and willing to consider variables, such as those conditions unique and specific to a company and the possible existence of alternative quality routes, in order to make fair and effective evaluations. Examiners must also be cautious, because actions taken by an organization often appear to follow the intent of the guidelines but really do not. These "false representations" become evident when Examiners compare how companies claim to employ Baldrige core values with what really happens in practice, and when "cross-validation" tests are conducted among the category responses provided in the application.

Customer-Driven Quality

The emphasis on customer satisfaction or customer-driven quality is a major success of the quality management effort. "Just focusing on customers is important," said John West, Manager of Corporate Quality Improvement at Federal Express. Yet, most organizations struggle to fully understand and deploy the concept of quality as it is judged by the customer. A strategic concept, customer satisfaction is concerned with such achievements as customer retention and market penetration, and so it remains central to how an organization thinks. For example, a company concerned with customer satisfaction will make product and service features the domain of the Total Quality system rather than of just the engineering or marketing departments.

It is important to note, however, that in many instances a company cannot measure customer requirements and project customer responses. The development of basic technology lends validity to this argument. For instance, when companies plan for aspects of long-term product and service development, they can only do so through limited "customer" input: pure research is well ahead of application. Yet, this limitation does not excuse the lack of customer focus that has, for example, led to high-technology products entering the market touting expensive features that are of no use to many customers, or the expenditure by financial institutions during the 1980s on installing technology that did not coincide with customer service requirements.

During a site visit Examiners often discover that not all employees, especially senior management, believe in customer focus. Some managers feel that they are "going with the fad," waiting for the inevitable return to "sanity." If this lack of commitment to customer focus exists, then a full deployment of those concepts and quality conditions that ensure long-term maintenance is absent. In other words, although conditions may exist for short-term success, conditions for long-term success may not.

Leadership

While leadership is "the driver" in all types of organizations, quality management organizations require that radical deviations from the traditional attitudes and behaviors of senior managers occur. In order to succeed today, the Baldrige guidelines suggest that senior managers must feel and act as a coherent group and be seen personally developing, deploying, and reviewing "clear and visible quality values and high expectations" and the "strategies, systems, and methods for achieving excellence." These qualities constitute a notable contrast to the traditional practices of leadership.

The Examiner must be observant of valid changes in senior management beliefs and behavior. It is not easy to move from an authoritarian position to one of personal involvement and "support." Under adverse financial conditions, reversion back to an authoritarian role is easy. So, a Baldrige site team priority is usually to ensure that quality management leadership is in place: approach, deployment, and results in the sense of effectiveness (including in the sense that employees see and believe that change is occurring) must be observed.

Continuous Improvement and Learning

Acceptance that competitiveness requires a defined and rigorously implemented approach to continuous improvement and learning is central to quality management. Such continuous improvement is demanding, for it necessitates that an effective approach be deployed to all operations, units, and activities from which learning is attained. In the past, critics of the Baldrige guidelines have attacked the relatively heavy focus on continuous improvement. Admittedly, there are two cases in which too much emphasis placed on continuous improvement constitutes a problem, and therefore is of concern for Examiners:

- When there is continuous improvement of things that do not matter. For example, a process should be eliminated because its improvement will not add value. Sometimes a new process should replace the old one but does not.
- A distraction from the dominant requirement of design exists that prohibits development and ensures that future expectations and requirements will not be met.

For several years, NIST has attempted to place more emphasis in the Award guidelines on design and prevention, innovation and creativity, future requirements, and continuous learning.

Employee Participation and Development

The concept of employee participation and development is based on the assumption that all workforce members have the potential to make effective contributions to the organization's objectives, given the "right" conditions. This potential is achieved through personal involvement and empowerment. The Criteria place considerable emphasis on developing these "right" conditions, including a fully committed, well-trained, and involved workforce reinforced by a reward and recognition system.

Many Award recipients claim that the empowerment of employees and the more effective use of teams play important roles in the quality improvement process. The problem for Examiners is to distinguish between conditions that superficially demonstrate achievement of these conditions and what really exists in the "hearts and minds" of employees.

Establishing a quality management infrastructure and "stocking" it with people does not mean that the long-term goal of participation will be attained. For example, it is easy to establish a quality council and team structure that are not an integral part of managing the "real business" of the organization. Often, companies establish quality management as a staff function, while line functions operate almost uninterrupted in management practices. In essence, such companies are merely paying cursory attention to suggestions from the quality function. Unfortunately, this situation is common, and companies that act in this manner rarely succeed.

Fast Response

Speed is a "popular" feature associated with quality management (see also Chapter 13). The association is based on the assumption that success in competitive markets requires ever-shorter product and service development cycles and faster response to meet customer requirements. The notion of fast response is accentuated when organizations feel they are being left behind and must make up for lost time. Fast response often becomes a dominant quality attribute. It is represented in the values and day-to-day service response features and is extended to organizational change.

The issue for Examiners to consider is that a fast response may not always be the most desired condition for quality effectiveness or efficiency. Customers do not always prefer speed in service settings. For instance, some bank customers prefer slow lines and more teller attention. Similarly, the amount of time a service representative spends on the telephone in complaint resolution can reflect a concern for the customer. It is well established that an effective (not necessarily fast) response to a complaint often increases customer loyalty. Moreover, excessive priority given to speed for gains in the short term can lead to greater losses in the longer term, as is evidenced by premature software releases.

Design Quality and Prevention

The rationale for design quality is that it leads to reductions in "downstream" waste and difficulties. Therefore, focus on design quality improves both effectiveness, such as customer retention, and efficiency. A focus on design quality means that a simultaneous focus on prevention exists; that is, building quality into products and services and the processes by which they are produced wards off problems.

A fundamental problem associated with quality management is to determine what comes first: what to do or doing it well. For a company with highly developed customer satisfaction measurement and related quality improvement efforts, attaining results may mean doing a better job with a system that is missing the longer-term needs or adding valuable opportunities for customers. The apparent upward movement in key indicators may disguise weak underpinnings. Examiners must ensure that prevention is prioritized through design and validation and that management reviews are in place in order to move to a new design where appropriate, despite apparent improvement success.

Long-Range View of the Future

Focus on the long term, or a long-range view of the future, is well represented in the Award Criteria. The Award guidelines state that achieving quality and market leadership requires a future orientation and long-term commitments to customers, employees, stockholders, and suppliers. Strategies and resource allocations must consider future requirements for critical factors such as the development of employees, supplier relations, and technology.

The Criteria have been criticized for neglecting some long-term requirements. Long-term development is a major issue for Examiners, especially since U.S. companies are recognized for their short-term profit focus. In terms of quality leadership, at issue is whether or not the short-term and long-term balance really is inherent in all of a company's practices. The strategic planning system provides the preliminary evidence of institutionalizing the long term. Then, the Examiner must identify a history of resource allocations and other actions that clearly demonstrate a long-term commitment.

Management by Fact

Achieving company quality and goals requires making decisions based on reliable information and analysis, what is called management by fact. Basic information and data for quality development, improvement, and evaluation are of many types and derive from multiple sources, including customer, product and service performance, operations, competitive comparisons, supplier, employee-related, and cost and financial. The Baldrige examination process and Criteria increase a company's focus on measurement, and widespread deployment of measurement importance is a major contribution of the Award.

Award winners show substantial commitments to quantitative measurement that are lacking in many unsuccessful Award applicants and nonquality focused organizations. A lack of measurement indicates a misapprehension about the urgency of quality, the necessity for prevention, the need to assess progress, and the obligation to meet future requirements. Many companies have measures, but they are often not connected to customer satisfaction. Measurement is the network that holds together both the Award Criteria and the effective quality organization. Lack of integrated measurement is a major reason for the failures of many organizations to adopt Total Quality Management. Effectively using measurement means achieving several requirements, including:

- *Participation*—everyone must understand and be committed to measurement and its use through their involvement.
- *Integration*—measures from multiple sources must be linked, such as customer satisfaction evaluations and internal process metrics.
- *Planning*—clear measurement links must exist between processes and individual work to company goals and strategies.
- *Deployment*—everyone using the information must receive it in a usable, documented form, and in a timely manner.

The Examiner must be careful to understand the real meaning of management by fact: it is the widespread effective use of information. It is not just the presence of information.

Partnership Development

An arresting aspect of the Award is the role of partnering, or partnership development. The Award requires that winners share information, and so essentially, a partnership with all ensues. Companies are expected to build internal and external partnerships, thereby serving mutual and community needs. These partnerships are broad in scope, including those for labor-management cooperation, mutual collaboration with suppliers and customers, and relationships with public sector and educational organizations. The Award has promoted interindustry cooperation, as is evidenced by the dissemination of benchmark information.

A significant aspect of partnering is the recognition that sharing between groups helps both parties. Nowhere is this recognition reflected more clearly than within successful Total Quality Management organizations. Traditionally, the lack of horizontal relations generated by the function-based hierarchies has led to inefficient and ineffective operations and to dysfunctional polarization among business units and functions. The Examiner, though interested in external suppliers and customer partnering, must consider internal relationships since here lies the real "causal" roots of effective partnering.

Corporate Responsibility and Citizenship

A company's customer requirements and quality system objectives must include corporate responsibility and citizenship. The responsibility is broad, including business ethics, environmental awareness, social, health, and safety considerations, and the dissemination of quality information especially in "local" communities. An extension of this corporate responsibility is a company's personal responsibiiity to its employees to help them make personal societal contributions in their day-to-day life.

This concept is more difficult for an Examiner to access in practice than one might imagine. Understandably, a company will direct these community efforts toward financial benefit. Yet, the Award Criteria do require some altruistic contribution to both the community and employees through social responsibility programs. A waste reduction plan that both saves money and contributes to the environment meets this requirement. The Examiner also must look for a balance of activities, including those without financial gain, which demonstrates basic commitment (e.g., helping a nonprofit organization with process improvement).

Results Orientation

Results are an aspect of the Award that have caused confusion. The basic use of results, or results orientation, is in the scoring system where they are the outcomes when meeting the requirements of approach and deployment guideline Items. Here, results are an intervening measure used to ensure that individual approach-deployment specifications are being met. Intervening results measurement takes several forms such as documented successes or responses by employees on questionnaires. An example for leadership is the use of employee feedback to evaluate the understanding of quality values to assist senior management in improving their approach deployment efforts.

Category 6 specifically represents results, and here results are the outcomes of the Category 1-5 approach-deployment activities. The Criteria refer mainly to the consequence of effectively managing resources, including suppliers. Results of customer requirement performance (e.g., on-time delivery), of efficiency (e.g., waste reduction, employee absenteeism, and productivity improvement), of supplier performance, and of innovation (e.g., effective adoption of new technology) are measured. Success in achieving Category 6 results must precede success in achieving the planned customer behavior results referred to in 7.4 and 7.5 in Category 7, such as market share.

◆ IMPACT OF THE BALDRIGE AWARD

U.S. Industry and Government

The most outstanding impact of the Award has been the widespread use of Award Criteria and guidelines by U.S. industry and public sector organizations. This application has taken many forms, ranging from using the guidelines as an informational input to formally adopting the guidelines for continuous process evaluation, as has been done by AT&T. Companies have also used their experience with the Award Criteria to help both their external suppliers and customers to make quality-related progress.

Baldrige Board of Examiner members contribute significantly to building awareness of the importance of quality and to information transfer activities.

Considerable efforts are made by those administrating the Award program to encourage Examiners in information transfer through presentations in the public educational arena, activities in professional associations and within their own companies, and by inclusion in their consulting practices.

The unique advantages businesses attain by using the guidelines and participating in the Award process include:

- An evaluation of quality progress using nationally recognized Criteria
- An assessment of progress against world-class standards
- The opportunity to join other organizations sharing the same experiences (e.g., the Quest for Excellence Conferences)
- An occasion to enhance quality management understanding, communication, and cooperation throughout the company
- The opportunity to allocate resources more effectively for prevention and improvement

To these can be added other benefits such as sensitization to innovation, competitive distinctiveness, strategic planning that links directly to work, a highly motivated and amiable work environment, and the potential to make notable productivity gains.

During the first six years, Award recipients have shared information on their successful quality strategies with thousands of organizations, including educational institutions, trade and professional associations, government agencies, and health-care organizations. The Baldrige guidelines are also extensively used by nonapplicant organizations to guide their quality management efforts, including as a means to evaluate progress.

Some of the companies that won the Award experienced a revolution set in motion by a threat to survival. "The company was hemorrhaging," says Wayland Hicks, executive vice president of Xerox Corporation. But at the moment the greatest losses seemed to occur, some U.S. companies that moved down the Total Quality Management path made the greatest of all gains: survival and then financial success. Xerox is one of these organizations.

How does winning the Baldrige Award or meeting its criteria contribute to the profitability of the firm? Does following its criteria increase profits? The answer remains controversial. Many articles have been written claiming to demonstrate that adopting Total Quality Management does not produce direct financial success. Yet, these criticisms must be seen more in relation to how organizations have taken action rather than to how the Baldrige guidelines assess progress. According to most key market and financial indicators, Baldrige Award winners are companies that have progressed further than the average organization. In an interesting exercise, NIST examined the stock prices of publicly traded winners and considered what profits would have been made, relative to the rest of the market, if they had been purchased at the time of winning. The result, as of October 1994, was a notable outperformance of the Standard & Poors 500 stock index. This study supports the results obtained by Heller as reported in Chapter 1.

In the instance of federal government organizations, a 1992 report of the United States General Accounting Office reported that about 68 percent of federal installations were working on Total Quality Management implementation. Since that time, progress has continued to be accelerated as a result of President Clinton's 1994 initiative requiring "customer assessment."

The Characteristics of Successful Applicants

The answers given by Award winners to questions about what happened to them provide some interesting insights. Probably the most notable lesson to learn from them is that there are many ways to build a quality organization. The Baldrige application is a set of criteria, not a recipe for success. Each company must find its own path to quality.

Exhibit 3.10 has excellence indicators for each of the Baldrige categories based on experience from the applicant examination process. These indicators provide all companies with issues on which they can focus when they are developing their own organizations. However, these issues reflect the experiences of the past and must be considered carefully with respect to the future. For example, although empowerment is an issue today, the building of entrepreneurial-type conditions is an issue for the future.

Considerable efforts have been made to transfer information from successful applicants that can be used by other U.S. companies. The vehicles are Examiners, the winners (because they have opened themselves to benchmarking), and public presentations by the Award staff. The Award administration has also launched many initiatives to conduct public programs, such as the annual Quest for Excellence Conference, and to make available extensive materials.

The State Awards

An important outcome of the Baldrige Award is the rapid development of state awards; as of 1995 there are about 36 state awards. Most are based on or have fully adopted the Baldrige Criteria, which has been actively encouraged by NIST who sponsored the National Governor's Association 1992 report *Promoting Quality Business: A State Action Agenda*. In 1994 NIST initiated state and local quality award workshops to encourage information transfer and networking. This movement has made an important contribution, not only to encouraging smaller and more "local" organizations to adopt quality improvement, but also to promote education. Several state awards are associated with academic institutions, examples being the University of Lowell (Massachusetts) and the University of Mississippi.

Several state awards have had notable successes, such as those in Massachusetts, New Jersey, New York, and Mississippi. Let us look at the Massachusetts Award as an example. This Award, funded from corporate donations and application fees, was first conducted in 1992. The guidelines are based on the Baldrige Award but are simplified to encourage small and less "sophisticated" organizations to pursue

Exhibit

3.10

Characteristics of Successful Applicants: Key Excellence Indicators

CATEGORY	EXCELLENCE INDICATORS
Leadership	• Visible in establishing and attaining goals. • Personal involvement in regular reviews. • Close contact with customers. • Champion of quality. • Reinforce total commitment. • Ensure that quality concept is well defined. • Give quality issues top priority as criteria when making decisions.
Information and analysis	• Quantitative orientation. • Interlinking measures (internal and external). • Widely deployed and accessible in timely manner.
Strategic planning	• Formal planning function exists and is integrated into business planning. • Planning process emphasizes continuous quality improvement. • The plan is clearly linked to quality values. • The plan considers both shorter and longer term. • A means exist to link planning with its execution.
Human resource development and management	• All are involved in quality process with understanding. • Emphasis is on problem solving and teamwork. • The culture is where all are focused on continuous improvement. • All receive training and cross-training. • The work of teams is tracked to ensure effectiveness.
Process development	• Quality in design (prevention). • Focus on response time. • Quality is built into tasks. • Integration of prevention and correction with daily operations. • Linkage to suppliers and impacts their capabilities.
Business results	• Broad base of improvement trends: products, services, internal operations. • Results benchmarked to leaders with indication of leadership. • Improvement in supplier quality.
Customer focus and satisfaction	• Front-line empowerment. • Strategic infrastructure support for front-line employees. • Service standards derived from customer requirements. • Attention to hiring, training, attitude, and morale of front-line employees. • High levels of customer satisfaction. • Proactive customer systems. • Use of all listening posts. • Requirements of market segments. • Measurement beyond current customers

SOURCE: NIST training materials.

the quality path and apply for the Award. That is, there are seven categories, but specifications are limited to the Item level with details for areas excluded. In addition, the application report is limited to 35 pages. There is no limit on the type of Massachusetts-based organizations that can apply, representing a recognition of nonprofit organizations.

In the first year, there were 36 local applicants and three winners. Interestingly, one winner was also a Baldrige Award winner that year: AT&T Transmission Systems. The other 1992 winners were Screenprint, a small company, and Foxboro. In 1993, there was only one winner, but it was a service organization: Pioneer Services Corporation. Then in 1994, the first nonprofit won an award, Delta Dental, along with a manufacturer, Varian Vacuum Products.

With many large firms requiring that their suppliers undergo the Baldrige Award examination process, the implications of quality for small firms will become increasingly important: they must know as much as large companies about quality improvement.

Overseas Leadership

Growing interest in the Baldrige Award is occurring overseas. Not only are the Baldrige guidelines used by U.S. companies overseas, but they are adopted by foreign corporations as well. This interest has extended to national governments, which are now requesting and receiving assistance ranging from seminars explaining the guidelines to the actual adoption of the guidelines for national awards. Australia and Venezuela have recently adopted the Baldrige guidelines. The Australian guidelines are now based on Baldrige, and Australian "evaluators" have been trained by Baldrige Examiners. In Venezuela, the Baldrige Criteria serve as the model for the national award.

An interesting comparison can be made with the European Quality Award in its similarity to the Baldrige Award. Exhibit 3-11 shows the **European Quality Award** diagramatically. As can be seen, there are parallels for the seven Baldrige categories:

EUROPEAN QUALITY AWARD
- Leadership
- Impact on Society
- Policy and Strategy
- People Management
- Process
- Business Results
- Resources
- Information Systems
- Financial
- Internal
- Technology
- Cutomer Satisfaction

BALDRIGE AWARD
- Leadership (and Corporate Responsibility)

- Strategic Quality Planning
- Human Resource Development and Planning
- Process Management
- Quality and Operational Results

- Information and Analysis

- Customer Focus and Satisfaction

Exhibit
3.11

European Foundation for Quality Management Award

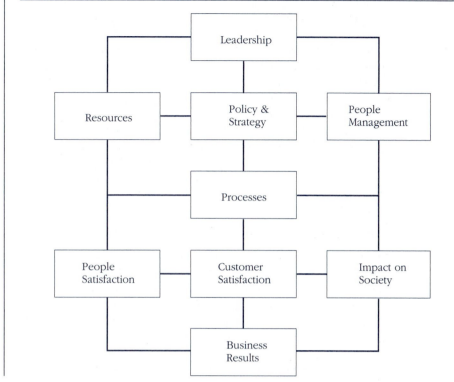

The feature that did distinguish the European Quality Award from the Baldrige Award was the European Award's focus on financial performance, but now the Baldrige Award has increased its emphasis on financial-related performance measures.

The Baldrige Award and ISO 9000 Standards

The ISO 9000 program, described in Chapter 2, was developed to meet the need to encourage international trade. The assumption is that if companies meet quality-related standards, then the quality of their output can be assured for buyers. Thus, the ISO 9000 view of quality is conformancy of specified operations to documented requirements. There are, at present, three requirement documents (ISO 9001, ISO 9002, ISO 9003) that specify the standards for third-party registration or other assessment schemes, and there are guidance documents (ISO 9000 and ISO 9004) such as for developing internal quality systems. Registration covers design and development, production, installation, and servicing.

Any company can successfully apply to be ISO 9000 registered. The multi-stage assessment process includes a document review, preassessment to identify possible noncompliance, and an on-site assessment by several auditors. If applicants successfully meet all requirements, they are registered and then are subject to "surveillance" in order to maintain this status.

The Baldrige Award program has different purposes. The main focus is to increase the competitiveness of U.S. companies by providing value to customers, with the intent of improving overall operational and financial performance. The program also aims to educate and transfer information for mutual (national) benefit. An examination of the coverage for both approaches shows that Baldrige is far more comprehensive.

The Baldrige Award and ISO 9000 programs differ notably in their purpose, procedures, and coverage. Yet, they are not at all in conflict, and both are relevant for most companies to use. The broad coverage and strategic focus of Baldrige makes it the global management approach for driving a total business while ISO 9000 is a subset focusing on specific requirements.

Use in Education

The Baldrige Award's most apparent educational contribution is professional development for the participants, both from applicant companies and members of the Board of Examiners. Through educational activities, these people have been able to transfer their understanding, experience, and enthusiasm to others. To this developmental benefit can be added the gains of networking and information transfer. When appointing members of the Board of Examiners, NIST has always encouraged academics. Consequently, several academic appointments have been made with a consequential deployment of the Award Criteria into educational institutions. This practice of encouraging academic institutions has extended into the state award programs.

The most apparent result has been the use of the Award Criteria in various academic courses. An example is making "quality" a major part of the Wharton MBA curriculum in the Fall of 1991. However, the effect has been farther-reaching, encouraging the development of quality management courses and programs. It is also evident that academic institutions have been affiliated with public award programs and quality-related activities, and many have actually begun using quality practices in the management of their own organizations.

◆ FUTURE OF THE AWARD AND CONTINUOUS IMPROVEMENT

The most apparent issue for the future is continuous improvement of the Award Criteria, examination process, and administration. Kurt Reisman of NIST has taken a strong position on continuous improvement: "The Baldrige Criteria are getting tougher much faster than U.S. businesses are getting better. We plan to keep raising the standards." There is a definite continuous improvement process that involves not only all members of the Board of Examiners, but also company representatives, experts, and members of the Award administration. An examination of the guidelines over time shows improvements each year.

The scoring results of Examiners have also changed over the six years, with the distribution of scores declining. That is, during a time when an understanding of Total Quality Management by applicants has increased, the Examiner's scores have declined. So, it does seem that the standards for conducting evaluations have risen.

With the Award's growing popularity, some have suggested that there is a danger that it could become an obstacle to quality by functioning as a distraction to the pursuit of quality in the future. That is, companies will be so caught up in pursuing the Award that they will not pursue other things that are more important to achieving excellence. This does not seem to be happening, however. The number of applicants each year is small, at 100 or less. In addition, the subsequent success of Award winners indicates that their actions have not proven to be distracting.

The Criteria have changed over the last six years through the Award's continuous improvement process:

- Less redundancy in the Items, with clarity of definition and fewer Items
- A notable improvement in the information provided so that applicants and Examiners can better understand the nature of the Items
- A reallocation of scores to place greater emphasis on areas such as results
- An increased emphasis on results, innovation, and recognition of future requirements
- Greater emphasis on linking, such as for planning, information, and process management

---

◆ Summary

The Award offers to all U.S. organizations a highly developed and validated means to systematically evaluate quality management progress. In addition, the Award is a valuable educational vehicle and provides a commonality of language that enhances information transfer. The Award's immediate effect is widespread. The most apparent effect is the motivation of individuals and companies and the generation of the related information transfer, including the fueling of state awards and college educational programs.

The Award is undoubtedly achieving its national competitive goal of contributing to a worldwide leadership in quality. Consequently, it seems reasonable to attribute some gains of the national productivity to efforts stimulated by the Baldrige Award and to take steps to ensure its viability and enhancement in the future.

◆ Key Terms

Board of Examiners	Goal (of quality process)	Senior Examiners
Corporate goal links	Examination Items	Judges
Core values and concepts	Areas to Address	Internal consistency
Driver	Scoring guidelines	Site visits
Systems	Scoring calibration	Feedback Report
Measures of progress	Examiners	European Quality Award

◆   Assignments

1. The Malcolm Baldrige Award Guidelines are subject to continuous improvement efforts. This includes reviews of their use and keeping them up-to-date about "best practices." Exhibit 3.12 offers the Strategic Planning Category 3.0 specifications for the 1995 Award Criteria, Exhibit 3.13 the Strategic Quality Planning 3.0 specifications for the 1991 Award Criteria. First read the 1995 specifications and then those for 1991. Outline the main differences in role, content, and presentation, and explain what may be the main reasons for these changes.

2. Fundamental to the Award Criteria are notions of "causality" and "linking." Exhibit 3.5 illustrates in overview this perspective. Based on the material provided in this chapter, explain causality and linking with an emphasis on planning and information (or measurement).

3. The Malcolm Baldrige Award had the term "quality" embedded throughout the Criteria in its initial years. Now it is difficult to find the word quality. What does this mean?

Exhibit **3.12**	**1991 Application Guidelines.** **3.0 Strategic Quality Planning (*60 pts.*)** The *Strategic Quality Planning* category examines the company's planning process for achieving or retaining quality leadership and how the company integrates quality improvement planning into overall business planning. Also examined are the company's short-term and longer-term plans to achieve and/or sustain a quality leadership position.

Exhibit

3.12

3.1 Strategic Quality Planning Process (35 pts.)

Describe the company's strategic quality planning process for short-term (1–2 years) and longer-term (3 years or more) quality leadership and customer satisfaction.

Areas to Address

a. how goals for quality leadership are set using: (1) current and future quality requirements for leadership in the company's target markets; and (2) company's current quality levels and trends versus competitors' in these markets

b. principal types of data, information, and analysis used in developing plans and evaluating feasibility based upon goals: (1) customer requirements; (2) process capabilities; (3) competitive and benchmark data; and (4) supplier capabilities; outline how these data are used in developing plans

c. how strategic plans and goals are implemented and reviewed; (1) how specific plans, goals, and performance indicators are deployed to all work units and suppliers; and (2) how resources are committed for key requirements such as capital expenditures and training; and (3) how performance relative to plans and goals is reviewed and acted upon

d. how the goal-setting and strategic planning processes are evaluated and improved

Notes:

(1) Strategic quality plans address in detail how the company will pursue market leadership through providing superior quality products and services and through improving the effectiveness of all operations of the company.

(2) Item 3.1 focuses on the process of goal setting and strategic planning. Item 3.2 focuses on actual goals and plans.

3.2 Quality Goals and Plans (25 pts.)

Summarize the company's goals and strategies. Outline principal quality plans for the short term (1–2 years) and longer term (3 years or more).

Areas to Address

a. major quality goals and principal strategies for achieving these goals

b. principal short-term plans: (1) summary of key requirements and performance indicators deployed to work units and suppliers; and (2) resources committed to accomplish the key requirements

c. principal longer-term plans: brief summary of major requirements, and how they will be met

d. two- to five-year projection of significant changes in the company's most important quality levels. Describe how these levels may be expected to compare with those of key competitors over this time period.

Note: *The company's most important quality levels are those for the key product and service quality features. Projections are estimates of future quality levels based upon implementation of the plans described in Item 3.2.*

SOURCE: 1991 Malcolm Baldrige National Quality Award Criteria.

Exhibit

3.13

1995 Application Guidelines.

3.0 *Strategic Planning (55 pts.)*

The *Strategic Planning* Category examines how the company sets strategic directions, and how it determines key plan requirements. Also examined is how the plan requirements are translated into an effective performance management system.

3.1 *Strategy Development (35 pts.)*

Describe the company's strategic planning process for overall performance and competitive leadership for the short term and the longer term. Describe also how this process leads to the development of key business drivers to serve as the basis for deploying plan requirements throughout the company.

Areas to Address

a. how the company develops strategies and business plans to strengthen its customer-related, operational, and financial performance and its competitive position. Describe how strategy development considers: (1) customer requirements and expectations and their expected changes; (2) the competitive environment; (3) risks; financial, market, technological, and societal; (4) company capabilities—human resource, technology, research and development and business processes—to seek new market leadership opportunities and/or to prepare for key new requirements; and (5) supplier and/or partner capabilities.

b. how strategies and plans are translated into actionable key business drivers which serve as the basis for deploying plan requirements, addressed in Item 3.2.

c. how the company evaluates and improves its strategic planning and plan deployment processes.

A D R
☑ ☑ ☐

Notes:

(1) Item 3.1 addresses overall company strategy and business plans, not specific product and service designs.

(2) The sub-parts of 3.1a are intended to serve as an outline of key factors involved in developing a view of the future as a context for strategic planning. Strategy and planning refer to a future-oriented basis for major business decisions, resource allocations, and companywide management. "Strategy and planning," then, addresses both revenue growth thrusts as well as thrusts related to improving operational performance.

(3) Customer requirements and their expected changes [3.1a(1)] might include pricing factors. That is, market success may depend upon achieving cost levels dictated by anticipated price levels rather than setting prices to cover costs.

(4) The purposes of projecting the competitive environment [3.1a(2)] are to detect and reduce competitive threats, to improve reaction time, and to identify opportunities. If the company uses modeling, scenario, or other techniques to project the competitive environment, such techniques should be briefly outlined in 3.1a(2).

Exhibit
3.13

(5) *Key business drivers are the areas of performance most critical to the company's success. They include customer-driven quality requirements and operational requirements such as productivity, cycle time, deployment of new technology, strategic alliances, supplier development, employee productivity and development, and research and development. Deployment of plans should include how progress will be tracked such as through the use of key measures.*

(6) *Examples of strategy and business plans that might be the starting points for the development of key business drivers are:*
- *new product/service lines;*
- *entry into new markets or segments;*
- *new manufacturing and/or service delivery approaches such as customization;*
- *new or modified competitive thrusts;*
- *launch of joint ventures and/or partnerships;*
- *new R&D thrusts; and*
- *new product and/or process technologies*

(7) *How the company evaluates and improves its strategic planning and plan deployment process might take into account the results of reviews (1.2c), input from work units, and projection information (3.2b). The evaluation might also take into account how well strategies and requirements are communicated and understood, and how well key measures are aligned.*

3.2 Strategy Deployment (20 pts.)

Summarize the company's key business drivers and how they are deployed. Show how the company's performance projects into the future relative to competitors and key benchmarks.

A D R
☑ ☑ ☑

Areas to Address

a. summary of the specific key business drivers derived from the company's strategic directions and how these drivers are translated into an action plan. Describe: (1) key performance requirements and associated operational performance measures and/or indicators and how they are deployed; (2) how the company aligns work unit and supplier and/or partner plans and targets; (3) how productivity and cycle time improvement and reduction in waste are included in plans and targets; and (4) the principal resources committed to the accomplishment of plans. Note any important distinctions between short-term plans and longer-term plans.

b. two to five year projection of key measures and/or indicators of the company's customer related and operational performance. Describe how product and/or service quality and operational performance might be expected to compare with key competitors and key benchmarks over this time period. Briefly explain the comparisons, including any estimates or assumptions made regarding the projected product and/or service quality and operational performance of competitors or changes in key benchmarks.

Exhibit

3.13

Notes:

(1) *The focus in Item 3.2 is on the translation of the company's strategic plans, resulting from the process described in Item 3.1, to requirements for work units, suppliers, and partners. The main intent of Item 3.2 is alignment of short- and long-term operations with strategic directions. Although the deployment of these plans will affect products and services, design of products and services is not the focus of Item 3.2. Such design is addressed in Item 5.1.*

(2) *Productivity and cycle time improvement and waste reduction [3.2a(3)] might address factors such as inventories, work-in-process, inspection, downtime, changeover time, set-up time, and other examples of utilization of resources—materials, equipment, energy, capital, and labor.*

(3) *Area 3.2b addresses projected progress in improving performance and in gaining advantage relative to competitors. This projection may draw upon analysis (Item 2.3) and data reported in results Items (Category 6.0 and Items 7.4 and 7.5). Such projections are intended to support reviews (1.2c), evaluation of planning (3.1c), and other Items. Another purpose is to take account of the fact that competitors and benchmarks may also be improving over the time period of the projection.*

SOURCE: 1995 Malcolm Baldrige National Quality Award Criteria.

Case Study

Overview

History and Nature of Our Business

Colony Fasteners, Inc. (CFI), is the world leader in the design and manufacture of fasteners. It has a distinguished history as the oldest fastener manufacturer in the United States, steeped in tradition dating back to 1877. The company started as a supplier of bolts, screws, rivets, and staples to the U.S. Army in the decade after the Civil War ended. Its original founders were two brothers, James and Thomas Pote, who served in the war as armorers. During their service, they were constantly frustrated with the quality and durability of the fasteners used for the artillery and undercarriages. They saw the need to supply a higher quality product to the Army and mobilized around the opportunity. With their background, experience, and service connections, they founded Colony Fasteners in Philadelphia, Pennsylvania.

The two brothers began the business with a credo founded in quality.

To All Customers, We Promise Service, Satisfaction, and Value.

To this day, this credo hangs in every CFI location worldwide. They instilled this spirit into employees, customers, and suppliers from the very beginning, believing that if they, and all their employees, lived true to these words, a successful enterprise would emerge. Today's business success is living testament that their vision was clear.

Originally, the product lines were limited to the types of fasteners used by the Army.

Quickly they expanded their products as new markets and customers were identified. Significant opportunities occurred in supplying the U.S. Navy's shipyards in Philadelphia and the surrounding areas. The company saw rapid growth with the defense building booms during the many wars and conflicts.

Significant growth occurred after World War II and during the Korean War. Offshore expansion began utilizing the tremendous leverage of inexpensive labor and facilities. Product lines grew when business segmentation began to occur. In the mid-'50s, CFI reorganized, establishing three significant business sectors: Consumer Products, Commercial and Automotive, and Defense and Aerospace. Each sector served a very distinct market. Customer segmentation occurred with new approaches to customer satisfaction emerging. Strong partnerships had been forged with the various branches of the defense establishment; ties to the automotive industry were deeply rooted; and CFI was leading the commercial market. Exhibit 3.14 shows how CFI is segmented according to business markets. Included in the business segments is the Corporate Support Sector, which is the organizational unit responsible for all corporate functions, such as Information Systems and Human Resources.

The Nuclear and Specialty sector was established in the late '50s with the advancement of the nuclear power industry and requirements for exotic materials and manufacturing processes. It was also the expansion of the aerospace environment that drove the requirement for special types of fastener devices that included explosive components and special processing.

---

*This case is extracted from a larger case used for training Baldrige Examiners. Only the relevant exhibits have been reproduced. Other exhibits would be in the items indicated in the larger case.

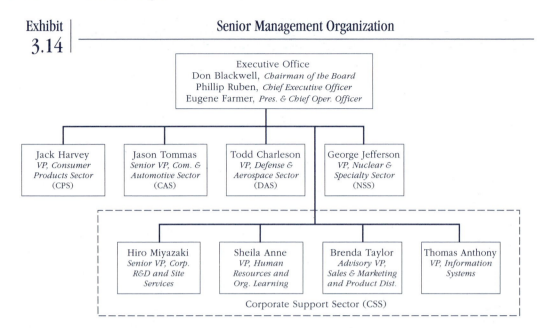

Exhibit 3.14 — Senior Management Organization

Executive Office
Don Blackwell, *Chairman of the Board*
Phillip Ruben, *Chief Executive Officer*
Eugene Farmer, *Pres. & Chief Oper. Officer*

Jack Harvey
VP, Consumer Products Sector
(CPS)

Jason Tommas
Senior VP, Com. & Automotive Sector
(CAS)

Todd Charleson
VP, Defense & Aerospace Sector
(DAS)

George Jefferson
VP, Nuclear & Specialty Sector
(NSS)

Hiro Miyazaki
Senior VP, Corp. R&D and Site Services

Sheila Anne
VP, Human Resources and Org. Learning

Brenda Taylor
Advisory VP, Sales & Marketing and Product Dist.

Thomas Anthony
VP, Information Systems

Corporate Support Sector (CSS)

Fasteners with strain gages embedded in the products were introduced by CFI.

During the '50s, CFI took a hard look at how it addressed its customers' needs. There were many staff members that had seen the successes of process control and began exploring new methods of process improvement and control. They were early converts of the teachings emerging from the universities and technology-based companies. During these years, many engineers and managers versed in quality principles, who are today's quality leaders and visionaries, were brought in to teach and share process improvement methodologies.

The '60s and '70s were business heydays. Growth was dramatic, with the defense and automotive sectors leading the contributions. Technology advancements were happening at blinding speed. Up to this time, CFI was a privately held company. In 1972, with growth and expansion driving the corporate direction, CFI went public on the New York Stock Exchange (NYSE symbol—CFI).

This was also a time when some of the customer focus was lost. The demands of new technology, growth and new market development, and the rapid expansion of the defense and aerospace business put a veil in front of the customer awareness. CFI lost ground relative to its customer satisfaction levels.

In the mid-'80s, it became apparent that something had happened. Customers were no longer first in the list of critical business priorities—or at least, so it seemed. Senior management at CFI stood back, reflected on the company's roots and determined that if this course continued, it would lose entirely its eroding market position. Ultimately, the company could suffer irreparable damage.

Senior management defined the elements of change in how the company would operate. Customers would again be placed first and foremost in everything employees do. Some of the old approaches to customer satisfaction were reinstalled. The notion of "Back to Basics" began to drive the company the way it was originally founded. These changes fortunately occurred in the mid-'80s. CFI's customers noticed the change in how they were being serviced and how their needs were again a driving force in the business relationships.

Customer Base

CFI's customer base is worldwide and extends from prime contractors for spacecraft manufacture to the average homeowner using its products to repair a lawnmower.

Each sector at CFI has a major customer base that it supplies. A brief description follows:

Consumer Products Sector—major customers include a large base of distributors, wholesalers, jobbers, and retail outlet chains.

Commercial and Automotive Sector—the major automotive manufacturers around the world are customers of CFI. The largest users of CFI products include the "Big 3" in the U.S. and the "Big 2" in Japan. Most of the smaller manufacturers in the U.S., Europe, South America, and Japan are also consumers of the same products supplied the major automotive manufacturers.

Defense and Aerospace Sector—literally all manufacturers of airframe, spacecraft and defense products purchase or contract CFI fabricated fasteners. Because the products are so specialized in construction and require extensive testing and qualification, CFI dominates this market.

Nuclear and Specialty Sector—there are few manufacturers in this market to contest CFI's presence. Most manufacturers of defense related aircraft use CFI products from this sector (e.g., explosive bolts for ejection systems). The nuclear power market is well served by the products from CFI. They are in almost all nuclear installations around the world.

Major Markets Served by CFI

Today, CFI is strong, reflecting a growth pattern that is unparalleled in its industry. The company is represented in all major industrialized countries in the world with manufacturing locations spanning from Asia to South, Central, and North America, and to European Economic Community (EEC) countries.

Products range from exotic to ordinary. CFI has products sitting on the moon, embedded in spacecraft heading out of this solar system, and holding together deep sea mining equipment 20,000 feet below the ocean's surface. Explosive products are included in most aircraft life-critical pilot ejection systems and in 85% of all automotive passive airbag restraint systems. Each and every nuclear reactor in the U.S. and most in the free world have CFI fasteners at critical locations in their systems. The defense sector provides fasteners to all branches of the U.S. military and most of the armies of the free world. CFI fasteners are used in critical locations from the compressor turbines of jet engines to the wheel studs supporting most of the rolling armament around the world. The ordinary products include pins, bolts, nuts, rivets, and screws used to assemble a wide variety of household products, from refrigerators and lawn mowers to cabinet hinges.

CFI's markets are segmented into 4 distinct sectors. Each sector serves a worldwide customer base that is serviced by a network of distributors, wholesalers, jobbers, and retail sales outlets. The four sectors are:

Consumer Product Sector—designs and manufactures simple screws, rivets, pins, and bolts of inexpensive materials and are sold at low cost for all types of uses.

Commercial and Automotive Sector—designs and manufactures fasteners used in industrial products and by all major automotive manufacturers.

Defense and Aerospace Sector—designs and manufactures high quality, high performance fasteners for special products used in airframe, spacecraft and defense products.

Nuclear and Specialty Sector—designs and manufactures fasteners for nuclear reactors, fusion devices and radiation hardened products. Also includes fasteners of extremely complicated design, materials, and applications like explosive bolts for ejection systems on fighter aircraft.

Quality Requirements

CFI's visibility occurred before the extensive scandal erupted concerning counterfeit bolts and fasteners illicitly distributed throughout the industry. It helped to prevent serious tainting of CFI's reputation. The scandal was a wake-up call to the industry and its customer base. CFI used this opportunity to further its already established reemergence of customer orientation. The scandal drove Congressional passage of the Fastener Quality Act of 1990 (FQA) for new regulations in the industry and placed a pall over all suppliers in varying degrees. Many of the data included in this application reflect this turbulent time in the industry.

Four years ago, a major customer initiated the need for suppliers to be oriented to the Malcolm Baldrige National Quality Award (MBNQA) Criteria, and CFI began proliferating the six sigma approach to its supplier base. This reinforced and placed further emphasis on CFI's process controls which had already begun in the '50s. Six sigma is now used in mainstream product production, support services, business services, and outreach to CFI's supplier base.

Position in the Industry

CFI is the leader in our industry. Because it has been in existence since the late 1800s, many strong bonds have been established between it and its customers. These bonds and partnerships contribute to its position in the industry. In many areas of the industry, CFI has hundreds of competitors, such as the Consumer Products sector. Most of these competitors are small and have a limited life span of five to 10 years. In the Commercial and Automotive areas CFI is a leader, but has strong competition from off-shore manufacturers supplying competitive products at very low prices. Some of these competitors have been in business for a very long time and have demonstrated their staying power. They are the ones offering the greatest challenge to maintaining and growing our current market share position. CFI has been supplying the defense industry for over 100 years and has clearly demonstrated in this market its willingness to meet ever changing and very demanding requirements. While there are many competitors, most of them are short lived and are driven through contract awards. CFI is the largest U.S. supplier of products to this market segment. Nuclear and Specialty sector products are driven, almost exclusively, by contracted specification and requirements. CFI has few competitors in this market segment. It has the leadership position in a small field of specialty fastener manufacturers. Often, the small manufacturer accepts a contract for specialty products then subcontracts the work to CFI because of our manufacturing capabilities and demonstrated design knowledge.

Employee Base

CFI has a unique culture, one that is recognized throughout the world by its customers and competitors alike. It is open, communicative, and constructively challenging. Employees openly talk and challenge each other. Managers and executives seek to ensure the highest quality products, in the least amount of time, and with the highest value for the customer. It is the highest embodiment of an "open door policy" seen in our benchmarking efforts on human resources and organizational development. Teams are actively involved throughout the world, driving CFI to excellence with a minimum of organizational barriers.

Exhibit 3.15 shows the growth, in terms of employees since the company's formation in

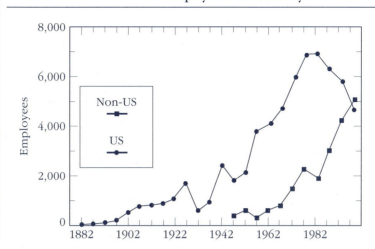

Exhibit 3.15

Employee Growth History

the late 1870's. The shift to off-shore labor is responsible for the transition between the U.S. and non-U.S. workers. The employee base at CFI contains hourly, salary nonexempt, and salaried contributors (approximately 61%, 18%, and 21% respectively). Most hourly workers have completed high school or its equivalent (92%). A large percentage (56%) of the salary nonexempt have some college education, a two-year degree or technical school credentials. Salaried employees have an expectation of being college graduates. While the majority of them have bachelors (83%), masters (32%), and doctorate degrees (14%), the small number (17%) are actively pursuing their academic goals using CFI's education support package.

Today's employees live a common vision while driving for higher levels of performance. The original credo of the two brothers forms the basis for all actions, internally and externally.

Major Equipment, Facilities and Technologies
World headquarters is in Philadelphia with manufacturing locations worldwide, including (by sector): Consumer Products (Juarez, Mexico; Sao Paulo, Brazil; Xiang, China; El Paso, TX); Commercial and Automotive (Dearborn, MI; Milwaukee, WI; Macon, GA; Jacksonville, FL; Oyama, Japan; Nagoya, Japan); Defense and Aerospace (Philadelphia, PA; Santa Ana, CA; Los Angeles, CA; Boston, MA); and Nuclear and Specialty (Los Angeles, CA; Philadelphia, PA, Salt Lake, UT [specializing only in explosive fasteners]; and Berlin, Germany). Other locations include sales offices in most major U.S. cities and significant cities around the world, a regulatory office in Washington, D.C., and regional sales hubs (East Coast office is Philadelphia, PA; West Coast office is Los Angeles, CA; Great Lakes office is Detroit, MI; Southeast office is Dallas, TX; Asia/Pacific office is Tokyo, Japan; Europe office is Calais, France). Note that the majority of employees assigned to a sales hub are located out of small offices and their homes to more conveniently locate them with their customers.

Supplier Base
CFI's supplier base is predominately composed of raw material suppliers and distributors. They supply materials such as wire, rod and bar stock, explosive components, and lubricants. Many suppliers additionally provide

the materials and equipment needed to turn raw materials into sellable products. These include: cutting tools, small and large manufacturing equipment, protective equipment for employees, and equipment used to test and evaluate the quality of the finished products. Some services are contracted by CFI such as maintenance, cafeteria, health services, and temporary workforce employees. Each supplier is expected to perform according to contract. They are measured and managed using these contract expectations.

Regulatory Environment

CFI is in a highly regulated industry in some market segments. Because it supplies products to the defense, aerospace, and nuclear market it is bound by a wide variety of requirements and regulations associated with each one. Additional regulations and requirements are imposed on CFI for the products it manufactures and markets outside of the United States.

Environmental regulations and requirements are similar to most manufacturing operations. CFI is regulated on the amount and type of effluents and waste discharge, safety considerations for its workers, and community safety activities.

There are some unique regulations and requirements imposed on the Salt Lake facility due to its processing of explosive materials. These include employee and community safety, testing and evaluation operations, and registration of some devices with bureaus of the U.S. and foreign governments.

Other Factors

The corporation started a profit-sharing program with its employees in the late 1980s. The approach annually splits corporate profits over a specified profitability value, pending a Board of Directors review: 50% for the corporation and 50% for the employees. The worldwide employee base shares equally in the division of its 50%.

In today's daily operations CFI is always focused on the future, especially in terms of customer needs and expectations and operational results. Throughout this application this is evident in the graphs, tables, and figures. Many of these show 1995 values; these represent the best foresight of the 1995 expected results.

Information and Analysis

2.1 Management of Information and Data

The CFI data system model is shown in Exhibit 3.16. At the core of the model is the worldwide data and information system and its five major database structures according to the sectors they support. Drawing data and information from the information system are the sectors, utilizing them to create unique applications and data structures. These, while unique, are accessible using various local area network and wide-area network technologies. The architecture and measurement of the effectiveness of this data system are the responsibility of the CSS Information Systems Group.

2.1.a Selection of data

CFI recognizes that the selection of proper data is essential to manage, monitor, and control the total business. It is important to collect all necessary data but not to collect too much data which would overload the process and result in lack of focus and concentration on the essential issues.

Data collected are related to the four product sectors and the one corporate support sector and are structured to lead to excellence in the five key business strategies of the company. Senior management determines which top-level data should be common to uniformly drive the excellence in the five key business strategies across the corpo-

Exhibit
3.16

CFI Data System Model

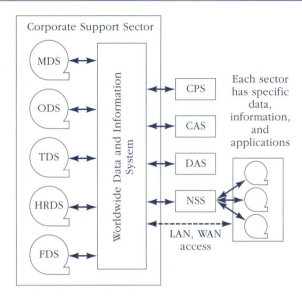

Corporate Support Sector

MDS

ODS

TDS

HRDS

FDS

Worldwide Data and Information System

CPS

CAS

DAS

NSS

Each sector has specific data, information, and applications

LAN, WAN access

ration, and which should be unique to ensure excellence in the sectors.

Foremost in the data selection process is a customer focus. The data collected provide information to reinforce the customer delight actions in each of the five business strategies.

The top-level data are decomposed to successively lower levels throughout the sectors down to the team level. Since employee involvement through teams is a key corporation strength, collection, analysis, and use of data at this level are the cornerstones to effectively managing by fact. The strong linkage of data up through all organizational levels enables appropriate action to be taken at the lowest possible level, as well as identification at all levels of connectivity and impacts to the five business strategies. From the team level upward, internal and external customers and suppliers are linked into the data stream to achieve the strong customer focus.

Benchmarking visits with process observations are utilized and adapted in the data selection and analysis review process as a vehicle to continually improve data management.

2.1.a(1) Types of data collected

Since the company depends heavily on process control of all products and support services, C_{pk}'s are prominent in the data items collected. This is true for both product-related as well as support service data. Some examples of the types of data collected are shown in Table 3.1. The sample data displayed are categorized in the business driver areas.

Each sector utilizes teams of concerned employees who are responsible for the selection of the data to be collected. These teams consist of users, developers, customers, suppliers, and Information Systems (IS) experts. They formally meet every Friday afternoon at 1:00 PM and hold informal meetings when special circumstances occur. The formal meetings are documented and ensure that each data task is often reviewed for continual improvement.

Table 3.1   Business-Related Driver Areas

Customer Related	Fig.
Response Time to Customer	
Queries	7.2.1
All Sector Customer Satisfaction	7.4.1
CAS Composite Customer	
Satisfaction	7.4.2
Technological Leader	7.4.5
CAS Customer Satisfaction	7.4.4
Customer Complaint Calls	7.4.6
Customer Retention	7.4.3

Product and Service Performance	
Percent Process Yield by Product	
Type	6.1.2
Percent of Critical Processes	
$C_{pk} > 1.5$	6.1.1
Operations Yield	6.1.3
Warranty Returns	6.1.4
Customer Problems Resolved in	
24 Hours	6.1.5
On Dock Performance	6.1.6

Internal Operations	
Operations Quality	6.2.3
Operational Productivity	
Non-Product	6.2.2
Product Design Cycle Time	6.2.8
Product Setup Cycle Time	6.2.9
Information Systems	6.2.10
Reduction in Solid Wastes	6.2.11
Employee Safety Record	6.2.13
Training Hours Per Employee	6.2.18
Employees Engaged in Teams	6.2.21
Corporate Citizenship Engagements	6.2.22

Supplier Performance	
Supplier Base Transitions	6.3.1
Supplier Receiving History	6.3.2
Certified Supplier Quality	6.3.3

Financial Performance	
Annual Sales Volume	6.2.5
Market Share	6.2.6
Profit Margin	6.2.7
Sector Gains and Losses in	7.5.5–
Market Share	7.5.8

2.1.a(2) Reliability and access of data

Data reliability is ensured by several means. CFI realizes that if data used for analysis of processes are not the best, best results will not happen. Most of the data are collected by automatic means and directly filed in the data system to ensure reliability.

Software utilized within the data system is designed to analyze the data as it is collected and immediately provide a flag if a large or significant variation occurs or erroneous entries are made. The flag alerts the operators to immediately review the situation as to the existence of poor data or a possible change in the process. The data teams regularly review the number of flags that occur for each data item. This reflects on both data collection and the actual process performance. By flagging wide variations, erroneous data inputs are corrected, and this results in further data reliability.

Daily, IS personnel back up all the data to ensure that loss does not occur if power outages or other disruptions occur. Weekly IS personnel also verify data accuracy through the use of automatic diagnostic routines.

Data are managed on a companywide Information System network using PC terminals for local use and a centralized mainframe in Philadelphia connected by satellite links. The local PC terminals are linked in local area networks so that all employees have access to real-time data anywhere in the world. In all locations, a minimum of 90% of the employees have a PC terminal readily at hand. Thus, data are accurate and reliable, real-time, and readily accessible.

Passwords, updated monthly, and authorized entry lists are randomly checked to verify security.

2.1.b Improvement of the data system

Semiannually, a formal top-down data review occurs. Starting at senior management and cascading through all levels of the organization, including customers and suppliers, the following questions are asked:

- Has the current data enabled us to make decisions and set priorities?
- Is the data actionable?
- Does the data enable us to determine the performance of the process?

Recommended changes from these reviews are fed to a Data Management Team for analysis. This multi-functional team, composed of management, process teams, IS, customers, and key supplier personnel, using the five business strategies as a guide to ensure data continuity, makes appropriate changes in the data management system.

The formal data review process is supplemented with informal data updates by IS management teams (with representatives from all sectors) which result from benchmarks and the continuous improvement process. Item 6.2 shows the improvements over the last ten years in the data systems.

2.1.b(1) Scope of information and data

In the data management team's formal analysis, as well as team activities within continuous improvement, one of the items addressed is whether the right data are reaching the right people. The teams analyze whether the results data show process outputs of importance to customers and whether in-process data enable prediction of output to gauge the performance of the process. Additionally, teams assess whether the recipients of the data are the appropriate persons for taking action on the data. As a means of canceling collection of data which is no longer of value, an additional consideration is: "Is this data being used?" CFI has found these analyses to be extremely valuable for ensuring that the right data gets to the right people while preventing data overload.

2.1.b(2) Use and analysis of data

With the aim of continual improvement of processes, improved C_{pk}'s are the desired result. However, the teams are continually refining the collection techniques to improve data reliability and timeliness as well as the effectiveness of the resulting data analysis.

At the top level of the company, Pareto and quadrant analyses are primary tasks at the team level. Cause-and-Effect Diagrams, the "5 Whys," and Pareto Charts are the most frequently used analysis tools.

The continuous improvement of C_{pk}'s across all functions, products, and support services is an indicator of the success of the process being utilized.

Item 6.1 shows the improvement in the percent of critical processes exceeding a C_{pk} of at least 1.5.

A technique widely used among the team members is electronic mail (E-mail) where all members are in an ongoing communication link. Many times a team member comes to work in the morning to find a solution or a well-defined occurrence that can be utilized to improve a process by reducing variability and cycle time.

2.1.b(3) Feedback from users

At the weekly meetings of the teams responsible for the data to be collected, users not assigned to the team are invited on a random basis and anyone interested has an open invitation. These non-team members are solicited to express concerns and make suggestions as to methods to make the data more available and useful to them.

All process operators, and this includes support functions, utilize their PC terminals to communicate with the other team members by electronic mail with addresses pre-loaded by name and function. Thoughts that occur to them on an ongoing basis, regardless of the time of day or circumstances, are easily captured and recorded for review and action.

An address is available to all employees on E-mail soliciting comments on data timeliness, accuracy, and clarity.

Many employees have PCs at home that are networked to the company data systems. These employees were helped in the purchase of the equipment. The company paid one-half the purchase cost and arranged for the purchase through the company, which reduced the cost another 15% as a result of the buying leverage. Additionally, the company pays for a dedicated telephone line to the employee's home to enable unencumbered communication service.

With communication capabilities in place, comments are continually received by the data teams. Many comments by electronic mail are received during the night-shift operations from employees with ideas that occur at home.

The comment may be as simple as "I don't understand the data." Whatever the comment, appropriate actions are taken. These comments often result in actions by the teams to request training sessions either on-the-job or in the classroom if the situation appears to be widespread. Often the teams will do the training design and sometimes the training itself.

The data are collected for the convenience of the users. All data teams realize the purpose of their existence is to be responsive to the user and for the improved operations of the company resulting in a greater personal profit share for the accomplishment.

2.2 Competitive Comparisons and Benchmarking
2.2a How required information is selected

CFI has pursued an aggressive benchmarking process since 1989 when Xerox, a Malcolm Baldrige National Quality Award (MBNQA) winner, demonstrated its success in using the technique. Since that time, many metric comparisons have been made. Most importantly, process changes have been accomplished that have significantly reduced variability and simplified processes throughout the company.

Early in the benchmarking process, training courses were established that described the total concept with the desired results. The training included process mapping techniques and how to modify processes to result in superior performance in cycle time reduction, quality improvement, and reduced variability.

To emphasize the importance of this new concept, a formal activity was initiated called *Pass Through Partnerships* (PTP). This concept is also utilized in working with suppliers and is described further in Item 5.4.

PTP is a process where complete cooperation between companies is established, and information that is non-proprietary is openly shared. As the process has matured, the partners have revised what was considered to be proprietary after realizing more is to be gained than lost in almost every information exchange.

The benchmarking activities were started in the Philadelphia headquarters. Quickly, responsibility was transferred to each of the four product sectors and corporate support sector, retaining a strong coordinating function to ensure full utilization of information access and to ensure focus on the real business issues. Each sector shares in the information gained by any of the sectors through the data systems.

The critical processes are identified during the strategic planning process and are continually monitored for continually improving results.

2.2.a(1) Needs and priority determination

The strategic planning process identifies areas of business where competition is great and the market share is low. The planning process causes the businesses to review capabilities in comparison with competitors in the market-place by collecting data primarily from public domain information. Analysis of this information is used in establishing goals and stretch targets and setting benchmark priorities.

The initial step in determining benchmark partnership needs is to make improvements in areas that will have the most immediate effect on the business or to provide a longer term capability that is necessary for continual growth.

The initial priority in benchmarking is to determine if the "best practice" is within one of the CFI sectors. If not, then outside bench-marking partners are searched for and found.

In the rapidly growing automotive market, the strategic plan indicated that the Commercial and Automotive Sector was not adequately responding to customer delivery demands of short-term increases in product quantities with little or no lead time. It was pointed out by the mutual customer that Hubler Electric was responsive in delivering electrical connectors overnight.

An arrangement with Hubler allowed a benchmarking team to review how the short-term increase was accomplished. The process was reviewed in detail. CFI's processes for storing and handling raw materials and the area layout were modified. Paperwork processes were also changed. CFI now can respond to doubling the delivery quantity on the next shift after a request, compared to what had been 14 days. This is one example of process improvement as a result of the PTP process. The overall improvement in deliver-on-dock results is seen in Item 6.1.

Each business sector establishes its own priorities for functions to benchmark. After individual sector priorities are established, a master priority list is formulated. Each sector

takes lead responsibility for two to three specific functions to benchmark. The ten or more functions are typically both product-related and non-product-related. Each year, this list is reviewed, and the top 10 functions are reestablished. Additional issues are added on an emergency basis if business conditions dictate. This usually adds about five more for each sector each year.

2.2.a(2) Criteria for information

Although the strategic planning process identifies the basic need, each specific instance requires different information. Gaps in knowledge of competitor performance or results are the highest target for gathering information. The second highest priority targets are processes which are critical competencies for our businesses. Within those critical competencies, our top priority is to determine our competitors' performance and then find those companies outside our industry whose process performance is better than ours and our competitors. Once found, CFI establishes a new partnering relationship to learn and understand how their processes are designed and perform.

2.2.a(3) How data are used

After the benchmark partnership is established, a team consisting of persons familiar with the process being examined and trained in the benchmark process is sent to observe in detail the process being used along with the metrics utilized. The team typically consists of a representative from Engineering, Operations, Information Systems from interested sections, plus members of Headquarters Administration to help ensure consistency and alignment with corporate directions.

The team, after the investigations, then returns to the home facility and modifies applicable processes, making changes and modifications to result in a simplified process with less variability, better quality, and reduced cycle time. The new process is documented and provided to the other business sectors within CFI through the corporate coordinator and the data system.

Team members are often called on to travel to another plant in another sector in order to ensure optimum application of the specific process steps. The process steps for the investigation and adaptation of processes from other companies have been well established from many repeat actions and are well documented. There is no longer a not-invented-here (NIH) attitude at CFI as far as applying processes from others.

Many support service process changes have been utilized across the company with few internal modifications. This demonstrates the confidence the various groups have built in the overall process. The result has been the multiplying of improvements of many routine common steps across the company. There have been many improvements in many applications with little additional costs.

2.2.a(4) Stretch targets
When conducting benchmark comparison analysis, both current and future gaps are established considering costs, process disruption, criticality of processes, and impact on other processes when setting stretch targets.

Process changes that have resulted from learning from other organizations in the PTP process have resulted in significantly improved results within CFI. Often the review of an individual process has resulted in modifying only a small part of an established process. Only a few individual steps are improved, and yet the overall results are substantially better.

In a heat treating process for fasteners for the Nuclear and Specialty sector, the PTP supplier being examined was treating the bolts in a manner that resulted in significantly better performance. Detailed examination showed that the improvement was primarily in the device that loaded and unloaded the bolts although the heating and quenching were not as good as what CFI was using. By changing only the handling device, we were able to achieve an overall tenfold improvement, five times better than the total process that was reviewed for benchmarking.

Besides the process improvements noted, metrics are gained that are utilized for goals to be attained. Many stretch goals have been selected through the PTP process.

Benchmarking successes have encouraged teams to be totally unencumbered with the past and to accept new processes that can be totally or partially applied.

2.2.b How the process is improved
A good measure of the results of the benchmarking process is seen during the annual strategic plan update. Competitive comparisons that are reviewed at that time show changes as the result of the improved processes throughout the organization. Market share increases, increased sales, and increased profits all relate to the benchmarking activities.

Measurements for competitive comparisons and benchmark metrics of best-in-class companies are continuously plotted for many activities. As actual results move toward the established stretch goals and best-in-class measures, satisfaction with results and methodology is determined. If the rate of change in the indicators is not aggressive enough to close the defined gap, changes activities are initiated for the process.

Since 1989 when the benchmarking activities started, the process has matured and grown. Initial benchmark partners were often selected on the basis of convenience of location or personal knowledge of some influential person in the potential partner. Today partners are selected on an objective basis of having the potential to significantly help the various businesses in their various processes. Best-in-class goals are utilized in the assessment and comparison of process results.

Similarly, experience has shown the importance of public domain searches before beginning formal benchmarking visits. This has been of significant help in the selection of the right benchmarking partners.

As processes have improved, the expectations have also improved. As more people have become familiar with what the benchmarking process can contribute, and as results have improved in the financial characteristics, there is more dissatisfaction with the present status and increased enthusiasm in doing things even better. The profit sharing by the employees is a great motivator.

Case Study

Colony Fasteners, Inc.

Assignment Requirement

The previous material was extracted from the 1995 Malcolm Baldrige National Quality Award training case. The purpose is to provide a means to understand how to make an assessment based on written material. The tasks are:

1. Read the case Overview section and list the business factors that you feel should be taken into account when evaluating this company.
2. Read the 2.0 Information and Analysis Criteria in Exhibit 1, noting the points assigned to the three Items. Examine the Scoring Guidelines in Exhibit 3.6 (in chapter) for how to apply the Criteria.
3. Read the Category 2.0 description from the case in its entirety.
4. Using the Criteria and Scoring Guidelines, carefully reexamine the content of Category 2.0 from the case, and complete these tasks:

(a) Provide a 0–100 point score for each of the three Items. Now, using the Item weights (shown as 45, 25, and 20), from the criteria you can calculate a single score based on 100 points. (Note: You must convert the three item weights to a base of 100.)
(b) List for each Item up to three Strengths and three Areas for Improvement. Reading Exhibit 3.9 (in chapter) will help you with the phrasing.
(c) List three issues that should be examined on a site visit. These may be to confirm a critical requirement, provide clarity, or test for something you think exists, but the written evidence is not adequate for a determination.

5. It is now useful to compare your conclusions with those of other people or groups.

<table>
<tr><td>Exhibit
1</td><td></td></tr>
</table>

| Exhibit 1 | ## Information and Analysis Criteria. |

2.0 Information and Analysis (75 pts.)

The **Information and Analysis** Category examines the management and effectiveness of the use of data and information to support customer-driven performance excellence and marketplace success.

2.1 Management of Information and Data (20 pts.)

Describe the company's selection and management of information and data used for planning, management, and evaluation of overall performance.

A   D   R
☑   ☑   ☐

AREAS to ADDRESS

a. how information and data needed to drive improvement of overall company performance are selected and managed. Describe: (1) the main types of data and information and how each type is related to the key business drivers; and (2) how key requirements such as reliability, rapid access, and rapid update are derived from user needs.

b. how the company evaluates and improves the selection, analysis, and integration of information and data, aligning them with the company's business priorities. Describe how the evaluation considers: (1) scope of information and data; (2) use and analysis of information and data to support process management and performance improvement; and (3) feedback from users of information and data.

Notes:

(1) Reliability [2.1a(2)] includes software used in the information systems.

(2) User needs [2.1a(2)] should consider knowledge accumulation such as knowledge about specific customers or customer segments. User needs should also take into account changing patterns of communications associated with changes in process management and/or in job design.

(3) Scope of information and data [2.1b(1)] should focus primarily on key business drivers.

(4) Feedback from users [2.1b(3)] might entail formal or informal surveys, focus groups, teams, etc. However, evaluations should take into account patterns of communications and information use, as users themselves might not be utilizing well the information and data available. Even though the information and data system should be user friendly, the system should drive better practice. This might require training of users.

2.2 Competitive Comparisons and Benchmarking (15 pts.)

Describe the company's processes and uses of comparative information and data to support improvement of overall performance.

A   D   R
☑   ☑   ☐

Exhibit
1

AREAS TO ADDRESS

   a. how competitive comparisons and benchmarking information and data are selected and used to help drive improvement of overall company performance. Describe: (1) how needs and priorities are determined; (2) criteria for seeking appropriate information and data—from within and outside the company's industry; (3) how the information and data are used within the company to improve understanding of processes and process performance; and (4) how the information and data are used to set stretch targets and/or encourage breakthrough approaches.

   b. how the company evaluates and improves its overall process for selecting and using competitive comparisons and benchmarking information and data to improve planning and overall company performance.

Notes:

(1) Benchmarking information and data refer to processes and results that represent best practices and performance.

(2) Needs and priorities [2.2a(1)] should show clear linkage to the company's key business drivers.

(3) Use of benchmarking information and data within the company [2.2a(3)] might include the expectation that company units maintain awareness of related best-in-class performance to help drive improvement. This could entail education and training efforts to build capabilities.

(4) sources of competitive comparisons and benchmarking information might include: (a) information obtained from other organizations such as customers or suppliers through sharing; (b) information obtained from the open literature; (c) testing and evaluation by the company itself; and (d) testing and evaluation by independent organizations.

(5) The evaluation (2.2b) may address a variety of factors such as the effectiveness of use of the information, adequacy of information, training in acquisition and use of information, improvement potential in company operations, and estimated rates of improvement by other organizations.

2.3 Analysis and Use of Company-Level Data (40 pts.)

Describe how data related to quality, customers and operational performance, together with relevant financial data, are analyzed to support company-level review, action, and planning.

A   D   R

☑ ☑ ☐

AREAS TO ADDRESS

   a. how information and data from all parts of the company are integrated and analyzed to support reviews, business decisions, and planning, Describe how analysis is used to gain understanding of: (1) customers and markets; (2) operational performance and company capabilities; and (3) competitive performance.

Exhibit

1

b. how the company relates customer and market data, improvements in product/service quality, and improvements in operational performance to changes in financial and/or market indicators of performance. Describe how this information is used to set priorities for improvement actions.

Notes:

(1) Item 2.3 focuses primarily on analysis for company-level purposes, such as reviews (1.2c) and strategic planning (Item 3.1). Data for such analysis come from all parts of the company and include results reported in Items 6.1, 6.2, 6.3, 7.4, and 7.5. Other Items call for analyses of specific sets of data for special purposes. For example, the Items of Category 4.0 require analysis to determine effectiveness of training and other human resource practices. Such special-purpose analyses should be part of the overall information base available for use in item 2.3.

(2) Analysis includes trends, projections, cause-effect correlations, and the search for deeper understanding needed to set priorities to use resources more effectively to serve overall business objectives.

(3) Examples of analysis appropriate for inclusion in 2.3a(1) are:
- How the company's product and service quality improvement correlates with key customer indicators such as customer satisfaction, customer retention, and market share; and
- cost/revenue implications of customer-related problems and problem resolution effectiveness.

(4) Examples of analysis appropriate for inclusion in 2.3a(2) are:
- trends in improvement in key operational indicators such as productivity, cycle time, waste reduction, new product introduction, and defect levels;
- financial benefits from improved employee safety, absenteeism, and turnover;
- benefits and costs associated with education and training;
- how the company's ability to identify and meet employee requirements correlates with employee retention, motivation, and productivity; and
- cost/revenue implications of employee-related problems and problem resolution effectiveness.

(5) Examples of analysis appropriate for inclusion in 2.3a(3) are:
- performance trends relative to competitors on key quality attributes; and
- productivity and cost trends relative to competitors.

(6) Examples of analysis appropriate for inclusion in 2.3b are:
- relationships between product/service quality and operational performance indicators and overall company financial performance trends as reflected in indicators such as operating costs, revenues, asset utilization, and value added per employee;
- allocation of resources among alternative improvement projects based on cost/revenue implications and improvement potential;
- net earnings derived from quality/operational/human resource performance improvements;

Exhibit
1

- comparisons among business units showing how quality and operational performance improvement affect financial performance;
- contributions of improvement activities to cash flow and/or shareholder value;
- trends in quality versus market indicators;
- profit impacts of customer retention; and
- market share versus profits.

SOURCE: 1995 Malcolm Baldrige National Quality Award Criteria.

◆ BIBLIOGRAPHY

1991 Award Criteria. Malcolm Baldrige National Quality Award, U.S. Department of Commerce, Technology Administration, NIST, Gaithersburg, Md., 1991.

1995 Award Criteria. Malcolm Baldrige National Quality Award, U.S. Department of Commerce, Technology Administration, NIST, Gaithersburg, Md., 1995.

GAO. "Management Practices—U.S. Companies Improve Performance Through Quality Efforts." GAO/NSIAD 91-190, U.S. Government General Accounting Office, Washington, D.C., 1991.

Lessons from the Malcolm Baldrige Award; Implications for Management Practice, Research and Education. SEI Center Reports, SEI Center for Advanced Studies in management, The Wharton School, Pittsburgh, Pa., February 8, 1991.

Promoting Quality Business: A State Action Agenda. National Governor's Association, 1992.

Reimann, Curt W., and Hertz, Harry S. *The Malcolm Baldrige National Quality Award and ISO 9000 Registration: Understanding Their Many Differences.* Office of Quality programs, NIST, Gaithersburg, Md. (unpublished manuscript, August 31, 1993).

Measures of Quality Product and Quality Process: The Traditional Approach

◆ ◆ ◆

*T*he president of a private northeastern college and his key advisers met with a renowned TQM consulting organization to map a quality program for the college. These leaders embraced the quality concept and felt it offered a tremendous benefit for the institution. The real problem was getting the faculty and staff to actively support the quality movement. The partner of the TQM consulting program proposed the following: "Why don't we develop the cost to the college of poor quality. We can conduct a simple study to get reasonable data. My suspicion is the costs will be about 25 percent of the annual college budget. This has been our experience. Given the fiscal pressures on higher education and the raging money debates on this campus, a cost of $12,500,000 (25 percent of the budget) will get everyone's attention."

◆ INTRODUCTION

The language of money serves as the basic medium for assessing economic achievement. Organizations communicate results in monetary terms. Senior managers measure performance of units (divisions, subsidiaries, or departments) with financial information. Ultimately, the stockholders of the corporation want assurances that the managers are operating the firm in a manner that creates wealth (a return on investment). Executives regularly evaluate the productive and efficient use of company resources in various facets of the business. Accountants produce, analyze, and present cost data to managers for measurement, economic justification, and valuation. Line managers make decisions based on the cost implications of the available choices.

Those directly involved and those benefiting from TQM also seek financial assessments of the program. They want to judge the overall impact of quality on their area of responsibility and to determine whether this has an effect on the total financial performance of the organization. At all levels of the organization, the cost associated with TQM can provide valuable feedback. It can help guide the various decisions surrounding the TQM process. A significant issue surrounding TQM is the assessment of the program costs and the benefits gained from implementing a Total Quality system. This evaluation requires the development of reliable costs associated with the effects of quality and a means of determining the resulting improvements.

This chapter explores the traditional concept of **Cost of Quality (COQ).** We will develop the history of its use and present the classic COQ model. We will also address the various legitimate concerns that managers have with the idea of using costs to measure quality and the limitation of the model. In Chapter 5, we present the emerging COQ model and other financial measures of quality that incorporate managers' reservations with the COQ tool. Chapters 4 and 5 combined provide a complete picture of the measures used to evaluate quality programs.

The basis of the interest and value of COQ measures is a manager's desire to understand what the delivery of the product or service costs. This is a critical element in guiding the organization toward profitability. Through their design and process, managers choose a level of product or service quality, or they may seek to improve their current level of quality. COQ offers managers a financial method to evaluate the level of their quality and the costs associated with different levels of quality.

The COQ is a well-recognized and often disputed tool used to understand the economic consequences of quality. Purchasing managers and discerning consumers are asking, "What are the costs related to quality?" Contractors are required to provide details of the costs due to quality for the products they sell to the government. The definition of COQ varies but, in general, is considered to be the costs (tangible and intangible) relating to the quality characteristics of a product or service.

Difficulties in Capturing the "True" Costs

Many quality experts recognize the difficulty of associating cost with the benefits of a quality program. They maintain that placing a cost figure on quality is difficult and that accounting is unable to capture the "true" costs of quality. Some fundamental concerns include the following:

- Quality costs do not readily appear in the accounting journals.
- Large timing delays between quality costs and benefits create distortions.
- Accounting rules (product and period costs) do not lend themselves to measuring quality.
- Numerous cost estimates are needed.
- There are hidden costs never captured.
- Matching future costs with historical costs is necessary.

As a result of these and other arguments, many observers have advocated the use of direct measures from operations such as statistical process control to measure a TQM program. We will fully explore this controversy and offer guidelines for choosing a measurement system that will fit the characteristics of a company-specific TQM program.

The value of COQ is actively disputed, with many TQM advocates believing that COQ has no place in a quality program, while others use this tool as a central measure of the results of good or poor quality. Much of this debate stems from the lack of a crisp and precise definition of quality and the elusive nature of cost measurement. We need to define quality before we measure the costs associated with attaining this characteristic or state of existence. For some, quality is based on the number of features and the attributes of a product. For example, a BMW is considered to be a better car than Nissan because it has more features. Others may make the same observation but base their decision on the reliability of the product. For example, a Chrysler is a better car than a Saab because it needs fewer repairs. We could continue with further examples, but there is some agreement as to the definition of quality. Fitness for use and conformance to specifications (Juran and Gryna, 1993) are the two prime dimensions used to define quality for COQ purposes. (Chapter 2 discusses these approaches further.)

Fitness for use consists of those product attributes that meet the needs of the customer and thus provide product satisfaction. Such product attributes as performance, reliability, durability, and aesthetics serve to meet the customer's expectations. Conformance to specifications refers to the degree to which a product meets the design specifications, or is built to the design. For example, a badly made BMW may have high fitness for use or meet customer expectations but a low quality of conformance. On the other hand, a well-made Nissan may have lower fitness for use but a high quality of conformance. Quality costs generally represent all costs associated with conformance to specifications or design; or, what are the costs that resulted from not making a product as designed?

The other approach to quality is conformance-based. As noted earlier, Crosby describes this approach as the "conformance requirements" specified by the engineering and product characteristics. Manufacturing is required to conform to the specifications. The closer the adherence to the manufacturing specifications, the higher the quality level. This approach lends itself to objective measures against standards, and the costs associated with conforming to these standards can be calculated. The customer, however, is ignored in these calculations of cost.

A third approach to measuring quality is the value approach. This is a customer-based subjective approach in which the balance between product cost and product value is determined. One can plot the consumer's preferences along the value and cost axis to determine a cost of quality.

Organizations collect cost by departments or by functions, and they know the costs related to the resources consumed to make a product. The costs associated with quality include both the direct and the indirect product costs (factory overhead) as well as administrative period costs. The latter costs relate not only to the manufacturing support to make the product, but also to servicing the customer during and after the sale. To complicate matters, often the costs related to quality are only a partial amount of a specific expense category. Generally accepted accounting principles and the structures of accounting records (ledgers and journals) do not lend themselves to capturing the cost related to quality.

◆ THE EVOLUTION OF COST OF QUALITY

During the post–World War II industrial boom, quality departments began to emerge in many organizations. These staff departments were created to aid the line departments with managing, measuring, and improving quality. The functional managers (i.e., engineering, assembly department, painting, etc.) were responsible for a budget. Strict budget management often required that departments sell their services to other departments. Managers were measured on conformance to budget. Their costs were budget related, and the departments that purchased services from other departments wanted to know exactly the value of the service rendered. The quality department was placed in the position of demonstrating the cost savings and benefits of their service. Thus, the common language of money entered the delivery of quality support. This forced the quality professional to think and argue in the common language of cost and monetary savings. Dr. J. M. Juran is often given credit for coining the concept of quality costs. He addressed the economics of quality in the first *Quality Control Handbook*, (1951) in which he used the famous analogy of "Gold in the Mine." He proposed that an optimal quality level could be found where the losses due to defects were equal to the costs of quality control. (Chapter 2 discusses the evolution of the quality concept in much greater detail.)

   Managers continued to struggle with applying cost to quality. Although they knew that quality-related costs were much larger than those shown in the accounting reports and often exceeded the reported product cost, they were not sure how to categorize or collect the relevant cost information. They needed the information to obtain a greater commitment to the benefits of quality and were aware that a positive cost trend would prove the economic value of quality. The traditional Cost of Quality model began to evolve with Masser (1957) who subdivided quality costs into prevention, appraisal, and failure costs. Freeman (1960) and Feigenbaum (1961) further developed the COQ model. Reporting and understanding quality costs became a requirement in 1963 for U.S. government contractors and subcontractors. The American Society for Quality Control (ASQC) formed the Quality Cost Committee in 1961, lending further validity to the concept. In 1967 this committee published *Quality Costs—What and How,* which established the traditional model.

◆ THE TRADITIONAL COST-OF-QUALITY MODEL

All quality costs are expenditures associated with ensuring that products conform to specifications or with the production of goods that do not conform. This model of quality cost refers only to the conformance specification's definition of quality;

it does not address the fitness for use definition of quality. This concern and other issues surrounding the use of the traditional Cost-of-Quality model are addressed later in the chapter. The model states that cost can be divided into two broad categories: conformance costs and nonconformance costs, each with two subcategories (conformance costs → prevention and appraisal; nonconformance costs → internal failure and external failure costs).

Conformance Costs

Conformance costs are those costs incurred to ensure that the manufactured products or delivered services conform to specifications. These costs are of two types:

Prevention Costs—costs associated with all activities designed to prevent defects in products or service. These include the direct and indirect costs related to quality training and education, pilot studies, quality circles, quality engineering, quality audits, supplier capability surveys, vendor technical support, process capability analysis, and new product reviews. These costs are used to build awareness of the quality program and to keep the costs of appraisal and failure to a minimum.

Appraisal Costs—the costs associated with measuring and evaluating the product or service quality to ensure conformance. These include the cost of inspection, test or audit of purchases, manufacturing or process operations, and finished goods or services. The direct and indirect costs of the various tests and inspections to determine the degree of conformity are included in this category.

Nonconformance

Nonconformance costs are associated with products or services that do not conform to the customer's requirement. They are often referred to as *failure* costs and consist of two types:

Internal Failure Costs—costs incurred prior to the shipment of the product or the delivery of the service. These costs are associated with defects that are found prior to customer delivery. They include the net cost of scrap, spoilage, rework and overhead, failure analysis, supplier rework and scrap, reinspection and retest, downtime due to quality problems, opportunity cost of product classified as seconds, or other product downgrades.

External Failure Costs—the costs of discovered defects occurring after product shipment or service delivery. These costs include warranty charges, customer complaint adjustments, returned merchandise, product recalls, allowances, and product liability. They also include the direct and indirect costs such as labor and travel associated with the investigation of customer complaints, warranty field inspection, tests, and repairs.

Developing the Cost-of-Quality Report

Managers develop quality cost reports using the above categories. They can be organized by division, product, or any appropriate business segment. Their frequency can vary from monthly to quarterly to annually. The cost definitions are customized for each organization and require the accountants' involvement to establish the level of detail and the association of activities to cost categories.

For example, the Joe Jones Company, using one of the many COQ software packages available, has established a Cost-of-Quality program. Their cost distribution report links the quality cost categories of appraisal, prevention, internal failure, and external failure (COQ) to the traditional cost structure of the company. Their quarterly report would appear as outlined in Table 4.1. This matrix reshapes the standard accounting cost data into the COQ cost elements.

With the assistance of the Accounting Department, the relationship between the regular cost structure categories and the Cost-of-Quality categories has been mapped through the accounting general ledger. Using the Joe Jones chart of accounts, the accountant can categorize each cost element pertaining to the Cost of Quality. Thus, the accountant, while recording costs, can also capture the Cost of Quality in the appropriate categories. The Joe Jones COQ matrix might look like the material shown in Table 4.2. Using the financial data developed in Table 4.1 managers can now look at the COQ cost elements by organizational function as shown in Table 4.3. This allows managers to determine and manage the actions that cause the various quality costs.

The key to producing this COQ report is the effort made to ensure that the Costs of Quality are properly captured. Often, these costs represent only a portion of an expense line item. For example, training costs are the prime element of the cost of prevention. In reality, both quality awareness and skills training are covered in dedicated specific quality improvement sessions and as part of other

Table 4.1

Cost of Quality Account Matrix

STANDARD ACCOUNTING COST ELEMENTS	COQ Cost Elements				
	PREVENTION	APPRL	INT FAIL	EXT FAIL	TOTAL
Direct Material	###	###	###	###	####
Direct Labor	###	###	###	###	####
Indirect Material	###	###	###	###	####
Indirect Labor	###	###	###	###	####
Misc Fixed	###	###	###	###	####
Sale & Admin	###	###	###	###	####
Total	###	###	###	###	####

Table 4.2

COQ Cost Elements

COMPANY FUNCTIONS	PREVENTION	APPRAISAL	FAILURE (I & E)
Development	Design review	Prototype Inspection Design test	Re-design Scrap
Purchasing	Supplier assessment Supplier inspection	Product Inspection	Corrective action on supplier failures Parts rejection
Production	Quality team training Quality process audit	Work in process Inspection	Rework Scrap
Sales	Sales team quality Training	Order entry Inspection	Reshipment due to shipping error
Orders			Reprocessing

general training efforts. The issue then is how does one accurately capture the expenses relating to the cost of prevention and not all of the Joe Jones training costs? Similar accounting issues surround the other COQ categories. Appraisal and internal failure costs are quite straightforward with distinct cost categories corresponding to the normal chart of accounts. The real problem arises with the cost related to external failure.

Many of the external failure costs are part of the normal field service and sales activities and are not designated as separate costs related to quality. How do you capture the costs (primarily labor time) related to resolving a customer problem? Sales personnel, customer service representatives, engineers, and others do not normally divide their time between efforts to make a sale and efforts to resolve customer problems. Many firms use educated estimates based on some internal time and cost study. Senior managers often get involved in resolving major customer problems. How are these costs captured? Many critics of this concept are concerned that hidden costs surrounding external failures are not reported. Lost opportunity, customer dissatisfaction, and negative customer referrals are certainly cost relating to poor quality.

It is important to remember that the Cost of Quality is, at best, an educated estimate of the costs and not a precise measure. Extensive use of estimates and the input from many diverse functions is necessary to capture the essential data. This requires the cooperation of the organization and an Accounting Department willing to support the company's quality movement. Agreement between the quality, operational, and accounting managers should be reached before the COQ data are collected. Critiques of the COQ model often cite the "soft numbers" as a real concern when using this tool for measurement or evaluation.

Table 4.3	Cost of Quality		
TYPE OF COST		AMOUNT	PERCENT
Prevention			
Plant training (locally delivered)		$ 300,924	12
Quality training consultant		$ 48,000	2
Training and display material		$ 36,841	2
Quality audit		$ 27,694	1
Total		$ 413,459	17
Appraisal			
Incoming inspection		$ 102,689	4
Internal inspection		$ 226,823	8
Statistical process control cost		$ 52,951	2
Quality engineering support		$ 239,510	10
Total		$ 621,973	24
Total Conformance Costs		$1,035,522	41
Internal Failure			
Scrap		$ 117,850	4
Rework		$ 141,950	5
Downgrading due to defects		$ 13,280	1
Plant downtime due to defects		$ 56,320	2
Reshipments (freight cost)		$ 20,000	1
Total		$ 349,400	14
External Failure			
Warranty adjustments		$ 610,450	24
Field repairs		$ 259,520	10
Product liability claim payments		$ 175,000	7
Additional customer discounts (due to field quality complaints)		$ 120,000	4
Total		$1,164,970	45
Total Nonconformance Costs		$ 1,514,370	59
Grand Total		$2,549,892	100

Using the report outlined in Table 4.1, Joe Jones can show the following: (1) the impact of the Total Cost of Quality demonstrating the need for quality improvement; (2) the COQ relationship to sales as a percentage, profit as a percentage, or in comparison to other financial reference points; and (3) the interrelationships between the various COQ categories and their trend over time.

Using the Cost-of-Quality Report

There is the popular story of how the manager of quality at AT&T seized the opportunity to point out to the chairman during a brief encounter in the elevator that the company's Cost of Quality was in excess of 25 percent of sales. Stunned by the size, the chairman's interest was raised, and he wanted to know more. The Cost of Quality as a percentage of sales demonstrated the magnitude of both the problem and the opportunity for AT&T. It served as the catalyst, driving the senior managers to take the quest for quality seriously. The literature and documented practices indicate that one of the strongest attributes of COQ is its ability to stimulate awareness and generate interest in quality. One consultant said: "We don't need a crisis to generate interest in a quality program. If they do not see the business value, we can use the Cost of Quality to get their interest."

Financial ratios are the generic reference for measuring performance. A number of companies report the percentage of Cost of Quality as it relates to total sales on a quarterly basis. A company with an excellent reputation for quality reports the internal failure costs (primarily scrap and rework) as a separate line item compared to the company's profit. Many public companies are discussing the attributes of their various TQM programs and are using both accounting and operational data to demonstrate to the stockholders the progress they are making. Currently, a number of companies are using **Return on Quality (ROQ)** to evaluate quality programs. Managers want to know if they are going to make money as a consequence of improving quality. (Chapter 5 discusses this concept further.)

Useful information can be gained by comparing the subtotal of the various Cost-of-Quality categories. The interrelationship between conformance costs, prevention and appraisal, nonconformance costs, and internal and external failure provide managers with an indication of the economic impact of their quality program. In most firms, the nonconformance or failure costs are several times those of the conformance costs. Managers can use this form of Cost-of-Quality analysis to measure the influence of prevention and appraisal expenditures on reducing internal and external failure costs. For example, to reduce the large cost of failures, managers are encouraged to increase expenditures in appraisal costs. This, coupled with modest increases in prevention costs through building awareness of quality, should result in a measurable reduction of both internal and external failure costs.

The Traditional Cost-of-Quality Model

The study of the relationship of the COQ categories led to the development of a significant body of economic literature offering various models to explain the interrelationship of the COQ categories. Exhibit 4.1 represents the original or classical model. In this case, the costs of prevention and appraisal are zero with a 100 percent failure rate. The costs of prevention and appraisal rise to infinity as perfection (no failures) is reached. This hypothetical model shows that total quality cost is higher when quality is low and falls as quality improves. According to the model, a company producing poor quality (i.e., defective) products can greatly reduce failure costs by adding relatively low-cost prevention and appraisal measures. As prevention and appraisal expenditures continue to rise, the rate of improvement begins to diminish until additional expenditures produce little decrease in failure cost.

The model suggests that a relationship exists between conformance and nonconformance quality costs, with a minimal total quality cost at the optimal balance. Implicit in this model is the tradeoff of conformance costs for nonconformance costs to achieve the lowest total quality cost. There is a level beyond which additional prevention and appraisal expenditures will only increase the total quality cost (the law of diminishing returns). Using this model, managers can monitor the amount of cost tradeoff over time. The model implies that a company with poor quality can reduce the Total Cost of Quality by spending on relatively inexpensive preventive and appraisal measures. At a certain point, however, these additional costs will only increase total quality costs as shown in Exhibit 4.1.

Exhibit 4.1 **Traditional Model of Quality Costs**

Behavior of Cost Components During TQM Implementation

The general behavior of the four quality cost components for a company starting TQM is as follows: Prevention costs remain relatively consistent as the awareness of TQM is built and maintained. Appraisal costs will initially increase as inspection programs are initiated but should eventually level off. Internal failure costs will initially increase as the inspection programs are implemented, but should then gradually decrease with learning. External failure costs should continue to fall as various TQM programs are brought on line.

A critical consideration is the intended application of the COQ information in the quality process. A major southwestern electronic component manufacturer incorporates the COQ data with the four categories in its monthly financial reporting material. It is a mature, financially driven company embarking on a major quality improvement effort. The financial reporting of the quality effort is natural and part of the firm's culture. The financial managers worked with operations and functional managers to properly define the cost category and to establish a simple and efficient data collection regime. At the start, COQ reporting was viewed as yet another number for judging performance.

Over time, the quarterly reports of COQ correlated with both the operational quality indicators and the divisions' financial performance. Managers were working to improve quality and saw the trend in the corresponding quality costs. Prevention and appraisal costs trend up, while the internal and external failure costs trend down. Most importantly, the Total Cost of Quality was trending down, thus confirming what the managers observed in other operational measures of quality such as defect rates, yields, and customer complaints.

Managers are comfortable with COQ reports when they are *not* used as a "hammer." COQ is part of the total company picture and a confirming indicator, not an absolute target number. Managers use the data to confirm the cost benefits of their quality program and to address the long-term trends of the company's quality improvements.

Although the COQ reporting process worked well for this electronics company, there are more cases of firms abandoning COQ reporting than those sustaining the measure. Many of the reasons are linked to the implementation process. Companies without a financial culture or in a very dynamic market find the historical nature of COQ incompatible with their operation. Other firms use COQ as an absolute measure and judge managers' performance against COQ targets.

◆ LIMITATIONS TO COST OF QUALITY

The Cost-of-Quality model is theoretical and assumes a static production environment with an unchanging production process over time. In reality, the production improves over time with the addition of technology, process improvements, and workforce improvements. The relationship between conformance and nonconformance costs is dynamic, with companies using technology and knowledge to improve quality. This model appears at length in quality manuals and textbooks as a basis for explaining quality costs. It encourages managers to monitor their spending in each COQ category and for their relationship. Managers believe that spending for the cheaper prevention and appraisal dollars will save the more expensive failure dollars. The literature is also full of critics of the COQ model and the use of cost in evaluating the progress of a quality program. The limitations of the Cost-of-Quality concept include the following:

1. Cost-of-Quality measurements do not solve quality problems. Many question the practical value of using COQ, maintaining that these data do not solve any of the problems that produce the cost of poor quality. The historical nature of the accounting data does not tell managers or operations people what needs fixing or what to do to improve quality. For example, Deming does not subscribe to Juran's notion that quality costs can be minimized at some nonzero number of defects (the classic tradeoff model above). Both Crosby and Deming believe that the cost of selling defective products is so high that quality costs will be minimized only at 100 percent conformance, or zero defects. Quality managers look for evidence of actions to improve quality. Knowing the costs does not provide any hints to this action.

2. Publication of the cost figures does not stimulate cost reduction. Managers quickly point out that decisions and actions are necessary if changes are to be implemented to affect the costs of quality. The cost numbers provide a relative reference point. It is up to the line managers to determine the steps necessary to reduce these costs.

3. Cost-of-Quality reports do not provide specific actions. Managers must decide the cost investments for each of the various categories. There is the belief that increased prevention and appraisal costs will lead to a reduction of failure costs. The specific actions are up to the individual manager. In addition, there is the belief that excess spending in prevention and appraisal will lead to increased total quality costs, for they will not be counterbalanced with the proportionate reduction in failure costs.

4. Cost-of-Quality calculations do not capture all of the cost. There are implied and hidden costs that make COQ useless. Feigenbaum points out that the COQ calculation ignores indirect and intangible failure costs. Extra production to compensate for failures, queuing time in the production process due to rework or excessive finished goods inventory to compensate for field failures, and excessive handling due to suboptimal production layouts are good examples of these costs. Garvin had similar concerns and was particularly interested in the involuntary costs that arise whenever customers choose alternative suppliers because of actual or perceived quality deficiencies.

5. Accounting conventions such as capital spending and rules for defining period and product cost render COQ of little use for evaluating a quality program. Cost of Quality looks at spending to improve quality and the assessment of the spending in the various cost categories during a given time

period. Much of the quality spending is capital in nature, where large expenditures for equipment are for up-front training conducted in order to have a stream of benefit. Investment for the future and depreciation of capital expenditures make accounting assessment of quality very difficult.

6. Important costs can easily be omitted from the COQ calculation. Both Feigenbaum and Garvin expressed concern about the integrity of the accounting data collection in the organization. They showed that numerous costs are not captured but, in fact, influence the Cost of Quality. The Joe Jones example above demonstrates the difficulty of accurately capturing the costs. Errors of omission as well as faulty estimation are quite possible.

7. There is a time delay between cause and effect, and a COQ report may not capture all the changes in the same period. Often the effects of quality training and the building of an awareness of quality in an organization are measured in years. The prevention spending in year one may only show its effect in year three, thus overlapping the conventional year-to-year Cost-of-Quality analysis.

8. Quality costs are subject to judgment and estimation, which can cause distortion. Many of the cost calculations for the categories mentioned above are a function of both line and accounting staff judgment. There are often no clear single-account numbers derived from the firm's chart of accounts to capture the COQ accounting data. The available accounting databases need to be assessed, and the costs relating to quality should be estimated.

9. COQ has a tendency to be short term. Many investments in quality are long term such as test equipment, process re-designs, or quality awareness training for all employees. There are very large initial costs with a stream of benefits over many years. The traditional model does not relate the stream of benefits to the costs associated with the benefit.

The following is an example of the management discussions surrounding a typical company's use of COQ:

Joe Jones manufactures, markets, and sells computer disk drives. Their quality costs for the previous year are reported by the controller as follows.

The first general observation is that the COQ report is a historical document that does not solve quality problems or provide the specific actions necessary to improve quality. The general manager asks, If we spend more money on training and inspections, will we be able to reduce the large external failure? If so, what type of training? Will the training take effect in this year and drive failure costs down? Will we be able to reduce the inspection time as the "quality-caring" attitudes of the employees improve? This report does not provide insights to answer these questions. The COQ report, however, can aid in setting priorities. It will highlight for managers the areas in which investments will have the greatest effect.

At the same review meeting, the quality manager expresses her surprise at the dollar size of the various cost categories. She questions the controller regarding the source of the numbers. Are the costs fully loaded, and do they include the fully burdened labor hours? The field repairs seem very high; where did these numbers come from? Do not forget that our technical field people make many types of customer calls and are an integral part of marketing our disk drives. They are not there just to solve quality problems. Can you separate their costs related to quality alone? Who makes these estimates, and what data do they use? She is just not very comfortable with the dollar values. They are using so many estimates, how do they know the difference between real progress and just estimating error?

The production manager then adds his concerns with the report. We recently purchased a new disk drive tester for $4.5 million. It not only does the routine operational testing, but it also provides design feedback and maintains its own SPC charts for the critical features of the disk drive. How are the costs calculated for the internal inspection? It appears that the equipment costs are not included in the internal inspection number; are they? He goes on, "I have another issue that bothers me: Our production batches always include extra disk drives to compensate for possible rejections. Can I back these costs out of my standard costs and put them in the Cost of Quality? Where would we capture this cost item? We should not charge the full cost of the equipment to inspection costs." The design feedback feature is very valuable and gives us useful information.

The controller, along with the financial analysts who compile the COQ report, was compelled to respond to the barrage of questions. "We make educated guesses and estimates to assign the costs to the proper category. Your Cost-of-Quality categories do not fit well with our current chart of accounts. The most difficult problem is the splitting of costs between quality and some other activity. It is quite difficult to estimate the cost split of the field technical visits. Sometimes we ask the technical representative, or, otherwise, we just guess. We can't spend all of our resources chasing these costs. This is our best estimate until you people give us more guidance."

From this example, one can see that determining the Cost-of-Quality is as much an art as a science. The numbers are not "hard" but rather "soft" in nature. Not all of the costs over time can be captured from the accounting records. Cost of Quality does provide an indication or general model of how we spend the firm's quality dollars. Companies know it takes resources to establish a TQM program, and managers need some feedback as to their effectiveness. When the COQ data are combined with other operational measures such as SPC trends, yields, defect rates, and customer complaints, a clearer picture of the measures of our quality program progress is developed for management to evaluate its effectiveness.

The meeting at Joe Jones produced a lively dialogue centering on the costs related to quality. There was the debate over the validity of the numbers, but the managers knew that the cost data were valuable as one of the assessments of the TQM program. What is important to note is that the COQ numbers were not used as a "hammer" or some absolute target for achievement. Rather, they were used for indication and as a means of setting priorities.

◆ Summary

This chapter focuses on the traditional economic model of Cost of Quality. The Cost of Quality can be divided into conformance and nonconformance costs. The conformance cost elements are prevention and appraisal costs. Nonconformance costs consist of internal and external failure costs. In the COQ model, a manager is encouraged to balance the costs of conformance with the cost of nonconformance. An optimal total quality cost is achieved when these two cost categories are balanced.

We showed how companies can use the COQ model. The COQ cost elements can be obtained from the accounting records, and managers can monitor the behavior of the quality cost elements over time. While this cost behavior provides managers with valuable insight, there are limitations to the use of the model. We outlined a number of limitations to COQ as a measuring device for a TQM program.

◆ Key Terms

Cost of Quality (COQ)	Prevention costs	External failure costs
Conformance costs	Appraisal costs	Return on Quality
Nonconformance costs	Internal failure costs	(ROQ)

◆ Assignments

1. What are the two cost elements of conformance cost? List three examples of each.
2. What are the two cost elements of nonconformance cost? List three examples of each.
3. What are the difficulties in attempting to measure the Cost of Quality?
4. Explain how the tradeoff between conformance costs and nonconformance costs works.
5. List and explain the limits to the use of the COQ tool.
6. How can companies use COQ to help manage their TQM process? Provide company examples to support your position.

Case Study

Matthews-Thornton Manufacturing Company

Early in 1992, Larry Matthews was flying home from a business trip to Portland, Oregon. He had just been to visit one of his oldest customers and, Larry hoped, his newest customer, Beaver Chainsaws. Matthews-Thornton Manufacturing (MTM), the company founded by his father and an army "buddy," was a manufacturer of aircraft-grade aluminum alloy bolts. Beaver had been one of the first customers to use these bolts in consumer products, and now, perhaps, it would be a regular customer, again.

Larry recalled a similar flight that he had taken five and a half years earlier. On that flight, he was returning from Portland after having been "fired" by Beaver. He had gone to convince them to retain MTM as a prime supplier but had been shocked to find out that Beaver's management had not been happy with MTM's quality and reliability for some time. He was also chagrined to find out that a competitor had offered to sell to Beaver bolts of demonstrated higher levels of quality and reliability at a slightly higher price. They had convinced Beaver's management that it was cheaper to pay a little more for better quality and reliability.

That trip had been an epiphany of sorts for Larry. He returned to Ohio determined to find out whether MTM's quality was really all that bad, and, if so, why it was bad. Finally, he wanted to understand the relationship between the price of quality and the cost of operations.

MTM manufactured tie-down bolts and fasteners for a variety of applications. The original selling point of these products was their light weight. Later, applications calling for corrosion resistance and absence of chemical reactiveness were added to the list of core markets for MTM's products. Many of the bolts and tighteners were designed to be driven with hex or torque wrenches. The nature of the way these products were tightened required close tolerances in the hexagonal or torx-star holes in the heads of the bolts. Thus, MTM had paid particular attention to the design and execution of bolt heads. Larry was at a loss to see how the reliability and quality could be improved at only marginal cost increases. As it turned out, that was not the source of Beaver's annoyance. The quality/reliability issue there was the absence of threads on about 3 percent of the delivered bolts and the tendency for about 0.5 percent of the bolts to snap under high torsion due to the acceleration of the drive wrenches.

Before MTM had even discovered the nature of these problems, Larry had taken two major steps to forestall further market erosion. First, he tripled the level of postmanufacturing inspection. Second, he instituted a "double money back" guarantee on MTM products. MTM quickly saw how expensive quality guarantees could be. Sight inspection for "blanks" was effective but labor intensive. Testing for faults in the bolts related to the snapping problem was far too expensive to be done on all bolts. Instead, x-ray test failures on statistical samples led to the rejection of entire job lots of bolts, which would have to be melted and reprocessed.

At about this time, however, a golf partner brought Larry's attention to a book by Phil

Printed with permission from Fred Nanni.

Matthews-Thornton Manufacturing Company (Continued)

Crosby that proclaimed, Quality Is Free! Larry read the book and immediately began a five-year quality improvement program (QIP) at MTM. Larry had seen that quality products could actually command a higher price. If MTM could learn to produce quality for free, it could become a much more profitable company.

The QIP began with an audit of quality-related costs in 1987. The goal for the program was to cut quality costs as a percentage of sales in half. The quality cost audit and measures of quality costs in ensuing years revealed the data given in Tables 4.4 and 4.5. In 1991, the fifth year of the program, the

budgeted costs related to quality were slightly exceeded, as shown in Table 4.6. The budget is based on the notion that prevention costs are fixed but all other quality costs are variable.

The reports generated from the quality data normally included annual and quarterly Cost-of-Quality performance reports showing quality cost budget variances. Some quality spending areas seemed always to have variances, whereas others were nearly always right on target. However, the trends in quality costs were generally in the right direction, and the level of revenues had

Table 4.4	Five-Year History of Revenues and Quality Costs, 1987–1991		
YEAR	SALES REVENUES	QUALITY COSTS	QC AS A % OF SALES
1987	$11,700,000	$2,269,800	0.1940
1988	$11,700,000	$2,042,820	0.1746
1989	$12,870,000	$2,059,200	0.1600
1990	$14,285,700	$2,101,840	0.1471
1991	$15,999,984	$1,522,659	0.0952

Table 4.5	Breakdown of Quality Costs as a Percentage of Annual Revenues, 1987–1991				
			Internal	External	
YEAR	PREVENTION	APPRAISAL	FAILURE	FAILURE	TOTAL
1987	0.0097	0.0291	0.0679	0.0873	0.1940
1988	0.0194	0.0388	0.0582	0.0582	0.1746
1989	0.0243	0.0388	0.0485	0.0485	0.1600
1990	0.0232	0.0524	0.0429	0.0286	0.1471
1991	0.0200	0.0411	0.0170	0.0170	0.0952

Matthews-Thornton Manufacturing Company (Continued)

Table
4.6

Quality Cost Detail by Category

COST CATEGORY	BUDGETED '91	ACTUAL '91	ACTUAL '90
Prevention costs			
Quality planning	$170,235	$170,235	$158,886
Quality training	22,698	22,698	22,698
Quality reporting	11,349	13,619	13,619
Process improve	90,792	113,490	136,188
Appraisal costs			
Visual inspection	567,450	590,148	658,242
Testing	56,745	68,094	90,792
Failure costs			
Internal rework	91,454	93,969	211,431
External allowances	265,117	272,000	408,571
Equipment overhaul	32,419	35,136	79,057
Equipment downtime	63,490	62,646	140,954
Scrap	85,012	80,624	181,402
Total quality costs	$1,456,761	$1,522,659	$2,101,840
Total Revenues	$15,748,768	$15,999,984	$14,285,700

steadily increased during the QIP period. The Cost-of-Quality data encouraged Larry. No new products had been introduced over the last five years, so he felt that any increases in profits were directly traceable to improved quality. Until his visit to Portland, Larry was basically optimistic about MTM's future.

As Larry reflected on his visit with Beaver, he felt a twinge of anxiety about the rate of quality improvement MTM had experienced. Were MTM's products good enough now? Had quality become free at MTM? Certainly, Beaver's management had not jumped at MTM's suggestion of a 5 percent undercut of their current supplier's price. They had agreed to consider MTM's offer, but Larry

was sure that they would be talking to the current supplier about his offer. He felt that a reanalysis of the Cost-of-Quality trends at MTM was in order.

CASE QUESTIONS

1. Plot the QIP trends and the quality cost trends. What do these data show?
2. What should Larry recommend to MTM?
3. What type of costs are driving the change in COQ?

ɔr Quality Control. *Accounting for Quality Costs*. Milwaukee, Wis.:

ls. *Quality, Productivity, and Competitive Position*. Cambridge, Mass.:
dvanced Engineering, 1982.
nd V. "The Challenge of Total Quality Control." *Industrial Quality*
57): 17–23.
nd V. *Total Quality Control*. 3rd ed. New York: McGraw-Hill, 1983.
w to Put Quality Costs to Work." *12th Metropolitan Section All Day*
tember 1960).
Competing on the Eight Dimensions of Quality." *Harvard Business*
ɩer–December 1987): 101–109.
anaging Quality: The Strategic and Competitive Edge*. New York: Free

nk M. Gryna. *Quality Planning and Analysis*. New York: McGraw-Hill,

ɔuality Manager and Quality Costs." *Industrial Quality Control* (October

Roth, and K. M. Poston, *Measuring, Planning, and Controlling Quality*
N.J.: National Association of Accountants, 1987.

Measures of Quality Product and Quality Process: The Emerging Cost-of-Quality Model

◆ ◆ ◆

*T*he general manager of a major division of a Fortune 50 corporation spoke in frustration at the monthly quality review meeting. "People will not get serious about quality if they don't believe the numbers. My sense is that you don't trust the COQ report. Jim (the controller) tells us every department has their own rules for collecting COQ data. Now, George (production manager) is admitting he changed the cost definitions so he won't get burnt by the COQ report. What is going on? Are we wasting our time with COQ?"

◆ INTRODUCTION

The limitations of the cost model discussed in Chapter 4 coupled with the manufacturing and process changes of today's organizations have led to a slightly different COQ model. As depicted in Exhibit 5.1, greater emphasis is placed on prevention and appraisal. Prevention spending is very important in building the quality mindset and instilling a sense of caring in the workforce. New technologies have reduced the inherent failure rates of materials and limited the direct labor content of most products. Automation of the process and testing routines has changed the shape of the COQ curve. This revised model looks at the Total Cost of Quality rather than the unit cost. It suggests that voluntary prevention and appraisal costs are relatively fixed over time rather than directly proportional to changes in the level of nonconformance, as shown in the more static traditional model.

This chapter explores the recent changes in the cost model and discusses the use and implementation of both accounting-based and operational-based measures of quality. We offer both successful and unsuccessful examples from industry and address the limitations of the COQ tool. We outline the support that accounting and information systems can provide to a TQM program. Finally, we

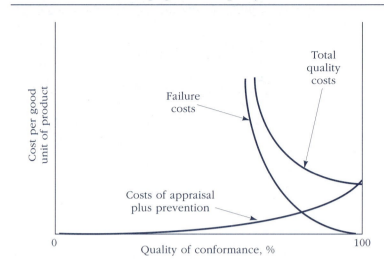

Exhibit 5.1 — Emerging model of quality costs

propose recommendations for choosing a measurement system to evaluate a TQM program for sustained success.

The **emerging COQ model** recognizes that total quality costs include indirect and intangible costs. These costs are probably not minimized at less than 100 percent conformance (Schneiderman,1986). Because of the high multiplier effect of perceived quality deficiencies, intangible failure cost may linger, even though the actual quality of conformance deficiencies has been totally eradicated. Cost minimization is also contentious, for it implies the existence of a specific optimal level. In reality, optimization is a moving target owing to technology breakthroughs and competitive pressures (Morse, Roth, and Poston, 1986). Prevention and appraisal costs are also subject to cost reduction through experience factors and market competition. The emerging model indicates that some amount of prevention and appraisal must be maintained to preserve the earlier quality improvements. This model does not encourage tradeoffs.

The concept of loss, rather than nonconformance, better encompasses the total business cost of out-of-pocket, indirect, and intangible failures. Minimizing quality loss acknowledges the multiplier effect of intangible failure costs and recognizes the need to sustain the quality improvement effort beyond the minimization point of out-of-pocket costs.

◆ **OTHER METHODS FOR MEASURING THE COST OF QUALITY**

As illustrated above, a number of problems are associated with producing accurate Cost-of-Quality numbers. It is very difficult to capture these costs in a precise manner. Managers, however, recognize the importance of having an economic measure of the progress of the quality program. Managers expect performance measures in financial terms. The emerging practices recognize the difficulty and theoretical nature of seeking the optimal COQ using the tradeoffs between conformance and nonconformance quality costs. The classic model gives a reasonable general model of classification but does not reflect how these costs behave. We still need to know the level of our costs of poor quality. Managers want to compare the costs in various areas before quality programs are installed in order to correct various identified deficiencies. There is the belief that accounting data can be incorporated in a measurement scheme for Cost of Quality.

There are several well-documented field-based studies (Carr, 1992, Carr and Tyson, 1992; Ittner, 1994) which outline the various innovative techniques utilized by such companies as IBM, Xerox, Tennant, Ford, Westinghouse, Pacific Bell, and others. These companies employ COQ calculations as an integral part of their quality program. They are flexible with the use of quality cost definitions, comfortable with cost estimations, and practical with presenting the information. In general, the Accounting Department takes an active role and assists the company with calculating the economic effect of poor quality.

Hale, Hoelscher, and Kowal (1987) implicitly refute the traditional model by recommending a different proportional distribution as the target for the quality cost categories. They describe how the Tennant Company has significantly improved product quality and reduced total quality costs. Tennant's Total Cost of Quality decreased from 17 percent of sales in 1980 to 7.9 percent by 1986, with a further reduction to 2.5 percent of sales in 1988. Average annual sales growth of 11 percent accounted for some but not all of the cost reduction. The proportional distribution of costs changed among the quality cost categories over the eight-year time period. Failure costs decreased from 50 percent in 1980 to 15 percent in 1988, while prevention costs increased from 15 to 50 percent during the same time period.

Clearly, Tennant does not endorse a model that depicts the location of optimal quality cost expenditures at the intersection of voluntary and involuntary costs. Nor does the company target cost minimization if this occurs at less than 100 percent conformance. According to a Tennant executive, no one really knows where the minimum cost of quality is: "There may be a theoretical answer to that issue, but not a practical answer. I feel that message is out-of-date and belongs in the same category as engineers that still use slide rules."

Despite the fact that only 15 percent of total quality costs are now represented by out-of-pocket failures, Tennant Company continues to incur additional voluntary quality cost expenditures. The company believes that backsliding will occur unless a steadfast commitment to quality improvement is maintained. Regarding their company's ongoing commitment, Hale, Hoelscher, and Kowal (1987, p. 53) write: "The quest for quality never ends. A company can make progress, and even reach the point where it has no quality problems. But unless quality improvement is a continual activity, all the progress that has been made will be lost."

An example of the policy conflict regarding the reduction of quality cost versus the reduction of failure rates is the Texas Instruments (TI):Materials & Controls Group case (Ittner, 1989). The division instituted a COQ program in response to a corporate program entitled "Total Quality Thrust." At the division level, COQ was designed to highlight the high cost of quality and demonstrate the impact on overall corporate profits.

TI used the Juran COQ model, with an emphasis on seeking the most efficient tradeoff between cost and quality levels. The COQ program did gain the immediate attention of division management as the COQ data were integrated with the regular financial reporting system. However, management expressed great reservations about the "soft numbers" used to estimate the external failure costs and were bothered by the difficulty in taking proper action utilizing the COQ data. The COQ reports did not suggest specific action and did not offer a solution to a quality problem. The cause and effect of specific quality actions and costs could not be accurately determined. In this case, COQ data served as a motivator, but their limits as a performance measure were evident.

Texas Instruments (TI) continues to track COQ data and report this information internally. However, the vice president of People and Asset Effectiveness understands the "softness" and incomplete nature of the cost data. Consequently, TI has gone to "hard" statistical process control numbers to manage quality at the Materials and Control group. They have ceased improving quality in some processes because it is not considered economically feasible given the existing process equipment.

Xerox Corporation, the winner of the 1989 Baldrige award for quality, strongly advocates total quality, with COQ playing a major role in its quality program. Xerox has modified the traditional COQ model by incorporating lost opportunity cost and the benchmarking process. Quality management considers prevention and appraisal cost as fixed over the short run and necessary for obtaining conformance and conducting business. Management views internal and external failure costs as COQ opportunities.

In the U.S. marketing division alone, 11 COQ opportunities, totaling $250 million, were identified for project management action. The costs of nonconformance for projects such as excessive spare parts usage, sales personnel turnover, and maintenance strategy were estimated, and empowered multifunctional teams were created to reduce the cost of nonconformance. In 1989 a $53 million cost savings for the 11 projects was achieved, which correlated with the division's income statement. The thrust of this program was not a tradeoff of prevention and appraisal costs for failure costs as the traditional COQ model suggests, but rather a project management process that seeks to continually reduce the cost of nonconformance.

In January 1989 IBM Corporation launched a companywide quality program called Market Driven Quality (MDQ). Under the leadership of John Akers, the chairman, IBM had been striving to restore its image and preserve its leadership position in the computer industry. Senior management identified poor quality as the root cause for many of the company's recent problems and, in response to these problems and with the full support and commitment of Chairman Akers, initiated the MDQ program.

The MDQ program has three major components: setting of initiatives, a system of quality measurements, and process reviews. The program's target, as stated by Jack Kueler, president of IBM, "is to reduce defects to near zero." At the 1989 senior managers meeting, Akers stated that "this (quality improvement) really is a survival issue" and indicated that the full force of the company was behind the MDQ program. Macrolevel targets were identified as improved product quality and increased customer satisfaction; specific targets included the minimization of product defects to the six-sigma level and the reduction of cycle time. The focus of this program is clearly continuous improvement toward **zero defects,** and not quality cost minimization.

The role of quality costs within the MDQ quality program was debated during recent discussions with IBM management at a major IBM production facility. The production line manager indicated that the Cost of Quality was an issue for the finance people and something in which he (operations) did not get involved. "They come around on occasion, but we have never seen any data." Apparently, IBM does not use COQ data to motivate the firm to improve quality. Instead, as the central focus of its quality improvement efforts IBM has chosen a specific nonfinancial target, the reduction of defects to the **six-sigma level.** (This implies a defect rate of 3.4 parts per million, as discussed in Chapter 8 in more detail.) Achieving the targeted six-sigma quality level, however, is used by many IBM operations as justification for additional capital investment.

Some Caveats When Using Cost of Quality

Used properly and as one of many measures, COQ can provide valuable information. The following caveats, however, should be considered when using COQ:

1. Direct tradeoffs between conformance and nonconformance expenditures are economically difficult to measure. Accounting justifications require subjective estimates and an underlying belief that a tradeoff does exist. This approach will not help evaluate the effectiveness of the expenditures.
2. The optimal level of the tradeoff is a theoretical point that is probably not at the 50/50 intersection point. It is nearly impossible to know when this point has been exceeded. Continuous process improvement and the reduction of quality cost expenditures make the theoretical optimal a moving target and impractical.
3. Zero defects or six-sigma programs require significant expenditures and capital investment. Improved quality takes time to develop and may be realized in higher customer satisfaction rather than in increased short-term profits. These programs often have a greater impact on market share than on improved returns.
4. Accounting data many not accurately capture and distinguish between the various cost categories. As a result, incorrect expense analysis may lead to inappropriate policy recommendations.

We have discussed how managers often use the initial calculation of Cost of Quality (COQ) to generate excitement for a quality program. They can create a perceived need for quality, for COQ gives quality an economic value. It measures the cost factors related to the quality issues facing an enterprise. Many firms, however, abandon the use of COQ after establishing their quality program. Managers replace the "soft" COQ numbers with "hard" operational numbers such as statistical process control data for use as a measurement of quality. Various nonaccounting quality measurement systems serve as the guide for attaining a certain level of TQM. The push for continuous improvement, or attainment of a specific quality defect level like six sigma, limits the use of COQ for firms pursuing these quality plans. Many argue that COQ fails to provide insight for solving quality problems.

◆ SUSTAINING COST OF QUALITY: THE XEROX STORY

Despite the limitations, firms continue to find value within the COQ concept. As discussed earlier, Xerox applied the Cost-of-Quality principles to its United States Sales and Marketing group (USCO) realizing an outstanding COQ savings of $53 million in the first year. The improvements were relatively painless and did not involve layoffs or drastic cost cutting. Many line managers, initially skeptical of COQ, began to appreciate the value of this tool. Could they sustain the benefits of this successful COQ program?

Over the subsequent four years, Xerox achieved over a $200 million savings in quality costs, overcoming severe business pressures and organizational distractions. These diversions alone were sufficient to dilute any COQ effort; nonetheless, the program prospered. Xerox made COQ an integral part of its Leadership Through Quality program and defines quality as 100 percent customer satisfaction. With the funding and support of the division chief financial officer, USCO created a separate COQ reporting system. It used COQ data as a tool and guide for selecting and organizing a priority system for quality improvement projects. The COQ savings improvements for the years 1989–1992 are shown in Table 5.1. Today this impressive example of sustained COQ is the benchmark for the corporation.

Table 5.1	COQ Savings, 1989–1992	
	YEAR	SAVINGS
	1989	$53 million
	1990	$77 million
	1991	$60 million
	1992	$20 million

USCO continues to use COQ with multifunctional, empowered teams to call attention to areas of cost savings opportunity. They focus on the business process to identify mechanisms that are not working well or appear inefficient. The first assessment in 1989 of the total potential COQ was $1.05 billion. Further analysis revealed a realistic potential of $253 million. The major difference was that USCO concentrated on only the business processes they fully controlled. They do not manufacture the product, and over 50 percent of the total potential COQ relates to product made by a separate division. These quality cost savings opportunities did not require significant cash investment and were totally controlled by USCO. The initial COQ projects represented the glaring problems in the company.

During the five COQ program years, the list of major projects for COQ process improvement has changed. Four of the 11 initial projects were completed in the first or second year. Team members identified new projects through open "brainstorming sessions" and added these to the list. Concurrently, the other project teams continued to work on reducing the Cost of Quality and found a continuing stream of quality savings within their business processes. They sought a targeted savings based on process improvements, or they used benchmarking to reference an attainable level of performance. In all cases, they based the cost savings calculations on financial estimates and provided only annual project assessments.

The COQ projects fit the Xerox quality culture, and the division faced continued pressure to reduce costs and respond to intensive competitive pressure. The personal energy and actions of the program managers ensured that project teams met regularly and identified cost savings opportunities. They sponsored brainstorming sessions for new COQ ideas and encouraged middle management involvement.

The finance quality manager inspired the search for new quality cost savings opportunities. Many of the successful COQ projects had matured, and the program produced excellent results. The COQ opportunities rewarded the company with significant initial savings. Project team member turnover hampered the sustained momentum. This, coupled with the less frequent and less formal project meetings, led to a sporadic identification of new COQ projects. There was a clear need for an injection of program enthusiasm.

Linking COQ to Problem Solving

To understand the Xerox COQ program, we should look at the details of one of their more successful COQ projects. The Excess/Cancel COQ project was part of the initial 11 company COQ projects. The project focused on the excessive annual replacement parts writeoff expense. The team met once a week, and the members included the parts and supplies controller, the manager of nonequipment inventory, the manager of parts planning, and several inventory analysts. The annual accounting provision, or expense, for excess and obsolete spare parts was over $22 million, or 7.3 percent of receipts. By any measure this was an enormous annual amount.

Using TQM Problem Solving Process (PSP), a Xerox quality tool (similar to the seven-step method discussed in Chapter 6), the team met weekly to identify the actions necessary to reduce the annual accounting provision. The structured process consisted of six steps:

1. Identification–Select the problem.
2. Analyze the problem.
3. Generate potential solutions.
4. Select and plan solutions.
5. Implement solutions.
6. Evaluate solutions.

The team benchmarked (techniques are discussed in Chapter 15) other companies and other Xerox operations in order to authenticate the desired state and to frame the size of the problem. They felt that a target of 2.1 percent of receipts was the level the company needed in order to achieve world-class status. A gap of 5.2 percent of receipts, or a Cost-of-Quality opportunity of $16 million, existed. Note, that Xerox uses COQ and quality opportunity cost interchangeably. The team then focused on identifying the causes of the excess. Using the fishbone diagram (Exhibit 5.2), they structured the root causes of the problem.

The problems and solutions identified were the following:

1. Excess inventory at field sites caused planners to order more parts because they were too far down the chain to have control over the inventory. There was no system for effective inventory use, and no disciplined inventory control process was in place. The solution was to establish a comprehensive field inventory management system.
2. The spare parts failure rate was too high based on the stated engineering specifications. The solution was to change the spare parts management process by making engineering responsible for the failure rates. Engineering was also financially responsible for the excesses created by the incorrect failure rates. This encouraged "getting it right the first time," one of the cornerstones of the Xerox quality program.
3. There was no strategy for product end of life. Product planners did not communicate with the parts planners. The solution was to establish a communication network between product and parts planners. This enabled better parts ordering as well as a centralized parts logistical system to support the old equipment remaining in the field.
4. The parts planners set parts activity trends using product leading indicators and product trend factors. The solution included the data from repair activity and customer service engineering, which contained specific parts usage. They updated the revised consolidated parts planning database monthly for the planners review.

Exhibit
5.2

U.S. marketing group customer service

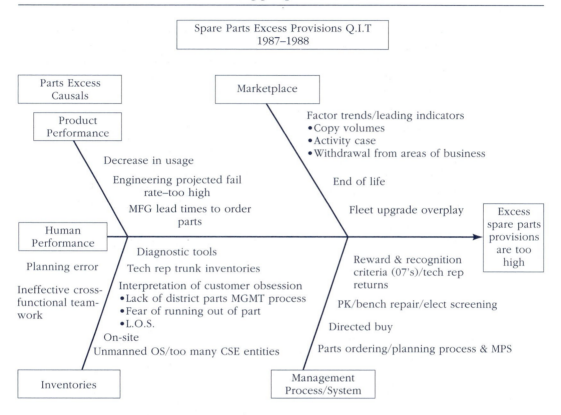

Spare Parts Excess Provisions Q.I.T
1987–1988

Parts Excess Causals

Product Performance

Decrease in usage

Engineering projected fail rate–too high

MFG lead times to order parts

Human Performance

Planning error

Ineffective cross-functional team-work

Diagnostic tools

Tech rep trunk inventories

Interpretation of customer obsession
•Lack of district parts MGMT process
•Fear of running out of part
•L.O.S.
On-site
Unmanned OS/too many CSE entities

Inventories

Marketplace

Factor trends/leading indicators
•Copy volumes
•Activity case
•Withdrawal from areas of business

End of life

Fleet upgrade overplay

Reward & recognition criteria (07's)/tech rep returns

PK/bench repair/elect screening

Directed buy

Parts ordering/planning process & MPS

Management Process/System

Excess spare parts provisions are too high

The cross-functional team used an array of quality tools adopted by Xerox to study the problem. They initiated a number of needed process changes; improved the data collection and analysis system; and changed some organizational accountability to match responsibilities. The cost of the solution implementation was minimal, and the potential savings were substantial. The 1988 saving was $5.5 million. The results pleased the team, those involved with the parts program, and the internal Xerox customers (the vice presidents of Service, Logistics and Distribution, and Finance).

The COQ Excess/Cancel Parts team continued to operate beyond the initial year. The team felt that additional implementation efforts were necessary to realize fully the solutions identified. In addition, further refinement of the solutions would move the operation closer to the benchmark target of 2.1 percent. As shown in Exhibit 5.3, the team continued to work the process and make additional change recommendations. They exceeded the benchmark after five years and are currently operating at a theoretical level of 0.5 percent of receipts.

As the team members became more comfortable with each other and as they became more familiar with the problem, they were able to creatively challenge the parts logistical system. The meetings became less formal, and each member enlisted the assistance of their colleagues to solve the problem. The project results overcame the high turnover of team members. The new people, familiar with the Xerox quality process, recognized the project accomplishments and enthusiasm. They understood the level of importance given to it by management. The other projects operated in a similar manner with structured meetings, team empowerment, and an extensive use of the various quality tools.

They did not have a rigid project protocol. Projects could be cross-functional or part of a single function. The goal was to solve the division's business problems which offered a cost savings to the organization. The finance quality manager drove the excitement and provided the energy to sustain the program.

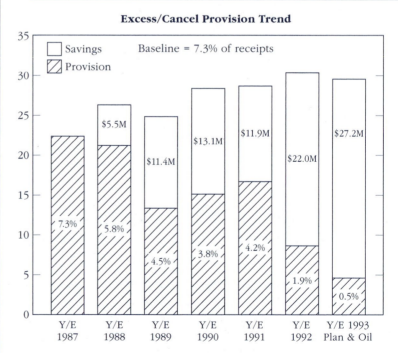

Exhibit 5.3

U.S. customer operations western hemisphere logistics and distribution cost of quality

Excess/Cancel Provision Trend

Baseline = 7.3% of receipts

Legend: □ Savings ▨ Provision

Y/E 1987: 7.3%
Y/E 1988: 5.8%, $5.5M
Y/E 1989: 4.5%, $11.4M
Y/E 1990: 3.8%, $13.1M
Y/E 1991: 4.2%, $11.9M
Y/E 1992: 1.9%, $22.0M
Y/E 1993 Plan & Oil: 0.5%, $27.2M

Key Message: Cumulative Savings of $91.1M in E/C Provision 1988 through 1993
(Based on continuing at the 7.3% of receipts level)

Diffusing COQ to the Field Sales Offices

Management is working more closely with the field sales and sales support of the 65 district offices. USCO is a sales organization and should be able to identify worthwhile COQ projects and form COQ teams at the districts. It is a natural extension to move the successful COQ program from the central headquarters to the field. The sales districts expenses were increasing, and there was the suspicion that nonconformance costs were contributing to this negative trend. Sandra Schiffman, the current manager of Quality and Customer Satisfaction, said: "The districts will buy into the program. We have shown Xerox COQ is not a measurement hammer, but rather a good process improvement tool."

Part of Xerox's COQ strategy for the 1990s was a commitment to quarterly COQ reporting for the sales districts. The firm examined lost opportunity (synonymous with COQ) due to quality from three areas:

1. Revenue (lost sales due to quality).
2. Process (costs due to business process inadequacies).
3. Expense (costs due to wasteful or excessive business expenses).

Xerox based the calculations on estimates and available accounting data. Internal benchmarks within the three areas served as the comparison to determine the COQ or lost opportunity.

Based on continuous improvement, or the kaizen approach, the performance of the top 10 sales districts comprise the internal benchmark for improvement. Xerox did a gap analysis for each opportunity area and provided assistance to the sales districts as needed. The graphic display of the quarterly performances motivated district performance and provided a very credible internal comparison. The internal benchmark created a custom and accepted reference for the Xerox field sales operational performance.

The company recognized the costs of not meeting as well as exceeding customer requirements. Sandra Schiffman said: "The district COQ program may have the wrong label (COQ) with their use of a revised set of quality cost definitions. The well-organized data, however, is a tool to help management identify areas that can improve revenue or reduce costs. We will continue to support the program." The COQ program provided an instrument to help the empowered sales districts attain success.

Using COQ as an Enabler

The unique implementation method of Xerox's COQ program sustained the stream of positive results. The COQ program is consistent with the well-established division and corporate quality culture. The quality process is second nature for the managers. The various quality tools such as fishbone diagrams, problem-solving process, and especially the mindset of continuous improvement provide the correct atmosphere for COQ combustion. COQ is not used as a measurement hammer or for individual performance evaluation. The company evaluates managers based on their knowledge and support of the Xerox Leadership Through Quality program of which COQ is an element. Achieving specific COQ project cost savings targets is not the responsibility of a specific manager, nor is any one group held accountable. There is a process owner who benefits from an empowered cross-functional team performing COQ as a collateral assignment.

Xerox uses the COQ program exclusively for identifying opportunities and setting priorities. It is an enabler. Managers realized that there would be few identified cost savings opportunities if people were held individually accountable and measured for a specific achievement level. No one wants to be penalized for identifying a cost savings opportunity. Early in the program, management considered using COQ as an additional performance measurement but quickly rejected the idea. The existing traditional budget-based financial performance measurement system works well. The extensive use of estimates and one-time annual reporting was not conducive for measurement purposes.

The division financial organization made extensive use of estimates calculating COQ. This required considerable change in as much as the various controllers are accountants who are, by nature and training, precise and want an audit trail of documented evidence. Sandra Schiffman remarked: "This was the most difficult adjustment for us. Only after we saw managers were using the cost information as a guide to set priorities rather than an absolute measure did we become comfortable with using estimates." Managers have accepted and are comfortable with the COQ metrics.

Xerox has made the definition and use of quality costs part of its business operation. As the business processes have changed or as the organization has been restructured, the definitions and uses of COQ have also changed. There remains, however, the universal reference of 100 percent customer satisfaction. Both internal and external benchmarks serve as a reference for calculating the opportunity cost or COQ of achieving the desired operational level. The absence of accounting rules, project team empowerment, extensive training, the use of estimates, and Pareto analysis techniques made COQ user friendly. COQ is a dynamic concept providing a useful economic metric of the overall business process improvement. It provides a broad indicator of progress.

The most important sustaining factor is the very strong top management support. The CFO, Phil Fishbach, who is often called "Mr. Cost of Quality," is a vigorous supporter of the program. His organization has taken over leadership of the program and committed significant financial human resources to achieve the project results, also ensuring that finance keeps the estimated numbers honest.

Sustaining COQ Through Maturity

The recent modest COQ results and the difficulty of identifying the potentially future valuable projects have created a real challenge for the organization. Transfers between divisions, normal attrition, and employee turnover, especially at the branches, require a renewed training effort. The less frequent COQ team meetings, the nonperformance measurement aspect of COQ, and the lack of COQ knowledge threaten the program.

As the program matures, estimated costs can start to exceed gains, or the cost savings opportunities can exceed customer requirements. Identifying opportunities for early breakthrough becomes more demanding, and finding new project champions is more difficult. Distractions and other projects contribute to the loss of discipline in assessing COQ opportunities.

◆   LESSONS FROM XEROX

The Xerox COQ program is difficult to replicate. The quality culture and corporate value system provide the atmosphere for COQ to flourish. Sustaining COQ takes a great deal of energy and senior manager support. It also requires the friendly atmosphere of a sound quality culture where the quality process is second nature and quality tools are abundant. Managers need to be comfortable with the use of estimates and trust the judgment of the financial managers. Most importantly, a sustained program must avoid the temptation of using COQ as an individual or department performance measure. The results of process change take time before they register economically. The COQ projects have their own life and often do not fit into a single functional area.

The Xerox Cost-of-Quality program may have a cost label, but in reality at USCO, it is the way they conduct business. It is part of the managers' fiber and fits very nicely in the companywide quality culture. The company eliminates the mystique of cost measurements with the COQ system, providing the division with an excellent way to confirm continuous improvement. It also allows management to set COQ targets and establish priorities for continuous improvement. The manufacturing operational data and SPC (statistical process control) information do not fit into a sales and marketing organization. COQ helps corroborate this service division's performance. It is the Xerox way of doing business.

Xerox has plucked the low-hanging COQ fruit during the last five years. It will require greater energy and resources to harvest the remaining cost opportunity fruit. Because of the continuous improvement culture, one would expect to see positive results persist. It will certainly be more difficult and will require the full support of senior managers.

◆   ACCOUNTING SUPPORT OF TQM

The controller or accountant can take one of four possible approaches when evaluating the cost implications of a Total Quality Management program. They are the following:

1. Use Cost of Quality as part of the regular reporting and control process. The traditional or emerging COQ model can be used, and the quality costs are collected by the cost categories. Most firms do not seek an optimal cost point. Rather, they assess the total quality costs and match the cost with the changes in quality as a result of the various TQM efforts.

2. Focus the accounting and control efforts on nonconformance costs (internal and external failure) reduction. Xerox and Tennant Corporation are good examples of companies that concentrate on nonconformance costs. The conformance costs are a natural part of the TQM program and can be considered a fixed cost of quality. Economic gains come from changing processes to reduce failure costs.

3. Support the operation with their focus on specific nonfinancial "hard SPC numbers" to monitor the progress of TQM. In essence, the firm has chosen to ignore the Cost of Quality and to rely on operational data as the real measure of success. SPC, yield rates, waste amounts, and defect percentages provide managers with the data to measure the progress of the TQM program. There is the assumption that these data correlate well with improved economic performance.

4. Do not use Cost of Quality. Aid the company with their focus on the general, overall nonfinancial measures of conformance such as six sigma to monitor the progress of TQM. IBM and Motorola are strong proponents of this approach. They drive the company to achieve a specific level of quality performance and make the necessary investment to achieve the target.

These four avenues of involvement for the accountant in the TQM program vary greatly in the level of activity. Using cost of quality in options 1 and 2 offers the best course for active participation in the TQM process.

◆ OTHER MEASURES OF TQM

Managers continue to seek innovative and creative means of demonstrating the value of TQM. These measures help direct activities and resources to solve problems, and they serve as a means of reporting the progress to higher levels of the organization. The measures, normally centered on important issues facing the company, serve to provide valuable feedback for performance improvement. They can be part of the regular TQM or financial reporting scheme, or they may be used as a separate reporting process. The following are examples of some of the creative measurement schemes.

Many firms recognize the large hidden cost of losing customers owing to some quality problem driven by customer dissatisfaction. Xerox and others refer to this as **lost opportunity cost**. They have developed measurement systems to measure the number and expected business loss of customers who do not order or who significantly reduce their business activity with the firm. A computer company refers to this as "defection analysis" and places a value on the stream of lost revenue. This loss is part of its cost of poor quality. Other companies employ outside consultants to conduct customer surveys that rank the firm's performance. In the automobile industry, the J. D. Powers customer quality survey is used as the standard of performance excellence. IBM has its consultant survey on 100,000 internal and external customers per quarter to determine the quality level of service. In order to get the customer's perspective of quality (meeting expectations), companies are increasingly relying on external surveys to provide the reliable data for analysis.

Analog Devices employs a **half-life model** for evaluating TQM progress. Art Schneiderman, the originator of the program, observed that any defect level subjected to legitimate quality improvement process decreases at a constant rate. When plotted on semi-log paper against time, it falls on a straight line. He developed a model based on extensive data that for each type of defect the defect level drops 50 percent over a specific level of time. For example, if the initial defect level were 10 percent and the defect half-life were six months, then after the first six months the defect level would be down to 5 percent, after the next six months the defect level would be at 2.5 percent, and so on.

The company adopted the half-life system as an integral part of its division performance score card to balance the strictly financial point of view. It measured such items as on-time delivery, outgoing defect level, lead time, manufacturing cycle time, process defect level, yield, and time to market. The managers found these data very useful in measuring the movement in continuous improvement, or *kaizen*. This measurement device continues to serve the company well.

The new innovative measures normally involve the use of time, a willingness to use outside data sources, and flexibility with the sources and mixture of data. The traditional historical accounting records do not capture the dynamics of most organizations or the complexity of their process. Operational data alone do not give the manager the economic consequence of their decisions. In order to gain a complete view of the impact of TQM, a holistic approach involving all of the stakeholders is necessary. Thus, we are observing more reliance on the quality assessment of the customer. Operating managers want measures that make sense, provide valuable feedback, and fit the nature of the business being assessed. The mix is based on what is appropriate.

Companies are rapidly learning that measuring performance using financial measures alone can distort performance and mislead management. Many companies are turning to the **balanced score card** approach. They incorporate measures from accounting, operations, human resources, customers, and other stake holders to arrive at a more integrative and holistic measure of performance. This trend also apples to measuring the impact of a TQM program. It is natural, for TQM is designed to influence the total organization. The Xerox COQ measurement system outlined above is a good example of a balanced score card. Analog Devices, while placing a heavy emphasis on the operational numbers, sought to balance the strict financial measures of quality. Exhibit 5.4 demonstrates how this can work.

The use of operational measures for TQM provides the flexibility needed to adjust the company's measurement system to a quality emphasis. For example, possible measures for a Taguchi (design quality in, see Chapter 8 for a detailed discussion) process would be the number of parts in a product; the percentage of common versus unique parts; or the number of suppliers required.

<table>
<tr><td>Exhibit
5.4</td><td colspan="3" align="center">Balanced measures of TQM</td></tr>
</table>

TQM ELEMENT	FINANCIAL MEASURE	NONFINANCIAL MEASURE
Customer satisfaction	External failure cost Field service expense	Customer satisfaction survey results On-time delivery Number of customer complaints
Internal performance	Appraisal cost Internal failure cost Prevention cost	Defect rates Yields Lead times Idle capacity Unscheduled machine downtime

In some cases, the quest for quality has led to disappointing financial results. The most famous example, Wallace Company, the 1990 Malcolm Baldrige award winner, filed for Chapter 11 (bankruptcy) two years later. Obsession with quality does not guarantee success. We want to make sure TQM programs have a pay-off. **Return on Quality (ROQ)** is a new evaluation method whereby managers can balance the cost of improved quality with the benefit (better financial results).

This measure goes beyond assessing TQM benefits in only cost-saving terms. It requires managers to realize the quality cost savings from the market. Companies must earn a return on their quality spending from their customers. We cannot just spend for the sake of quality. We must now put our quality program gains to the economic test. Will the customers buy more or pay more for our goods or services as a result of our quality spending? This requires that a customer focus on the quality cost savings and that ROQ correlate well with the ROI companywide performance measure.

Managers need to look for the quality programs valued by the customer. Hampton Inns, ATT, UPS, GTE, and Federal Express are using ROQ to evaluate TQM projects. They are seeking cost-effective solutions to quality problems identified by their customers. For example, Hampton Inn offered a money-back guarantee for any reason to a dissatisfied customer. Everyone, maids, desk clerks, and so on, were empowered to offer the money back. Company morale soared, but $1.1 million was returned in the first year. Management, however, attributed a $11 million increase in the same year to the program (*Business Week,* August 8, 1994). This is quite an acceptable ROQ!

ROQ gives added meaning to quality spending. At the same time, it offers an economic measure to those companies relying solely on operational measures to evaluate TQM.

◆ INFORMATION SYSTEMS SUPPORT

A central element of any comprehensive measurement process is the systems support needed for accurate and timely data collection. The data need is not complex but does come from diverse parts of the organization. There is not one system that can readily supply all the needed data. The accounting systems with some modification can capture the financial data. Operational systems such as MRP II production planning can deliver most of the operational data. SPC and other quality information systems can add another dimension to the nonfinancial measures. External data such as customer satisfaction surveys need collection and analysis. Finally, sales and marketing data captured at the point of sale or return need to be included. Clearly, a holistic measurement system requires an array of data sources. A data warehouse concept lends itself very well to providing a comprehensive set of TQM measures. (See Chapter 14 for more information on the systems support issues.)

A number of software packages are available that will develop the Cost-of-Quality calculations and graphs for a firm. In essence, they ask you to rearrange your chart of accounts so that the appropriate cost information is placed in the proper COQ category. This can be accomplished by making some custom modifications to an existing account system and adding the graphic support. In both cases, the critical issue is the assignment of costs to a specific COQ category. This can be arbitrary, for in many cases the costs associated with quality do not neatly fall into one account.

◆ IMPLEMENTATION

There is no set lockstep process for implementing a TQM measurement or Cost-of-Quality program. They are not standalone systems. The measurement program must be fully integrated into the total TQM process. The first implementation step is gaining the complete support of senior management and the active participation of the financial manager. Remember, the key to measurements is providing reliable data for process feedback. This allows managers to assess the progress of the TQM process and to make changes as appropriate. The senior managers will monitor the information, and the financial manager is key in developing the appropriate costs.

The second stage of implementation is obtaining the cross-functional involvement of the TQM team. Clearly, the finance and accounting personnel are critical for cost calculations. Input from the various personnel in manufacturing and marketing is important for developing a set of operational metrics that will capture the effect of TQM.

There are other caveats that are key to implementation, notably:

- Use reliable estimates. Precise measures may be too costly to obtain.
- Use the TQM measures for process indication. Avoid the temptation to use the measures for performance evaluation.

- Use a team approach in determining the perimeters of the measures.
- Remember that the rhythm of the reports can vary from daily to yearly. It takes time for TQM to make a measurable difference. Most firms opt for the longer reporting time of quarterly or annually.
- Emphasize training, which is key to understanding the meaning of the measures.
- Establish the measures by natural business unit such as a subsidiary, a specific plant, or an independent division. Keep the measures within the TQM operation.
- Set realistic expectations.
- Be flexible and change with the shift in TQM focus.

◆ Summary

As a firm's TQM program develops, the approach to COQ reporting can take one of the following four approaches:

1. Use Cost-of-Quality analysis as a regular management reporting and control tool
   - Consistent with Juran
   - Used by Ford in the 1980s
   - Used by TI until 1990
2. Focus on reducing the price of nonconformance, including opportunity losses.
   - This approach assumes that conformance costs (in Crosby's terminology) will continue at a high level and will be managed by budgets and continuous improvement programs.
   - If spending on conformance remains consistently high, the reporting focus can switch to nonconformance costs, with specific inclusion of the opportunity cost of bad quality. The goal is the steady reduction of nonconformance costs to zero.
   - This approach has been adopted by many firms committed to TQM (Xerox, Westinghouse, and Tennant Company).
3. Focus on nonfinancial, production information to monitor TQM progress with an emphasis on **input measures** and SPC.
   - This approach deemphasizes formal COQ reports.
   - It is used by TI (Materials & Control group) and Daishowa Paper (Japan).
4. Focus on nonfinancial, production information to monitor TQM progress, with an emphasis on **output measures** of conformance.
   - Examples include Motorola, IBM, and Analog Devices.
   - This approach deemphasizes formal COQ reports.
   - It is customer focused.

Assessing the economic impact of TQM can take many forms. The classic COQ model provides a reference point for understanding the theoretical behavior of these quality costs. The emerging model reflects the modern view of the behavior of quality costs with a continuous investment in prevention. Using these measures is difficult because of the practicality of gathering the cost data and the accuracy of the accounting information. Many firms recognize these difficulties and ignore any measures of Cost of Quality. Various stake holders, however, continue to ask how much TQM is costing the organization and whether it is worth it.

Significant value is gained by being able to frame the impact of a TQM program in financial terms. This requires active participation by the accounting group and their creativity and flexibility. Each system should be designed specifically for the individual firm. The operational forces driving the quality costs are unique for each firm and reflect their complexity and method of competition. Finally, COQ is not a standalone measure; rather, it is best used in conjunction with other TQM measures. It is not designed to be an absolute measure or to be used as a hammer. It is in a indicator of progress or lack thereof, it provides a general reference level of spending, and it can verify the economic impact of quality.

◆ Key Terms

Emerging COQ model	Lost opportunity cost	Input measures
Zero defects	Half-life model	Output measures
Six-sigma level	Return on Quality	
Balanced score card	(ROQ)	

◆ Assignments

1. How is the newly emerging COQ model different from the traditional COQ model?
2. What are the caveats for using the new models of COQ?
3. What were the keys to Xerox's success in sustaining the Cost-of-Quality program?
4. Outline the four approaches the controller of a company can take to support a TQM program.
5. Discuss and provide an example of another method to measure the progress of a TQM program.
6. What is the balanced score card, and how can it be used to measure a TQM program?

Cost-of-Quality Assignment

The objective of this assignment is to determine the Cost of Quality for a typical workday that you experience. The exercise should also give you a good understanding of the several elements of Cost of Quality as they may apply to a service business.

On the attached sheet, log the activities that are performed in each 15-minute increment. During some of these time intervals, you will actually be doing more than one activity. Write down the activity that took up most of the time during that period. Activities that take more than one period can be noted simply with ditto marks.

For each activity note the "customer." For some activities, the customer may be yourself.

For the process column, generic descriptions are enough. Examples may be prepared for meeting, study, and networking.

In the activity column, provide a little more detail regarding the specific task. This makes it easier to complete the next column.

Assign a Cost-of-Quality category as:

- Essential for tasks that add value and are being performed for the first time. These are directly related to the job and are performed for a specific customer. If they were not done, the job would not be satisfactorily done. That is, you should be able to identify a customer who pays the organization for doing this work. If you cannot, the task could be for an internal customer, and it would fall into one of the Cost-of-Quality categories.
- Prevention for tasks that are likely to prevent a failure from occurring. Examples may be updating the appointment book or filing papers.
- Appraisal involves reviewing one's work. An example may be checking one's work and finding errors.
- Internal failures involve correcting the work before it has reached the "customer." An example would be correcting errors in a project report and reprinting it.
- External failures involve correcting work after the "customer" has pointed out the errors. These have additional costs related to customer satisfaction, but we will not be including these costs in this assignment.

Questions

1. Did all activities have a customer?
2. What proportion of the time was spent on activities classified as essential?
3. What percentage of time was spent performing tasks in each of the four Cost-of-Quality categories?

TIME PERIOD	"CUSTOMER"	PROCESS	ACTIVITY	COST-OF-QUALITY CATEGORY
		COST-OF-QUALITY LOG		
NAME				
8:00				
8:15				
8:30				
8:45				
9:00				
9:15				
9:30				
9:45				
10:00				
10:15				
10:30				
10:45				
11:00				
11:15				
11:30				
11:45				
12:00				
12:15				
12:30				
12:45				
13:00				
13:15				
13:30				
13:45				
14:00				
14:15				
14:30				
14:45				
15:00				
15:15				
15:30				
15:45				
16:00				
16:15				
16:30				
16:45				
17:00				
17:15				
17:30				
17:45				
18:00				
18:15				
18:30				
18:45				
19:00				

Case Study

Materials and Controls Corporation

Background

Materials and Controls Corporation (MCC) has become the third largest of seven business groups in its industry. Headquartered in Newton, Massachusetts, the group operates in four domestic and nine foreign countries. MCC has two main technologies—Metallurgical Materials, which produces industrial and thermostatic clad metals used in cookware, coins, cable, and integrated circuits; and Control Products, which integrates with the manufacture of sensors, relays, and switches.

The MCC group is organized into Product Customer Centers (PCC), which have individual profit and loss (P&L) responsibility. Each PCC has its own Marketing, Engineering, Finance, and Manufacturing functions. Corporate support includes Research & Development, Finance, Personnel Services, and the People and Asset Effectiveness Departments.

Getting Started

In 1950 MCC was proactive in productivity improvements, work simplification programs, and team building. But it was not until the early 1980s that the company committed itself to a Total Quality Thrust. This was brought on by a Hewlett-Packard study (HP was one of MCC's major customers). The study's message was clear: the United States' best suppliers were inferior to Japan's worst suppliers. MCC's competitive success required a commitment to quality improvement. The theme "Do it right the first time" was adopted as a performance requirement and would be measured.

Using Cost of Quality (COQ) as an integral part of its strategic business planning came about as MCC was losing market share to Japan, Italy, and Brazil. MCC realized that improved quality, reliability, and service coupled with price reductions was the only way to regain market share and stay on top.

A Cultural Change—Training

A top-down training program on the fundamentals of quality and the need for quality improvement was undertaken. MCC's top managers, including production personnel, were sent to quality training courses. Additional training was conducted for all salaried employees within MCC to instill awareness and to help communicate management's commitment to quality improvement.

Cost-of-Quality Implementation

The benefits of using COQ to supplement existing financial indicators became clear. In 1981 a "Quality Blue Book" was created showing indices such as product reliability, customer quality feedback, and COQ figures. The COQ measure was intended to highlight the costs of poor quality (i.e., the cost of *not* doing it right the first time) to bring attention to the problems, with no real intent to measure the return on prevention expenditures.

MCC's COQ system gained momentum as a key component of the Total Quality Thrust. By measuring quality in financial terms, COQ supported a cultural change by using familiar language—($$) dollars wasted. The COQ "buy-in" was beginning to take hold.

Based on work of Chris Ittner. Reprinted with permission.

Materials and Controls Corporation (Continued)

Full-scale COQ implementation within MCC began in late 1981. The Quality Assurance (QA) Department performed a preliminary COQ calculation using data provided by Finance. This COQ figure was published in the Quality Blue Book.

Over the next few reporting periods (months), QA and Finance worked to reclassify 77 COQ line items down to 19, as semantic overlaps and multiple definitions were found. The 19 line items became a working standard, which were then classified into the four major COQ categories: Prevention, Appraisal, Internal Failure, and External Failure costs.

Problems Encountered

As the COQ program matured, it became apparent that the current system excluded costs that were considered part of the manufacturing process—for instance, in-process checking by hand. The PC managers argued about "Engineered Scrap" (scrap that was left over after the stamping press punched out the required diameter). "Wasn't that inherent to the process?" they asked. How could Finance collect the cost of support departmental personnel who repeated tasks because of problems like undershipments, late deliveries, or clerical errors? How could indirect quality costs in the "Hidden Company" be captured? Although these problems were realized, it was easier to use data that already existed in the accounting system.

A desire to maintain consistency over time so that trends would be visible made it difficult to add new measures for indirect, or "white-collar" quality costs. Managers wanted to see COQ go down quickly, so adding more "Hidden Company" costs only made the problem appear worse. Attempts to improve the system by making it more accurate and relevant by including "hidden costs" appeared to be in conflict with the need to maintain "comparability" across reporting periods.

It took time and patience to convince COQ users, but by 1987 the value of using COQ to manage the improvement process became apparent. Two main factors contributed to widespread acceptance:

1. Managers began presenting COQ figures with emphasis on improvement. It was accepted that figures could be dynamic month-to-month, depending on business conditions.
2. No "hammering" was allowed. The Quality Blue Book was not used as a personnel performance indicator. Rather, quality measures were focused on long-term trends and opportunities for improvement. Team improvements became important.

The Blue Books were distributed to senior staff and to the responsible company and managers on a monthly basis. Although not formally distributed to operating personnel, the information was available to them. "Cost-of-Quality numbers provide the single best indicator that problems have arisen . . . problems that cause a poor P & L performance," says Carl Sheffer, a group vice president. "The reports now go to all of my managers and team members. I take personal interest in COQ and ask for the numbers. I highlight product lines that have improved and lines that have deteriorated. We focus primarily on Internal Failure and RMRs (Returned Material Reports) because they are the hard numbers. The others are more helpful for trends."

Materials and Controls Corporation (Continued)

MCC's quality gains and cost reductions were directly linked to management commitment and willingness to invest in improvement projects. It was sometimes difficult to justify subjective benefits like improved employee morale and customer perception. MCC's success in implementing COQ was achieved by making COQ part of the quality improvement and financial planning process. Quality Improvement Teams (QITs), which included representation from organizations like Marketing, Engineering, Materials, Production, Quality, and Finance, met to establish and determine which COQ projects would be worked on, using COQ numbers to establish project priorities.

Attainable savings were estimated and incorporated into the product line's profit forecast. COQ project tracking was assigned to the Manufacturing Engineering product line management department.

The identification and implementation of COQ projects is the key to instilling quality awareness and improving quality performance," says Bob Porter, vice president of Quality and Reliability. The "process of getting management involved in identifying the opportunities for quality improvement, establishing priorities, helping ensure resources are available, and monitoring progress is the critical issue. We need to speak the right language . . . and COQ is the language of management. Without COQ numbers this process wouldn't work.

The Bottom Line

From its inception in 1982 through the year ending 1987, MCC's COQ as a percentage of net sales billed decreased from 10.7 to 7.8 percent of net sales billed, as shown in Table 5.2.

The Motivation

MCC's COQ system focuses increased management attention on the results of poor quality as measured in monetary terms. "COQ is most helpful for middle managers to see the consequences of poor quality on overall income," says Carl Sheffer. "It gives one number that focuses several things together. If we focused just on scrap, we would get lower scrap costs, but would go out of business as we passed scrap onto the customer. You have to improve the whole, not just pieces at a time."

Having a COQ system has proven to be an attention getter at MCC. It has forced priority setting, and it has stimulated quality improve-

Table 5.2	COQ as a Percentage of Net Sales Billed					
TYPE OF COST	1982	1983	1984	1985	1986	1987
Prevention	2.3	2.0	2.0	2.1	2.3	2.3
Appraisal	2.2	1.9	1.7	1.9	1.9	1.8
Internal failure	5.3	4.8	4.5	4.2	3.6	3.3
External failure	0.9	0.7	0.6	0.4	0.4	0.4
Total COQ	10.7	9.4	8.8	8.6	8.2	7.8

Materials and Controls Corporation (Continued)

ment activities. It has been a "scoreboard for improvement." MCC's success in using COQ to better manage the improvement process has led the way to future quality improvement projects, and has shown management that COQ does pay high dividends if properly implemented.

CASE QUESTIONS

1. List three positive observations.
2. List three negative observations.
3. List three things you would do differently.
4. Why did COQ work at MCC?

◆ Bibliography

American Society for Quality Control. *Accounting for Quality Costs* Milwaukee, Wis.: ASQC, 1991.

Atkinson, H., Hamburg, J., & Ittner, C. *Linking Quality to Profits: Quality-based Cost Management*. Milwaukee, Wis.: ASQC Press, 1994.

Carr, Lawrence P., "Applying Cost of Quality to a Service Business." *Sloan Management Review* (Summer 1992): 72–79.

Carr, L. P., "How Xerox Sustains the Cost of Quality", *Management Accounting*, August 1995, pp. 26–32.

Carr, L. P., and L. Penemon. "Managers, Perceptions About Quality Costs." *Journal of Cost Management* (Spring 1992): 65–71.

Carr, L., and T. Tyson. "Planning Quality/Cost Expenditures." *Management Accounting* (October 1992): 52–56.

Deming, W. Edwards. *Quality, Productivity, and Competitive Position*. Cambridge, Mass.: MIT Center for Advanced Engineering, 1982.

Feigenbaum, Armand V. "The Challenge of Total Quality Control." *Industrial Quality Control* (May 1957): 17–23.

Feigenbaum, Armand V. *Total Quality Control* 3rd ed. New York: McGraw-Hill, 1983.

Garvin, David A. "Competing on the Eight Dimensions of Quality." *Harvard Business Review* (November–December 1987): 101–109.

Garvin, David A. *Managing Quality: The Strategic and Competitive Edge*. New York: Free Press, 1988.

Hale, Roger L., Douglas R. Hoelscher, and E. Kowal. 1987. *Quest for Quality*. Minneapolis, Minn.: Tennant Co., 1987.

Ittner, C. "Texas Instruments: Cost of Quality [A]," Harvard Business School, 9-189-029.

Juran, J. M., and Frank M. Gryna. *Quality Planning and Analysis*. New York: McGraw-Hill, 1980.

Morse, W. J., H. P. Roth, and K. M. Poston. *Measuring, Planning, and Controlling Quality Costs,* Montvale, N.J.: National Association of Accountants, 1987.

"Quality: How to Make it Pay," *Business Week,* Aug 8, 1994. By David Greising and bureau reports.

Schneiderman, Arthur M. "Optimal Quality Costs and Zero Defects: Are They Contradictory Concepts?" *Quality Progress* (November 1986): 28–31.

Continual Improvement: Basic Tools

◆ ◆ ◆

T he essence of KAIZEN is simple and straightforward: KAIZEN means improvement. Moreover, KAIZEN means ongoing improvement involving everyone, including both manager and workers. The KAIZEN philosophy assumes that our way of life—be it our working life, our social life, or our home life—deserves to be constantly improved.

Masaaki Imai, Kaizen *(1986, p. 3)*

◆ OVERVIEW OF CONTINUAL IMPROVEMENT

The quality-oriented organization makes customer satisfaction its main focus. To deliver quality products, process owners must determine who their customers are (both internal and external), as well as the needs, requirements, and expectations of those customers. Then they must ensure that process outputs meet customer needs.

In the context of quality, *kaizen* means continuous improvement: a systematic approach to the closing of gaps between customer expectations and the characteristics of process outputs. It is a philosophy that the Japanese have developed, and their mastery of this philosophy has been one of the most influential factors in their productivity and in the competitiveness of their products and services.

Exhibit 6-1 should be helpful in understanding these concepts. Organizations involve a myriad of processes, and virtually all processes are linked to other processes. For any process (let us call it Process A so that we may refer to it), the inputs to that process are outputs of other processes in the organization (the **internal suppliers** of Process A) or of **external suppliers** to the organization. The output of Process A, in turn, goes either to another process within the organization (an **internal customer** of Process A) or to an **external customer** of the organization. So Process A is a supplier to the next customer and a customer to its suppliers.

The customer of Process A has some **requirements, needs,** or **expectations** for the output of Process A. On the other hand, the output of Process A has some characteristics that are relevant to these customer expectations. These are technically called the **quality characteristics** of the output. To the extent that there is a gap between these characteristics and the customer's expectations, there is a quality

Exhibit
6.1

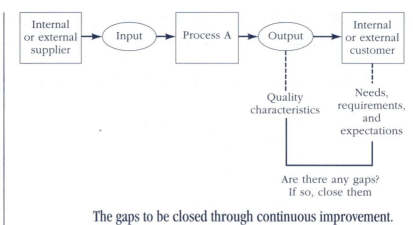

The gaps to be closed through continuous improvement.

problem. This quality problem is the responsibility of the **owner** of (the person re-sponsible for) Process A. Continuous improvement is a frame of mind that continu-ally forces us to systematically search for those gaps and systematically close them as long as it is feasible to do so. In this case, it would force the owner of Process A to close whatever gaps exist, to the extent that it is feasible to close them.

One gains a better understanding of continuous improvement by contrasting it with other approaches. Continuous improvement requires a proactive, systematic, fact-based, and continually ongoing approach to the solution of quality problems. This approach may be contrasted with reactive activities, which deal with prob-lems as they occur in haphazard fashion. One example of this proactive approach is the tight control the Japanese exert over operations through **foolproofing** (sometimes called, using the Japanese terms, *bakayoke* or *pokayoke*). Garvin (1988, p. 212) writes:

> In that approach [foolproofing] an operation or process was designed to make human error impossible. At one plant, fans were attached to subassemblies using a torque wrench hanging from the ceiling; it was located so that bolts could not be overtight-ened. At another plant, each unit on the assembly line was accompanied by its own box of parts. Incorrect attachments were thus eliminated, even during changeovers.

Shingo (1986) presents many examples of foolproofing that will help trigger one's ideas on what and how to foolproof.

The Japanese practice of ongoing, small-scale continuous improvement has also been often contrasted with the typically American search for large-scale breakthroughs. These two approaches to problem solving were thought for some time to be rather mutually exclusive (as the result of different and perhaps in-compatible mental frameworks) but many observers now consider them to be complementary. Exhibit 6-2a shows the results of continuous improvement alone,

Exhibit
6.2

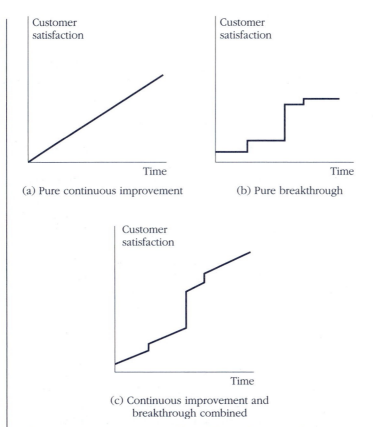

(a) Pure continuous improvement   (b) Pure breakthrough

(c) Continuous improvement and
breakthrough combined

Continuous improvement and breakthrough approaches to customer satisfaction. The two approaches are not mutually exclusive and, when combined, usually result in faster improvement of customer satisfaction.

Exhibit 6-2*b* the results of pure breakthrough, and Exhibit 6-2*c* the better results of the combined approach which Deming has called continual improvement.

The Center for Quality Management was founded in 1990 by seven leading firms in the Boston area with the purpose of promoting quality awareness and the sharing of ideas on quality management among member companies. The Center views TQM as the amalgamation of three main activities throughout an organization: customer focus, continual improvement, and total participation. If any of these basic activities is missing, true TQM does not exist. Thus, continual improvement is one of the three fundamental cornerstones in the Center's conceptual model of TQM. We wholeheartedly agree with that model.

Relationship of Chapters 6, 7, and 8 to Continual Improvement

In *Quality, Productivity and Competitive Position* Deming (1982, p. 47) states:

Management's new job is embodied in the 14 points. It is necessary for management to learn also some rudiments of statistical theory and applications. Education in simple but powerful statistical techniques is required of all people in management, all engineers and scientists, inspectors, quality control managers, management in the service organizations of the company, such as accounting, payroll, purchase, safety, legal department, consumer service, consumer research. Engineers and scientists need rudiments of experimental design.

This chapter presents a brief overview of some basic tools, mostly statistical, that are necessary for continual improvement as well as for managing by facts. Management by facts is one of the key requirements of the Baldrige Award. This requirement implies that *your responsibility to quality includes applying these tools not only to quality improvement, but also to general management.* In this chapter we also discuss in detail the seven-step method for continuous improvement, and we illustrate it with a case that shows the integrated use of the basic tools.

Chapter 7 focuses on control charts and statistical process control. All tools and concepts in Chapters 6 and 7 are widely applicable to the improvement of both service and manufacturing activities. Rather than being arcane, these tools and concepts are simple and easy to learn. They should be in the bag of any manager who is interested in continuous improvement and wishes to manage by facts. Finally, in Chapter 8 we cover several of the more advanced tools used in continual improvement.

It is important for you to know about all of these tools not only so that you will be able to use them, but also so that you will be able to interface with others who use them. These basic tools are those Ishikawa advocated be taught to all employees. Today they are considered essential for organizations practicing TQM. As a manager, it will be your job to monitor and give feedback to quality improvement teams that use these tools in their reports and oral presentations. A knowledge of the tools and concepts will make your job a lot easier.

◆ DATA TYPES AND SUMMARIES

Types of Data

The process of continual improvement is fact-oriented, and data often have to be collected to ascertain those facts. Some of the data pertain to variables such as delivery times, the ages of customers, or the weights of bags of sugar one might be in the business of producing, which are numeric in nature. These variables and data are known as **numeric** or **quantitative.** Other data, such as the state of origin of our clients, the different types of customer complaints about our service, or the types of defects in automobile paint jobs, pertain to variables that are not numeric. These variables and data are known as categorical or qualitative.

It is crucial to ensure accuracy and consistency when data are collected and handled. As part of this effort, it is important to establish appropriate **operational de-**

finitions of terms and concepts. It is also important that these definitions be understood and followed by everyone involved in data collection and analysis. For example, you could send people out to visit households and collect data on the number of telephones in each household they visit. They could ask the question, "How many telephones are there in this household?" and be answered "Four." Of the four, two might be connected and in use, one might be an old telephone that is now inside a box in the attic, and a fourth might be a toy telephone that little Jimmy plays with. Perhaps only two of these four telephones are of concern to you. The people who collect data for you must have an operational definition of "telephone in the household," and the person who provides the answer must also be made aware of this definition. Specifications such as "a weight of 10 pounds" or "a defective shirt" have little meaning unless these terms are appropriately defined.

The tools we describe in this chapter are used in the analysis of data. Some are used only for numeric data, others only for categorical data, and still others are used for both.

Populations and Samples

Statistical work often involves a group of items (usually large) that have one or more characteristics that are of interest. This large group is generically called a **population,** although often the items are not people. The number of items in the population is denoted N and is called the **population size.**

In order to learn about the characteristics of interest, you could examine every item in the population. This, however, is often impractical, so instead you normally resort to taking a relatively small **sample** from the population (the number of items in the sample is denoted n and is called the **sample size**), observing how the characteristics of interest behave in the sample, and based on what you observed, making a good guess about the behavior of the characteristics of interest in the whole population. This distinction between populations and samples will be useful when we introduce some of the concepts and notation in this section. We discuss these ideas in more detail in Chapter 7.

Data Summarization

Austral, a domestic Argentine airline, is working on improving the response for its flight reservation system. As part of its effort, the airline collected a sample of 102 telephone calls from those received during a one-week period. Table 6-1 shows the duration of these calls in minutes.

Raw data such as these can be summarized so that they convey more meaning to people using them and so that they may be more easily compared to other data sets. (Do call lengths get substantially different as we approach the year-end holidays?) The larger the amount of raw data, the harder it is to digest it in raw form and the more important it becomes to summarize it. Quantitative and qualitative data can be summarized either by tables or graphically. Quantitative data can also be summarized numerically.

Table 6.1	Duration in Minutes for a Sample of 102 Telephone Calls Received by the Flight Reservation System of Austral					
	5.1	8.6	4.7	5.9	12.4	7.8
	7.2	7.2	3.6	4.0	9.2	5.2
	4.9	8.6	3.6	7.5	7.4	6.2
	8.0	10.9	5.5	3.9	5.3	7.2
	6.3	3.9	6.9	5.4	2.0	8.0
	5.8	3.5	8.4	4.4	7.0	8.3
	9.0	4.6	5.7	9.8	4.0	6.0
	10.9	6.8	5.9	8.7	3.8	7.6
	15.6	7.0	5.0	6.9	4.7	7.5
	6.4	9.4	6.9	2.7	10.0	4.7
	7.3	10.4	4.7	4.2	6.7	4.6
	7.1	6.7	4.9	5.3	4.4	2.5
	8.3	4.4	5.5	1.9	2.1	7.4
	6.5	3.7	6.8	4.8	8.4	4.7
	9.8	1.8	7.6	7.2	7.1	5.7
	8.6	8.2	4.3	2.5	7.8	5.3
	5.5	3.9	6.7	7.9	7.0	7.4

In this chapter we first describe the most common ways of summarizing data by tables and graphically. We then provide an overview of how to summarize data numerically.

Table 6-2 presents a taxonomy of the main methods for summarizing data. This table will provide a useful framework as you read through the chapter.

◆ TABULAR AND GRAPHIC SUMMARIZATION OF NUMERIC DATA

Tabular Summaries for Numeric Data: Frequency Distributions

The frequency distribution is the most common way of summarizing numeric data by means of a table. Exhibit 6-3 shows a tally sheet for the call lengths given in Table 6-1. A suitable number of *cells (classes, bins,* or *intervals* are terms also used) was chosen, and the 102 data values were systematically tallied, one by one, into these cells.

Notice that all cells have the same width. Cells are adjacent to one another but do not overlap, and they collectively cover all values in the data set: the smallest data value is 1.8 and the largest value is 15.6, so the first cell extends below the smallest value and the last cell extends above the largest value. The number of cells one

Table
6.2

Main Methods for Summarizing Data

			Quantitative	Qualitative

One variable	Tabular		Frequency distribution
			    absolute frequencies
			    relative frequencies
			    percentages
			Cumulative distribution
				Similar to quantitative

	Graphic		Tally Sheet Histogram/Dot plot Stem and leaf Run chart	Tally sheet Location plot Bar chart Pie chart Pareto diagram
	Numeric	Location	Mean Median	
		Spread	Range Variance Std. deviation Percentiles	
		Multiple	Box plot	

Two variables			Tally sheet
			Scatter diagram
				Tally sheet
				Cross tabulation
				    or contingency
				    table

SOURCE: "Total Quality Management: What it Means Today"
Copyright © Ismael Dambolena, Babson College, Wellesley, MA, 1992. Reprinted by permission

chooses is usually somewhere between 5 and 20, and it often depends on the number of data values that are being tallied. By and large, the more data the more cells.

Table 6-3 shows an *absolute* **frequency distribution** for the call lengths shown in Table 6-1. The *absolute frequencies* in this table are counts of the tallies in Exhibit 6-3.

Also often used are *relative frequency distributions,* which display the absolute frequencies of the cells divided by the total number of values, as shown in Table 6-4, and *percentage distributions,* where the relative frequencies multiplied by 100 are displayed for each cell. Relative frequencies are also called **proportions** and always add up to 1. Percentages always add up to 100. One advantage that both relative frequencies and percentages have over absolute frequencies is that they allow you to directly compare a variety of distributions obtained from different sample sizes.

Exhibit
6.3

Call Length in Minutes	Tally
[1,2)	II
[2,3)	HHT
[3,4)	HHT III
[4,5)	HHT HHT HHT I
[5,6)	HHT HHT HHT I
[6,7)	HHT HHT III
[7,8)	HHT HHT HHT HHT
[8,9)	HHT HHT I
[9,10)	HHT
[10,11)	IIII
[11,12)	
[12,13)	I
[13,14)	
[14,15)	
[15,16)	I

Tally sheet for the call lengths in Table 6-1.

Table 6-5 shows a *cumulative* **frequency distribution** for the call lengths. The cumulative frequency for each cell is the sum of the absolute frequencies for that cell and for all cells above it. Cumulative relative frequencies and cumulative percentages are also often displayed.

Cumulative distributions simplify many computations. If you had to find out how many of the calls took no more than 10 minutes, using the absolute frequency distribution you would have to add the first nine absolute frequencies in Table 6-3. You could obtain the same answer by simply picking the ninth cumulative frequency in Table 6-5. Many statistical procedures require the use of cumulative distributions, and many statistical tables are presented in cumulative form.

All of these distributions present basically the same information in different form, and any of them conveys more immediate information about the 102 call lengths than the raw data did. Even more impact, however, is carried by a graphic display, as we show next.

Graphic Summaries for Numeric Data: Histograms and Stem-and-Leaf Displays

One picture is said to be worth one thousand words, and you had better believe it. A **histogram** is a picture that summarizes numeric data. The histogram in Exhibit 6-4 displays graphically the information in the frequency distribution in Table 6-3. The horizontal axis represents the variable we are summarizing (in this case the length of telephone calls), and the cells are represented as intervals on that axis.

Table 6.3	Absolute Frequency Distribution for the Call Lengths in Table 6-1	
CALL LENGTH IN MINUTES	ABSOLUTE FREQUENCY	
1.0 to under 2.0	2	
2.0 to under 3.0	5	
3.0 to under 4.0	8	
4.0 to under 5.0	16	
5.0 to under 6.0	16	
6.0 to under 7.0	13	
7.0 to under 8.0	20	
8.0 to under 9.0	11	
9.0 to under 10.0	5	
10.0 to under 11.0	4	
11.0 to under 12.0	0	
12.0 to under 13.0	1	
13.0 to under 14.0	0	
14.0 to under 15.0	0	
15.0 to under 16.0	1	
Total	102	

The vertical axis is suitably scaled so that it can accommodate the largest cell frequency. The bars represent the frequencies in each cell. Instead of absolute frequencies, the vertical axis sometimes displays relative frequencies or percentages.

By just taking a quick look at the histogram, we learn that short calls take one or two minutes; once in a while a call will take over 15 minutes, but most calls take no more than 10 minutes, three-fourths of calls between four and nine minutes, and so on. The 16-minute call is clearly seen to be an **outlier** (a call substantially longer or shorter than the bulk of the remaining calls). The average call seems to take about six or seven minutes to complete.

We next show how some of these ideas are used in the monitoring of quality. In Chapter 8 we will see them used in an integrated fashion as part of a case study on quality improvement.

The histograms in Exhibit 6-5 show shrinkage in speedometer casings before and after a product improvement experiment. The actual experiment is discussed in detail later in this book. The first histogram shows post-extrusion shrinkage for a sample of 100 casings under old processing methods, and the

Table
6.4

Relative Frequency Distribution for the Call Lengths in Table 6-1

CALL LENGTH IN MINUTES	RELATIVE FREQUENCY
1.0 to under 2.0	0.020
2.0 to under 3.0	0.049
3.0 to under 4.0	0.078
4.0 to under 5.0	0.157
5.0 to under 6.0	0.157
6.0 to under 7.0	0.127
7.0 to under 8.0	0.196
8.0 to under 9.0	0.108
9.0 to under 10.0	0.049
10.0 to under 11.0	0.039
11.0 to under 12.0	0.000
12.0 to under 13.0	0.010
13.0 to under 14.0	0.000
14.0 to under 15.0	0.000
15.0 to under 16.0	0.010
Total	1.000

other shows shrinkage under improved processing conditions. Here the histograms clearly and effectively show a drastic reduction in shrinkage (one of the goals of the experiment) as well as a more uniform product, with less variation in shrinkage (a second goal).

Stratification is the separation of a group into two or more subgroups according to a given factor. Exhibit 6-6*a* shows the percentage of nitrogen in 62 batches of fertilizer produced by Agro, together with the specification limits (10 ± 0.3 percent). Several batches are out of specifications. The fertilizer was produced by two different production lines. When the batches were stratified according to production line and separate histograms were developed for each line (Exhibit 6-6*b* and 6-6*c*) it was noticed that only one line seemed to have problems in meeting specifications. That line was targeted for improvements.

Several new techniques for data analysis, collectively called **exploratory data analysis** (EDA), were developed by John Tukey (1977). Some of these techniques are used extensively and are nowadays included in most statistical packages. One of them is the **stem-and-leaf display.**

Table
6.5

Cumulative Frequency Distribution for
the Call Lengths in Table 6-1

CALL LENGTH IN MINUTES	CUMULATIVE FREQUENCY
1.0 to under 2.0	2
2.0 to under 3.0	7
3.0 to under 4.0	15
4.0 to under 5.0	31
5.0 to under 6.0	47
6.0 to under 7.0	60
7.0 to under 8.0	80
8.0 to under 9.0	91
9.0 to under 10.0	96
10.0 to under 11.0	100
11.0 to under 12.0	100
12.0 to under 13.0	101
13.0 to under 14.0	101
14.0 to under 15.0	101
15.0 to under 16.0	102

Exhibit
6.4

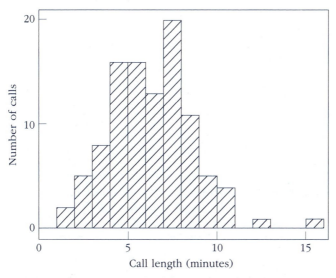

Histogram of the call lengths in Table 6-1. Just a quick look
at the histogram gives us much information about the raw
data it summarizes.

Exhibit
6.5

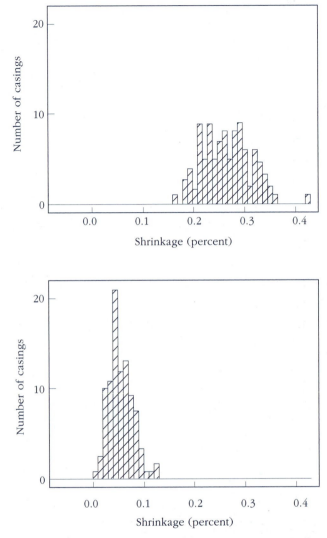

Shrinkage in speedometer casings before (*top*) and after
(*bottom*) a product improvement experiment. Notice the
reduction in both average shrinkage and spread. Both reductions were goals of the experiment.

Exhibit 6-7 shows a stem-and-leaf display for the 102 call lengths in Table 6-1.
The values in the second column of the display are the *stems*. The stem in a row
represents the leading digits of the data values in that row. The third column
shows the *leaves*. Each leaf in a row represents the trailing digit for a data value
in that row. The leaves are sorted in ascending order. For example, the 9 on the

Exhibit
6.6

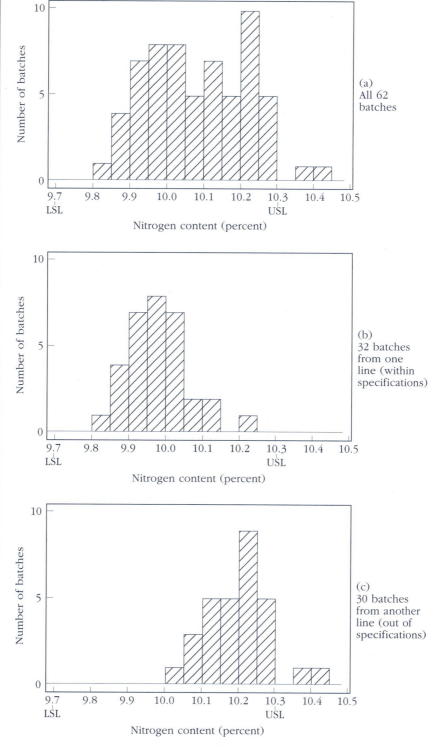

Histograms showing the percentage of nitrogen in batches of fertilizer. The specification limits are also shown. When all batches (*top*) were stratified by production line, it was noticed that in one line (*middle*) nitrogen content was quite acceptable while in the other (*bottom*) the average content was too high.

Exhibit
6.7

MTB > stem c3

STEM-AND-LEAF OF C3	N = 102
LEAF UNIT = 0.10	

2	1 89
7	2 01557
15	3 56678999
31	4 0023446677777899
47	5 0123334455577899
(13)	6 0234577788999
42	7 00011222234445566889
22	8 00233446667
11	9 02488
6	10 0499
2	11
2	12 4
1	13
1	14
1	15 6

Stem-and-leaf display for the call lengths in Table 6–1.
The stem-and-leaf display, though similar to a
histogram, contains more information about the
individual values.

first row (a leaf) and the 1 on that same row (the stem) represent the value 1.9, which is the second lowest value in the data set that the diagram summarizes. The 1 on the second line (a leaf) and the 2 on that same line (the stem) represent the value 2.1, which is the fourth lowest value in the data set.

The values in the leftmost column are called *depths* and represent the number of leaves in that row "and beyond to the nearest end." For example, the 15 in the leftmost column of the third row tells you that the total number of leaves in that row and above is 15. The 1 in the leftmost column of the next to the last row tells you that the total number of leaves in that row and below is 1. The depths in row 4 (31) and row 5 (47) tell you that there are 16 leaves in row 5 (since 47 - 31 = 16). The one exception to this convention occurs when the median observation belongs entirely within one row. In these cases, the depth is shown in parentheses, and it represents a count of the leaves in the row that contains the median.

Notice that the histogram and the stem-and-leaf display are similar in shape. The leaves in the stem-and-leaf display, however, contain information on the individual data values that is lost when the histogram is used.

◆ OTHER GRAPHIC TOOLS

Graphs carry much more impact than tables or data lists, so they are very widely used (a random check of the *Wall Street Journal* can reveal more than 20 graphs in it). You should strive to use graphs whenever you analyze data or communicate facts based on data.

Histograms are just one of the many different types of graphs available for representing data. Here we show a few other types of graphs that are very often used.

Graphs for Categorical Data: Bar Charts, Pie Charts, and Pareto Diagrams

Table 6-6 shows the percentages of total time that fifth graders spent on different subjects in Japanese and U.S. schools during the early 1980s.

The **bar chart** in Exhibit 6-8 and the **pie chart** in Exhibit 6-9 are graphic representations of the categorical data for U.S. schools. The bar chart is most helpful in comparing the percentage in one class with percentages in any of the other classes. The pie chart, where the sizes of the different slices are proportional to the percentages in the classes, is preferable in showing how the percentage in any class compares with the whole. The **paired bar chart** in Exhibit 6-10 is helpful in directly comparing the data of the two countries.

Every reader will agree that one often faces many problems that need to be worked on. This state of affairs is common in companies that are in the early stages of implementing a quality improvement program: as they measure more, they discover many problems that were not apparent before, and they are sometimes shocked by their magnitude. **Pareto diagrams** are bar charts that provide information on the relative importance of problems. This information helps select the most crucial problems for earlier action, and thus it helps in choosing the ar-

Table 6.6	Percentages of Total Time That Fifth Graders Spent on Different Subjects in Japanese and U.S. Schools (early 1980s)		
SUBJECT		JAPAN	UNITED STATES
Language		24	42
Mathematics		23	18
Social science		13	15
Music		8	4
Art		10	6
Moral education		5	1
Other		17	14

SOURCE: Harold Stevenson, "Making the Grade: School Achievements in Japan, Taiwan and the United States." 1983 Annual Report, Stanford, Calif.: Center for Advanced Study in the Behavioral Sciences, 1983.

Exhibit

6.8

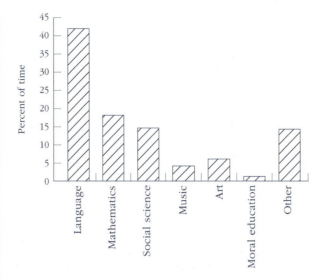

Bar chart showing the percentage of total time that
fifth-grade students in U.S. schools spent on different
subjects (early 1980s).

Exhibit

6.9

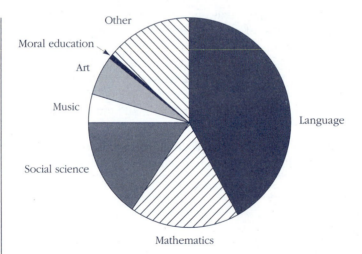

Pie chart showing the percentage of total time that fifth-grade students in U.S. schools spent on different subjects (early 1980s).
The pie chart does a better job than the bar chart in showing
how the percentage in any category compares to the whole.

Exhibit
6.10

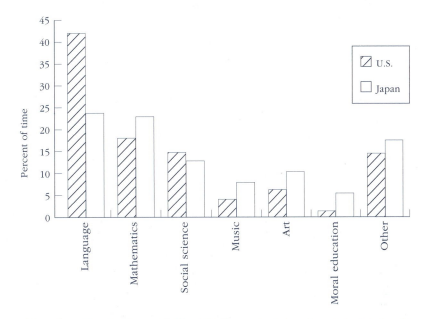

Paired bar chart for the data in Table 6-8. The paired bar chart is helpful in directly comparing the same data for the two countries.

the most crucial problems for earlier action, and thus it helps in choosing the areas where quality improvement efforts should initially be concentrated.

Vilfredo Pareto (1848–1923) was an Italian-born Swiss sociologist and economist who researched the distribution of income and wealth late in the nineteenth century. Not surprisingly, he found that a relatively small number of people received most of the total income and held most of the total wealth. The **Pareto principle** states that in many instances a small proportion of items account for a large percentage of some variable linked to those items. For example, a relatively small group of highly populated states account for a large percentage of all U.S. electoral votes, relatively few customers account for a large percentage of total sales in many businesses, and a few problem types often account for most of the complaints a company gets from customers. In dollar terms, people sometimes refer to this as the 80–20 rule, which says that approximately 80 percent of costs are accounted for by 20 percent of the items. One should not consider this 80–20 breakdown as fixed, since it really may change substantially from one situation to another.

Table 6-7 shows absolute frequencies, percentages, cumulative frequencies, and cumulative percentages for defects of different types found in speedometer decals during inspections over a one-month period.

The absolute frequencies in Table 6-7 were developed by aggregating the daily tallies for each type of defect over one month. The types of defects were then arranged in decreasing order of occurrence, and the absolute frequencies were

Table
6.7

Different Types of Defects Found in Speedometer Decals
During a One-Month Period

DEFECT TYPE	ABSOLUTE FREQUENCY OF OCCURRENCE	PERCENT OF ALL DEFECTS	CUMULATIVE FREQUENCY	CUMULATIVE PERCENTAGE
Pinholes	332	41	332	41%
Registration	265	33	597	74
Scratches	78	10	675	84
Sharpness	58	7	733	91
Wrong color	45	6	778	97
Finish	15	2	793	99
Blots	12	1	805	100
Total	805	100		

Exhibit
6.11

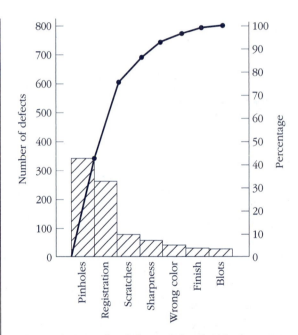

Pareto diagram for defects in decals. The bars reflect the magnitude of the different problems. The
ogive shows cumulative frequencies. The diagram
separates the "vital few" (here pinholes and registration problems) from the "trivial many." The
steepness of the ogive gives an indication of how
much disparity exists, in frequency of occurrence,
between the vital few and the trivial many.

transformed into percentages (by dividing them by the total number of defects and multiplying by 100). Finally, the cumulative columns were developed by accumulating both absolute frequencies and percentages.

The Pareto diagram in Exhibit 6-11 is a graphic representation of these data. The different types of defects are shown as classes in the horizontal axis, where they are arranged in the same order as in the table, with the most frequent defect shown on the left. The bar for a class represents both the number and the percentage of defects for that defect type. The number of defects is read on the left scale (where absolute frequencies are indicated) and the percentage on the right scale. The line graph that moves up from left to right (called an *ogive*) shows cumulative numbers (reading on the left scale), or cumulative percentages (on right scale), up to and including any given class.

The Pareto diagram shows that two types of defects (pinholes and registration problems) account for almost three-quarters of the defects. Significant reductions in any of these two types of defects will cause a substantial decrease in the overall defect rate. On the other hand, even a complete elimination of blots would not make a major dent in the overall rate. This does not imply that blots should not be worked on. If with little effort you could get rid of them, you should go ahead and do that immediately. However, other things being equal (such as level of difficulty in problem solving), pinholes and registration problems should concern you more initially.

In the above example, it made good sense to work directly with the number or percentage of defects because each type of defect is equally costly (the scrapping of a decal). However, in many instances the different types of defects (or other problems) have substantially different costs. In these cases, it makes more sense to work

Table 6.8	Distribution of Defects and Costs for Printed Circuit Boards				
DEFECT TYPE	NUMBER OF DEFECTS	AVERAGE SCRAP AND REPAIR COST PER DEFECT	AVERAGE WEEKLY COST	PERCENTAGE OF TOTAL COST	CUMULATIVE PERCENTAGE
Defective components	105	12.60	1323.00	45%	45%
Component out of alignment	210	4.75	997.50	35%	80%
Improper solder joint	32	8.75	280.00	10%	90%
Solder balls	76	3.25	247.00	9%	99%
Component missing	8	2.50	20.00	1%	100%
Totals			2867.50	100%	

Exhibit
6.12

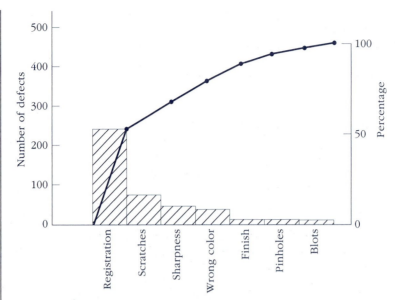

Pareto diagram for defects in decals after process improvement efforts. Comparing this Exhibit to exhibit 6-11, we can clearly notice the improvement.

with costs rather than with numbers of defects. Table 6-8 shows frequencies of occurrence for different types of defects in printed circuit boards. These frequencies were multiplied by average unit costs of repairing or scrapping these boards.

It is left to you in a problem at the end of the chapter to develop a Pareto diagram based on average weekly costs rather than the number of defects. In cases where unit costs are difficult or impossible to estimate, one may instead use a subjective factor that reflects the seriousness of the problem or defect.

Pareto diagrams are useful in assessing the effectiveness of quality improvement efforts. After looking into the problem of pinholes and finding a solution for it (a detailed problem-solving procedure for doing this systematically is discussed later in the chapter), data on decal defects were collected again for one month and the Pareto diagram in Exhibit 6-12 was drawn. The resulting improvements are obvious by comparing this diagram with the diagram in Exhibit 6-11. The number of pinholes has been drastically reduced, and as a result the overall defect rate has also improved substantially. Notice that the *left scales* are the same in both figures (the diagram before and the diagram after the problem-solving effort), while the *right* scale has been shrunk to reflect the improvement. It is improper, though often done, to leave the *right* scale unchanged. If one does this, then the improvement, which should be apparent in the comparison, does not really show.

Not only are Pareto diagrams useful in assigning priorities to problems that need work, as we showed above, but they are also helpful in finding the causes of problems and thus making it easier to solve them. As Mary Walton (1986, p. 107) writes in an excellent book on Deming:

> At the printed circuit board plant, management organized a safety campaign at the employee's request. A team gathered data on accidents, then used a Pareto to diagram the findings. Eye injuries were more common than any other. The team then researched causes and again made another Pareto chart. The largest number of eye accidents occurred during the process of clipping the wire leads of components after they were soldered to the printed circuit board. In this fashion, Pareto charts can be used to narrow down problems.

Better eye protection during wire-lead clipping and better monitoring of proper use were thus singled out as possible solutions to eye-injury problems.

Pareto diagrams also have many applications in areas other than quality management. The ABC inventory management systems, for example, are based on a Pareto analysis of the annual usage, in dollars, of the different parts that a company carries in inventory. A relatively small number of parts (Class A items) tend to account for a fairly high share of the total annual usage and receive the closest scrutiny. On the other hand, a large number of parts (Class C items) tend to account for a fairly small share of total usage and are therefore managed much more loosely. Class B items fall in the middle both in terms of their share of total usage and the attention that they are paid.

Graphs for Time-Ordered Data: Run Charts

Exhibit 6-13 shows a histogram for the weekly number of late deliveries by KitCo, a major kitchen appliance manufacturer. The data were collected during a 16-week period, while improvements in the delivery system were being implemented, so there are 16 weekly data values in the histogram. Exhibit 6-13 also shows a **run chart** or **time series plot** for the same data. In a run chart the horizontal axis represents time, and the vertical axis represents individual observations of a numeric variable of interest. The chart is useful in examining the behavior of the variable over time. The time dimension is often crucial: notice how potentially important information on the trend of the variable is captured by the run chart but missed by the histogram. Every time you use data that were collected over time you should plot them on a run chart to learn more about its features. Later on we will discuss control charts, which are among the most widely used tools in quality management. The run chart looks in many ways like a control chart, but, as we shall see, it is different from it in at least one major respect: it does not include control limits.

Flow Diagrams

A **flow diagram** or **flowchart** provides a very effective graphical description of how something works. These diagrams are used widely in many fields. In quality

Exhibit
6.13

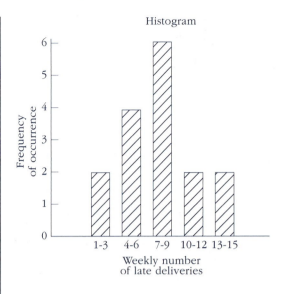

Histogram

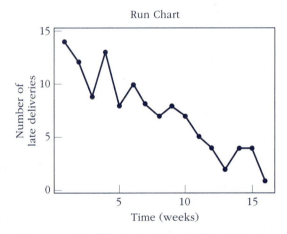

Run Chart

Histogram (*top*) and run chart (*bottom*) for the weekly number of late deliveries of kitchen appliances by a major manufacturer. The run chart shows important information on trend that is not apparent from the histogram. Whenever you use data that were collected over time, you should plot it on a run chart to learn about its features.

management, they are used to describe processes during continual improvement efforts and also in other contexts.

Exhibit
6.14

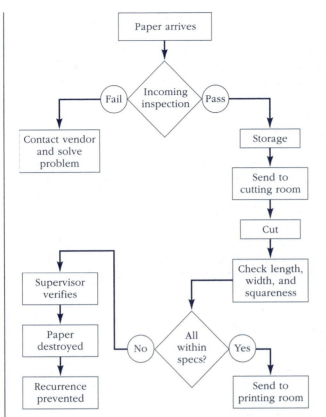

Flow diagram for the processing of incoming paper at a printing press. The flow diagram is invaluable in describing processes.

Exhibit 6-14 shows a flow diagram for the processing of incoming paper prior to printing decals at a printing press, in the analysis of which one of us was involved. The diagram shows the different steps of the process and the sequence in which they take place. Receivers, inspectors, storeroom clerks, cutting press operators, and different supervisors would typically be consulted in order to develop such a diagram. More detail could be added to the diagram in further refinements. Specialized symbols are sometimes used instead of the simple boxes and diamonds shown here.

Flow diagrams should almost invariably be used to describe processes that are to be improved. A thorough understanding of how a process currently works is essential to one's ability to improve it, and in most cases this understanding is best gained through the development of a flow diagram.

If one asked two persons involved with a process to independently develop flow diagrams for it, it would not be uncommon to have as a result two substantially different flow diagrams. Agreement on how a process actually operates is also essential to the ability to improve it, and here, too, the flow diagram is extremely useful. Finally, the flow diagram helps document a process once it is improved.

Again, as in all modeling, developing a flow diagram is in itself valuable and instructive. It is particularly useful in the services, where the flow of paperwork and information may not be as obvious as is the flow of materials in manufacturing processes. In our consulting, we often ask our clients to make a flowchart of the relevant processes. It helps them better understand the way their processes operate, it saves them money, and it improves our communications. In fact, if through practice you become familiar with how to develop flow diagrams, you will find them invaluable in communicating many ideas and processes to others.

In Chapter 7 we use a flow diagram to describe the general procedure followed in the developing of control charts. Flow diagrams will also be used later on, not only in our discussions of continual improvement but also in Chapter 15 when benchmarking is discussed.

Cause-and-Effect Diagrams

A **cause-and-effect diagram** is a graph that shows the relationships between a problem and its possible causes. These tree diagrams, originally developed by Kaoru Ishikawa in 1953, are used during brainstorming sessions where possible solutions for a problem are being sought. In this context, they provide a model for the connections between the problem (usually a quality characteristic that is not meeting customer needs) and factors that affect it. The problem is called the *effect,* and the factors that affect it are called the *causes.* Cause-and-effect diagrams are helpful in eliminating problems by tackling their causes, and they are also useful in understanding the effects that several factors have on a process. They are also known as **fishbone diagrams** or **Ishikawa diagrams.**

Exhibit 6-15 shows a cause-and-effect diagram for poor barbecue quality. The effect (poor barbecue quality) is shown on the right, and the possible causes (or factors) and their interrelations are shown on the left.

In order to develop a diagram such as this, the problem would first be agreed upon and defined precisely. Then, in a brainstorming session, people familiar with cooking barbecues would suggest the different possible causes. Finally, the causes would be grouped together, and their interrelations would be shown by the appropriate diagram.

Notice how primary causes feed into the main horizontal line of the diagram, secondary causes feed into main causes, tertiary causes into secondary causes, and so on. In spite of the fact that it is also called a fishbone diagram, a cause-and-effect diagram that looks like the skeleton of a fish (only primary causes feeding into a main line) is not an appropriate model for a complex problem.

Exhibit
6.15

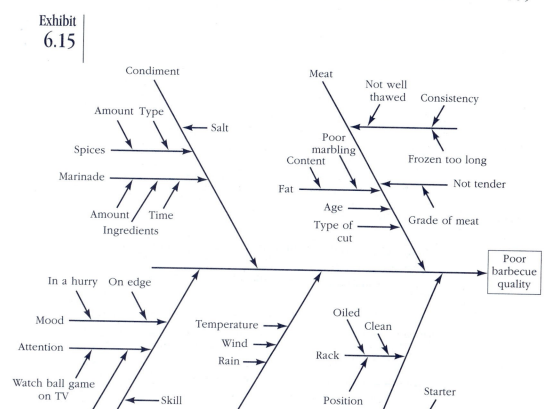

Cause-and-effect diagram for poor barbecue quality.

To facilitate the grouping of causes, several major generic categories have often been suggested. For production processes the suggested major categories, known as the four Ms, are manpower, machines, materials, and methods. For service or administrative processes they are known as the four Ps: people, plant and equipment, policies, and procedures. In many instances, most causes will fall into one of these major categories. This general procedure is just one of several that may be followed to develop a cause-and-effect diagram.

In *Guide to Quality Control,* Ishikawa (1982) points to several fringe benefits of using cause-and-effect diagrams. The process of developing them is educational in itself; they give you a framework for discussion; they force you to actively look for the causes of problems and to collect data; they are a guide to concrete action; and the more you use them, the more effective they become as an

Exhibit
6.16

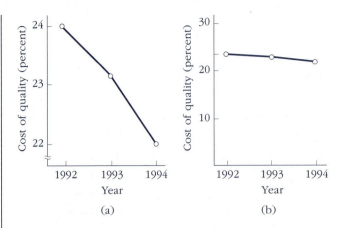

Two ways of graphing reductions in the cost of quality as a percentage of total production costs. Some people may be misled by the graph on the left.

improvement tool. We would add that, as with all modeling, once the model has been properly designed, the problem is much better understood. Cause-and-effect diagrams have been found useful in many problem-solving activities outside the realm of quality improvement, but, unfortunately, they are not used very often in contexts other than quality management.

Cautionary Note on Graphs

One should be careful not to be misled by some graphs and not to mislead with them. A quick glance at Exhibit 6-16a might make you believe that drastic reductions in the cost of quality are being achieved. Exhibit 6-16b puts those reductions in a better perspective.

Facilitating Data Collection: Check Sheets

Check sheets are special types of forms for data collection. They make it easier to collect data, they tend to make the data collection effort more accurate, and they automatically produce some sort of data summarization which is often very effective for a quick analysis. There are two main types of check sheets: **tally sheets** and **location plots.**

We already used a tally sheet in tallying our call lengths in Exhibit 6-3. The tally sheet contains the information presented later in the frequency distribution (Table 6-3) and histogram (Exhibit 6-4) of the call lengths.

Tally sheets may also be used for categorical variables. Exhibit 6-17 shows a tally sheet for defects found in speedometer decals on a one-day period. The data

Exhibit

6.17

No. _____

Decal type: _____   Date: _____

Specifications: _____   Remarks: _____

Lot number: _____

Defect type	0	5	10	15	20	25	30	35	Total frequency
Registration	||||| ||||| ||							12
Finish										1
Wrong color	||								2
Pinholes	||||| ||||| |||||							16
Blots										1
Sharpness	|||								3
Scratches	||||								4

Tally sheet for defects found in speedometer decals during a one-day period.

were collected by tallying during inspections. An aggregate of these data over one month was used to develop a Pareto diagram for these defects.

Exhibit 6-18 shows a tally sheet on which two categorical variables—type of defect and shift where the defect occurred—were cross tabulated. The **cross-tabulation** shows the marginal distributions for the two variables. From one of these marginal distributions we learn about the incidence of the different defect types, and from the other we learn how defects are shared among the three shifts. The cross-tabulation also shows the interrelationships between the two variables. We learn from it that most of the pinholes and registration problems occur during the evening shift, and this information offers a clue as to where to start looking when one tries to solve these problems. Later in this chapter we discuss scatter diagrams, which help analyze the relationships between numeric variables.

Exhibit 6-19 shows a location plot for defects that occurred in the production of tires by a major manufacturer. For each defect found, its position was indicated in the location plot. The plot helps identify the cross-sectional location of the defect (left graph) and its location around the tire (right graph), starting at the tread joint. When many defects were plotted this way, the concentration of a large proportion of them on a particular area in the location plot served as a clue to a problem in the manufacturing process that caused most of the defects. Location plots

Exhibit
6.18

Type of defect	Shift Day	Shift Evening	Shift Night	Total
Pinholes	||	ЖТ III	||	12
Registration		ЖТ II	||	9
Scratches	||	||	III	7
Sharpness		||	ЖТ I	8
	4	19	13	36

Cross-tabulation of type of defect and shift where the defects occurred. Cross-tabulations such as this show the relationship between two categorical variables as well as the distribution of each variable individually.

for traffic accidents are routinely used by state and local authorities to improve the system of road signals, change the setting of speed limits, and emphasize the enforcement of traffic regulations in critical areas. Tally sheets have many uses in areas other than quality management. A location plot for murders committed in Boston over the past three years will send you a clear signal about areas that you should try to stay away from if you can manage to do so.

NUMERIC DATA SUMMARIZATION

Quantitative data can be summarized numerically by producing a few summary numbers that describe key characteristics of the data, such as their *location* (what is a typical value for these data?) or their *spread* (how far apart are these data?).

Measures of Location: The Mean and the Median

The **mean** (the average value) is the most common measure of location for a quantitative data set. It is computed by adding the values in the data set and dividing by the number of values. The sum of the 102 call lengths in Table 6-1 is 648.0, so their mean is 6.353 minutes: the average call takes a little less than six and a half minutes to complete. Find this mean in the horizontal axis of the histogram for these data (Exhibit 6-4) and notice how central it is to its distribution. The mean of a population is denoted μ, and the mean of a sample

Exhibit
6.19

Location Plot
for Tire Defects

Tire Model P195/75 R14 M+S X2

Inspected by Jim Philips

Date 11-5-94

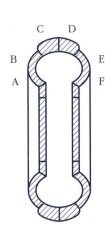

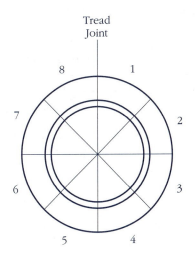

Tread
Joint

	Circumference							
Cross Section	1	2	3	4	5	6	7	8
A					||			
B	|||							~~HHT~~ ||||
C				||				
D								
E	~~HHT~~							||||
F								

File: h:TIRES

A location plot for tire defects. Many tallies on a cell in the table provided a clue to the manufacturing problem that caused the defects.

distribution. The mean of a population is denoted μ, and the mean of a sample is usually denoted $\overline{X}$.

The **median** (the value in the middle after the values have been arranged in ascending or descending order) is also used often. To find the median we first sort the values. If the number of values is odd, the median is the single value in the middle; if the number of values is even, the median is the average of the two values in the middle. Table 6-9 shows the 102 call lengths in Table 6-1 sorted in ascending order. Since the two values in the middle are 6.4 and 6.5, the median is 6.45. The median is not influenced by outliers, and this makes it preferable to the mean in many applications.

Table 6.9	The Call Lengths in Table 6-1 Sorted in Ascending Order					
	1.8	1.9	2.0	2.1	2.5	2.5
	2.7	3.5	3.6	3.6	3.7	3.8
	3.9	3.9	3.9	4.0	4.0	4.2
	4.3	4.4	4.4	4.6	4.6	4.7
	4.7	4.7	4.7	4.7	4.8	4.9
	4.9	5.0	5.1	5.2	5.3	5.3
	5.3	5.4	5.4	5.5	5.5	5.5
	5.7	5.7	5.8	5.9	5.9	6.0
	6.2	6.3	6.4	6.5	6.7	6.7
	6.7	6.8	6.8	6.9	6.9	6.9
	7.0	7.0	7.0	7.1	7.1	7.2
	7.2	7.2	7.2	7.3	7.4	7.4
	7.4	7.5	7.5	7.6	7.6	7.8
	7.8	7.9	8.0	8.0	8.2	8.3
	8.3	8.4	8.4	8.6	8.6	8.6
	8.7	9.0	9.2	9.4	9.8	9.8
	10.0	10.4	10.9	10.9	12.4	15.6

Measures of Spread: The Standard Deviation, Variance, Range, and Percentiles

The **variance** and its square root, the **standard deviation,** are the most commonly used measures of spread. The variance of a set of numbers is the average of their squared deviations from their mean. For a *population* of N numeric values, the variance, denoted σ^2, is computed using the formula

$$\sigma^2 = \frac{\sum_{i=1}^{N}(X_i - \mu)^2}{N}$$

where X_i is the ith value in the sample. For a sample of n numeric values, on the other hand, the variance is denoted S^2 and computed as follows. [*Note:* There are statistical reasons for dividing by n - 1 rather than by n in this formula for the sample variance. One often samples from a population and computes the variance of the sample in order to estimate the population variance. If in computing the sample variance we divided by n, we would systematically underestimate the population variance. When we divide by n - 1, we make an adjustment so that, on average and in the long run, the sample variance neither underestimates nor overestimates the variance of the population.]:

$$S^2 = \frac{\sum_{i=1}^{n}(X_i - \bar{X})^2}{n - 1}$$

As we mentioned above, the standard deviation is the square root of the variance. The symbol for the standard deviation of a population is σ; for a sample the symbol is S.

For the call lengths in Table 6-1 the variance is

$$S^2 = \frac{(5.1 - 6.35)^2 + (8.6 - 6.35)^2 + \ldots + (7.4 - 6.35)^2}{102 - 1} = 5.48$$

The standard deviation of the call lengths is the square root of this variance, or 2.34. This standard deviation represents, again roughly speaking, the average deviation of the 102 call lengths from their mean.

Also used as a measure of spread for a set of numeric values is their **range,** the difference between the largest and the smallest values. The range is very often used in statistical process control: as we shall see later, the range chart is the most prevalent tool for controlling the spread of a measurable quality characteristic. For the call lengths in Table 6-1, the largest value is 15.6 and the smallest value 1.8, so their range is 13.8. The term *range* is also used to refer to the span between the smallest and largest data values, so one could say that the call lengths range from 1.8 to 15.6.

The median, as we saw before, divides an ordered set of values into two halves. The quartiles divide these halves again in half. The **first quartile** or **lower quartile** is, roughly, a value such that one-fourth of the observations lie below it and three-fourths lie above it. The **third quartile** or **upper quartile** leaves, roughly, three-fourths of the values below it and one-fourth above it. The median and the quartiles are particular cases of a more general idea: the **percentiles.** The first quartile is the 25th percentile, the median is the 50th percentile, and the upper quartile is the 75th percentile. You are 95th percentile IQ-wise in the United States if your IQ is higher than those of 95 percent of people in this country. The term percentile is commonly used in quality management and in many other fields.

Exhibit
6.20

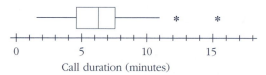

A box plot for the call durations in Table 6-1.
This graph depicts the main numeric summary measures for the data set.

The lower and upper quartiles for the call lengths in Table 6-1 are 4.70 and 7.65, respectively. By referring to the ordered values in Table 6-7, you can verify that the first quartile, 4.70, is one-fourth of the way down the list. (There are actually five 4.70s, and one of them is one-fourth of the way down the list.) The third quartile, 7.65, lies between the 77th and 78th ordered observations, three-fourths of the way down the list. The distance between quartiles is the **interquartile range,** a measure of spread for the data. The interquartile range for the call lengths is 2.95 (7.65 − 4.70). Virtually all statistical packages and many spreadsheets have commands or functions that automatically compute all these numeric summary measures.

A Graphic Display of Numeric Summaries: The Box Plot

We have already referred to exploratory data analysis when we discussed stem and leaf displays. The **box plot** (or **box-and-whisker plot**) is another widely used tool of exploratory data analysis. It presents in graphic form the main numeric summary measures for a data set. Exhibit 6-20 shows a box plot for the 102 call lengths in Table 6-1. The rectangle is the box, which extends between the first and the third quartiles. The vertical line within the box indicates the location of the median.

The two horizontal lines extending beyond the ends of the box are the whiskers, which cover the range of the data except for possible outliers, such as those represented by the asterisks beyond the right whisker. [*Note:* In terms of exploratory data analysis, an outlier is an observation that lies more than 1.5 interquartile ranges beyond a quartile.] Box plots are particularly useful in the comparison of several data sets, as shown in Exhibit 6-21.

Graphing the Relationship Between Two Variables: The Scatter Diagram

Scatter diagrams or **scatter plots** are graphs that depict the joint behavior of two quantitative variables and are useful in investigating their possible relationship. Table 6-10 shows tensile strength and hardness measurements for a sample of 25 pieces of an alloy.

Exhibit 6-22 shows a scatter diagram for the 25 pairs. For each piece of the alloy, its hardness was located on the scale in the horizontal axis, its tensile strength

Exhibit

6.21

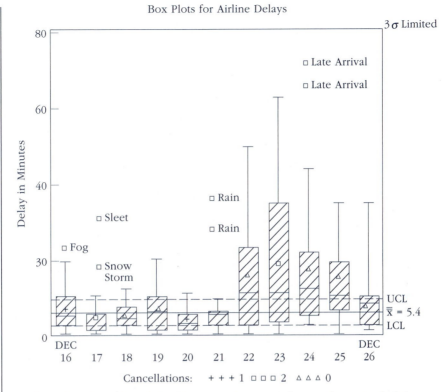

Box plots for airline delays during a time period around a major holiday.
Longer delays are clearly noticeable immediately around the holiday.

Exhibit

6.22

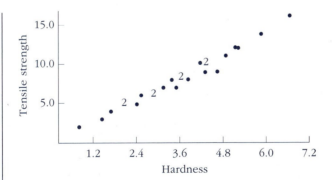

Scatter diagram for the data in Table 6-10. The close
relation between the two variables suggests that a
nondestructive test for hardness could be substituted
for a destructive test for tensile strength.

Table	
6.10	

Tensile Strength and Hardness Measurements for a Sample of 25 Pieces of an Alloy

SAMPLE NUMBER	TENSILE STRENGTH	HARDNESS
1	10	4.27
2	8	3.59
3	8	3.56
4	12	5.26
5	6	2.50
6	8	3.79
7	12	5.16
8	9	4.27
9	7	3.10
10	10	4.32
11	7	3.51
12	5	2.08
13	9	4.69
14	14	6.13
15	10	4.19
16	3	1.41
17	4	1.73
18	6	2.87
19	11	4.97
20	2	0.82
21	16	6.76
22	8	3.40
23	5	2.45
24	5	2.08
25	6	2.87

was located on the scale in the vertical axis, and a point was plotted on the scatter diagram to represent this pair of values.

The scatter diagram shows a fairly tight linear relationship between tensile strength and hardness. The test for tensile strength is destructive, but hardness can be measured through a nondestructive test. This way one can accurately estimate tensile strength at considerable savings. Moreover, through a regression analysis one can determine the equation of a straight line that describes well the relationship between these two variables:

$$\text{Tensile strength} = 2.29 * \text{Hardness} - 0.172$$

Draw this line in Exhibit 6-22 and notice how well it represents the relationship. The equation may now be used to transform values of hardness into tensile strength equivalents. Through regression analysis, one can also quantify the "tightness" of the relationship between the two variables and the magnitude of the error one is likely to make in using hardness as a proxy for tensile strength.

The run chart is one particular type of scatter plot, with time as the variable plotted on the horizontal axis.

◆ THE SEVEN-STEP METHOD FOR CONTINUOUS IMPROVEMENT

We have already discussed continual improvement as a central concept and fundamental cornerstone of Total Quality Management, and we have also gained an understanding of the basic tools used for continuous improvement. We now turn to the *process itself* of continually improving services and products. How do you go about actually improving and closing those gaps between what you are now doing and what you should be doing? How do you solve the problems that stand in the way of your efforts to improve quality?

The **seven-step method** is an efficient and systematic procedure for solving problems and improving quality. The procedure consists of a standard sequence of steps that induce an in-depth analysis of a problem, its relevant factors, the possible causes, the possible solutions, and their effectiveness. The basic tools are used extensively, as necessary, as part of the seven-step method.

This section discusses in detail the seven-step method and its condensed version, the **PDCA cycle** (the Plan-Do-Check-Act cycle), also called the **Shewhart cycle.** These procedures are applicable to general problem solving as well as to continually closing gaps between the characteristics of process outputs and the needs of customers.

There are many variants of the seven-step method. Florida Power and Light, (FP&L), the first non-Japanese company to win the Deming Prize in 1989, has its "quality improvement story" (a name that derives from a "storyboard" format used for reporting quality improvement activities at Komatsu, the Japanese tractor company). The story's seven steps are (1) reason for improvement, (2) current situation, (3) analysis, (4) countermeasures, (5) results, (6) standardization, and (7) future plans. [*Note:* In *Deming Management at Work,* Mary Walton (1990) gives an account of what went on at FP&L during the four years preceding the award. She also describes in detail three quality improvement stories from those days. FP&L is a leader in the field of quality improvement. Its quality improvement program, the core of which is the quality improvement story, has been used as a benchmark by Xerox and others.] AT&T has an "eight-step improvement cycle." Their eight steps are (1) select improvement area, (2) identify outputs and customers, (3) determine customer expectations, (4) describe current process, (5) focus on improvement opportunities, (6) determine root causes, (7) trial and implement solutions, and (8) hold the gains. Shoji Shiba, a Japanese consultant to the Center for Quality Management in Boston, uses a "WV model" in which a proactive improvement phase—which includes problem sensing, problem exploration, and problem formulation—precedes the usual seven steps. Brian Joiner, a well-known U.S. quality consultant, has his own version which is described in detail in an article from *Quality Progress* at the end of this chapter. Art Phipps, president of Lifeline Systems, winner of the Shingo Prize, gave a talk at Babson College not long ago and used a version of his own. Wherever you look, you find yet another model for continuous improvement, each one with its own little twist. These variants of the seven-step method are all somewhat different from one another, but in essence they are all very similar. The description of a typical variant might look very much as follows.

The Seven Steps

Step 1. Select a problem and describe it clearly.

A meaningful and relevant problem is selected. The problem is defined in terms of a gap between what is currently happening and what would be happening under ideal circumstances. The importance and relevance of the problem are underscored. Any preliminary data that are relevant to the problem are put forth. Metrics that will be used to measure progress are determined. Any necessary operational definitions are developed. Goals are set, a team is formed, a leader is chosen, and a schedule is developed.

Step 2. Study the present system.

The present system is flowcharted. Data are collected on how the current system operates, including data on the metrics that were selected for measuring progress. Variables that may be related to the problem are identified, and data are collected on those variables. All data are examined to find any relevant relationships.

Step 3. Identify possible causes.

Potential causes for the problem are identified through brainstorming by workers familiar with the process. A cause-and-effect diagram is developed. Most likely causes are singled out by those same experienced workers.

Step 4. Plan and implement a solution.

A list of possible solutions is developed, also through brainstorming. The solutions are evaluated. One or more solutions are selected for implementation. The implementation is planned and the solutions are implemented.

Step 5. Evaluate effects.

Data on the metrics selected for measuring progress are collected again. Other relevant data are also collected. The data are analyzed, and a determination is made on the effectiveness of the solutions that were implemented.

Step 6. Standardize any effective solutions.

Solutions that proved effective are adopted permanently. They are made part of standard operating procedures. The possibility of instituting those better methods elsewhere is considered and analyzed.

Step 7. Reflect on process and develop future plans.

The problem-solving effort just completed is reviewed in order to draw as many useful general conclusions as possible. A summary is made of what was learned. A decision is made on whether further improvement is needed on the problem that was just tackled; if not, other problems on which work is needed are identified.

Relation to the PDCA Cycle

The seven-step method is an offspring of the PDCA cycle (Plan-Do-Check-Act cycle) or Shewhart cycle, a more concise model first developed by Walter Shewhart to provide a framework for the design of experiments:

Plan the experiment.
Do it (perform the experiment).
Check the results of the experiment.
Act according to what you observed.

Deming generalized the PDCA cycle to any type of improvement activity and made it an integral part of quality improvement. He liked to represent the cycle by the drawing in Exhibit 6-23. In *Out of the Crisis* Deming (1986) recommends the PDCA cycle as a model for improvement and as a procedure for finding special causes of variation. [*Note:* Deming points out that he called it the Shewhart cycle when he introduced it in Japan in 1950 and later on, but the Japanese put it into immediate use under the name of Deming cycle and have called it that ever since.] The Japanese Union of Scientists and Engineers (JUSE) expanded it into the seven-step method more than 20 years ago. The PDCA cycle and the seven-step method correspond as follows:

PDCA SEVEN-STEP METHOD

Plan   1. Select and describe problem.
          2. Study present system.
          3. Identify possible causes.

Do   4. Plan and implement solution.
Check   5. Evaluate effects.
Act   6. Standardize solution.
           7. Reflect on process and develop future plans.

Exhibit
6.23

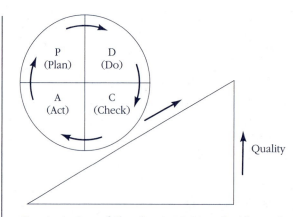

Deming's view of Shewhart's PDCA cycle. Through
continued application of the cycle, the organization gets to higher and higher quality levels.

Shiba, Graham, and Walden (1993, p. 57) describe continuous improvement
and its engine, the PDCA cycle, as follows:

> If you are sailing a boat with the intent to intercept another boat, you periodically re-
> calculate the course to the target. Each time you make the best calculation you can.
>   What you don't do is follow the initial course calculation without correction until the
> calculation indicates that you have reached the target. You realize that despite your best
> initial efforts to calculate the course to the target, the target may be moving in unfore-
> seen ways, and the currents and winds in which you are sailing may carry you off
> course. You follow the principle of seeking frequent feedback about your position and
> the target's position in relation to your course.
>   In business, however, people tend to think that they should be able to develop the
> correct plan or procedure for meeting business needs without trial and feedback.
>   The PDCA principle of iteration gives you a system for making improvements in a
> step-by-step way, doing the best job you can within relatively short improvement cy-
> cles. In that way you can try an improvement and get real feedback regarding the di-
> rection and distance of targets or goals. It is important to get improved products or ser-
> vices rapidly to markets or in the hands of the next process, in order to get this user

feedback. In addition, PDCA is a system for making continuous improvements to achieve the target or ever-higher performance levels.

The PDCA cycle is always shown as a circle to indicate the continuous nature of improvement. All types of improvement and improvement maintenance require iteration.

An article from *Quality Progress*, "Accelerating Improvement," reprinted later in this chapter, presents a simple and easy to follow example of how a restaurant owner used the seven-step method as part of her continuous improvement efforts. Then a case study at the end of the chapter illustrates the use of the seven-step method for process improvement by workers at Motorola Codex. The practice of continuous improvement and the use of the seven-step method at Xerox and Analog Devices were described in Chapter 5 when the cost of quality was discussed. The use of these techniques to improve the service to patients and physicians in a hospital is discussed in Chapter 11.

◆ Summary

In this chapter we have discussed the basic tools, most of them statistical in nature, used for continuous improvement. These tools are also used in managing by facts—one of the key requirements of the Baldrige Award.

One main thrust of the chapter was how to summarize the most important characteristics of a large data set. Data summarization is essential to the intelligent use of data. We learned that data may be summarized by means of tables, graphs, or numbers. Graphs carry a lot of impact, so whenever possible you should use them to compare data sets or communicate your findings. Whenever you deal with data that were collected over time, a run chart is likely to disclose features that would otherwise be hard to discover. Graphs, as we have seen, are also very handy in depicting the relationship between variables. The chapter also discussed the seven-step method for problem solving and continuous improvement.

As a manager, you will be responsible for direct quality improvement as well as for monitoring and giving feedback to quality improvement teams that report to you. A mastery of the basic tools will make both of these jobs much easier.

◆ Key Terms

Internal supplier	Internal customer	Requirements, needs, or
External supplier	External customer	expectations

Quality characteristic
Owner
Continuous improvement
Foolproofing
Numeric or quantitative
   data
Categorical or qualitative
   data
Operational definitions
Population
Population size
Sample
Sample size
Raw data
Frequency distribution
Proportion
Histogram

Outlier
Stratification
Exploratory data analysis
Stem-and-leaf display
Bar chart
Pie chart
Paired bar chart
Pareto diagram
Pareto principle
Run chart or time series
   plot
Flow diagram or
   flowchartCause-and-
   effect, fishbone, or
   Ishikawa diagram
Check sheet
Tally sheet

Location plot
Cross-tabulation
Mean
Median
Variance
Standard deviation
Range
Quartiles
Percentile
Interquartile range
Box plot (box-and-
   whisker plot)
Scatter diagram or scat-
   ter plot
Seven-step method
PDCA cycle, or
   Shewhart cycle

◆ Assignments

1. The following table shows the contents in fluid ounces of 60 randomly selected cans of soda:

12.05	12.02	12.04	11.97	11.97	12.03
11.99	11.94	11.95	11.93	12.01	11.93
12.06	11.98	12.00	12.10	11.96	12.02
11.97	11.97	11.93	12.06	11.96	12.05
12.04	12.00	11.97	11.95	12.02	12.05
11.95	12.08	12.01	12.02	12.01	11.99
12.01	12.02	12.04	11.97	11.98	12.01
11.97	12.00	11.94	11.97	12.01	11.95
12.03	11.98	12.03	12.00	11.97	12.00
11.98	11.98	12.02	12.01	11.99	11.94

In the work below, use a leftmost cell boundary at 11.90 fl.oz. and a cell width of 0.05 fl.oz. If an observation falls exactly on a boundary, place it in the cell that will appear in the histogram immediately to the right of that boundary (the cell with values higher than the boundary; this is what most statistical packages actually do).

a. Develop an absolute frequency distribution for the data.
b. Develop a relative frequency distribution.
c. Develop a cumulative frequency distribution.

d. Develop an absolute frequency histogram and use it to prepare a brief summary of the main features of the data.
e. The specifications for this variable are 12.00 +/− 0.15 fl.oz. How well does the process output seem to satisfy those specifications?
f. Could this data be related to quality management?

2. The data in Assignment 1 are shown below sorted in ascending order.

11.93	11.93	11.93	11.94	11.94	11.94
11.95	11.95	11.95	11.95	11.96	11.96
11.97	11.97	11.97	11.97	11.97	11.97
11.97	11.97	11.97	11.98	11.98	11.98
11.98	11.98	11.99	11.99	11.99	12.00
12.00	12.00	12.00	12.00	12.01	12.01
12.01	12.01	12.01	12.01	12.01	12.02
12.02	12.02	12.02	12.02	12.02	12.03
12.03	12.03	12.04	12.04	12.04	12.05
12.05	12.05	12.06	12.06	12.08	12.10

a. Develop a stem-and-leaf display for the data.
b. Develop a box plot.
c. What are the range and the interquartile range for the data?
d. What are the 30th and 80th percentiles?

3. A bank manager keeps records of the weekly number of complaints by customers. For the last 10 weeks the record shows the following data:

$$4 \quad 0 \quad 2 \quad 6 \quad 1 \quad 0 \quad 2 \quad 4 \quad 2 \quad 3$$

a. Find the following statistics for this sample:
   i. The mean
   ii. The median
   iii. The range
   iv. The variance
   v. The standard deviation

b. Develop a run chart for the data.
c. Could these data be related to quality management?

4. Below are breaking strengths, in pounds, for a sample of blank gears from a new supplier:

    1976 2425 2003 2138 2198 2322 2110

Find the following statistics for this sample:

a. The mean
b. The median
c. The range
d. The variance
e. The standard deviation

5. The following distribution shows the distances traveled last year by 160 cars owned by a car rental company:

DISTANCE TRAVELED (MILES)	NUMBER OF CARS
40,000 to under 50,000	4
50,000 to under 60,000	22
60,000 to under 70,000	35
70,000 to under 80,000	49
80,000 to under 90,000	33
90,000 to under 100,000	17

a. Draw a histogram for these data.
b. Develop a cumulative frequency distribution.
c. Which of the six cells in the distribution contains the first quartile? The median? The third quartile? The 70th percentile?

6. Below is information on the causes of fire for a random sample of 182 residential fires in a major U.S. city last year:

CAUSE OF FIRE	NUMBER OF FIRES
Open flames	10
Electrical wires	21
Electrical appliances	12
Children who played with fire	15
Heating	27
Smoking	49
Cooking	17
Other	31

a. Develop a Pareto diagram for these data and prepare a brief summary of your findings.
b. Develop a pie chart for the data.
c. Could these data be related to quality management?

7. Develop a Pareto diagram for the average weekly costs of defects in printed circuit boards shown in Table 6-8 in the text.

8. Collect hourly data on your pulse rate (beats per minute) over a 14-hour period starting early in the morning and plot the data on a run chart. Does your pulse rate seem to change during the day? Does there appear to be some systematic variation?

9. Prepare a flow diagram for the process you tend to follow from the time you wake up until the time you finish breakfast on a day when you have a morning class.

10. Develop a cause-and-effect diagram for the causes of possibly not doing well in an exam. Is "not doing well in an exam" related to quality management? Explain briefly.

11. Develop a cause-and-effect diagram for the causes of possibly getting late to class. Explain briefly how "getting late to class" is related to quality management.

12. Go to the library and collect data from the *Wall Street Journal* on daily percent changes in the Dow Jones Industrial Average and the S&P 500 Index. (These are listed on page 1 of the Money and Investing section.) Collect these data for 15 days in the recent past. Plot the data on a scatter diagram and comment on any relationship that seems to exist between changes in the two indices.

Case Study

Accelerating Improvement

BY MARIE GAUDARD, ROLAND COATES, AND LIZ FREEMAN

The following article includes a case study showing how the seven step method was followed by a team of workers to reduce long waits by restaurant customers at peak times. It also offers additional insights on issues related to the seven-step method and benefits derived from its use.

Reprinted by permission from *Quality Progress,* October 1991, pp. 81–88.

CATCH UP? PEOPLE INQUIRE HOW LONG it will take America to catch up with the Japanese. . . . Does anyone suppose that the Japanese are going to sit still and wait for someone to catch up? How can you catch up with someone that is all the time gaining speed?"—W. Edwards Deming, Out of the Crisis.

The need to improve quality has captured the attention of American industry. The need to accelerate the improvement process, however, is just now being realized, and ways to accelerate it are just beginning to be explored. The Seven Step Method and the Project Team Review Process are related techniques that, in the proper management setting, can accelerate process improvement.

The Seven Step Method is a structured approach to problem solving and process improvement. It leads a team through a logical sequence of steps that force a thorough analysis of the problem, its potential causes, and possible solutions. The structure imposed by the Seven Step Method helps a team focus on the correct issues rather than diffuse its energy on tangential or even counterproductive undertakings. The Seven Step Method has been used successfully by U.S. and Japanese companies for several years.

The Seven Step Method is most successful when accompanied by regular project reviews performed by managers with a vested interest in the project's outcome. In many organizations, project teams are not reviewed until a solution or recommendation is to be presented—the notion of a status review is foreign. However, there is a formal review process in which peers and superiors guide, support, and monitor project teams while they are working on problems. This Project Team Review Process structures a session so that it becomes a productive meeting with positive consequences, thereby providing teams with support and focus.

The Seven Step Method and Project Team Review Process were part of a program

Accelerating Improvement (Continued)

designed to help a small printing company, which will be called Sprinters, with its organizational change. When designing this program, we drew from our own experience working with companies and from the Seven Step and Project Team Review models developed by Joiner Associates Inc.[1,2] These models emphasize interaction between the project team and a guidance team.

Sprinters employs about 150 people, and its management group consists of 13 people. In December 1989, we helped form the management group into three project teams, each with a loosely defined problem to solve. Each team was supplemented, as appropriate, by employees who were not part of the management group. The result was three teams, one of five members, one of six, and the third of seven members. Over the next eight months, these teams were trained in and practiced using basic group process skills, the Seven Step Method, and the Project Team Review Process.

The Seven Step Method

The value of the Seven Step Method lies in the discipline and logic that it imposes. The seven steps are briefly described in Table 6.11.

Table 6.11.   The Seven Step Method

Step 1   Define the Project

1. Define the problem in terms of a gap between what is and what should be. (For example, "Customers report an excessive number of errors. The team's objective is to reduce the number of errors.")

2. Document why it is important to be working on this particular problem:

- Explain how you know it is a problem, providing any data you might have that supports this.

- List the customer's key quality characteristics. State how closing the gap will benefit the customer in terms of these characteristics.

3. Determine what data you will use to measure progress:

- Decide what data you will use to provide a baseline against which improvement can be measured.

- Develop any operational definitions you will need to collect the data.

Step 2   Study the Current Situation

1. Collect the baseline data and plot them. (Sometimes historical data can be used for this purpose.) A run chart or control chart is usually used to exhibit baseline data. Decide how you will exhibit these data on the run chart. Decide how you will label your axes.

2. Develop flowcharts of the processes.

3. Provide any helpful sketches or visual aids.

4. Identify any variables that might have a bearing on the problem. Consider the variables of what, where, to what extent, and who. Data will be gathered on these variables to localize the problem.

5. Design data collection instruments.

6. Collect the data and summarize what you have learned about the variables' effects on the problem.

7. Determine what additional information would be helpful at this time. Repeat substeps two through seven until there is no additional information that would be helpful at this time.

Step 3   Analyze the Potential Causes

1. Determine potential causes of the current conditions:

Accelerating Improvement (Continued)

- Use the data collected in step two and the experience of the people who work in the process to identify conditions that might lead to the problem.

- Construct cause-and-effect diagrams for these conditions of interest.

- Decide on most likely causes by checking against the data from step two and the experience of the people working in the process.

2. Determine whether more data are needed. If so, repeat substeps two through seven of step two.

3. If possible, verify the cause through observation or by directly controlling variables.

Step 4   Implement a Solution

1. Develop a list of solutions to be considered. Be creative.

2. Decide which solutions should be tried:

- Carefully assess the feasibility of each solution, the likelihood of success, and potential adverse consequences.

- Clearly indicate why you are choosing a particular solution.

3. Determine how the preferred solution will be implemented. Will there be a pilot project? Who will be responsible for the implementation? Who will train those involved?

4. Implement the preferred solution.

Step 5   Check the Results

1. Determine whether the actions in step four were effective:

- Collect more data on the baseline measure from step one.

- Collect any other data related to the conditions at the start that might be relevant.

- Analyze the results. Determine whether the solution tested was effective. Repeat prior steps as necessary.

2. Describe any deviations from the plan and what was learned.

Step 6   Standardize the Improvement

1. Institutionalize the improvement:

- Develop a strategy for institutionalizing the improvement and assign responsibilities.

- Implement the strategy and check to see that it has been successful.

2. Determine whether the improvement should be applied elsewhere and plan for its implementation.

Step 7   Establish Future Plans

1. Determine your plans for the future:

- Decide whether the gap should be narrowed further and, if so, how another project should be approached and who should be involved.

- Identify related problems that should be addressed

2. Summarize what you learned about the project team experience and make recommendations for future project teams.

Here is a simple case study that generally illustrates the use of the method:

A restaurant caters to business travelers and has a self-service breakfast buffet. Interested in customer satisfaction, the manager constructs a survey, distributes it to customers over a three-month period, and summarizes the results in a Pareto chart (Exhibit 6.24). The Pareto chart indicates that the restaurant's major problem is that customers have to wait too long to be seated. A team of employees is formed to work on this problem.

Step one: define the project. With the survey as the background, the team undertakes the first step. The problem is that customers wait too long to be seated. They should not have to wait at all. The problem is important because customers have complained,

Accelerating Improvement (Continued)

Exhibit

6.24

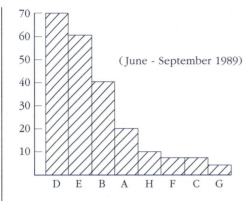

(June - September 1989)

Code	Reason
A	Room too drafty
B	Table not clean
C	No dietetic sweetener provided
D	Had to wait for seats
E	Buffet table not well organized
F	Missing utensil at place setting
G	No ashtray on table
H	Had to wait long time for coffee

Pareto chart of complaints

Exhibit

6.25

Run chart of percent of customers waiting in excess of one minute to be seated.

Accelerating Improvement (Continued)

Exhibit

6.26

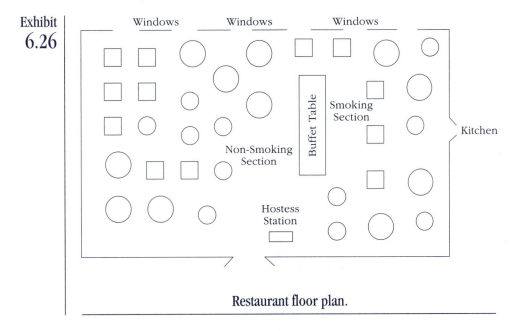

Restaurant floor plan.

and this is supported by the Pareto chart constructed from the survey data. Most of the customers are business travelers who want either a speedy breakfast or a chance to conduct business during breakfast. Decreasing the wait to be seated will increase the restaurant's ability to respond to these key quality characteristics. Pro-gress can be measured by the percent of the customers each day who have to wait in excess of, say, one minute to be seated. The team develops an operational definition of "waiting to be seated" to answer such questions as: When does the wait start? When does it end? How is it measured?

Step two: study the current situation. The team collects baseline data and plots them (Exhibit 6.25). At the same time, it develops a flowchart of seating a party. The team members feel that a floor diagram might be helpful, so they produce one (Exhibit 6.26). The variables they identify as potentially affecting the problem are: day of the week, size of the party, reason for waiting, and time of the morning. Data relating to these variables are collected.

From the baseline data, the team learns that the percent of people served who have to wait is higher early in the week and decreases during the week, with only a small percent waiting on weekends. This is reasonable, since the restaurant's clientele primarily consists of business travelers. The size of the party does not appear to be a factor, because parties of all sizes wait approximately the same proportions. A histogram of the number of people waiting by the time of the morning reveals nothing surprising: more people wait during the busy hours than during the slow hours (Exhibit 6.27). The reason

Accelerating Improvement (Continued)

Exhibit

6.27

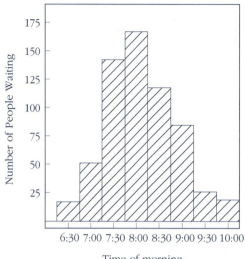

Histogram of the number of customers
waiting in excess of one minute by the time
of morning.

for waiting, however, is interesting. Most people wait because a table is not available or because they have a seating preference (as opposed to the hostess not being around to seat customers or customers waiting for friends to join them).

At this point, it would be easy for the team to jump to the solution of putting more staff on early in the week and during busy hours in the morning—but analyzing causes is not done until the next step.

The team decides additional information is needed on why tables are not available and how seating preferences affect waiting. After data are collected, it learns that tables are generally unavailable because they are not cleared (as opposed to being occupied) and that most of the people who have a seat-

ing preference wait for a table in the non-smoking area.

Step three: analyze the potential causes. A cause-and-effect diagram is constructed for "Why tables are not cleared quickly," with particular emphasis on identifying root causes (Exhibit 6.28). This diagram, together with the rest of the data the team has gathered, leads the team to conclude that the most likely cause is the distance from the tables to the kitchen, particularly in the nonsmoking area.

Step four: implement a solution. The team develops a list of possible solutions. Since the team has not been able to verify the cause by controlling the variables, it chooses a solution that can be easily tested: set up temporary workstations in the nonsmoking area. No other changes are made. The team

Accelerating Improvement (Continued)

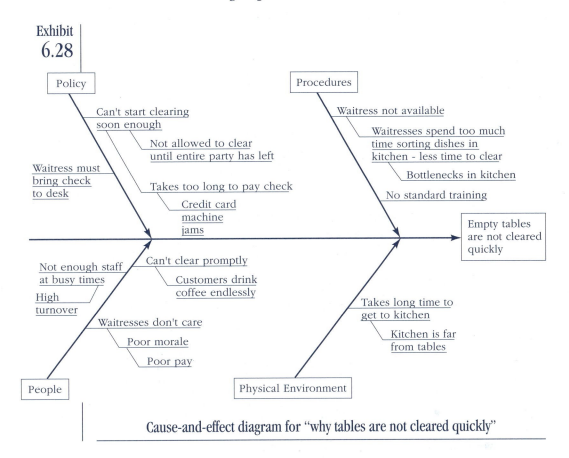

Exhibit 6.28

Cause-and-effect diagram for "why tables are not cleared quickly"

continues to collect data on the percent of people waiting longer than one minute to be seated.

Step five: check the results. After a month, the team analyzes the data collected in step four. As Exhibit 6.29 shows, the improvement is dramatic.

Step six: standardize the improvement. The temporary workstations are replaced with permanent ones.

Step seven: establish future plans. The team decides that the next highest bar in the Pareto chart of customer complaints—buffet table not well organized—should be addressed.

The purpose of the seven steps

The overall purpose of the Seven Step Method is to facilitate process improvement. Each step has a specific purpose, and these are given in Table 6.12.

Table 6.12   The Purpose of the Seven Steps

Step 1   Define the Project

To show the importance of the project and to indicate why energy should be spent here (instead of elsewhere) in order to use resources efficiently, obtain the support of management, and motivate the team.

Accelerating Improvement (Continued)

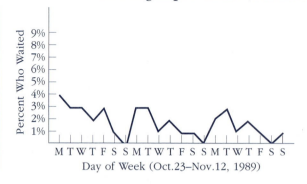

Exhibit 6.29

Percent Who Waited

9%
8%
7%
6%
5%
4%
3%
2%
1%

M T W T F S S M T W T F S S M T W T F S S
Day of Week (Oct.23–Nov.12, 1989)

Run chart of percent of customers waiting in excess of one minute to be seated.

To reach an agreement on how success will be measured.

Step 2   Study the Current Situation

To use data (rather than opinion) to narrow the focus and to refrain from jumping to possibly incorrect solutions or causes.

To develop baseline data to be used to verify solutions.

Step 3   Analyze the Potential Causes

To find root causes (rather than symptoms) of the problem.

To narrow the focus in order to change the most fundamental causes that can be changed.

Step 4   Implement a Solution

To find the best possible solution, plan its implementation, and implement it (preferably on a small scale).

Step 5   Check the Results

To determine whether the preferred solution is effective.

To decide whether to standardize the solution or return to an earlier step.

Step 6   Standardize the Improvement

To ensure that the problem stays fixed.

Step 7   Establish Future Plans

To determine whether more work needs to be done on this particular problem.

To promote the practice of continuous improvement in terms of organizational and team effectiveness.

Since the plan-do-check-act (PDCA) cycle also has process improvement as its goal, it seems natural to ask how it and the Seven Step Method are related. W. Edwards Deming's thoughts on the PDCA cycles are presented in *The Team Handbook*.[3] The "plan" step consists of planning a change or test aimed at improvement; the "do" step consists of carrying out the change or test, preferably on a small scale; the "check" step involves studying the results to understand what has been learned; and the "act" step consists of adopting the change, abandoning it, or repeating the cycle.

Accelerating Improvement (Continued)

It seems clear that much of the PDCA thinking is imbued in the Seven Step Method. The PDCA cycle, however, is a broad paradigm for process improvement that applies in situations where the Seven Step Method does not. The Seven Step Method is appropriate when a deep understanding of the problem is needed to determine and plan an effective solution. A team acquires this understanding through the data-based localization and cause analysis in steps two and three. In these steps, the team is continually restrained from jumping to solutions. Only in step four does the team formulate and implement a solution. This step is similar to the "plan " and "do" steps in the PDCA cycle. In step five, which is comparable to the PDCA cycle's "check" step, the team check its results. After checking, the team either standardizes it findings (step six) or returns to a prior step to obtain an even deeper understanding of the problem or possible solutions—a process much like the "act" step of the PDCA cycle. In addition to reflecting on its experience in terms of tasks, group processes, and organizational issues, in step seven the team identifies future needs. Identification of these needs continues the PDCA cycle, if appropriate, those needs are addressed using the Seven Step Method.

The Seven Step Method is directed at analytic rather than enumerative studies. In an enumerative study, an existing population is studied; an analytic study focuses on prediction.[4] In analytic situations, the key is to learn about the cause systems that underlie the processes of interest to understand the effects of various conditions. Since organizations are usually interested in learning about the future, almost all problems in industry—and certainly the most important ones—are of an analytic nature. The Seven Step Method helps solve analytic problems efficiently because it focuses on understanding causal relationships, as evidenced in steps two through five.

The method's value

After the management group at Sprinters had been using the Seven Step Method in their project teams for about three months, we asked them, at a training session, to brainstorm what they had learned as a result of the method. The managers overwhelmingly found the method's focus and restraint to be difficult but valuable. They also valued the way the method provides organization, logic, and thoroughness. They were impressed by the use of data instead of opinions. A number of people commented on how they were listening to each other more carefully and respecting each other's ideas more and on how, perhaps because of the focus on data, there had been a lowering of territorial fences and a promotion of cooperation and trust. The managers' perceptions concerning the method were also shaped by the group process skills they had been practicing and the project reviews they had undertaken.

As consultants, we viewed the benefits to the project team members in the same light and were impressed by what seemed to be a significant cultural change. In addition, we felt that the team members learned a great deal about each other and about the organization during their struggles with various tasks and issues.

Difficult issues

The three project teams found several concepts in the first two steps extremely difficult. The first was arriving at a problem statement.

Accelerating Improvement (Continued)

The initial tendency was to frame a solution as a problem. The analog of this in the restaurant case study would be to state the problem as "There aren't enough tables" or "The waitresses and waiters need to work harder" instead of "The customers wait too long." Once this hurdle was crossed, there were others. One team needed to agree on several operational definitions before it could even begin to formulate a problem statement. Another team kept revising its problem statement during the first four months before settling on one that was consistent with what the team was doing. The third team arrived at a problem statement relatively easily by comparison, but even they struggled.

Localization—the process of focusing on smaller and smaller vital pieces of the problem—is another task that the teams found difficult. Localization is usually achieved by stratifying data using Pareto charts with categorical data and run charts with continuous data. Localization is what makes a problem tractable. Although team members could see the value of localization in solving sample problems, they found it hard to internalize this in solving their own problems. Realizing that their own problems were not overwhelming but instead tractable through localization was an important achievement for the project teams.

There were other issues that proved difficult. It was much easier for the teams to justify the importance of the problem in terms of internal considerations rather than in terms of the customer's key quality characteristics. We sensed that this occurred because the team members had not yet internalized the idea that improvement should be driven by customer requirements, not internal indicators. Some team members could

not see the benefits of collecting data accurately and consistently, so they resisted devising ways to accomplish this. The teams had trouble understanding how baseline data would be used to validate a solution. Causes of the problem often crept into discussions where they did not belong. The teams had difficulty keeping an open mind about potential causes. For example, they resisted investigating the effects of variables that they felt were not causes. The teams needed a significant amount of coaching in how to obtain information in a nonthreatening way (through interviews or surveys) from the people who work in the system. The teams also faced several organizational challenges, such as finding the time to work on their projects, arranging meetings to accommodate second- and third-shift employees, and getting support from line workers who were to collect the data.

Project Team Review Process

The Project Team Review Process was introduced to the teams when they had been working on their projects for only a month. We felt it best to introduce this process early to emphasize the value of communication among teams, to keep the teams apprised of each other's progress, and to promote a supporting environment. Reviews were then conducted about every two months. An outline of the review process appears in Table 6.13.

Table 6.13   The Review Process

1. Team Presentation

2. Preparation for Review

   • Brainstorm positive comments, and agree on two.

Accelerating Improvement (Continued)

- Brainstorm questions about the logic and data, and agree on two.
- Brainstorm ideas on the premise "If I could ask the team to do one more thing, it would be to. . .," and agree on one. While the reviewers are preparing, the presenting team reflects on its presentation.

3. Review of Team

- Each reviewer gives two positive comments.
- Each reviewer asks two questions about logic and data.
- Each reviewer asks the team to do "one more thing."

4. Presenting Team Reflects on Review

- What were the main messages the team heard?
- How did it feel to be reviewed?

Figure 1. Pareto Chart of Complaints

Figure 2. Run Chart of Percent of Customers Waiting in Excess of One Minute to be Seated

Figure 3. Restaurant Floor Plan

Figure 4. Histogram of the Number of Customers Waiting in Excess of One Minute by the Time of Morning

Figure 5. Cause-and-Effect Diagram for "Why Tables Are Not Cleared Quickly"

Figure 6. Run Chart of Percent of Customers Waiting in Excess of One Minute to be Seated

The review-consisting of positive feedback, clarifying questions, and "one more thing" suggestions—was designed by Joiner Associates. For our purposes, we made three innovations: using it in a context where project teams had held only one or two meetings, and compressing the time for the review.

The three Sprinters teams were reviewed during a four-hour meeting. Each team was asked to make a 10-minute presentation of its progress. After this presentation, the other two teams and a team of three consultants brainstormed independently to come up with:

- positive comments about the presenting team's efforts, choosing two to share with the team.
- clarifying questions about the presenting team's logic and data, choosing two to share.
- suggestions in the form of "If there were one more thing we could ask you to do, it would be. . .," choosing one to share.

Each reviewing team was given 15 minutes to select an individual to present that team's review and to prepare for it. Meanwhile, the presenting team was asked to reflect on its presentation. Seven minutes were allotted for each review, during which the reviewer shared the two positive comments, two clarifying questions (to which the presenting team responded), and the "If I could ask you to do one more thing" suggestion.

After the three teams had conducted their reviews, the presenting team members spent 15 minutes debriefing. In the debriefing, they brainstormed the main messages they had heard and discussed how it felt to be reviewed.

The purpose of the review process

Because most organizations conduct reviews after a solution is found, the term "review" has a negative connotation. Consequently, such organizations find it difficult to accept that team reviews are conducted to stimulate communication, promote a supporting environment, and keep teams focused and on track. Since the individuals on the Sprinters

Accelerating Improvement (Continued)

management team would eventually be directing teams of their subordinates, we felt it critical that they should experience the value of team reviews and learn to perform productive reviews. In addition, we felt that if they experienced reviewing and being reviewed, they would be more sensitive to the needs of their employees when reviewing them in the future.

The approach we used is very structured both in terms of time content. The rationale for limiting the time was to make the point that, with discipline, a team review need not be a lengthy undertaking. Thus managers would view reviews as tractable and be willing to review projects frequently. The rationale for the structure was to give the managers exposure to a good process, one they could use as a model when conducting their own reviews. The rationale for limiting a reviewing team to only two positive comments, two clarifying questions, and one suggestion was that it forced the team members to focus on the most vital issues.

By beginning the review with positive comments, both the reviewers and the presenting team must acknowledge the good aspects of what the team has accomplished; thus, the review builds on the team's strengths. The clarifying questions help both the reviewers and the team being reviewed understand and clear up any ambiguities, misunderstandings, or misconceptions. The final suggestion allows the reviewers to direct the presenting team while acknowledging the considerable efforts the team has already expended.

The review's value

The team's reactions to the review process have been and continue to be very positive.

Although beginning the review with positive comments might be perceived by some onlookers as artificial, the teams do not view it as such. Team members are interested in the particular aspects of their work that the reviewers single out as worthy of praise. These positive comments generate a system of values within the organization. For example, if reviewers often praise teams for resisting jumping solutions, it is perceived as desirable behavior and thus an organizational value. When the teams felt frustrated with their tasks, the reviews gave them support and renewed their enthusiasm. This was partially due to the reviewers' understanding, born out of the experiences on their own project teams, that they shared with the team being reviewed. Part of it was also due to the direction and guidance the reviews provided.

Like any learning tool, the review process surfaced difficulties from which the teams learned. The reflection sessions were of great value in teaching managers what does and doesn't work well in a review and in helping them be more sensitive during a review. For example, during an early review, a presenting team perceived one clarifying question— "Aren't you jumping to conclusions by doing. . . ?"—as accusatory. In their reflection period, the presenting team members revealed that this question dampened their enthusiasm for the rest of the review. The teams then discussed the question and concluded that it is important to frame questions, especially sensitive ones, in a positive and open context. A better strategy would have been to refocus the presenting team's attention using a statement such as "Please explain again the logic of how you got from your data to your conclusion."

Perhaps the greatest benefit of the review process to the three management-based teams at Sprinters was its influence in form-

Accelerating Improvement (Continued)

ing the managers into a team. When the company began its quality improvement effort, the managers were territorial and defensive. The review process was quite successful in promoting and communicating support among the three management-based teams. In fact, after one of the early review sessions, an influential manager said, "It sounds to me as if we [the people on the three project teams] have become a team!" Although overstated, this comment indicated a breakthrough in the managers' ability to envision themselves working as a team. The managers continue to struggle toward that goal, consistently growing in their shared values and support for each other.

Instructional considerations

Our philosophy of training is that it should be given on a just-in-time basis, because people learn methods and techniques better when they have an immediate application for them. Thus, we covered only the methods and techniques the teams needed when they needed to use them.

Our work with the teams began with a one-day introduction to the Deming management philosophy. This orientation stressed the value of process management vs. hierarchical management; discussed the notion of operational definitions and the customer's key quality characteristics; introduced the concept of process variability, process stability, and control charts; and demonstrated the consequences of tampering with the process.

In another one-day program, the teams were introduced to a process for brainstorming and consensus decision making. The work on the projects was launched with a half-day introduction to the Seven Step

Method during which the teams worked through steps one to three in the restaurant case study. Half-day training sessions were then held at one-month intervals, and the topics included meeting skills, run charts, special and common causes, process stability, classical flowcharts, top-down flowcharts, deployment flowcharts. Pareto charts, localization, check sheets, collecting data, involving people who work in the process as resources, interviews, surveys, stem-and-leaf plots, histograms, stratification, and scatter plots.

Pedagogical approach

The pedagogical approach we used is based on the constructivist perspective, which assumes that learning occurs when an individual interacts with the environment to construct his or her own knowledge.[5,6] In such a model, the individual or team builds on existing concepts. Because learning results from resolving conflicts or fulfilling needs, the individual or team is the primary decision maker and is in charge of the progress. The instructor is a facilitator who guides participants as they set their own pace.

As mentioned earlier, the teams were trained on a just-in-time basis, an approach that is consistent with the constructivist perspective. At half-day monthly meetings, we addressed the needs common to all the teams. We also regularly met with the teams individually to monitor their progress, to learn of any training needs (sometimes providing the training to meet a particular need), and to give guidance. These meetings also provided the teams with observations on their use of group process skills.

Whenever appropriate, we modeled the behavior we were teaching. For example, when teaching the teams how to review each

Accelerating Improvement (Continued)

other, we became a reviewing team our-selves and participated in the review process alongside the other teams. While attending team meetings, we often behaved as team members, participating in the group process, asking questions, and making observations relevant to the task.

In formal teaching sessions that intro-duced new techniques almost all the exam-ples were from the primary industry and Sprinters' data were used whenever possible. In fact, data that the teams had gathered for their projects were used whenever appropri-ate. This was especially valuable because the teams could relate to the revealed peculiari-ties of the data-gathering process. Most of the example were followed with exercises re-quiring the teams to apply the technique be-ing learned to their own problems.

Speeding the transition

The goal in introducing the Seven Step Method and the Project Team Review Process at Sprinters was to speed the transi-tion to a management culture that enabled employees to implement Deming's princi-ples, thereby accelerating improvement. The necessary infrastructure involved strong management commitment, including top managers' willingness to form the first pro-ject teams and receive training and coaching in group process and meeting skills. Our pri-mary objective was to provide them with a learning experience in team and problem-solving processes. From what we have seen, these managers have developed a sound ap-preciation of the factors involved and will be able to make the transition to guiding project teams composed of their own subordinates with relative ease and success.

The synergistic effect of the Seven Step Method and the Project Team Review

Process has contributed value to both the project teams at Sprinters and to the educa-tional goals set for the company's top man-agers. The three management-based teams are steadily making progress in solving their problems, and the managers are applying what they have learned to other areas of their management responsibilities. We feel strongly that the progress of the teams and of the organizational change effort has been ac-celerated by the Seven Step Method, which provides a road map for solving difficult problems, and by the Project Team Review Process, which bolsters commitment and elicits support and guidance.

References

1. We were first exposed to the Seven Step Method and the review process through Joiner Associates, a consulting firm in Madison, WI. Joiner Associates is actively de-veloping and promoting these powerful tools.

2. A seven-step model that resembles the one developed by Joiner Associates is given in Hitoshi Kume, *Statistical Methods for Quality Improvement* (Tokyo: Association for Overseas Technical Scholarship, 1985).

3. Peter R. Scholtes and other contribu-tors, *The Team Handbook* (Madison, WI: Joiner Associates, 1988), pp. 5–31.

4. W. Edwards Deming, *Out of the Crisis* (Cambridge, MA: MIT Center for Advanced Engineering Study, 1982).

5. E. Von Glaserfeld, "Learning as a Constructive Activity," in J. C. Gergeron and N. Herscovics, editors, *Proceedings of the Fifth Annual Meeting of the North American Chapter of the International Group for the Psychology of Mathematics Education,* 1983, Vol. 1, pp. 41–69.

6. Joan Ferrini-Mundy, Marie Gaudard, Samuel D. Shore, and Donovan Van Osdol,

"How Quality Is Taught Can Be as Important as What Is Taught,"*Quality Progress,* January 1990, pp. 56–59.

Marie Gaudard is an associate professor in the Department of Mathematics at the University of New Hampshire in Durham. She received a doctorate in statistics from the University of Massachusetts in Amherst. Gaudard is a member of ASQC.

Roland Coates is the president of Coates Freeman Associates in New Ipswich, NH. He received a bachelor's degree in psychology from Middlebury College in Middlebury, VT. Coates is an ASQC member.

Liz Freeman is the vice president of Coates Freeman Associates in New Ipswich, NH. She received a master's degree in adult learning from Boston University in Boston, MA.

Case Study

Motorola-Codex

Codex Corporation was founded in 1962, and at that time it became the first company to apply its expertise in information theory, coding, and data compression to commercial communications products. Fifteen years later Codex was acquired by Motorola as a strategic component of its worldwide integrated communications capability. The company has operated under the name Motorola Codex since 1991. Motorola's net sales in 1993 were $16,963 million, and employment at the end of that year was 120,000.

In recent years, Motorola Codex has introduced several new products that represent cutting-edge advances in the field of network communications. Examples are the first integrated, OSI-based network management system, which allowed users to incorporate multiple technologies (1987); a frame relay interface, which permitted access to high-speed digital networks while providing the benefits of fast packet switching on the backbone (1990); the 9800/SNMP processor, which integrated LAN and WAN network information for quick diagnoses and problem resolution (1991); and the first high-speed dial modem based on proposed V.fast technology, with synchronous transmission speeds of 24 Kbps and asynchronous transmission speeds of up to 115.2 Kbps (1992). In 1993 Motorola Codex unveiled a set of strategic product and service goals based on a family of architected platforms combining general-purpose processors with protocol-specific software modules. The aim was to provide a practical network migration path for the global enterprise.

In 1987 Motorola initiated six sigma, a pioneering, corporatewide quality improvement process. In the following year the organization won the first Malcolm Baldrige National Quality Award. At the beginning of 1992 a team of workers at Motorola Codex embarked on a plan to reduce the defect rate in the modem circuit board production line. The *seven-step method,* a standardized pro-

Prepared by Ismael Dambolena and Laura Horton
© Copyright, Ismael Dambolena, Babson College
Wellesley, Massachusetts (USA)

Motorola-Codex (Continued)

Exhibit
6.30

LEADER: GERALD A. MESOLELLA
SPONSOR: LEO COTE
FACILITATOR: HARRY MCGRATH

TEAM MEMBERS

KATHY BOGOSH
FRANK CACCAVELLI
BETTY DAVIDSON
CHRIS EVANS
JAN GAUTHIER
RAY GAUTHIER
PAT GULLENS

TEAM MEMBERS

BRIAN JARDIN
ANN MCNAUGHTON
THU PHAM
MIKE PHILLIPS
INA PINETTE
CONNIE ROUILLAR
GREG SPELLMAN
VANG XIONG

The Post-IR Hammers.

cess improvement tool, was chosen as the TQM vehicle for this project.

The Team

Fifteen people from various process stations and engineering support were selected as team members (see Exhibit 6-30). All three shifts of the production line were represented on the team, and meetings were held for one hour once or twice a week. The first and the second shifts met at 2:30 P.M., the second and third shifts at 11:00 P.M., and the third and first shifts met at 6:00 A.M. This allowed team members from different shifts the opportunity to meet with each other and exchange ideas. The team members were excused from the production line during the meetings, and members often arrived an hour before their shift started or stayed an hour after their shift ended. Team members had received training on continuous improvement tools and

processes. The team chose as its name, for reasons that will soon become apparent, "The Post-IR Hammers," and proceeded as follows.

In broad terms, team members had the feeling that too many defects occurred because when problems were found in the test station at the end of the production line, the feedback on those problems did not get quickly enough to the workstations where the problems generated. With this general insight in mind, they started concentrating their energies on defining the problem in further detail.

Exhibit 6.31 shows a flowchart of the circuit board production line. Each workstation along the production line is the customer of the previous workstation. Infrared reflow (IR) is the workstation where the actual soldering of components occurs in a heated chamber (220 degrees centigrade). Components that are heat sensitive (IR-incompatible devices) are manually inserted

Motorola-Codex (Continued)

Exhibit
6.31

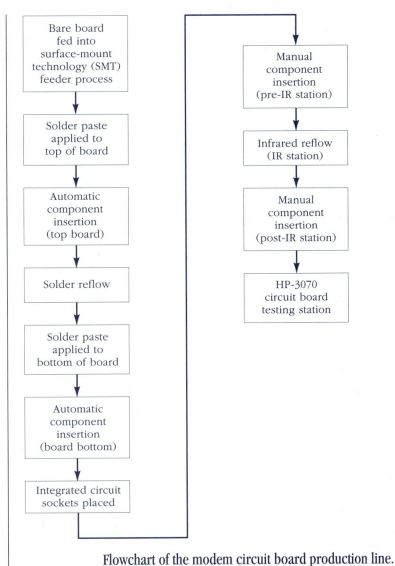

Flowchart of the modem circuit board production line.

and hand soldered at a post-IR workstation. This workstation also handles the manual insertion and hand soldering of components that cannot be automatically inserted onto the circuit board. The components then go from the post-IR workstation to a circuit board testing station. This testing station is the customer of the post-IR station.

Motorola-Codex (Continued)

The time it took the circuit boards to reach the test station after leaving the IR station was too long. Therefore, while the test station was identifying defects when they occurred, it was unable to provide timely feedback on the defects to the manufacturing process so that the necessary corrections and changes in the process diagnosed by the tests could be made immediately. The team felt that this problem resulted in an unduly high defect rate. Thus, it was determined that the problem to focus on was the long cycle time at the post-IR station.

Defects per unit and defects per million opportunities were quality metrics used by the test area, and the team decided to use them for the purpose of benchmarking progress. In addition, cycle time and cost savings would also be used.

Project Goals

The team leader, Gerald Mesolella, led the team to a choice of goals that he felt were at-tainable, and that would correct some of the existing problems and significantly improve the process. The team's goals, to be completed by December 1992, were the following:

1. Reduce cycle time in the post-IR area by 15 percent.
2. Achieve a reduction in costs of at least $250,000 using IR-compatible devices.
3. Reduce by 50 percent the number of defects per unit and the defects per million opportunities.

A flowchart of the process was developed (this flowchart, shown in Exhibit 6-31, is called an AS-IS map by people at Motorola), and a layout plan of the assembly line was completed (Exhibit 6.32). The team then asked workers from the circuit board test station, "What are your problems, and how can we improve the input you are receiving?" After recording all the responses, several basic analysis techniques were used. The team also introduced a logbook at each workstation so that all operators would

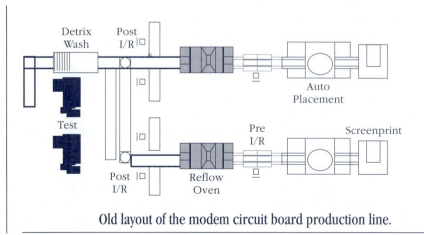

Exhibit 6.32

Old layout of the modem circuit board production line.

Motorola-Codex (Continued)

record the assembly and material problems they encountered.

Problems Found

Among the problems identified by the above data collection efforts were the following:

- Too many parts were installed and hand soldered at the workstations.
- Station setups made the identification of parts difficult.
- The number of operators was insufficient to keep up with production volume.
- An excessive number of solder balls had to be removed, thus extending cycle time.

- SPC charting of defects was too time consuming.
- No standard operating procedures had been developed.

The factory reporting system (FRS), a barcode on-line data-collection and information-generating system, was used to determine current quality (in January 1992) in terms of defects per million opportunities and number of defects per unit. In addition, the process time was investigated by function and graphed. The resulting Pareto diagram (Exhibit 6.33) showed the team that post-IR was responsible for 60 percent of the total process cycle time. These baseline data were collected to be used later as a reference point for measuring progress.

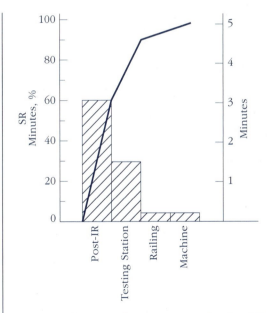

Pareto diagram of process times for the different functions. The post-IR process time accounted for about 60 percent of total time.

Motorola-Codex (Continued)

Since the post-IR function is completely operator dependent while the rest of the manufacturing line is automated to one degree or another, it was felt that the post-IR cycle time would be relatively easy to improve if the root causes were identified and problems were solved. As part of this work, the team also benchmarked other processes within the same plant.

The team brainstormed to identify root causes for the backlog at post-IR. They used the AS-IS map, the factory layout plan, quality reports, and cycle time reports in this identification stage. Using all the information collected, they developed the cause-and-ef-

fect diagram shown in Exhibit 6.34. Team members deemed several of the causes to be likely culprits.

Simulation Modeling

A simulation model was used to determine the optimal number of operators at post-IR. This simulation confirmed that an increase in the current number of operators was necessary. As a result, dedicated workstations were set up. Each production line incorporated color-coded part bins to make the workstations more uniform.

Exhibit 6.34

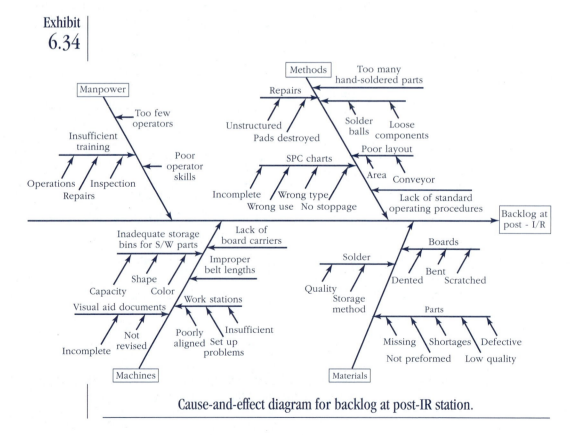

Cause-and-effect diagram for backlog at post-IR station.

Motorola-Codex (Continued)

Many problems were identified concerning the lack of operator training. Solutions to this issue were derived, such as training classes and on-the-job training, to enhance the skills necessary to continue to produce a quality product.

Because too many parts were manually installed and hand soldered at the post-IR stations, component and manufacturing engineering reviewed the component specifications to determine which components could be made IR compatible and thus eliminate their manual insertion. After the engineers made this determination, they modeled and manufactured the new devices. By moving the IR-compatible devices to the pre-reflow station, the testing area was allowed to receive assemblies at a more efficient rate. This also allowed the post-IR operators more time to ensure that the quality of the assemblies coming from the previous operations was at an acceptable level.

Since there was no standard operating procedure to systematically guide the post-IR operators to complete their job requirements, the team members and quality engineering worked together to develop one. This procedure focused on manufacturing techniques to clearly define the assembly methods. Also included in the procedure was a classification of minor and major repairs. Minor repairs would be identified and repaired at the post-IR station, whereas major repairs would be made at a designated repair station.

The old conveyor layout contributed to a long, non-value-added cycle time which delayed the delivery of the product to the test station. Team members and manufacturing engineering worked together to modify the layout and align workstations so that each process line had a direct route to the test station, thereby reducing cycle time.

Finally, manufacturing engineering and the post-IR operators worked together to improve or eliminate other problems, such as excess solder balls and the cleaning of circuit boards.

Goals Achieved

After measuring progress, it was clear that the team had, by and large, achieved its goals. Devices that were moved from post-IR to pre-reflow during 1992 resulted in cost savings of $243,000 during 1993. The 15 components that were made IR compatible resulted in additional savings of $91,000, for total savings of $334,000 in 1993. The team is committed to continuing the effort during 1994 and expects to save $683,000 this year.

Moving the insertion of several parts from post-IR to pre-reflow and automating this insertion not only resulted in cost savings; it also contributed to a reduction in cycle time. The average cycle time per assembly in January of 1992 was 5.12 minutes. The present average cycle time is 4.45 minutes, which represents a reduction of 13 percent. This reduction was achieved, and deliveries were made on time, in spite of the fact that the number of assemblies processed per month increased from 21,000 in January to 30,000 in October and 35,000 in December (Exhibit 6.35).

When the team first collected data on defects per unit (dpu) and defects per million opportunities (ppm) in January 1992, they observed average levels of 0.04 dpu and 704.4 ppm. By the end of the year, the average levels were down to 0.017 dpu and 287.5 ppm (see run charts in Exhibit 6.36). These new levels represent a reduction of almost 60 percent in defects.

Additional benefits were realized, such as an improved and timely feedback from the

Motorola-Codex (Continued)

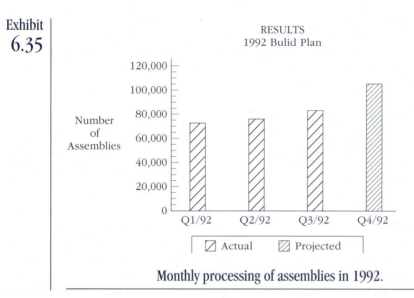

Exhibit
6.35

RESULTS
1992 Bulid Plan

Number
of
Assemblies

Monthly processing of assemblies in 1992.

test area, a standardized operating procedure for all post-IR manufacturing operations, and an improved statistical process control (SPC) procedure that triggers process stoppages when out-of-control conditions occur.

Visual aid documents, which illustrate the component locations for manufacturing operators, are now being revised on an ongoing basis. In July 1992 the team tested and approved a new operating procedure for all post-IR operators as well as the new layout of the post-IR process area shown in Exhibit 6.37. The SPC process specification for post-IR was revised, and operator training was completed in August 1992. A training program was developed and implemented with assistance from educational services in the last quarter of 1992. Finally, engineering change orders (ECOs) were approved and implemented for nine of the new parts that are IR compatible.

After finishing their project, the team felt a great sense of accomplishment, but they also realized that early on they had problems focusing on continuous improvement. Looking back, they recognize that things were tough at the beginning. Then momentum developed, and they were better able to handle all tasks. They gained confidence and now feel sure that they will succeed in future endeavors. A number of new operators became part of this year's team, and the group believes this will result in additional strength. The team feels they learned how to work together and how to arrive at a consensus that can bring about change. They are enthusiastic about the progress they have made and are excited about the possibility of continuing to improve processes using the seven-step method and other tools of Total Quality Management.

Questions

1. What fit is there between the work done by The Post-IR Hammers and the

Motorola-Codex (Continued)

Exhibit
6.36

Run charts for defects per unit (DPU) and defects per million opportunities (PPM) during 1992.

seven-step method described in the text? Can you clearly identify the seven steps in their work?

2. Can you also identify the four phases of the PDCA cycle in the work of The Post-IR Hammers?

3. Which basic tools did The Post-IR Hammers use in their work? Which basic tools were not used? Could any of these have been used?

Motorola-Codex (Continued)

Exhibit
6.37

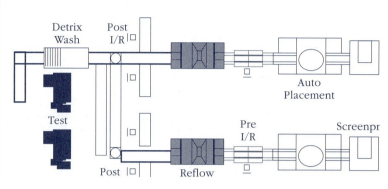

Improved layout of the modem circuit board production line.

◆ Bibliography

Deming, W. Edwards. *Quality, Productivity and Competitive Position.* Cambridge, Mass.: MIT Center for Advanced Engineering Study, 1982.

Deming, W. Edwards. *Out of the Crisis.* Cambridge, Mass.: MIT Center for Advanced Engineering Study, 1986.

Garvin, David. *Managing Quality.* New York: Free Press, 1988.

Imai, Masaaki. *KAIZEN: The Key to Japan's Competitive Success.* New York: Random House, 1986.

Ishikawa, Kaoru. *Guide to Quality Control.* (2nd rev. ed.). Tokyo: Asian Productivity Organization, 1982.

Shiba, Shoji. Alan Graham, and David Walden. *A New American TQM: Four Practical Revolutions in Management.* Portland, Oreg.: Productivity Press, 1993.

Shingo, Shigeo. *Zero Quality Control: Source Inspection and the Poka-Yoke System.* Stamford, Conn.: Productivity Press, 1986.

Tukey, John W. *Exploratory Data Analysis.* Reading, Mass.: Addison-Wesley Publishing Co., 1977.

Walton, Mary. *Deming Management at Work.* New York: G. P. Putnam's Sons, 1990.

Walton, Mary. *The Deming Management Method.* New York: Dodd, Mead, 1986. A paperback version is available from Putnam Press, 1993

Continual Improvement: Statistical Process Control

◆ ◆ ◆

T he central problem in management and in leadership, in the words of my colleague Lloyd S. Nelson, is failure to understand the information in variation. He that possesses even a fuzzy understanding of the contents of this chapter would understand . . . that the type of action required to reduce special causes of variation is totally different from the action required to reduce variation and faults from the system itself; would understand the meaning of the capability of a process and of a system of measurement; . . . would understand that leadership that takes aim at people that are below average in production, or above average in mistakes, is wrong, ineffective, costly to the company; that the same holds for a leader that supposes that everyone could be an achiever. He would understand why it is that costs decrease as quality improves. It is essential, however, in industry and in science to understand the distinction between a stable system and an unstable system, and how to plot points and conclude by rational methods whether they indicate a stable system. The points might show (e.g.) weekly figures on sales, quality incoming and outgoing, complaints of customers, inventory, absenteeism, accidents, fires, accounts receivable, beneficial days.

W. Edwards Deming, Out of the Crisis *(1986, p. 309)*

◆ INTRODUCTION

This chapter is about control charts and statistical process control. We will learn "how to plot points" and by looking at these plots, conclude, as Dr. Deming suggests whether we are facing a stable or an unstable system. The difference is crucial because, as Dr. Deming points out, the type of action suitable in the first case is totally different from the type of action required in the second case.

Before our detailed discussion of control charts, we link them to the basic tools in Chapter 6 through a brief comment on Ishikawa's *seven basic tools*.

The Seven Basic Tools

If one had to single out the person in Japan who best epitomizes the shift in that country toward a quality philosophy, the choice would most likely be Kaoru Ishikawa. He was instrumental in extending Feigenbaum's total quality control concepts from their original spanning of the organization across functional areas to their inclusion of everyone in the organizational hierarchy from top to bottom, and their spreading along the product life cycle from start to finish. He was deeply involved in the early development of quality circles and other quality activities in Japan. He has won the prestigious Deming Prize.

Ishikawa was the author of two of the best known books on quality: *What Is Total Quality Control? The Japanese Way* (Ishikawa, 1985) and *Guide to Quality Control* (Ishikawa, 1982). The 1982 work was originally published in Japan in 1968 and describes the basic tools that have been found most useful in the improvement of quality by Japanese quality circles. It became a popular text for quality circle members and leaders who wanted to refine their understanding and use of those tools. In spite of its simplicity, the book has received wide praise from statisticians. Ishikawa's book covers the following tools:

Histograms
Check sheets
Pareto diagrams
Graphs
Scatter diagrams
Cause-and-effect diagrams
Control charts

Quality practitioners refer to these tools as the **seven basic tools** or **seven basic statistical tools** for quality improvement.

The first six tools on the list were discussed in Chapter 6. Control charts, which are covered in this chapter, are used almost exclusively in the area of quality management and continuous improvement, although they could find many applications elsewhere. These tools are simple and find applications in both service and manufacturing activities.

◆ CONTROL CHARTS

Sources of Variation

All process outputs exhibit some variation. If you own a restaurant, your Irish stew will be a little different from day to day. If you manufacture integrated circuits, the percentage of defective circuits you manufacture will vary somewhat from hour to hour. If you manage a bank, the number of mistakes your bank makes in crediting and debiting accounts will change from day to day. If you make pencils, their diameter will be different from pencil to pencil. If your measurements tell you that all pencil diameters are the same, all you need in order to see some variation is a new measuring instrument that will measure those diameters more precisely.

Some of the variation in the output of any process is natural to that process. It is always present to some degree, and it is the aggregate result of many relatively small factors, such as minor variations in environmental conditions, the quality of raw materials, or the performance of an operator. Given the way the process currently operates as a function of technical or economic limitations, these **common causes of variation** are essentially uncontrollable. This type of variation is called **inherent, controlled, chance,** or **common variation**. Processes for which the output exhibits only common variation are said to be **in statistical control** or, for short, **in control.**

On the other hand, a process may from time to time be subject to some additional variation, which is relatively large and is caused in many instances by only one factor and occasionally by a few factors. Examples are the use of an inferior raw material from a new supplier, a machine that has been incorrectly set up, or a standard that is not being followed. This type of variation, which is usually sporadic, is called **uncontrolled, assignable,** or **special variation**. Processes for which the output exhibits special variation (in addition to the omnipresent common variation) are said to be **out of control.**

Recent thinking (prominently by Deming, among others) maintains that common variation accounts for about 85 percent of the problems in processes, while special variation only accounts for the remaining 15 percent. Current thinking also maintains that common variation is the responsibility of management, since in order to reduce it the process itself must be changed and this can only be done through management action. Examples of such action are more training, better machines, or a better environment. Tinkering by workers can only exacerbate the problem by introducing additional variation. Special variation, on the other hand, stems from **special causes** or **assignable causes** which should be identified and corrected. Appropriately empowered workers can in most cases do this more effectively because they are closer to the process and know it better than managers. The reduction of common variation by management and the identification and elimination of special variation mostly by workers are two important facets of continuous improvement efforts. The remainder of this chapter deals with the identification of special variation. The assessment of common variation is dealt with in Chapter 8.

Introduction to Control Charts

How do you know when special variation is present? This question was answered by Walter A. Shewhart of Bell Laboratories in the 1920s when he developed the concept of a control chart. A **control chart** is a chart used to monitor outputs or inputs of processes. The use of control charts in monitoring processes is called **statistical process control** (SPC).

INTCO, an integrated circuit manufacturer, produces many different types of computer chips. Among them is model FX-486. A quality characteristic for this type of chip is the proportion of defective chips produced. Based on current technology and under operating conditions that are stable and consistent over time (in our new terminology: with the process in control), about one-tenth of the chips produced are expected to be defective in the long run and in a random way. In order to monitor whether this proportion of defective chips produced by the process remains stable over time (that is, in order to monitor whether the process remains in control), production workers at INTCO sample 100 chips every half hour and observe the number of defective chips in those periodic samples.

Statistical theory tells us that if the process is in control (operating normally, in stable and consistent fashion, and randomly producing 10 percent defective chips in the long run), then there is an overwhelming chance that the number of defective chips in any random sample of 100 chips will be somewhere between 1 and 19 chips. INTCO may therefore monitor the *proportion of defective chips produced by the process* by observing the *number of defective chips in samples of this fixed size*. Any sample of size 100 with more than 19 defective chips in it would give INTCO a very strong indication that the long-term proportion of defective chips that the process is producing has gone up from the usual one in ten. In other words, they would have a very strong indication that the process is out of control, and the special causes for this special variation should be found and corrected.

A control chart for this quality characteristic (the proportion of defective chips being produced by this process) is shown in Exhibit 7.1. This particular chart applies only to samples of size 100 from this process. The vertical axis provides a scale for the proportion of defective chips observed in any sample of this size. Two **control limits** and a **center line** have been drawn across the chart. The *lower* control limit (LCL) is one defective chip per hundred, or 0.01, and the *upper* control limit (UCL) is 19 defective chips per hundred, or 0.19. The center line is midway between them, at 10 defective chips per hundred, or 0.10. The horizontal axis provides a scale for successive samples to be taken over time. For each sample, the number of defective chips will be observed, and the proportion defective will be computed and plotted on the chart.

As long as the plotted values stay within the control limits and do not show any other abnormal trends or patterns to be discussed later, there will be no evidence that special variation is present and thus workers at INTCO will believe that the process remains in control. In this case, the variation shown by the control chart represents the common variation in the process. Workers should not reset or adjust a process when only common variation is present, since this would actually add more variation to the process. Only management action can reduce common variation when this reduction is deemed economical.

On the other hand, whenever a plotted value falls outside the control limits or any other abnormal trends or patterns appear, then workers will have found evidence of special variation in the process. If this is the case, they will work toward finding and eliminating the causes for this special variation.

Exhibit
7.1

p chart for monitoring the proportion of defective microchips produced by INTCO. This chart applies only to samples of size 100 and a long-run proportion defective of 0.10 when the process is in control. Sample proportions that fall outside the control limits or other abnormal patterns would show strong evidence of special variation.

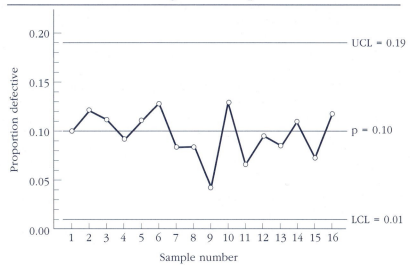

Processes where only common variation is present are *in control*. These stable processes have several advantages: their future behavior may be predicted (in a statistical sense and as long as the process remains in control), their capability to meet requirements may be assessed (we will discuss the assessment of process capability in Chapter 8), costs with the present system are minimized, and the effects of changes implemented in an attempt to improve the system may be accurately measured. This is, in a nutshell, the essence of control charts.

The ability to distinguish between common and special variation is important not only for workers, but also for managers, public officials, the media, and citizens in general. There may well be an upward trend in the planet's temperature, but two or three hot summers in a row are not necessarily an indicator of that trend. A 10 percent decline in the crime rate in a city from one year to the next does not necessarily indicate that crime is being brought under control. The variation in both cases may well be common, and if this is the case the indication is not there. This is the main point Deming makes in the passage we quoted earlier in this chapter.

Attributes and Variables

Many different types of control charts are used. Therefore, in order to understand which type of control chart ought to be used in any given situation, it is useful to categorize them. The first and broader split depends on the nature of the quality characteristic one is monitoring. The quality characteristic may be either an attribute or a variable.

Variables are quality characteristics such as weight, length, time, temperature, voltage, tensile strength, shrinkage, or any other characteristic that you *measure*. They are numeric characteristics, and the values that you record when you observe them may be fractional (you will hear people say that the values "vary continuously" or "vary over a continuum"). You may measure a dimension, for example, to the nearest thousandth of an inch, a time to the nearest hundredth of a second, or a voltage to the nearest tenth of a volt.

Attributes are quality characteristics for which, when you observe them, you concentrate on defects. A fluorescent lamp that you manufacture will either work or not work. A transaction that a bank processes may either be correctly or incorrectly processed. A shirt that is inspected may be defective or may have no defects. A typed page may have no errors, one error, two errors, or more. In any of these cases, you are either classifying production units or service transactions according to whether they are "good" (conforming to a set of well-defined criteria) or "defective" (nonconforming), or you are counting how many defects each unit or transaction has.

We will define a **defect** as a fault or nonconformity whereby a product or service fails to meet customer requirements. A **defective item** is an item with one or more defects.

◆ CONTROL CHARTS FOR ATTRIBUTES

In the next two sections, we discuss the uses and main features of the four most widely used control charts for attributes: *p* charts, *np* charts, *c* charts, and *u* charts. Details on how the charts are developed and their statistical basis are discussed later in the chapter. Examples are from manufacturing, but several applications to the services are provided in the assignments.

p Charts and *np* Charts

The **p chart,** or **control chart for proportion defective,** is used to monitor the proportion of defective items being turned out by a process. This monitoring is done by observing the proportion of defective items in periodic samples. It is the most often used control chart for attributes.

Proportions are by tradition frequently used in process control. Recall that "proportion" means the same as "relative frequency." In either case, we are referring to the number of defective items produced divided by the total number of items produced during a given time span. Proportions fluctuate between zero and one, and by multiplying them by 100 one can easily transform them into everyday percentages.

The chart in Exhibit 7.1, used by INTCO for monitoring the defective chips they produced, is an example of a p chart. The chart in this example is to be used with samples of size 100, and it assumes a long-run proportion defective equal to 0.10 (a 10 percent defective) when the process is in control. The center line is at 0.10 (the long-run proportion defective), the upper control limit at 0.19, and the lower control limit at 0.01. If either sample size or long-run proportion defective changed, the center line and control limits would change. The long-run proportion defective when the process is in control is denoted p (hence the name of this chart), so for the above example p is 0.10.

If on a given day workers at INTCO took periodic samples of 100 chips every half hour and obtained the data shown in Table 7.1, then they would plot in the chart the proportion defective in each of those samples (column 3). These data have been plotted in Exhibit 7.1. Points outside the control limits or other irregularities would provide them with strong evidence that special causes of variation exist.

The term *fraction defective* is sometimes used instead of *proportion defective.* If you hear someone talk about a **control chart for fraction defective**, they are referring to a p chart.

Table 7.1	Results of 16 Samples of 100 Microchips Each Taken by Workers at INTCO to Monitor Their Process		
	SAMPLE NUMBER	NUMBER DEFECTIVE	PROPORTION DEFECTIVE
	1	10	0.10
	2	12	0.12
	3	11	0.11
	4	9	0.09
	5	11	0.11
	6	13	0.13
	7	8	0.08
	8	8	0.08
	9	4	0.04
	10	13	0.13
	11	6	0.06
	12	9	0.09
	13	8	0.08
	14	11	0.11
	15	7	0.07
	16	12	0.12

In our discussion we have assumed that p, the long-run proportion defective when the process is in control, was 0.10. In practice, p is seldom known and has to be estimated from data. Later in this chapter, we explain the procedure for estimating p and for developing the control limits for the p chart.

The control chart in Exhibit 7.2 is called an **np chart** or **control chart for number defective**. This type of chart is sometimes used instead of a p chart. In the **np** chart, the vertical scale represents the *number* of defective items per sample instead of the *proportion* of defective items. The data from Table 7.1 (column 2) are plotted in Exhibit 7.2. Notice how similar this chart is to the p chart in Exhibit 7.1. Some people find numbers more readily interpretable than proportions, and to them *np* charts make more sense than p charts. As we discuss later on, however, p charts can be used with variable sample sizes, but *np* charts should not be used.

c Charts and u Charts

We have dealt with the monitoring of processes through *charts for proportion defective* (p charts) or *charts for number defective* (np charts), and we did that monitoring through a periodic repetition of the following steps:

- We took a sample of several items from the process output.
- We classified each item in the sample as either good (no defects in the item) or defective (one or more defects in the item).
- We recorded the *number of defective items in the sample* or the *proportion*

Exhibit 7.2 | *np* chart for monitoring the number of defective microchips produced by INTCO. Notice the differences and similarities between this chart and the p chart in Exhibit 7.1.

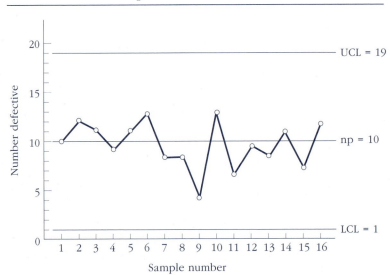

of defective items in the sample, and used this value to monitor the process by means of a control chart.

This monitoring method is applicable mainly when the process output consists of individual items that are relatively simple and inexpensive. When the process output is complex or continuous in nature, then a different approach is more applicable. Although an individual chip might be classified as good or defective, and if defective it might be discarded, one would hardly use the same procedure for the whole computer or even for a circuit board. For any of these more complex items, any defects are likely to be corrected, and "How many defects were there?" becomes a relevant question. A similar approach would be taken with a roll of metal sheet. A single defect will not, in most cases, make the entire roll unusable, but many defects may cause it to be downgraded or scrapped. Here, again, the number of defects plays an important role.

One often monitors defects in processes with complex or continuous outputs through *charts for number of defects*. Here the monitoring is done as follows:

- Periodically, either a single item or several items are sampled.
- The *total number of defects in this single item or group of items* is observed and recorded, and this value is used to monitor the process by means of a control chart.

There are two types of control charts for number of defects: **c charts** and **u charts**. The type of chart used depends on whether the *area of opportunity* for defects to occur stays essentially the same or varies from one item sampled to the next. If we are monitoring the number of air pockets in 5-gallon bottles to be used by a distributor of mineral water, or the number of defects in a speaker system of a given type, then the area of opportunity remains the same from each item inspected to the next and a *c* chart would be used in monitoring. If we are monitoring the number of typographical errors in typed documents, then the area of opportunity (the length of the document) changes from one document to the next and a *u* chart would be used.

Table 7.2 shows defect data for 25 rolls of coated paper. Each roll was inspected, and the total number of defects was recorded. All the rolls were of the same size, so the area of opportunity for defects to occur remained constant from roll to roll.

Table 7.2

Number of Defects in 25 Rolls of Coated Paper

Roll no.	1	2	3	4	5	6	7	8	9	10	11	12	13
No. of defects	5	6	3	5	3	6	6	7	5	5	4	3	5
Roll no.	14	15	16	17	18	19	20	21	22	23	24	25	
No. of defects	4	9	11	3	7	5	5	12	4	6	7	3	

Total no. of defects: 139

A *c* chart developed from these data by a statistical package and with the data values plotted on it is shown in Exhibit 7.3. This chart is used to monitor future production by counting the total number of defects in rolls to be produced and plotting those numbers on the chart. Points outside the control limits or nonrandom patterns in the chart would offer significant evidence of an out-of-control process.

Table 7.3 shows data on blemishes for 25 countertops. Each countertop was inspected, and the total number of blemishes was recorded. Because the countertops were of different sizes, the table also shows the area of each countertop.

| Exhibit 7.3 | *c* chart for monitoring the number of defects in coated paper rolls of the same size. |

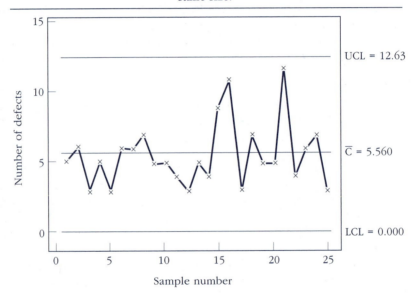

Table 7.3

Area and Number of Blemishes in 25 Countertops

Countertop no.	1	2	3	4	5	6	7	8	9	10	11	12	13
Area (sq.ft.)	18	19	17	37	47	23	28	26	27	38	25	24	29
No. of blemishes	4	10	1	9	14	3	9	12	3	10	4	8	8
Countertop no.	14	15	16	17	18	19	20	21	22	23	24	25	
Area (sq.ft.)	28	30	29	38	40	25	26	29	31	19	50	42	
No. of blemishes	14	8	13	8	12	6	8	13	9	5	8	17	

Total area: 745 sq.ft.

Total no. of defects: 216

Since the area of opportunity here changes from each countertop to the next, a *u* chart was developed for it through a statistical package. This chart is shown in Exhibit 7.4. Defects per square foot are recorded in the chart for each sample. Notice that the control limits are variable. They change as a function of the area of opportunity, with smaller areas resulting in wider limits. Also notice that the vertical axis in this chart represents the number of blemishes per unit area. In monitoring future countertops, one would divide the number of defects observed in every sampled countertop by the area of the countertop and plot this value on the chart.

◆ CONTROL CHARTS FOR VARIABLES

Variables (quality characteristics that you *measure*, such as weights or times) are controlled by monitoring both their average level and their spread. Exhibit 7.5 shows why: either a shift in the average level of a variable or an increase in its spread (or a combination of both) may result in output that does not satisfy requirements. So control charts for variables come in pairs: one for controlling average level and one for controlling spread. In the next two sections, we discuss the uses and main features of the most widely used control charts for variables. Details on how the charts are developed and their statistical basis are discussed later in the chapter.

Exhibit
7.4

u chart for monitoring the number of blemishes per square foot in countertops of different sizes.

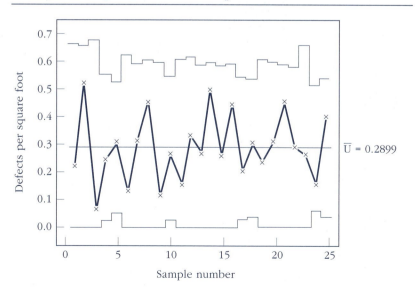

$\bar{U} = 0.2899$

Exhibit

7.5

The top histogram shows all sample values of a variable well within specifications. A shift in the average level of the variable (*middle histogram*) or an increase in its spread (*bottom histogram*) results here in output that fails to meet specifications.

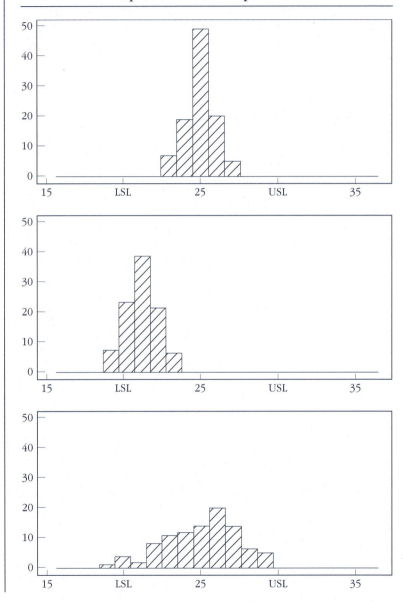

X-bar Charts and R Charts

The **X-bar chart** for average level and the **R chart** for spread are the most often used pair of charts for controlling variables. Other charts are used sometimes, such as the median chart or the midrange chart for average level and the standard deviation chart for spread.

PLASTEX produces, among many other products, a variety of plastic cords. One of these is a thin plastic cord with a nominal tensile strength of 80 pounds. Table 7.4 shows data from 25 samples, each consisting of four pieces of cord, taken at hourly intervals. In statistical process control terminology, each of these samples of four pieces of cord is called a subgroup. Each piece of cord was tested, and its tensile strength was recorded. The table shows these tensile strengths, the mean and range for each subgroup of four pieces, the average of the 25 means, and the average of the 25 ranges.

An X-bar chart and an R chart developed from these data are shown in Exhibit 7.6. The X-bar chart has the 25 subgroup means plotted on it, and it will be used for monitoring the future average level of the process by continuing to observe hourly subgroups of size four and plotting the mean of each subgroup on the chart. Future subgroup ranges will be plotted on the R chart to monitor the process spread. As usual, points outside the control limits or nonrandom patterns in either chart would offer significant evidence of an out-of-control process.

Control Charts for Individuals

There are many instances when, in the monitoring of a variable, only one value of the variable is naturally available at any one time. This is the case, for example, in the monitoring of the viscosity (or any other quality characteristic) of a chemical produced in batches, the temperature or humidity in a climate-controlled room, or the monthly telephone costs in an organization. These variables are monitored through *control charts for individuals*. A **chart for the individual measurements** is used to control the average level of the variable, and a **moving range chart** is used to control the spread.

Table 7.5 shows accounts receivable balances of Marnec Ltd., a large wholesaler of building materials. These receivables were determined at the end of each week for a 25-week period. The moving range for any given week is the absolute value of the difference between the receivables for that week and the receivables for the prior week.

The moving range chart and the chart for the individual measurements for these data are shown in Exhibit 7.7. The charts may be used to monitor receivables in future weeks by determining receivables at the end of each week, computing the moving range for that week, and plotting these two values on the corresponding charts. Points outside the control limits in either chart or nonrandom patterns in the chart for individual measurements would offer significant evidence of an out-of-control process.

Table	Tensile Strengths for 25 Samples of Plastic Cord Produced by PLASTEX					
7.4						

SAMPLE NUMBER	SAMPLE VALUES (TENSILE STRENGTH)				SAMPLE AVERAGE (X-BAR)	SAMPLE RANGE (R)
1	75	78	85	81	79.75	10
2	83	84	76	80	80.75	8
3	81	82	79	74	79.00	8
4	77	81	89	79	81.50	12
5	79	76	82	78	78.75	6
6	83	77	85	85	82.50	8
7	87	79	83	75	81.00	12
8	80	85	76	76	79.25	9
9	86	79	82	80	81.75	7
10	74	82	80	84	80.00	10
11	80	74	75	81	77.50	7
12	76	81	79	78	78.50	5
13	77	86	77	84	81.00	9
14	83	78	72	86	79.75	14
15	79	85	75	78	79.25	10
16	81	84	82	81	82.00	3
17	80	84	81	81	81.50	4
18	80	77	83	77	79.25	6
19	78	75	74	85	78.00	11
20	79	78	79	80	79.00	2
21	88	77	81	72	79.50	16
22	79	74	82	80	78.75	8
23	84	79	84	81	82.00	5
24	75	78	80	77	77.50	5
25	79	85	82	85	82.75	6
			Averages		$\overline{\overline{X}} = 80.02$	$\overline{R} = 8.04$

◆ **OUT-OF-CONTROL PATTERNS**

Although any points that fall outside the control limits in a control chart offer a clear significant evidence of an out-of-control process, other patterns or trends in the data may also be indicators of potential trouble. For example, systematic cycles or trends in the time-ordered data—even if the points are within the control

Exhibit
7.6

X-bar chart (*top*) and *R* chart (*bottom*) for monitoring the average level and spread of tensile strength (in pounds) of cords produced by PLASTEX.

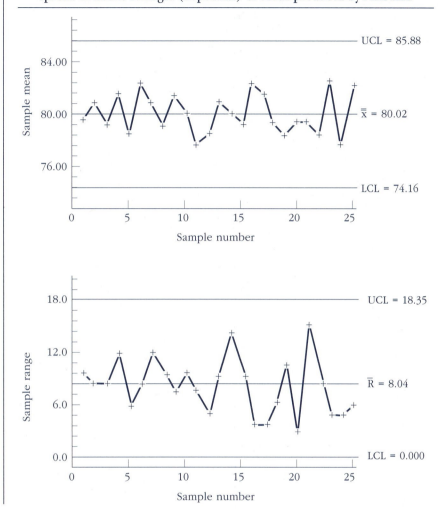

limits—would indicate that some nonrandom, external sources of variation are likely to be affecting the process. Whenever external sources of variation are present, we want to find them and remove them, so we must be alerted. Thus we need to take these patterns into account.

Most of the original work on these patterns and the development of rules to recognize them was done at Western Electric (now AT&T) many years ago, and a wealth of detail on this subject may be found in AT&T's *Statistical Quality Control Handbook* (AT&T, 1956). This handbook, which despite its age is still very much alive and widely used, is an excellent source on the interpretation and use of control charts.

<table>
<tr><td>Table</td><td colspan="3">Twenty-five Consecutive Weekly Accounts Receivable
Balances for Marnec Ltd.</td></tr>
</table>

WEEK	ACCOUNTS RECEIVABLE BALANCES (000)	MOVING RANGE
1	47.0	
2	41.3	5.7
3	64.3	23.0
4	83.3	19.0
5	48.0	35.3
6	87.8	39.8
7	65.3	22.5
8	40.8	24.5
9	55.5	14.7
10	50.8	4.7
11	47.8	3.0
12	66.3	18.5
13	39.0	27.3
14	31.5	7.5
15	48.3	16.8
16	47.1	1.2
17	63.0	15.9
18	51.3	11.7
19	72.6	21.3
20	58.9	13.7
21	33.5	25.4
22	42.3	8.8
23	62.8	20.5
24	87.6	24.8
25	42.3	45.3
	$\overline{X} = 55.14$	$\overline{R} = 18.79$

Nowadays every major company, author, or computer package seems to have its own set of rules for detecting out-of-control patterns. Each set of rules has its own little twists, but in essence they are all very much alike. Here we give the rules advocated by Western Electric. As most sets of rules, they are based on dividing the spread between the control limits into six zones of equal width, as

Exhibit 7.7 | Moving range chart (*top*) and individual measurements chart (*bottom*) for monitoring the weekly balances (in thousands of dollars) of accounts receivable at Marnec Ltd.

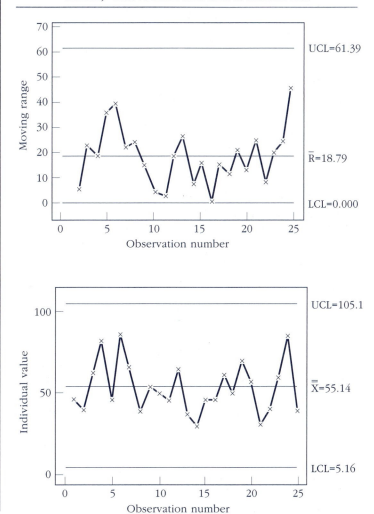

shown in Exhibit 7.8, and in a strict sense they are applicable only to control charts where the control limits are symmetric about the center line. The rules suggest that a process is out of control if any of the following conditions occur:

1. Any point falls outside the control limits.
2. Two out of three consecutive points fall in zone A and on the same side of the center line.

Exhibit

7.8

Zones for out of control patterns.

UCL ———————

                 Zone A

- - - - - - - - - - - - - - - -

                 Zone B

- - - - - - - - - - - - - - - -

                 Zone C

Centerline ———————

                 Zone C

- - - - - - - - - - - - - - - -

                 Zone B

- - - - - - - - - - - - - - - -

                 Zone A

LCL ———————

3. Four out of five consecutive points fall in zones A or B and on the same side of the center line.
4. Eight consecutive points fall on the same side of the center line.

We suggest that whenever you choose a set of rules, you choose one that includes just a few simple rules.

◆ THE DEVELOPMENT OF CONTROL CHARTS

The general procedure for developing control charts is in many ways similar regardless of the type of chart. This general procedure is described by the flow diagram presented in Exhibit 7.9. The procedure is followed for the initial development of a center line and control limits for an attribute or variable. It is also used again, to assess potential effects, every time the process undergoes a change.

In this section we explain *how* control charts are developed. We first give a fairly detailed description of how p charts are developed to illustrate the general procedure; then we give more succinct descriptions for other types of charts. This knowledge will allow you to develop and use the charts. In subsequent sections of this chapter, we introduce several statistical concepts that are necessary for understanding *why* things are done this way, and finally we apply these concepts to the understanding of those whys.

The Development of p Charts

Step 1.

Select at least 20 (if possible 25 to 30) periodic samples each of size n. It is preferable to select n, the sample size, so that the average number of defectives per sample will be at least 3. In other words, n times your guess for p should be at least 3. In this example we will select 25 samples each of size $n = 100$.

Exhibit
7.9

Flow diagram showing the general procedure for developing control charts.

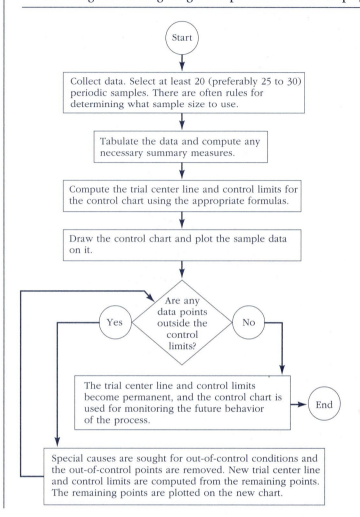

Step 2.

Observe the number of defective items in each sample and tabulate the data as shown in Table 7.6.

Notice that the proportion defective was computed for each sample. The overall proportion defective for all samples, $\bar{p}$, was also computed as follows:

$$\bar{p} = \frac{\text{Total number defective}}{\text{Total number inspected}} = \frac{245}{2500} = 0.0980$$

This overall proportion defective is called a *trial estimate* of p.

Table
7.6

Data on Defective Items for 25 Samples of Size 100

SAMPLE NUMBER	NUMBER OF DEFECTIVE ITEMS	PROPORTION OF DEFECTIVE ITEMS
1	10	0.10
2	5	0.05
3	10	0.10
4	13	0.13
5	14	0.14
6	9	0.09
7	8	0.08
8	9	0.09
9	7	0.07
10	15	0.15
11	10	0.10
12	7	0.07
13	8	0.08
14	10	0.10
15	12	0.12
16	10	0.10
17	12	0.12
18	9	0.09
19	6	0.06
20	5	0.05
21	10	0.10
22	16	0.16
23	13	0.13
24	5	0.05
25	12	0.12
	Sum = 245	Avg = 0.098

Step 3.

Compute *trial control limits* for the p chart.

$$\text{UCL} = \bar{p} + 3\sqrt{\bar{p}(1 - \bar{p}) / n} = 0.098 + 3\sqrt{(0.098)(0.902) / 100} = 0.1872$$
$$\text{LCL} = \bar{p} - 3\sqrt{\bar{p}(1 - \bar{p}) / n} = 0.098 - 3\sqrt{(0.098)(0.902) / 100} = 0.0088$$

If the value obtained through this formula for the lower control limit is negative, then the lower control limit is set equal to zero.

Step 4.

Draw the control chart with $\bar{p}$ as center line and the trial control limits, and plot on it the proportions defective from the k samples, as shown in Exhibit 7.10.

Step 5.

(a) If all points are within the control limits and there is no other evidence of non-random behavior, then the trial center line and control limits are transferred to a control chart that is used to monitor the process.

(b) If some points are outside the control limits, then the special causes are sought, the out-of-control points are removed, and a new center line and control limits are computed from the remaining points. The remaining points are plotted, and if more points now fall outside the new limits (this may happen sometimes, since the new limits will be narrower), then the search for special causes and removal of offenders is repeated. Eventually, a center line and control limits are developed and used to monitor the future behavior of the process.

Sometimes the number of items sampled varies from sample to sample. This occurs, for example, when the whole output for each day is used as a sample and the output volume varies from day to day. In this case, the control limits vary from sample to sample (much as they do for the u chart in Exhibit 7.4) as a function of the changing sample sizes in the denominator of the formulas for control limits.

Exhibit 7.10

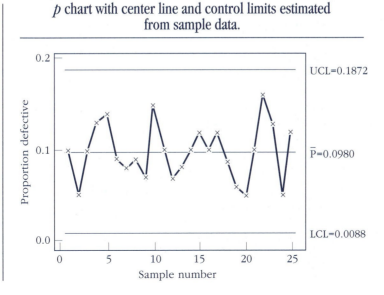

p chart with center line and control limits estimated from sample data.

np Charts

From the data in Table 7.6 we compute

$$\bar{p} = \frac{\text{Total number defective}}{\text{Total number inspected}} = \frac{245}{2500} = 0.098$$

The center line for the np chart is

$$\text{Center line} = n\bar{p} = 100(0.098) = 9.8$$

This value represents an estimated long-run average of 9.8 defectives per sample of 100. The control limits are computed as follows:

$$\text{UCL} = n\bar{p} + 3\sqrt{n\bar{p}(1 - \bar{p})} = 100(0.098) + 3\sqrt{(100)(0.098)(0.902)} = 18.72$$
$$\text{LCL} = n\bar{p} - 3\sqrt{n\bar{p}(1 - \bar{p})} = 100(0.098) - 3\sqrt{(100)(0.098)(0.902)} = 0.88$$

If the value obtained through this formula for the lower control limit is negative, then the lower control limit is set equal to zero. For np charts the sample size should remain constant from sample to sample.

c Charts

From the data in Table 7.2 we can compute the average number of defects per roll:

$$\bar{c} = \frac{\text{Total number of defects in all rolls}}{\text{Total number of rolls inspected}} = \frac{139}{25} = 5.56$$

The center line for the control chart is set at $\bar{c}$, and the control limits are

$$\text{UCL} = \bar{c} + 3\sqrt{\bar{c}} = 5.56 + 3\sqrt{5.56} = 12.63$$
$$\text{LCL} = \bar{c} - 3\sqrt{\bar{c}} = 5.56 - 3\sqrt{5.56} = -1.51 \rightarrow 0$$

If the value obtained through this formula for the lower control limit is negative, then the lower control limit is set equal to zero.

u Charts

From the data in Table 7.3 we can compute the average number of defects per unit area of opportunity (per square foot in this case):

$$\bar{u} = \frac{\text{Total number of defects observed}}{\text{Total area inspected}} = \frac{216}{745} = 0.2899$$

The center line for the chart is set at $\bar{u}$, and the control limits are

$$\text{UCL}_i = \bar{u} + 3\sqrt{\bar{u}/a_i}$$
$$\text{LCL}_i = \bar{u} - 3\sqrt{\bar{u}/a_i}$$

where a_i is the area of the ith countertop. Here the control limits change from countertop to countertop as a function of the countertop area: the larger the area, the narrower the limits. If the value obtained through this formula for the lower control limit is negative, then the lower control limit is set equal to zero.

For the first countertop, for example, the control limits are

$$\text{UCL}_1 = 0.2899 + 3\sqrt{0.2899/18} = 0.6706$$
$$\text{LCL}_1 = 0.2899 - 3\sqrt{0.2899/18} = -0.0908 \rightarrow 0$$

Notice that these are the control limits shown in Exhibit 7.4 for the first countertop in the sample.

X-bar Charts

The computation of center line and control limits is based on the data in Table 7.4. Subgroups of size $n = 4$ or $n = 5$ are very often used.

The center line for the X-bar chart is set at $\bar{\bar{X}}$, the overall average. The computation of control limits requires a factor, A_2, which depends on the subgroup size. Values of A_2 for common subgroup sizes are included in Table 7.11. The control limits are computed as follows:

$$\text{UCL} = \bar{\bar{X}} + A_2\bar{R} = 80.02 + 0.729(8.04) = 85.88$$
$$\text{LCL} = \bar{\bar{X}} - A_2\bar{R} = 80.02 - 0.729(8.04) = 74.16$$

The R chart should be developed before the X-bar chart. The reason for this is that $\bar{R}$ is used in the development of the X-bar chart, so that the range must be in control before the X-bar chart can be developed.

R Charts

The computation of the center line and control limits for the R chart is based on the data presented in Table 7.4. The same data are used for the R chart and the X-bar chart.

The center line for the R chart is set at $\bar{R}$. The computation of control limits requires two factors, D_3 and D_4, which depend on the subgroup size. Values of D_3 and D_4 for common subgroup sizes are included in Table 7.11. The control limits are computed as follows

$$UCL = D_4 \overline{R} = 2.282(8.04) = 18.35$$
$$LCL = D_3 \overline{R} = 0(8.04) = 0$$

As already mentioned, subgroups of size $n = 4$ or $n = 5$ are very often used to monitor variables. On occasion larger subgroup sizes are used. If the subgroup size is $n = 10$ or larger, then the S chart, based on the standard deviation, should be used instead of the R chart. The books cited later under references have details on S charts.

Control Chart for Individual Measurements

From the data in Table 7.5 we can compute

$$\overline{X} = \text{average of the 25 individual measurements} = 55.14$$
$$\overline{R} = \text{average of the 24 moving ranges} = 18.79$$

The center line is set at $\overline{X}$, and the control limits are

$$UCL = \overline{X} + 2.66 \overline{R} = 55.14 + 2.66(18.79) = 105.12$$
$$LCL = \overline{X} - 2.66 \overline{R} = 55.14 - 2.66(18.79) = 5.16$$

The moving range chart should be developed before the control chart for individual measurements. The reason why is that the average moving range is used in developing the control chart for individual measurements, so one must ensure that the range is in control before developing the control chart for individual measurements.

Moving Range Control Chart

$\overline{R}$ is computed as for the control chart for individual measurements. The center line is set at $\overline{R}$, and the control limits are

$$UCL = 3.267 \overline{R} = 3.267(18.79) = 61.39$$
$$LCL = 0$$

◆ STATISTICS, PROBABILITY, AND RANDOM VARIABLES

Inferential Statistics

Statistics deals with the collection of data, their analysis, and the interpretation and presentation of results. The field is often classified into two parts: **descriptive statis-**

tics and **inferential statistics,** or **statistical inference.** Descriptive statistics entails the tabular, graphic, and numeric summarization of data we discussed in Chapter 6.

Statistical inference involves a usually large group of items that have a characteristic that is of interest to you (see Exhibit 7.11). As we mentioned in Chapter 6, this large group of items is generically called a population, although the items, more often than not, are not people. Examples of populations are all single-family homes in Chicago, all automobiles in the United States, all trees in New England, and all accounts in a large corporation. The number of items in the population is denoted N and called the population size.

In order to learn about the characteristic of interest, you could examine every item in the population. This, however, is often impractical. In many cases, the population is so large that it would take too long and cost too much to examine each item. In some cases, the examination destroys the item. For example, to find out how long light bulbs last, you must burn them. So instead of examining each item in the population, you normally resort to the following approach.

1. You take a relatively small sample from the population. The number of items in the sample is denoted n and called the sample size.
2. You observe how the characteristic of interest behaves in the sample.
3. Based on what you observed, you make a good guess about the behavior of the characteristic of interest in the whole population.

Example

Suppose you wanted to find out how many adults in the Greater Boston area are single (see Exhibit 7.12). In this example N, the number of adults in the Greater

Exhibit 7.11	The general problem in statistical inference.

Characteristic of interest

Large group of items
(N items)

POPULATION

1. Take a relatively small <u>sample</u> of n items (n called <u>sample size</u>).

2. Observe how the characteristic behaves in the sample.

3. Make good guess about behavior of the characteristic in the population.

Exhibit

7.12

An example of statistical inference.

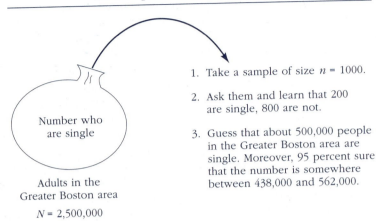

Number who
are single

Adults in the
Greater Boston area

$N = 2,500,000$

1. Take a sample of size $n = 1000$.

2. Ask them and learn that 200 are single, 800 are not.

3. Guess that about 500,000 people in the Greater Boston area are single. Moreover, 95 percent sure that the number is somewhere between 438,000 and 562,000.

Boston area, is about 2.5 million, and it would take a long time to ask everyone. So you could do the following:

1. Randomly select 1000 adults from the Greater Boston area ($n = 1000$).
2. Find from the sample the number that are single. Say this turns out to be 200.
3. From these data you guess that about 20 percent of the adults in the Greater Boston area (some 500,000 people) are single. With some further analysis, you could also say that you are approximately 95 percent sure that the number is somewhere between 438,000 and 562,000.

When we make a statistical inference we are making a good guess about a characteristic of a population based on a statistical analysis of a sample taken from that population.

Random Sampling

Samples are usually taken in a random way. This tends to make the sample representative of the population and allows the use of the many statistical techniques that are based on the assumption that the sample is random. There are several different ways of sampling randomly. The most commonly used method is simple random sampling. In a **simple random sample** of size n, every subset of n items in the population has the same probability of being selected.

Enumerative and Analytical Studies

The study we just discussed, conducted on the marital status of adults in the Greater Boston area, is an example of an **enumerative study**. Enumerative studies deal with populations that remain relatively unchanged while we study them and will also stay relatively unchanged in the future as we apply the knowledge we gained in our study. When, based on enumerative studies, you make predictions about these populations in the relatively near future, you can accurately assess the possible errors involved in such predictions.

Contrast this with the study of a manufacturing or service process. Here conditions, and consequently process output, often change significantly even over a short time span. This makes it much harder to assess the precision and accuracy of predictions about the future behavior of those processes based on present and past observations. Studies of processes whose outputs are subject to significant change over time are called **analytical studies**. It is important to distinguish between these two types of studies because the applicability of the methods one may use depends on the type of study one is facing.

Probability

As we all know, probability is a measure of the likelihood that something will happen. What you may or may not know is that probability is measured on a scale that ranges from zero to one, where zero denotes impossibility and one denotes certainty. So the probability that I'll be happy if my soccer team loses is close to zero, the probability that the tree outside my window will still be there tomorrow is close to one, and the probability that I will get a head when I toss a fair coin is 0.5. This last probability is written

$$P[H] = 0.5$$

In determining the probability of a head, we used an **a priori** or **classical** approach. When we use this approach, we determine the probability logically, based on the symmetry or geometry of the situation at hand. Here we actually argued, without even noticing, that the coin had two faces, that the fairness of the coin made them equally likely to occur, and, therefore, that the certainty of something happening (probability equal to one) had to be equally split between the two faces.

If the coin is bent so that both faces are no longer equally likely to occur, we could now estimate the probability of a head by using the **relative frequency** approach. We would toss the coin a large number of times, count the number of heads we obtained, and divide this count by the number of times we tossed the coin to obtain an estimate of the probability. If we tossed the coin 1000 times and obtained 387 heads, we would estimate the probability of a head as

$$P[H] = \frac{387}{1000} = 0.387$$

This estimate of the probability will tend to be better and better the more we toss the coin.

In determining the probability that Joe Smith will get elected in an upcoming election, or that the Dow Jones will be higher at the end of the month than it is now, neither of the previous two approaches would be of much help. We would then resort to a **subjective** assessment of the probability.

Random Variables and Probability Distributions

A **random variable** is a variable that takes on numeric values in a way that cannot be exactly predicted. Random variables are denoted by capital letters, often with subscripts. Here are a few examples:

X_1 = the number of heads obtained when two coins are tossed
X_2 = the number of employees absent on any given day at the Boston offices of Hingham Investments
X_3 = the number defective out of 20 parts sampled from an incoming shipment

Let us look at X_1 in more detail. The possible values that X_1 can take on are 0, 1, or 2. If you repeatedly toss two dimes, and record the number of heads each time you toss them, you will see that in the long run you will get no heads about one-fourth of the time, exactly one head about half the time, and two heads about one-fourth of the time. This way you would estimate the probabilities of X_1 taking on the values 0, 1, and 2 to be approximately 0.25, 0.50, and 0.25. Using an a priori approach—which we will not discuss here—it is possible to establish that the probabilities of these three values are *exactly* 0.25, 0.50, and 0.25. We therefore may write:

$$P[\text{no heads}] = P[X_1 = 0] = 0.25$$
$$P[\text{one head}] = P[X_1 = 1] = 0.50$$
$$P[\text{two heads}] = P[X_1 = 2] = 0.25$$

These probabilities of the possible values of a random variable are often displayed in a **probability distribution**, as shown in Table 7.7. The possible values are listed in one column and their corresponding probabilities in another column to their right. The probabilities must always add up to one, as they do in this case. Exhibit 7.13 shows a graph of the distribution, where the possible values of the random variable are plotted along the horizontal axis and the probabilities are shown in the vertical axis. Vertical lines (or sometimes bars) over the different values indicate their probabilities.

To estimate the probability distribution of X_2 the number of employees absent on any given day at the Boston offices of Hingham Investments, you would need data on absenteeism. You could collect data for the past year (250 working days), tally the values, and obtain the frequency distribution shown on the left of Table 7.8. An estimate of the probability distribution of X_2 is shown on the right side of the same figure. The probability estimates in the probability distribution are simply rel-

Table
7.7

The Probability Distribution of the
Random Variable "The Number of
Heads Obtained When Two Coins
Are Tossed"

i	$P[X_1 = i]$
0	0.25
1	0.50
2	0.25
	1.00

Exhibit
7.13

Graph of the distribution of the random variable "the
number of heads obtained when two coins are
tossed."

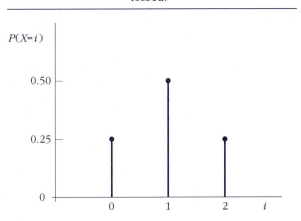

ative frequencies, derived from the frequency distribution by dividing the frequencies by the total count. Since absenteeism is a process that takes place over time and is possibly subject to significant seasonalities or other changes in surrounding conditions, this should be the subject of an analytical rather than an enumerative study. The distribution in Table 7.8 applies only if the process is in control.

The Expectation of a Random Variable

The concept of expectation of a random variable is one of the most useful concepts in decision making. Intuitively, the expectation represents the *long-run av-*

Table
7.8

Frequency Distribution for Daily Absenteeism and an Estimated Probability Distribution for the Number of Employees Absent

NUMBER ABSENT	FREQUENCY	i	$P[X_2 = i]$
0	14	0	0.056
1	34	1	0.136
2	77	2	0.308
3	85	3	0.340
4	36	4	0.144
5	3	5	0.012
6	1	6	0.004
Total	250		1.000

erage of the random variable. In other words, it is the average of all values over (infinitely) many occurrences of the random variable.

How would you find the expectation of X_1, the number of heads obtained when two coins are tossed? Perhaps by thinking of what would happen if you tossed two coins many, many times? Let us suppose that you toss the two coins 10,000 times. After recalling the distribution of X_1 (see Table 7.7), you will agree that in about 2500 of these repetitions no heads will appear, in about 5000 of them one head will appear, and in about 2500 of them two heads will appear. So, roughly, how many heads will you see altogether? Well, let's do some accounting of what you will see:

NUMBER OF HEADS	IN ABOUT	FOR A TOTAL OF
0	2500 repetitions	0 heads
1	5000 repetitions	5000 heads
2	2500 repetitions	5000 heads
		10,000 heads

So you will see about 10,000 heads in the 10,000 repetitions, or an average of about one head per repetition. Therefore, the expectation of X_1 should be about one. In fact, as we will see next, it is exactly one.

The **expectation, expected value,** or **mean** of a random variable is easily computed by multiplying each possible value of the random variable times its probability of occurrence and adding all those products. So a formula for the expectation of a random variable X is

$$E[X] = \Sigma \; i \; P[X = i]$$

where the summation is performed over all possible values of the random variable (all possible is). Both $E[X]$ and μ are used as symbols for expectation.

Using this formula, you can compute the expectation of X_1 by multiplying pairwise the values in each row of the distribution and then adding all these products:

$$E[X_1] = (0)(0.25) + (1)(0.50) + (2)(0.25) = 1$$

The value you obtain this way is the same value you obtained intuitively.

If you go back to Exhibit 7.13 and plot this expectation on the horizontal axis of the graph, you will notice that the distribution balances around this point. The expectation is a *measure of location* for the probability distribution: many values of the random variable will always "jump around it." The following example illustrates how the expectation of a random variable is used in decision making.

Example

Two fair dice are rolled. If their sum is either 5 or 6, you will win $350; otherwise you will lose $100. Would you play?

To find out whether playing would be advantageous to you, you could roll two fair dice 10,000 times. In about 2500 of these rolls the sum would be either 5 or 6, and you would therefore estimate the probability of the sum being either 5 or 6 to be about 0.25. (The probability that the sum is either 5 or 6 can be found to be exactly 0.25 by the a priori method.) You could then define a random variable

$$Y = \text{Your winnings in one play of this game (in dollars)}$$

The possible values of Y are either 350 or -100, and the probabilities of these two values are 0.25 and 0.75. Therefore, the distribution of Y is

i	$P[Y = i]$
-100	0.75
350	0.25

and the expectation of Y is

$$E[Y] = (-100)(0.75) + (350)(0.25) = 12.5$$

How do you interpret and use this value? If you were to play this game a large number of times, then your average winnings per play would be around $12.50. If you were allowed to play this game many times, you would definitely play it, particularly if you had enough money to guard against a possible string of early losses. You know that in the long run you would come out ahead. But many people would play the game even if they were allowed to play it only once, arguing that a positive expectation means that the game is favorable to them.

In business decision making, where investment alternatives usually have uncertain returns, expected returns are computed for the different alternatives in very much the way we just did. These expected returns are then used as one of the main criteria in comparing alternatives and making decisions.

The Variance and Standard Deviation of a Random Variable

The monitoring of variation is central to quality work when quality is defined as conformance: other things being equal, the less the variation the higher the quality. Therefore, in addition to measuring the general location of random variables, which we do through their expectation, we also want to measure their spread. You will not be surprised by learning that we measure the spread of a random variable by its variance and standard deviation. The **variance** is computed as follows:

$$\text{Var}[X] = \Sigma \, (i - E[X])^2 \, P[X = i]$$

where the summation is performed over all possible values of the random variable. So we must first compute the expectation, then subtract this expectation from each possible value of the random variable, square all these differences to make them all positive, weigh them with the probabilities of the different values, and add all these results. The task sounds formidable, but it is actually fairly simple, as we will see in the example below. Both $\text{Var}[X]$ and σ^2 are used as symbols for the variance. The **standard deviation** is, as before, the square root of the variance, and it is denoted $S[X]$, or σ.

Example

To compute the variance of X_1, the number of heads obtained when two coins are tossed, we first recall that we already computed the expectation and its value is 1. We then compute

$$\text{Var}[X_1] = (0-1)^2(0.25) + (1-1)^2(0.50) + (2-1)^2(0.25) = 0.50$$

The standard deviation of X_1 is

$$S[X_1] = \sqrt{0.50} = 0.707$$

Discrete Versus Continuous Random Variables

Random variables are classified into two main categories: discrete random variables and continuous random variables. The distinction is important because the two types of random variables are modeled differently.

To determine whether a random variable is discrete or continuous, you look at the possible values that the random variable can take on. If there are *gaps* between the possible values, then the random variable is a **discrete random variable**. The random variable X_1, the number of heads obtained when two coins are tossed, can only take on the values 0, 1, and 2. There are gaps between these three values, in the sense that the random variable cannot take on any values between them. Therefore, X_1 is a discrete random variable, and so are all the other random variables we have discussed thus far.

By contrast, think of the random variable

X_4 = the time it takes a bank clerk to service the next customer

Here the possible values range over a continuum, so the gap between any two possible values depends only on how accurate an instrument you use to measure time. When there are no gaps between the possible values of a random variable, as in this case, the random variable is a **continuous random variable**. The following are other examples of continuous random variables:

X_5 = the diameter of a randomly selected engine piston
X_6 = the cost of repairing your car the next time it breaks down

As we have seen, we describe the distribution of discrete random variables by means of a table that assigns a probability to each possible value. This assignment is sometimes made by means of a formula rather than a table, but the idea is always the same: *if the random variable is discrete, the distribution is specified by assigning a probability to each possible value of the random variable.*

For continuous random variables, the above method for describing the distribution does not work. In a sense there are too many possible values for us to be able to assign a probability to each. So for continuous random variables we describe the distribution by means of a curve, as shown in Exhibit 7.14. This curve is called the *density* of the random variable and has the following properties:

1. The curve never drops below the *x*-axis.
2. The total area under the curve is equal to one.
3. Probabilities are represented by *areas under this curve.* More precisely, the shape of the curve is such that the probability that the random variable will take on a value within an interval equals the area under the curve and over the interval. The height of the curve does *not* represent the probability of a value.

The expectation and variance of continuous random variables can be computed, through calculus, in ways analogous to those used for discrete random variables. Their interpretations are the same as for discrete random variables. With these ideas about continuous random variables now clear, we turn to a discussion of the most widely used distribution in statistics.

Exhibit 7.14	The density of a continuous random variable. The total area under the density is one. The shaded area represents the probability that the random variable will take on a value between *a* and *b*.

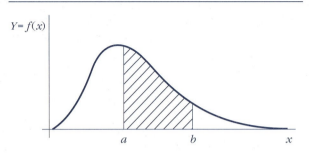

◆ THE NORMAL DISTRIBUTION

If you examine the weather records for New York City (or almost any other place of your choice) and obtain data on the average daily temperatures for all days in the month of June for each of the last 10 years, you will notice that a histogram of the resulting 300 values is fairly symmetric, bell-shaped, and relatively smooth. If you randomly select 500 adult females (or adult males, or seven year olds) born in this country and measure their heights, you will notice that a histogram of the 500 heights is also fairly symmetric, bell-shaped, and smooth. You will find similar results in histograms for the diameters of engine pistons, for the contents of 12-oz. beer bottles (there will be variation here too, if you measure precisely), and for many other random variables around you. Most random variables with bell-shaped histograms are modeled by means of a continuous, symmetric, and bell-shaped curve called the **normal distribution**.

The location and spread of the normal distribution are controlled by two *parameters*, its *mean*, μ (which may have any value), and its *standard deviation, σ* (which must be positive). If, for example, we choose $\mu = 3$ and $\sigma = 0.5$, the curve looks as shown in Exhibit 7.15. This curve has the following features, which are common to all normal curves:

1. The curve reaches its highest point when $x = 3$, our choice for the mean. The curve is symmetric about this value.
2. As you move away from the mean in either direction, the curve dwindles down, and after you have moved three standard deviations away (to 1.5 on the left and 4.5 on the right) it almost touches the *x*-axis. There is practically no area under the curve beyond those points. (The curve never actually touches the x-axis, but keeps getting closer and closer to it.)
3. The whole area under the curve is one. A rectangle of unit area is shown in Exhibit 7.15 for reference purposes.

| Exhibit 7.15 | The density of the normal distribution with mean 3 and standard deviation 0.5. The total area under the curve is one. A rectangle of unit area is shown for comparative purposes. |

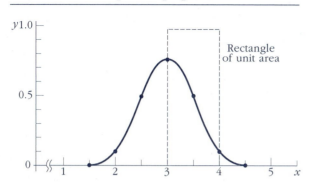

If we choose $\mu = 100$ and $\sigma = 10$, then the curve looks as shown in Exhibit 7.16. This new curve is centered around 100, and it dwindles down so that when we move three standard deviations away from 100 in either direction there is virtually no area under the curve outside that range. The whole area under the curve is again one.

The Standard Normal Distribution and Normal Probability Tables

The normal distribution with $\mu = 0$ and $\sigma = 1$ is called the **standard normal distribution**. A graph of its density is shown in Exhibit 7.17. It is centered around zero, and the interval from -3 to $+3$ contains practically all the area under the density. A normal random variable with mean 0 and standard deviation 1 is called

| Exhibit 7.16 | The density of the normal distribution with mean 100 and standard deviation 10. IQ test results follow this distribution. |

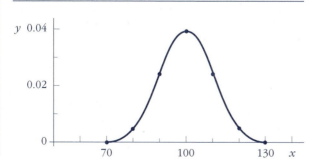

Exhibit

7.17

The standard normal density.

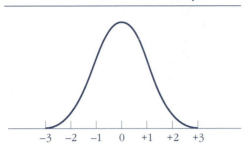

a *standard normal random variable*. The notation Z is often used for standard normal random variables.

Areas under the standard normal density have been tabulated. Through these tables it is easy to find probabilities for standard normal random variables. Once you learn how to find probabilities for standard normal random variables, it is a simple matter to find probabilities, in general, for a normal random variable with any mean and standard deviation. We will first learn how to use the standard normal table, and then, with this knowledge in hand, we will learn how to find probabilities for any other normal distributions.

Areas under the standard normal density are obtained from Table 7.9. Let Z be a standard normal random variable. For any positive value x you find $P[0 < Z < x]$, the shaded area in Exhibit 7.18, by following these two steps:

Step 1

Find x in the table margins: You select a table *row* by entering the left margin of the table with the integer part and first decimal digit of x, and a table *column* by entering the top table margin with the second decimal digit of x.

Step 2

Read the probability inside the table at the intersection of the row and column you entered in step 1.

We will now illustrate the use of the table through some examples. *It is very useful to draw a picture of the distribution with which you are dealing every time you must find a normal probability.*

Example

Find the following probabilities for a standard normal random variable Z.

(a) $P[0 < Z < 1]$

| Table 7.9 | The Standard Normal Distribution |

X	0.00	0.01	0.02	0.03	0.04	0.05	0.06	0.07	0.08	0.09
0.0	0.0000	0.0040	0.0080	0.0120	0.0160	0.0199	0.0239	0.0279	0.0319	0.0359
0.1	0.0398	0.0438	0.0478	0.0517	0.0557	0.0596	0.0636	0.0675	0.0714	0.0753
0.2	0.0793	0.0832	0.0871	0.0910	0.0948	0.0987	0.1026	0.1064	0.1103	0.1141
0.3	0.1179	0.1217	0.1255	0.1293	0.1331	0.1368	0.1406	0.1443	0.1480	0.1517
0.4	0.1554	0.1591	0.1628	0.1664	0.1700	0.1736	0.1772	0.1808	0.1844	0.1879
0.5	0.1915	0.1950	0.1985	0.2019	0.2054	0.2088	0.2123	0.2157	0.2190	0.2224
0.6	0.2257	0.2291	0.2324	0.2357	0.2389	0.2422	0.2454	0.2486	0.2517	0.2549
0.7	0.2580	0.2611	0.2642	0.2673	0.2704	0.2734	0.2764	0.2794	0.2823	0.2852
0.8	0.2881	0.2910	0.2939	0.2967	0.2995	0.3023	0.3051	0.3078	0.3106	0.3133
0.9	0.3159	0.3186	0.3212	0.3238	0.3264	0.3289	0.3315	0.3340	0.3365	0.3389
1.0	0.3413	0.3438	0.3461	0.3485	0.3508	0.3531	0.3554	0.3577	0.3599	0.3621
1.1	0.3643	0.3665	0.3686	0.3708	0.3729	0.3749	0.3770	0.3790	0.3810	0.3830
1.2	0.3849	0.3869	0.3888	0.3907	0.3925	0.3944	0.3962	0.3980	0.3997	0.4015
1.3	0.4032	0.4049	0.4066	0.4082	0.4099	0.4115	0.4131	0.4147	0.4162	0.4177
1.4	0.4192	0.4207	0.4222	0.4236	0.4251	0.4265	0.4279	0.4292	0.4306	0.4319
1.5	0.4332	0.4345	0.4357	0.4370	0.4382	0.4394	0.4406	0.4418	0.4429	0.4441
1.6	0.4452	0.4463	0.4474	0.4484	0.4495	0.4505	0.4515	0.4525	0.4535	0.4545
1.7	0.4554	0.4564	0.4593	0.4582	0.4591	0.4599	0.4608	0.4616	0.4625	0.4633
1.8	0.4641	0.4649	0.4656	0.4664	0.4671	0.4678	0.4686	0.4693	0.4699	0.4706
1.9	0.4713	0.4719	0.4726	0.4732	0.4738	0.4744	0.4750	0.4756	0.4761	0.4767
2.0	0.4772	0.4778	0.4783	0.4788	0.4793	0.4798	0.4803	0.4808	0.4812	0.4817
2.1	0.4821	0.4826	0.4830	0.4834	0.4838	0.4842	0.4846	0.4850	0.4854	0.4857
2.2	0.4861	0.4864	0.4868	0.4871	0.4875	0.4878	0.4881	0.4884	0.4887	0.4890
2.3	0.4893	0.4896	0.4898	0.4901	0.4904	0.4906	0.4909	0.4911	0.4913	0.4916
2.4	0.4918	0.4920	0.4922	0.4925	0.4927	0.4929	0.4931	0.4932	0.4934	0.4936
2.5	0.4938	0.4940	0.4941	0.4943	0.4945	0.4946	0.4948	0.4949	0.4951	0.4952
2.6	0.4953	0.4955	0.4956	0.4957	0.4959	0.4960	0.4961	0.4962	0.4963	0.4964
2.7	0.4965	0.4966	0.4967	0.4968	0.4969	0.4970	0.4971	0.4972	0.4973	0.4974
2.8	0.4974	0.4975	0.4976	0.4977	0.4977	0.4978	0.4979	0.4979	0.4980	0.4981
2.9	0.4981	0.4982	0.4982	0.4983	0.4984	0.4984	0.4985	0.4985	0.4986	0.4986
3.0	0.4987	0.4987	0.4987	0.4988	0.4988	0.4989	0.4989	0.4989	0.4990	0.4990

SOURCE: Generated using MINITAB.

Exhibit
7.18

Use of the standard normal table.

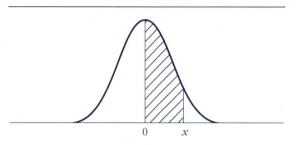

To find the shaded area:
1. Enter with x in the table margins.
2. Read the desired area inside the table.

Exhibit 7.19 shows the area to be found. Here $x = 1.00$, so you enter the left margin with 1.0 (the integer part and first decimal digit of x) and the top margin with 0.00 (since the second decimal digit of x is 0). Inside the table you find 0.3413, the probability you wanted.

(b) $P[-2.35 < Z < 0]$

Exhibit 7.20 shows the area to be found. By symmetry, the area between -2.35 and 0 is the same as the area between 0 and $+2.35$. Therefore, you enter the left margin with 2.3 and the top margin with 0.05. Inside the table you find 0.4906, the desired probability.

(c) $P[-0.33 < Z < 1.27]$

Exhibit 7.21 shows the area to be found. Here the area straddles the mean, so you divide it into two parts: the area between -0.33 and 0, and the area between 0 and 1.27. To find the first of these two areas, using symmetry again, you enter the table with 0.3 on the left and 0.03 across the top. Inside the table

Exhibit
7.19

Finding $P[0 < Z < 1]$.

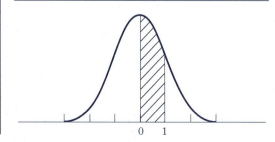

Exhibit
7.20

Finding $P[-2.35 < Z < 0]$.

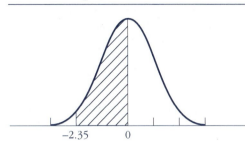

Exhibit
7.21

Finding $P[-0.33 < Z < 1.27]$.

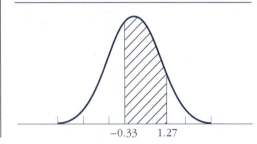

you find 0.1293. The second area, entering the table with 1.2 on the left and 0.07 across the top, is found to be 0.3980. The total area is the sum of these two areas, or 0.5273.

(d) $P[1 < Z < 1.85]$

Exhibit 7.22 shows the area to be found. You find this area by finding the difference between the area from 0 to 1.85 and the area from 0 to 1. The first of these areas is 0.4678 and the second is 0.3413. Therefore, the area you want is 0.1265.

Exhibit
7.22

Finding $P[1 < Z < 1.85]$.

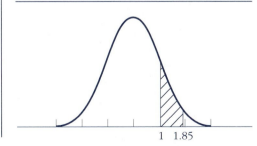

(e) $P[Z > 1.17]$

Exhibit 7.23 shows the area to be found. Since the whole area to the right of 0 is 0.5, you can find the area to the right of 1.17 by subtracting the area between 0 and 1.17 (which is 0.3790) from 0.5. The area you want is $0.5 - 0.3790 = 0.1210$.

Finding Probabilities for Normal Distributions: The General Case

Now that you know how to use the standard normal table, you are well prepared to learn how to find probabilities for a general normal random variable with any mean and standard deviation. To find these probabilities we use the following standardization rule:

If X is a normally distributed random variable with mean μ and standard deviation σ, then in order to find

$$P[a < X < b]$$

where a and b are any two values, one calculates

$$P\left[\frac{a - \mu}{\sigma} < Z < \frac{b - \mu}{\sigma}\right]$$

where Z represents a standard normal random variable.

Example

The time it takes to refuel flight LH-152 at Kennedy Airport is approximately normally distributed with mean 22 minutes and standard deviation 2 minutes. What is the probability that the next time the flight is refueled it will take between 20 and 23 minutes to complete the task?

 Exhibit 7.23

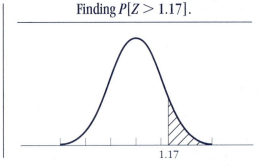

Finding $P[Z > 1.17]$.

1.17

If you let

$$X = \text{time in minutes to refuel the flight}$$

then X is normal with $\mu = 22$ and $\sigma = 2$. You want to find the probability

$$P[20 < X < 23]$$

which is represented by the shaded area in Exhibit 7.24.
To find this probability all you must do is compute

$$P\left[\frac{20 - 22}{2} < Z < \frac{23 - 22}{2}\right] = P[-1.0 < Z < 0.5]$$

This probability is represented by the shaded area under the standard normal density in Exhibit 7.25. This area has value 0.5328 and is approximately the probability we wanted (since the distribution of X is only approximately normal).

It is important to notice the similarity between the two figures in this example (Exhibits 7.24 and 7.25). They underscore the fact that the area between 20 and

| Exhibit 7.24 | Finding $P[20 < X < 23]$. |

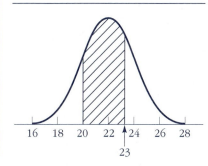

| Exhibit 7.25 | $P[-1.0 < Z < 0.5]$. |

23 under the distribution of X is the same as the area between -1.0 and 0.5 under the standard normal density.

The value -1.0 in the standardized figure reflects the fact that the value 20 is one standard deviation *below* the mean (negative sign) in the distribution of X, while the value $+0.5$ in the standardized figure reflects the fact that the value 23 is half a standard deviation *above* the mean (positive sign) in the distribution of X.

Example

The life of a new battery you just bought for your car is approximately normal with mean 60 months and standard deviation 10 months. What is the probability that you will not have to buy another battery if you plan to keep your car four more years?

If here you let

$$X = \text{battery life in months}$$

then X is normal with $\mu = 60$ and $\sigma = 10$.
You want to find

$$P[X > 48]$$

the shaded area in Exhibit 7.26. To find this probability you use a one-sided version of the normal probability rule:

$$P\left[Z > \frac{48 - 60}{10}\right] = P[Z > -1.2]$$

This probability is represented by the shaded area under the standard normal density in Exhibit 7.27. This area is 0.8849. This is, approximately, the probability you wanted.

Exhibit	Finding $P[X > 48]$.
7.26	

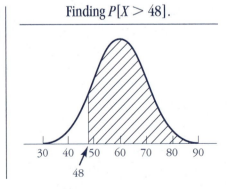

Exhibit
7.27

$P[Z > -1.2]$.

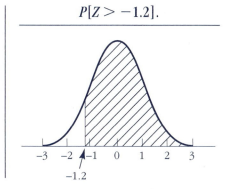

Problems Where Areas Are Given

Problems that deal with normal random variables fall into two categories. In some problems you must determine a probability, whereas in others a probability is an input to your problem and there is something else to be determined. We already saw how to deal with problems of the first type by means of the standardization rule. Problems of the second type, where a probability is an input to the problem, are best tackled through a different approach.

Example

The demand for each issue of the Sunday *Times* during the month of June is approximately normal, with mean 350,000 copies and standard deviation 12,000 copies. On a given Sunday in June the publisher wants to satisfy 90 percent of the demand. How many copies should be printed?
Here we let

$$D = \text{June demand for each issue of the Sunday } Times$$

We know D is approximately normal with $\mu = 350,000$ and $\sigma = 12,000$. Exhibit 7.28 shows the distribution of D. In order to have a 90 percent probability of satisfying demand, one must produce x newspapers, and the whole area left of x must be 0.90.

In this type of problem, where an area is given, we recommend the following step-by-step approach. It is based on good reasoning rather than the blind plugging of values into a formula.

1. *Transform the given area into an area between the mean and a point away from the mean.* For our problem the shaded area in Exhibit 7.29 is 0.40.
2. *Find the closest value to this area inside the table and read the corresponding value from the margins.* The value closest to 0.40 inside the table is 0.3997. The corresponding value in the margins is 1.28.

Exhibit
7.28

The distribution of demand for an issue of the
Sunday *Times* during the month of June.
Producing *x* newspapers there will be a 90 per-
cent probability that the demand will be satisfied.

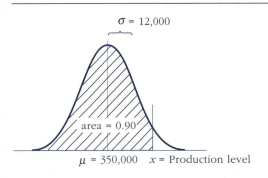

$\sigma = 12,000$

area = 0.90

$\mu = 350,000$ *x* = Production level

Exhibit
7.29

The shaded area in Exhibit 7.28 has been transformed into an area between the mean and a
point away from the mean. These are areas one
finds *inside* the standard normal table.

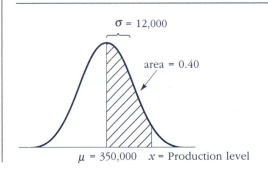

$\sigma = 12,000$

area = 0.40

$\mu = 350,000$ *x* = Production level

3. *Interpret the value in the margins.* By now the following key statement
should not come as a surprise to you: *Regardless of the normal distribution
with which you are dealing, the area between the mean and a point that is
1.28 standard deviations away from the mean is 0.40* (actually 0.3997).

So the distance between the mean and *x* is

$$1.28 \ \sigma = 1.28 \ (12,000) = 15,360$$

It follows, as shown in Exhibit 7.30, that

$$x = 350,000 + 15,360 = 365,360$$

Exhibit
7.30

If a normal area between the mean and a point away from the mean is 0.40, then the point away from the mean *must* be 1.28 standard deviations away. If the Sunday *Times* produces 365,360 newspapers, they will have a 90 percent probability of satisfying demand.

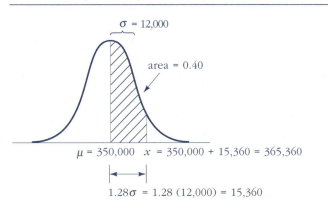

$\sigma = 12,000$

area = 0.40

$\mu = 350,000$ $x = 350,000 + 15,360 = 365,360$

$1.28\sigma = 1.28\,(12,000) = 15,360$

This approach not only solves the problem; it also gives you an additional insight into the normal distribution: *in terms of standard deviations away from the mean all normal distributions act alike.*

◆ THE BEHAVIOR OF SAMPLES

In statistical process control we periodically sample some of the output of a process and observe the quality of the sample. We then decide, based on what we observed, whether the process appears to be operating as it should (the process is in control, let's not tinker with it) or abnormally (the process is out of control, let's find the causes and fix the problem). In doing this, we are doing inferential work: we look at a sample, and, based on what we observe (the characteristics of the sample), we make a guess about the process from which the sample came. In order to understand the whys of this inferential work, we must first get acquainted with how samples behave. In this section we will learn a few general facts about the behavior of samples that come from populations whose characteristics we know. Once we learn how samples from known populations behave, we will be able to turn things around, look at a sample, and make a good guess about the unknown characteristics of the population the sample came from.

Recall that in process control two different types of quality characteristics are monitored. In some cases, the characteristic can be measured, and the possible values of the measurement vary over a continuum. Quality characteristics of this type are called variables and are controlled by assessing both the average and the variation of the values in a sample. In other cases, the quality characteristic cannot be measured. Quality characteristics of this kind are called attributes and are controlled either by classifying items or transactions in a sample according to whether they are good or defective, or by counting how many defects occur in each item or transaction in the sample.

In this chapter we first explore the behavior of sample means in order to gain some knowledge that will be useful in understanding how to control variables. Then we explore the behavior of sample proportions, and this way we will gain knowledge useful in understanding the controlling of attributes.

The Behavior of Sample Means: The Central Limit Theorem

The central limit theorem is so called because of the central role it plays in statistics. It deals with the behavior of sample means, and a good deal of statistical inference is based on this theorem and on other similar theorems. The theorem can be proved mathematically, but all we will do here is get a good intuitive grasp of what the theorem says.

Consider a large population of numbers, such as the weights of all adult people in this country, the hourly wages of construction workers in Munich, or the monthly rents of single-family homes in the Greater Boston area. Notice that each of these populations consists of many *items* and each item has a *number* attached to it; this is what we mean when we talk about a population of numbers. Regardless of which of these populations you are considering, the population has a mean, μ, and a standard deviation, σ. Both of these *parameters* could actually be computed.

Suppose that from this population you randomly draw a sample of n items (so you get n numeric values), compute the mean of this sample, $\overline{X}$, and put the items back in the population. Suppose you repeat this procedure a large number of times, say 1000 times. After doing this you will have computed 1000 different $\overline{X}$s. Is there anything you can reasonably say about these 1000 $\overline{X}$s even before you go through this whole procedure? In fact, we can say the following:

1. A histogram of the 1000 $\overline{X}$s will be centered around μ, the mean of the population that the samples came from. In other words, *the average of the 1000 $\overline{X}$s will be close to μ*. This is an intuitively appealing fact.
2. The standard deviation of the 1000 $\overline{X}$s will be close to $\sigma/\sqrt{n}$. What this says is that *the more spread there is in the population the more spread there will be in the 1000 $\overline{X}$s, and the larger the size of each of the 1000 samples the less spread there will be in the 1000 $\overline{X}$s*. This fact is also intuitively appealing.
3. If the values in the population are normally distributed, then the 1000 $\overline{X}$s will also be normally distributed. Their histogram will be bell-shaped, and histogram frequencies will be closely matched by areas under the normal distribution. This is again intuitive.
4. A not so intuitive but important fact: If n (the size of each of the 1000 samples) is large enough, then the 1000 $\overline{X}$s will be at least approximately nor-

mally distributed regardless of the distribution of the values in the population. In other words, *if you are sampling from a population whose histogram has any shape and if you use a large sample size, a histogram of the 1000 $\overline{X}$s will be bell-shaped and histogram frequencies will be closely matched by areas under the normal distribution.*

This is the **central limit theorem**. It is one good reason for the widespread use of the normal distribution. Let us illustrate it through an example.

Example

You are facing a population of 6 million marbles, each labeled with a digit from 1 to 6 with each of these digits equally represented. So there are 1 million ones, 1 million twos, and so on up to 1 million sixes. Randomly drawing one marble from this population is equivalent to rolling a fair die. A histogram for this population is shown in Exhibit 7.31. The mean of this population is $\mu = 3.5$ (just locate the value 3.5 along the *x*-axis of the histogram in Exhibit 7.31 if you need to convince yourself of this), and the population standard deviation is $\sigma = 1.71$ [*Note:* The mean and variance of a numeric population are the same as the mean and variance of the random variable "a single value randomly drawn from that population." This random variable has distribution

i	$P[X = i]$
1	1/6
2	1/6
3	1/6
4	1/6
5	1/6
6	1/6

Exhibit 7.31 A histogram for our population of six million marbles.

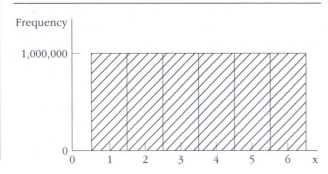

and therefore, since its mean is 3.5, its variance is

$$\text{Var}[X] = (1-3.5)^2(1/6) + (2-3.5)^2(1/6) + \ldots + (6-3.5)^2(1/6) = 2.92$$

Hence the population variance is also 2.92, and its standard deviation is $\sigma = \sqrt{2.92} = 1.71$.]

If from this population you randomly drew a sample of 30 marbles (or if you rolled a fair die 30 times), if you computed the sample mean (or the average of the 30 rolls), replaced the marbles, and if you then repeated this procedure 1000 times, thus obtaining 1000 sample means, according to the central limit theorem you should then expect the following:

1. An average for the 1000 $\overline{X}$s close to $\mu = 3.5$.
2. A standard deviation for the 1000 $\overline{X}$s close to $\sigma/\sqrt{n} = 1.71/\sqrt{30} = 0.312$.
3. Although our population is not normally distributed, with a sample size as large as this we should expect the 1000 $\overline{X}$s to produce a histogram well in agreement with the normal distribution. [*Note:* The population is not normal since its histogram is flat rather than bell-shaped. In order for a population to be normally distributed, a histogram of the population (and therefore also a histogram of a fairly large sample from the population) must be smooth and bell-shaped. Relative frequencies in the histogram must match areas under the normal distribution.]

You could now start rolling a die to verify all this, or you could use the computer to simulate the rolling of dice and keep track of results. We used a statistical package to simulate the generation of 1000 $\overline{X}$s under these conditions. The 1000 simulated $\overline{X}$s, which behave exactly as $\overline{X}$s computed from the actual rolling of dice, were analyzed. This analysis is shown in Exhibit 7.32. The histogram of the 1000 $\overline{X}$s is bell-shaped, their average, 3.4991, is very close to 3.5, and their standard deviation, 0.3019, is quite close to 0.312.

The use of computers to simulate real-life random processes, in very much the way we have done here, is widespread in industry. Computer simulation models are often developed for complex business situations, and decisions are based largely on the results of those simulation models.

What we have just learned can now be paraphrased a bit more concisely in the following terms. Suppose you are facing a large population of numbers that have mean μ and standard deviation σ. Suppose that from this population you take a random sample of n items and compute their mean, $\overline{X}$. Then this sample mean is a random variable. (Recall that a random variable is a variable that takes on numeric values in a way that cannot be exactly predicted.) We have just learned that if the population is normally distributed or n is large, many values of this random variable $\overline{X}$ have a bell-shaped histogram centered around μ and with a standard deviation $\sigma/\sqrt{n}$. Another way of saying this is to state that *if the population is normal or the sample size is large, then means of random samples coming from*

Exhibit 7.32

Analysis of the 1000 sample means produced by simulation. Notice that the histogram is bell-shaped and that the mean and standard deviation of the 1000 sample means are very close to the values that one could predict theoretically.

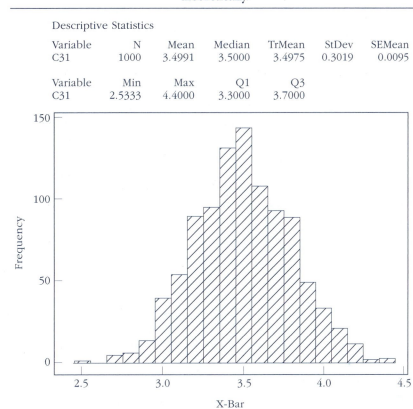

Descriptive Statistics

Variable	N	Mean	Median	TrMean	StDev	SEMean
C31	1000	3.4991	3.5000	3.4975	0.3019	0.0095

Variable	Min	Max	Q1	Q3
C31	2.5333	4.4000	3.3000	3.7000

X-Bar

that population are normally distributed with mean μ and standard deviation $\sigma/\sqrt{n}$. This is the central limit theorem.

How large does the sample size, n, have to be in order for the sample mean to be normally distributed? It depends on the distribution of the population that you are sampling from. For populations that are fairly "well behaved" (unimodal and rather symmetric), sample sizes as small as 4 or 5 will suffice. For very skewed populations, on the other hand, sample sizes of 30, and occasionally even more, are necessary to produce sample means that are approximately normal. In process control work, one often finds that quality characteristics are fairly well behaved, so it is common to use samples of sizes as small as 4 or 5 when the central limit theorem is applied to the development of control charts.

A widely used rule of thumb says that "If n is 30 or more, sample means are normally distributed." This rule is almost always at least nearly true. A sample size of 30 guarantees the approximate normality of sample means for samples coming from most populations. One should realize, however, that the rule is conservative, in the sense that for many well-behaved populations the means of much smaller samples will also be approximately normal.

Example

When filling machines are working properly, the distribution of contents of beer bottles is fairly well behaved. The average bottle content is 12.07 oz., and the standard deviation of the contents is 0.02 oz. A sample of nine bottles is randomly drawn from a production line. If the machine in that line is working properly, how likely is it that the average of the nine contents will be below 12.05 oz.?

Since the distribution of the population of contents is fairly "nice," samples of size $n = 9$ from a machine that is working properly will produce sample means that are approximately normally distributed with mean 12.07 oz. and standard deviation $0.02/\sqrt{9} = 0.0067$ oz. The distribution of these means is shown in Exhibit 7.33. The probability we want is the area under the extreme left tip of this distribution. It can be found through the standardization rule:

$$P[X < 12.05] = P\left[Z < \frac{12.05 - 12.07}{0.0067}\right] = P[Z < -3.00]$$

Entering the standard normal table with 3.00 in the margins, we find inside the value 0.4986. Subtracting this value from 0.5, we obtain the desired probability:

$$P[Z < -3.00] = 0.5 - 0.4986 = 0.0014$$

Exhibit	The distribution of mean contents for random samples of
7.33	size 9 from a population. The contents in the population are fairly well behaved; they have mean 12.07 oz. and standard deviation 0.02 oz.

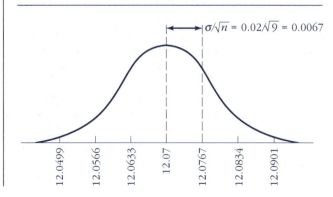

The general reasoning we used here will be applicable to our discussion of the statistical basis for the development of X-bar charts.

The Behavior of Sample Ranges

Consider again a large population of numbers with mean μ and standard deviation σ. Suppose that from this population we draw a random sample of size n, compute the sample range, R, and repeat this procedure many times. There is not much we can say about normality for the distribution of the many ranges we obtain this way. However, something we can say is that both the mean and the standard deviation of the distribution of these ranges are directly proportional to σ, the standard deviation of the population from which we are sampling. We will use these facts in our discussion of the statistical basis for the development of R charts.

The Behavior of Sample Proportions

We just examined the behavior of means of samples drawn from a *large population of numbers.* We learned that, under conditions that are met quite often, the means of those samples are normally distributed. This knowledge is applicable to the control of *variables.*

We will now examine the behavior of samples drawn from a *large population of items of two kinds: some good and some defective.* The knowledge we gain in doing this will be applicable to the control of attributes.

Suppose you are facing a large population of N items, some of them good and some defective. Let us denote by p the proportion of defective items in this population:

$$p = \begin{array}{c} \text{Proportion} \\ \text{defective} \\ \text{in the} \\ \text{population} \end{array} = \frac{\text{Number defective in the population}}{N}$$

Notice that p is a parameter for this population in the same sense that μ and σ are parameters for a large population of numbers.

Suppose that from this population you randomly draw a sample of n items for which you compute

$$p_s = \begin{array}{c} \text{Proportion} \\ \text{defective} \\ \text{in the} \\ \text{sample} \end{array} = \frac{\text{Number defective in the sample}}{n}$$

Suppose you put these items back in the population and repeat this procedure a large number of times, say 1000 times, and this way you get 1000 different values of p_s. Is there anything you can reasonably say about these 1000 values of p_s, even before you actually go through the whole procedure? There are three things we can say, very similar to the four things we said for means of samples coming from a large population of numbers.

1. A histogram of the 1000 values of p_s will be centered around p, the population proportion defective. In other words, the average of the 1000 values of p_s will be close to p. This is an intuitively appealing fact.
2. The standard deviation of the 1000 values of p_s will be close to

$$\sqrt{\frac{p(1-p)}{n}}$$

This says that the spread of the 1000 sample proportions bears some relationship to p and is inversely related to n, the size of each of the 1000 samples.
3. If n is large enough, then the 1000 values of p_s will be approximately normally distributed.

The question arises again: "How large does n have to be?" The answer here depends on the value of p. For values of p close to 0.5, a sample size as small as 20 is sufficient, whereas as p departs substantially from 0.5 in either direction, larger and larger sample sizes are necessary. A widely used rule requires that n and p satisfy the following three conditions:

$$n >= 20$$
$$np >= 5$$
$$n(1-p) >= 5$$

This is an empirical rule that works fairly well in practice. The first condition states that the sample size must always be moderately large, whereas the other two conditions require an even larger sample size when p departs substantially from 0.5, so either p or $1-p$ becomes very small.

Example

You are dealing with a population of 10 million glass lenses, 1 million of which are defective. Suppose that from this population you drew a sample of 100 lenses, computed the proportion of defective lenses in the sample, and put the lenses back in the population. Suppose that you then repeated this procedure 1000 times, thus obtaining 1000 sample proportions of defective lenses. According to what we just discussed, you should expect these 1000 sample proportions to exhibit the following characteristics:

1. The proportion of defective lenses in the population is

$$p = \frac{1,000,000}{10,000,000} = 0.10$$

so the average of the 1000 sample proportions should be close to 0.10.
2. The standard deviation of the 1000 sample proportions should be close to

$$\sqrt{\frac{p(1-p)}{n}} = \sqrt{\frac{0.10(0.90)}{100}} = 0.030$$

3. Since

$$n = 100$$
$$np = 100(0.10) = 10$$
$$n(1 - p) = 100(0.90) = 90$$

all three conditions in the empirical rule are satisfied. Therefore, the 1000 sample proportions should have a histogram that conforms to the normal distribution.

As before, we produced 1000 sample proportions under these conditions by simulation. An analysis of the results is shown in Exhibit 7.34. As expected, the histogram of the 1000 sample proportions is bell-shaped, and frequencies in the histogram conform well with normal probabilities. Also as expected, the average (0.10165) and standard deviation (0.02892) of the 1000 sample proportions are quite close to 0.10 and 0.030.

We can summarize what we learned by saying that *if the proportion of defective items in a population is* p *and if* n, *the size of a random sample from that population, satisfies the following three conditions*

$$n >= 20$$
$$np >= 5$$
$$n(1 - p) >= 5$$

then the proportion of defective items in the sample is approximately normally distributed with mean p *and standard deviation*

$$\sqrt{\frac{p(1-p)}{n}}$$

Exhibit
7.34

Analysis of the 1000 sample proportions produced by simulation. Notice that the histogram is bell-shaped and that the mean and standard deviation of the 1000 sample means are very close to the values that one could predict theoretically.

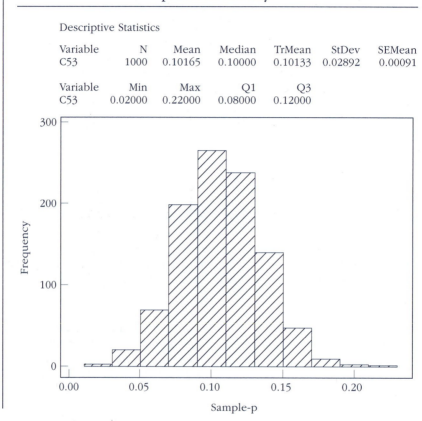

Descriptive Statistics

Variable	N	Mean	Median	TrMean	StDev	SEMean
C53	1000	0.10165	0.10000	0.10133	0.02892	0.00091

Variable	Min	Max	Q1	Q3
C53	0.02000	0.22000	0.08000	0.12000

Example

Under normal operating conditions, a machine produces microchips, 8 percent of which are defective. If 100 microchips are randomly sampled from the output, what is the probability that there are more than 15 defective chips in the sample?

The proportion of defective chips in this population is $p = 0.08$, so for this sample size we have

$$n = 100$$
$$np = 100(0.08) = 8$$
$$n(1 - p) = 100(0.92) = 92$$

The three conditions in the empirical rule are satisfied, so the proportion defective in this sample, p_s, is approximately normal, with mean 0.08 and standard deviation

$$\sqrt{\frac{p(1-p)}{n}} = \sqrt{\frac{0.08(0.92)}{100}} = 0.0271$$

Having more than 15 defective chips in the sample is equivalent to having a proportion defective in the sample that is 0.15 or more, so we want

$$P[p_s >= 0.15]$$

This probability is the shaded area under the distribution of p_s, shown in Exhibit 7.35. To find this probability, we use the standardization rule:

$$P[p_s >= 0.15] = P\left[Z > = \frac{0.15 - 0.08}{0.0271}\right] = P[Z >= 2.58]$$

Entering the margins of the standard normal table with 2.58, we obtain the value 0.4951 inside the table, so the probability we want is

$$P[Z >= 2.58] = 0.5 - 0.4951 = 0.0049$$

The general reasoning we used here will be applicable to our discussion of the statistical basis for the development of p and np charts.

Exhibit 7.35	The distribution of proportions defective for random samples of size 100 from a population where the proportion defective is 0.08.

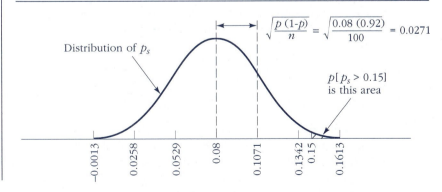

◆ STATISTICAL BASIS FOR THE DEVELOPMENT OF CONTROL CHARTS

In an earlier section (The Development of Control Charts), we gave a general description of how control charts are developed as well as specific formulas for computing the center line and control limits for the control charts that are most widely used. With some further statistical background, we are now in a position to give details on why limits are set that way.

p Charts

Let us return to the monitoring of defective microchips by INTCO which we discussed earlier in this chapter when we first looked at *p* charts. Suppose that INTCO's process is in control and that the long-run proportion defective is 0.10 (in other words, 10 percent of their microchips are defective in the long run). Suppose that every half hour workers in the production line randomly sample 100 chips and inspect them, and that for each sample they compute

$$p_s = \begin{array}{c} \text{Proportion} \\ \text{defective in} \\ \text{the sample} \end{array} = \frac{\text{Number defective in the sample}}{100}$$

What should you expect about the behavior of many of these sample proportions of defective chips? How can you apply to this situation what you just learned about the behavior of samples? Think about it before reading further.

In this example we have

$$n = 100 >= 20$$
$$np = 100(0.10) = 10 >= 5$$
$$n(1 - p) = 100(0.90) = 90 >= 5$$

Since the three conditions in the applicable empirical rule are satisfied, sample proportions of defective chips are approximately normal with mean $p = 0.10$ and standard deviation

$$\sqrt{\frac{p(1 - p)}{n}} = \sqrt{\frac{0.10(0.90)}{100}} = 0.03$$

The distribution of these sample proportions is shown in Exhibit 7.36.

Now suppose that in one of their periodic samples of 100 chips the workers at INTCO find 22 defectives. What should they conclude? Well, the proportion defective in this sample is 0.22. Looking at Exhibit 7.36 and noticing how far out the value 0.22 lies relative to the distribution, they could argue that if the long-run proportion of defective chips were still 0.10, then obtaining a sample as extreme

Exhibit

7.36

The distribution of proportions of defective microchips in random samples of size 100 from a process that is in control and produces 10 percent defective chips in the long run.

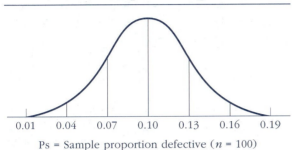

| 0.01 | 0.04 | 0.07 | 0.10 | 0.13 | 0.16 | 0.19 |

Ps = Sample proportion defective (n = 100)

as this would be *extremely* unlikely. In fact, the probability that a normally distributed value lies four or more standard deviations away from the mean in either direction is only 0.00006. The workers could therefore conclude that it seems extremely likely that the proportion of defective chips has gone up from the usual 0.10. In other words, workers at INTCO have found very strong evidence that their process is *out of control*.

How far out in the tail does the sample have to be in order for the evidence the workers find to be strong enough? It has been traditional in the United States to set the limits three standard deviations away from the mean. In doing so, if the distribution of the sample is normal, as it is in this example, and as long as the process is in control, there is a 0.997 probability that a sample will fall inside these *three-sigma* limits. (You can verify this by entering the margins of the standard normal table with 3.00 and finding inside the value 0.4986. Since you are moving away from the mean in both directions, you should multiply this value by 2.) Therefore, the probability of obtaining a sample result outside the limits if the process remains in control is less than one-third of 1 percent.

The limits we just discussed are the control limits for the control chart. It follows from our discussion that if p, the long-run proportion of defective items, is known, then the center line is set at p and the control limits are set at

$$\text{UCL} = p + 3\sqrt{p(1 - p)/n}$$
$$\text{LCL} = p - 3\sqrt{p(1 - p)/n}$$

In cases where p is not known (a vast majority of the cases), $\bar{p}$ is computed from several samples as discussed earlier and used as an estimate of p. Then the center line is set at $\bar{p}$ and the control limits are set at

$$\text{UCL} = \bar{p} + 3\sqrt{\bar{p}(1 - \bar{p})/n}$$
$$\text{LCL} = \bar{p} - 3\sqrt{\bar{p}(1 - \bar{p})/n}$$

To summarize, when setting the control limits this way and as long as the process remains in control, virtually all sample proportions of defective items (99.7 percent of them) will fall between the control limits. On the other hand, sample proportions of defective items outside the control limits provide overwhelming evidence of a process that is out of control. For the 99.7 percent to apply with three sigma limits, we must have a sample size large enough for the three conditions in the empirical rule to be satisfied.

np Charts

The theory behind np charts is very similar to the theory that underlies p charts. Let's start by restating verbatim something we learned in an earlier section, The Behavior of Sample Proportions. If the proportion of defective items in a population is p and if n, the size of a random sample from that population, satisfies the following three conditions:

$$n >= 20$$
$$np >= 5$$
$$n(1 - p) >= 5$$

then the proportion of defective items in the sample is approximately normally distributed with mean p and standard deviation

$$\sqrt{\frac{p(1 - p)}{n}}$$

We should note that np charts deal with the *number* rather than the *proportion* defective in the sample. These two variables are very closely linked, however, since the proportion defective is just the number defective divided by the sample size (a constant). Therefore it takes only minor modifications for our statement from The Behavior of Sample Proportions to apply to the *number* of defective items in a sample:

If the proportion of defective items in a population is p and if n, the size of a random sample from that population, satisfies the following three conditions:

$$n >= 20$$
$$np >= 5$$
$$n(1 - p) >= 5$$

then the *number* of defective items in the sample is approximately normally distributed with mean np and standard deviation

$$\sqrt{np(1 - p)}$$

It follows that in the usual cases where p is not known and $\bar{p}$ is used instead, the center line for the control chart is set at $n\bar{p}$ and three-sigma control limits are set at

$$UCL = n\bar{p} + 3 \sqrt{n\bar{p}(1 - \bar{p})}$$
$$LCL = n\bar{p} - 3 \sqrt{n\bar{p}(1 - \bar{p})}$$

c Charts and u Charts

These charts for number of defects are based on the Poisson distribution, a discrete distribution that we have not discussed. For c charts and u charts the number of defects in the sample is assumed to follow the Poisson distribution, an assumption that is often well approximated in practice. For the Poisson distribution, the mean and the variance always have the same value.

For c charts this value is estimated by $\bar{c}$. Therefore, if the Poisson assumption is satisfied, then the number of defects in a sample is Poisson distributed with estimated mean $\bar{c}$ and estimated standard deviation $\sqrt{\bar{c}}$. Hence the center line for the c chart is set at $\bar{c}$, and the three-sigma control limits are set at

$$UCL = \bar{c} + 3 \sqrt{\bar{c}}$$
$$LCL = \bar{c} - 3 \sqrt{\bar{c}}$$

For u charts the statistical basis is similar.

X-bar Charts

Let us return to the monitoring of the strength of plastic cords produced by PLAS-TEX which we originally discussed in the section Control Charts for Variables. Suppose that the production process is in control, the mean tensile strength is $\mu = 80$ lb., and the standard deviation of tensile strength is $\sigma = 3.6$ lb. Suppose that every hour workers in the production line randomly sample four cord pieces, measure their tensile strength, and compute $\bar{X}$, the mean tensile strength for the sample. What should you expect about the behavior of many of these sample means?

For this process, as for many production processes, the variation in output is likely to be fairly well behaved (unimodal and rather symmetric; in practice, you should actually verify that this is the case). Therefore, according to what we learned earlier, means of samples of size 4 are likely to be approximately normally distributed with mean $\mu = 80$ lb. and standard deviation $\sigma/\sqrt{n} = 3.6/\sqrt{4} = 1.8$ lb. The distribution of these sample means is shown in Exhibit 7.37. Following the same line of thought we followed earlier in this section about three-sigma limits for p charts, we would set the center line for the control chart at 80 lb. and the three-sigma control limits at 74.6 lb. and 85.4 lb.

Exhibit
7.37

The distribution of mean tensile strength in samples of size 4 from a process that is in control. For this process the mean tensile strength is 80 lb. and the standard deviation is 3.6 lb.

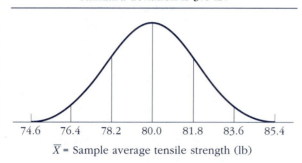

| 74.6 | 76.4 | 78.2 | 80.0 | 81.8 | 83.6 | 85.4 |

$\overline{X}$ = Sample average tensile strength (lb)

For a process with known mean and standard deviation, the reasoning we just followed would lead us to set the center line for the control chart at μ and the three-sigma control limits at

$$\text{UCL} = \mu + 3\,\sigma/\sqrt{n}$$
$$\text{LCL} = \mu - 3\,\sigma/\sqrt{n}$$

When the mean and standard deviation are not known, we collect data as shown in Table 7.10. Notice that this table is very similar to Table 7.4, which we used earlier when we discussed the development of X-bar charts. In Table 7.10, however, there is an additional column on the right with sample standard deviations that is not part of Table 7.4. This column was added so that we can give an intuitive rationale for the way X-bar charts are developed. Given the data in Table 7.10, it would seem natural to estimate μ by $\overline{\overline{X}}$, estimate σ by $\overline{S}$, and set the center line for the control chart at $\overline{\overline{X}}$ and the control limits at

$$\text{UCL} = \overline{\overline{X}} + 3\,\overline{S}/\sqrt{n} \tag{7.1}$$
$$\text{LCL} = \overline{\overline{X}} - 3\,\overline{S}/\sqrt{n} \tag{7.2}$$

However, it is interesting at this point to examine the scatter diagram in Exhibit 7.38. This scatter diagram depicts the relation between the sample ranges and sample standard deviations in Table 7.10. We notice how closely these two variables are related. For the small sample sizes often used in the development of X-bar and R charts ($n = 4$ or $n = 5$), this close relation between sample ranges and sample standard deviations is the norm. Therefore, either of them is a good proxy for the other, so R, which is much easier to compute, is used instead of S in X-bar charts when the sample size is small. $\overline{R}$ is then used instead of $\overline{S}$ as an estimator of σ. Notice from the scatter diagram or from Table 7.10 that the R in each sam-

Table 7.10

Tensile Strengths for 25 Samples of Plastic Cord Produced by PLASTEX

SAMPLE NUMBER	SAMPLE VALUES (TENSILE STRENGTH)				SAMPLE AVERAGE (X-BAR)	SAMPLE RANGE (R)	SAMPLE STANDARD DEVIATION (S)
1	75	78	85	81	79.75	10	4.27
2	83	84	76	80	80.75	8	3.59
3	81	82	79	74	79.00	8	3.56
4	77	81	89	79	81.50	12	5.26
5	79	76	82	78	78.75	6	2.50
6	83	77	85	85	82.50	8	3.79
7	87	79	83	75	81.00	12	5.16
8	80	85	76	76	79.25	9	4.27
9	86	79	82	80	81.75	7	3.10
10	74	82	80	84	80.00	10	4.32
11	80	74	75	81	77.50	7	3.51
12	76	81	79	78	78.50	5	2.08
13	77	86	77	84	81.00	9	4.69
14	83	78	72	86	79.75	14	6.13
15	79	85	75	78	79.25	10	4.19
16	81	84	82	81	82.00	3	1.41
17	80	84	81	81	81.50	4	1.73
18	80	77	83	77	79.25	6	2.87
19	78	75	74	85	78.00	11	4.97
20	79	78	79	80	79.00	2	0.82
21	88	77	81	72	79.50	16	6.76
22	79	74	82	80	78.75	8	3.40
23	84	79	84	81	82.00	5	2.45
24	75	78	80	77	77.50	5	2.08
25	79	85	82	85	82.75	6	2.87

Averages $\overline{\overline{X}} = 80.02$ $\overline{R} = 8.04$ $\overline{S} = 3.59$

Exhibit
7.38

Scatter diagram for the ranges and standard deviations of the 25 samples in Table 7.10.

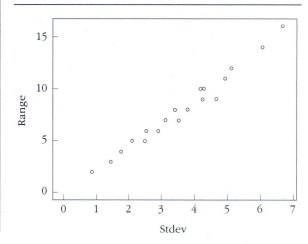

ple seems to be about twice as large as S. In fact, for samples of size $n = 4$, as we are using in this example, R is 2.059 times as large as S on average in the long run. The long-run average ratio of R to S depends on the sample size one uses. This ratio is denoted d_2, and its value is given in Table 7.11 for commonly used sample sizes. Substituting $\bar{R}/d_2$ for $\bar{S}$ in Eqs. (7.1) and (7.2), we get the following three-sigma control limits for the X-bar chart:

$$\text{UCL} = \bar{\bar{X}} + 3\ (\bar{R}/d_2)/\sqrt{n} \qquad (7.3)$$
$$\text{LCL} = \bar{\bar{X}} - 3\ (\bar{R}/d_2)/\sqrt{n} \qquad (7.4)$$

Table
7.11

Control Chart Factors

SUBGROUP SIZE	A_2	D_3	D_4	d_2	d_3
2	1.880	0.000	3.267	1.128	0.853
3	1.023	0.000	2.574	1.693	0.888
4	0.729	0.000	2.282	2.059	0.880
5	0.577	0.000	2.114	2.326	0.864
6	0.483	0.000	2.004	2.534	0.848
7	0.419	0.076	1.924	2.704	0.833

For our example, with $X = 80.02$, $\overline{R} = 8.04$ and $d_2 = 2.059$, the control limits are

$$UCL = 80.02 + 3 \cdot (8.04/2.059)/\sqrt{4} = 85.88$$
$$LCL = 80.02 - 3 \cdot (8.04/2.059)/\sqrt{4} = 74.16$$

These are the same values that we obtained for the control limits earlier in this chapter. However, if you compare Eqs. (7.1) and (7.2) with the formulas we used for developing control limits for X-bar charts, you will notice that they are different. Both types of formulas are commonly used in industry and in the literature, and it is easy to reconcile them. Through simple algebraic manipulation, Eqs. (7.3) and (7.4) may be rewritten as follows:

$$UCL = \overline{\overline{X}} + (3/d_2 \sqrt{n})\,\overline{R} \tag{7.5}$$
$$LCL = \overline{\overline{X}} - (3/d_2 \sqrt{n})\,\overline{R} \tag{7.6}$$

The factor in parentheses, $3/d_2\sqrt{n}$, depends only on n, the sample size we are using, and is denoted A_2. Substituting A_2 for the factor in parentheses in Eqs. (7.5) and (7.6), we obtain the formulas presented in the section The Development of Control Charts. We remind you that values of A_2 for commonly used sample sizes are given in Table 7.11. Also remember that the R chart should be developed before the X-bar chart.

R Charts

We learned earlier that both the mean and the standard deviation of the distribution of the sample range, R, are proportional to the standard deviation of the population that the sample came from. More precisely, the expected value and standard deviation of R are

$$E[R] = d_2\,\sigma \tag{7.7}$$
$$S[R] = d_3\,\sigma \tag{7.8}$$

where d_2 and d_3 are constants that depend on the size of the sample. Values of d_2 and d_3 for selected sample sizes are given in Table 7.11.

Equation (7.7) may be rewritten

$$\sigma = E[R]/d_2 \tag{7.9}$$

so if one knows $E[R]$ one can use Eq. (7.9) to find out the value of σ. It makes good intuitive sense that $\overline{R}$, the average of many ranges all computed from samples of size n from a given population, is a good estimator of $E[R]$, the expected value of the distribution of R for a sample of the same size from that same population. Therefore, again referring to Eq. (7.9), we can see that an *estimate* of σ, which we will denote $\hat{\sigma}$, can be obtained as follows:

$$\hat{\sigma} = \overline{R}/d_2 \tag{7.10}$$

We may now substitute $\hat{\sigma}$ for σ in the right-hand side of Eq. (7.8) to obtain an estimate of $S[R]$, which we will denote $\widehat{S[R]}$:

$$\widehat{S[R]} = d_3\,\hat{\sigma} = d_3\,\overline{R}/d_2$$

In developing the control chart for R, we use $\overline{R}$, our estimator of $E[R]$, as the center line, and the three-sigma control limits are computed as follows:

$$\text{UCL} = \overline{R} + 3\,\widehat{S[R]} = \overline{R} + 3\,d_3\,(\overline{R}/d_2) = \left[1 + 3\frac{d_3}{d_2}\right]\overline{R} \tag{7.11}$$

$$\text{LCL} = \overline{R} + 3\,\widehat{S[R]} = \overline{R} - 3\,d_3\,(\overline{R}/d_2) = \left[1 - 3\frac{d_3}{d_2}\right]\overline{R} \tag{7.12}$$

The factors in brackets on the right-hand sides of Eqs. (7.11) and (7.12) are functions of subgroup size only and are denoted D_4 and D_3, respectively. Substituting D_4 and D_3 for the factors in brackets, we obtain the formulas we presented in The Development of Control Charts. We remind you that values of D_4 and D_3 for commonly used sample sizes are given in Table 7.11.

Control Chart for Individual Measurements

In order to understand the rationale for setting the center line and control limits for the control chart for individual measurements, it is instructive to compare the procedures followed here with those that are followed for X-bar charts.

First, we notice that in both cases we use the average of all our observations as the center line. Second, we recall from Eqs. (7.3) and (7.4) that the control limits for the X-bar chart may be written as

$$\overline{\overline{X}} \pm 3\,(\overline{R}/d_2)/\sqrt{n} \tag{7.13}$$

This same formula is used in the chart for individual measurements. Since our samples are of size 1, n must be assigned the value 1. Because we are computing moving ranges from two observations, we must use $d_2 = 1.128$ for a sample of size 2 from Table 7.11. Substituting these two values in (7.13), we obtain

$$\overline{X} \pm 3\,(\overline{R}/1.128) = \overline{X} \pm 2.66\,\overline{R}$$

which is the expression for the control limits we used in The Development of Control Charts.

Moving Range Control Chart

The formulas for the center line and control limits for the moving range chart are the same as those for the regular R chart. The center line is set at $\overline{R}$, and the control limits are set at

$$UCL = D_4 \overline{R}$$
$$LCL = D_3 \overline{R}$$

Since we are computing moving ranges from two observations, we must use $D_4 = 3.267$ and $D_3 = 0$ for a sample of size 2 from Table 7.11. These were the values used in The Development of Control Charts.

References

Statistical process control is a fairly complex and technical area, and there are many books with extensive materials on the development and use of control charts. Among the best, we feel, are those by Grant and Leavenworth (1988) and Wheeler and Chambers (1986). Grant and Leavenworth's book is a classic, first published in 1946 and now in its sixth edition. Wheeler and Chambers's book is excellent and very readable.

Wheeler (1993) has also written a less technical book on statistical process control, from which we have reprinted a very interesting example as a case at the end of this chapter. We also recommend this book very strongly as further reading on the subject.

◆ Summary

Control charts, developed by Walter Shewhart, are the battlehorse of statistical process control and allow you to know whether special variation is present in the output of a process. If that is the case, it should be found and eliminated. If only common variation is present, tinkering with the process will make the problem worse because additional variation will be induced that way. Control charts are among Ishikawa's seven basic tools for quality improvement.

Common variation is the responsibility of management and according to Deming, accounts for about 85 percent of problems. Special variation, which accounts for the remaining 15 percent, is the responsibility of workers. They are best acquainted with the process and, thus, best equipped to find potential causes.

Control charts are used almost exclusively in quality improvement but could profitably be used in many other areas. Managers, government officials, news reporters, and many others would make better decisions and have better opinions if they learned to distinguish between common and special variation.

◆ Key Terms

Seven basic tools
Common causes of variation
Inherent, controlled, chance, or common variation
In statistical control
Uncontrolled, assignable, or special variation
Out of control
Special causes or assignable causes
Control chart
Statistical process control
Control limits
Center line
Variable
Attribute
Defect
Defective item

p chart, control chart for proportion defective
control chart for fraction defective
np chart or control chart for number defective
c chart
u chart
X-bar chart
R chart
Chart for individual measurements
Moving range chart
Descriptive statistics
Inferential statistics or statistical inference
Simple random sample
Enumerative studies
Analytical studies

A priori or classical probability
Relative frequency
Subjective probability
Random variable
Probability distribution
Expectation, expected value, or mean (of a random variable)
Variance and standard deviation (of a random variable)
Discrete random variable
Continuous random variable
Normal distribution
Standard normal distribution
Central limit theorem

◆ Assignments

1. Small electrical assemblies are produced in lots of size 144. The table below shows the number of defective assemblies in 24 lots that were sampled, each at the end of a 30-minute period, to control the process.

Lot Number	Number Defective	Lot Number	Number Defective
1	3	13	8
2	2	14	5
3	0	15	0
4	1	16	1
5	3	17	2
6	4	18	4

LOT NUMBER	NUMBER DEFECTIVE	LOT NUMBER	NUMBER DEFECTIVE
7	5	19	2
8	2	20	0
9	1	21	6
10	3	22	3
11	3	23	1
12	0	24	0

a. Develop a p chart for this process. Does the process appear to be in control?

b. Develop an np chart for the process and contrast it with the p chart you developed in part (a). What are the differences and the similarities?

2. The table below shows weekly data on the total number of shipments and the number of late shipments for a mail-order company.

WEEK	TOTAL SHIPMENTS	LATE SHIPMENTS	WEEK	TOTAL SHIPMENTS	LATE SHIPMENTS
1	915	36	11	910	37
2	255	8	12	933	30
3	616	28	13	760	18
4	321	8	14	685	29
5	233	7	15	522	21
6	610	22	16	540	17
7	645	37	17	480	19
8	532	21	18	703	37
9	707	18	19	871	42
10	513	23	20	959	40

Develop an appropriate control chart for this data. Does the process seem to be in control?

3. A bank is analyzing its savings transactions. Use the data below to determine whether the proportion of transactions that involve savings accounts appears to be in control.

DAY	TOTAL	SAVINGS	DAY	TOTAL	SAVINGS
1	635	128	14	625	133
2	725	133	15	781	190
3	561	108	16	706	119
4	650	165	17	645	135
5	685	105	18	704	148
6	823	152	19	641	120

	TRANSACTIONS			TRANSACTIONS	
DAY	TOTAL	SAVINGS	DAY	TOTAL	SAVINGS
7	771	181	20	720	124
8	650	130	21	636	131
9	731	173	22	745	121
10	625	134	23	820	153
11	553	125	24	730	121
12	685	159	25	599	131
13	772	98	26	623	115

4. A process is currently being monitored with a p chart with the center line at 0.125, sample size 200, UCL at 0.195, and LCL at 0.055. What are the center line and control limits for the equivalent np chart?

5. The following table shows data on defects in electronic organizers manufactured by COSCO.

ORGANIZER NUMBER	NUMBER OF DEFECTS	ORGANIZER NUMBER	NUMBER OF DEFECTS
1	4	15	2
2	1	16	5
3	6	17	0
4	0	18	4
5	3	19	5
6	7	20	1
7	0	21	0
8	4	22	6
9	3	23	2
10	1	24	7
11	4	25	11
12	7	26	2
13	5	27	1
14	4	28	4

Develop an appropriate control chart to determine whether this process seems to be stable over time.

6. A chain of office-supply stores has the following on-the-job accident record for the past 18 months:

MONTH	EXPOSURE IN THOUSANDS OF WORKER-HOURS	NUMBER OF ACCIDENTS
March 1993	121	10
April	117	8

MONTH	EXPOSURE IN THOUSANDS OF WORKER-HOURS	NUMBER OF ACCIDENTS
May	126	9
June	125	3
July	126	18
August	125	13
September	119	6
October	111	6
November	110	12
December	108	8
January 1994	109	6
February	107	17
March	141	11
April	128	3
May	136	10
June	138	24
July	137	13
August	139	27
September	134	16
October	130	13
November	128	12
December	121	15
January 1995	121	5
February	120	10

Develop the appropriate control chart to verify whether there are assignable causes for the variation in the number of accidents over time.

7. Twenty-five samples of size 4 yielded the following coded data:

SUBGROUP NUMBER	X1	X2	X3	X4
1	54	62	40	76
2	68	62	93	99
3	69	21	68	105
4	90	81	76	53
5	60	42	53	37
6	70	75	41	54
7	80	81	63	95
8	37	77	56	62
9	80	65	82	45
10	61	60	55	35

SUBGROUP NUMBER	X1	X2	X3	X4
11	70	42	95	90
12	75	97	82	99
13	52	61	72	88
14	44	35	38	31
15	61	52	37	71
16	36	54	43	61
17	48	71	38	41
18	56	39	75	68
19	78	66	57	93
20	31	38	34	45
21	94	75	36	51
22	60	43	36	54
23	68	99	99	92
24	73	38	36	68
25	62	36	79	55

Develop the appropriate control charts for this process.

8. Twenty-four hourly temperatures for a climate-controlled room are shown below. Develop a moving range chart and a chart for individual measurements for the data and determine whether temperature appears to be in control during this 24-hour period.

TIME	TEMPERATURE (DEG C)	TIME	TEMPERATURE (DEG C)
4 am	18.6	4 pm	19.2
5 am	18.5	5 pm	18.1
6 am	18.3	6 pm	18.4
7 am	19.4	7 pm	18.7
8 am	18.3	8 pm	18.5
9 am	19.0	9 pm	18.6
10 am	18.5	10 pm	18.8
11 am	18.3	11 pm	18.5
noon	18.5	midnight	18.3
1 pm	18.4	1 am	18.2
2 pm	18.9	2 am	18.4
3 pm	19.5	3 am	18.5

9. What type of control chart would you use to control the following process?

LOT NUMBER	NUMBER INSPECTED	NUMBER OF UNITS OUTSIDE SPECS
1	1050	26
2	685	53

LOT NUMBER	NUMBER INSPECTED	NUMBER OF UNITS OUTSIDE SPECS
3	139	32
4	72	23
5	210	30

10. What type of control chart would you use to control the following process?

DAY	BOLTS OF CLOTH PRODUCED	NUMBER OF DEFECTS
1	40	28
2	42	35
3	65	30
4	44	36
5	44	30

11. What type of control chart would you use to control the following process?

BATCH	HARDNESS (CODED)
1	0.403
2	0.408
3	0.406
4	0.405
5	0.409

12. Juicy Fruit produces bottled fruit juice with six bottling machines. A sample of 200 days yielded the following data:

Number of machine failures	0	1	2	3	4
Number of days observed	74	68	32	20	6

a. Use these data to develop an estimate of the probability distribution of the random variable X = the number of machine failures on a given day. Draw a graph of the distribution.

b. Find the expected value of X and draw it on the graph.

c. Find the variance and standard deviation of X. Relate the standard deviation to the graph. Is it roughly the long-run average distance to $E(X)$?

d. What is the probability of at least two machine failures on any given day?

e. What is the probability of more than two machine failures on any given day?

13. By rolling two fair dice many times, you can determine that the probability of their sum being either 5, 6, or 7 is approximately 0.42. Would it be to your advantage to play the following game?

You will pay the house $100, and then two fair dice will be rolled. If their sum is 5, 6, or 7 you will get back $220 (the $100 you paid plus another $120); otherwise you will lose the $100 you paid.

14. What is the minimum amount you would have to get back from the house in Assignment 13 in order for the game to be advantageous to you?

15. Find the area under the standard normal curve between these values:
    a. 0 and 0.6
    b. 0 and 1.63
    c. 0 and −1.25
    d. −0.34 and 2.03
    e. 0.85 and 1.33
    f. −0.62 and −1.79

16. Find the following areas under the standard normal curve:
    a. To the right of 0.89
    b. To the left of −1.24
    c. To the right of −1.49
    d. To the left of 1.96

17. Find a value k such that
    a. $P(Z > k) = 0.10$
    b. $P(Z < k) = 0.30$
    c. $P(Z > k) = 0.80$
    d. $P(-k < Z < k) = 0.90$

18. A normally distributed random variable X has mean 100 and standard deviation 30. Find the following probabilities:
    a. $P(100 < X < 115)$
    b. $P(80 < X < 130)$
    c. $P(X > 145)$
    d. $P(X < 120)$

19. The time to first failure of an electronic component is approximately normally distributed with a mean of three years and a standard deviation of six months. If this electronic component has a 24-month warranty, what percentage of them will require repairs under warranty?

20. The amounts dispensed by an automatic bottle-filling machine are approximately normal with mean 12.07 oz. and a standard deviation of 0.05 oz. What percentage of the bottles filled by the machine will contain at least 12 oz.?

21. The standard deviation of a normally distributed variable is 10. What must the mean be if 3 percent of the distribution must be less than 60?

22. A normally distributed variable has mean 150. What must the standard deviation be in order for 90 percent of the distribution to be more than 110?

23. The time to first failure of an electronic component is approximately normally distributed with a mean of three years and a standard deviation of six months. This electronic component has a 24-month warranty. If the mean time to first failure remains the same, what reduction in the standard deviation of the time to first failure is necessary so that only 1 percent of the components will require repairs under warranty?

24. The amounts dispensed by an automatic can-filling machine are approximately normally distributed, centered around whatever value the machine is set to and with a standard deviation of 0.05 oz. How should the machine be set in order for 95 percent of the cans to contain at least 16 oz.?

25. Dairy Sun produces half-gallon cartons of milk. State regulations require that at least 95 percent of cartons labeled half gallon contain at least 64 fl. oz. The fillings are normally distributed, centered around whatever value the filling machines are set to. If the standard deviation of the fillings is 0.2 fl. oz., what average value should the machines be set to in order to comply with state regulations?

26. Refer to Assignment 25. Dairy Sun could buy new filling machines that are much more accurate. The standard deviation of fillings with the new machines would be 0.02 fl. oz., one-tenth of the standard deviation with the present machines. The new fillings would also be normally distributed.
    a. What average value should the new machines be set to in order to comply with state regulations?
    b. If the cost to Dairy Sun of a fluid ounce of milk is 1 cent, and total annual sales are 50 million cartons, what are the expected annual savings from the purchase of the new machines? (These savings and other factors are, of course, to be weighed against the cost of the new machines.)

27. The breaking strength of the grocery bags used by Maxi Markets is normally distributed with mean 15 lb. and a standard deviation of 2 lb.
    a. If a single bag is randomly selected, what is the probability that its breaking strength is below 14 lb.?
    b. If a random sample of three bags is selected, what is the probability that the average breaking strength of the three bags is below 14 lb.?

28. Diamond Industries manufactures and sells artificial diamonds in boxes of 100. The diamonds have a mean weight of 3 carats and a standard deviation of 0.4 carat. Each box contains a random sample from Diamond Industries' output. Newton Manufacturing Company has just purchased one box. What is the probability that the average weight of the diamonds in this box is between 2.95 and 3.05 carats?

29. A can-filling machine dispenses fills that are normally distributed with mean 12.1 fl.oz. and a standard deviation of 0.2 fl.oz. If a random sample of nine

cans is selected by a state inspector, what is the probability that the average fill is below 12 fl.oz.?

30. An operator in Nashua Engines checks the output of an automatic machine that manufactures piston rings. The machine has been set up so that the rings have an external diameter of 600 mm. The outside diameters are normally distributed and have a standard deviation of 0.03 mm. Every hour this operator randomly selects four rings, measures their outside diameters, and computes the average of the four diameters. If the average is below 599.96 mm or above 600.04 mm, the operator resets the machine. If the mean external diameter of the rings being produced is actually 600 mm, what is the probability that the operator will reset the machine based on what he observes in a sample?

31. The time to failure of an electronic component has mean 4000 hours and standard deviation 500 hours. If a batch of 50 randomly selected components is sold to a customer, what is the probability that the average life of the units in the batch will exceed 3900 hours?

32. If 45 percent of voters in the state are voting for a candidate, what is the probability that in a random exit poll of 200 voters across the state, over half of those polled have voted for the candidate?

33. Eight percent of 50-lb. bags of fertilizer manufactured by Agro Biz are underweight. If you buy 100 of these bags, what is the probability that over 10 percent of them will be underweight?

34. Twelve percent of the pieces produced by a machine are defective. If a random sample of 200 pieces is taken, what is the probability that there are at least 10 percent defective pieces in the sample?

35. A state has an actual unemployment rate of 8 percent. An economic adviser to the governor monitors the unemployment rate monthly through a random sample of 500 potential workers. What is the probability that the monthly sample will show an unemployment rate of 6 percent or less?

C a s e   S t u d y

We have pointed out in the introduction to this chapter that control charts are used almost exclusively within the realm of quality management, although they could be profitably used in many other settings. "Understanding the Trade Deficits" gives us an excellent example of their use in a different setting.

It is essential to understand the difference between common and special variation so as not to unduly react to the common but duly react to the special. This is the core of Deming's message at the beginning of this chapter.

This case was reprinted from an excellent book by Donald Wheeler, *Understanding Variation: The Key to Managing Chaos*, which we strongly recommend as further reading in statistical process control.

Understanding the Trade Deficits

BY DONALD J. WHEELER

U.S. Trade Deficits for the first ten months of 1987 are given in Figure 1. In this period the deficit got worse (increased) relative to the preceding month six times, and it improved (decreased) only three times. While the year started with a deficit of $10.7 billion, by October this had worsened to a deficit of $16 billion. Surely this is justification for gloom and doom.

As each of these values was reported in the news media, they would be invariably ac-

companied by statements like "the U.S. trade balance deficit increased (or decreased) last month to a value of—billion dollars." According to the news, the trade balance is always increasing or decreasing. It hardly ever stays the same. But how much of this churning around is signal, and how much of it is just noise?

We begin by placing the data for 1987 on a control chart. The use of one year's worth of data is essentially arbitrary, but we have historically used the calendar to arbitrarily sub-divide all sorts of time series, and we shall, no doubt, continue to do so in the future. There is nothing magic about the use of a year's worth of data.

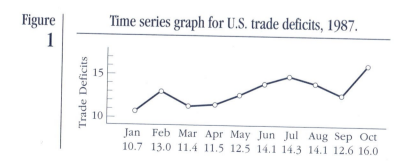

Figure 1 | Time series graph for U.S. trade deficits, 1987.

	Jan	Feb	Mar	Apr	May	Jun	Jul	Aug	Sep	Oct
Trade Deficits	10.7	13.0	11.4	11.5	12.5	14.1	14.3	14.1	12.6	16.0

Understanding the Trade Deficits (Continued)

The average deficit for 1987 was $12.75 billion. Using the technique which is described in the next chapter, it can be seen that, based on the amount of month-to-month variation, the deficit could vary from 8.32 billion to 17.18 billion without representing a real departure from the average of 12.75 billion.

The chart in Figure 2 shows no evidence of a sustained trend. The deficits are not systematically getting better, nor are they systematically getting worse. For the year as a whole, this chart shows no clear-cut evidence of change. Some months *appear* to be better than others, but this chart indicates that it will be a waste to analyze any one month to see what is different from preceding months. One should treat *all* the months of 1987 as if they came from the same system.

The data for 1988 are shown in Figure 3 below. These values could be plotted against the limits shown in Figure 2.8 above. This is done in Figures 4 and 5.

Figure 4 shows that by March of 1988 there was definite evidence of an improve-

Figure 2 — Control chart for monthly U.S. trade deficits in 1987.

Figure 3

Monthly U.S. Trade Deficits, 1988 ($ billion).

	JAN	FEB	MAR	APR	MAY	JUN	JUL	AUG	SEP	OCT	NOV	DEC
1988	10.0	11.4	7.9	9.5	8.0	11.8	10.5	11.2	9.2	10.1	10.4	10.5

Figure 4 — Control chart for U.S. trade deficits, 1987–early 1988.

Understanding the Trade Deficits (Continued)

Figure
5

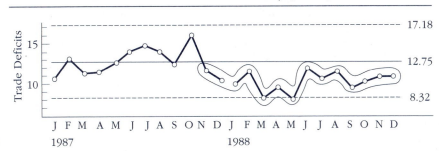

Control chart for U.S. trade deficits, 1987–1988.

ment in the deficit. The March value is below the lower limit of 8.32.

Before a single month can be said to signal a change in the time series, that single value must go beyond one of the two limits. This happens in March of 1988. Now that one has definite evidence of a change, how does one interpret the chart? One method is to look at the sequence of points adjacent to the out-of-control point which are are also on the same side of the central line as the out-of-control point. This sequence is shown in Figure 5. The interpretation of this sequence could be expressed as follows. A change is clearly indicated in March of 1988—it may have begun as early as November of 1987—and it continued throughout the rest of 1988.

Thus, there is definite evidence that the trade deficit improved during 1988, com-

pared with 1987. One could now re-compute limits for 1988 and use them to evaluate further monthly values for signs of improvement or deterioration.

CASE QUESTIONS

1. Compute the center line and control limits for the trade deficit data for 1987. Verify that you get the values shown in Figure 2.
2. Provide three examples from everyday life where people react to common variation as if it were special variation. (Think of business managers, government officials, and, particularly, news media.)

◆ Bibliography

AT&T. *Statistical Quality Control Handbook*. Indianapolis, Ind.: Western Electric Co., 1956. Available from the American Society for Quality Control.

Deming, W. Edwards. *Out of the Crisis*. Cambridge, Mass.: MIT Center for Advanced Engineering Study, 1986.

Grant, Eugene L. and Richard S. Leavenworth. *Statistical Quality Control*. 6th ed. New York: McGraw-Hill Book Co., 1988.

Ishikawa, Kaoru. *Guide to Quality Control*. 2nd rev. ed. Tokyo: Asian Productivity Organization, 1982.

Ishikawa, Kaoru. *What Is Total Quality Control? The Japanese Way*. Englewood Cliffs, N.J.: Prentice-Hall, 1985.

Wheeler, Donald J. and David S. Chambers. *Understanding Statistical Process Control*. Knoxville, Tenn.: Statistical Process Controls, 1986.

Wheeler, Donald J. *Understanding Variation: The Key to Managing Chaos*. Knoxville, Tenn.: Statistical Process Controls, 1993.

Continual Improvement: Some Advanced Tools

◆ ◆ ◆

*W*hen the soldiers of Desert Storm crouched in the sand to scout Iraqi troops, they took their night-vision goggles for granted. But their advantage hadn't come easily. In 1989, the manufacturer, ITT's Electro-Optical Products Division, had struggled with leaky seals on the goggles' phosphor screens. ITT fixed the problem—which was due to variations in a ceramic sealing compound—with the help of a design technique pioneered by Genichi Taguchi, one of Japan's quality masters.

Miller and Woodruff, Business Week (1991, p. 24)

◆ INTRODUCTION

Chapter 6 introduced you to basic tools for continual improvement. Later in that chapter you learned how to solve problems and achieve improvement by means of the seven-step method, which requires use of the basic tools in an integrated way. In Chapter 7 you learned how to use control charts for detecting the presence of special variation. The methods of Chapter 6 are used to eliminate special variation and bring processes into statistical control. This state of statistical control has several important advantages; including the predictability of process output and the minimization of costs with the current system. In Chapter 7 you also learned another extremely important concept: management should not react to common variation as if it were special variation.

In this chapter we discuss several other tools, by and large of a more sophisticated nature, that are also used in continually improving products and services. Among them are experimental design techniques such as those used by ITT to fix their problems with leaky goggles, and also affinity diagrams, electronic brainstorming, the assessment of process capability, and Taguchi's loss function.

◆ ENHANCING THE SEVEN-STEP METHOD

The seven-step method we discussed in Chapter 6 usually results in incremental improvements. Generally, a quality improvement team is assembled to go over the seven steps when management observes that a system is no longer performing the way it should and is seeking some solutions. In these cases, the problem statement is clearly defined, and management is just taking a *reactive approach* to an unacceptable situation.

When management adopts a *proactive approach* to problem solving, the problem statement is not immediately evident to everyone:

- A company suspects that its strategy needs to be reviewed. A team is assembled to identify weaknesses and recommend improvements.
- A manager wants to define his department's mission and the scope of its responsibilities.
- A product manager seeks to gather some new insights into the needs of the customer to suggest product improvements.

In each of these cases, there is no clear problem. A marketing manager describing the weaknesses she sees in the corporate strategy may list a number of them from her perspective. The chief financial officer may have a different list, and the operating manager would have a third perspective. Often the data they present are qualitative and based on events they have experienced. The team then has to structure this information and arrive at a consensus.

The process consists of two distinct stages. The first is to generate ideas and communicate them to the rest of the team. The second is to assemble these ideas into a coherent form so that priorities can be determined.

One technique that has been touted over the years as an effective means of generating ideas is **brainstorming.** The team members assemble and, with the help of a facilitator, quickly generate several ideas. In order to encourage the flow of ideas, the facilitator specifically discourages evaluation of the ideas until all ideas have been recorded. Proponents of brainstorming are enthusiastic about the number of ideas generated. The concept has great intuitive appeal—if several people get together, exchange ideas freely, and build on them, there should be a significant synergy.

Recent studies, however, have shown that the process may not be as effective as claimed (see, for example, Mullen et al., 1991). Several groups were studied as brainstorming groups and as groups of individuals and were asked to generate ideas on their own. Invariably, the groups of individuals generated more useful and "better" ideas. In addition, although brainstorming generates ideas, it is not always effective in providing a coherent structure to them. Two enhancements of traditional brainstorming try to overcome these deficiencies:

- The affinity diagram or structured brainstorming
- Electronic brainstorming

The **affinity diagram or structured brainstorming** is based on the work of Jiro Kawakita, a Japanese anthropologist. Kawakita needed a way to assemble qualitative sociological data. TQM practitioners noted the similarity of his sociological data to the qualitative data in businesses and adopted the technique. Companies in the United States find it useful in building consensus.

Today the affinity diagram is one of the *seven management tools* or *seven new tools* for proactive problem solving. Japanese executives have used these tools since the mid-1970s for strategic planning and at lower managerial levels. Some of the tools are new, some are old. Some were originally developed in the United States and some in Japan. They were first introduced in the United States in the late 1980s by Michael Brassard (1989). In addition to the affinity diagram, the seven management tools include the *relations diagram,* the *systematic diagram,* the *matrix diagram, matrix data analysis,* the *process decision program chart,* and the *arrow diagram method.*

Electronic brainistorming uses groupware and concepts developed by J. Nunamaker. Later, other companies created software to make meetings more efficient as well as to enable meetings between people who were dispersed over a large geographical area. The most well known of these is Lotus Notes. Kirkpatrick (1992) observes that more companies are relying on groupware to achieve flatter and more team-focused organizations.

Developing an Affinity Diagram

Exhibit 8.1a shows an example of a completed affinity diagram (see Exhibit 8.1b for an overview). In this case, a group of six faculty members and two administrators were assembled to identify the weaknesses of the existing system for advising students. Early on, it was clear that the discussion would require several meetings. Prior attempts to discuss the advising system had resulted in fruitless discussions in meetings spread throughout the academic year. Even though it would have been ideal to gather everyone for an extended meeting and reach a conclusion, this was not practical. In all, the process took 10 hours (five meetings of two hours each).

We next describe the five standard phases in the development of an affinity diagram. Following the generic description of each phase, we illustrate it with the analysis of the student advisement system.

Phase 1: Select the theme.

The theme should be within the authority of the team to effect, and it should be tied to the mission of the organization. So the first step is to identify the mission and determine whether the team is suited to the task. Once this is established, a question needs to be posed as a stimulus for the brainstorming. It is often best to state the question in terms of a weakness. For example, what are the weaknesses of our current product offerings?

***The advising team first came up with a mission statement for the advising system: "Students bear the ultimate responsibility for their own academic success.

The purpose of the faculty advising system is to help students develop intellectually through informed, accurate, and sustained advice about their academic experience." Before proceeding, this mission statement had to be accepted by the vice president and the Faculty Review Board. Once they agreed, the team formulated the theme for the affinity diagram as "What are the weaknesses of the existing advising system?"

Phase 2: Brainstorming.

In this phase team participants generate a list of their ideas. The ideas are written on cards so that they can be moved around to form groups later in the process. This phase usually starts with a brief discussion of the issue. Then each person responds to the theme with several statements, each on a card, posting them so that others can see them. During this period there is no discussion of the cards. Once all the cards have been posted each statement is discussed until everyone in the team understands it. This is called scrubbing. During scrubbing it is critical to make sure all statements are factually based. Exhibit 8.2 provides some examples of opinion-based statements and the "scrubbed"statement.

***The advising team discussed the issue and then broke up with instructions to poll other students and faculty. The comments were sent to the team leader by e-mail or campus mail. The team leader and another member of the team edited all of the labels for clarity and rewrote them on Post-It notes. Unclear comments were clarified by calling the author. If a comment contained more than one thought, it was rewritten on two labels. The author's name was added to each label. When the team met next to "scrub" the labels, the authors provided explanations as needed.

Phase 3: Grouping.

The team collectively groups the cards. The tendency is to place the cards in logical groups. If the team is searching for a new insight, it tries to group according to underlying themes or images. The first-level groups are in turn collected to form the next level of groups, until there are about six distinct upper-level groups.

***Once the labels were "scrubbed," the Post-It notes were attached to a large sheet on a wall. Every member of the team got up and started to group the labels. Some labels represented distinct thoughts and were placed in their own category. The first level of grouping resulted in 15 groups. The team next created titles for these groups. This process was repeated for two more levels, finally resulting in five upper-level groups. Participation levels of individuals varied significantly during this period. Certain people were more active when forming the groups; others were more active when creating the labels.

Exhibit
8.1a

Affinity diagram for exploring weaknesses in the student advisement system. (detail.)

ADMINISTRATIVE STRUCTURE
AND SUPPORT NEEDS
IMPROVEMENT

ADMINISTRATION OF THE
PROGRAM NEEDS WORK

- A -

THE ADVISING PROGRAM
HAS TECHNICAL/
MECHANICAL PROBLEMS.

* Some advisers do not know
how to handle a drop situation.

* Advisers are not aware of
Registration seats available
during Registration period.

* There are no mechanicals
for advisers to learn of student
progress.

* "Advise" program on the
VAX is too slow.

- B -

THE PROGRAM
IS NOT RUN
BY FACULTY.

- C -

RELATIONSHIP OF
ADVISING PROGRAM AND
ADMINISTRATIVE
COMPONENT IS UNCLEAR.

* Student confusion about
relationship between
undergraduate office and
Student Affairs.

* Advisers' role vis-à-vis
Student Affairs.

* Some advisers unaware of
their role vis-à-vis that of
Registrar and Dean.

- D -

RELATIONSHIP BETWEEN
ADVISING PROGRAM AND
ORIENTATION NOT
CLEAR.

* Faculty advising not
coordinated with
Orientation program.

* Many students did not
read the book assigned
for summer.

Exhibit

8.1a

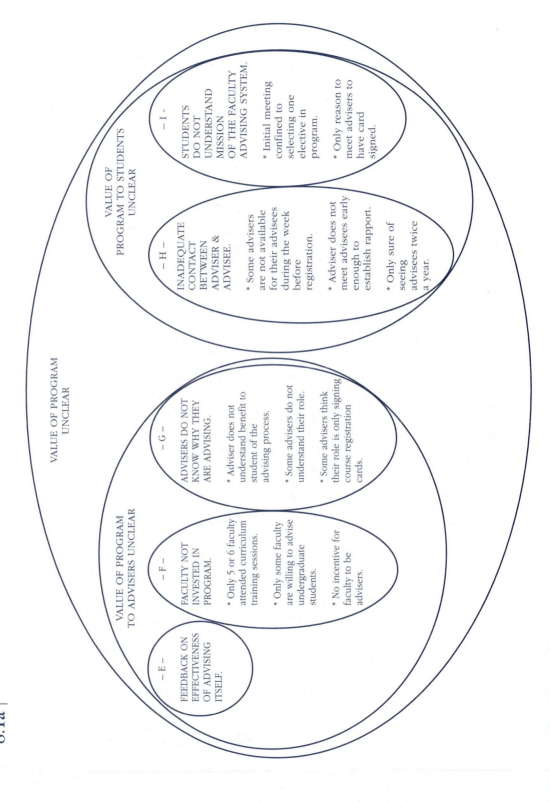

VALUE OF PROGRAM
UNCLEAR

VALUE OF
PROGRAM TO STUDENTS
UNCLEAR

- I -

STUDENTS
DO NOT
UNDERSTAND
MISSION
OF THE FACULTY
ADVISING SYSTEM.

* Initial meeting
confined to
selecting one
elective in
program.

* Only reason to
meet advisers to
have card
signed.

- H -

INADEQUATE
CONTACT
BETWEEN
ADVISER &
ADVISEE.

* Some advisers
are not available
for their advisees
during the week
before
registration.

* Adviser does not
meet advisees early
enough to
establish rapport.

* Only sure of
seeing
advisees twice
a year.

VALUE OF PROGRAM
TO ADVISERS UNCLEAR

- G -

ADVISERS DO NOT
KNOW WHY THEY
ARE ADVISING.

* Adviser does not
understand benefit to
student of the
advising process.

* Some advisers do not
understand their role.

* Some advisers think
their role is only signing
course registration
cards.

- F -

FACULTY NOT
INVESTED IN
PROGRAM.

* Only 5 or 6 faculty
attended curriculum
training sessions.

* Only some faculty
are willing to advise
undergraduate
students.

* No incentive for
faculty to be
advisers.

- E -

FEEDBACK ON
EFFECTIVENESS
OF ADVISING
ITSELF.

Exhibit

8.1a

Affinity diagram for exploring weaknesses in the student advisement system (detail.)

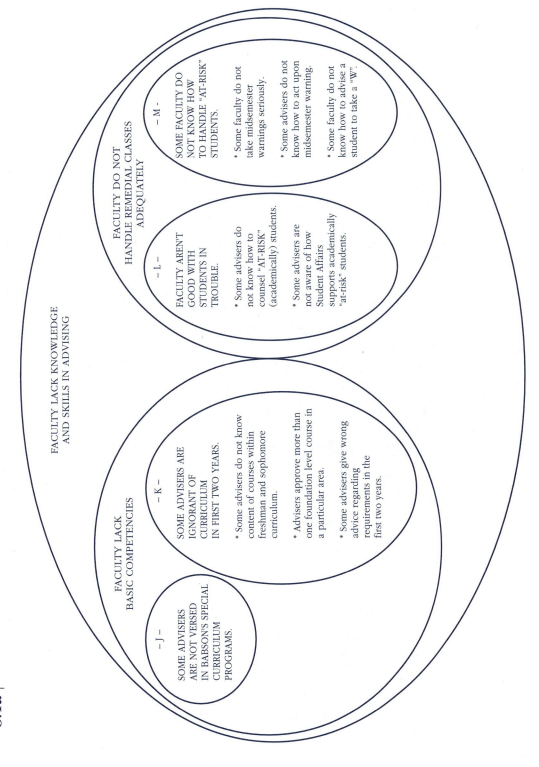

FACULTY LACK KNOWLEDGE
AND SKILLS IN ADVISING

FACULTY LACK
BASIC COMPETENCIES

– J –

SOME ADVISERS
ARE NOT VERSED
IN BABSON'S SPECIAL
CURRICULUM
PROGRAMS.

– K –

SOME ADVISERS ARE
IGNORANT OF
CURRICULUM
IN FIRST TWO YEARS.

* Some advisers do not know
content of courses within
freshman and sophomore
curriculum.

* Advisers approve more than
one foundation level course in
a particular area.

* Some advisers give wrong
advice regarding
requirements in the
first two years.

FACULTY DO NOT
HANDLE REMEDIAL CLASSES
ADEQUATELY

– L –

FACULTY AREN'T
GOOD WITH
STUDENTS IN
TROUBLE.

* Some advisers do
not know how to
counsel "AT-RISK"
(academically) students.

* Some advisers are
not aware of how
Student Affairs
supports academically
"at-risk" students.

– M –

SOME FACULTY DO
NOT KNOW HOW
TO HANDLE "AT-RISK"
STUDENTS.

* Some faculty do not
take midsemester
warnings seriously.

* Some advisers do not
know how to act upon
midsemester warning.

* Some faculty do not
know how to advise a
student to take a "W".

315

Exhibit 8.1a

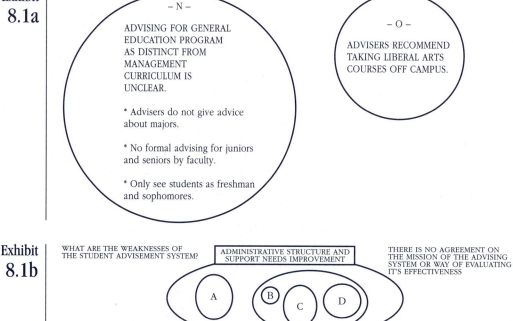

– N –

ADVISING FOR GENERAL
EDUCATION PROGRAM
AS DISTINCT FROM
MANAGEMENT
CURRICULUM IS
UNCLEAR.

* Advisers do not give advice about majors.

* No formal advising for juniors and seniors by faculty.

* Only see students as freshman and sophomores.

– O –

ADVISERS RECOMMEND
TAKING LIBERAL ARTS
COURSES OFF CAMPUS.

Exhibit 8.1b

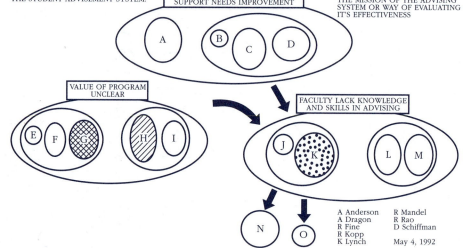

WHAT ARE THE WEAKNESSES OF
THE STUDENT ADVISEMENT SYSTEM?

ADMINISTRATIVE STRUCTURE AND
SUPPORT NEEDS IMPROVEMENT

THERE IS NO AGREEMENT ON
THE MISSION OF THE ADVISING
SYSTEM OR WAY OF EVALUATING
IT'S EFFECTIVENESS

VALUE OF PROGRAM
UNCLEAR

FACULTY LACK KNOWLEDGE
AND SKILLS IN ADVISING

A Anderson   R Mandel
A Dragon   R Rao
R Fine   D Schiffman
R Kopp
K Lynch   May 4, 1992

Phase 4: Prioritizing.

The upper-level groups are first linked by "causal" arrows. Causal arrows indicate that one group of weaknesses may be caused by another group. Constructing this framework linking the weaknesses helps the team establish the priorities. The next step is to decide as a team which of the first-level groups represent the most significant issues and to rank them.

***Up to this point each member of the team was providing input. But some people like to dominate discussions and actually enjoy the free-wheeling approach of

Exhibit
8.2

Some examples of opinion-based statements and the corresponding "scrubbed," fact-based statements.

OPINION	FACT-BASED STATEMENT
Company X is very successful.	Sales revenues for Company X have increased each of the last ten years.
Company Y is not responsive to customers.	Company Y contests every product liability suit.
Demand for this product is very robust.	This product's sales have increased 33 percent over the last year.
Dealers were unhappy with the supplying process.	One dealer complained that recent deliveries took two to six weeks instead of one week.

many meetings where they are able to stray from the agenda. This team also had members reluctant to follow the process. The objections came in several forms.

- "I dislike the structure that is being forced on us."
- "I think many of these issues are of equal importance, so why do I have to choose which is more important?"
- "But the solution is going to solve many of these problems, so why do we have to prioritize them?"

The team leader/facilitator had to take a firm stand insisting that the process be followed. The team leader was willing to accept suggestions to improve the process but only after the prescribed process had been completed. He also pointed out that this was one turn of the PDCA wheel. So, if the proposed solutions did not address some problems members felt were important, the team could tackle them but only after the high-priority items selected by the team were handled.

Phase 5: Wrap-up.

During the wrap-up, the group's conclusion is articulated along with the significant issues that support the conclusion. An important aspect of this phase is to have the group also review the process they used to reach their conclusion. What were the weaknesses of the process they used, and what could be done to improve it the next time?
***The completed affinity diagram was circulated to the team. Then it assembled for a sixth session to suggest solutions to the top priority problems. As expected, the solutions addressed several additional issues as well. The recommendations were presented to the vice president and the Faculty Review Board which implemented them the following year.

Appendix 8.1 gives a fairly detailed explanation of the steps followed in the development of an affinity diagram, and it should prove helpful in developing one. More details on affinity diagrams are available in Brassard (1989) and in "Step by Step KJ Method: A Problem Solving Tool for Organizing Qualitative Data" (1990).

Electronic Brainstorming

Although the affinity diagram is an effective approach, many companies have begun to use groupware to support brainstorming (see, for example, Gallupe and Cooper, 1993; Kirkpatrick, 1992; and Tyran et al., 1992). This approach has several advantages:

- It is effective for larger teams. Tyran et al (1992) mention group sizes of 30, and Gallupe and Cooper (1993) mention group sizes of 50.
- When group members are dispersed geographically, the groupware can permit a brainstorming meeting. Kirkpatrick (1992) notes that some companies are beginning to use this approach.
- The technique encourages communication across different levels of the organization since ideas are entered anonymously.

Phase 1: Idea Generation.

The theme for the meeting is distributed earlier when the participants are invited. When they arrive at the electronic meeting room, each sits at a terminal. They see a blank page on the screen and start to type in an idea. As soon as the idea has been entered, a new page is presented. This page shows the ideas that other participants have entered. But none of the ideas can be traced to an individual. Some systems will also display the ideas on a large screen for all to view. These ideas can prompt other ideas, or they may generate comments. The research indicates that people can be highly productive in this phase.

Phase 2: Categorization.

The participants review all of the ideas and define categories to which they would belong. Then they examine each comment and assign it to a category. Redundant comments can be removed at this stage.

Phase 3: Prioritization.

Participants are then required to rank order the categories. The software tabulates the rankings and computes the ranking for the entire group. As in the idea generation phase, the prioritization is done anonymously. In some cases, it may be desirable to evaluate the categories based on several criteria. When the results are presented, the group discusses the results and decides whether some of the lower priority categories should be dropped from further consideration.

Phase 4: Action Planning.

Each category, beginning with the highest ranked, is presented on the screen. Participants then discuss and decide

- The action to be taken
- The inhibitors/obstacles
- Who has the responsibility
- Milestone dates
- How success will be measured

The action plan is recorded in the category file along with the comments and ideas that were generated earlier. In this phase, the groupware is used only for recording the results of the discussion that takes place verbally.

Although the groupware is an effective means for idea generation, it is less effective as a method for creating an action plan. At this stage, participants invariably appear to resort to verbal discussion. Tyran et al. (1992) note that some of these discussions may occur at another time and away from the electronic meeting room. There are some additional shortcomings:

- Participants with better keyboard skills are able to enter more ideas. And if some have inadequate keyboard skills, the method may prove too intimidating.
- Some senior people may dislike the approach because the anonymity makes it more difficult for their ideas to be accepted. Earlier, the group may have accepted their ideas because they knew who was offering them.
- When too many ideas are generated, the editing and categorization can be a frustrating task.
- The costs of the equipment can be high especially for small companies. In addition, groups often find it useful to hire a facilitator, which may add to the expense.

In the remainder of this chapter, we discuss several other tools of a more advanced nature that are used in continuous improvement: the assessment of process capability, six-sigma quality, Taguchi's loss function, and the design of experiments.

◆ PROCESS CAPABILITY AND SIX-SIGMA QUALITY

An important issue that must often be considered in assessing the performance of a process is the degree to which its output conforms to specifications. Process capability indices provide a quantitative measure of this conformance. The Japanese have used these indices for many years in order to quantify one of the main goals in quality management: the reduction of variation in process output.

The output of virtually every process has some variation. If you believe that the output of a process is always the same, chances are that you will change your mind if you measure finer or observe more closely. If you measure a quality characteristic on a fairly large number of units from the output of a process, those measurements will show variation. A *dot plot* (similar to a histogram) for the pH levels of 300 jars of wool dye from a process that is in control is shown in Exhibit 8.3. The values are spread over a range (4.05 to 4.39) that is also shown in Exhibit 8.3. It is common to measure this **natural spread** for the likely values of a variable by measuring the standard deviation of the variable and multiplying it by six. The standard deviation of the 300 values in this example is 0.062, so six standard deviations amount to 0.372. Notice that this value is quite close to the range (4.39 − 4.05, or 0.34) over which the 300 values are spread. If the data have a smooth, bell-shaped dot plot, a six-standard-deviation span centered around the mean will in most cases include virtually all the observations. For normally distributed data it will include 99.7 percent of the observations in the long run.

On the other hand, measurable quality characteristics are often subject to **specification** or **tolerances** that represent requirements on that characteristic. The pH level for the dye in our example has a *lower specification limit* (LSL) of 3.98 and an *upper specification limit* (USL) of 4.48. The level of acidity of the dye (which the pH measures) must be within this range in order for the dye to do its job properly on the wool. It should be emphasized that conceptually, these specification limits are entirely different from the control limits developed for control charts. The specification limits are design requirements, whereas the control limits depend on how the process actually operates.

The C_p Index

Exhibit 8.4 shows the dot plot for the pH values, their natural spread, the specification limits for the pH, and the **tolerance spread** (the range from the lower to the upper specification limits). This figure shows that the natural spread of this variable is substantially narrower than the tolerance spread. This implies that, as long as the process continues to operate this way, there is little likelihood of pro-

| Exhibit 8.3 | Dot plot for the pH levels of 300 jars of wool dye that also shows the natural spread of the variable. |

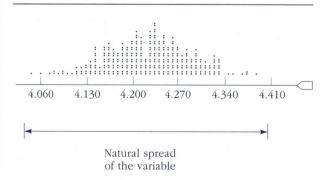

Natural spread
of the variable

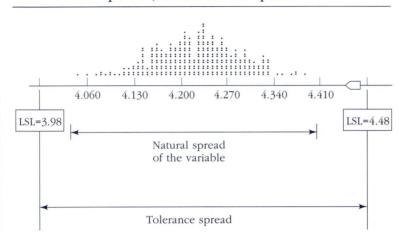

Exhibit
8.4

Dot plot for the pH levels of 300 jars of wool dye showing the natural spread for the process, the lower and upper specification limits for the pH level, and the tolerance spread.

ducing dye jars with a pH level that is out of specifications. If the natural spread and tolerances were as shown in Exhibit 8.5, on the other hand, the situation would be troublesome.

The relation between the tolerance spread and natural spread for a process variable is often quantified by computing a **process potential index** or C_p **index** using the following formula:

$$C_p = \text{Tolerance spread/Natural spread} = (\text{USL} - \text{LSL})/6\,S$$

For our example, the process potential index is computed as follows:

$$C_p = \text{Tolerance spread/Natural spread} = (\text{USL} - \text{LSL})/6\,S$$
$$= (4.48 - 3.98)/6(0.062) = 0.50/0.372 = 1.34$$

A C_p value greater than 1.00 shows a tolerance spread wider than the natural spread and is therefore an indicator of a capable process, whereas C_p values lower than 1.00 are indicators of poor process capability. The C_p for our example, 1.34, tells us that the tolerance spread is 34 percent wider than the natural spread of our variable. C_p values above 1.33 are commonly required in industry.

The C_{pk} Index

For processes that are not centered between the specification limits, the C_p index may be misleading. Exhibit 8.6 presents an extreme example of a process with a

Exhibit
8.5

A process in which a substantial proportion of output is
out of specifications: the natural spread is wider than
the tolerance spread.

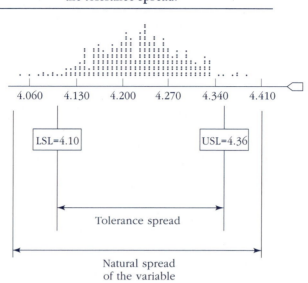

high C_p, showing great *process potential* (since the natural spread is much narrower than the tolerance spread), but poor *actual process performance* in the
sense that a good deal of the output is out of specifications. To overcome this limitation a second index, called the **process performance index** or C_{pk} **index,** is
also very often used:

Exhibit
8.6

A process with excellent process potential (the natural spread is much narrower than
the tolerance spread) but poor process performance (the process is not centered).

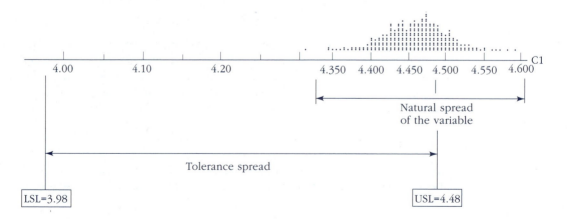

C_{pk} = Distance from the mean to the nearest specification limit/3 S

For our 300 pH measurements the mean is 4.22. This value is closer to the lower specification limit (3.98) than to the upper specification limit (4.48), so we would compute our process performance index as follows:

$$C_{pk} = (4.22 - 3.98)/3(0.062) = 0.24/0.186 = 1.29$$

Our process, though not perfectly centered within the specification limits, was not far from being centered so the C_p and C_{pk} are not so different. For a process that is very out-of-center, such as the process in Exhibit 8.6, the difference would be much larger. For perfectly centered processes, the C_p and C_{pk} indices are equal. For processes that are not centered, the C_{pk} index is always smaller than the C_p index. For some processes, tolerances are one-sided, and in these cases one-sided indices are used.

A process must be in statistical control before its capability is measured. Processes out of control fluctuate and are thus unpredictable; trying to measure their capability would not make any sense. Kane (1986) gives further details on process capability.

Six-Sigma Quality

Six-sigma quality was a concept originally developed by Motorola in 1987 as a quality improvement goal. It called for a drastic reduction in the defect rates of products and processes throughout the company by the year 1992. Many companies, including Boeing, Caterpillar, Corning, Digital Equipment, IBM, and Raytheon, have subsequently started six-sigma programs as part of their continuous improvement efforts.

A process with output centered between specification limits and a process capability index equal to two, such as that shown in Exhibit 8.7, would be called a *centered process with six-sigma quality* by people at Motorola. The "six-sigma" derives from the fact that the specification limits are six-process-standard-deviations

| Exhibit 8.7 | A centered process with six-sigma quality: the tolerance spread is twice as wide as the natural spread. |

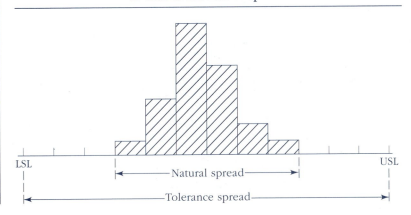

away from the targeted midpoint of the tolerance range. If the process output is normally distributed, then in the long run only about two units per billion would be out of specifications. A centered process with three-sigma quality would have a process capability index equal to one and, if normally distributed, would produce about 2700 units per million that are out of specification.

A more realistic definition of six sigma takes into account potential shifts in the process average. This allows for two-sided shifts in the mean of the distribution as shown in Exhibit 8.8. The average magnitude of these shifts is assumed to be one and a half times the standard deviation of the process. Research indicates that this assumption is consistent with shifts in the process mean that commonly occur in industrial processes. Processes with a process potential index equal to two, with a mean that is in the long-run average centered between the specification limits, and where these shifts in the process mean occur, are called *six-sigma processes with mean shifts*. If the process output is normally distributed, under these conditions about 3.4 parts per million would be out of specifications in the long run. Table 8.1 shows the relation between different sigma levels and the long-run proportion of units that are out of specifications. For more information on six-sigma quality, see Dambolena and Rao (1994).

| Exhibit 8.8 | The effect of shifts in the average level of a process: the boundaries of the natural spread get closer to the specification limits. This results in a higher proportion of output that does not meet specifications. |

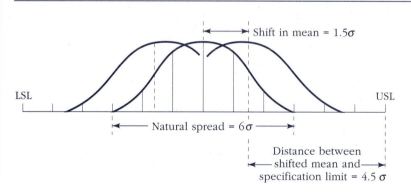

Table 8.1	Sigma Quality Levels

Nonconforming Units per Million

SIGMAS	WITHOUT SHIFT IN MEAN	WITH SHIFT IN MEAN
3	2,700	66,803
4	63	6,200
5	0.57	233
6	0.002	3.4

◆ TAGUCHI'S LOSS FUNCTION

Not long ago, just maintaining the dimensions of products within their specification limits was paramount. **Taguchi's loss function** challenged this concept by postulating that for most measurable quality characteristics, such as length, weight, or density, there is a target value and any deviations from that target are undesirable. Moreover, the loss function allows us to evaluate the costs of deviating from target. In doing so, it lets us make financial comparisons between production methods that have varying degrees of precision.

The Goal-Post View of Quality

The Industrial Revolution brought with it specialization of labor and interchangeability of parts. Prior to that time artisans, individually or in groups, manufactured the whole product and ensured that pieces fitted together properly. With the specialized production of interchangeable parts, it became necessary to ensure that parts fitted together well when they were assembled. Specification limits were the means to this end. In order for a peg to fit into a hole, neither too tightly nor too loosely, specifications were defined for both the hole and the peg. Go/no-go gages were used to make sure both hole and peg were within specifications. As long as both holes and pegs were within specifications things went well,; when either was out of specifications things were wrong. This approach implied the *goal-post* view of costs shown in Exhibit 8.9a. According to this view, as long as a measurable quality characteristic is within specifications all is well, we are happy with the state of things, and there is no implicit cost to us. When the measurement is out of specifications, things are wrong, we are unhappy with the state of things, we scrap or rework, and we incur a cost.

Some problems are associated with this goal-post view. One problem is exemplified by the following anecdote. A study found that U.S. consumers preferred television sets made by Sony in Japan over those made, also by Sony, in the United States. This finding was puzzling because both the Japanese and U.S. factories used identical designs and specifications. Further study showed that the distributions of color density for sets made in the two counties were like those shown in Exhibit 8.10. The distribution for sets made in the United States was virtually all within specifications but had many values near the specification limits. For sets made in Japan, on the other hand, a slight percentage was out of specifications, but the distribution had a much lower variance and most values closely hugged the target. This difference in goals, manufacturing to meet specifications versus manufacturing as close to target as possible, was the cause of the difference in customer preferences. Deviations from target resulted in inferior performance for too many sets manufactured in the United States.

Another problem with the goal-post view is the quantum jump from no cost for a measurement that is barely inside specifications to a substantial cost for a

Exhibit
8.9

The conventional or goal-post view of poor-quality losses (*top*) and Taguchi's view (*bottom*).

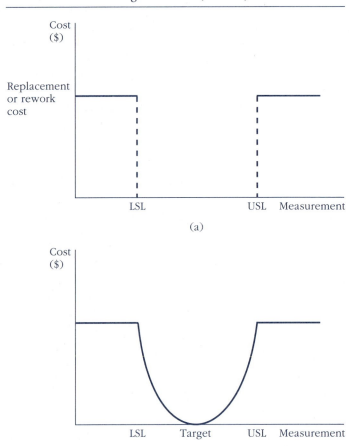

(a)

(b)

measurement that is barely outside of specifications. This drastic jump makes little intuitive sense and is one of the problems Taguchi solves with his loss function.

The Loss Function

Exhibit 8.9b shows the loss-function counterpart to the goal-post view of losses that we showed in Exhibit 8.9a. In order to produce the curve in Exhibit 8.9b, Taguchi uses the function

$$y = k(x - \text{target})^2$$

Exhibit
8.10

Distribution of color density for TV sets made by Sony in Japan and the United States. The lower variance for sets made in Japan means better quality.

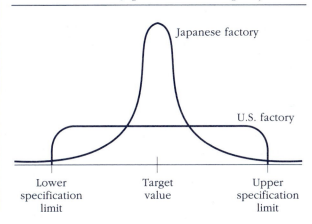

where
    y = the cost or loss incurred by a measurement on an item
    k = a constant, to be determined for each application
    x = the actual measurement on the item
    target = the most desirable or optimal value of the measurement

For example, if the weight of a bag of sugar should be 1 lb. and a particular bag you produce weighs 0.998 lb., then $x = 0.998$ lb., and y is the cost you incur because the weight of the bag is 0.998 lb. rather than 1 lb.

Notice the following features of this function:

1. When the measurement is equal to the target value, the resulting cost or loss is zero.
2. When the measurement is not on target, the cost incurred is proportional to the square of the distance to the target.

This idea of quantifying error, cost, or variation by measuring squared distances to the target has found widespread use. We have used it in computing the variance. It is also used to compute the mean squared error with which one evaluates the precision of a forecasting model, to produce the least-squares line in regression modeling, and in many other applications.

We now show how the loss function is developed and used.

Example.

The specifications for the diameter of an axle are 25.00 mm $\pm$ 0.25 mm. If the diameter is out of specifications, the axle must be scrapped at a cost of $4.00. What is the loss function for this application?

Since our target value is 25.00 mm, we know the loss function has the form

$$y = k(x - 25.00)^2 \tag{8.1}$$

For each application we need to determine the value of k. In order to do so, we must know the cost or loss associated with any particular measurement that is out of target. Here we know that the cost incurred when the measurement is at the specification limits (that is, when $x = 24.75$ or $x = 25.25$) is $4.00. [*Note:* Technically speaking, the cost is the same at the limits and "just barely beyond them," when the measurement gets out of specifications. In addition, the specification limits should be such that at that point, on the margin, the "overall cost to society" of keeping the part in use starts exceeding the cost of scrapping the part. This "overall cost to society" is one of Taguchi's most influential and profound concepts. He uses it as his definition of quality, or rather of the lack thereof. To Taguchi, "Quality is the loss a product causes to society after being shipped, other than any losses caused by its intrinsic functions" (Taguchi, 1986). The cost to society includes inferior product performance and consequent customer dissatisfaction, environmental impact, and similar factors. Kackar (1986) has written an excellent essay touching on these and other issues.]

We may, therefore, substitute this cost and any of the two specification limits in Eq. (8.1) to obtain:

$$4.00 = k(25.25 - 25.00)^2$$

Then we may solve for k:

$$k = 4.00/(25.25 - 25.00)^2 = 4.00/(0.25)^2 = 64$$

Knowing the value of k, we may write down the complete loss function for this application:

$$y = 64(x - 25.00)^2$$

Finally, we may use this loss function to compute the costs associated with any measurements of our choice. For example, for a few selected values of x we may compute:

x	Cost
25.25 (USL)	$64 (25.25 - 25.00)^2 = \$4.00$
24.75 (LSL)	$64 (24.75 - 25.00)^2 = \$4.00$
25.20	$64 (25.20 - 25.00)^2 = \$2.56$
25.10	$64 (25.10 - 25.00)^2 = \$0.64$

Graphing these costs as well as a few others that we may compute similarly, we obtain the curve shown in Exhibit 8.11. We may now use either the function or the curve to compare the costs of production methods with different precision and in this way determine how much we can afford to spend in order to reduce variation. We next illustrate how to do this.

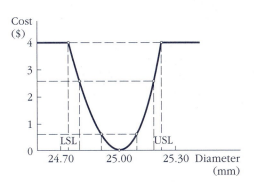

Exhibit
8.11

Loss function for axle diameter. The loss function allows us to compare the cost of production methods that have different precision.

Example.

Two different methods were tested for producing the axle discussed in our previous example. One thousand axles were produced using each method, and their diameters were recorded. The resulting relative frequency histograms are shown in Exhibit 8.12. (These histograms are rather coarse to simplify our explanation. You should recognize, however, that in practice you would develop histograms with more and narrower cells to increase your precision.) It is clear that method B has lower variability than method A, but, in dollars and cents, how much better is it? One million of these axles are manufactured every year. What are the annual losses with each method?

We will use the midpoint of each cell as the "typical value" for that cell and will compute costs as if all measurements in a cell were located at the midpoint. This is often done to simplify computations, and, as the number of cells increases, the error likely to be committed eventually becomes practically negligible. The following table summarizes our calculations. The loss per part for each cell midpoint is computed by evaluating the loss function at that midpoint. The annual volume for each cell midpoint is obtained by multiplying the total number of parts produced per year (one million) times the relative frequency for that midpoint (which is read from the relevant histogram). The annual loss for each cell midpoint is the product of the loss per part for that cell times the annual volume for that cell.

The annual losses incurred by not meeting the diameter target are twice as large for method A than they are for method B, and there is more than half a million dollars at stake.

In an article worth reading, Lawrence Sullivan (1986), a former manager of reliability at Ford and chairman of the American Supplier Institute, tells us about three quality improvement projects at Nippondenso involving a rotor shaft machining process, a metal plate boring process, and a material shaft press-fit

Exhibit
8.12

The distribution of axle diameters for two different production methods.
Method B has lower variability. How much better is it in dollars and cents?

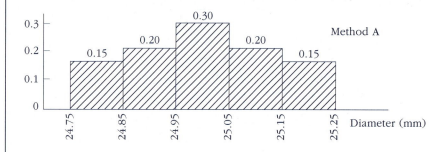

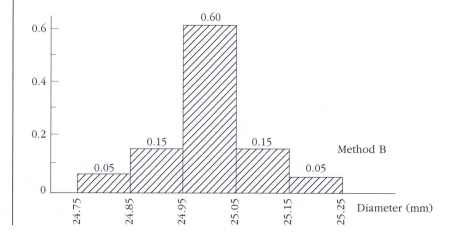

	Method A			Method B	
CELL MIDPOINT	LOSS PER PART	ANNUAL VOLUME	ANNUAL LOSS	ANNUAL VOLUME	ANNUAL LOSS
24.80	$2.56	150,000	$384,000	50,000	$128,000
24.90	0.64	200,000	128,000	150,000	96,000
25.00	0.00	300,000	0	600,000	0
25.10	0.64	200,000	128,000	150,000	96,000
25.20	2.56	150,000	384,000	50,000	128,000
Total annual losses			$1,024,000		$448,000

process. The aggregate savings for these projects were estimated by traditional methods at 8.6 million yen. The loss function, on the other hand, yielded an estimate of 85.5 million yen, an almost tenfold increase. Quality improvement projects that would not have been considered financially feasible using traditional costing methods were deemed viable using the correct approach to estimate their savings.

◆ DESIGN OF EXPERIMENTS[1]

An American manufacturer of casings for speedometer cables had an after-processing shrinkage problem that made the speedometer cable assembly noisy. Process engineers believed that any or all of 15 different process variables could potentially affect the shrinkage. Through some experimentation, they found that only eight of the 15 process variables truly affected shrinkage, while the remaining seven were immaterial to the problem. The eight significant variables included the type of braided wire used, the wire diameter, and the outside diameter and material of a plastic liner. By setting these eight significant variables properly the engineers were able to reduce the average shrinkage by 80 percent and also to cut in half the variation in shrinkage from casing to casing. In this way, they refined their product so that it became much better on average and also much more consistent. We will look further into this case later in this chapter.

A Japanese manufacturer of tiles had problems with the uneven size of the tiles baked in their new $2-million kiln (Byrne and Taguchi, 1987). This variation in size was caused by differences in temperature inside the kiln. Tiles baked near the sides of the kiln tended to have a larger average size and more variation in size than those baked near the center of the kiln. A kiln redesign would have solved the problem at a cost of about half a million dollars, but a better solution was found. Brainstorming by engineers and chemists familiar with the process identified seven variables likely to affect tile dimensions. Among them were the content of limestone, the fineness of additive, the content and type of agalmatolite, and the content of feldspar. Experimenting with these seven variables, they discovered that the content of limestone was most crucial and that some of the other variables also had a significant effect on final tile size. By increasing the limestone content from 1 to 5 percent and by setting appropriately the other significant variables, they were able to reduce the percentage of tiles with size problems from 30 percent to less than 1 percent. Fortunately for the company, limestone was the least expensive material in the tile. The experimentation also showed them that they could reduce the content of agalmatolite, the most expensive material, without adversely affecting tile characteristics. The expensive kiln redesign was avoided, and, besides, variable costs of production were reduced.

---

[1]This section and the following one were adapted from *Experimental Design Primer.* Copyright © Ismael Dambolena, Babson College, Wellesley, MA, 1993.

A German manufacturer had serious problems with surface blemishes that occurred during the production of photoreceptors (copier drums). The blemishes required a microscopic examination of 100 percent of the product and resulted in 35 percent rework. Ten relevant variables were identified through brainstorming. They involved raw materials, an evaporation process, and tooling design. Experimentation showed that seven of the variables had significant effects. By appropriately setting those seven variables, surface blemishes were reduced by 94 percent (from an average of 8.8 per drum to an average of 0.52 per drum) and an annual rework cost of 420,000 deutsche marks was avoided. Process capability increased more than 30 times (Heil et al., 1986).

The marketing manager for an airline identified several variables that might potentially influence the choice of flights by people flying to Paris on business: the carrier, the type of aircraft, the flight departure time, the likely timeliness of the arrival, the likely passenger load, the attitudes of flight attendants, and the entertainment offered during the flight among others. Experimentation with customers showed that only four of the variables had a significant effect on the passenger choices while the others had little effect. From the experimental results management concluded, for example, that money would be better spend on improving scheduling and the attitudes of flight attendants than on the replacement of older aircraft (Green and Wind, 1975).

These examples are all illustrations of the use of **design of experiments** to select from an initial set of variables (called *factors*), any of which may have an effect on another variable (called the *response*), the ones that actually do have an effect (the *significant factors*). When the design of experiments is used for quality, the response is usually a quality characteristic that the experimenters want to improve. Based on the results of the experiment, these significant factors may then be appropriately set so that the response is improved. The nonsignificant factors may be set so that costs are reduced. The design of experiments had its origins during the early 1920s. Ronald Fisher, one of the foremost statisticians of all times, developed its fundamental ideas as part of his efforts to find better ways to grow crops at an agricultural research station. These methods were subsequently transferred to industry, where they now find widespread application in the improvement of product and process designs. They also form the basis of conjoint analysis, a relatively new statistical tool widely used in cutting-edge marketing (see Chapter 9).

Many experts believe that the widespread use of experimental design may well be one of the main factors influencing the high quality of Japanese products. A few years ago, a group of well-known American quality specialists who were visiting Japan observed what was being done there in different areas that affect manufacturing quality, and reported their findings upon their return. They were very impressed by how widely experimentation was used in Japanese companies. In one company they visited, more than 6000 experiments had been conducted in one year. In another company, while a product was designed and developed over a three-year period, 48 experiments were conducted. "The chief engineer of this product told us that the use of planned experiments was the most important factor in developing such a high-quality product. Multifactor experiments seem to be an integral part of the design process in Japanese companies" (Box et al., 1988, p. 39).

Turning to domestic use of experimental design, Sullivan (1987) reports that by mid-1987 there were over 6000 case studies from American companies on the application of Taguchi methods. One of the centerpieces of "Taguchi methods" is a set of special techniques for doing the design of experiments. They were developed by Genichi Taguchi, a Japanese engineer and consultant, and have been used for a long time in Japan where they are credited for the wide diffusion of experimental design. In recent years they have also generated a great deal of interest in the United States. In the same article Sullivan (1987, p. 77) states that "In quantifying the results of these case studies, quality (i.e., defects) is rarely used as a measure of success; results are usually evaluated on the basis of annual cost savings."

Sullivan cites results reported by three companies of very different sizes: ITT, which since 1983 has trained approximately 1200 engineers in Taguchi methods and has completed over 2000 case studies for savings estimated at $35 million; Sheller Globe, which has trained 120 engineers and completed 225 case studies for savings of $10 million; and Flex Products, which trained 12 engineers and completed 75 case studies for savings of $1.4 million.

In the following section we discuss a case, included at the end of this chapter, in which the design of experiments is used to solve a quality problem. The discussion will give you a good grasp of some of the basic principles involved. We feel that experimental design is a superb tool that is not being used in the United States as much as it should be. We also feel that if managers understood more about it, then it would be used more to everyone's benefit. The ideas presented here are understandable even without a strong statistical background. Read the case "Product Improvement by Application of Taguchi Methods" at the end of this chapter, try to understand as much as you can about it, and then come back to the following section for a discussion.

◆ CASE DISCUSSION: PRODUCT IMPROVEMENT BY APPLICATION OF TAGUCHI METHODS

The case deals with the post-extrusion shrinkage of a speedometer cable casing manufactured by Flex Products, a General Motors supplier. A schematic detailing the components of the casing is shown in Figure 1. (All figure numbers in this section refer to figures in the case at the end of this chapter.) Excessive casing shrinkage may cause noise in the assembly, and this has been a major problem with this type of assembly in the past. The shrinkage is quantified by expressing the reduction in length as a percentage of the original length of the casing. Many experiments varying one factor at a time were done in the past to try to reduce shrinkage. These experiments were costly but did not produce useful results. In contrast, the new approach will rely on simultaneously changing all factors under consideration in a systematic way. This approach is more efficient in terms of the information it yields.

As you go through these sections, think of roles you could play as a manager. In particular, you should be able to visualize a role when the factors are listed and the results are analyzed. In addition, it is important for a manager to know when to call on others for expert help. For example, if a large number of experiments have to be done in order to gain some insight, and they are going to take an inordinately long amount of time, it would be prudent to obtain the help of an expert statistician. This person may be able to reduce the number of experiments significantly without materially affecting the validity of the insights.

The Factor Listing

Information from customers, production workers, quality employees, and engineers was used in identifying 15 factors which, it was felt, were likely to affect casing shrinkage. The factors are listed in Figure 4. These 15 factors are related to all three stages of the manufacturing process: production of the inner liner, of the braided wire that goes around it, and of the exterior coating. Two *levels of experimentation* were then selected for each factor. For factor A, for example, the outside diameter of the inner liner, a decision was made to run some tests using its current nominal dimension and to run other tests using a different dimension (carefully chosen but not specified in the paper). These levels were arbitrarily called "level 1" and "level 2," respectively. It is common to select either two or three levels at which to experiment with each factor. The levels of experimentation for all factors are listed in Figure 4.

The Orthogonal Array and Experimental Results

Figure 5 has information on the experiment itself. Each row in that figure shows on the left (columns A through O) an experimental setup under which four tests were made, and on the next four columns the results obtained in the four different tests using the setup. Looking at the first row of numbers in that figure, for example, we see 15 ones in columns A through O, which tells us that for the tests reported in this row all 15 factors were set at level 1. Four tests were made at these settings (i.e., four casings were produced with all 15 factors at level 1). Each of the tests made using fixed setting is called a *replication,* so these four tests are four replications made under the same experimental conditions. The percentage shrinkage in the casings was measured for each of these four tests, and the shrinkage was recorded in the next four columns (0.49, 0.54, 0.46, and 0.45). The last column in the table shows a signal-to-noise ratio, an indicator of quality that is computed from the test results. Later we will discuss the meaning and purpose of signal-to-noise ratios. The 16 rows of ones and twos in columns A through O, which describe the different experimental setups used in the experiment, are the *orthogonal array* for this experiment.

An Analogy

In order to bring these ideas closer to home, let us use them in a more familiar environment. Let us suppose that we are interested in producing high-quality popcorn. First, we would ask ourselves, "What factors affect popcorn quality?" After some thinking, we would come up with factors such as the type of kernels used, the type of oil, the oil temperature, the stirring method, the amount of oil used, and the type of pan among others. Suppose that, to make things simple, we decide to experiment with only two of these factors: the oil temperature and the kernel type. Reasonable oil temperatures for popping corn, we find out, are in the range 325 to 375 degrees Fahrenheit. We therefore choose the two end-points of this range as the two levels of oil temperature that we will experiment with. We also choose two different kernel types: Regular and Supreme. Using the notation and terminology in the case, we would say that we have selected two factors: A = oil temperature and B = kernel type. Our equivalent for Figure 4 would be

FACTOR LISTING
A. Oil temperature   A1 = 325 °F   A2 = 375 °F
B. Kernel Type   B1 = Regular   B2 = Supreme

Two factors, each of which can be set at any two levels, give us the four possible different factor-level combinations shown below

OIL TEMPERATURE	KERNEL TYPE
325 (level 1)	Regular (level 1)
325 (level 1)	Supreme (level 2)
375 (Level 2)	Regular (level 1)
375 (level 2)	Supreme (level 2)

This table may now be abbreviated in a form similar to that in Figure 5:

FACTOR A	FACTOR B
1	1
1	2
2	1
2	2

We now prepare four batches of popcorn using the factor-level combination in the first row (a temperature of 325 degrees and Regular corn) and rate the popcorn quality of each batch on a well-predefined scale ranging from 0 (awful) to 10 (excellent). These four ratings would then be entered on the first row as shown here:

FACTOR A	FACTOR B	TEST1	TEST2	TEST3	TEST4
1	1	6	8	7	6
1	2				
2	1				
2	2				

After repeating this procedure with the other three rows, we would have a table that looks very much like the one in Figure 5 except for the signal-to-noise ratios.

Randomization and Fractional Factorial Experiments

Two points should be made here. First, the 16 different tests should be performed in random order (we used a sequential order in our explanation to make it less cumbersome). This *randomization* reduces or eliminates any systematic bias in the observations and is an extremely important feature in experimental design.

Second, in our popcorn experiment we tried all possible factor-level combinations. Experiments where all possible factor-level combinations are tried are called *full-factorial* experiments. With two factors each at two possible levels there were only four combinations. If we added another factor, also at two levels, then the number of possible factor-level combinations doubles: there are eight of them. For n factors each tested at two levels, the number of all possible factor-level combinations is 2^n. For the 15 factors in the speedometer cable casing, the number of possible combinations is $2^{15} = 32,768$. With four replications at each possible combination, the total number of tests would be over 131,000. This quick growth in the number of possible level-factor combinations as the number of factors grows prevents experimenters from trying all possible combinations when there is a large number of factors, since it would be too costly and time consuming to do so. In these cases just some of the combinations are carefully selected and used. Experiments in which only some of the combinations are used are called *fractional-factorial* experiments. Only 16 (carefully selected) of the 32,768 possible combinations were used in the speedometer cable casing experiment. With four replications per combination, a total of 64 tests were made. This procedure, of course, yielded less information than one would have obtained from a full factorial experiment, but it was deemed necessary here and, as we will see, still yielded very substantial information. Fractional factorial experiments are often used in industry.

The Signal-to-Noise Ratio

Experimentation was done at 16 different factor-level combinations. Here we are trying to find combinations that produce low shrinkage and, since consistency is always one of the key components of quality, we also try to have little variation in the output. By casually looking at the test results, can you identify some of the better combinations and some of the worse ones? The second combination and the last combination look pretty bad (with shrinkage around 0.5 to 0.6 percent), while the third combination looks pretty good (shrinkage around 0.1 percent). Notice also that the signal-to-noise ratio is low for the bad combinations, while it is high for the good combination. We learned before that signal-to-noise ratios are indicators of quality. We are learning now that higher signal-to-noise ratios are indicators of better quality.

Taguchi uses the signal-to-noise ratio to summarize experimental design results. The ratio was computed for each experimental row, based on the four test results obtained in that row, using a procedure that is explained in detail in Appendix 8.2. The formula used here for computing the ratio is such that either a *lower average shrinkage* for the four test results in a row or a *lower variance* for the four shrinkages will produce a higher ratio. Higher ratios are, therefore, indicators of both lower shrinkage and lower variation, so the higher the ratio for a row, the better the settings in that row. If we had to choose one from the 16 settings in Figure 5, we would choose the settings in the third row. However, there are well over 32,000 possible settings that we have not explored, so choosing the best from these 16 is not good enough. (This is true in spite of the fact that the 16 were carefully selected; the careful selection was based on other considerations.) In order to improve our choice of settings, we must analyze our test results further. We start by analyzing the individual effect of each factor on shrinkage.

Analysis of Results

Using the information in Figure 5, are you able to tell which of the two experimental levels is better for factor A? You could argue as follows.

Factor A was set to level 1 in the first eight experimental settings (the first eight rows) and to level 2 in the last eight rows. The sum of the signal-to-noise ratios is 105.88 for the first eight rows and 87.59 for the last eight rows. So, on average, the first eight rows produced higher ratios than the last eight rows. Since higher ratios are desirable, level 1 of factor A (which was used in the first eight rows) seems better than level 2 (used in the last eight rows). The same analysis could be done for other factors. For factor C, for example, the sum of ratios for the first four and last four rows (level 1) is 87.61, while the sum of ratios for the middle eight rows (level 2) is 105.86. Therefore, level 2 seems better than level 1 for factor C.

This analysis was done for all 15 factors, and the results are shown in Figure 7. Notice that each factor is set to level 1 in eight rows and to level 2 also in eight rows, so sums of ratios at level 1 are in all cases directly comparable to sums at level 2. Notice also that every factor is in a sense "independent" of every other factor. Consider, for example, factors A and B. Factor A is set to level 1 in the first eight rows. Factor B is set to level 1 in four of those rows and level 2 in the other four rows. Similarly, when factor A is set to level 2 (last eight rows), factor B is set to level 1 in half the cases and to level 2 in the other half. Therefore, the levels of factor B "affect us equally" when we are evaluating the levels of factor A. The orthogonal array in columns A through O has the property that this "independence we have just noticed for factors A and B also holds true when any two factors are selected.

Looking again at Figure 7, we see that for some factors the sum of rations at level 1 is quite different from the sum at level 2, whereas for other factors there is little difference between the two sums. Most of these smaller differences are likely to be caused by experimental randomness, whereas most of the larger differences are likely to be indicators that the setting of the factor really has an impact on the signal-to-noise ratio. The analysis of variance table in Figure 8 summarizes a statistical analysis of the data. This analysis shows that for the eight factors with the largest differences (factors A, C, D, E, F, G, H, and K) the setting is likely to have an impact, while for the other seven factors, in all likelihood, the setting does not really matter.

Conclusions

Figure 9 graphs the data in Figure 7 for the eight significant factors (those for which the settings matter). Since there are eight ratios at each level for each factor, the values in Figure 7 were divided by 8 to produce *average* signal-to-noise ratios at the different levels. In this figure we clearly see that factor E is the most significant and that it performs better at level 2 (higher average ratio). The second most significant factors is factor G, and it should also be set at level 2. The best levels for all significant factors are the following:

Factor:	E	G	K	A	C	F	D	H
Level:	2	2	1	1	2	2	1	1

Some of the techniques that Taguchi uses in experimental design have been criticized by specialists in the field. One criticism is that his fractional factorial experiments are often excessively fractionated and therefore do not allow the study of possibly significant interactions between factors. Taguchi's advocates respond by pointing out that Taguchi recommends *confirmation runs* after his experiments. After setting the eight significant factors to the levels at which the experiment indicates they perform best, 100 cable casings were produced and their shrinkage was compared to that of 100 cable casings produced at the old settings. Figure 11 and Figure 12 show the results of these comparisons. The average shrinkage has been reduced by more than 80 percent, and the standard deviation of the shrinkage has been cut in half. As a consequence, the signal-to-noise ratio has more than doubled. It is interesting to notice that the settings used for the significant factors in the confirmation experiment were unlike any of the 16 settings used in the original experiments and that the signal-to-noise ratio for the confirmation experiment is higher than it was for any of the 16 settings tested in the original experiments.

Taguchi's approach to experimental design has been criticized in other ways. Critics point out that some of his results have been shown to be suboptimal, some of his designs are not as efficient as they could be, and some problems have been found with the amalgamation of "signal" (mean level) and "noise" (variation) into a single signal-to-noise ratio. Taguchi himself has been criticized for not giving proper credit to those who, decades ago, developed many of the designs he uses. On Taguchi's behalf it should be said, foremost, that his approach to experimental design is relatively uncomplicated. This simplicity seems to have "popularized" the use of these techniques in Japan and to have resulted in more overall improvement (less improvement, perhaps, in each single use but many more uses) than would otherwise have occurred. This is actually in line with Japanese philosophy: when they approach improvement, they would rather improve by 10 percent the effectiveness of many, many processes than improve by 50 percent the effectiveness of just a few.

Experimental design is a very helpful tool in the design and redesign of products and processes. If you feel like exploring these ideas further, Lochner and Matar (1990) have written a very readable and clear book. A book by Box, Hunter, and Hunter (1978) is, in our opinion, the best on the subject; however, it requires a solid grasp of statistics even though it is not too mathematical. Phillip Ross's book (1988) gives a detailed account of Taguchi's techniques.

◆ Summary

In this chapter we have discussed several techniques used in continual improvement that tend to be newer or more advanced than those discussed in the last two chapters. Many people find brainstorming to be an effective approach to generating ideas. Electronic brainstorming has been shown to encourage a freer flow of ideas. It also enables people to share ideas when it is difficult to meet face to face, and it can support large groups. The additional structure provided by electronic brainstorming encourages a team consensus and the development of an action plan. However, in some cases it is not as effective as the affinity diagram approach, which works best with smaller teams. Over the next few years we can expect to witness the development of new techniques that will combine the best features of both methods.

An important issue that must often be considered in assessing the performance of a process is the degree to which its output conforms to specifications. Process capability provides a quantitative measure of this conformance. The C_p index may be used for centered processes, but the C_{pk} index provides a better reflection of performance when processes are not centered. Six-sigma quality, a concept originally developed by Motorola, uses process capability targets as a quality improvement goal.

Plain conformance to specifications implies a goal-post view of the costs incurred by process output that is off-target. Taguchi's loss function recognizes that any deviation from target has adverse cost implications. Its use provides a better assessment of the savings that would result from reducing variance in process output.

Many experts feel that widespread use of experimental design may well be one of the main factors influencing the high quality of Japanese products. Experimental design models allow you to determine which variables are likely to have a significant effect on a quality characteristic. By setting those variables at the proper level, you may improve that quality characteristic.

◆ Key Terms

Brainstorming
Affinity diagram or struc-
   tured brainstorming
Electronic brainstorming
Natural spread
   (of a variable)

Specifications or
   tolerances
Tolerance spread
Process potential index
   or C_p index

Process performance
   index or C_{pk} index
Six-sigma quality
Taguchi's loss function
Design of experiments

◆ Assignments

1. Prepare an affinity diagram using one of the following themes:
   a. What are the weaknesses of meetings you have attended?
   b. What are the weaknesses of the registration system in the college?
   c. What are the obstacles to initiating Total Quality Management in your orga-
      nization?
   d. What are the weaknesses of the Management Information Systems curriculum?

2. Argo Industries purchases one type of spring from a supplier in Ohio. The specification limits for spring elongation under a force of 300 g are 13.0 cm ± 1.0 cm.
   The elongations under that force for a sample of 50 springs are shown below.

13.4	13.4	13.2	13.5	13.3	13.4	13.4	13.3	13.5	13.2
13.1	13.6	13.4	13.4	13.8	13.2	13.4	13.5	13.2	13.2
13.4	13.1	13.6	13.5	13.6	13.5	13.4	13.2	13.3	13.4
13.5	13.5	13.0	13.3	13.3	13.4	13.3	13.2	13.1	13.2
13.4	13.2	13.6	13.7	13.3	13.2	13.2	13.1	13.5	13.0

   The process is in statistical control.
   a. Develop a histogram for the sample data. Guess, by examining the his-
      togram, what the mean and the standard deviation of this sample are.
   b. As you may verify by using the pertinent formulas from Chapter 6, the mean
      of this sample is 13.348 and the standard deviation is 0.178. Based on this
      knowledge, what are your estimates of the C_p and C_{pk} indices for this
      process?
   c. How good are these values of C_p and C_{pk}? How could they be improved?

3. Two processes are under consideration to produce frictional clutch plates for
   an automatic transmission. The annual production level is approximately

100,000 plates. The drawings specify an overall thickness of 0.125 in ± 0.002 in. The cost of scrapping a plate is $25. Below are histograms of plate thickness for each process.

a. Develop the loss function for the thickness of this plate.

b. What are the approximate annual losses for each of the two processes? In other words, up to how much more can you afford to spend annually in order to use Process B rather than Process A? Use the cell midpoints as "typical values" for all the observations in a cell, recognizing that in practice you would select narrower intervals and thus be more accurate (and in doing this you would also spend some extra time).

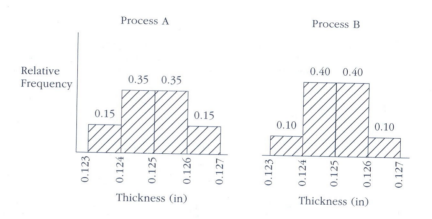

Product Improvement by Application of Taguchi Methods

BY JIM QUINLAN

1 The Product Under Test

The product under test in this experiment was extruded thermoplastic speedometer casing, shown in *Figure 1*. This product is used to cover the mechanical speedometer cable on automobiles. The product consists of an extruded polypropylene inner liner, a layer of braided wire, and a coextruded casing.

This product has been produced for over fifteen years. Prior to manufacture by Flex Products, the casing under test had been produced by a division of General Motors Corporation. That division had conducted much one factor at a time experimentation with high costs and disappointing results.

2 The Quality Characteristic

The quality characteristic of concern is the post extrusion shrinkage of the casing. Excessive shrinkage can cause noise in the

Product Improvement by Application of Taguchi Methods (Continued)

Figure 1 The Product

Extruded Thermoplastic Speedometer Cable Casing.

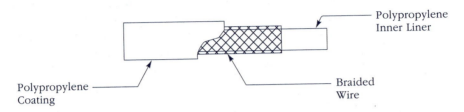

Polypropylene
Inner Liner

Polypropylene
Coating

Braided
Wire

Figure 2 The Quality Characteristic

Percent Shrinkage after a two hour heat soak test.

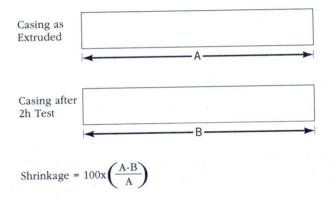

Casing as
Extruded

A

Casing after
2h Test

B

$$\text{Shrinkage} = 100\text{x}\left(\frac{A\text{-}B}{A}\right)$$

assembly, which has been one of the larger problems with mechanical speedometer cable assemblies. The post extrusion shrinkage is approximated with a two hour heat soak test, as shown in *Figure 2*.

The percent shrinkage is obtained by measuring a length of casing that has been properly conditioned, placing that casing in a two hour heat soak in an air circulating oven, reconditioning the sample, and measuring the length. The post test length is then subtracted from the original length, divided by the original length, and then mul-

tiplied by 100 to obtain a percent result. The approximate length of the samples is 600 mm.

3 The Process

The production process for this product is to (1) extrude the polypropylene liner, cool it and coil it, (2) uncoil the liner and braid wire around the liner and recoil it, and (3) uncoil the wire coated liner and extrude the coating onto it and then cut the product to the finished length.

Product Improvement By Application of Taguchi Methods (Continued)

Figure 3 The Cause and Effect Diagram for the Experiment

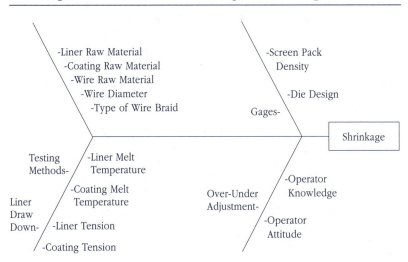

There are three separate operations. Most of the efforts at reducing post extrusion shrinkage had been directed at the final operation, since many of the characteristics were specified by the engineering drawing. In addition, in discussions regarding post extrusion shrinkage, the final operation seemed the most logical operation in which factors that significantly effect shrinkage would exist.

4 The Cause and Effect Diagram for the Experiment

In the preliminary design of the experiment, cause and effect diagrams are the most useful manner in which to generate a listing of the factors for test. Cause and effect diagrams lend more structure to ideas than the traditional brainstorming methods. *Figure 3* in the text is a greatly abbreviated version of the actual C-E diagram.

In this experiment, we obtained the opinions of our customers, the production personnel, the quality personnel, and the engineers involved in the product and process to develop a list of factors that could contribute to post extrusion shrinkage. By obtaining input from all informed personnel, the probability of conducting a successful experiment is increased dramatically.

This large diagram of potential factors was then reduced to the 15 most likely candidates by a consensus process

5 The Factor Listing

The final result was a listing of the fifteen, two level factors shown in *Figure 4*. Note that four factors concern the first step of the production process, the next three concern wire braiding, and the final eight concern the coating process.

A number of these factors concern design specified characteristics. Liner outer diameter, liner raw material, wire braid type, wire

Product Improvement by Application of Taguchi Methods (Continued)

Figure 4 Factor Listing

Liner	**A.** Liner O.D.	**A1** = Existing	**A2** = Changed
Process	**B.** Liner Die	**B1** = Existing	**B2** = Changed
	C. Liner Material	**C1** = Existing	**C2** = Changed
	D. Liner Line Speed	**D1** = Existing	**D2** = 80% of Existing
Wire	**E.** Wire Braid Type	**E1** = Existing	**E2** = Changed
Braiding	**F.** Braiding Tension	**F1** = Existing	**F2** = Changed
	G. Wire Diameter	**G1** = Smaller	**G2** = Existing
	H. Liner Tension	**H1** = Existing	**H2** = More
	I. Liner Temp.	**I1** = Ambient	**I2** = Preheated
Coating	**J.** Coating Material	**J1** = Existing	**J2** = Changed
Process	**K.** Coating Die Type	**K1** = Existing	**K2** = Changed
	L. Melt Temperature	**L1** = Existing	**L2** = Cooler
	M. Screen Pack	**M1** = Existing	**M2** = Denser
	N. Cooling Method	**N1** = Existing	**N2** = Changed
	O. Line Speed	**O1** = Existing	**O2** = 70% of Existing

diameter, and coating raw material are all designed into the product.

The levels of the factors were selected by personnel familiar with the process. This group was essentially the same as that which participated in the cause and effect diagram, with the exception that our customer's personnel were not included.

6 The Layout and Results Using L16 Orthogonal Array

Figure 5 shows the L16 array, the four separate shrinkage results, and the signal to noise ratio. The L16 array allows the testing of up to 15, two level factors. Of course, this type of design runs the risk of confounding the interactive effects with the factorial effects. To eliminate this risk entirely is only possible if all of the 32,768 combinations of the factors were tested. To minimize the risk, the experiment must be tested for reproducibility.

Since a minimum of 3,000 feet of finished product was the smallest quantity that could be manufactured at a given combination of factors, 48,000 feet of product was committed to this experiment.

The experiment itself was quite complicated to run through our extrusion plant. In an effort to minimize the confusion, summary sheets for each operation were provided to the foreman and operators. These sheets listed the combination of the factors and the orders of production, which were randomized as much as possible.

Even with the use of the summary sheets, the conduct of this experiment was not easy. The management and production operators at our extrusion facility deserve much of the credit for the success of this experiment.

After randon samples were selected for each three thousand foot sample, there were then four separate short term heat soak tests performed. One test was performed each

Product Improvement by Application of Taguchi Methods (Continued)

Figure 5 Layout Using Orthogonal Array L_{16}

A	B	C	D	E	F	G	H	I	J	K	L	M	N	O		TEST1	TEST2	TEST3	TEST4	S/N RATIO
1	1	1	1	1	1	1	1	1	1	1	1	1	1	1		0.49..	0.54..	0.46..	0.45..	6.26
1	1	1	1	1	1	1	2	2	2	2	2	2	2	2	...	0.55..	0.60..	0.57..	0.58..	4.80
1	1	1	2	2	2	2	1	1	1	1	2	2	2	2	...	0.07..	0.09..	0.11..	0.08..	21.04
1	1	1	2	2	2	2	2	2	2	2	1	1	1	1	...	0.16..	0.16..	0.19..	0.19..	15.11
1	2	2	1	1	2	2	1	1	2	2	1	1	2	2	...	0.13..	0.22..	0.20..	0.23..	14.03
1	2	2	1	1	2	2	2	1	1	2	2	1	1	1	...	0.16..	0.17..	0.13..	0.12..	16.69
1	2	2	2	2	1	1	1	1	2	2	2	2	1	1	...	0.24..	0.22..	0.19..	0.25..	12.91
1	2	2	2	2	1	1	2	2	1	1	1	1	2	2	...	0.13..	0.19..	0.19..	0.19..	15.05
2	1	2	1	2	1	2	1	2	1	2	1	2	1	2	...	0.08..	0.10..	0.14..	0.18..	17.67
2	1	2	1	2	1	2	2	1	2	1	2	1	2	1	...	0.07..	0.04..	0.19..	0.18..	17.27
2	1	2	2	1	2	1	1	2	1	2	2	1	2	1	...	0.48..	0.49..	0.44..	0.41..	6.82
2	1	2	2	1	2	1	2	1	2	1	1	2	1	2	...	0.54..	0.53..	0.53..	0.54..	5.43
2	2	1	1	2	2	1	1	2	2	1	1	2	2	1	...	0.13..	0.17..	0.21..	0.17..	15.27
2	2	1	1	2	2	1	2	1	1	2	2	1	1	2	...	0.28..	0.26..	0.26..	0.30..	11.20
2	2	1	2	1	1	2	1	2	2	1	2	1	1	2	...	0.34..	0.32..	0.30..	0.41..	9.24
2	2	1	2	1	1	2	2	1	1	2	1	2	2	1	...	0.58..	0.62..	0.59..	0.54..	4.68

TOTAL .. 193.47

day. Shrinkage was calculated from the above formula and recorded.

7 The Signal to Noise Ratio

Dr. Taguchi has extended the audio concept of signal to noise to multivariate experimentation. The formulae for signal to noise are so designed that the experimentor can always select the highest value to optimize the experiment. Therefore, the method of calculating the signal to noise ratio differs depending on whether a larger response, a smaller response, or an on target response is desirable.

In cases such as this where the smaller amount of shrinkage is better, the formula is shown in *Figure 6*. In this case, either a reduction in the mean shrinkage and/or a reduction in the variability will improve the situation. The figure shows the improvement in signal to noise ratio when either of those characteristics improve.

8 The Totals for Each Factor Level

The first step in the analysis of all multivariate experiments is to sum all the results containing one level of a factor and comparing it

Product Improvement by Application of Taguchi Methods (Continued)

Figure 6 Signal to Noise Ratio When Smaller Response Is Better

Formula:

$$S/N = -10 \times \text{Log} \left[1/n \sum_{i=1}^{n} y_i^2\right]$$

Examples:

Case	Avg.	Y_1	Y_2	Y_3	Y_4	S/N
1...	.50	.56	.44	.54	.46	5.94
2...	.15	.21	.09	.19	.11	16.00
3...	.15	.15	.16	.14	.15	16.47

CASE 3 IS BEST—SAME AVERAGE AS CASE 2 BUT LESS VARIABILITY

Figure 7 S/N Totals for each Factor Level

A1 = 105.88	E1 = 67.96	I1 = 92.82	M1 = 94.97
A2 = 87.59	E2 = 125.51	I2 = 100.64	M2 = 98.50
B1 = 94.40	F1 = 87.89	J1 = 99.40	N1 = 94.51
B2 = 99.07	F2 = 105.58	J2 = 94.07	N2 = 98.96
C1 = 87.61	G1 = 77.74	K1 = 106.25	O1 = 95.01
C2 = 105.86	G2 = 115.73	K2 = 87.22	O2 = 98.46
D1 = 103.19	H1 = 103.24	L1 = 93.50	
D2 = 90.28	H2 = 90.22	L2 = 99.97	

**THE GREATER THE DIFFERENCE IN LEVEL TOTALS FOR A FACTOR,
THE GREATER THE SIGNIFICANCE OF THAT FACTOR**

to the other level of the factor. If level one of factor A, for example, either decreased the average shrinkage or substantially reduced the variability, then the total Signal to noise ratio for A1 would be larger than that for A2.

Since the experiment was conducted using an orthogonal array, each total for a factor level contain eight signal to noise ratios. By definition the totals for both levels of a given factor equal the total of the experimental results, i.e. 193.47. By reviewing the numbers in *Figure 7,* a feeling for the effect of each factor can be obtained by noting the

difference in signal to noise totals for a given factor level. The greater the difference between level 1 and level 2 for a factor, the greater that factor's effect.

9 The Analysis of Variance Table

Figure 8 is the ANOVA table for the experiment. The analysis is performed by noting the sources of variation in the lefthand column, which are, of course, the fifteen factors under test in the experiment. The column labelled df indicates the degrees of freedom for

Product Improvement by Application of Taguchi Methods (Continued)

Figure 8 Analysis of Variance Table

Source	df	S	V	F	S'	(%)
A	1	20.9128	20.9128	11.87*	19.1513	4.6
B	[1]	[1.3612]	1.3612 Pooled		-	-
C	1	20.8282	20.8282	11.82*	19.0667	4.6
D	1	10.4171	10.4171	5.91*	8.6556	2.1
E	1	207.0275	207.0275	117.53**	205.2660	49.5
F	1	19.5625	19.5625	11.11*	17.8010	4.3
G	1	90.1788	90.1788	51.19**	88.4173	21.3
H	1	10.5963	10.5963	6.02*	8.8348	2.1
I	[1]	[3.8226]	3.8226 Pooled		-	-
J	[1]	[1.7765]	1.7765 Pooled		-	-
K	1	22.6350	22.6350	12.85**	20.8736	5.0
L	[1]	[2.6146]	2.6146 Pooled		-	-
M	[1]	[0.7782]	0.7782 Pooled		-	-
N	[1]	[1.2355]	1.2355 Pooled		-	-
O	[1]	[0.7418]	0.7418 Pooled		-	-
e	7	12.3304	1.7615	-	26.4222	6.4
T	**15**	**414.4886**	-	-	**414.4886**	**100.0**

* = Significant at 95% Confidence, $F(0.05, 1, 7) = 5.59$

** = Significant at 99% Confidence, $F(0.01, 1, 7) = 12.20$

the factor. The next column, labelled S, is the sum of squares for the factor. The column labelled V is the mean sum of squares, i.e the sum of squares for the factor divided by the degrees of freedom in that factor. The column labelled F is the results of the traditional Fisher test for significance; and an asterisk denotes whether the factor was significant at 95 or 99 percent confidence.

Notice that seven degrees of freedom, seven factorial effects in this case, have been pooled into an estimate of error. This esti-

mate of variance, or mean sum of squares for error, is used as the denominator of the F test.

The column labelled S' is the pure effect of each factor. Since all multivariate experiment designs assume that error is allocated equally over all the degrees of freedom within the experiment, each significant effect contains an amount of error which must be subtracted out. The error is added to our estimate of error in the S' column. Notice that St and S't are equal—the total variation within the experiment is constant. The final

Product Improvement by Application of Taguchi Methods (Continued)

column is the S' value for each significant factor divided by the total variation S't. This column indicates the percent of contribution to variance by each factor.

From this table, it is easy to see that Factors E and G are the most important in terms of shrinkage. These two factors account for more than 70 percent of the experimental variance.

10 The Graphs of Significant Effects

To obtain a clear idea of the experimental results, the effect of each significant factor is graphed. The factors are arranged so that the most significant is on the left. These graphs indicate what was observed in the table of summary results—that the greater the differ-

Figure 9 Graphs of Significant Effects

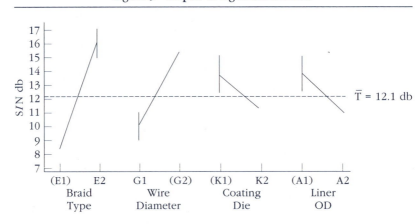

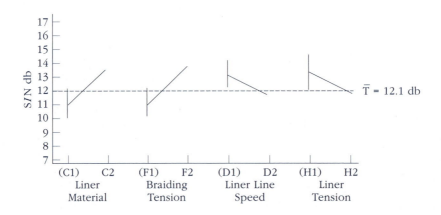

[ ] = Existing Condition

Product Improvement by Application of Taguchi Methods (Continued)

ence between levels, the greater the effect. The points are calculated by taking the total of the factor level shown in *Figure 7* and dividing the number of data points in that total to obtain an average effect. In the case of E1 for example, the average effect is 67.96 divided by 8, or 8.5 db. The experimental average of 12.1 db is obtained by dividing the total for the experiment (193.47) by the number of data points (16).

The vertical bar is the 90% confidence range for the estimate of the factor level's mean. This is based on our estimate of error and the degrees of freedom therein.

Since the higher signal to noise ratio is more desirable, it can be seen that the best level of the factors under test were being used in five of the eight significant cases. The most significant factor, however, was specified by the engineering drawing at an undesirable level.

11 Existing versus Optimum Conditions

If each factor were selected for the best signal to noise ratio, what would be the effect on post extrusion shrinkage as measured by the two hour test? And, since the actual production condition was not tested in this experiment, what does the experiment predict our shrinkage to be in production as it was currently being run?

These questions can be answered using a simple formula for prediction from the experimental results. Since the assumption has been made that each factor is independent, i.e. no significant interactions exist, the factorial effects are assumed to be independent. *Figure 10* shows these calculations and their results.

Note that the term optimum reflects only the optimum levels of the factors as defined by this experiment. The true optimum combination of these factors could be widely different than the combination shown in *Figure 10*. This optimization is based only on the knowledge obtained from the experiment.

A 90% confidence band is shown on both estimates—this band again reflects the estimate of error within the experiment and the degrees of freedom on which that estimate of mean is based. The term of the sum of

Figure 10 Calculation of Existing Versus Optimum Mean S/N Ratio.

I. Existing = A1 C1 D1 E1 F1 G2 H1 K1

$\hat{u}$ = A1 + C1 + D1 + E1 + F1 + G2 + H1 + K1 $-7 \times$ T

$\hat{u}$ = 13.24 + 10.95 + 12.90 + 8.50 + 10.99 + 14.47 + 12.91 + 13.28 $-$ 84.64

$\hat{u}$ = 12.60 $\pm$ 4.18

$$\frac{1}{n}\sum_{i=1}^{n} y^2_i = 0.0595$$

II. Optimum = A1 C2 D1 E2 F2 G2 H1 K1

$\hat{u}$ = A1 + C2 + D1 + E2 + F2 + G2 + H1 + K1 $-$ 7 $\times$ T

$\hat{u}$ = 13.24 + 13.23 + 12.90 + 15.69 + 13.20 + 14.47 + 12.91 + 13.28 $-$ 84.64

$\hat{u}$ = 24.28 $\pm$ 4.18

$$\frac{1}{n}\sum_{i=1}^{n} y^2_i = 0.0037$$

Product Improvement by Application of Taguchi Methods (Continued)

squares divided by the number of sample is calculated from the estimated mean as well. Since this is basically an estimate of the average squared plus the square of the standard deviation, it will be used later in our discussion of the loss function.

12 The Actual Results versus the Prediction

To test the results of our experiment, a comparison was made between the predictions and the actual results. Had these not compared within the 90% confidence range, the experimental results would be suspect. Either a significant hidden factor could exist, the conduct of the experiment might be flawed, or a strong interactive effect could exist.

As can be seen in *Figure 11,* the experiment successfully predicted the actual signal to noise ratio of the process both at the existing and the optimized condition.

The effect this had on the distribution of post extrusion shrinkage can be seen in *Figure 12*. This dramatic improvement, it should be noted, was only achieved by

Figure 11 Actual Results in the Process

	$\bar{X}$	S	S/N	Predicted Range
Before	0.26	0.05	11.64	8.42/16.78
After	0.05	0.025	25.05	20.10/28.46

Figure 12 Short-Term Shrinkage in Percentage

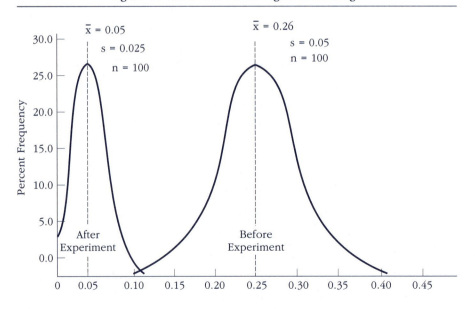

Product Improvement by Application of Taguchi Methods (Continued)

changing one of the design criteria of the product. The control charting efforts that had been assiduously applied to this process and product could not have been successful in reducing the average post extrusion shrinkage by the amount shown.

13 The Loss Function

One of Dr. Taguchi's concepts that has been gathering slow acceptance is that of the loss function. Since quality is defined by Dr. Taguchi as the loss a product causes to society, both producer and consumers costs must be considered. In most cases, lower producer costs lead to higher consumer costs and the sum of those two costs to society can be approximated by $L = k\sigma^2$.

Using this formula allows reduction in variability to be a quantified gain. This formula is used to calculate the gain to society caused by a process improvement.

While much of this formula is approximation, I feel more and more comfortable with its use. The savings shown in *Figure 14* go

somewhere, either to the producer or to the consumer. By minimizing the cost of our products to society. American manufacturers can continuously improve their competitive position in world markets.

CASE QUESTIONS

1. What is a factorial experiment? When is it used? How do you improve quality by using a factorial experiment?
2. What is a signal-to-noise ratio? What are the different types of signal-to-noise ratios used? How are signal-to-noise ratios used as part of Taguchi's approach to experimental design?
3. You will be using a factorial experiment to improve the aroma of a coffee blend.
   a. What factors would you use?
   b. Suppose your answer to part (a) involves six factors. If you run a full factorial experiment using two levels per factor and two replications per factor-level combination, how many tests would you have to run?

Figure 13 Loss Function for Speedometer Casing

If Shrinkage = 1.50%, then Customer Complains.

Warranty Cost to Replace Cable Assembly = $80.

Therefore:

   $K = (80/(1.5^2)) = \$35.56$

And:

   $L = k\sigma^2$ (For Smaller the Better $\sigma^2 = \bar{y}^2 + s^2$)

Therefore:

   Existing Condition $L_e = 35.56 \times 0.0595 = \$2.12$ per unit.

   Optimum Condition $L_o = 35.56 \times 0.0037 = \$0.13$ per unit.

Product Improvement by Application of Taguchi Methods (Continued)

Figure 14 Loss Function

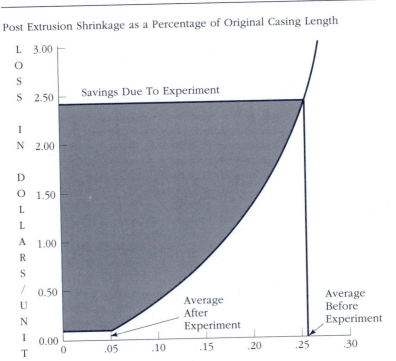

Post Extrusion Shrinkage as a Percentage of Original Casing Length

Steps For Building
an Affinity Diagram

◆ ◆ ◆

The instructions below are intended for use by a team of people (not more than 10). The group intends to create the affinity diagram on a sheet of paper. Usually, this worksheet is made up of two sheets of paper from a flip chart attached to each other. Ideas generated in the brainstorming session are written on a 3-by-3 Post-It note. When these ideas are grouped, the label representing the group is written on a 3-by-5 Post-In note. One person in the group is nominated as facilitator. This person's task is to make sure the group follows the steps of the exercise.

It is important to keep the process moving forward. Groups often tend to return to an earlier step in an effort to "make it perfect." A device that is effective in maintaining the momentum is to conduct a small ceremony at certain critical steps. The ceremony consists of all members of the group assembling in a circle and shouting "Yo-One" with a loud clap. It is done after Steps 3, 4, 5, 6, and 9. The intent is to provide a clear dividing line and implicitly get everyone's agreement not to return to steps done before the ceremony.

Step 1. State the Issue.

The team should agree on the issue that is being considered. The statement describing the issue is often stated in the form of a weakness. For example, "What are the weaknesses in our new product development process?" or "What weaknesses do we have in communicating our commitment to TQM principles through the organization?" The issue is written on the top left-hand corner of the worksheet.

Step 2. Initiate Brainstorming.

First, have everyone in the room voice their ideas in a concise way. Each person is allotted 30 seconds before moving on. This stage can continue for several minutes until the facilitator senses it is time to move along. With a six-person group three rounds seem to be enough, and they last a maximum of 10 minutes.

All members of the team write their ideas down on a 3-by-3 Post-It note, one idea per note. The idea should be stated as a sentence in response to the issue wrriten on the worksheet, and it should not exceed seven words. As the notes are written, the facilitator places them on the worksheet and reads them out aloud to the group. No criticism of the idea is allowed at this stage. There should be at least 20 distinct ideas, otherwise this is a trivial exercise.

Step 3. "Scrub" the Ideas.

Once all of the ideas have been written down, review each idea in turn. The group should evaluate the idea of redundancy and clarity. Ideas considered to be redundant should be discarded (the author of the note must agree). To ensure the idea is clear, it is useful to have the author provide an illustrative example.

Step 4. Group the Ideas.

All members of the team gather around the worksheet for this part of the exercise. The individual notes are spread over the worksheet by the facilitator. Then each person takes notes that they feel have an affinity and put them together. If another person disagrees, they can simply take the notes apart and place them with others. This is best done as a silent process; no reasons need be given for putting notes together. If there is a disagreement, the facilitator can allow some discussion. The purpose is to group notes based on "feel," not necessarily on an obvious logical connection. There should be no more than three cards per group, but not all cards have to be in a group.

Step 5. Create Headers.

Write on a 3-by-5 Post-It note a header statement that captures the meaning of the cards in each group. Headers do not have to be written for "loners" that do not belong to any group. The header should be written as a sentence responding to the issue statement. Try not to include any words that have been used in the labels in that group.

Step 6. Prepare Higher-level Grouping.

Before moving to the next level of groupings, take a look at the ideas generated so far and add any that may have been omitted. Then assemble the groups of notes and cover them with the header label. At this point, the only ideas visible on the worksheet would be the header labels and the loners. Continue grouping labels and writing headers until the total number of groups and loners are five or less.

Step 7. Establish the Relationships.

Place the five or less groups randomly on the worksheet. Draw arrows indicating the relationships between the groups. Do this in pencil or on a Post-It note. If one group is the cause of problems represented by another group, an arrow should be drawn from the first group to the second. If two groups contradict each other use the symbol ">——<".

Step 8. Draw the Completed Diagram.

Place the groups on the worksheet so that enough space is available to make all of the cards underneath the group header visible. Keep some space free at the top right-hand corner of the worksheet. Place all of the cards in position and glue them to the worksheet. Show the relationship of the first-level titles by drawing a red circle around them. Then show the relations of the second level groupings by circling with a blue marker. Continue using different colors to represent each level of groupings. Finish by drawing the connecting arrows between the top-level groupings. These should be bold, and all should have the same color.

Step 9. Establish Priorities.

Each member of the group is given three votes to indicate their evaluation of the relative importance of each group. Sticky dots are good for documenting the votes. Each person gets a red (most important), blue and green (least important) dot. Each person places the dot on one of the first round headers or a loner. Once everyone has voted, the priority is established by totaling the points. The red dots are worth three points, the blue two, and the green one. The group with the largest number of points is the most important. Highlight this circle by filling it with a red cross-hatch. The next most important would be highlighted with a blue single hatch and the third with a green dotted fill.

Step 10. Summarize the Results.

Write a statement capturing especially the three most important issues in the top right-hand corner. Write a one-page summary consisting of two parts. Summarize the conclusions, the three most important issues, and the causal relationships.

Review the process and record the weaknesses the group perceived. Include any suggestions for improvement.

How Signal-to-Noise Ratios Work

◆ ◆ ◆

One characteristic of Taguchi's approach to experimental design is his use of signal-to-noise (S/N) ratios. The S/N ratios combine, in a single measure, information on both the average level and the spread of a variable.

Taguchi uses three main types of S/N ratios:

1. "Lower-is-better" ratios apply to variables, such as the force required to close a door or the warp in lumber, where a lower value is preferable.
2. "Higher-is-better" ratios apply when you are trying to maximize a variable, such as the yield of a process, the satisfaction level for a service, or the energy efficiency of an engine.
3. "Nominal-is-best" ratios apply to variables for which there is a target value and deviations in any direction are undesirable, as is the case for the diameter of an axle or the phosphate content in a fertilizer.

Regardless of whether you are trying to minimize, maximize, or be as close as possible to a target, you also want to reduce variation as much as possible.

In our case study, shrinkage is to be as small as possible, so the lower-is-better ratio is used. The following formula is used to compute lower-is-better ratios:

$$\text{S/N} = -10 \log_{10} \left[\frac{1}{n} \sum y_i^2 \right]$$

In this formula, n represents number of observations for which we are computing the S/N ratio (four in our example) and y_i represents the ith observation for which we are computing the ratio.

To see what this formula does, we will apply it to the following three rows of data (not our experimental data but, rather, data suitably chosen to show the properties of S/N ratios). In each data row there are four observations, their average, their standard deviation, and a S/N ratio computed from the four observations according to the formula we just presented. A graph of the observations is also shown below.

Row	Y_1	Y_2	Y_3	Y_4	Average $\overline{Y}$	Standard Deviation S	S/N Ratio
1	0.56	0.44	0.54	0.46	0.50	0.059	5.98
2	0.21	0.09	0.19	0.11	0.15	0.059	16.00
3	0.15	0.16	0.14	0.15	0.15	0.008	16.47

Row	0.1	0.2	0.3	0.4	0.5	0.6
1				○	○ ○	○
2		○ ○	○ ○			
3		○○○○				

If these observations represented shrinkage, which row would have the best results and which would have the worst? If you observe the averages and standard deviations for the three rows, and recall that shrinkage is to be minimized and its variation is to be reduced as much as possible, you should conclude the following:

- Row 3 has the best results (since it has the lowest standard deviation and no other row has a lower average).
- Row 1 has the worst shrinkage (high average and high standard deviation).

The S/N ratios in the last column confirm this, since *higher S/N ratios are always better*. All S/N ratio formulas are such that this is always true. Regardless of whether you are using the lower-is-better, the larger-is-better, or the nominal-is-best formula to compute an S/N ratio for a set of observations, the higher value of the S/N ratio, the better the observations.

We next show how the S/N ratios are computed. We use as an example row 1, where the four observations are

$$y_i = 0.56 \qquad y_2 = 0.44 \qquad y_3 = 0.54 \qquad y_4 = 0.46$$

Using these four values, we compute

$$\Sigma y_1^2 = 0.56^2 + 0.44^2 + 0.54^2 + 0.46^2 = 0.3136 + 0.1936 + 0.2916 + 0.2116 = 1.0104$$

Therefore, with $n = 4$, we have

$$S/N = -10 \log_{10} \left[\frac{1}{n} \Sigma y_i^2 \right] = -10 \log_{10} \left[\frac{1}{4} (1.0104) \right]$$

$$= -10 \log_{10} (0.2526) = -10 (-0.5976) = 5.976$$

The S/N ratios for the other two rows are computed similarly.

Higher-is-better and nominal-is-best ratios are computed as follows (Kackar, 1986):

Higher is better:

$$S/N = -10 \log_{10} \left[\frac{1}{n} \Sigma \frac{1}{y_i^2} \right]$$

Nominal is best:

$$S/N = 10 \log_{10} \left[\frac{\bar{y}^2}{s^2} \right]$$

where $\bar{y} = \dfrac{\Sigma y_i}{n}$

and

$$s^2 = \frac{\Sigma (y_i - \bar{y})^2}{n - 1}$$

are the mean and variance of the y values.

◆ Bibliography

Box, George, William G. Hunter, and J. Stuart Hunter. *Statistics for Experimenters*. New York: John Wiley and Sons, 1978.

Box, G., R. Kacker, V. Nair, M. Phadke, A. Shoemaker, and J. Wu. "Quality Practices in Japan." *Quality Progress* (March 1988): 37–41.

Brassard, M. *The Memory Jogger Plus +*. Methuen, Mass.: GOAL/QPC, 1989.

Byrne, Diane M, and Shin Taguchi. "The Taguchi Approach to Parameter Design." *Quality Progress* (December 1987): 19–26.

Dambolena, Ismael, and Ashok Rao. "What Is Six Sigma Anyway?" *Quality* (November 1994): 10.

Gallupe R. B., and W. H. Cooper. "Brainstorming Electronically." *Sloan Management Review* (Fall 1993): 27–36.

Green, Paul E. and Yoram Wind. "New Way to Measure Consumers' Judgments." *Harvard Business Review* (July–August 1975): 362–371.

Heil, H., B. Hofmann, N. Schmidt, and J. Segain. "Photoreceptor Optimization via Taguchi Methods." Dearborn, Mich.: American Supplier Institute, 1986.

Kackar, Raghu N. "Taguchi's Quality Philosophy: Analysis and Commentary." *Quality Progress* (December 1986): 21–29.

Kane, Victor. "Process Capability Indices." *Journal of Quality Technology* (January 1986): 41–52.

Kirkpatrick, D., "Here Comes the Payoff from PCs." *Fortune,* March 23, 1992, pp. XX.

Lochner, Robert H., and Joseph E. Matar. *Designing for Quality*. White Plains, N.Y.: Quality Resources, 1990.

Miller, K. L., and D. Woodruff. "A Design Master's End Run Around Trial and Error." Special issue of *Business Week,* October 25, 1991.

Mullen, B., C. Johnson, and E. Salas. "Productivity Loss in Brainstorming Groups: A Meta-analytical Integration." *Basic and Applied Social Psychology* 12 (1991): 3–23.

Ross, Phillip J. *Taguchi Techniques for Quality Engineering*. New York: McGraw-Hill Book Co., 1988.

"Step by Step KJ Method: A Problem Solving Tool for Organizing Qualitative Data." Cambridge, Mass.: Center for Quality Management, 1990.

Sullivan, L. P. "The Seven Stages in Company-Wide Quality Control." *Quality Progress* (May 1986): 77–83.

Sullivan, Lawrence P. "The Power of Taguchi Methods." *Quality Progress* (June 1987): 76–79.

Taguchi, Genichi. *Introduction to Quality Engineering: Designing Quality into Products and Processes*. Tokyo: Asian Productivity Organization, 1986.

Tyran, C. K., A. R. Dennis, D. R. Vogel, and J. F. Nunamaker, Jr. "The Application of Electronic Meeting Technology to Support Strategic Management." *MIS Quarterly* (September 1992): 313–334.

Chapter 9

Customer Measurement I: Traditional Multi-Attribute Methods

◆ ◆ ◆

*I*t is the mid-1980s, and consumer perceptions of automobiles in the U.S. market are summarized by the perceptual map shown in Exhibit 9.1. While car buyers consider a broad array of **customer attributes** (product features) in selecting a new car, the **perceptual map** focuses on two "macro" dimensions that are judged to be key drivers of choice and that, in fact, summarize many other more specific features. These dimensions are: conservative/older *versus* sporty/youthful; *and* classy/status symbol *versus* practical/affordable. *Despite its apparent simplicity, this perceptual map yields some very important conclusions:*

- *Chrysler's* entire product line—Chrysler, Plymouth, and Dodge—appeals to the conservative/older market segment. Thus Chrysler's CEO, Lee Iacocca, faces a situation in which the company is underrepresented in the more youthful, sporty market positioning.
- *Mercedes Benz* faces a major "youth gap" in its ongoing competition with BMW. While the Mercedes marque's older, more conservative positioning is considered by some to be a company hallmark, Mercedes Benz marketing managers recognize the youth gap to be an obstacle to growth.

*W*ith hindsight, it can be seen that both Chrysler and Mercedes moved to repair product line weaknesses as revealed by the **positioning map.** In particular, Chrysler focused on the Dodge marque to spearhead its repositioning efforts. Dodge introduced more youthful, sporty models in constant succession: Dodge Daytona (mid-1980s); high-performance/niche models under the Carroll Shelby/Daytona name in the late 1980s; Dodge Stealth in 1991; Dodge Viper in 1992; and the Dodge Avenger to replace the Daytona in 1995–1996. Consumer advertising reinforced the repositioning effort with upbeat, youthful advertisements. Similarly, Mercedes has taken a major step to broaden its market appeal through the introduction of the 190E and, more recently, the C Class to compete directly with the BMW 3 Series.

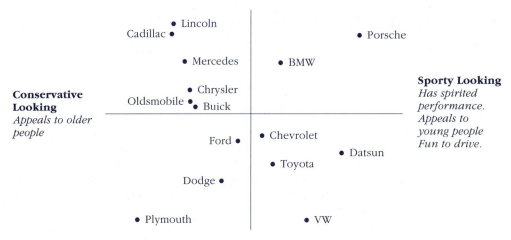

Exhibit
9.1

Perceptual Map of U.S. Automobile Market, 1984

Like Chrysler and Mercedes Benz, all marketers need to give high credence to the customer's perception and definition of quality. This chapter and the next will present a group of customer measurement techniques—multi-attribute measurement methods—which will help the product development team in hearing the Voice of the Customer.

◆ INTRODUCTION

Just as identifying and satisfying customer needs is basic to Total Quality Management, it has historically been a central tenet for the marketing and marketing research functions. The Marketing Department should be able to bring to the product design a clear set of specifications on what it will take to meet customer needs. Then it is marketing's job to join a multifunctional team in translating stated needs into actionable, technical specifications. The end goal is detailed specifications for a product that can be produced to meet cost and performance targets.

As the preceding example illustrates, perceptual mapping is an excellent tool for understanding how customers view the market—what in TQM parlance has been labeled the Voice of the Customer. Basically, perceptual maps provide direction for new product development, product improvement, and marketing communications programs, all geared toward the goal of creating higher customer satisfaction. Of course, marketers have always been concerned with identifying and satisfying customer needs and have, over time, developed a rather standard set of measurement techniques toward these ends. This chapter introduces the multi-attribute model and describes traditional research approaches for putting it into practice. In what follows we use interchangeably the terms *attributes, customer attributes, benefits, features,* and *product characteristics.*

In a broader sense, the tools described in this and the following chapter serve to define what is meant by marketing-driven quality. Although "marketing types" have traditionally been criticized for decision-making-by-the-seat-of-the-pants and for lacking support data, the tools explicated here should, we believe, add credibility to Marketing's ongoing role in collecting the Voice of the Customer and in communicating it throughout the organization. To be sure, the traditional techniques covered in this chapter have predated the rise of TQM and its codification. Nevertheless, these tools have long served as a means of capturing and interpreting the Voice of the Customer, a TQM building block, and their influence is clearly imprinted on the more modern TQM approaches that follow in Chapter 10.

◆ MULTI-ATTRIBUTE MODEL

Experienced marketers are constantly alternating between two different, but complementary, perspectives on the nature of a product offering, that is,

- *Gestalt or holistic view*—the meaning of the brand as a whole. Consider the overall images conjured by such brand names as Mercedes Benz (functionally brilliant, a mark of status), Campbell's Soup (traditional, nourishing), Crest Toothpaste (effective, conservative), and the Democratic party (for large government, populist).
- *Multi-attribute view*—the brand as a **bundle of benefits,** a constellation of want-satisfying attributes. For example, a Mercedes excels in comfort, styling, safety, durability, and resale value.

For TQM purposes, the multi-attribute view is the more useful of the two, although it is advantageous for the product design team to keep in mind the Gestalt view as it labors over the task of defining product specifications. The **multi-attribute model** of buying behavior originated in the field of psychology as a means of

Exhibit
9.2

Examples of Core Benefit Propositions

BRAND	CBP
Prudential Insurance	Large and financially solid ("A Piece of the Rock")
Toyota	High quality/no defects; high resale value
American Express Card	High status; travelers' friend in foreign countries
Disney World	Clean; friendly; fun; for the whole family
Home Depot	Low prices; staff offers expert advice
Steven Spielberg	Brings imagination to the screen; old-fashioned thrills

explaining how individuals acquire specific beliefs and attitudes (Engel, Blackwell, and Miniard, 1993). Multi-attribute thinking is quite simple. That is, consumers are seen as buying products for the functions or benefits they deliver; and *the consumer will select that brand that delivers important performance attributes in a superior way.*

In multi-attribute thinking, a product *is* the bundle of key benefits delivered to the customer. Urban and Hauser (1993) have given the label, **Core Benefit Proposition (CBP)** to the statement of important attributes that provide value for the customer and that differentiate the product from its competitors. Since a good deal of advertising is devoted to communicating a brand's CBP, the reader will be familiar with the examples presented in Exhibit 9.2.

Working toward the definition of an effective CBP via traditional multi-attribute methods requires that several steps be carried out:

1. Identify important attributes.
2. Plot existing objects in attribute space; employ data-reduction techniques to improve interpretation.
3. Measure consumer perceptions via rating scales.
4. Determine the importance weights of attributes.
5. Base new product design on filling gaps in the perceptual space.

A sixth step, translating the CBP into technical specifications, represents an extension of the above and is covered in the next chapter. A discussion of steps 1-5 follows.

Identify Important Attributes

The first step in putting into practice any of the multi-attribute approaches in this and the next chapter is to develop a complete list of customer needs expressed as desirable product attributes. For the purposes of traditional consumer measurement techniques, this list typically numbers 10 to 30 attributes; the newer,

Quality Function Deployment technique (Chapter 10) may generate far more customer features, as many as 100 to 200. The process of compiling the list of attributes is a major part of the research phase labeled **exploratory research.** Typically, exploratory research employs secondary sources, qualitative research techniques, and expert judgment in setting up the structure of a formal questionnaire. Thus the exploratory phase leads to the creation of a questionnaire which, after pretesting and modification, becomes the data-collection instrument. Specifically, a list of attributes may be generated by the following:

1. *Secondary sources*
   - Literature review—published articles, government data, and past research.
2. *Qualitative research*
   - Focus groups
   - One-on-one interviews
3. *Competitors' promotion*—sales literature, advertising, and packaging
4. *Expert judgment*—for example, conversations with dealers, salespeople, and the like

A full discussion of exploratory techniques is beyond the scope of this text, but suffice it to say that none of the above should be ignored in laying the groundwork for multi-attribute measurement. Focus groups are a particularly interesting method for generating attribute lists. Intuitively, we think they allow for group synergies—that is, ping-ponging of ideas among participants. However, recent research indicates that these group synergies are not present and that one-on-one interviews perform as well as focus groups in generating a list of customer attributes (Griffin and Hauser 1993).

Two techniques for eliciting product attributes are to ask respondents to relate product problems that have been bothersome (e.g., "The kids love chocolate, but within minutes it's all over the furniture!") and to use the **Repertory Grid.** The Repertory Grid takes triads of brands and asks respondents to describe which two are most similar and which two are most dissimilar, and why. Product attributes for the instant hair-conditioner category are listed in Exhibit 9.3.

Plot Existing Objects in Attribute Space; Employ Data-Reduction Techniques to Improve Interpretation

The data collected in steps 1 and 2 above are highly useful in their raw form; nonetheless, the decision maker may want to employ data-reduction techniques to summarize the data in a more interpretable format. To illustrate, we will borrow an example from Urban and Hauser (1993). Exhibit 9.4 indicates customer ratings of how well five communications methods deliver on 25 customer needs. Examination of the **snake plot** yields the following conclusions: personal visits are superior on many measures but are more expensive than the telephone or teletype; closed-circuit

Exhibit

9.3

Product Attributes of Instant Hair Conditioners

FACTOR	RELATIVE IMPORTANCE	ATTRIBUTES COMBINED TO FORM THE FACTOR
Conditioning	33%	Nourishes dry hair.
		Restores moisture.
		Keeps control of split ends.
		Makes dry hair healthy looking.
		Conditions hair.
		Helps keep hair from breaking.
		Penetrates hair.
Clean	27%	Leaves hair free of residue/flakes.
		Leaves hair grease- and oil-free.
		Leaves hair clean looking.
		Rinses out easily/completely.
Manageability/effects	23%	Makes hair more manageable.
		Leaves hair shiny/Lustrous.
		Leaves hair soft and silky.
		Gives hair body and fullness.
Fragrance	17%	Has pleasant fragrance while using.
		Leaves hair with nice fragrance.

SOURCE: Darral G. Clarke, "Johnson Wax: Enhance (A)," Harvard Business School, case (#9-583-046), 1982, p. 8. Copyright © 1982 by the President and Fellows of Harvard College. Reprinted by permission.

television (CCT) is seen as a "hassle" and as being expensive (these are clear signals for possible product improvements!); all methods suffer from low ratings on "plan in advance" and "eliminate red tape."

Exhibit 9.5 presents the five communications methods plotted in "reduced space" created by utilizing a technique called **factor analysis.** In essence, factor analysis has identified subgroups of attributes within the original list of 25. "Ease of use" is a combination of attributes, 2, 3, 6, 10, 13, 14, 21, and 22; "effectiveness" is numbers 1, 4, 7, 9, 11, 15–20, and 23. Factor analysis works by detecting correlations among items on the list. It combines highly correlated subgroups and weights the original scores to yield a new score for each object (product) on the new combined attributes. Exhibit 9.5 is commonly labeled a perceptual map or positioning map. Other techniques that achieve data reduction include discriminant analysis, cluster analysis, and correspondence analysis. The positioning map in Exhibit 9.5 represents an improvement in interpretation over the snake plot in the previous table. The superior effectiveness of personal visits is clearly shown, as is CCT's deficiency in ease of use. Of course, the decision maker can be grossly misled if the attribute plotting employs the respondents' average scores from

Exhibit
9.4

Customer Ratings of Five Communications Methods ("Snake Plot")

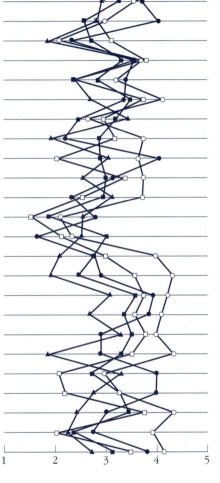

1. Effective information exchange
2. Find and reach the right person
3. Save time
4. Not need visual aids
5. Not get trapped
6. Eliminate paper work
7. Persuade
8. Focus on issues
9. All forms of information
10. No hassle
11. Control impression
12. Good for security/privacy
13. Must plan in advance
14. Eliminate red tape
15. Monitor people and operations
16. High level of interaction
17. Solve problems
18. Express feelings
19. Not misinterpret
20. Good for group discussion
21. Inexpensive
22. Quick response
23. Enhance idea development
24. Works well for commitment
25. Can maintain contact

1   2   3   4   5

- • Telephone
- ○ Personal Visit   □ Closed-Circuit Television
- ■ Narrow Band Video Telephone   ▲ Teletype

SOURCE: Glen L. Urban and John R. Hauser, *Design and Marketing of New Products,* 2nd ed., p. 209. © 1993. Reprinted by permission of Prentice-Hall, Inc., Englewood Cliffs, NJ.

Exhibit 9.5 | Perceptual Map of Five Communications Methods in "Reduced" Attribute Space

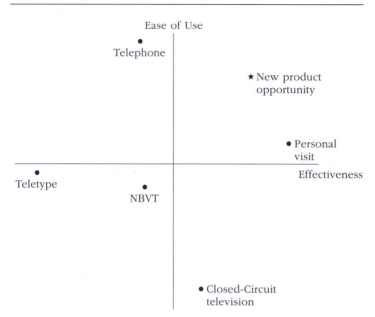

SOURCE: Glen L. Urban and John R. Hauser, *Design and Marketing of New Products,* 2nd ed., p. 211. © 1993. Reprinted by permission of Prentice-Hall, Inc., Englewood Cliffs, N.J.

widely dissimilar market segments. Thus, assuming adequate sample size, the analyst should test *a priori* segmentation schemes (e.g., grouping customers by demographics) or can employ cluster analysis to detect natural customer groupings.

Measure Consumer Perceptions Via Rating Scales

Attribute lists such as the one presented in Exhibit 9.3, are easily transformed into rating scales. One way is simply to ask consumers to rate brands they are familiar with on a scale of poor–excellent in delivering the particular attribute. Another way is to make a qualitative statement about the attribute asking consumers to respond on an agree-disagree scale. A third alternative is to create a rating scale, called the **semantic differential,** in which the end-points are bounded by opposite adjectives. For example, consumers might be asked to rate airline companies on dimensions such as good service–poor service, modern–old fashioned, cheap–expensive, and convenient schedules–inconvenient schedules. Exhibit 9.6 shows the actual **rating scales** used to measure instant hair-conditioner attributes from Exhibit 9.3.

Exhibit
9.6

Example of Multi-attribute Rating Scales

Brand: _____

Please rate the above brand of creme rinse, hair conditioner, or balsam conditioning product on each of the items below. The *best possible rating* you can give is a 7, the *poorest possible* rating is a 1. Circle *one* number for each item listed. Even if you have never used the product yourself, we would like your impression of what it is like based on what you have seen or heard.

	Best Possible Rating						Poorest Possible Rating
1. Nourishes dry hair.	7	6	5	4	3	2	1
2. Leaves hair free of residue, film, and flakes.	7	6	5	4	3	2	1
3. Gives hair body and fullness.	7	6	5	4	3	2	1
4. Rinses out easily/completely.	7	6	5	4	3	2	1
5. Restores moisture.	7	6	5	4	3	2	1
6. Keeps control of split ends.	7	6	5	4	3	2	1
7. Leaves hair feeling soft and silky.	7	6	5	4	3	2	1

SOURCE: Darral G. Clarke, "Johnson Wax: Enhance (A)," Harvard Business School, case (#9-583-046), 1982, p. 29. Copyright © 1982 by the President and Fellows of Harvard College. Reprinted by permission.

The advantage of closed-end rating scales is that consumers can easily respond by simply "checking the box," thus permitting the rating of several brands (sometimes including an "ideal product") on several attributes. The clear disadvantage in the approach is the garbage in/garbage out principle that limits the responses to the questions asked. Thus, although multi-attribute rating scales enable the collection of a substantial amount of information which can then be manipulated by various statistical programs, the application of these surveys produces few surprises. At the same time, the sheer volume and coverage of the information provides an excellent starting point for creative sessions designed to transform the market, create new attributes, define new competitive strategies, and the like. As is noted below, the Japanese have traditionally taken a different viewpoint than U.S. researchers on the tradeoff of statistical significance versus depth.

The attribute data gathered via numerical rating scales will, for data analysis purposes, probably be treated as though they were true interval data. In fact, in a strict sense, rating scales provide only data of an ordinal nature. However, in our view, the fact that the "interval assumption" is made so often with apparently good results indicates that statistical techniques such as multiple regression and factor analysis are sufficiently robust. On the other hand, there exist statistical methods such as correspondence analysis and binary factor analysis which make far less stringent demands on the data.

Determine the Importance Weights of Attributes

Attributes that are salient, that is, considered in product choice, but that have little relative importance to the customer should receive less priority in product development and communications programs. For example, in the presidential campaign of 1984, Walter Mondale committed a positioning error by stressing deficit reduction, a relatively unimportant attribute compared with taxes and crime. And importance weight can vary by market segment. For example, a study of female fashion apparel customers revealed the following differences in important attributes. (See Exhibit 9.7.)

Attribute importance may be determined by *direct methods* in which respondents indicate importance weights, say, for example, on a rating scale ("Not at all Important" to "Very Important"); and **revealed importance** methods in which importance weights are derived via statistical techniques but are not given directly by respondents. **Conjoint analysis** and **preference regression** are two revealed importance methods; conjoint analysis is discussed later in this chapter. While researchers have generally seen revealed importance measures as superior, a recent reexamination of the issue indicates that this may not be so (Griffin and Hauser 1993). In any case, the best discussion of measuring attribute importance is to be found in Urban and Hauser (1993, Chapter 10).

Base New Product Design on Filling Gaps in the Perceptual Space

Snake plots and perceptual maps reveal clear opportunities for improving existing product offerings. To complete the example from Urban and Hauser, a "new product opportunity" is identified in Exhibit 9.5 as a communications method that

Exhibit
9.7

Important Store Attributes Sought by Female Fashion Apparel Shoppers

IMPORTANT ATTRIBUTES	Segment			
	PRICE SHOPPER	YOUNG CAREERS	SENIOR SHOPPER	FASHION ELITE
	Low prices	Up-to-date fashions	Easy to get to store	Quality merchandise
	Easy to get to store	Latest fashions	Knowledgeable clerks	Up-to-date fashions
	Good markdowns	Exciting display	Lots of salespeople	Latest fashions
				Lots of salespeople

SOURCE: Kopp, Eng, and Tigert (1989).

combines high effectiveness with ease of use. Scanning back and forth between the perceptual map and the raw ratings in Exhibit 9.4, the design team can begin to draw up specifications for a new or improved product.

◆ MARKET SEGMENTATION

In marketing, market segmentation is everything. Segmentation simply means breaking up a total market into smaller groups that differ in their response to some marketing variable. For example, market segments can be defined by their differences on basic product benefits desired (benefit segmentation), geographic variables, demographics (age, income, occupation, etc.), psychographics (activities, interests, opinions, lifestyles), and usage rate, for example, heavy versus light users. In industrial markets, segmentation bases usually include the customer's industry classification, company size, and location.

Segmentation can also be described according to price and promotion sensitivities. For example, consumers who will not buy without a coupon are termed a "deal-prone" segment. And many segmentation schemes show differences along several of the above variables simultaneously.

Theoretically, segmentation *always* produces higher customer satisfaction; however, the key tradeoff is that dividing high-volume mass markets into smaller segments may increase the costs of production and marketing. For example, upscale automobiles like BMW, which use selective media, face higher costs than mass market brands that can buy broad media such as network TV. Thus, in TQM terms, segmented, customized products will always be better matched to customer needs. The key question is: Are these customers willing to pay for the extra costs involved in tailoring the product mix? (*Note:* When customization can be achieved at no cost, segmentation becomes a "no brainer." To borrow a phrase from Nike, just do it!)

For product designers, benefit segmentation is the most powerful basis for segmenting markets. The Telecom case example below illustrates the importance of benefit segmentation, for it shows how different groups of customers value different product features. To accomplish benefit segmentation in any perceptual mapping study, simply divide the sample into segments and test the hypothesis that they differ significantly.

◆ CASE STUDIES

Johnson Wax Enhance Conditioner

This is an excellent case study written by Darral G. Clarke, a noted management scientist. As part of research conducted in conjunction with Assessor, a pretest market simulation model, the attributes in Exhibit 9.3 were factor analyzed to yield the

Exhibit
9.8

Perceptual Map of Instant Hair-Conditioner Market

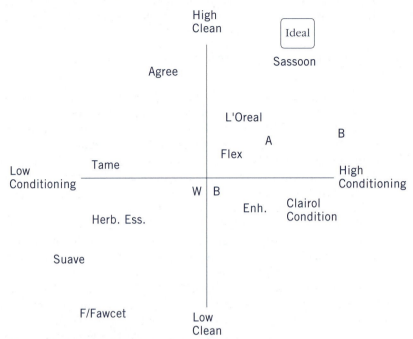

Enh. = Enhance; WB = Wella Balsam

SOURCE: Darral G. Clarke, "Johnson Wax: Enhance (A)," Harvard Business School, case (#9-583-046), 1982, p. 16. Copyright © 1982 by the President and Fellows of Harvard College. Reprinted by permission.

four factors (also indicated in Exhibit 9.3) conditioning, manageability, fragrance, and clean. Consumers rated the leading instant conditioner brands on the attributes, and the results were plotted on a series of perceptual maps that displayed the four factors two at a time. Exhibit 9.8 contains a plot of the "conditioning" and "clean" dimensions for a subset of brands popular at the time of the case (1979). Note also that the positioning of the "ideal" brand is also shown; brands closer to the ideal are presumed to garner a higher share of consumer preferences. From this simple display of data, several implications are apparent. First, it appears that Clairol's Condition brand has in fact achieved the positioning implied by its brand name. Similarly, Agree, whose tagline is "stops the greasies," has indeed achieved an excellent positioning on the "clean" dimension. The map also allows a new product development team to speculate on a possible Core Benefit Proposition (CBP) for possible new brands. For example, point "A" implies a new product with the *"Popular price of Flex, yet delivers more benefits"*; or point "B" would be: *"Unsurpassed conditioning, yet leaves hair feeling clean."* This latter CBP might even work as a *repositioning* for Clairol Condition. In sum, Johnson Wax used positioning maps such as these to target and evaluate its positioning efforts for Enhance, a new conditioner originally positioned toward the problems of dry hair.

Suzuki Samurai

In the mid-1980s, Suzuki Motor Corporation employed the perceptual map in Exhibit 9.9 to contemplate possible positionings for a new four-wheel-drive vehicle it was planning to launch in the United States. The perceptual map was created by *Newsweek* magazine, which gathered ratings on 35 automobile attributes. These were reduced by factor analysis to seven underlying dimensions: *everyday driving, passenger comfort, quality/durability, styling, off-road/snow driving, capacity,* and *gas mileage.* The map shown in Exhibit 9.9 plots several existing sport utility vehicles and pickup trucks on the "off-road" and "everyday" attributes. The situation faced by Suzuki was an interesting one. Management was convinced by various pieces of research and previous marketing of the product in other places that the Samurai was, in fact, a versatile product that could take on any of three possible positionings: that is, an off-road/sport-utility vehicle, a compact pickup truck, or a replacement for a subcompact automobile.

The CBP would vary depending on the usage situation targeted. One of the factors Suzuki management had to contend with was whether and how far each of the positionings would possibly diverge from what the physical product could actually deliver. In fact, subsequent research indicated that consumers perceived the Samurai as being much more off-road and not well suited for everyday driving. Thus, in a sense the company was faced with making a comparison between two multi-attribute maps—that is, one based on perceptions and one based on real product function

Should Suzuki have chosen an "everyday driving" CBP, product engineers would probably have had to modify the vehicle's design. In fact, Suzuki's advertising agency recommended what they termed an "unposition"; that is, advertising that would, by design, not define the product or the consumer but would allow different customer segments to adopt the positioning that best suited its needs and perceptions. Beyond this, the multi-attribute framework itself is of obvious advantage to product designers interested in seeing what current positions have been captured by specific brands as well as in discovering possible gaps to be filled.

Telecom Inc.

Telecom Inc. was a large telecommunications company (name disguised) that desired to enter the market for nonintelligent computer terminals. A multi-attribute study revealed 30 attributes that were reduced via factor analysis to 14 underlying dimensions (Exhibit 9.10). In the study, the sample of potential customers was divided into four major segments by means of cluster analysis. The four segments differed in their sensitivities to the various attributes as shown in the exhibit; segment names were assigned by the researchers. In essence, the study found that each of

Exhibit
9.9   Perceptual Map of Sport Utility Vehicles and Pickup Trucks

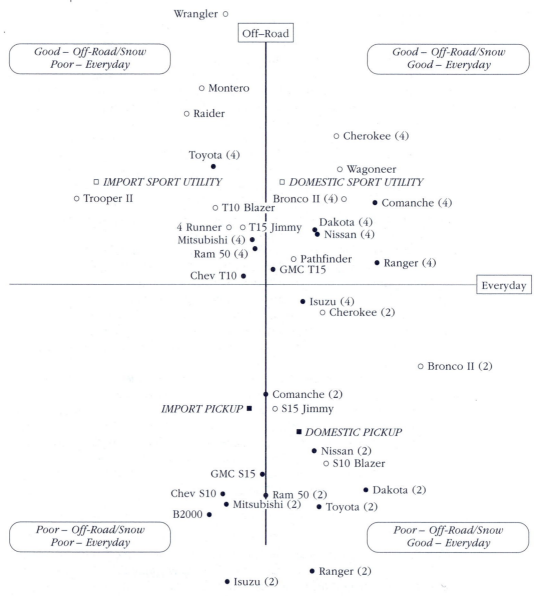

Wrangler ○

Off–Road

Good – Off-Road/Snow
Poor – Everyday

Good – Off-Road/Snow
Good – Everyday

○ Montero

○ Raider

○ Cherokee (4)

Toyota (4)
●   ○ Wagoneer

□ IMPORT SPORT UTILITY   □ DOMESTIC SPORT UTILITY

○ Trooper II   Bronco II (4) ○   ● Comanche (4)
                    ○ T10 Blazer
4 Runner ○   ○ T15 Jimmy   Dakota (4)
Mitsubishi (4) ●   ● Nissan (4)
Ram 50 (4) ●
                    ○ Pathfinder   ● Ranger (4)
Chev T10 ●   ● GMC T15

Everyday

● Isuzu (4)
○ Cherokee (2)

○ Bronco II (2)

● Comanche (2)
IMPORT PICKUP ■   ○ S15 Jimmy

■ DOMESTIC PICKUP

● Nissan (2)
○ S10 Blazer

GMC S15 ●

Chev S10 ●   ● Ram 50 (2)   ● Dakota (2)
      ● Mitsubishi (2)   ● Toyota (2)
B2000 ●

Poor – Off-Road/Snow
Poor – Everyday

Poor – Off-Road/Snow
Good – Everyday

● Ranger (2)

● Isuzu (2)

● Perceptions of *specific* brands/models of *pickup trucks*
○ Perceptions of *specific* brands/models of *sport utility vehicles*
■ Perceptions of the *category of pickup trucks*
□ Perceptions of the *category of sport utility vehicles*

SOURCE: Tammy Bunn Hiller and John A. Quelch, "Suzuki Samurai," Harvard Business School, case (#9-589-028), 1988, p. 13. Copyright © 1988 by the President and Fellows of Harvard College. Reprinted by permission.

Exhibit 9.10	Benefit Segmentation of Nonintelligent Terminal Market			
BENEFITS SOUGHT	HARDWARE BUYERS (N = 79)	BRAND BUYERS (N = 75)	PEOPLE BUYERS (N = 171)	ONE-STOP SHOPPERS (N = 159)
Speed	.88*	.93*	1.03*	1.06*
Operator	.86	.89	1.13	.98
Aesthetics	.97	.86	1.10	.98
Compatibility	.99	1.00	1.00	1.00
Service	1.02	1.07	.95	1.01
Delivery	1.14	.95	1.03	.92
Absolute price	1.15	.94	.97	.98
Price flexibility	1.34	.94	1.00	.86
Software	.90	1.10	.90	1.11
Broad line	.86	1.09	.91	1.12
Manufacturer visibility	.89	1.52	1.00	.81
Manufacturer stability	1.03	1.10	1.02	.92
Sales competence	.75	.90	1.21	.94
Reliability	.97	1.05	.97	1.02

*All numbers are indexed to 1.00. For example, read like this: "Speed is 22 percent (1.00 − .88) *less* important to hardware buyers, as compared to all respondents surveyed." Or like this: "Service is 2 percent (1.02 − 1.00) *more* important to hardware buyers, as compared with all respondents."

SOURCE: Rowland T. Moriarty and David J. Reibstein, "Benefit Segmentation: An Industrial Application," Report No. 82-110, Marketing Science Institute, Cambridge, Mass., 1982, p. 21. Copyright © 1982 Marketing Science Institute. Reprinted by permission.

the four segments desired a different mix of features. In other words, the definition of "quality" varied considerably across the groups. For example, "Hardware Buyers" are relatively unconcerned about ancillary services; they desire a functional product at a "no frills" price. "Brand Buyers" will probably be reluctant to try a new, untested brand name. Armed with these data, Telecom would then have to decide which segment to target, a decision that would be based on, among other things, segment size, accessibility by the current sales force, and fit between attribute preferences and Telecom's ability to meet these customer needs in a superior way. In any case, the market research study clearly demonstrated that each of the four segments required a different Core Benefit Proposition.

◆ CONJOINT ANALYSIS

Conjoint analysis (or **tradeoff analysis**) is a very clever multi-attribute technique that draws upon and extends some of the principles developed above. Conjoint analysis was popularized in marketing roughly two decades ago, and the 1975 *Harvard Business Review* article by Green and Wind is still worth reading. Conjoint analysis provides a bridge between traditional multi-attribute methods and the newer Quality Function Deployment technique to be covered in the next chapter. Following are features of conjoint analysis:

1. *Preference versus perceptions*—Conjoint analysis puts the respondent in a choice mode as opposed to a perceptions or rating-scale mode. Respondents select the most preferred choice between pairs of attribute bundles.
2. *Revealed preference*—In much the same way that preference regression derives the customers' attribute importance weights, the output of conjoint analysis is imputed customer utility weights for discrete levels of each attribute. Thus the technique decomposes customer preference into the value placed on attributes and attribute levels, while not asking the customer to "intellectualize" these through introspection. Thus the customer reveals his or her underlying reason for preference without being directly asked to do so.
3. *Identifying the product specifications*—Conjoint analysis goes further than rating scales in translating customer desires into product design specifications.
4. *Market share estimate*—Utility measures developed in conjoint analysis can be used to simulate the share of choices that a hypothetical new product design would achieve. For example, assuming a conjoint study of a product with five attributes measured at three levels each (e.g., high, medium, low), a conjoint study could provide a market share estimate for the $(3^5) = 243$ new product combinations contained in the analysis.

While a detailed explanation of conjoint analysis is beyond the scope of this chapter, the following rudimentary example by Robert Eng (1994, based on Dolan, 1990) will illustrate the basic features of the technique.

Assume that customer satisfaction for candy bars is determined by two attributes, "chocolatiness" and "crunchiness." Assume also that consumers can react to chocolatiness at three levels (high-medium-low) and crunchiness at two levels (low-high); thus there are $(2 \times 3) = 6$ possible combinations of these attributes. Next, we array the six possibilities and ask a consumer to indicate her rank-order preference for these combinations (see Exhibit 9.11). Using only this ranking, we then compute an average utility score for each level of each attribute as shown in Exhibit 9.12. Taking these utilities, we then compute a total utility for each of the original six-attribute combinations; in so doing, we hope that the rank order of total utilities reproduces the consumer's original rank order of choices. In Exhibit 9.13 we have carried out these calculations, and we see that the utility scores almost exactly reproduce the original choice rank, with the exception that there is a tie between attribute combinations ranked 3 and 4. Having satisfied ourselves that the utility weights reasonably reflect the consumer's underlying choice process, we then plot the utilities on the graphs in Exhibit 9.14 to present a dramatic visualization of the value added by var-

Exhibit
9.11

Conjoint Analysis: Candy Bar Attribute Combinations With Customer Preference Ranking

% Chocolate	% Crunchy	Choice Rank
High	Low	5
Med	Low	4
Low	Low	6
High	High	2
Med	High	1
Low	High	3

SOURCE: Eng (1994).

Exhibit
9.12

Conjoint Analysis: Computation of Attribute

Utility Weights

Chocolate	Crunchy Low	Crunchy High	Average
High	5	2	3.5
Med	4	1	2.5
Low	6	3	4.5
Average	5	2	

SOURCE: Eng (1994).

ious attribute levels. Clearly, in this example, the most satisfying product would be one with high crunchiness and medium chocolate; and we could then give this new product description to the product development team for further development.

The above example indicates how conjoint analysis transforms a respondent's ranking of actual choice alternatives into utility weights (or part-worths) for each discrete level of each attribute. Actual conjoint studies are much more complicated than this and employ statistical techniques such as analysis of variance and regression in order to determine the utilities. Since the utilities are often calculated for each individual in the sample, the product designer can then run numerous

Exhibit 9.13 | **Conjoint Analysis: Total Utility Scores —Comparison of Choice Rank with Desired Rank**

	% Chocolate	% Crunchy	Value Score Chocolate Crunchy			Value Rank	Choice Rank
A	High	Low	3.5 + 5	=	8.5	5	5
B	Med	Low	2.5 + 5	=	7.5	3.5	4
C	Low	Low	4.5 + 5	=	9.5	6	6
D	High	High	3.5 + 2	=	5.5	2	2
E	Med	High	2.5 + 2	=	4.5	1	1
F	Low	High	4.5 + 2	=	6.5	3.5	3

SOURCE: Eng (1994).

Exhibit 9.14 | **Conjoint Analysis: Graphic of Utility Weights**

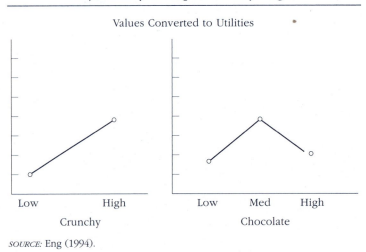

Values Converted to Utilities

SOURCE: Eng (1994).

hypothetical attribute combinations through the derived utilities in order to determine which combination receives the highest score from the most respondents. This share of respondent's first choices can be translated into an estimate of ultimate market share. An important addition to the above is a derivation of a price elasticity function as well as a consideration of manufacturing cost levels. When these are added to the analysis, which includes several levels of many attributes, the resulting output can be very useful indeed to product developers. Of course, one of the major shortcomings of the technique—that is, that the attribute levels have not been defined in precise terms—is a problem addressed by Quality Function Deployment in the next chapter.

In a case study often used to teach conjoint analysis (Clarke 1981), a manufacturer of fork lift trucks, Clark Equipment, has measured customer utility for the following attributes: performance (three levels), reliability (three levels), durability (three levels), parts availability (three levels), transmission type (three levels), brand name (four levels), and selling price (from $15,000 to $20,000). The market share results of several hypothetical attribute configurations were simulated. The most promising designs were cost-estimated by Clark's manufacturing group. Based on this, a target design was derived, which optimized market share and profit contribution. Clark's product engineering group was then given the target specifications to develop into an actual new model.

Conjoint analysis, as well as the other multi-attribute techniques described in this and the following chapter, can be readily applied to service offerings. For example, Marriott Corporation employed conjoint analysis in the design of three successful extensions to its hotel product line: Courtyard by Marriott, Fairfield Inn, and Marriott Suites (Wind et al., 1989). Exploratory research found that consumer preference for lodging could be explained by 50 attributes in seven groups (macro-attributes): *external factors* (e.g., building shape, landscape design), *rooms* (e.g., size, decor, amenities), *food-related services, lounge facilities, services* (e.g., reservations, registration, checkout), *leisure-time facilities,* and *security factors.* When alternative, feasible levels of each of the 50 attributes were considered, the design matrix consisted of almost 170 attribute-level combinations. For example, *in-room entertainment,* one of nine attributes under *rooms,* could be offered at *four* different levels. In a conjoint variant called hybrid conjoint analysis, respondents were asked to rate the importance of each attribute, as well as to select a preferred attribute bundle (complete hotel design) from among an array of choices. The final design (see Exhibit 9.15) was in the authors' words (p. 37), "quite different from the original design idea of a small Marriott [hotel], but it reflected the highest expected share from the target business traveler."

Since its early applications over two decades ago, conjoint analysis has undergone considerable development until it has emerged in the 1990s as a very useful research technique. Urban and Hauser report that hundreds of conjoint applications are conducted in industry each year (1993, 278). A major disadvantage of the technique is that the number of possible attribute combinations can mushroom quickly, thus placing an onerous burden on respondents. This problem has been successfully addressed by computer-assisted interviewing, combined with

Exhibit 9.15   Conjoint Analysis Applied to a Service: Complete Design of New Hotel Offering

EXTERNAL FACTORS

Building Shape
  L-shaped w/Landscape
  Outdoor courtyard
Landscaping
  Minimal
  Moderate
  Elaborate
Pool type
  No pool
  Rectangular shape
  Indoor/outdoor
Pool location
  In courtyard
  Not in courtyard
Corridor/View
  Outside access/re-
    stricted view
  Enclosed access/unre-
    stricted view/bal-
    cony or window
Hotel size
  Small (125 rooms, 2
    stories)
  Large (600 rooms, 12
    stories)

ROOMS

Entertainment
  Color TV
  Color TV w/movies at
    $5
  Color TV w/30 chan-
    nel cable
  Color TV w/HBO,
    movies, etc.
  Color TV w/free
    movies
Entertainment/Rental
  None
  Rental Cassettes/in-

room Atari
  Rental Cassettes/stereo
    cassette playing in
    room
  Rental Movies/in-room
    BetaMax
Size
  Small (standard)
  Slightly Larger (1 foot)
  Much larger (2 1/2
    feet)
  Small suite (2 rooms)
  Large suite (2 rooms)
Quality of Decor (in
  standard room)
  Budget motel decor
  Old Holiday Inn decor
  New Holiday Inn
    decor
  New Hilton decor
  New Hyatt decor
Heating and Cooling
  Wall unit/full control
  Wall unit/soundproof/
    full control
  Central H or C
    (seasonal)
  Central H or C/full
    control
Size of Bath
  Standard bath
  Slightly larger/sink
    separate
  Much Larger bath
    w/larger tub
  Very large/tub for 2
Sink location
  In bath only
  In separate area
  In bath and separate
Bathroom Features
  None

Shower Massage
Whirlpool (Jacuzzi)
Steam bath
Amenities
  Small bar soap
  Large soap/shampoo/
    shoeshine
  Large soap/bath gel/
    shower cap/sewing
    kit
  Above items + tooth-
    paste, deodorant,
    mouthwash

FOOD

Restaurant in hotel
  None (coffee shop
    next door)
  Restaurant/lounge
    combo, limited
    menu
  Coffee shop, full menu
  Full-service restaurant,
    full menu
  Coffee shop/full menu
    and good restaurant
Restaurant nearby
  None
  Coffee shop
  Fast food
  Fast food or coffee
    shop and moderate
    restaurant
  Fast food or coffee
    shop and good
    restaurant
Free continental
  None
  Continental included
    in room rate
Room service
  None

Phone-in order/guest
  to pick up
Room service, limited
  menu
Room service, full
  menu
Store
  No food in store
  Snack items
  Snacks, refrigerated
    items, wine, beer,
    liquor
  Above items and
    gourmet food items
Vending service
  None
  Soft drink machine only
  Soft drink and snack
    machines
  Soft drink, snack, and
    sandwich machines
  Above and microwave
    available
In-room kitchen facilities
  None
  Coffee maker only
  Coffee maker and
    refrigerator
  Cooking facilities in
    room

LOUNGE

Atmosphere
  Quiet bar/lounge
  Lively, popular
    bar/lounge
Type of people
  Hotel guests and
    friends only
  Open to public—gen-
    eral appeal

Open to public—many
singles
Lounge nearby
None
Lounge/bar nearby
Lounge/bar w/enter-
tainment nearby

SERVICES

Reservations
Call hotel directly 800
reservation number
Check-in
Standard
Pre-credit clearance
Machine in lobby
Check-out
At front desk
Bill under door/leave
key
Key to front desk/bill
by mail
Machine in lobby
Limo to airport
None
Yes
Bellman
None
yes
Message service
Note at front desk
Light on phone
Light on phone and
message under door
Recorded message

Cleanliness/upkeep/
management skill
Budget motor level
Holiday Inn level
Nonconvention Hyatt
level
Convention Hyatt level
Fine hotel level
Laundry/Valet
None
Client drop off and
pick up
Self-service
Valet pick up and drop
off
Special Services
(concierge)
None
Information on restau-
rants, theaters, etc.
Arrangements and
reservations
Travel problem
resolution
Secretarial services
None
Xerox machine
Xerox machine and
typist
Car maintenance
None
Take car to service
Gas on premises/bill
to room
Car rental/Airline reser-
vations

None
Car rental facility
Airline reservations
Car rental and airline
reservations

LEISURE

Sauna
None
Yes
Whirlpool/jacuzzi
None
Outdoor
Indoor
Exercise room
None
Basic facility w/weights
Faculty w/Nautilus
equipment
Racquet ball courts
None
Yes
Tennis courts
None
Yes
Game room/
Entertainment
None
Electric games/pinball
Electric games/pin-
ball/ping pong
Above + movie the-
ater, bowling
Children's playroom/
playground

None
Playground only
Playroom only
Playground and
playroom
Pool extras
None
Pool w/slides
Pool w/slides and
equipment
Pool w/slides, water
fall, equipment

SECURITY

Security guard
None
ll a.m. to 7 p.m.
7 p.m. to 7 a.m.
24 hours
Smoke detector
None
In rooms and through-
out hotel
Sprinkler system
None
Lobby and hallways
only
Lobby/hallways/rooms
24-hour video camera
None
Parking/hallway/pub-
lic areas
Alarm button
None
Button in room, rings
desk

NOTE: The table lists 167 attribute-level combinations. Underlined attributes represent the final design of Courtyard by Marriott as determined by conjoint analysis and other techniques.

SOURCE: Reprinted by permission of Wind et al., "Courtyard by Marriott: Designing a Hotel Facility with Consumer-Based Marketing Models," *Interfaces* 19, 1, Jan–Feb 1989, Operations Research Society of America, and the Institute of Management Sciences, 290 Westminster Street, Providence Rhode Island 02903, USA.

clever research designs that greatly reduce the number of choices required of respondents. Together, these methods serve both to *motivate* respondents and to *customize* the questioning to individual attribute weightings.

◆ IMPLICATIONS AND DISCUSSION

Segmentation and positioning are old marketing topics that have important implications for TQM. A key component of product quality is conformance to customer needs. Multi-attribute research methods serve to identify product deficiencies versus competitors and to define promising gaps in attribute space. These situations represent a clear opportunity for product development. Multi-attribute output such as snake plots and perceptual maps are effective tools for defining a new or revised Core Benefit Proposition as input to the workings of a multifunctional product-design team. A good part of product quality is delivering high levels of important benefits. Multi-attribute methods are invaluable in this regard.

Segmented products *always* produce better conformance to needs, assuming that costs and price held equal. *Product options* and *line extensions* are common means of providing customization under an overall product-line umbrella. But product-line proliferation can place marketing and manufacturing at loggerheads. Line extensions and product variants require shorter production runs and more frequent changeovers, and generally complicate the design, manufacturing, procurement, and distribution processes. In short, marketing's desire for product customization often conflicts with the goal of operational groups to deliver low costs.

Traditional multi-attribute methods have several major shortcomings.

1. *Large sample research may sacrifice depth.* The advantages of large sample sizes are representativeness, reduction in sampling error, and ability to segment and conduct statistical tests. The disadvantage is that these studies don't allow respondents to give "out of the box" replies and do not bring the designers into intimate contact with the customer.
2. *A perceptual map or conjoint study is a snapshot of the current market, yet superior product quality is often achieved by adding new attributes.* Auto-focus in cameras and airbags in automobiles are examples of new features that added value and changed the basis for competition in the market. Thus the perceptual map should be reviewed not only as indicating gaps in the current market, but also as the starting point for creative exploration of new features.
3. *Perceptual maps can be distorted by price differences.* Maps often show high-priced, high-quality products to be closer to the "ideal" when, in fact, a low-attribute, low-priced product may be equivalent in terms of customer value. To place different-priced products on an equal footing, the analyst may re-scale the map by dividing the product's attribute ratings by its price, producing what is termed a "dollar-scaled" perceptual map. Conjoint analy-

sis does a better job of incorporating price because price is usually included in the attribute bundles that respondents are required to trade off.

4. *Multi-attribute research may do well at capturing tangible product performance dimensions but less well at measuring emotional end benefits.* As a consequence, attribute scaling needs to be supplemented by a qualitative understanding of customers' emotional triggers. Advertising agencies have historically maintained an expertise in understanding the language, signs, and symbols that add to the customer's psychological satisfaction. For example, low calorie beer presented as a diet product had little appeal. Presented as being "less filling" (so you can drink more), it was a huge success.

The final problem associated with traditional multi-attribute studies is that the Core Benefit Proposition is expressed at a level of generality that may not be helpful for product designers. This problem is addressed in the next chapter.

◆ Summary

Multi-attribute measurement plays an important role in capturing the Voice of the Customer and in setting quality targets for products and services. In selecting among competitive products or brands, the customer is choosing the "bundle of benefits" that best satisfies her needs. Identifying and fulfilling these needs is the key to the customer's perceiving the product offering as "high quality." Simply put, the producer should aim for a Core Benefit Proposition that delivers superior levels of important customer benefits.

Traditional multi-attribute techniques include perceptual mapping and conjoint analysis. In general, multi-attribute measurement involves five essential steps: (1) Identify salient attributes; (2) measure consumer perceptions via rating scales; (3) plot existing objects in attribute space; (4) determine attribute importance weights; and (5) base new product design on filling gaps in the perceptual space.

Perceptual mapping presents a broad overview of customer needs and competitive positioning. Perceptual maps have clear implications for new product development, product improvement, and communications efforts. In addition, perceptual maps may provide a foundation for creative exploration of new attributes.

Conjoint analysis hones in more precisely in assigning weights to discrete attribute levels. These data enable product developers to make crucial tradeoffs in product design. If costs are known, conjoint measurement permits a determination of those features that add the greatest additional utility per dollar in production costs.

For all their diagnostic power, traditional multi-attribute measures fall short in translating the Voice of the Customer into the language of the engineer. This problem is directly addressed by a newer multi-attribute method, Quality Function Deployment, the topic of the following chapter.

◆ **Key Terms**

Customer attributes	Exploratory research	Revealed importance
Perceptual map	Repertory Grid	Conjoint analysis
Positioning map	Snake plot	Preference regression
Bundle of benefits	Factor analysis	Tradeoff analysis
Multi-attribute model	Semantic differential	
Core Benefit Proposition	Rating scales	

◆ **Assignments**

1. Begin with the automobile perceptual map in Exhibit 9.1. Identify one or more additional "macro" dimensions that are *not* captured on this map from 1984. Identify the specific product features that comprise the new macro dimension. On judgment, determine where several well-known automobile marques are positioned on your new dimension. Which marques seem to be leaders in creating and capturing new customer attributes?

2. Taking your results from Question 1, identify the role played by advertising in creating new consumer choice dimensions. Does being "first in the mind" convey to customers that the brand is "first in function?"

3. For the positioning maps in Exhibits 9.1, 9.5, 9.8, and 9.10, name three strengths and three weaknesses of these maps (as a whole) as a tool in developing superior products.

4. Why was Chrysler so successful with the "Minivan" when Chrysler products do not usually excel on "quality" and "low frequency of repair"?

5. Marketing experts say that to be a market leader, a brand must "own" the customer's mind on the key customer attribute (CA); The CA lays the foundation for the Core Benefit Proposition (CBP). For the following, give your perception of the single key CA "owned" by the brand. What is the CBP? Compare your perceptions with those of your classmates. Where do you agree? Disagree? Where has the same CA/CBP been identified with a different word? Brands: **Bounty** paper towels, **Advil** pain reliever, **Tylenol** pain reliever, **Aleve** pain reliever, **Midas** mufflers and brakes, **IBM, Apple, Compaq, Volvo, Saturn, Lexus, Jeep, Federal Express.**

6. For extra credit, name the advertising tagline that captures the CBP identified in Question 5.

7. Which is considered superior for "everyday driving" (Exhibit 9.9)—imported sport utility or domestic (U.S.) sport utility? Can you venture a guess as to why?

8. Using the directions on a compass (N, S, E, W, NE, NW, SE, SW), indicate the direction in which the designated brand would move on Exhibit 9.8 given the product development move listed. (*Hint:* you must refer to Exhibit 9.3!)
   - Tame is improved on "restores moisture."
   - Enhance's attempt to improve fragrance results in a worsening of "rinses out easily."
   - L'Oreal improves itself on cleaning and "controls split ends."

9. You perform a conjoint analysis on a product that has three customer attributes—warranty, torque, and resistance. The customer utility weights are on a 1–10 scale, with 10 the highest. Your task now is to configure the best product you can (highest total utility) while keeping the cost at $1000 or under.

WARRANTY	NONE	ONE YEAR	TWO YEARS
• UTILITY	1	3	5
• COST	$0	$200	$300
TORQUE	LOW	MED	HIGH
• UTILITY	4	7	9
• COST	$200	$400	$500
RESISTANCE	LOW	MED	HIGH
• UTILITY	3	5	7
• COST	$100	$300	$450

10. Working in groups, first select an industry. Gather advertisements from several competitors. Based on the ad themes, derive the key Customer Attributes, create a perceptual map (or maps), and plot each competitor with respect to advertised strengths. What are the opportunities for new product development or product improvement? Define a promising new Core Benefit Proposition.

C a s e   S t u d y

ABC Snacks*

Bill Jones, product manager at ABC Snack Company, was reviewing the results of a market research study conducted some years earlier. Bill had a very small budget to conduct original research of his own, and thus he wondered how the prior, published study might be of use. At the least, he wished to

*This case study is hypothetical and is based on data and techniques described in *Market Structure Analysis* by James H. Myers and Edward Tauber, American Marketing Association Monograph, 1977, Chapter 4. Used by permission of American Marketing Association, Chicago.

gain a deeper understanding of consumer motivations to purchase kids' snack foods as the basis for doing brainstorming sessions to develop some new snack concepts. The prior study had been conducted as follows:

1. Focus groups were conducted among mothers of elementary school-age children in order to generate a list of customer choice attributes. The result was a list of 14 attributes (see Exhibit 9.16); the researchers concluded that the list was all-inclusive. That is, this was a virtually complete inventory of all factors

Exhibit 9.16

CHARACTERISTICS	FACTOR LOADINGS FOR DIMENSION I	II	MEAN IMPORTANCE RATING
1. Filling/not filling	.317	.073	2.90
2. Fattening/not fattening	.424	−.009	2.64
3. Juicy/dry	.301	.125	3.28
4. Bad/good for complexion	.645	.104	2.19
5. Messy/not messy to eat	.204	.664	2.67
6. Expensive/inexpensive	.244	.347	2.43
7. Good/bad for teeth	.762	.056	1.53
8. Oily/not oily	.516	.240	2.65
9. Gives/doesn't give energy	.541	.165	2.21
10. Easy/hard to eat out of hand	−.069	.796	2.83
11. Nourishing/not nourishing	.565	.116	1.70
12. Stains/doesn't stain clothing, furniture	.250	.664	2.55
13. Easy/hard to serve	.046	.747	2.87
14. My children like it/dislike it	.071	.243	1.86

Scale: 1=extremely important; 2=very important, 3=fairly important; 4=of little importance.

SOURCE: Myers and Tauber (1977), p. 46.

ABC Snacks (Continued)

that mothers considered in selecting a snack for their children.

2. A list of snack food types was developed by the researchers for examination in the study. The list encompassed 10 popular snack food categories: apples, oranges, raisins, milk, ice cream, snack crackers, cookies, peanut butter sandwich, potato/corn chips, and candy.

3. Armed with the list of customer attributes and snack food types, the researchers asked mothers to give two kinds of ratings:

   • Each attribute was rated on a 1–4 important scale where: 1 = extremely important; 2 = very important; 3 = fairly important; and 4 = of little importance. Next, respondents rated each of the snack foods on each characteristic using a seven-point "poor-to-excellent" rating scale.

   • Mothers were asked to indicate their frequency of serving each food as a

snack for their children age 12 or under.

   • Additional information on demographics, eating habits, and diet factors were gathered.

4. The importance ratings were factor analyzed to determine attribute redundancy and to uncover the presence of underlying "macro" dimensions. The results of this factor analysis, as well as data on the mean importance rating, are presented in Exhibit 9.16.

5. Combining the factor analysis with the mothers' ratings of each snack food, a positioning map in Exhibit 9.17 was developed.

As Bill Jones looked at the data collected, many issues crossed his mind. First, he noticed that the attribute dimensions on the positioning map had been omitted and that he would need to reinterpret the factor analysis in Exhibit 9.16 in order to derive his

Exhibit 9.17 | **ABC Snacks: Perceptual Map of Snack Food Market**

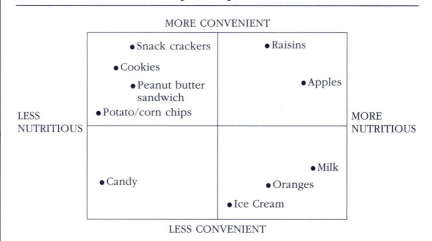

SOURCE: Myers and Tauber (1977), p. 47.

ABC Snacks (Continued)

Exhibit
9.18

Attributes Defining "Factors"

FACTOR 1	FACTOR 2
1. Fattening/not fattening	1. Messy/not messy
2. Bad/good for complexion	2. Easy/hard to eat out of hand
3. Good/bad for teeth	3. Stains/doesn't stain
4. Oily/not oily	4. Easy/hard to serve
5. Gives/doesn't give energy	
6. Nourishing/not nourishing	

SOURCE: Myers and Tauber (1977), p. 47.

own version of these dimensions. To accomplish this task, Bill knew the key was a proper interpretation of the factor loadings in Exhibit 9.16. Referring back to an old statistics book from his college days, Bill proceeded to perform this analysis as follows:

• He remembered that the factor loadings represented the degree of correlation between the individual product characteristic and the unknown, yet-to-be-named, factor represented by the Roman numeral columns. For ease of interpretation, the factor analysis had been run with the constraint that it produced only two dimensions. The advantage of this technique was that the results would be easily displayed on a two-dimensional product positioning map. The possible disadvantage of this approach was that two dimensions may not completely capture all of the key consumer purchase drivers, and thus the map would present an incomplete picture of consumer behavior in the snack food category.

• Bill knew that the correlations (factor loadings) could range between minus 1.0 and 1.0, with loadings closer to the extremes representing higher correlations. A factor loading near zero would indicate

that this characteristic was *not* strongly related to the underlying dimension.

After some thought, Bill chose a cutoff of 0.40 to differentiate between high and low factor loadings. Having made this decision, he proceeded to circle all loadings, 0.40 or above in columns 1 and 2 of Exhibit 9.16. Having done this, he was faced with defining the two factors as being related to the product characteristics in Exhibit 9.18.

Now Bill knew he would have to find labels for the two factors, a procedure that the statistical technique, factor analysis, does *not* perform automatically. In labeling the dimensions, Bill knew that he must answer the following:

1. *Common thread*—Did the items highly correlated with each factor in fact have a common theme running through them? Consumer survey research is subject to many types of errors that might produce uninterpretable factors—that is, groups of customer attributes that do not hang together. Three common error factors were: poor exploratory research (e.g., focus groups), which produced a faulty or poorly worded list of customer attributes; poor

ABC Snacks (Continued)

or confusing questionnaire wording; and respondent fatigue, often related to an overly long survey instrument.

2. *Semantic label*—Naming the factors was a highly judgmental and subjective process. Since these labels would affect the interpretation of the positioning study results by all who used the positioning map as a decision input, the original labeling decision had to be taken carefully.

In studying the two attribute clusters, Bill was relieved to find what he thought to be a clear common thread running through each list. After some thought, he settled on the following alternatives for Factor 1: healthy/unhealthy, nutritious/not nutritious, and nourishing/not nourishing. For Factor 2 he considered: convenient/not convenient and easy/hard to serve. Finally, Bill settled on nutritious/not nutritious and convenient/not convenient as factor labels, and he transferred these to the positioning map in Exhibit 9.17.

As Bill looked at the resulting fully labeled perceptual map, he felt that it would give excellent guidance to ABC's product improvement and new product development efforts. The map clearly showed "winners" and "losers" on each of two very important consumer choice dimensions. Although the published version of the snack food study did not indicate a specific "ideal point," Bill felt that consumers would probably want maximum amounts of nutrition and convenience, and he penciled an ideal point into the upper right-hand corner of the positioning map. Upon doing this, Bill had a vaguely uneasy feeling that something was missing. With the *ideal point* drawn as described, the positioning map clearly indicated that raisins and apples were the snacks closest to the ideal. Bill knew from his own experience how difficult

it was to get kids to choose wholesome and convenient snacks over perennial favorites such as cookies, candy, snack chips, and ice cream! Bill quickly found a clue to the discrepancy back in Exhibit 9.16. Here he found that the fourteenth attribute, "My children like it/dislike it" was the third most important attribute overall as indicated by the mean importance ratings, yet this dimension was not included at all on the positioning map. While Bill imagined that the full data from the snack food study had considered kids like it/dislike it and expensive/inexpensive as the third and fourth choice dimensions, he unfortunately did not have these data. Therefore, Bill redrew the positioning map on judgment, with "kids like it" as the third dimension plotted against nutrition (Exhibit 9.19) and convenience (map not shown). Having done so, Bill realized that the ideal point was maximum nutrition, convenience, and kids like it, and in the re-drawn three-dimensional space, such snacks as candy and ice cream fared much better in their closeness to the ideal.

Having satisfied himself that he had a reasonably good picture of the snack food market in the mid-1970s, Bill wondered what changes had come about in the last two decades. Specifically, he made a list of specific marketing moves implemented by several snack food manufacturers. If he found these moves to be consistent with his map, this would give him confirmation that the perceptual mapping technique was valid and valuable. That is, Bill felt that if major strategic moves in the marketplace could be well explained by the perceptual maps in Exhibits 9.17 and 9.19, he would recommend that ABC Snacks undertake to conduct its own updated version of the study as a guideline to overall product improvement and new product development programs at the company. In comprising his list, Bill noted that marketing moves

ABC Snacks (Continued)

Exhibit

9.19

ABC Snacks: Perceptual Maps—Nutrition vs. "Kids Like"

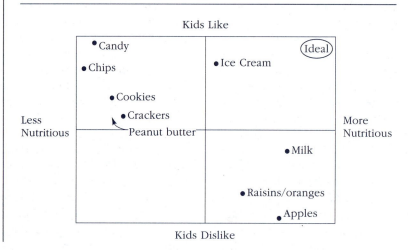

consisted of both new product development and marketing communications initiatives. Was the common objective of all these moves to bring perceptions closer to the ideal point?

1. *Apple chips*—These looked like potato chips but were made from apples. In Bill's mind, this was clearly an attempt to combine nutrition and kids like it dimensions.

2. *M&M's*—Bill felt that candy's poor convenience perception was based primarily on the messiness of chocolate. Given this problem, M&M's was clearly a positioning success and would be perceived as much more convenient than normal chocolate candy. The product's long-standing slogan, "Melts in your mouth not in your hand," was, in Bill's view, a clever and memorable evocation of the "convenience" positioning.

3. *"Good for you snacks"*—In addition to apple chips, other new products appeared to be clearly positioned to combine "good for you" (higher nutrition

dimensions) with high "kids like it" scores. Fruit Rollups, Frookies (naturally sweetened cookies), and juice-based snack drinks were three such examples of this new product genre.

4. *California raisins*—The outstanding commercials employing the claymation animation technique were, in Bill's view, a direct attempt to improve the overall "coolness" of raisins as a kid's snack; or in positioning terms, to bring raisins from the bottom to the top of Exhibit 9.19 with improved perceptions on "kids like it."

5. *Peanut butter*—Bill had been so impressed by new product and communications moves within the peanut butter category that he was frankly surprised at how poor peanut butter's nutrition perceptions were in the mid-1970s. Skippy had launched a "nutrition" campaign featuring former Mouseketeer Annette Funicello. In a series of commercials, Annette explained to kids (and Moms watching) that

ABC Snacks (Continued)

peanut butter is to be favored for its high protein content. In addition, "reduced fat" and "reduced sugar" line extensions that had appeared in the peanut butter category were clear attempts to drive the product from left to right on the positioning map.

Were all of the above consistent with the dimensions, customer perceptions, and ideal point as illustrated in his final perceptual map? Could each of the marketing actions above be interpreted as a logical program to push consumers toward the ideal point? What could Bill Jones hope to achieve by updating the Snack Food Positioning Study?

CASE QUESTIONS

1. Assess the perceptual mapping exercise undertaken by Bill Jones. Is the technique useful to him?
2. What are the strengths and weaknesses of the perceptual map that Bill Jones has derived? What key pieces of additional data does he need?
3. What key dimension has been omitted from the perceptual maps? Does it make a difference?
4. Under what circumstances would you prefer to have a snake plot of all snacks on all 14 dimensions?

5. In your view, does the perceptual map enhance or inhibit creativity—for example, development of advertising themes, new product ideas, or new customer attributes/perceptual dimensions?
6. Use the positionings in Exhibit 9.17 and 9.19 to create a third perceptual map with the dimensions, convenience and kids like it. Assign values to the perceptual maps from −5 to +5 with 0,0 as the origin. For example, the ideal point would be 5,5.
7. For extra credit, create a three-dimensional map. Use a flat square piece of Styrofoam as the base with the length and width to represent nutrition and convenience. (Just superimpose the perceptual map in Exhibit 9.17 on this.) For kids like it, cut straws or pipe cleaners or sticks with longer straws corresponding to higher values of kids like it. For example, the length for apples will be roughly one-tenth that of candy. Make the longest straw the same length as the length of the base. You will have a cube with origin at 0,0,0. (Remember that the zero point on kids like it is 5 units above the base! The base now has a kids like it value of − 5.) Attach a piece of cardboard to the end of each straw to label the product. Place a straw at 5,5,5 and label this "ideal."

◆ Bibliography

"Car Makers Use Image Map as a Tool to Position Products." *The Wall Street Journal,* March 22, 1984, p. 33.

Clarke, Darral G. "Clark Material Handling Group—Overseas: Brazilian Product Strategy, (A)." Case study, Harvard Case Clearinghouse (#9-581-091), 1981.

Clarke, Darral G. "Johnson Wax: Enhance (A)." Case study, Harvard Case Clearinghouse (#9-583-046), 1982.

Dolan, Robert J. "Conjoint Analysis: A Manager's Guide." Technical note, Harvard Case Clearinghouse (#9-590-059), 1990.

Eng, Robert J. "Conjoint Analysis." Presentation given to American Marketing Association, Boston Chapter, Bentley College, March 1994; based on Dolan, above.

Engel, James F., Roger D. Blackwell, and Paul W. Miniard. *Consumer Behavior.* 7th ed. Fort Worth, Tex.: Dryden Press, 1993, Chapter 11.

Green, Paul E., and Yoran Wind, "New Way to Measure Consumers' Judgments." *Harvard Business Review* (July-August 1975): 107–117.

Griffin, Abbie, and John R. Hauser. "The Voice of the Customer." *Marketing Science* 12, no. 1 (Winter 1993): 1–15.

Hiller, Tammy Bunn, and John A. Quelch. "Suzuki Samurai." Case study, Harvard Case Clearinghouse (#9-589-028), 1988.

Kopp, Robert J., Robert J. Eng, and Douglass Tigert. "A Competitive Structure and Segmentation Analysis of the Chicago Fashion Market," *Journal of Retailing,* Winter 1989, 496–515.

Moriarty, Rowland T., and David J. Reibstein. "Benefit Segmentation: and Industrial Application." Report No. 82-110, Marketing Science Institute, Cambridge, Mass., 1982.

Myers, James A., and Edward Tauber. *Market Structure Analysis.* Chicago: American Marketing Association, 1977.

Urban, Glen L., and John R. Hauser. *Design and Marketing of New Products.* 2nd ed. Englewood Cliffs, N.J.: Prentice Hall, 1993, Chs. 8–10.

Wind, Jerry, Paul E. Green, Douglas Shifflet, and Marsha Scarbrough. "Courtyard by Marriott: Designing a Hotel Facility with Consumer-Based Marketing Models." *Interfaces* 19, no. 1 (January-February 1989): 25–47.

Customer Measurement II: Quality Function Deployment

◆ ◆ ◆

*T*he only things that are preventing Quality Function Deployment (QFD) from becoming recognized as the most important product development tool of the century are the unpronounceable name tag and the fact that QFD cannot be learned in an afternoon. From all evidence, the technique is spreading like wildfire, the strong implications from users is that competitors who are not employing QFD are at a distinct disadvantage. In any case, success stories abound. And while this chapter reveals that QFD received mixed reviews from many organizations, most of the problems with the technique can be addressed through careful planning, experience, and realistic expectations. In short, QFD is so conceptually sound that the technique should be strongly considered for inclusion in any Total Quality Management effort.

*A*pparently, QFD played an important role in one of the major turnarounds in U.S. industrial history. Ford Motor Company—which entered the 1980s weakened and as a takeover candidate—employed QFD to design the Taurus/Sable, a model largely credited with its turnaround. Press reports at the time buzzed at the volume of customer input that had been fed to Ford design engineers. Today, Ford is introducing its new "world cars," the Contour/Mystique, which were designed with a large amount of QFD input. Introduced first in Europe as the Mondeo, the car was said by Britain's Daily Mail to be "setting a mid-90s benchmark in advanced engineering, safety and comfort . . . never has a new Ford car been such a pleasure to drive and ride in" (Kemp, 1993, 31).

*F*ord has also challenged Chrysler's lead in mini-vans through the introduction of the Windstar, which cost $500 million in design, engineering, and testing. Design team members "believe Windstar has benefited from more market research and **Voice of the Customer** (QFD) input than any other Ford vehicle to date" (Brooke, 1994, 40).

*A*lthough Ford is an oft-cited avatar of QFD in the United States, marketers as disparate as AT&T (development of new ATM system), York International Corporation (central environmental systems), Florida Power and Light, and Hewlett-Packard have recently reported QFD efforts. HP used the technique in the design of a new digit multimeter, the model 34401A. The project team consisted of members from marketing, manufacturing, R&D, and industrial design. The Voice of the Customer was collected by focus groups, followed by in-depth personal interviews and then telephone interviews conducted by 10 members of the team. The surprise was the level of dissatisfaction expressed with current HP meter offerings. The data gathered on the Voice of the Customer were used by the project team as the input to a QFD. The result was the model 34401A. In the final analysis, QFD was credited with being an excellent tool. In particular, QFD was credited with forestalling the temptation to add extra product features that would have substantially increased costs but contributed little to customer-valued functions.

◆ INTRODUCTION

In the previous chapter we introduced the multi-attribute framework of product design. Multi-attribute thinking helps to define the Core Benefit Proposition (CBP), which serves to establish the product's unique reason for being. Quality Function Deployment then provides a check on the CBP and guides the process of implementing the CBP through product design and manufacturing. Positioning maps are more strategic in that they broadly define areas of unmet customer needs. QFD charts are more specific because they translate the product definition into the Voice of the Engineer. For example the perceptual map in Exhibit 9.5 indicates that a successful new personal communications technique should be *effective and easy to use* (the CBP). Logically, this would be followed by a QFD exercise to enumerate the necessary design components.

To reiterate: the traditional market measurement techniques described in Chapter 9 have long been known and are extremely useful, but fall short in translating customer needs, broadly defined, into specific operations and product design specifications. For example, assume that a positioning map indicates that a particular college is inferior to its competitors on the "campus social life" dimension. Armed with knowledge of "what" the consumer wants, product designers need a clear enumeration of the "how's" in delivering the "social life" benefit. Is the answer a new student union building, more school-sponsored parties, name entertainers to appear on weekends, or more informal, outside-of-class contact with faculty? Next, the designer needs to know the cost-benefit tradeoff of adding discrete levels of each "how" and which **"hows"** are synergistic (more of one leads to more of another) and which are negatively correlated.

A relatively new technique, Quality Function Deployment (QFD), has emerged, which effectively relates the **"whats"** and "hows" of product design, and in so doing translates the voice of the customer from the marketer's language. QFD is a multi-attribute measurement method that incorporates a significant organizational behavior component. That is, in order to build the **House of Quality**—a big part of QFD—personnel from engineering, manufacturing, marketing, and sales must convene to hammer out a mutually agreed upon work plan. Thus, QFD is per se a powerful integrative device. It works best if there is an ongoing history of cross-functional cooperation; if there is not, QFD will *force* integration if only on a project-by-project basis. In product design, *ad hoc* integration is superior to *no* integration.

◆ QFD AND THE HOUSE OF QUALITY

Quality Function Deployment was developed in 1972 at Mitsubishi's Kobe shipyard. The technique was first used in the United States by Ford and Xerox in 1986. Since then the technique has gained wide acceptance in the United States, having been adopted by such companies as Hewlett-Packard, Digital Equipment, Eaton Controls, Texas Instruments, and the U.S. Army. In essence, QFD promises to provide better products at more favorable cost. In addition, one observer (Vasilash, 1989) cites the following additional advantages:

- Engineering changes are cut by 30 to 50 percent.
- Design cycles are shortened by 30 to 50 percent.
- Startup costs are reduced by 20 to 60 percent.
- Warranty claims are cut by 20 to 50 percent.

Quality Function Deployment is extremely intuitive, does not incorporate statistics (a strength and a weakness), and results in a prioritized list of specific product design targets. QFD involves the development of four "Matrices," or "Houses," which step down the product design and manufacturing process into ever increasing levels of specificity. Following is a brief description of the four Houses:

1. The Planning Matrix or House of Quality (HOQ), which will be the focus of this chapter. The HOQ sets forth product design specifications, or **engineering characteristics** (ECs), in terms of their relative importance and **target values** to be achieved in design and manufacturing.
2. The Product Deployment Matrix in which design specs from the planning matrix are stepped down to the subsystem and component level. Critical relationships between component and product characteristics are flagged.
3. The Component Development Matrix which illuminates the exact parameters of component design.
4. The Operator Instruction Sheet, the final key document, defines operational requirements, the process plan checkpoints, and the quality control plan chart.

As does this chapter, most of the literature on QFD focuses on the Planning Matrix. Although the reader could begin to reap the benefits of QFD by following the templates prescribed here, it is likely that additional guidance will be desired. Organizations that can assist in implementing QFD include the Center for Quality of Management and Goal/QPC in Massachusetts. In addition, there are companies that provide QFD software, which makes it easier to construct the House of Quality, such as ITI in Ohio.

◆ AN OVERVIEW OF QFD

Why *Quality Function Deployment?* Wallace (1992, 89) claims that QFD is a "Japanese phrase which didn't translate very well." He translates the word "quality" as "attributes," and "deployment" as "development." For him, QFD means Development of Product Characteristics. According to Larry Smith (1991, 369) of Ford: "The Japanese word 'deployment' refers to an extension or broadening activity." QFD exemplifies *broadening* in two ways:

- The focus on **customer attributes** (CAs) of traditional marketing research is broadened in QFD to include the translation of these into the language of the product designer.
- The House of Quality, the focus of this chapter, is the first of several QFD matrixes—King's (1989) version contains 30—which step down the HOQ, or quality matrix, into levels of increasing specificity. In this way, the Voice of the Customer is *deployed* throughout the multiple company functions (e.g., manufacturing, parts, quality control, R&D), which ultimately must coalesce in producing the final, customer-pleasing product.

Before we look in detail at all the elements of Exhibit 10.1, let us first step back to gain a conceptual overview of the HOQ technique. First, HOQ employs traditional multi-attribute logic in capturing the Voice of the Customer. Like perceptual mapping, inputs into HOQ include (1) enumeration of salient *customer attributes* (CAs), (2) measurement of attribute importance, and (3) attribute ratings of our brand and competitors. To this basic framework, HOQ adds the following extensions and modifications:

- Customer attributes (the "whats" of customer desires) are enumerated at a higher level of specificity. While perceptual maps handle 10 to 30 CAs, HOQ may employ as many as 200 to 300.
- The attributes are weighted for importance. This can involve using a questionnaire and evaluating the responses.
- CAs are translated into engineering characteristics (ECs) that underlie them. ECs are the technical "hows" to the consumer "whats."
- ECs are prioritized via an ingenious, but straightforward, weighting procedure. The product development team knows what to work on first.

Exhibit
10.1
House of Quality for Foundry Coke

Product Planning
Foundry Coke

Relationships:
◎ Strong
○ Medium
△ Small

Internal Technical Requirements

↑ Max   ↓ Min   ○ Target

Customer Requirements / Customer Importance (B)

Customer Requirements	Importance	1 SHATTER	2 ABRADABILITY	3 PULVERIZATION	4 BULK DENSITY	5 SIZE GRADING	6 CARBON CONTENT	7 SULFER CONTENT	8 VOLATILES	9 ASH CONTENT	10 MOISTURE	11 BLENDING RATIO	12 DRYING TIME	13 TEMPERATURE	14 LENGTH	15 WARM UP TIME	16 SCREEN SIZE	17 SULFER	18 MOISTURE	19 HARDNESS	20 WASH TIME	Complaints
CONSISTENT SIZING	5											◎		○	◎	◎	◎			◎		3
BIG COKE	3					◎									◎		◎					
LITTLE BREAKAGE	4	◎																				
HIGH STRENGTH	4	◎	◎	○	△							◎										
FEW FINES/TOO BIGS	5																◎					2
NO BREEZE	4	◎																				1
BURNS WELL	4						◎										◎					
GOOD RESULTS FROM USE	4	○					◎	◎				○										
COMPENSATE FOR SCRAP VAR	2						◎					△					◎					
NO CONTAMINATION	4																					7
HIGH FIXED CARBON	3						◎							○								
LOW SULFER CONTENT	2							◎										◎		◎		
LOW VOLATILES	2								◎													
LOW MOISTURE	2										◎		◎						◎			
CONSISTENT DENSITY	3					◎																
NO MEALY COKE	2													○	◎	○						1
NO GREEN COKE	3												△		◎							2
LOADS CERTIFIED	2																					
GOOD COLOR	2													◎	◎							

Customer Assessment: 1 2 3 4 5

Target Values (I)

Technical Assessment (G) × = Us   ● = Them   (scale 5 4 3 2 1)

Here is a House of Quality filled out. Notice how the data are weighed so that the members of the QFD team can figure out just what's important.

Important Control Items

Weights		1	2	3	4	5	6	7	8	9	10	11	12	13	14	15	16	17	18	19	20
Absolute		120	36	12	31	99	99	18	18		18	95	21	29	144	57	135	18	18	72	18
Relative																					

SOURCE: Gary S. Vasilash, "Hearing the Voice of the Customer," *Production* (February 1989): 66–68. Reprinted by permission.

- Synergies and tradeoffs among ECs are clearly identified.
- Cross-functional communication is encouraged (really, is deemed mandatory) by the process of "building" the HOQ.

QFD probably had its biggest boost in the United States with the highly touted application by Ford in the development of the Taurus/Sable. The product introduced in 1986 has been a tremendous success. The media reported that Taurus was the result of an innovative new product development process that emphasized customer feedback. Later, the technique was revealed to be QFD. David Muthlier, who while at Ford participated in the Taurus/Sable program, said that Ford discovered that QFD is the "best way to design, develop and launch a [new] product." (Vasilash, 1989, 66). Presently, all of the big three U.S. automakers use QFD. At Toyota Autobody, QFD is credited with reducing startup and preproduction costs by 60 percent from 1977 to 1984 (Hauser and Clausing, 88). The method then received a huge boost in awareness with the publication of Hauser and Clausing's (1988) *Harvard Business Review* article, "House of Quality" which is still a must-read for those new to QFD.

Although many published QFD applications have been in manufacturing, it has proven to be a very effective tool in the development of software and in other service businesses. Akao (1990) provides several illustrations:

- CSK, a major software company in Japan, generated customer demands using a brainstorming technique. The raw Voice of the Customer was translated into functional requirements. For example, the customer asked for "output that is easy to see." This was understood to mean that the size of the output could be changed at the customer's request. Then an Affinity Diagram (see Chapter 8) approach was used to categorize the demands. A questionnaire was designed and used to categorize the customer attributes into the three Kano categories (described later in this chapter in Research Methodology Issues). Next, these abstract requirements were made more concrete by defining measurable characteristics. So, "easy to see output" could consist of measurable characteristics such as "report available on several sizes of paper," "variety of available font sizes," and "ability to move graphics to separate page." These were inputs to the HOQ by which the software engineers designed the product.
- The Yaesu Book Center is one of the largest bookstores in the world. In deciding what needed to be done to satisfy the customer, the store managers started by collecting the Voice of the Customer. Starting with vague expressions such as "pleasant service," they created measurable characteristics such as "percent of sales clerks knowing location of books," "speed of checkout," "availability of person to talk to customer in their native language." Customers were asked to complete a questionnaire so that the characteristics could be assigned importance weights. One that stood out was customers wanting "a classification scheme that was easy to understand." This

led Yaesu to come up with a new way of classifying books, patrolling the store to check books and reclassify if necessary, and providing point-of-purchase clerks at the edge of sections to help direct customers.

◆ BUILDING THE HOUSE OF QUALITY: AN EXAMPLE

Exhibit 10.1 is a completed House of Quality for the product, foundry coke, taken from Vasilash (1989). Tracking through this example illustrates the components of the HOQ.

Customer Inputs/Voice of Customer

Customer attributes (CAs) are enumerated in the HOQ's left-hand wall, **A**. CAs should be arranged in a hierarchy of two to three levels—that is, primary, secondary, and tertiary benefits. Average customer importance ratings are given in Column **B**. Customer ratings of our brand versus one or more competitors are given in the right-hand wall, **C**. This particular HOQ has been modified to include a column labeled "customer complaints," which flags the frequency of reported product problems.

Technical Inputs

Engineering characteristics (ECs) are enumerated in the HOQ's ceiling, **D**. The two large grids, one comprising the HOQ's "rooms" (**E**) and another comprising its "roof" (**F**), indicate correlations. The rooms comprise what has been labeled the **relationship matrix,** which reveals correlations between the CAs and ECs. Following convention, three levels of correlation are derived and are given the following symbols/weighting values:

SYMBOL	WEIGHT
Δ	1
O	3
◉	9

The roof, dubbed the **correlation matrix,** gives correlations, both positive and negative in sign, between pairs of ECs. Negative correlations often flag potentially difficult tradeoffs between ECs, that is, more of one in the pair can be obtained only by sacrificing the other. (Even positive correlations can have unwanted consequences if having higher values of an EC is undesirable.) An additional technical input is shown in the technical assessment (**G**) where our brand is compared with those of competitors on technical "goodness," in this case on a five-point scale.

Key Output: EC Weights and Target Values

The HOQ's foundation or "basement" contains the key output of the Planning Matrix. With the customer and technical inputs in place, we can now calculate the absolute weights of ECs (see **H**). The weights are simply the sum of correlations given in the relationship matrix (rooms), each multiplied by its corresponding customer weight. For example, the absolute weight for the EC "carbon content" is [(9 × 4) + (9 × 4) + (9 × 3)] = 99. The relative weight of ECs is simply the rank ordering of the absolute weights. Finally, the new product team must agree on target values, **I**, for each EC, or at least for the most important ECs where technical feasibility permits. (Some HOQs add a row entry for "technical feasibility" to the basement display.)

Implications

The completed HOQ in Exhibit 10.1 points to the following findings and conclusions. The reader should carefully track through and confirm each of these:

1. The most important EC is the "length of heating during processing," which has an absolute value of [(9 × 5) + (9 × 3) + (3 × 3) + (9 × 2) + (9 × 3) + (9 × 2)] = 144.
2. The least important EC is "pulverization," which has a value of (3 × 4) = 12. (Actually, "ash content" with a value of zero is *not* related to *any* customer attribute!)
3. Customers see our product as being far superior in having "big coke" and as being far inferior on "no contamination." The two do not counterbalance because contamination is more important than big coke.
4. We do better technically on the EC "shatter," and should be—but are not— perceived as superior on "little breakage." Breakage is important to customers, and, a marketing communications effort to correct this misperception should probably be undertaken.
5. The correlation matrix (roof) contains mostly good news! Correlations between shatter/length, sulfur/sulfur, and moisture/moisture are strongly positive, a desirable result. The negative correlation (#) between carbon content/ash is desirable. (The reader should confirm why.) Finally, the impact of the weak positive correlation between volatiles/temperature cannot be ascertained without more information about the direction of movement of a possible new temperature target.
6. All things being equal, the design team should address in order: length of heating, screen size, and shatter strength. Target values for these ECs must be determined to complete the HOQ.

◆ RESEARCH METHODOLOGY ISSUES

Companies report that, when looked at as a marketing research technique, QFD has two clear benefits. First, customer needs are recorded in *respondents' own words*. Second, the data are *gathered and analyzed by cross-functional groups*. An important benefit of the new approach is that "It takes the Voice of the Customer (that is, customer needs stated in the language of the customer) and preserves it—insulates it against the traditional problem of reinterpretation as it's converted into internal technical requirements to meet those needs" (O'Neal 1991, 9).

For example, during Ford's initial research for the Taurus in the early 1980s, it was found that drivers wanted fuel-injected engines. Later, QFD studies revealed that they really wanted *more powerful* engines. The latter specification, derived from customers' own words, was found to be more accurate and more useful to design engineers. Similarly, BBN Communications Corporation, a maker of communications equipment, found through QFD that a key component in "ease of use" was having ports on both the front and back of the product. Finally, QFD helped guide Hewlett-Packard in the development of a new palmtop PC. "We wanted to get the customer's words for what they wanted rather than our own words," said the HP marketing manager (Burrows, 1991, 73).

The following subsections discuss specific methodological issues in collecting customer input for the House of Quality.

Developing a List of CAs

In Chapter 9 we described a number of exploratory research techniques for generating attribute lists in multi-attribute research. In QFD, CAs in the customer's language (Voice of the Customer) are generated either by focus groups or one-on-one interviews. After analyzing two studies, Griffin and Hauser (1991) concluded that **one-on-ones** were more efficient than focus groups, although either technique is effective, and that 10 to 20 one-on-one interviews were needed to generate more than 80 percent of all possible CAs. In a study of portable food coolers conducted by the same authors, 30 interviews generated 90 percent of all possible CAs.

Grouping and Labeling CAs

For the long list of CAs characteristic of building the HOQ, there is the issue of how to group these into categories. The two competing methods are: (1) affinity chart (see Chapter 8), in which the product development team agrees on categories, and (2) a customer sort technique that combines customer judgments with cluster analysis. Griffin and Hauser have analyzed research (some of it their own) comparing the two techniques and have concluded that the customer sort method is superior. They report favorable (qualitative) results from a hybrid research protocol in which the product development team completes the sorting task in parallel with consumers. Differences in the two grouping/labeling solutions are then discussed and debated.

Measuring Attribute Importance

Griffin and Hauser compared three measures of attribute importance: (1) a direct nine-point rating scale, (2) a constant sum scale in which customers allocate points among customer needs, and (3) an anchored scale in which the customers allocate 10 points to the most important need and up to 10 points to all other needs. All three measures correlated highly with separate measures of interest and preference, and no clear winner emerged. The authors themselves prefer the anchored scale followed by constant sum.

Qualitative Research Emphasis

For marketing scholars steeped in the lore and science of traditional multi-attribute "attitude" research, the small-sample approach of QFD sends up a red flag. After all, a sample size of 200 produces proportions that are accurate to only plus-or-minus seven percentage points; at a sample size of 30, the error balloons to plus-or-minus eighteen percentage points! And all of this assumes that sample selection is random, not a convenience sample of customers chosen because they are friendly or local. These are issues that receive scant attention in the QFD literature (with the exception of Griffin and Hauser). Thus to embrace QFD, marketers must readjust to what Burrows (1991, 73) calls a "new wave in market research [which] emphasizes qualitative input over sheer numbers." Of course, the term *qualitative* carries with it the promise of *greater depth* in the research method. The preference for depth over sample size appears to pervade the Japanese view of marketing research (see Johansson and Nonaka, 1987). For example, much of the data on the needs of luxury car buyers employed to develop the Lexus was conducted by researchers who literally *moved into the neighborhood,* not to collect statistics, but to observe the target market at close range. Black and Decker employed a similar approach when they designed handheld tools. They observed people using the tools around their houses and then improved the design.

The Kano Questionnaire

When assigning importance weights to customer attributes, Kano (see Chapter 2) provided an intriguing insight. He proposed that customer attributes could be divided into three categories:

- **Must-bes**—These are characteristics the customer expects to be present. If they are absent, the customer is deeply dissatisfied. But if they are present, they do not contribute significantly to customer satisfaction.
- **One-Dimensional**—These are characteristics for which the customer looks. The better the product or service performs on these attributes, the happier is the customer.
- **Attractors**—Also known as **delighters,** these are characteristics that excite the customer because they were unexpected and they are very useful to have.

As an example, consider a stay at a deluxe hotel. The visitor expects the hotel to be clean; this is a must-be characteristic. Checking-in to the hotel takes time.

The faster it is done, the more satisfied, the visitor is; this is a one-dimensional characteristic. An attractor characteristic could be a bottle of wine sent up to the room shortly after the visitor arrives.

Kano devised a questionnaire that helps categorize the different characteristics. The questions are organized as pairs, each with five possible responses. For example, a question about seat-belts in a car may be formed as:

1. If the belt is easily adjusted, how do you feel?
    1. I like it that way.
    2. It must be that way.
    3. I am neutral.
    4. I can live with it that way.
    5. I dislike it.
2. If the belt is not easily adjusted, how do you feel?
    1. I like it that way.
    2. It must be that way.
    3. I am neutral.
    4. I can live with it that way.
    5. I dislike it.

Notice that one question deals with the characteristic in a positive manner, and the twin deals with it not functioning. When the responses are compiled, it is possible to categorize the characteristic using the following table:

		NEGATIVE				
		1. Like	2. Must-be	3. Neutral	4. Live with	5. Dislike
	1. Like	Q	A	A	A	O
	2. Must-be	R	I	I	I	M
POSITIVE	3. Neutral	R	I	I	I	M
	4. Live with	R	I	I	I	M
	5. Dislike	R	R	R	R	Q

If the majority of responses for a specific pair are in a cell marked A, then that is an attractor. If the cell is marked O, it is one-dimensional; if it is marked M, it is a must-be. Characteristics in cells marked I are those for which customers show no preference. If the majority fall in a cell marked R, it indicates that the customers would not like that characteristic. In other words, the questions had been interpreted so that the characteristic not being present would be preferred. This could indicate a problem in the way the question was presented or a fundamental misunderstanding of the desired characteristic. Responses in cells marked Q indicate that some customers would like the characteristic to be present and also not to be present. This probably indicates that the item for the response was improperly formulated.

Once characteristics are categorized, products can be designed to meet the important requirements. In selecting these, it is important to select all of the "must-bes" and meet them at least at a minimum threshold level. One-dimensional items are those that are typically articulated by customers as a functionality they would desire. The specifications for these would be based on what the competition has achieved. Finally, the attractors are selected. The practice is to select one or two of the attractors. Succeeding enhancements would include additional attractors. The objective is to specify requirements for a series of products, enabling a succession of new products to be brought to market.

◆ IMPLEMENTING QFD—THE MANAGER'S VIEW

Most of the descriptions of QFD which have reached the literature speak favorably of the technique. On the other hand, Burrows (1991, 70) reports "horror stories of frustrating, time-wasting days in front of wall-size QFD matrices . . . many a company (including Digital Equipment Corporation) have ended up with 100-by-100 matrices—that's 10,000 cells to fill in—wasting months of precious time. Team members get caught up in the details of the exercise while the market window closes on them." Similarly, a QFD veteran at Hewlett-Packard sounds a cautionary note: "It's worse to oversell [QFD] than to give people a realistic view of what it can do. If it backfires—as it has—you can end up killing off something that could have been a great product because a bunch of people got bogged down" (Burrows, 1991, 74).

David L. Muthlier, the senior manager at Ernst & Whinney, agrees that "a lot of companies aren't ready for [QFD]." He says that the company must in a larger sense be already oriented toward focusing on customer needs, top management must be committed, and QFD participants should have a working knowledge of problem-solving techniques (e.g., the Affinity Diagram) and be capable of working in teams. Muthlier suggests that as an initial project, "select something that's not too complex, but not too trivial—an area where [the company] is presently doing well. Stack the deck for success" (Vasilash, 1989, 68).

According to Burrows (1991), organizations can improve implementation of QFD if they keep the following eight points in mind:

1. Assume a time limit of about three months for each QFD exercise. Bravener (1992) says that "major projects require 50–60 hours of meetings, and most work happens outside of meetings."
2. Keep the team size ideally between five and eight members, and always less than ten.
3. Limit the number of elements in each matrix to less than 50-by-50.
4. Use the customer's exact words. Translations or paraphrases can end up mimicking the engineer more than the customer.

5. Stick to paper. While QFD software programs exist, many experts say that working with pencil and paper encourages interaction and helps build consensus and team understanding.
6. Start off slow, on a subsystem or on a upgrade rather than on a brand-new product. Experience is the best teacher here.
7. Appoint a "facilitator"—normally a nontechnical staffer with strong interpersonal skills and a clear understanding of the process—to shepherd the team. Don't try to learn it from a book.
8. Don't expect miracles. Research shows that only about 20 percent of QFD users realize identifiable short-term advantages in the marketplace, but over 80 percent get strategic benefits such as increased understanding of the customer, increased communication and shared vocabulary among divisions, fewer downstream engineering changes, and faster decision making.

Research by Griffin and Hauser (1992) appears to confirm the numbers in point 8 above. Their study of 35 projects in nine firms found that QFD provides strategic benefits in 83 percent of the projects and yields tactical, short-term benefits in only 27 percent of the projects (see Exhibit 10.2). Key variables influencing the success of QFD were (1) that QFD be viewed as an investment rather than a cost, (2) that both management and development team members were committed to the process, and (3) that QFD was used to solve a specific product or process goal. The same article by Griffin and Hauser strongly suggests that a HOQ incorporate 200 to 300 customer needs; this puts their advice in conflict with Burrows' point 3 above.

Organizational Behavior Implications

The requirement that QFD be implemented by a cross-functional team highlights the importance of management techniques which, in their own right, have

	Successes and Failures of QFD (35 projects in nine companies)		
Exhibit 10.2	TACTICAL SUCCESS CATEGORY	NO.	% WITH STRATEGIC BENEFITS
	Tactical success	7	100%
	No change	7	100%
	Mixed results	8	100%
	QFD failures	4	50%
	No information	9	56%
	Total	35	83%

SOURCE: A. Griffin, J. R. Hauser, "The Marketing and R&D Interface," WP 3350-91-MSA, MIT, Cambridge, MA.

gained wide adherence. Cross-functional participation and overlap in the timing of development steps are favored over the traditional model in which the nascent new product is passed along from one functional fiefdom to the next. No longer is new product development seen as a sequential process where marketing input is "thrown over the wall" to designers who, in turn, toss product specifications to procurement, manufacturing, and quality assurance. The benefits of the newer cross-functional/parallel approach can be enhanced if team members are carefully selected, if a committed project champion is present, and if suppliers and customers are deeply involved throughout the process. Chapter 13 provides more detail about cross-functional approaches to product development.

The case study of Northern Telecom's development of the Norstar key system product illustrates this point. The challenge was to develop a key system (telephone switching exchange for small businesses) with greater functionality and dramatically lower costs than the existing model. Fortunately, Northern management recognized that the company's substantial financial commitment to the new product would need to be matched by a parallel commitment to overhauling its internal new product development process. Like many companies, Northern in 1988 still created new offerings through a traditional, sequential process. In fact, the major development functions were physically separated by the vast distances that are typical of Canada. First, the project leadership itself was selected to be cross-functional: an engineer and a product marketer were selected to co-direct the development process, Next, the co-leaders insisted on the co-location of the design team. Customers and suppliers were intimately involved in the process. Use of various types of marketing research techniques such as focus groups, beta tests, and simulations was intensive.

A study by Griffin and Hauser confirms that QFD enhances intracompany communication. They found that overall communication among the product development group was increased substantially in a QFD project as compared with a traditional, phase-review, new-product process.

◆ CASE STUDIES

Puritan-Bennett Spirometers

A spirometer is a medical device that measures lung capacity. Puritan-Bennett (PB) market share had been halved over the 1988–1990 period. Competition had intensified as rival Welch Allyn (WA) had introduced a basic, no frills model at less than half of PB's price of $4500. PB, a technological leader, needed to react quickly and directly to emerging threats like WA at the low end. With the help of a consultant, QFD was employed, and a HOQ was built around 26 CAs and 56 ECs. Exhibit 10.3 reproduces a small portion of the House of Quality. Note the following:

- Overall customer importance is a combination of two measures: raw customer importance measured on a 100 point scale, multiplied by "sales points," a judgmental weight often used in HOQ.
- In printout quality, PB *is tied for last* among five competitors. This CA is driven by three ECs: printer resolution, fade resistance, and paper feed failure rate.
- Price is the most important CA. (This confirmed rumblings from the sales force and marketplace!)

The result of PB's QFD effort was an innovative, modular product named Renaissance, which was very portable, could be networked to the customer's existing office printers, and carried a base price (without printer) of $1590. Market acceptance of the new line was rapid and positive. The case's author comments:

[S]uccess depended on the skill of the people involved and on PB's expertise and experience in spirometry. But the method did ensure that technical tradeoffs reflected the needs and desires of the customer and that the customer-contact people understood the framework for making decisions. It suggested areas of investigation and provided a means to evaluate potential solutions. It provided a common language (a customer's language) to discuss and resolve alternative approaches. It made sure that the right information got to the right people at the right time. In short, it enhanced communication and focused the design process on the customer. (Hauser, 1993, 66)

Bharat Earth Movers Ltd.

The HOQ in Exhibit 10.4 was developed to guide ongoing development of Bharat's earth mover equipment line. The HOQ is simple and straightforward, and it highlights some of the key components of HOQ which set it apart from more traditional multi-attribute methods. The "basement" points developers toward high-priority ECs and clearly outlines target values. Note also the roof matrix (p = positive correlation; n = negative), which flags potentially difficult tradeoffs. For example, increasing payload requires high brake capacities; reducing power steering noise places demands on spherical bearing mountings. The example indicates how even very simple HOQs can assist in new product development and design.

◆ CLOSING THOUGHTS

QFD is unique because it is one of the few marketing research techniques that seems to have a companywide following. Bob King's QFD manual (1989) stresses the technique's advantage in reducing redesign and thereby reducing overall design time. Design engineers support QFD because it lends credibility to their ongoing efforts to collect customer feedback. Marketers see QFD as a way of implementing new product development or product improvement directives in order to gain true (and promotable!) advantages over competitors. QFD exercises

Exhibit 10.3a — House of Quality for Puritan-Bennett Spirometers

GENERAL PRACTICE/SMALL HOSPITAL
PRODUCT DEFINITION MATRIX

WHATs vs. HOWs Legend
- Strong ●
- Moderate ○
- Weak △

HOWs (columns):

1. Mechanical design
2. Aesthetic rating (panel of judges)
3. # hands required to carry system
4. System footprint (sq cm)
5. Printer
6. Printer resolution (dots/liter, etc.)
7. Fade resistance (years)
8. Paper loading time (sec)
9. Printer noise (db)
10. Paper feed failure rate (units ?)
11. Measurement accuracy
12. ATS waveform accuracy (% errors and SD)
13. Average vs expert tech test results (% diff)
14. Inspiratory accuracy (% error)
15. Sputum induced error (% error)
16. Accuracy vs flow entry conditions (% error)
17. Accuracy vs environmental condx (% error)
18. Report
19. Average vs expert physician diagnosis (% diff)
20. # of report items not used
21. # of report items missing
22. Time to Prepare record for filing
23. Ease of use
24. Time to perform print a 3 FUC best sum report
25. Initial setup time (min)
26. Time for new tech to do test first time
27. Time to enter patient data
28. Data entry error rate
29. Time to correct data entry error
30. Calibration

WHATs (rows) and relationships (column : symbol):

#	WHAT	Relationships
1	**Basic Unit**	
2	Product is affordable	
3	Appearance of unit	2:●
4	Portability	3:● 4:●
5	Reliability	
6	Printer Quality	6:○ 7:● 8:● 9:●
7	Provides accurate readings	12:● 14:○ 15:○ 16:○ 17:○
8	Eliminates tech variability	13:●
9	**Output**	
10	Diagnostic info meets needs	20:○ 21:○
11	Easy to interpret diagnostic info	19:● 20:○ 21:○
12	Effective data/retrieval	
13	Convenient sized output	22:●
14	Printout quality	6:● 7:● 10:○
15	**Ease of use**	
16	Set up first time	6:○ 25:●
17	Easy to operate	6:○ 14:○ 24:○ 26:● 27:○ 28:○ 29:○
18	Fast to use	15:○ 24:● 27:○ 28:○ 29:○
19	Easy to calibrate	16:○
20	**Patient interface**	
21	Easy to hold	
22	Right size for patient	
23	Sanitary	
24	Easy to clean	
25	Low cost supply	
26	Environmentally safe	
27	**Service and support**	
28	Quick response time	
29	Availability mach/supp	
30	Good training/education	26:○ 27:○
31	Cost of repairs/service	
32	**Company requirements**	
33	Passes PB environmental test	17:○
34	Available to ship mid-1981	
35	Reusable design	

Bottom rows (by HOW column):

Col	Direction of movement (Max. Min. Tg)	Objective target values	Absolute technical importance	Rank importance
2	^	693 A	693	25
3	v	2 Hands	531	36
4	^	Less than PB 900A	531	36
6	^		855	15
7	^	20 years	855	15
8	v		878	14
9	v		693	25
10	v		978	10
12	v	<3% Vol. <5% Flow	900	12
13	v		1260	3
14	v	<3% Vol. <5% Flow	300	42
15	v		890	27
16	v		640	32
17	v		540	32
19	v		810	17
20	v	None	540	32
21	v	None	540	32
22	v		756	21
24	v		1200	4
25	v		1005	7
26	v		1410	1
27	v		680	28
28	v		680	28
29	v		680	28

Exhibit
10.3b

House of Quality for Puritan-Bennett Spirometers

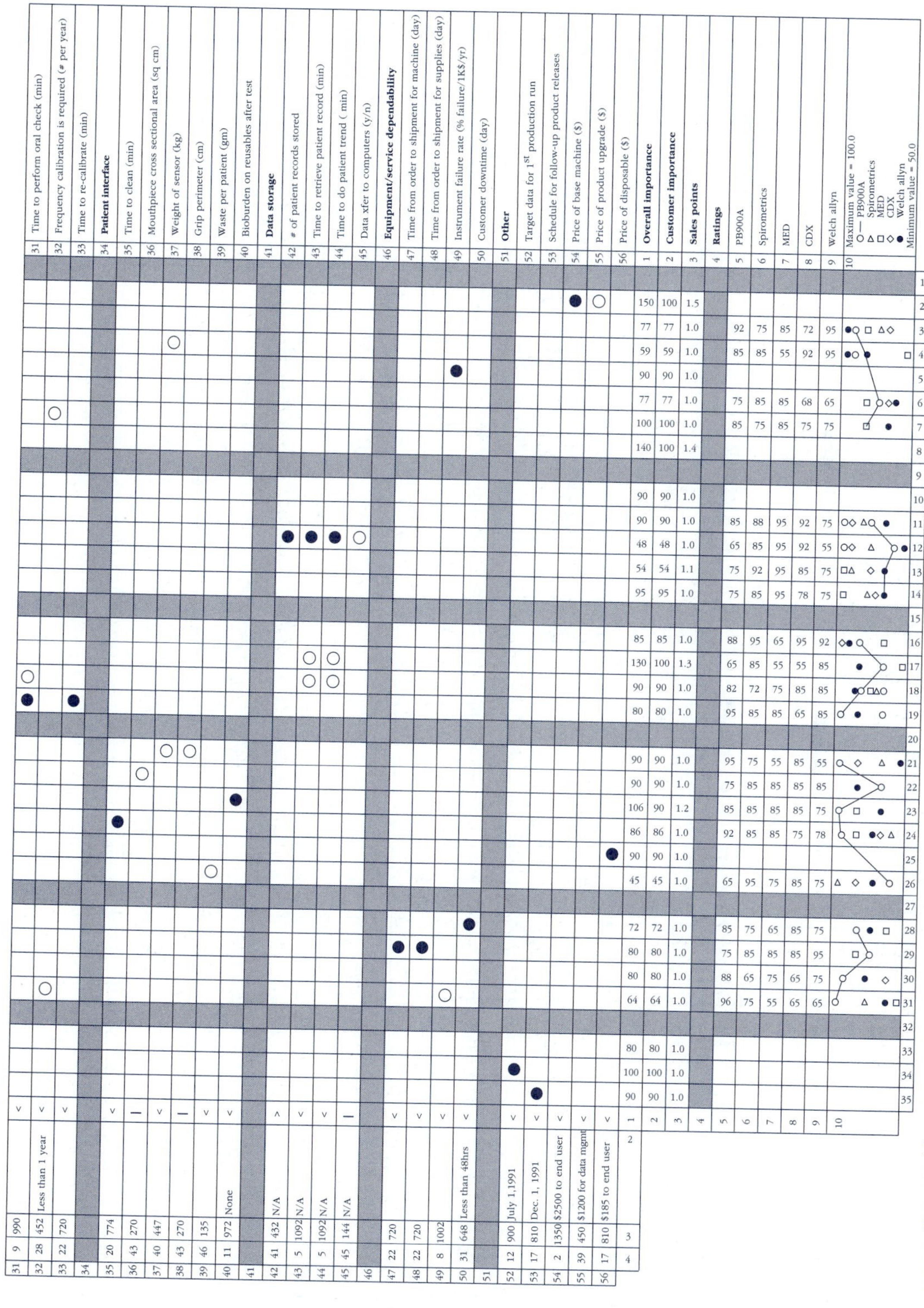

Column labels:

31 Time to perform oral check (min)
32 Frequency calibration is required (# per year)
33 Time to re-calibrate (min)
34 **Patient interface**
35 Time to clean (min)
36 Mouthpiece cross sectional area (sq cm)
37 Weight of sensor (kg)
38 Grip perimeter (cm)
39 Waste per patient (gm)
40 Bioburden on reusables after test
41 **Data storage**
42 # of patient records stored
43 Time to retrieve patient record (min)
44 Time to do patient trend (min)
45 Data xfer to computers (y/n)
46 **Equipment/service dependability**
47 Time from order to shipment for machine (day)
48 Time from order to shipment for supplies (day)
49 Instrument failure rate (% failure/1K$/yr)
50 Customer downtime (day)
51 **Other**
52 Target data for 1st production run
53 Schedule for follow-up product releases
54 Price of base machine ($)
55 Price of product upgrade ($)
56 Price of disposable ($)
1 **Overall importance**
2 **Customer importance**
3 **Sales points**
4 **Ratings**
5 PB900A
6 Spirometrics
7 MED
8 CDX
9 Welch allyn
10 Maximum value = 100.0
   ○ PB900A
   △ Spirometrics
   □ MED
   ◇ CDX
   ● Welch allyn
   Minimum value = 50.0

#	Overall importance	Customer importance	Sales points	PB900A	Spirometrics	MED	CDX	Welch allyn
2	150	100	1.5					
3	77	77	1.0	92	75	85	72	95
4	59	59	1.0	85	85	55	92	95
5	90	90	1.0					
6	77	77	1.0	75	85	85	68	65
7	100	100	1.0	85	75	85	75	75
8	140	100	1.4					
10	90	90	1.0					
11	90	90	1.0	85	88	95	92	75
12	48	48	1.0	65	85	95	92	55
13	54	54	1.1	75	92	95	85	75
14	95	95	1.0	75	85	95	78	75
16	85	85	1.0	88	95	65	95	92
17	130	100	1.3	65	85	55	55	85
18	90	90	1.0	82	72	75	85	85
19	80	80	1.0	95	85	65	85	
21	90	90	1.0	95	75	55	85	55
22	90	90	1.0	75	85	85	85	85
23	106	90	1.2	85	85	85	85	75
24	86	86	1.0	92	85	85	75	78
25	90	90	1.0					
26	45	45	1.0	65	95	75	85	75
28	72	72	1.0	85	75	65	85	75
29	80	80	1.0	75	85	85	85	95
30	80	80	1.0	88	65	75	65	75
31	64	64	1.0	96	75	55	65	65
33	80	80	1.0					
34	100	100	1.0					
35	90	90	1.0					

Bottom row values:

31 9 990
32 28 452 Less than 1 year
33 22 720
34
35 20 774
36 43 270
37 40 447
38 43 270
39 46 135
40 11 972 None
41
42 41 432 N/A
43 5 1092 N/A
44 5 1092 N/A
45 45 144 N/A
46
47 22 720
48 22 720
49 8 1002
50 31 648 Less than 48hrs
51
52 12 900 July 1,1991
53 17 810 Dec. 1, 1991
54 2 1350 $2500 to end user
55 39 450 $1200 for data mgmt
56 17 810 $185 to end user
1 / 2
3 / 4

Exhibit 10.4 — House of Quality for Bharat Earth Movers

CUSTOMER NEEDS	RANKINGS	Center of gravity	Turning cycle	Suspensions	Operator cabin	Dashboard	Payload/GVW	Computer designed	Fatigue tested	Service brakes	Emergency brakes	Power steering	Telescopic hoist	Planetary axle	Spherical Brng. Mtgs.	Engine	Transmission	Refilling capacities	Tractive effort	Dumping efficiency
Stability	5	5	5	1	0	1	5	5	0	5	5	0	5	5	1	3	3	0	5	5
Riding comfort	3	1	1	1	3	1	1	1	0	3	3	3	1	5	3	1	1	0	5	5
Automation	3	1	0	1	3	5	1	5	0	3	3	1	5	5	0	3	3	3	5	5
Productivity	5	3	1	1	1	3	5	5	3	5	5	3	5	5	1	5	5	5	5	5
Long life	5	0	1	1	1	1	3	3	3	5	5	3	3	5	3	5	5	3	5	0
Safety	5	5	5	3	5	5	5	5	3	5	5	5	5	5	1	1	1	1	5	5
Steering	3	5	5	5	5	0	5	5	0	1	1	5	0	5	0	1	0	0	5	1
Compactness	3	3	1	3	3	5	5	3	3	3	3	5	5	5	1	5	5	5	0	0
Performance	5	3	3	3	3	5	5	5	5	5	5	5	5	5	3	5	5	5	5	5
Low operating cost	3	0	1	3	0	5	5	1	1	3	3	1	1	5	3	5	5	5	0	5
Serviceability	3	1	1	3	3	5	5	3	3	5	5	3	3	5	5	5	5	5	0	0
Maneuverability	3	5	5	3	1	0	5	3	0	1	1	5	1	5	0	0	0	0	5	3
RATINGS		128	117	102	104	138	196	178	178	182	182	149	163	200	81	155	152	124	185	157
		Possible low	~14.75	~5 CPS	Ergonomics	Electronics	~0.55	Maximum	2.5 M Cycles	12000 Kgs.	12000 Kgs.	No noise	Compact	No failures	~6°	~450 Hp.	~16:1	Optimum	~26 tons	~50°

DESIGN FEATURES

Comparative Analysis: Worse — Same — Better

SOURCE: Omnamasivaya Maduri, "Understanding and Applying QFD in Heavy Industry," *Journal for Quality and Participation* (January–February 1992): 64–69. Reprinted with permission from *The Journal for Quality & Participation*. Copyright The Association for Quality and Participation, Cincinnati, Ohio.

give R&D engineers an opportunity to demonstrate to marketers and others that new produce features are constrained by considerations of technical feasibility and tradeoffs against cost. Operations people applaud QFD because it allows them to communicate "manufacturing realities" to designers much earlier in the development process than was the case heretofore.

King sees QFD as a way of breaking down departmental barriers that were a natural outgrowth of the industrial era in the first half of the century. Simply put, organizational specialization brought with it the creation of departmental feifdoms. In fact, one of the purposes of quality control—a function added in the 1920s and 1930s—was to compensate for the fact that designers and manufacturing personnel no longer talked to each other. King says that by the 1970s, "we have fortified the walls and we have the great American pastime of throwing Molotov cocktails over the wall and wiping out the other department" (King, 1989, 1–5).

Just as the traditional multi-attribute model can be readily adapted to nonmarketing decisions such as choosing a college (or even choosing a mate!), QFD can be useful in decisions beyond new product development or product improvement. Other applications cited include determining an optimum employee benefits package and the best strategy to avoid government regulators, or even selecting the best food service for the company cafeteria (King in Burrows, 1991, 74).

By now the reader should be convinced that marketers' interest in QFD has a conceptually sound basis. The "marketing concept" can be reduced to three words: customers, integration, and efficiency. That is, marketers must listen to the Voice of the Customer, integrate the activities of multiple business functions (don't pass projects over the wall), and make the tough cost-benefit tradeoffs in product design which pave the way for profits. Matched against these criteria, QFD emerges as a very potent tool. According to William Walsh (1990, 34) of Eaton Controls: "[I]n terms of the overall positive impact on a new product development program, the Quality Function Deployment technique probably has no equal as a managerial tool. For the very process of making sure that all valid customer needs have been included also begins to build essential total organizational commitment to the project."

◆ Summary

Quality Function Deployment and its first house, the House of Quality, represents a powerful tool in integrating the new product development team and focusing it on the Voice of the Customer. The HOQ builds on and extends traditional multi-attribute methods by defining the crucial link between customer needs (CAs) and product design specifications (ECs). Additional houses under the QFD umbrella step the Voice of the Customer down further into the component and manufacturing design areas.

Originated in Japan by Akao, QFD was introduced to the United States in the mid-1980s and has since gained wide acceptance. This is not surprising given the intuitive nature of the technique, its foundation in traditional multi-attribute logic, and the overall heightened concern for TQM arising from intensified global competition. Although QFD has many enthusiastic supporters, the technique requires a strong commitment to overcome startup costs in management time, the normal pain in organizational learning, and the reported lack of demonstrable short-run results (at least for companies in the initial stages of adoption).

The emergence of QFD has caused researchers to reconsider a number of issues in research methodology. These include: how to group and label attributes, how to measure attribute importance, and how to conduct the exploratory research phase. Fortunately, this research has borne fruit. In addition, QFD users have shared their experiences in the literature and have provided helpful advice to novices desiring to try this technique.

While we have attempted to highlight some of the newer ideas incorporated in QFD, none of the individual components of the process represents a radical breakthrough. "QFD does nothing that people didn't do before, but it replaces erratic, intuitive decision making . . . with a structured methodology," says a GenRad marketing manager. "It helps you make sense of it all so that everyone is working in the same direction" (Burrows, 1991, 70).

◆ **Key Terms**

Voice of the Customer	Target values	Must-be
"How" vs. "Whats"	Customer attributes (CAs)	One-dimensional
House of Quality	Relationship matrix	Attractor
Engineering	Correlation matrix	Delighter
characteristics (ECs)	One-on-ones	

◆ **Assignments**

1. How is QFD similar to perceptual mapping? How is it different?

2. Marketing has always focused on the "Voice of the Customer." Given this fact, what is unique about QFD?

3. What is the significance of a negative correlation in the "roof" or correlation matrix?

4. To generate CAs, which would you use—focus groups or one-on-one personal interviews? Why?

5. Why is QFD inherently more of an "involving" technique—organizationally speaking—than perceptual mapping?

6. From the chapter, what do you think is the most difficult aspect of implementing QFD in your company?

7. How successful is QFD in the short run? Is the technique worth the effort? What are the risks in implementing QFD?

8. Referring to the Puritan-Bennett House of Quality in Exhibit 10.3, confirm that the absolute technical importance weight for the most important EC equals 1410 (*Hint:* This is computed as the sum of the customer **importance weights** multiplied by the relationship weight given in the Whats versus Hows legend. Since the most important EC affects *two* customer attributes, your expression will look as follows.

$$\text{Absolute tech. importance} = [(\text{Overall importance CA}_1 \times \text{Correlation}) + (\text{Overall importance CA}_2 \times \text{Correlation})]$$

9. For the most important EC (see no. 8 above), how does Puritan Bennett stack up competitively on the two CAs affected?

10. Again, referring to Exhibit 10.3, the column "Sales Points" is a multiplier that indicates the relative power of the customer attribute in persuading customers to purchase. From an examination of the chart, describe numerically how sales points figure into the absolute technical importance ratings in the basement of the house.

11. You are designing a fast-food restaurant. In discussions with focus groups and your other research, you have identified three characteristics about the counter service that appeal to your customers:
    • Server establishes eye contact.
    • Server is neatly dressed.
    • Server speaks up.
    (a) Add another characteristic you feel may be an attractor.
    (b) Create a Kano questionnaire and obtain responses from others in the class. Try to get at least 10 responses.
    (c) Categorize the characteristics as must-be, one-dimensional, or attractor.

12. Translate the following Voice of the Customer statements into measurable characteristics (you may have more than one characteristic per statement):
    (a) I can never find help when I run into a problem on the word processor.
    (b) I would like better tasting varieties of peanut butter in the stores.
    (c) I get tired being on my feet for hours while shopping.
    (d) I want class to be a fun experience.

◆ Voice of the Customer Assignment

In this exercise you are the supplier. The customer is represented by companies seeking to hire college graduates in the industry where you plan to work.

This exercise is to listen to the Voice of the Customer. The next exercise is to build a House of Quality. We will focus on the initial interviews, skip the design and administration of the survey instrument, and go directly to constructing a House of Quality.

Work in groups of five. Two of you should go on each interview for a total of five interviews. It is recommended that one person take comprehensive notes about what is said. The other asks questions and notes nonverbal gestures that are made in response. Each interview should last only about half an hour. A set of sample questions is provided below. Immediately after the interview, get together for a debrief session. Remember to send the interviewee a note of thanks.

1. Select two people to interview. Ideally, they should be the type of people you will be working for, not recruiters or personnel people.
2. Develop questions. Examples are:
    Q1. When you have just hired someone, what images come to mind about the person at work?
    Q2. What are the weaknesses you see in the MBAs you hire?
    Q3. What do you look for in the resume (during the interview) when recruiting?
    Q4. Describe the ideal candidate, from your perspective, that you could envision in the next two years.
    These questions are just intended as a sample to get you started in your own development of questions. It is acceptable to have questions that differ from these.
3. Conduct interviews. Two should be enough for our purposes. Allocate 30 minutes each. After the first interview, you will find it useful to go quickly through steps 4–6 below for the first interview before meeting with the second person. During the interviews:
    • Remember that you are there to listen, not to sell.
    • Collect qualitative data, not quantitative data.
    • Obtain specific personal experiences, not generalizations (low level of abstraction).
    • Be flexible. If you see a line of question opening up that is different from what you had planned, feel free to follow it.
    • Try to get facts, not opinion.
4. Make a tree chart of the "image" statements. You will find that the statements are at different levels of abstraction. As a result, some statements may in fact become the heading for others. Form these into a tree diagram with each level of the tree being a different level of abstraction.
5. Using stickers of red/green/blue pens, vote on the importance of all statements at the lowest level of abstraction. All statements that members of the group feel to be important are used. For a real product this is a minimum of 20 items. In order to keep *this* exercise manageable, just pick six.
6. Translate the Voice of the Customer. This is a critical part of the QFD process. You may end up with more than one quality requirement for each of the statements you selected in the previous step. This part is critical to developing a good House of Quality. Here are some rules of thumb:

a. Write from a positive perspective. Avoid words such as should or must. Use present tense verbs such as is or are.

b. Avoid statements that describe how to do things. For example, a statement like "Recruit should have a course in communications" describes a "how to." A better translation would be "Recruit is able to make presentations."

c. Avoid abstractions such as quality and good. For example, the statement above could be made a lower level by splitting as
"Recruit is able to present prepared talks to large groups."
"Recruit is able to articulate ideas extemporaneously at meetings."

d. Use multivalued, not 0–1 thinking. For example, the first statement could be:
"Recruit is able to present prepared talks to most of the large groups we work with."
This indicates that the recruit should be able to make sales presentations but may not be required to make presentations to senior management.

7. These quality requirements form the left side of the house—the CAs. They describe what the customer wants. At this point you would create a Kano questionnaire, test it, and then distribute it to several customers. Research seems to indicate 20 people is sufficient. Based on the analysis of these results, you would establish the rate of importance for each of the customer demands. For this exercise, estimate the rate of importance based on your own experience. Use a scale of 1 to 5, with 5 being the most important.

8. Next to this column, again on a scale of 1 to 5, estimate the skills of your group. This is an evaluation of where the company is now. You would then list how competitors are doing. That is not relevant in this example, so skip to the next step.

9. The next two columns are company and improvement ratio. In the company plan column, write in on a 1 to 5 scale where you would like your group's skills to be upon finishing the MBA program. The improvement ratio is calculated by dividing the number in the company plans column by the number in the company now column.

10. In the next column you enter the sales points: 1.5 for a strong sales point; 1.2 for moderate; and 1 for a weak point. Follow this by calculating the absolute quality weight in the next column. This is a product of the rate of importance, the rate of improvement, and the sales point. The last column is the demanded quality weight. It is obtained by converting the absolute quality weight into a percentage. So, while the total of the absolute weights could be any number, the total of the demanded weights will always be 100.

◆ Constructing the House of Quality Assignment

The next part of building the house is to generate the quality characteristics (ECs), or how you can meet the customer's demands. These characteristics are intended to be a valid measure of the customer's demanded quality requirement and also something you will be able to measure to determine how well you have implemented.

1. For each quality requirement, brainstorm an exhaustive list of alternative measures. Evaluate each measure. If you feel it is ambiguous, you may need more than one measure. List all measures without consideration for their feasibility or validity.
2. For each quality requirement, assess its validity (how valid is this as a measure of the quality characteristic?) and its feasibility (how feasible is it to measure this requirement?). Use the following code:

VALIDITY (FEASIBILITY)	CODE
Strong	⦿
Moderate	○
Weak	Δ
None	blank

For each quality requirement, select the smallest set of feasible and valid quality characteristics. These quality characteristics are placed on top of the "house."

3. Make the roof of the house. Quality characteristics that support each other are noted by a tick, and those that contradict each other by an x. Before you do this, you will find it useful to fill in each room of the house. Entries in each room indicate how well the quality characteristic relates to the customer demand. Use the same code as in the previous step.
4. Finally, finish the foundation. First enter a number in each room that shows some correlation. This is a product of the correlation strength (9 for strong, 3 for moderate, 1 for weak) and the absolute weight. The two rows at the foundation of the house consist of the total and the percentage.
5. Below the percentage row, add a row listing the current value for each characteristic for your group. This would be followed by rows showing what the competition does, but we will ignore that for this exercise. The last row shows the target value your group wishes to achieve for each characteristic.

You have now built a complete House of Quality. If you were doing this at a company, the most important characteristics and their target values would be used by the design engineers (some of whom would have been on your QFD team) as a priority list. In this context, in the next stage you would put together a mix of courses and experiences that would enable your group to achieve these quality characteristics.

Quality Function Deployment at Knight Inc.: A Manufacturing Application of QFD

It was early in 1992, and Hank Deer, general manager of R&D for Knight Inc.'s Textile Business Unit, was thinking about a number of questions that he knew had to be answered in a meeting he was to have with the new vice president, Bob Wall. Wall oversaw the management of the Textile Business Unit, and he had recently replaced Jack Hatch, the previous vice president. The purpose of the meeting was to decide how and when to apply quality management tools to R&D's processes and how R&D's resources were to be utilized. As far as applying quality management tools was concerned, within the past 18 months Deer had spearheaded a multifunctional team that had applied the QFD (Quality Function Deployment) tool to the development of a new product. In Deer's mind, the QFD exercise had been very successful but had also raised some questions. Although this exercise had resulted in an improved product that had increased market share in its niche market from 5 to 35 percent, three problems had been encountered along the way: (1) The need to establish a technical database was identified, an undertaking that would be costly and time consuming; (2) the Sales Department viewed QFD as being too time intensive and as redundant of its ongo-

This case was prepared with the cooperation of the company by Matthew Cook (MBA student), Ashok Rao (professor of operations management), and Robert J. Kopp (associate professor of marketing), all of Babson College, Wellesley, MA 02157. The case is intended to provoke classroom discussion and is not meant to represent either effective or ineffective handling of an administrative situation. The names of the company, all individuals, and certain data have been disguised.

© 1992 Matthew Cook, Ashok Rao, and Robert Kopp.

ing efforts in collecting customer feedback; and (3) similarly, R&D saw QFD as academic—R&D was well satisfied with its current approach to new product development, even though cycle times were extremely variable, ranging from one to seven years.

Company Background

Knight Inc. was a Fortune 500 company. In 1982 the company's president decided that the corporation needed to adopt the quality management process. Phillip Crosby's Quality Management Process was selected as the methodology to follow. During 1982, 400 to 500 key managers were sent to Crosby's Quality College in Florida. Over the next six to seven years, the Quality Process had a number of starts and stops throughout the company. One of the problems was lack of commitment to the process by middle and upper management. In spite of this, the president's office never let the vision die. By the end of the 1980s, persistence appeared to be paying off; Knight's culture had changed. Quality management had become an integral part of doing business at Knight.

The Textile Mill Supply Business

One of the businesses of Knight Inc. was its Textile Mill Supply Business Unit. This was a relatively small business unit for Knight, but it was a business the company had been in for 50 years. The primary products manufactured and sold by this business unit were rubber rollers (cots) and rubber cord reinforced endless belts (aprons). These products were used on textile spinning frames.

Quality Function Deployment at Knight Inc.:
A Manufacturing Application of QFD (Continued)

Both the cot and apron were used in the drafting zone on the spinning frame. Spinning frames take fiber, such as cotton, and spin it into thread, which is then used to make fabric. The cot and apron are in actual contact with the fiber and are critical components used to turn fiber into thread.

During the early 1950s, Knight developed a rubber formulation that was patented. This patent gave Knight a significant product performance advantage over the competition. The advantage was so significant that by the late 1960s Knight had over a 90 percent market share. In 1969 the patent expired; by 1985 market share was down to about 75 percent.

The Competition

In the late 1960s and throughout most of the 1970s, Knight had no real competition. In the late 1970s one U.S. competitor began to invest in R&D. This resulted in a major improvement in the performance of the competitor's products and an increase in its new product introductions in the 1980s. By the mid-1980s, the Japanese also began to enter the U.S. market. The Japanese cot and apron manufacturers entered the U.S. market for two reasons: (1) A number of U.S. textile mills in the 1980s were purchased by the Japanese during the industry shakeout; and (2) the Japanese had become original equipment manufacturers of textile spinning frames, selling a large number of frames in the U.S. market.

For this thread-making process to work smoothly, cots and aprons must maintain the proper surface friction and smoothness, and must also be able to dissipate a static electrical charge. The textile mill wants an apron and a cot that will provide it with world-class

quality thread. Thus, suppliers like Knight were challenged not only with identifying target values for optimum surface friction and smoothness, but also with finding technical solutions to achieve these goals.

Origins of Change in the Textile Business Unit

By the beginning of 1989, the managers of this business unit knew that serious problems were on the horizon. Market share was eroding much more quickly than it had been—it was now at 68 percent. Knight had generated no new products in four years, and the quality of the product being produced by the plant was coming under attack by the customer. Competitive products were now challenging Knight's historical leadership position in product performance. Finally, the marketplace was starting to believe that cots and aprons were commodity products; increasingly, customers were buying on the basis of price.

A presentation was made to the vice president, Mr. Hatch, who was responsible for this business unit as well as for two other business units in the company. The presentation was rejected because of the up-front costs—Mr. Hatch stated that first the profit budget had to be met for 1989, and then he would decide whether money would be released for capital and R&D expenditures.

The management team of the business unit knew that they had to prove the need for R&D if a reversal of the current business trend was to occur. Making the 1989 profit budget was not realistic for the reasons stated above. Mr. Hatch had to be convinced that spending money now on R&D was the only hope of making profit in the future. It was at this point that Hank Deer, the general man-

Quality Function Deployment at Knight Inc.:
A Manufacturing Application of QFD (Continued)

ager of R&D, suggested the use of the quality management tool, Quality Function Deployment (QFD). Deer felt that the business unit could not afford to waste the limited R&D resources it had; to complicate matters, a quick success with a new product would also be needed. Deer had attended a seminar on QFD. If what he had heard was accurate, this tool could better define what the customer wanted and how Knight could deliver those requirements. If done correctly, QFD could significantly reduce the product development cycle time.

The QFD Exercise

The key managers of the Textile Business Unit decided that to turn this business around, the strategy had to change. A strategic plan was developed focusing on the quality management process. The strategy called for increased R&D efforts and process improvement at the manufacturing facility, supplemented by capital investment.

The Textile Business Unit management team decided to use QFD for the development of an apron for the Kaneda spinning frame. The Kaneda frame was introduced in the early 1980s. Running 10 times faster than conventional spinning frames, this equipment was relatively new technology for the textile industry. In the past couple of years, the number of machines in the United States had grown to 1000, with each machine having 250 spindles. Because of the high speeds, standard aprons had an unacceptably short life. Knight had tried on and off for seven years to develop a product for the Kaneda, but without success. Not only was Knight not participating in the sales opportunity, but also as the industry leader for cots and

aprons, it was in the embarrassing position of not having developed a product for this new type of frame. In addition, Knight management believed that the knowledge gained from the development of a Kaneda apron could be applied to the development of new aprons for conventional spinning frames.

To start this QFD exercise, Hank Deer asked the sales group for an initial list of customer "whats" (customer attributes or CAs) for the Kaneda apron. With this list of "whats," an initial meeting was held consisting of technical people from the plant, R&D personnel, marketing and sales representatives, and the division quality management manager. From this meeting a more comprehensive list of customer requirements was developed (see Exhibit 10.5).

The QFD team, under Deer's leadership, next developed a list of customers to contact. The list was intended to give a cross section of the industry and viewpoints on customer needs. The OEM was selected, Kaneda-North America, as well as a large customer, a small customer, an integrated customer, and a sales yarn customer. Each customer was contacted and asked if it would be willing to participate in this fact-finding exercise.

The QFD team felt it had a comprehensive list of customer "whats," so the questionnaire that was developed focused on problems with current Kaneda aprons in the market, general customer requirements, and features that would delight a customer. The visitation team consisted of Deer, a sales representative, and the technical manager from the manufacturing facility. As part of the visitation, each customer was asked to give a performance rating on each attribute. Because customers tended to rate all attributes as a "5"—extremely important—the Knight interviewers had to prod re-

Exhibit	Customer Rating Form with Revised List of CAs/What's
10.5	

	IMPORTANCE RATING 1 (NOT VERY IMPORTANT) TO 5 (EXTREMELY IMPORTANT)
ATTRIBUTES	RATING

Performance

Nontagging	_____
Long life	_____
Crack-resistant	_____
Groove-resistant	_____
No friction change OD	_____
6-week life expectancy	_____
Consistent yarn quality	_____
Proper tracking	_____
No build up	_____
Chatter-resistant	_____
Nonfelting	_____

Appearance

Smooth cut	_____
Uniformity of color	_____
OD surface	_____
Smoothness	_____
Texture uniformity	_____
Homogeneity	_____
ID surface uniformity	_____
Clear identification	_____

Dimension

Meets OEM spec	_____
Uniformity of dimension	_____
Size stability	_____

Customer Service

Competitive price	_____
Fast 50 availability	_____
Technical sales service	_____
Professional service	_____

Packaging

Durable package	_____
Appearance	_____

Quality Function Deployment at Knight Inc.:
A Manufacturing Application of QFD (Continued)

spondents to differentiate among levels of importance (see Exhibits 10.5 and 10.6). Each customer also rated Knight's and each competitor's Kaneda apron against the "whats" list (see Exhibit 10.6).

At this point, Deer began to construct an apron "House of Quality" with the CAs as the left wall and the customer ratings as the right wall (see Exhibit 10.6). Next, he convened a meeting of manufacturing and R&D personnel to sketch out the "ceiling" of the house. This consisted of the engineering characteristics (ECs) or the "hows" of producing the customer attributes. In the same meeting the House of Quality's interior "rooms" were filled in as the group determined the degree of relationship between each pair of CAs ("hows") and ECs ("whats"). In QFD three standard symbols are employed to indicate whether the relationship is weak, medium, or strong (see legend in Exhibit 10.6), with a blank denoting "no relationship."*

A similar exercise was conducted at this meeting to define the "roof" of the house, in which correlations between pairs of ECs were identified. Positive correlations would mean that changing the value of one attribute in a pair would change the other attribute in the same direction. Negative correlations meant that a given EC could be improved only at the expense of the other EC in the pair. In short, negative correlations signaled that some difficult tradeoffs might have to be made in production or design. Finally, target

values for various ECs were decided upon to form the house's foundation.

Next, it was a straightforward task to calculate the importance weights at the very bottom of the house. For example, the value for "wall thickness variability" was calculated as $[(3 \times 5) + (1 \times 3) + (9 \times 5) + (3 \times 4) + (9 \times 4) + (9 \times 5) + (9 \times 5) =]$ 201.

It was at this meeting that many surprises occurred. In Deer's words: "As we went through the exercise, many of us were surprised at how little we really knew about the 'hows'. For example, for 'consistent yarn quality' we had a devil of a time deciding the 'hows'. We had such a hard time coming to a group consensus that we simply took a vote. In retrospect, the problem we encountered pointed to the fact that we had been allocating very little R&D effort to this type of research."

Other surprises also emerged. *Life expectancy*, which with the very high-speed Kaneda machine had declined from between 12 and 18 months to just six weeks, was not as important now as absolute reliability over the six-week life span. Since the new machine incorporated a narrow channel to hold the apron, *proper tracking* had become less of a design issue. Conversely, the narrow channel increased the likelihood of *tagging* (or fraying), a problem that was addressed by improving the *smooth edge cut* of the apron. Knight was at a competitive disadvantage on the *no buildup* attribute, a problem that had been identified earlier by the sales force. The QFD exercise, however, had given this problem more credibility with R&D.

Hank Deer recognized that the "textbook" application of QFD would require designing experiments to test and quantify the relationships shown in the "rooms" and "roof" of the

---

*The use of the terminology *customer attributes/CAs* and *engineering characteristics/ECs* is taken from the seminal article, "The House of Quality" by John Hauser and Don Clausing, *Harvard Business Review* (May-June 1988): 63–73.

Exhibit
10.6   Knight, Inc.: Apron House of Quality

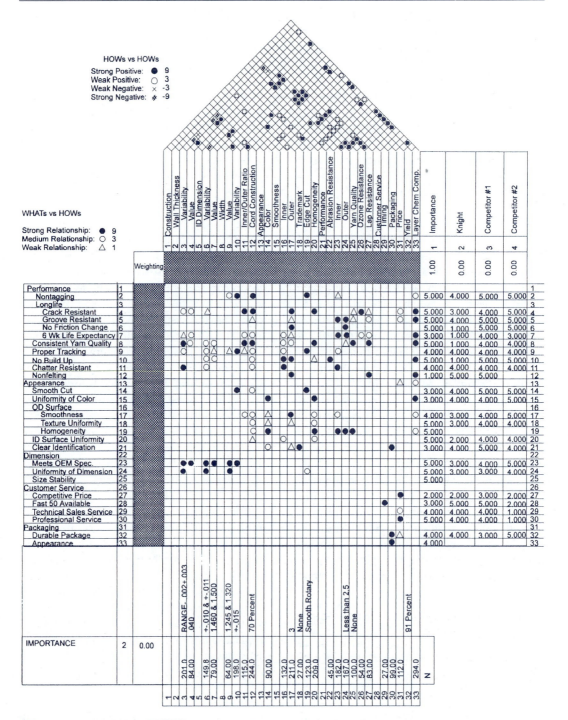

Quality Function Deployment at Knight Inc.:
A Manufacturing Application of QFD (Continued)

house. Such experiments not only would produce more accurate data, but would also serve to avoid the frequent disagreements that arose when conducting the exercise on a judgment basis. Unfortunately, with market share eroding, Knight managers viewed experiments as desirable but not essential.

With the House of Quality constructed, the team then highlighted specific areas to address. These items were: wall thickness variation; width variability; cord construction; smoothness outer; abrasion resistance inner; and layer chemical composition. The target ECs were selected based on two criteria: their importance weight and the team's judgment on the feasibility of improvement. Each area was assigned to a production team and/or a technical team. These teams assessed potential negative impacts as detailed by the roof of the House of Quality. Initially, Hank Deer tried to get these teams to continue to build the Houses of Quality back through the manufacturing and R&D processes. This did not prove to be as successful; however, manufacturing used statistical process control techniques to improve the areas they were assigned.

Results

In the beginning of 1991, a new Kaneda apron was introduced by Knight Inc. This product had a new compound for the inner liner, with significant improvement in abrasion resistance. The wall thickness variation and smoothness of the outer jacket were greatly improved through capital investment and statistical control of the finish grinding operation. Capital was spent to improve the width variation, and in the assembly operation changes were made to control the cord

construction. With this new product, 1991 sales results showed an increase of 235 percent over those of 1990. This exercise also led to the realization that Knight did not have the know-how to achieve a number of design requirements. For this QFD exercise, it took a year to introduce the new product. Knight was fortunate in that some of the more complicated design requirements did not have to be delivered to allow Knight to have an impact in the marketplace.

Looking Ahead

In Hank Deer's view, the QFD exercise on aprons had demonstrated the value of the technique—not only as a means of effecting specific product improvements, but also as a tool for creating an ongoing base of technical knowledge. However, Deer recognized that others at Knight viewed QFD as time-consuming and overly academic. It was a luxury the company could ill afford given the fact that R&D and manufacturing were already stretched to the limit. He was also aware that some in the Sales Department maintained that the priorities uncovered in the QFD process were those that Sales had already been requesting for some time. Also, Sales was always calling for new products. Would doing product improvements, such as the apron project, take away from overall output of the new product development effort?

As he prepared for his presentation to Bob Wall, Hank Deer knew that he would be asked to take and defend a position on several key questions. With the pressure from the marketplace, could R&D afford to put forth the resources and to take the time to develop the technical database? It could take

Quality Function Deployment at Knight Inc.:
A Manufacturing Application of QFD (Continued)

two to five years to develop a truly comprehensive knowledge base. Should R&D resources be spent continuing traditional product development approaches? Was the application of the QFD tool as successful as Hank felt it was? Should R&D continue to use the QFD tool now or in the future? What did the reactions of the Sales group and the R&D personnel tell Bob Wall about the Total Quality Management process in Knight's Textile Business Unit? With the pressures of the marketplace for new products, did Bob Wall have to sacrifice some of his commitment to the TQM philosophy?

◆ Bibliography

Akao, Yoji, ed. *Quality Function Deployment QFD: Integrating Customer Requirements into Product Design*. Cambridge, Mass.: Productivity Press, 1990.

Bravener, Lee C. "QFD: The Proper Tool for the Job." Presentation to Eighth International Congress on CIM Databases, 1992.

Brooke, Lindsay. "1994 Ford Windstar." *Automotive Industries* 174, no. 1 (January 1994): 40.

Burchill, Gary, Diane Shen, Erik Anderson, David Boger, Chris Bolster and Bill Fetterman. *Concept Engineering*. Center for Quality Management, Document No. 71, 1992.

Burrows, Peter. "In Search of the Perfect Product." *Electronic Business* (June 17, 1991): 70–74.

Coate, L. Edwin. "TQM at Oregon State University." *Journal for Quality and Participation* (December 1990): 90–101.

Graessel, Bob, and Pete Zeidler. "Using Quality Function Deployment, To Improve Customer Service." *Quality Progress* (November 1993): 59–63.

Griffin, Abbie, and John R. Hauser. "The Marketing and R&D Interface," In *MS/OR in Marketing*. Gary L. Lilien and Jehoshua Eliashberg, eds. Amsterdam, The Netherlands: Elsevier, 1992.

Haavind, Robert. "Hewlett-Packard Unravels the Mysteries of Quality." *Electronic Business* (October 16, 1989): 101–104.

Hauser, John R. "How Puritan-Bennett Used the House of Quality." *Sloan Management Review* 34, no. 3 (Spring 1993): 61–70.

Hauser, John R., and Don Clausing. "The House of Quality." *Harvard Business Review* (May–June 1988): 63–73.

Johansson, Johny K., and Ikujiro Nonaka. "Marketing Research the Japanese Way." *Harvard Business Review* (May–June 1987): 16–18, 22.

Kemp, Michael. "In the Nick of Time—Ford Comes Up with a Winner." *Daily Mail* (February 6, 1993), 31.

King, Bob. *Better Designs in Half the Time: Implementing QFD in America*. 3rd ed. Methuen, Mass.: Goal/QPC, 1989.

Maddux, Gary A., Richard W. Amos, and Alan R. Wyskida. "Organizations Can Apply Quality Function Deployment As Strategic Planning Tool." *Industrial Engineering* (September 1991): 33–37.

Maduri, Omnamasivaya. "Understanding and Applying QFD in Heavy Industry." *Journal for Quality and Participation* (January–February 1992): 64–69.

O'Neal, Charles R. "It's What's Up Front That Counts." *Marketing News* (May 4, 1991): 9, 28.

Reid, Robert P., Jr., and Margaret R. Hermann. "QFD . . . The Voice of the Customer." *Journal for Quality and Participation* (December 1989): 44–46.

Rice, Valerie. "Spreading the Gospel: Quality Is Everybody's Business at TI." *Electronic Business* (October 16, 1989): 121–125.

Simpson, David. "Becoming a More Responsive Team: York International Corp. Central Environmental Systems." *Appliance* 51, no. 4 (April 1994): Y9.

Smith, Larry R. "QFD and Its Application in Concurrent Engineering." Proceedings, Designed Productivity International Conference, Honolulu, February 6–9, 1991, 369–373.

Strassberg, Dan, "Get It Right with Quality Function Deployment." *EDN* 37, no. 20 (October 1, 1992): 62.

Urban, Glen R., and John R. Hauser. *Design and Marketing of New Products.* 2nd ed. Englewood Cliffs, N.J.: Prentice-Hall, 1993, Chapter 13.

Vasilash, Gary S. "Hearing the Voice of the Customer." *Production* (February 1989): 66–68.

Wallace, Thomas F. *Customer-Driven Strategy: Winning Through Operational Excellence.* Essex Junction, Vt.: Oliver Wight Publications, 1992, pp. 89–96.

Walsh, William J. "Get the Whole Organization Behind New Product Development." *Research Technology Management,* 33, no. 6 (November/December 1990): 32–36.

Initiating TQM: Managing Change

◆ ◆ ◆

*T*he manager of a hospital CT (computerized tomography) Department was the unwilling participant in delivery of poor service to patients and physicians. Patients were arriving for appointments but were usually late. The late arrivals completely disrupted the schedule for the department. Patients were angry because inevitably they were kept waiting for important diagnostic procedures. Doctors were upset because they could not get the diagnostic information they required in a timely fashion. Finally, the CT staff itself was upset because of the volume of complaints they were receiving. Something had to be done!

Using TQM techniques, such as those described in Chapter 6, a **cross-functional team** composed of representatives from each area served by the CT area met and developed ways to solve their problem. Within one year, they had changed the CT procedures so that instead of having 20 percent of the patients on time, 85 percent were on time. Patients were happy, doctors were satisfied, and the CT process team received awards for their work on the process. Most organizations have problems like this, but very few know how to solve them.

◆ INTRODUCTION

The keys to the successful utilization of the tools and techniques in this book lie in your ability to change the organizational culture so that paying attention to quality is a normal part of the behavior of the organization. However, sustaining the methods of organizational change necessary to transform an organization so that quality becomes a way of life is the hardest part of the TQM process. This chapter provides an overview of the theories and processes of **organizational change** and the ways leaders at all organizational levels can implement TQM so that it becomes part of the organization.

◆ THEORIES OF ORGANIZATIONAL CHANGE

Most corporate leaders today would agree that the only constant in business life is change. This change can be large or small, rapid or slow, planned or unplanned, controllable or not controllable. It occurs in all aspects of organizational life, from the implementation of new information systems or new organizational structures for a Total Quality program to the implementation of new business strategies in order to become customer focused. The cost of ignoring the need for change can be high. For example, suppose TQ company (and its customers) existed in an environment where the cycle time for new product development was two years. Everyone was satisfied with the status quo. The customers were satisfied, the firm was complacent. All of a sudden, a competitor began to offer a better, lower-cost product, custom-designed in half the time. TQ company has to experience major internal change to meet this competitive threat. The cost of not changing may be the business itself. Although this may be an extreme example, most companies increase their capacity to respond and adapt to changing demands and opportunities by learning to manage change through understanding the situation in which the organization finds itself, by paying attention to the implementation process itself, by involving the people affected by the change, and by learning to deal with future changes (Jick, 1993). How organizations learn to do this is quite complicated, and yet, it is intuitively obvious. We will highlight the ways organizations make change in this chapter.

In the 1970s and early 1980s, the pace of organizational life was slower than it is today. Although leaders and managers recognized that organizations had to change to keep pace with changing times, the pace of the change was gentler and more manageable, and making change was relatively simple. In order to implement change, managers had to decide to develop new behaviors, hopefully through a systematic analysis of the organization's problems. Then, they had to decide the appropriate solution to the problem. During the implementation of the change, they had to "unfreeze" the organization from old habits, make the change (implement the new performance systems, restructure, reorganize the manufacturing process, etc.), and then "refreeze" the organization so that the new behaviors would be followed (Bennis, Benne, and Chin, 1985). Unfortunately, in today's complex organizations people don't unfreeze, change, or refreeze as readily as the leaders of change may wish. Therefore, more complex methods of managing change have been proposed.

A convenient way to begin thinking about implementing change is to understand the model described below. The model involves the dimensions that are most critical for managers. Once practitioners have assessed the organization along the dimensions described, they can make some critical decisions about the specific actions they can take to make the desired change. The model is multiplicative. If one aspect required for successful change approaches zero, then the entire formula approaches zero. (In essence, one should not attempt change at that time.) The model (Beer, 1980) is a simple formula, with broad ramifications:

Amount of Change = (Dissatisfaction × Model × Process) > Cost of Change

The change is the product of the amount of dissatisfaction with the status quo, the new model (vision) for managing within the organization, and the planned process for making change. The product of these elements must be greater than the cost of the change to the affected groups and individuals in the organization.

◆ TYPES OF CHANGE

The amount of change is the magnitude of the desired change. Organizations make many types of changes all the time (Ackerman, 1986). This change can be **developmental**, the fine-tuning of an existing organizational process. It can be **transitional**, where the organization evolves slowly through reorganizations, mergers, or the introduction of new processes or technologies. While the end result may not be clear at the outset, temporary arrangements, pilots, or phases are appropriate during the process. Finally, change can be **transformational**, where the organization completely rethinks its mission, culture, activities, and critical elements for success. Clearly, it is more complicated to make transformational change than it is to make developmental change. In addition, transformational change may incorporate both developmental and transitional change, transitional change may necessitate developmental change, and transformation may occur as a variety of transitional changes. Therefore, it is imperative to determine the kind, depth, and complexity of the necessary change before beginning the process. For many organizations, instituting TQM programs involves transitional change because taking the steps necessary to initiate TQM programs occurs incrementally. For example, an organization that has always paid attention to customer requirements may simply need to make transitional changes such as forming of cross-functional teams for new product development. However, an organization that has resisted entrusting employees with the management of their work would need to experience a transformation in its key values and activities.

Todd Jick (1990) outlines some key questions to consider when assessing the type and amount of change required:

1. How extensive should the change be? If extensive, transformation may be required.
2. Is the change really needed? Is the organization simply choosing the easiest thing to change? This entails an accurate diagnosis of organizational problems and a sound change plan.
3. What kinds of results are desired, long or short term? Short term may be more transitional; longer term may require transformation.
4. What kind of change is the organization able to make? Some organizations are more difficult to change than others.
5. What kind of implementation plans are currently in place? These plans need to be evaluated to make sure that they fit with new plans and programs.
6. What are the consequences of not changing at all? Massive organizational change can be very traumatic for firms; sometimes the costs of the change may be too high.

Knowing the answers to these questions is the first step in developing the steps for instituting and implementing the change necessary to begin a TQM program. The preceding model is useful for diagnostic purposes.

◆ UNDERSTANDING THE MODEL FOR CHANGE: CREATING DISSATISFACTION WITH THE STATUS QUO

Dissatisfaction with the status quo (D) is essential for any change to occur. Sources of dissatisfaction range from a simple desire to do things better to taking advantage of an apparent opportunity to managing through an anticipated or current crisis to dealing with an impending disaster. Although it is intuitively obvious that it is easier to change an organization before it is in a crisis situation, most organizations wait to change until crisis is upon them. One manager likened organizations to frogs; if one puts a frog in boiling water, the frog will sense the water is hot and dangerous, and jump out. If the frog is in cold water, it happily swims. However, if the frog is in cold water, and the water temperature slowly rises till it boils, the frog dies, for it cannot recognize the transition from comfort to danger. Much is the same for organizations; often they don't realize the heat is on until they are dying (or dead). They simply continue with things as they are, and they don't recognize either changing competitive forces, customer requirements, or opportunities until it is too late. The dissatisfaction required for smooth change to occur should come when the frog is in cold water. While happily swimming, our organizational "frog" is constantly scanning the environment for information about the environment, customers, and employees.

Dissatisfaction can stem from a variety of sources. Most dissatisfaction that drives transitional or transformation change may not originate in the CEO's office (Shetty and Butler 1990). Any level of dissatisfaction can be used to identify how processes or products can be changed. Customers can be dissatisfied with the levels of service they receive. A new product development team can be dissatisfied with the barriers to cross-functional work within an organization. The president can be dissatisfied with the way the organization is adapting to new competitive challenges. Whatever the source, dissatisfaction forces people in organizations to recognize that both the industry and the organization provide major sources of opportunities and challenges. While dissatisfaction can be negative and demoralizing, it can also be positive and stimulate a desire for change in parts of the organization where change may be resisted. It can be used as a motivator or as a source of new ideas. Finally, it can be used as a message to the organization that change must occur. Whatever its source, dissatisfaction *must* be present in order for change to occur. If not present, then it can be generated by organizational members from any level. Beer, Eisenstadt, and Spector (1990) have discovered that the most effective change programs grow from dissatisfaction that occurs from organizational "outposts" and are driven by people who are not part of the traditional senior headquarters management team. Usually, these programs arise from dissatisfaction with a product or process. Unit leaders develop programs to change the product or process, focusing on the work itself. If they are successful, the word of the success spreads throughout the organization, and the program is adopted by more and different units.

For TQM programs, dissatisfaction can originate from many sources. Customers are increasingly demanding in their standards; they want no defects, and they also want on-time delivery at reasonable prices. If they don't get that from suppliers (internal and external), they will take their business elsewhere. As a result, many companies begin TQM programs as a response to customer concerns or complaints. Others recognize that quality and productivity are critical to costs, sales, and profitability. They believe that instituting quality programs reduces costs (reducing scrap, rework, work-in-process, warranty claims, etc.), and that it increases sales and market share through improved reputation and the potential for higher prices. The most important aspect of this type of dissatisfaction is spreading the word of it throughout the organization.

There are many ways to generate the needed levels of dissatisfaction. Analytically, organizations can look at data that show them market-segment, business system analysis. They can do technology studies or analyses of the current skill sets present in the organization. Techniques that have been very effective are Cost-of-Quality studies (described in Chapters 4 and 5) and benchmarking (described in Chapter 15). All these techniques will provide the manager with useful data about what is going wrong and about possible areas to change. However, if direct analytic data providing evidence of dissatisfaction are not present, there are other ways managers can generate dissatisfaction, ways that may appeal to the more intuitive side of an organization. These techniques may make the situation more obvious to those who do not view the situation as problematic. Several of these methods find their base in TQM philosophy. One is to use the Baldrige framework (described in Chapter 3) or the ISO 9000 guidelines (described in Chapter 2) to evaluate the organization's capabilities. Some companies apply for the Baldrige or the ISO 9000 in order to have objective outsiders highlight areas that are in need of improvement. Simple conversations with customers, focus groups or joint meetings, or other methods as described in Chapters 9 and 10 can help managers discover areas that need improvement. Role playing of situations as a competitor can help people in organizations see the world another way. Finally, just as in fishbone diagrams, continually asking *why* events occur often helps the organization generate dissatisfaction with the status quo. (In some organizations, support for questioning current modes of operation may be necessary.) Generating dissatisfaction is difficult in organizations where questioning has not been encouraged; employees have not been encouraged to speak up, to give notice of problems, or to ask why things are done in a particular way. TQM programs often provide a platform through which to generate healthy levels of dissatisfaction.

Dissatisfaction, therefore, must be nourished in an organization seeking to make change. It requires an external, learning orientation, a questioning of existing management techniques, and an analysis of things that have gone wrong in the past. Organizational leaders, regardless of level, must be willing to examine their own behaviors as well as the organizational processes that occur, and must seek to understand rather than blame. Particularly where an organization is moving toward a TQM philosophy, it is critical that all managers begin to generate questions and dissatisfaction with the status quo because it helps people see the current situation as detrimental to internal and external customers.

◆ UNDERSTANDING THE MODEL FOR CHANGE: THE NEW MODEL OF MANAGING

The **new model of managing (M)** is the strategic and organizational vision, the image of the future operations of the organization. The vision is the attempt to articulate the desired company of the future, in often grandiose terms. Visions provide a framework for action and an emotional appeal for organizational members. Many organizations have vision statements and mission statements; for example, "we strive to be 'close to the customer' in all our actions" (Richards and Engle, 1989). Vision statements adopted by other companies are as follows:

> North American Phillips: We . . . are totally committed to achieving corporatewide excellence. This means that each of us must understand and meet the requirements of our customers and co-workers. We all must continually strive for improvement and error-free work in all we do . . . in every job . . . on time . . . all the time.
> Shell: Our objective is to supply products, services, and technology that meet the customer's requirements every time without error.
> Hewlett-Packard: Our intent is to provide products and services of the highest quality and the greatest possible value to our customers, thereby gaining and holding their respect and loyalty.
> Ford Motor Company: Our mission is to improve continually our products and services to meet our customers' needs, allowing us to prosper as a business and to provide a reasonable return for our shareholders, the owners of our business.
> AT&T: Quality excellence is the foundation for the management of our business and the keystone of our goal of customer satisfaction. It is, therefore, our policy to consistently provide products and services that meet the quality expectations of our customers . . . and to actively pursue ever-improving quality through programs that enable each employee to do his or her job right the first time.

There is a difference, however, between the vision articulated by the senior managers and the actions that are taken. In an organization searching for ways to change to incorporate more quality into its style, managers at all levels should be focusing and searching for ways to make the vision articulated by senior managers a reality. Organizations often begin the development of a vision by asking their leadership to write out what they believe the organization will, and should, look like in the next five years, and how they presume to get there!

Good visions can articulate what is important, unique, and exciting about what the organizations do. They serve as guides for the decision rules employees make about behavior. A company in which an employee stops shipment of a poor quality product, because the vision statement emphasizes the importance of manufacturing quality products, illustrates just how strongly well-communicated visions can guide behavior. Good, effective visions are, according to Jick (1990):

- Clear, concise, easily understandable
- Memorable
- Exciting and inspiring
- Challenging
- Excellence-centered
- Stable but flexible
- Implementable and tangible

These visions tend to include an orientation to customers, a focus on employees, a statement of organizational competencies, and particular organizational standards and criteria for excellence. However, they need to be viewed as tangible, real, and implementable. For example, one insurance company had a vision, "to be the best in customer service and in all we do." While employees were excited by the process of doing better than they had before, they had no way of translating the vision of being the best into action. Visions need to specify the key success factors for customer satisfaction, the values and principles the employees stand for and rally behind, the capabilities that have enabled the organization to perform in the past, and will in the future, and the standards for performance that appeal to the pride and efforts of all those who affiliate with the organization.

Visions can be developed by the CEO/leader, by the CEO/senior team, or from the bottom up. Rational activities can guide an organization in the development of a vision. Alternative strategic concepts can be tested. Special task forces, studies, or pilot projects can be initiated which test the vision. The implications of alternative visions can be tested in places where the organization is receptive to change. Selective changes in the management team can be made to promote or strengthen key supporters of the vision or remove key resistors. For example, in their 1991 annual report for General Electric Company, John F. Welch, chairman and chief executive, and Edward E. Hood, Jr., the vice chairman and executive officer, defined leadership behavior in the GE they envisioned. In fact, according to the *New York Times* (March 4, 1992), they acted on that assertion by removing key business unit leaders who did not epitomize the new values of the corporation.

Organizational leaders arrive at visions by constantly asking what-if questions, by shopping for people with new ideas, by listening and encouraging initiative, and by talking constantly with people inside and outside the organization. They sketch out alternatives, and then they listen to the reactions and comments of employees and customers. They look for good examples, and they support experiments. Champions of the new behaviors ultimately emerge and should be supported. By beginning with small wins and showcasing people who facilitate the wins, organizations can encourage people to behave in line with the new vision. Initiatives should be encouraged, and ideas and views should be discussed. Multiple experiments, often running in parallel, should be encouraged.

This process should end with a clearly articulated understanding of the direction the organization wishes to take, a committed top management team, convinced that changing the company to achieve the tenets of the vision are critical, and a growing group of change champions within the organization. For example, Florida Power & Light's vision—to become the "best managed utility, and recognized as such"—drives a sustained effort to communicate its TQM program to other companies. An engine manufacturer asks employees to sign a commitment, which links the overall corporate vision to specific behaviors that will help achieve TQM goals (Holpp, 1989). Finally, and most important from a change and TQM perspective, is the examination of the organization to ask, "What will it take" to get from here to there? This enables the next phase in the change model, the implementation plan, to be designed.

◆ UNDERSTANDING THE CHANGE MODEL: IMPLEMENTATION

Implementation plans (P) need to establish momentum in order to accomplish the desired change. The implementation plans are sequences of events, programs, meetings, and activities designed to help employees learn new perspectives, skills, attitudes, and behaviors. Several strategic initiatives can be executed which specify assignments, objectives, and outcomes for particular programs. For TQM programs, different elements of organizational design, the tasks, the people, and the structures in place, may have to be altered in order to accomplish the strategic objectives. We will focus on implementation specifics in more detail later in this chapter. For example, reward systems that previously rewarded quantity of output alone may have to be revised to include measures of quality.

Behavioral changes that are possible implementation steps include managers who continually monitor customer concerns to ensure that the changes being implemented are in fact appropriate. Managers should always stay open to new ideas, approaches, and the need to change the implementation plan. Active use of themes, symbols, and celebrations can keep the spirit of implementation alive. For example, Paul Revere Insurance Company arranged large company meetings in order to reward successful quality teams publicly. These celebrations served to keep the spirit of change constant within the organization.

Managing an effective implementation process is critical to the success of any change program. Intel Corporation's Computer Service Division (Clark et al., 1993) tried several times to implement a Quality program without success. The vision was clear, the plan was in place, and all signs pointed to success. However, internal organizational frictions surfaced because there was no clear vision for setting the importance of TQM into the organization. No matter how well everyone worked together during the training periods, everyone reverted to old ways when back in the work environment. New systems, structures, and processes were not adequately modeled or planned to make real change. Intel management eventually made the commitment to apply for the Baldrige National Quality award. As we will see later in this chapter, the program designed to focus on a unifying goal, winning the Baldrige, helped Intel implement TQM across the organization.

Larry Alexander cites several implementation problems that occur in organizations during times of change (Alexander, 1985). They are particularly appropriate to examine when initiating TQM programs.

1. Implementation takes more time than organizational leaders initially thought. For example, most managers believe that getting people to change behavior will be easy once they realize the problems the organization faces. Unfortunately, because people often resist change regardless of the rationale, time must be spent educating and communicating the reasons for change. Successful acceptance of TQM programs often takes several years and a few starts.

2. Problems in implementation often surface that had not been identified beforehand. Murphy's law is often applicable: whatever can go wrong will, particularly in change programs. Most managers don't realize that organizations are systems, so that when one part is changed, other parts change as a result of the first change. This problem often occurs in organizations implementing TQM programs when there are changes in structures (e.g., team-based operations) but no corresponding change in measurement (e.g., individual-based rewards).

3. Coordination of implementation activities is not always effective, for a variety of reasons. Often, competing activities and crises take precedence, distracting the leaders' attention from the implementation itself. Senior managers may not always have the time to examine the implementation progress of TQM programs. When committing Teradyne to a TQM program, Alex D'Arbeloff, the CEO, recognized the time commitment it would require on his part and publicly announced he planned to allocate 50 percent of his time to the effort.

4. Employees are at times insufficiently and inadequately trained or are otherwise incapable of initiating the desired program. Education of all employees is a key component of TQM programs (see Ishikawa's philosophy in Chapter 2). A common measure of progress in the early stages of introducing TQM is the number of people who have been to a TQM class.

5. Unforeseen environmental circumstances often have an adverse effect on the implementation process. One business unit transformed its new product development cycle from three years to 18 months by paying careful attention

to business process design. Unfortunately, the unit produced components for the Defense Department, and the market declined as defense spending went down. No quality improvement will substitute for market decline!

6. Other implementation difficulties stem from interpersonal problems occurring within the organization itself. For example, some managers never win the appropriate support for their plan. They may not involve all those affected by the change, and they are quick to dismiss anyone's misgivings as "resistance." (We will examine resistance later in the chapter.)

◆ UNDERSTANDING THE CHANGE MODEL: COST OF THE CHANGE

Good change managers recognize that some cost is involved in introducing change in organizations. TQM proposes new values and attitudes. As the change leaders and managers are reinforcing and consolidating this philosophy in the company and its supporting organizational structures, organizational leaders are looking for sustained achievement of results. Although many "analytic" changes are made at this time, in systems, corporate policies, managerial assignment and performance criteria, other more behaviorally oriented changes are occurring as well.

Managers must continue to talk to customers and to focus on the competitive environment, not on the situation internally. They must travel the organization, spreading the news of change in story and symbol. Many powerful communication tools are available for managers to use at this time (internal newspapers, videos, conferences, picnics, etc.). Finally, managers must continually interpret success and enable problem solving to occur. A key activity is for managers to coach their employees as they apply the problem-solving techniques learned in their education program. Florida Power and Light used a standard checklist. Managers would view the presentations of the quality team and congratulate the team on good application of tools and encourage them when the application was weak. Incentive programs must focus on attainment of strategic objectives, and support for experimenting must continue. Finally, the problems that occurred and the affected stakeholders must be examined. Only then can the cost to employees and stakeholders be assessed.

When change occurs, crucial organizational dynamics usually shift at the same time. Power can change from one group to another. When Ford Motor Company transformed its culture, the finance group went from being the critical action group to playing support roles. At the same time, someone previously seen as a maverick was seen as "just what we need around here; a free-thinker who's not wedded to old ideas." Definitions of competence shift. Relationships between organizational members change; as teams become cross functional and fluid, established networks of support (and resistance) become obsolete. Rewards and identities change as well; change may be seen as a demotion or as punishment. Successful change leaders should do their utmost to guard against that phenomenon.

Once the change has been made, and the organization has fully adapted to the new vision while remaining open to further change as needed, reinforcement and consolidation of the change must occur so that the new behavior becomes routine. Sustained achievement of intended results and continual actions in accordance with the new vision and values should be routine. Systems (performance appraisal systems, management information systems) that support the goal need to be finalized. One manager stated, "People around here need to get 'thumped' if they don't make the kind of adaptations necessary to be more competitive." Behaviorally, continual conversations with customers and focused managerial attention on customers and competitors will emphasize the need for change to become routine. Understanding and interpreting the reasons for success and problems, and continual use of themes and symbols, are critical so that the organization can look at the problems and the possibilities for the next go-round of change.

◆ THEORY TO PRACTICE: IMPLEMENTING TQM

Although there are many suggestions for success in implementing change, there is no tried and true way to ensure a successful change experience. Because each organization and each set of managers implementing the change is unique, organizations seeking to make a change have many different options available. However, in a recent book, Kanter, Stein, and Jick (1992) outlined what they call the "Ten Commandments for Change," a list that is an "inventory of ingredients" for successful change. We will use this framework to develop a list of guidelines for introducing TQM and implementing organizational change.

THE TEN COMMANDMENTS OF CHANGE
1. Analyze the organization and its need for change.
2. Create a shared vision and common direction.
3. Separate from the past.
4. Create a sense of urgency.
5. Support a strong leader role.
6. Line up political sponsorship.
7. Craft an implementation plan.
8. Develop enabling structures.
9. Communicate, involve people, and be honest.
10. Reinforce and institutionalize the change.

1. Analyze the Organization and Its Need for Change.

This analysis, performed at several levels of the organization, should cover the organization's history, its operations, its functioning, its strengths, and its weaknesses. Any analysis should also discern the effect the proposed changes have on the organization. Who will support the change? Who will resist it? Analysis should point to particular levers of action change that implementors should take to initiate the process. For example, an organization that has a history of employee participation in decision making should continue that tradition when implementing change.

Many tools for organizational diagnosis exist. Weisbord (1978) defines four steps in organizational problem identification and solution development. This type of Action Research begins with data collection, the gathering of bits of information from which a diagnosis may be made. These data include not only formal customer and employee surveys, but also informal conversations and simple observation. Data can be gathered by people from many organizational levels and departments. General Electric Company began a transformational change in 1988 with its WORKOUT program. Designed so that each organization would act with speed, simplicity, and self-confidence, the program instituted 'town meetings' within business units to hear the strategy of the business unit presented by senior management, to diagnose problems that might be present, and to develop team and cross-functional solutions to those problems. One reason why General Electric Company's WORKOUT programs were so effective at diagnosis of business unit problems was that people from across the organization were brought together to present and discuss vast amounts of qualitative and quantitative data and create the diagnosis from those data. Data about organizational processes, measurements, and procedures were discussed along with assessments of the political processes that drive behavior one way or another. While they started at senior management level, gradually, as the results appeared and problems were solved, more and more people across the business units began to have "work-outs" in their departments.

Diagnosis is the use of the data to identify gaps between what currently exists and what should be. The diagnosis is the conclusion about what the data mean. When a gap between what is and what should be is determined, a diagnosis has been made. Diagnosis is a critical step in determining what the meaning, priority, and relationship are to the facts. For example, in one organization, management was concerned that purchasing managers were expediting incoming parts, costing the organization thousands of dollars in air freight. The organization's internal audit managers spent a great deal of time gathering data on the types of expediting, the parts that were being shipped, the production process, and so forth. They determined that the production scheduling process was the source of the expediting problem. Only by putting the facts together was the organization (in this case, purchasing and plant managers from across the company) able to make a real diagnosis: that the organization's evaluation of purchasing agents based on their low in-plant quarterly inventory was causing them to delay the acceptance of parts for processing toward the end of the quarter, leading to the expediting after the inventory had been measured. The diagnosis was not that the process was bad, but that the measurement system was not assessing the correct behavior. Low inventory should not have been the issue; rather, having the correct parts on hand should have been.

Accurate diagnosis led to correct problem identification at that company. Action, the next step in organizational diagnosis, is the planning and implementation of steps that can be taken to improve the situation. In the previous example, the Human Resource organization worked with the purchasing and production managers to develop a new performance measurement system that would accurately measure their key job requirements. Evaluation, the final step in the diagnostic cycle, revealed that expediting disappeared as the appropriate changes in measurement were made. Weisbord's approach is simply another way of outlining the Plan-Do-Check-Act, or the PDCA cycle described in Chapter 6. Data collection and diagnosis correspond to Plan; Action corresponds to Do, and Evaluation corresponds to Check and Act.

Problem analysis is not a clean, well-defined process. It is often an iterative, incomplete, messy, ambiguous set of activities, examining formal and informal processes that occur within organizations.

2. Create a Shared Vision and Common Direction.

We have established that a clear, engaging vision is critical to the change process, but the way the vision is presented to the employees affects the implementation itself. For example, some organizations merely publish the vision and expect people to adhere to it. Others, aware that vision will be a strong guide to people's behavior, take great pains to outline the business rationale, organizational benefits, and expected outcomes. This attention to detail enables employees to internalize the vision. Vision statements must be short and to the point, and must also possess a strong emotional component that everyone can support, according to Lawrence Holpp (1989). They must be linked to behaviors that can be picked out, reinforced, and practiced by employees. Uncorrected, intangible visions are blocks to implementing TQM programs as well.

3. Separate from the Past.

Although it is critical to hang on to some elements of organizational life that provide continuity, such as location, some legends, or heritage, it is also important to take a hard look at what routines and structures no longer work and seek to move beyond them. These discussions often occur in the time of vision-setting and design of implementation. For example, an organization had a very innovative product development history. However, the organization had not produced a new product successfully in 10 years because many procedures bureaucratized the process. In changing the organization to develop products quicker, the change leaders kept the legends of product development successes, but modified the structures and routines that no longer worked.

4. Create a Sense of Urgency.

This commandment is coupled with the generation of dissatisfaction with the status quo discussed earlier. Persuading an organization to change when things seem to be going well is difficult. Therefore, organizational change leaders need to generate a sense of urgency by carefully outlining the situation at hand and constantly communicating to the organization itself. TQM data about customer satisfaction, competitive forces, and the need for quality as a state of mind can be provided to organizational members so that they see the need to implement TQM programs. As mentioned earlier, two effective techniques that have been used are benchmarking and Cost of Quality.

5. Support a Strong Leader Role.

Executive actions speak louder than words. No organization should undertake a major drive for change, even for Total Quality programs, without the support of leaders who can serve as strategists for change. Top management is responsible for initiating and supporting a vision of a TQM culture (Blackburn and Rosen, 1993), aligning employees around a vision, and leading the drive to craft the necessary structures and systems that reward employees who work toward implementing the TQM culture. As we have seen, leadership in the change process can come from a variety of sources. (In fact, it is rare for one person to possess all the necessary qualities.) The employee involvement strategies implicit in the TQM process enable leaders to emerge from a variety of positions in the organization.

The role of the leader is particularly important in TQM organizations because the role of the supervisor/middle manager has changed. Leaders get lost in the shuffle and feel powerless as a result. Their traditional role as the authoritarian has changed, and they feel disenfranchised (and can be key resistors to any change). It is important that organizations ready to implement TQM programs recognize the changing role of the leader, and either give them new skills in the coaching and developing of work teams, or abandon their role entirely (Holpp, 1989). Making supervisors and middle managers responsible for building and maintaining their teams gives them a stake in the success of the process and a clearly defined role to play in the development of TQM programs.

Most organizations where the implementation of TQM programs has been most effective utilized the Human Resource managers within the organization. These managers generally are responsible for selection, training, and development, and so are in strong positions to facilitate moves toward TQM. They can assist in the diagnosis of readiness, value-chain analyses, restructuring of necessary performance measurement systems, and the long-term culture change necessary for TQM (Hendricks and Triplett, 1989). Human Resource managers who assist in the design and delivery of TQM programs can work strategically with the TQM office and committee to ensure satisfactory program design, delivery, and assessment.

6. Line Up Political Sponsorship.

Change implementors must have active, broad-based support for change from across the organization. The support of the strong leader will help in this process, but implementors must also have the acceptance of those who are "recipients" of the change. TQM's emphasis on communication, synergies, and employee involvement makes it possible for informal leaders across the organization to be "tapped" as key sponsors. An understanding of key supporters and key resisters is crucial at this stage; it is through building alliances and networks of supporters that resistance erodes. This understanding requires delving through several layers of analysis: force field analysis, stakeholder analysis, commitment charting, and understanding resistance.

One way to determine where support for change lies is through a technique called **force field analysis**. (This technique can also be used to analyze data in commandment 1.) What are the forces driving the change, and what are the forces against it? A simple listing of the forces driving change, and their relative strengths, are drawn and compared to the forces that prevent the change from occurring.

Understanding the forces that drive and restrain change can lead to an assessment of the key owners of the problem. These are the people who have an interest or investment (whether financial or not) in the problem, those whose commitment is necessary (or whose resistance should be minimized) for the change to succeed. A relatively simple technique to use in order to determine these key supporters is called **stakeholder analysis**. One lists key stakeholders and their interests in a particular problem or organizational situation. For example, in the previous expediting example, stakeholders include the purchasing managers themselves (their evaluations were their interest), the plant/production managers (who needed the parts to meet their schedule), the business unit managers (who wanted to meet productivity and profitability goals), the finance staff (whose credibility was on the line), the Human Resource staff (whose design of measurement was at issue), and the customers and stockholders of the company itself.

Beckhard and Harris (1987) suggest that change implementors develop a commitment plan after they have concluded their stakeholder analysis. This is another tool to ensure adequate political sponsorship. **Commitment charts** should enable the change initiator to understand the dynamics necessary to achieve the requisite commitment. For example, it lists the key stakeholders and the level of their commitment, and it enables the change initiator to use the chart to develop plans to achieve commitment and to assess progress.

People who are in the midst of a change can withhold their support for a variety of reasons. This resistance often appears irrational to the people who are initiating the change, but it is critical that the sources behind the resistance be understood. When the change leader understands the sources of the resistance of key stakeholders, he or she can develop plans to attain commitment and reduce the causes of the resistance. Then, the change can be achieved with minimal cost to the organization.

Kotter and Schlesinger (1979) have identified four common reasons why people resist changes: a desire not to lose something of value, a misunderstanding of the change and its implications, a belief that the change does not make sense for the organization, and a low tolerance for change itself. Understanding the reasons behind the resistance enables change leaders within organizations to develop implementation plans that might minimize the resistance. For example, if the resistance to implementing TQM programs comes from a lack of understanding of TQM, then educational programs can be developed. If a quality assurance department is afraid of losing control over a key process or area, an appropriate intervention can be made.

7. Craft an Implementation Plan.

Organizations need to have specific, nuts-and-bolts implementation plans that map out key events, steps, and processes. The plan should enable the organization to bridge the gap between what is and what should be. While the plan itself can be relatively simple (this allows for fine-tuning as events progress), essential elements must include specification of clear roles and responsibilities for all parties to the change. In addition, implementation plans must be designed with the needs of specific organizations in mind. No one plan is effective for all organizations, but some of the diagnostic tools previously cited can serve as guides to use in crafting implementation plans. Three main sets of problems have been found in the formulation and implementation of TQM programs (Krishan et al., 1993):

- Confusion arising from the pursuit of multiple quality initiatives, and lack of clarity and consistency of TQM goals.
- Implementation problems, an inability to translate broad quality goals into quantitative targets, difficulties over organizational design issues, and communication difficulties.
- Lack of consistency between TQM and other strategic initiatives being pursued by the organization.

The analytic tools we have discussed earlier can be utilized to minimize these problems.

The analysis of key stakeholders and resisters can be utilized so that plans deal with the sources of resistance (Kotter and Schlesinger, 1979). For example, an education and communication program can be ideal when resistance is based on inaccurate information. Involvement in some aspect of the implementation itself can reduce or eliminate resistance; employee involvement programs help managers deal with this issue. Coaching and training is an effective approach to reducing resistance, and one that is widely used when implementing TQM programs. Negotiations (and reexamination of union contracts in particular) are often keys to reducing resistance. This was a key starting point for Boston Edison, a utility company Finally, methods of reducing resistance that alters the political balance of power (cooptation, influence, coercion) can be utilized (however, only when the risks of these methods are fully understood by the change initiator; Kotter, 1977).

Blackburn and Benson (1993) studied the practices that most support a Total Quality culture. They found that, although a variety of options were available for those companies wanting to implement TQM programs, several policies were critical in order to set the context for TQM within the organization. These policies contributed to the achievement of a corporate culture based on collective effort, cross-functional work, managers who coached and enabled employees to perform their tasks well, and increased customer satisfaction and product quality. Attention was paid to communication of the change, to mechanisms for employee involvement, design of jobs, training for required job-related skills, performance measurement and evaluation systems, reward systems, safety and health programs, and recruitment, selection, and development programs. The Human Resource Department can play a critical role by developing implementation plans that form a collection of mutually supportive and interdependent processes, each appropriate for the organization in question.

An essential part of any TQM implementation program lies in training. TQM requires that employees learn more than simple job requirements. They must understand the values inherent in the organization's vision, the many informal influence techniques available to them (Bradford and Cohen, 1990), the dynamics of a heterogeneous workforce, the flexible organization design, and other qualitative issues. In addition, they must understand techniques and technologies unique to TQM—JIT, SPC, and so on (Holpp, 1989). Organizations are making tremendous investments in training so that employees understand what is expected of them and why. It is critical (Holpp, 1989) that training

- Be delivered on the job, with real-world relevance and application time.
- Be delivered as needed, coordinated with the needs of employees.
- Be conducted by line people, team members, leaders, supervisors, or managers.
- Be provided to employees at all levels simultaneously so that clear messages are reinforced all at once.
- Be skill-based, measurable, and with attainable outcomes.
- Be designed by the human resource organization in concert with management.
- Play an active role in need diagnosis, developing, and delivering the training.

In addition, training should teach people some qualitative skills, such as how to work and communicate in groups. In TQM programs, organizations become very dependent on teams and teamwork. Most people need to learn to influence each other and those over whom they have little, if any, control. Employees also need to learn how to handle team dynamics so that meetings can be effective, to increase involvement, and to aid the individual employee efforts in problem analysis and diagnosis. TQM is often based on employee actions; training in effective facilitation and support is critical. North American Phillips targeted everyone for 100 hours of training annually. The training was to cover such topics as awareness of TQM, environment for quality improvement, the management role, the team role, and managing customer satisfaction and supplier relationships. The training was conducted internally using a top-down approach. Corning also targeted everyone for training. They planned on 72 hours per person per year. Topics were focused on awareness, tools, and techniques.

8. Develop Enabling Structures.

Altering the status quo and developing new ways to organize, measure, and assess progress are critical for any organizational change. These enabling structures can include such practical ideas as pilot tests, workshops, or training, or more symbolic structures such as banners, meetings, or moving around office space at the request of a team.

For TQM to succeed, systems and structures must be in place that allow for a variety of perspectives on areas that should be discussed in order to make quality changes. Some consistency must be maintained between goals and performance measures. Developing systems to translate quality goals into quantitative performance targets was a critical requisite for success at Northern Telecom, for example. Only when departments were required to commit to specific performance targets were implementation problems overcome (Krishan et al., 1993).

Appropriate organizational structures should be in place for managing quality initiatives. While parallel learning structures (task forces, teams, etc.) can be effective, in some organizations this parallel structure presents a broad administrative burden. The key to success lies in the support of senior management in whatever process the organization chooses (Krishan et al., 1993).

The Henry Ford Health Care provides an example of a typical organization structure for facilitating TQM. At the top level a Corporate Quality Council consisting of senior managers was organized and reported to the Management Policy Committee. Each of the major divisions (such as the Henry Ford Hospital, the Wyandotte Hospital, and the Medical Group) established a Steering Committee. Reporting to these were the Quality Systems teams and the Quality Improvement teams.

Job designs should reflect each employee's discretionary decision-making ability. Performance reviews should emphasize progress toward facilitation of quality and teamwork. Compensation systems should reflect team-related contributions and skill mastery. Systems for generating employee ideas and suggestions must be in place. Selection, recruitment, and development systems should reflect the realities of the TQM workplace and screen out those who are not appropriate. Finally, informal structures (ceremonies, gatherings, recognition) should be in place to reinforce small and large gains.

When Corning initiated its TQM program, its recognition program included the following:

- Six individual outstanding contributor awards were given, each award for $3000.

- Each division would award 10 to 1000 cash awards ranging from $25 to $2500.
- Each division would have 10 to 20 team awards per year.
- Each location would present two awards to the Quality Person of the Year.
- Each location would hold dinners, picnics, and formal award ceremonies all year long.

9. Communicate, Involve People, and Be Honest.

Effective communication is critical from the beginning of a change effort. Every element of the change must be talked about, presented, and discussed, across levels of the organization. Managers should gauge people's reactions and be honest about contingencies and the consequences of making change.

Cohan (1990) has found that, generally, most corporations rarely establish the communications networks necessary to drive the information required to establish TQM programs throughout the company. Believable information, which stimulates enthusiasm and clearly demonstrates the reward for participation, is the key to successful communication about quality. When companies trumpet successes, publicize heroes, and celebrate those employees who epitomize the desired behaviors, the reward for participation in TQM programs becomes obvious. Communications about TQM can cover a broad range of activities, including face-to-face conversations, group or site visits, videotapes, brochures, booklets, company newsletters, advertising campaigns—anything that talks openly about the ongoing quality initiatives.

Because really successful TQM programs are customer-oriented, Cohan suggests beginning a TQM program with an objective customer survey, to get at the "unfiltered" truth. Sharing the results of the survey with employees is critical because they can use the data to make the diagnosis and plan the improvements that will change the customer's perceptions. Another way to approach this understanding of customer requirements is through direct conversation of employees with customers (a technique that also serves to reduce resistance to change as employees begin to be educated about the company's problems with quality).

Cohan also emphasizes that supervisors fully understand the program and be able to communicate it as coaches to employees. Managers must communicate the details and results of change programs often, and be visible and honest about results. Rewards must also be publicized. Employees in one company did not believe that their initiatives would be taken seriously in the firm's quality effort. Only when one group's efforts were praised and made the front page of the company's newsletter did other groups begin to take TQM initiatives seriously. Recognition must be consistent with the desired behavioral standards and business values. These efforts must be communicated across the organization as well.

A Japanese insurance company created a one-page poster to communicate its plan in a succinct manner. The top of the poster (about half a page) stated the guiding vision of the company, which emphasized customer focus followed by the five corresponding goals

1. Retain customers through perfect execution.
2. Achieve error-free processing of cash transactions.
3. Make computer systems more customer-oriented.
4. Apply office automation to improve internal operations.
5. Keep standard operating procedures up to date with customer needs.

These were followed by a timeline showing the entire fiscal year. Below this were graphic bars showing the activities of senior management, sales personnel, and cross-functional teams from the main and branch offices. The bottom section of the poster pictured the key events such as steering committee meetings, recognition events, and training schedules.

10. Reinforce and Institutionalize the Change.

Throughout any organizational change, the organizational leaders must prove their commitment to the change itself. We have talked about the formal and informal ways that can be done. By reinforcing the new behaviors, managers emphasize the importance of transformation. Senior management commitment to programs is palpable and is demonstrated daily.

Because change is an ongoing process, it is difficult to keep the tenth commandment. Particularly in TQM organizations, continuous improvement toward Total Quality is a permanent quest. Therefore, the process of adaptation and change is the behavior that should be reinforced and institutionalized, not the change itself. An organization should be able to reinvent itself as appropriate; and understanding the principles of change should make this possible.

TQM is a long-term improvement strategy for most organizations. Senior management teams often become nervous when results are not dramatic. Executives want to make sure that the investment in training, systems revision, process analysis, diagnosis, surveys, and all the tools has a good payout. After all, they have a "stake" in the success of the program, too. Integration of TQM into an organization's culture often takes at least five years, and the automobile companies have been working on it for almost ten (Brown, 1989). Motorola, a TQM pioneer, has been working to implement TQM for almost 20 years, and it anticipates continual efforts to institutionalize TQM as a way of organizational life.

It is often easy for organizations to address the obvious problems, the issues that everyone recognizes. These problems are much like "low-hanging fruit"—easy to get to and very tasty. However, harvesting only the low-hanging fruit neglects a large part of the crop! Organizations must resist the temptation to go on to the next field before the work is done (Beatty and Ulrich, 1990).

One of the problems associated with major organizational change efforts lies in the energy and commitment of the managers who are charged with implementing the change. Maintaining this commitment is critical for reinforcing and institutionalizing any change. However, when managers (or any level of employee charged with making or implementing change, from factory employee to vice president of operations) continually work on implementing change, they experience a variety of intense emotions, which they must understand. They will face massive resistance from diverse constituencies, no matter how close they are to the process or to the people who are affected by the change. They will be frustrated because change often takes longer than expected, or other things happen which impinge on the change effort. They will be lonely because they are often "out front," covering new territory or blazing new trails. They often experience a real sense of isolation as a result. They may also experience a great deal of pain, as they are often blamed for, and are feeling responsible for, the throes of change the organization is feeling. One manager described herself as "facing an insurmountable task" when made part of a change agent team charged with responsibility for examining and changing the organization's billing and order-taking process in order to become more customer oriented.

The feelings of pain also bring great energy, almost a "roller coaster" ride of emotions. There is the wonderful challenge that accompanies being part of an organizational improvement. A spirit of teamwork and collaboration across organizational boundaries pervades, and there is the sense that the group charged with implementing change is in it together. A great deal of growth and development of each individual's personal talents takes place. People involved with implementing change generally learn a great deal about the workings of business and themselves. Finally, there is an incredible sense of gratification and accomplishment. Most people charged with implementing change see it as a continual, incremental process where they, and their organization, "take two steps forward, and often one and one-half steps backwards . . . but even so it's forward progress!"

Linda Ackerman has described the predictable stages of organizational change in a way that maps out the emotional changes described above (Ackerman, 1986). It is when the morale and confidence of the organization become very high that the change is in most danger of failing, because expectations are very high. Organizations must learn to be realistic about just what can be accomplished, and to build change teams and efforts across and down.

◆ TQM AND ORGANIZATIONAL CULTURE

Understanding the mechanics and the emotional energies required to make the change needed to become a TQM organization is critical, but part of the difficulties inherent in making the move to TQM is a result of the potential conflicts with the culture of the organization. Culture is the common behavior and internalized codes of conduct that guide people's daily actions. Organizational behavior is shaped by the ways people internalize the assumptions and values that define, either explicitly or not, the culture of the organization. People quickly learn which actions are allowed and which are not. For example, an organization that has traditionally been a hierarchical one, with little autonomy or encouragement of initiative, exhorted its employees to become more oriented toward problem solving, cross-functional work, and discussion, as part of an ongoing TQM process. Unfortunately, this behavior violated long-standing cultural traditions and functional rivalries. Despite senior management's efforts and encouragement, the attempt was unsuccessful. The organization became paralyzed by the existing culture.

Cultures vary in their content (the set of basic assumptions) and in their strength (the intensity of behaviors) (Schlesinger and Schlesinger, 1993). Content is affected by the environment and the industry as well as by formal structures, policies, and plans. Many manufacturing organizations have as an unwritten (yet often inviolable) rule, "Get the goods out the door." Even if some of the goods were poor quality, the key driver of behavior was always to get the goods out and let the customer worry about quality. As organizations move toward TQM, production–ship targets can be missed as attention gets paid to shipping only quality products. This can be highly stressful to employees, particularly in an organization with a strong "let's ship it" attitude. Such programs often backfire, leaving management scratching their heads and wondering what went wrong. It is critical to understand the ways culture can be used to guide and direct the implementation of TQM programs, using the ten commandments and the change model as guides.

John Kotter and James Heskett (1992) studied the relationship between culture and performance, and found that only those cultures that value continuous and adaptive changes promote effective economic performance over time. Organizations successful in making transformational change have managers who pay close attention to environmental changes and who initiate changes in the organization's design and strategy in order to cope with environmental shifts. In addition, and for TQM purposes probably most important, these organizations value the needs of all who have a share in the organization, from employees to customers to shareholders. People and processes that manage toward continual change (read improvement) are equally valued, and valued highly.

Cultures can be changed by focusing on the actions of current members, by adding people who represent the new culture, and by socializing people to new behaviors. Informal mechanisms (stories, legends, celebrations) are as important as formal mechanisms. For example, one group of long-term employees redesigned a package to solve a long-standing packaging problem. They were thrilled because "it was the first time management had asked us to help." The organization was thrilled because a key variable in visual quality was addressed. The team became instant heroes, and their names were on the package, in the newsletter, on a plaque. The legend spread and more and more employees felt comfortable changing their behavior.

Kotter and Heskett identified some key behaviors which managers can use to create cultures that are adaptable to environmental shifts. Establishing a need for change, a sense of crisis, is the first step. In addition, establishing a new direction, based on the firm's core competencies and key constituencies, is required. Communicating the direction, modeling the behavior, and recognizing and rewarding failures and successes is also important. Finally, adaptive organizations must have managers who can balance adherence to the core values with flexibility in process, who establish organizational designs which "fit" with the environment and mission of the firm (systems, tasks, and people are in alignment), who promote leadership qualities in others, and who establish mechanisms that enable the emergence of leaders at all levels.

◆ IMPLEMENTING TQM PROGRAMS

If managers follow the rules for change presented in this chapter, why, then, do so many Total Quality Management programs fail? Krishan and his group (1993) have concluded that, while there is no recipe for success, many factors contribute to the failure of TQM programs. They cite three sets of problems encountered in the design and delivery of TQM:

1. Goals: confusion arising from the pursuit of multiple quality initiatives, with little clarity and consistency of goals.
2. Managerial inaction: an inability to translate broad quality goals into quantitative targets, difficulties over the appropriate organizational structures within which to implement programs, communication difficulties, and problems in managing the transition from individual to organizational learning.
3. Strategic confusion: an inconsistency between quality goals and other strategic initiatives, particularly the difficulties that arise in pursuing Total Quality Management while restructuring and/or downsizing.

Multiple Programs and Goals

Because there are as many ways to improve quality as there are companies that try it, finding the appropriate methodology is complicated. Appropriately setting the quality standards, whether based on internal (setting one's own targets for performance) or external (customer orientation) measures, then defining and sharing the definition of quality, is the first step in establishing clear goals and directions for the program. In fact, some organizations are successful at designing and co-ordinating one set of programs to accomplish many quality objectives.

Implementation Issues: Quantitative Targets

Quality goals should be linked to quantitative, measurable performance targets that are in turn linked to specific, realistic deadlines. However, there was even more variety between measures than between goals. These conflicting targets made the number and conflict between the goals cited above even more noticeable. In order to define goals more clearly and decrease goal conflict, organizations can translate quality goals into quantitative performance targets by committing departments to the targets. Discussion of the timing and importance of targets can resolve the goal conflict.

Developing Structures

Organizations struggle to develop the appropriate structures to use in order to manage quality initiatives. Informal networks of cross-functional or cross-departmental task forces can be very exciting, yet they provide no way to resolve conflicts between the informal quality management process and the formal structure. Initiatives can also be managed through the existing structures, but because coordination between programs is so critical, existing structures often make coordination more complicated. Sequential goal setting seems to be the most effective way to coordinate initiatives; the setting of a single performance goal for the company enables it to integrate across boundaries. In addition, the objectives of programs should not be too ambitious. Targets should be specific, measurable, and attainable within a well-defined period (Krishan et al, 1993). These incremental targets should be well communicated across the organization.

Communication

Communication across functions, departments, and other organizational boundaries is always difficult. Communicating TQM programs, objectives, and measures is no less problematic. Often, communication efforts improve when the focus is placed on the customer. The many ways to communicate effectively have already been addressed in this chapter.

Training

Training programs can be used to communicate the TQM message throughout the organization while employees are learning basic skills. In addition, while working together through the training, employees learn to talk to one another about problems and problem solving. Achieving a close link between training programs and TQM programs is made easier when a TQM program with one clear objective is achieved, because the training programs can be adapted in accordance with quality goals.

STRATEGIC GOALS

TQM programs seek to enhance competitiveness by paying attention to customer demands for quality products. These efforts mandate a change in the way organizations approach problem solving and employee involvement. As we will see in Chapter 12, employees are encouraged to become part of the process. Usually, this involvement can result in a relatively secure environment whereby employees are encouraged to take risks and innovate. When downsizing or restructuring occurs in organizations, often as a way to enhance competitiveness by lowering costs, layoffs and reorganizations can cause a drop in morale and a feeling of insecurity among employees. This prevents the atmosphere of trust required for involvement to be developed. In addition, quality improvement is long term, whereas restructuring is short-term, more radical action. The emotions of a restructuring often lead to a sense that the status quo should be protected; this feeling is incompatible with the changes required for TQM. Therefore, because the management process involved in TQM is different from that required by restructuring, Krishnan and his group suggest that companies try restructuring before beginning a TQM effort.

Essentially, three questions aid in the planning and delivery of TQM:

1. Is a quality management program appropriate? Yes, if the company is relatively stable strategically and looks to improve long-term performance through attention to product and customer satisfaction.
2. What goals and what programs are involved? Clarity over goals directed at multiple performance dimensions and stakeholders is the foundation for TQM, as we have seen in other chapters.
3. How should TQM be implemented? Because most change programs fail in the implementation, it is important to follow the rules outlined in this chapter.

◆ IMPLEMENTING TQM

Many organizations are implementing TQM programs, some with great success. Let's see how the principles outlined above have been utilized in two organizations. Intel Corporation's computer service division (Clark et al., 1993) was established to service its system-level products. Initially, the division had limited competition, low volume of work, and high margins. As the computer industry made the transition to products based more on personal computers, Intel and the service division had to change to support this transition. The group did not make the transition well; profit margins went down, and pressure was on to reduce costs. Reorganizations became continual, and layoffs and restructurings became routine. According to Clark, by 1988 the division had completely lost sight of customer requirements.

Quality training began between 1988 and 1990. Business processes were examined. TQM training occurred across the organization. Managerial groups got together to define key organizational procedures. Hopes were high for change, but all was in vain. People reverted to their old ways when the training ended (Clark et al., 1993). Clearly, neither customer dissatisfaction nor the model nor the process had been effective in making change. Something else had to be done.

Late in 1990, Intel decided to apply for the Baldrige award. The real drive for quality had begun. The company established a quality technology group, charged with developing tools for use in implementing a program outlining a new way of managing within Intel. The computer services group was one of the first to deploy the program.

The program began with a self-study course, the quality leadership series, which was designed to help map the existing processes and to determine the best way to use process improvements to fix any misfits between process elements. Senior managers kicked off the program by taking the course; it then cascaded to other organizational levels. Ultimately, everyone in the services division took the course. According to Clark et al. (1993), experiencing the course helped employees understand the division's problems and to find ways to make real improvements. The spreading of the dissatisfaction had begun.

The services organization presented a complete roadmap for the organization to use to implement TQM across the division. A cross-functional team got together to create 200 projects to support the program's strategic objectives. The rest of the organization tackled the projects with great enthusiasm.

By April 1991, however, little to no progress had been made in process improvement. In fact, most of the teams weren't even meeting. Commitment to the quality effort varied across the organization, and priorities and goals were unclear. In addition, business conditions and profitability were declining at a time when achieving profitability was critical. Senior management, recognizing that some managers were actively resisting the change in processes, decided to act (Clark et al., 1993). They brought together a core group of six top managers to review the goals and to reduce the number of projects. At the same time, upper level employees experienced restructuring and reduction in force. The services group thus began to develop a process for implementing TQM. The new management team was to support a Total Quality focus enthusiastically, all the while engaging employees in the process. Four critical process tactics were identified as targets. Finally, three process managers were selected who would be responsible for facilitation and for keeping the organization's improvement efforts coordinated. Teams were organized to work on the projects and to define customer satisfaction. Implementation of the four critical tactics became more realistic and attuned to the process itself (Clark et al., 1993).

During the execution phase, the cross-functional team met weekly and performed root cause analysis, using the tools described in Chapter 6. They developed plans with measurable milestones, and they worked hard to understand the formal and informal processes of the organization itself. Each team was responsible for reporting progress against each milestone, which encouraged accountability and responsiveness. By May of 1991, the organization began to see some visible improvements (Clark et al., 1993). Process improvements, employee involvement, and departmental morale soared. Early successes were used to generate more enthusiasm for the program, and, after seven months, dramatic improvement had been made in customer satisfaction (from 70 percent in May 1991 to 95 percent in December 1991) and outage (from 25 hours in May to 11 hours in December).

Clark and his group (1993) maintain that Intel's computer service division was successful because they learned many of the ideas we have addressed in this chapter. They learned to be prepared to make fundamental business changes and to realign the organization if and when necessary as the business changed. They learned to get commitment and to demonstrate enthusiasm, as well as to encourage and stimulate visibility, responsibility, and accountability among employees. They specifically defined tactics, and they selected those to implement the tactics who were dedicated to the change itself.

They also decided to support and nurture the employees as they went through the process. Essentially, they had the vision and commitment, a (revised, and now appropriate) model for change, and they paid attention to the informal and formal processes required within the organization to make things work.

Next, let's examine the ongoing process of change at a division of a financial services company (Schlesinger, personal communication). The company began a drive for quality to serve the customers better, in a division that processed over 100 million transactions and 3 million phone calls a year. The leader of the division initiated and designed the TQM program with help from the Corporate Quality Department (and a team of consultants). Their efforts were guided by an explicit corporate philosophy, which emphasized high-quality work at all organizational levels and reinforced that quality with built-in technical redundancy and professional bench strength. The company's quality philosophy was also explicit: that quality is a process, that senior management had to be committed to each initiative, that the involvement of employees in the process was critical, and that results had to be measurable, with meaningful rewards and recognition.

First, they developed a vision, and they outlined explicit business objectives, including decreasing client services costs, creating a responsive and flexible organization, and ensuring consistent, quality service for all clients. They accomplished these objectives by reorganizing the division, beginning business process redesign, rationalizing the introduction of new products and services, and converting their computer technology. The team started with a diagnosis of the situation, from the perspectives of both the internal and external customer. Then, they made no decisions for 90 days, and they spent the time developing a plan and talking about the changes with all of the organization's employees. After six months of diagnosing and communications, they began work on 200 action items and 28 key initiatives. Finally, the change began to have an impact. Assignments began to change, managers were relocated, problems and issues were confronted and resolved. Training in the new ways of working began, and the reward system and structure were changed to reflect the new quality focus. The change is ongoing.

The program this company initiated involved elements and techniques developed elsewhere in this book. The process for change, however, was, in the words of the change leader, critical for success. Real diagnosis of the problems, consistent sharing of leadership, and decision making from the senior managers to the employees were critical to the process. "Endless" communication across the organization was important. Monitoring the results (and changing the systems accordingly) enabled the employees to see the results and to know that they were important to the business. Finally, they celebrated with recognition and rewards that were designed to be meaningful to the business and the employees (for example, free trips and vacations).

The senior manager and leader of the change effort described the lessons learned as a guide to change agents.

1. Trust people, be patient, and have faith in people and the process.
2. Be unswerving in your goals.
3. Communicate everything, often, even when you don't have all the answers.
4. Recognize that not everything will go as planned; make midcourse corrections into learning opportunities.
5. Be visible, and constantly support and encourage.

◆ Summary

The tools outlined in this book give the background in Total Quality Management, and this chapter specifically gives an outline for implementation planning utilizing those tools. Institutionalizing and reinforcing the TQM process involves continuing change and becoming what Peter Senge (1990) calls a "learning organization." Leaders in these organizations must build shared visions, challenge existing models and processes for the ways work is done, and foster systemic patterns of thinking, very much as the leader in the financial services company described above. The organizations they lead are places where people are continually expanding their capabilities in order to change the future. That is the ultimate in Total Quality Management.

◆ Key Terms

Cross-functional team	Transformational change	Implementation plans (P)
Organizational change	Dissatisfaction with the	Force field analysis
Developmental change	status quo (D)	Stakeholder analysis
Transitional change	New model of managing (M)	Commitment charts

◆ Assignments

(These exercises are more generic but can be useful integrative summaries for a TQM class.)

1. Group Exercise on TQM

   In your study or task group, look through recent articles on implementation of TQM in organizations. What commonalities can you find across the literature? What differences do you perceive? What are the common themes about implementation and practice across the literature? Be prepared to present your analysis to the class.

2. Group or Individual Exercise on TQM

   In your study or task group, or individually, interview several practitioners who have been involved in TQM efforts within their organization. Find out as much as you can about the implementation process, promises, pitfalls, and opportunities. What common themes can you draw from these experiences? How transferable are these activities from one organization (or person) to another?

3. Group or Individual Exercise on TQM

   Review the five vision statements in the section "Understanding the Model for Change." Do these meet the criteria listed by Jick for good and effective visions? What changes would you suggest?

4. Individual Exercise on TQM Implementation

   One of the most important elements for successful implementation of any change is the change agent him or herself. List at least five skills you believe are essential for successful change agents. Thinking candidly about you and your skills, how many of these skills do you currently possess? If you do not have these skills, develop a plan to practice and learn the necessary skills.

5. Individual Exercise

   Below are four situations in which you are the Quality champion. Comment on the approach used by the Quality champion. How would you handle each situation?

Situation 1: You are in an organization that has committed itself to the Total Quality journey. A vice president for operations has been hired. This person is not committed to Total Quality. In order to educate him, you think it would be a good idea to take him on some trips to companies with exemplary TQM activities. You have already talked this over with the company president and the new VP. The new VP is cool to the idea of taking these trips. You examined his calendar and found dates when he would be available to take the trips. Then you wrote letters to the heads of companies you wish to visit and sent them to the VP for his signature.

Situation 2: The VP of Customer Service has invited you to a strategy session. Knowing the VP is not convinced that TQM tools are useful, you devise an agenda. The centerpiece of the agenda involves having the meeting participants create an Affinity Diagram (see Chapter 8 for a discussion of Affinity Diagrams). You show the agenda to the VP. She attaches it to the notice of the upcoming meeting she sent out to all of the participants.

Situation 3: Corporate has sent you to introduce TQM to the administrative area of a hospital. You need to establish credibility with the employees. So you get involved with some significant activities that help you become very visible. You make it a point to sit with them during lunch and to engage people in one-on-one chats, trying to find what problems exist that can be solved using TQM approaches. You organize a quality council consisting only of the administrative staff and try to involve them in some team-building.

Situation 4: The Sales Department manager has a short-term focus dictated by the quotas she has to meet. You have reviewed the performance of the department for the past several months and found the performance is sporadic. In a meeting with the manager, you ask if she would like to have the sales performance become more predictable with results above quota. You point out the problems salespeople experience as a result of poor support from the operations staff. You suggest putting together a cross-functional team of sales and operations people to examine the support process and suggest improvements. Your plan is to use the seven basic tools described in Chapter 6.

C a s e   S t u d y

Hank Snow and East Coast Electric: Instituting TQM

Hank Snow woke up excited and eager for the day to begin. Today was his six-month anniversary as the manager of Mechanical Engineering Services at East Coast Electric Supply. Hank was eager to begin stressing attention to quality in the department. He wondered just how he would be able to get his group of 250 engineers to embrace TQM in their work. He felt he understood the organization, the culture, and the nature of the work. He was eager to develop a plan as soon as possible and to start the challenges ahead.

East Coast Electric Supply

East Coast Electric Supply (ECE) is a small public utility in Long Bay which generates and transmits electric power and ancillary services to several cities and towns on the east coast of the United States. ECE employs

approximately 5000 people and is functionally organized. Relationships across the functions are harmonious; any conflicts are faced directly and settled amicably.

ECE has been operating for over 50 years in a regulated environment that favors competition. ECE has been able to meet those competitive challenges successfully. However, in the last 10 years, other issues have caused ECE management to be concerned about their operations. These issues include increased environmental concerns, load management and conservation concerns, fluctuations in fuel supply and cost, and the significant cost increases incurred in normal business operations, including significant costs in pensions, health care, and competitive salaries. ECE's management, headed by President and CEO Ben Yawkey, has been focusing on long-term strategic planning, controlling costs, expand-

Hank Snow and East Coast Electric: Instituting TQM (Continued)

ing revenue options, and consolidating key business functions and operations. These new actions began at a time of reduced revenues for ECE. These circumstances are quite a change for the formerly sleepy utility. Suddenly, people have had to recognize that the environment is really changing.

ECE and Quality

Part of ECE's efforts to revitalize itself came from Yawkey's interest in TQM. He knew that Kansai Electric Power Company had received the Deming Award in 1987, and he was familiar with Florida Power and Light's Quality Program. He decided to bring TQM to ECE. In 1992 he pulled together 20 senior managers into a TQM task force. This task force benchmarked other TQM programs looking for the basic elements that enabled other organizations to implement TQM successfully. The task force concluded its work, and in 1993 ECE formally began a "Total Quality at ECE" program. Charles Rush was named VP of Quality, and a memo was issued to the organization which outlined the quality improvement process.

Over the first four months of the program, 150 senior executives received Total Quality training. Hank had heard that each of the executives was enthusiastic about the program and that it would work if given the chance. Hank was pleased; there had been some concern around ECE that the senior managers, most of whom had long tenure in ECE, were not receptive to change.

The training focused on customer expectations, problem diagnosis and prevention, and building commitment to workplace quality. Finally, open decision-making and employee empowerment was key to the Total Quality effort. Essentially, training emphasized:

- Quality as consistent conformance to customer expectations internal and external customers meeting customers specifications and expectations doing the job right all the time—customer satisfaction indicators are measurements of quality
- Conformance to expectations 100 percent of the time, over time.
- Achievement of quality through prevention and specific improvement projects.
- Ongoing improvement.
- Prevention of mistakes and elimination of nonconformance.
- Management commitment as critical to the quality process.

The senior management training program was only a beginning, but Rush hoped that ultimately the entire organization would experience the training and begin to implement TQM.

Hank Snow

Hank Snow is 35 and has an undergraduate degree in engineering from East Coast University. He is a recent graduate of Eastern State University's Evening MBA program, where he concentrated on management and operations. He has worked in various capacities in other utilities. Married, with two children, Hank moved to Long Bay and joined ECE because he believed that he would be able to combine his engineering and his management skills to effect change in the utility. He also liked the community itself and the fact that his wife would be able to maintain her real estate career.

Hank had a quiet personality. With his gentle nature and warm smile, coupled with a quiet humor, he made friends easily. While

Hank Snow and East Coast Electric: Instituting TQM (Continued)

at Eastern, he had taken courses in operations and organizational change. Although he felt confident in his abilities to understand organizations and the obstacles and opportunities presented by making change, he knew that implementing change was harder than planning it! Hank had learned about TQM at school and had participated in TQM symposia, which had left him excited about the opportunities TQM provided. He was scheduled to take ECE quality training during his first month as head of the Mechanical Engineering Services Department.

ECE's Culture

Hank had attended a training session entitled "Managing ECE's Climate and Performance" during his first months at ECE. The session was presented to a wide spectrum of middle managers just like Hank. Mr. Yawkey opened the session with a statement of ECE's challenges, strategies, and opportunities. He clearly challenged the group to take an active part in improving the company. As the training proceeded, it became clear to Hank that two cultures were present within ECE. Each function regarded itself as team-oriented, a "family," and cooperative and productive. Each function saw ECE, on the other hand, as top-down, authoritarian, tense, and stagnant. The disparity led Hank to consider that there were many real cultural barriers to achieving the Total Quality culture which Yawkey desired. As he listened to the training, he made a list of cultural concerns:

1. Honesty—ECE had to be honest with its employees and the objectives of the quality program.
2. Trust—More trust was needed between management and the employees.

3. Communications—ECE needed to be careful about how things were communicated to employees.
4. Cross-functional rivalries—Each function needed to be aware that it belonged to the same corporation and had to cooperate to meet competitive challenges.
5. Authority—Middle management had responsibility, though not formal authority, to execute practice and to make decisions.

Hank was most concerned about the group's failure to take action to make any changes in their process or practice. The failure didn't seem to stem from an inability to diagnose the problems; rather, it came from a fear that upper management would react negatively and defuse any efforts. He left the meeting excited, but concerned about both reaching the members of his department and in keeping his immediate bosses informed and supportive.

The Mechanical Engineering Services Department (MESD)

The MESD provided engineering support and project management services to ECE (Exhibit 11.1). Its tasks ranged from support of long-range planning and design of major capital improvement projects to provision of technical expertise for special tasks and maintenance of power generating units. Project engineers usually followed MESD projects from start to finish and obtained services from within ECE or from outside it, depending on the problems involved. Each project engineer reviewed his or her project monthly to ensure both proper direction and strategy. Neither the project engineers nor

Hank Snow and East Coast Electric: Instituting TQM (Continued)

Exhibit

11.1

Mechanical Engineering Services: Key Activities

Assessment of existing conditions	Specifying and evaluating equipment
Feasibility studies	Outside vendor, contractor selection
Preliminary engineering report	Contract negotiations
Project cost estimating	Construction management
Economic justification	System startup
Project scheduling	Project turnover
Project design engineering	Project followup

Each project or report has standardized guidelines and methods. "Project design" documents are used as operation and procedural outlines for each engineer's work. These documents ensure that MESD delivers the project within approved methods and specifications. It clearly defines the project and the technical design, and states clearly the many levels and stages of project review.

the other members of the services unit had attended any quality training when Hank took over; however, they had heard of it.

Hank's Activities

Hank began to stress quality almost immediately. He believed that each project should strive to be of the highest quality, on schedule, and on target for cost estimates (Exhibit 11.2). "Our projects are constant; they never go away," he said. "It doesn't make any sense to have anything less than acceptable quality. They are expected to operate trouble-free for 25 years; we have to do everything we can to make that happen!"

After a month on the job, Hank began the process of discussing quality with the 4 key leaders of the department (Exhibit 11.3). As part of their weekly department meetings, Hank began to talk about TQM. He first reviewed quality as a concept, showing humorous but hard-hitting videotapes to illustrate what quality means. Then he gave an

overview of the ECE quality program and the potential positive effects on the business. He completed an analysis of the Cost of Quality, and the benefits of working with quality processes, to the group. Finally, he reviewed and discussed operations and guidelines, as well as ways to make improvements on methods of doing business.

The Project Design Document

Hank decided that the first TQM-oriented change he would initiate would be the use of a project design document, which would provide a checklist to ensure that all aspects of the project were maintained, to clearly define and protect the design, and to review and assess the project's process. This type of document is used by many engineering firms and is a valuable project management tool. Seven out of the ten project engineers were either neutral or favorable to using the project design document in their work. Hank urged two of the engineers, one who was beginning a

Hank Snow and East Coast Electric: Instituting TQM (Continued)

Exhibit
11.2

Hank's Ideas for Future Changes with MESD

1. Continue active communication and feedback on all engineering studies and projects.
2. Provide an engineering presence within each department to support the department.
3. Develop an itemization of all engineering activities and indicate the engineer responsible.
4. Provide in-plant inspections to guarantee preventative maintenance.
5. Demonstrate improvements in customer satisfaction.

Exhibit
11.3

Key Managers within MESD

Skip Connolly—50 years old, BSEE and MSEE from Eastern State University. Has been with ECE since he graduated from college. He is the keeper of the flame, the source of legends and stories about the way things "used to be." While he is not overtly resistant to Hank's changes and TQM in general, he carefully guards the existing methods because "they work . . . and always have." He is well-liked within the department. Skip works on a very important long-term project.

Ralph Norton—45 years old, BSEE, MSEE, and newly minted MS in Environmental Studies from Eastern State. Has been at ECE for 10 years and has been frustrated at times with the complacency at ECE. He would like to focus on making the company more efficient but is unclear about just how to do that. He is highly regarded for his technical skills.

Jennifer Goldman—35 years old, BSEE from Massachusetts Institute of Technology. Comes to MESD from the President's Office, where she worked on special engineering projects. Her direct style and competence sometimes threaten others in MESD; however, the engineering talent and interpersonal skills she brings to projects often result in success where everyone had anticipated failure.

Allan Faherty—40 years old. Has been at ECE for two years. His project had recently attracted considerable attention because it came in on time and under budget. A strong believer in TQM, he had seen what it could do when he'd worked at Florida Power and Light. His brusque style tended to aggravate his co-workers, but he was trying to calm down.

project and another who was ending one, to use the document. He provided the initial details and templates, and he was careful to include and specify issues that were troubling the engineer. In each situation, both the client and the engineer found the document helpful for project planning. Hank felt that, with time and help, more project engineers would use the project design document.

Hank reviewed the MESD operations and the ways they met ECE's Total Quality prospectives with the case writer.

We do a good job meeting project technical quality, but can improve in the perception of the way our services are provided. While we don't have good measures of project quality, we do measure project costs. We don't mea-

Hank Snow and East Coast Electric: Instituting TQM (Continued)

sure project schedules well, although it IS important to our customers. We also know whether projects have met or exceeded expectations after the project acceptance meetings, but not before. We try to work with our customers to develop achievable expectations, but this is not always possible. The way I see it, we can really make improvements in prevention and specific improvements, by doing more detailed engineering in the pre-project stage to obtain more accurate estimates, by developing useful guidelines (like the project design document), by developing technical guidelines, by improving documentation standards, and by improving our internal records and files. I know that I can show my commitment to the process, but our guys spend so much time with other departments and areas, I need to make sure they demonstrate this commitment as well. That's something they didn't teach me at ESU!

He sat back in his chair. "I know that senior management is supportive of this kind of effort, but I have some concern about what more I can do to demonstrate TQM. If it works, I will be assured of further advancement. If it fails, my career could be stalled." Yet, he felt that it was worthwhile to proceed. He just wondered just what he should do next.

CASE QUESTION

1. What steps do you think Hank should take to implement TQM within MESD?
2. What obstacles do you see? What opportunities do you see?

◆ Bibliography

Ackerman, Linda. "Development, Transition, or Transformation: The Question of Change in Organizations." *O.D.'s Practitioner* (December 1986): 1–8.

Alexander, Larry. "Successfully Implementing Strategic Decisions." *Long Range Planning,* 18, No. 3 (1985): 91–97.

Beckhard, Richard, and Reuben T. Harris. *Organizational Transitions: Managing Complex Change.* 2nd ed. Reading, Mass.: Addison-Wesley Publishing Co., 1987.

Beer, Michael, Russell A. Eisenstadt, and Bert Spector. "Why Change Programs Don't Produce Change." *Harvard Business Review,* (November–December 1990).

Beer, Michael, Russell A. Eisenstadt, and Bert Spector. *The Critical Path to Corporate Renewal.* Cambridge, Mass.: Harvard Business School Press, 1990.

Beer, Michael. *Organization Change and Development: A Systems View.* Glencoe, Ill.: Goodyear, 1980.

Beatty, Richard W., and David O. Ulrich. "Re-Energizing the Mature Organization." *Organizational Dynamics,* (Summer 1991): 16–30.

Bennis, Warren G., Kenneth D. Benne, and Robert Chin. *The Planning of Change.* 4th ed. Portsmouth, Ohio: Holt, Rinehart and Winston, 1985.

Blackburn Richard, and Benson Rosen. "Total Quality and Human Resource Management: Lessons Learned from Baldrige Award Winning Companies." *Academy of Management Executive.* 7, No. 3 (1993): 49–66.

Bradford, David, and Allan Cohen. *Influence Without Authority*. New York: John Wiley and Sons, 1990.

Brown, Mark Graham. "Commitment . . . It's not the Whether, It's the 'How To'." *Journal of Quality and Participation* (December 1989).

Clark, Tom, Larry Walz, George Turner, and Bish Miszuk. "Intel's Circuitous Route to Implementing Total Quality." *Quality* (February 1993) 25–31.

Cohan, George S. "Communications: Driving the Quality Train." *Quality* (December 1990).

Hendricks, Charles, and Arlene Triplett. "TQM: Strategy for '90's Management." *Personnel Administrator* (December 1989).

Holpp, Lawrence. "Ten Reasons Why Total Quality Is Less Than Total." *Training,* (October 1989): 93–103.

Jick, Todd D. "Note: The Challenge of Change," Harvard Business School, 1993, 490–016.

Jick, Todd D. "The Vision Thing." Harvard Business School, 1990, 490–019.

Kanter, Rosabeth Moss, Barry A. Stein, and Todd D. Jick. *The Challenge of Organizational Change: How Companies Experience It and Leaders Guide It*. New York: Free Press, 1992, pp. 382–384.

Kotter, John P. "Power, Dependence, and Effective Management." *Harvard Business Review* (July–August 1977).

Kotter, John P., and James L. Heskett, *Corporate Culture and Performance*. New York: Free Press, 1992.

Kotter, John P., and Leonard A. Schlesinger. "Choosing Strategies for Change." *Harvard Business Review* (March–April 1979).

Krishan, B., A. B. Shani, R. M. Grant, and R. Baer. "In Search of Quality Improvement: Problems of Design and Implementation." *The Academy of Management Executive* (November 1993).

The New York Times, March 4, 1992.

O. D. Resources. *Change Announcement Planning Guide*. Atlanta, Ga.: Paton, 1985.

Richards, Dick, and Sarah Engle. "After the Vision: Suggestions to Corporate Visionaries and Vision Champions." In John Adams, ed. *Transforming Leadership*. Alexandria Va: Miles River Press, 1989.

Schlesinger, Leonard, personal communication, 1994.

Schlesinger, Phyllis, and Leonard Schlesinger, "Designing Effective Organizations." In Allan R. Cohen, ed. *The Portable MBA in Management*. New York: John Wiley and Co., 1993.

Senge, Peter. "The Leader's New Work: Building Learning Organizations." *Sloan Management Review* (Fall 1990).

Shetty, Y. K., and Paul F. Butler, "Regaining Competitiveness Requires HR Solutions." *Personnel* (July 1990).

Ulrich, David, and Dale Lake. *Organizational Capability: Competing from the Inside Out*. New York: John Wiley and Sons, 1990.

Weisbord, Marvin. *Organizational Diagnosis: A Workbook of Theory and Practice*. Reading, Mass.: Addison-Wesley Publishing Co., 1978.

Employee Practices in Total Quality Management Organizations

◆ ◆ ◆

*E*nvision two similar companies, both beginning Total Quality programs. "We're driving towards achieving Total Quality in all our operations," the CEO of Company A announces proudly. He drives the TQM process from the top-down. When employees make suggestions, he (and his lieutenants) revise them to "be realistic." He encourages involvement, yet, six months, or even a year later, only the CEO and selected members of the executive team are part of the process of design and implementation. Middle managers have heard of the quality program, but aren't quite sure what it is. People on the shop floor have heard rumors, but are sure that whatever this new program is, it *ISN'T* good for them. The TQM program fades away, and the CEO scratches his head and tries another new program.

When Company B's CEO announces the TQM program, she emphasizes that the entire organization must work together to show concern for customers. While she and her senior management team have outlines for the progression of the program, she solicits (indeed, demands) ideas and suggestions from employees at all levels. She encourages changes in the status quo and builds cross-functional teams to work on key organizational problems. TQM is taught at cascading levels throughout the organization. In six months, the organization has uncovered, and solved, some key customer-oriented problems. Within a year, most functions have quality teams working on problem solving. Middle managers and shop employees are actively involved in the TQM program and are convinced that TQM/continuous improvement is the way of the future.

◆ INTRODUCTION

What is the difference between these two companies' experiences? Although some of the differences lie in the implementation process (see Chapter 11 for more details on implementing TQM), the major difference is in the involvement of employees across the organization. TQM programs that do not have management commitment and employee involvement are bound to fail. While management's role is critical to achieving Total Quality, it is often the most overlooked part of the process.

This chapter examines human resource management issues in TQM organizations. First, we examine the intricacies of employee involvement and its relationship to the TQM process. Next, we study the nature of organizational structures and boundary setting. Third, we discuss the measurement and reward of teams in TQM. Finally, we address employee involvement teams and their characteristics.

◆ EMPLOYEE INVOLVEMENT AND TQM: SIMILARITIES AND DIFFERENCES

Employee involvement (EI) evolved out of American business's need to improve performance. Managers and academicians believed that by involving employees in problem-solving, decision-making, and business operations, performance and productivity would increase. Many organizations, large and small, began to involve employees in participatory management programs, quality of work life programs, and democratic management programs. However, to be effective, employee involvement must be the overall approach to management in each organization in which it occurs. Essentially, employees should be encouraged, through culture, systems, and practice, to control their destiny and participate in the daily life and processes of the organization. In order to participate effectively, employees need power, information, knowledge, and rewards that are relevant to business performance. Only then will employees be able to make decisions that will affect productivity.

Generally, organizations begin EI programs because they are good business. As business conditions become more competitive, EI programs enable organizations to adapt to competition effectively. EI programs generally increase productivity because they increase the information flow in the organization. Organizations with involved employees have to share corporate performance and financial results, so that employees know the impact of their actions and work. They must share an understanding of technology (process) as well. Finally, they must have a climate where employee involvement is routine across the organization.

Organizations in which every employee is motivated and able to make changes that support the organization's strategic needs use several strategies to achieve this involvement. First, senior managers must be involved in modeling employee involvement. If senior managers don't let their employees be responsible for decisions and actions, then EI has little chance of succeeding down organizational levels. Second, any involvement and participation should direct employee inputs toward each business's strategic operational imperatives, so that employees can set priorities on decision making.

Enabling decision making down to the lowest level in the organization is another factor critical to employee involvement. This does not mean that all decisions must go to all levels; rather, it means only that each employee has the information, the perspective, the tools, and the power to make decisions that affect his or her performance. It also presumes that the prevailing organizational attitude toward people encourages people that care and are motivated and capable of making decisions. Reward systems that support participation by rewarding the initiation of change and the fostering of team building should be in place. One way to generate rewards is through a well-conceived method of accepting, and acting on, suggestions from employees. Training in the qualitative aspects of decision making and communication of real business information are also critical parameters in employee involvement.

When the Paul Revere Insurance Company instituted its Quality Has Value program, significant emphasis was placed on generating and rewarding suggestions. The objective was to change the culture so that people "listened down" instead of "listened up and proclaimed down." The program required that each person belong to a quality improvement team. At the home office there were 127 teams averaging 10 people per team. Training was provided on conducting meetings, facilitating idea-generation, and problem solving (primarily using brainstorming). As teams came up with ideas, these were logged into a computerized tracking program, along with estimated cost savings. At the end of each week, the Quality group would evaluate all ideas that had been implemented and certify if it could be counted toward an award. Awards were based on the number of ideas or the dollar savings. For example, 10 suggestions or a $10,000 saving would earn a bronze pin. Fifty suggestions, or $50,000 saving, would earn a gold pin. In the first year, 7109 ideas were logged and 4115 of these were implemented, for an annual savings of $3.25 million.

Lawler, Ledford, and Mohrman (1989) studied employee involvement practices in Fortune 1000 firms to determine whether companies had incorporated employee involvement into their managerial approaches. They asked about the degrees to which business information, training, power, and rewards for performance were spread throughout the organization. They wondered whether or not employees felt that they controlled their work, got information about their performance, and were rewarded for their performance—all important aspects of participatory management practice. True employee involvement requires that power, knowledge, information, and rewards be present at all levels of the organization, because when all these factors are present employees can see and understand the relationship between their efforts and organizational success or failure. The Baldrige award (described in Chapter 3) has an entire section devoted to Information and Analysis. As part of the review, examiners determine whether information is readily accessible to employee involvement teams.

The results of their survey were mixed. Although many companies had adopted practices that are associated with employee involvement, such as quality circles, gain-sharing, and self-managing work teams, usually these were only in part of the organization, with limited change as a result. For example, **suggestion-oriented practices** (quality circles, suggestion awards) were used more than self-managing work teams, as teams required that employees become more responsible for major decisions. It appears that, in 1987, companies were beginning to experiment with employee involvement programs and, satisfied with the results, were willing to expand them across the organization.

Lawler, Ledford, and Mohrman (1992) continued their survey of employee involvement practices in Fortune 1000 firms, including service and industrial firms. The results of the survey, while reflecting senior management's views and concentrating on large firms, are a good reflection of corporate activity in employee involvement and TQM.

◆ EMPLOYEE INVOLVEMENT: TECHNIQUE ADOPTION

Employee involvement programs have a positive effect on company performance and internal business conditions, according to Lawler and his group (1992). As more and more organizations delay and downsize to increase productivity and reduce costs, involving employees in their work reaps organizational rewards. With fewer layers of management to supervise work, and with the nature of managerial work changing to one of managing and facilitating development of leaders at all organizational levels (Kotter, 1990), organizations must have employees that can make decisions about their work. Thus, employee involvement programs can be seen as opportunities for organizations in today's competitive environment. Let's see how well companies do at adopting techniques that make EI possible.

There are some differences between large and small firms in their adoption of EI techniques. Large firms tend to be more procedural in their use of EI programs, in keeping with their more bureaucratic, hierarchical structures. Although these procedures are easier to communicate across the organization, hidden pockets of resistance are more prevalent in large firms. Small firms tend to adopt EI as a way of getting work done with limited resources; it is simply a way of doing business in small organizations.

Although sharing information about corporate performance is critical to attaining true employee involvement, some organizations perhaps do not share enough relevant information about organizational performance. Not having relevant information about corporate performance of course makes real employee involvement in decision making difficult, for they cannot be expected to be meaningfully involved in decisions affecting anything other than their relevant job responsibilities without real data.

Increasing employee knowledge and attainment of the skills needed to improve the business is critical to employee involvement because without the right skills, it is impossible for employees to participate in the business, or even perform their jobs well. Training, in both quantitative and qualitative areas, is required to make EI programs effective. However, Lawler and his group (1992) discovered that most Fortune 1000 corporations do a poor job of training employees on general business or interpersonal skills, anything other than skills directly related to each employee's job. This lack of training would, of course, have a direct impact on the effectiveness of EI programs across organizations.

Tying rewards into organizational performance is a way of ensuring that employees care and work to improve organizational performance. Performance-based rewards are critical to EI efforts because employees need to see the link between their behavior and corporate performance. Reward systems seem to be effective in improving performance because they see the rewards for their efforts. Individual performance measures that do not tie individual behavior to the success of the business are not generally supportive of EI programs. Other rewards that are clearly linked to performance are more appropriate. For example, team incentives support EI efforts because most EI work takes place in some kind of team. Profit sharing, because of its direct link to organizational performance, is a good reward for EI efforts. **Gainsharing,** which stresses involvement as a key to achieving the bonus system, is not widely used in companies despite its close link to EI. Flexible benefits, skill-based pay, an all-salaried workforce, and other reward and recognition plans are other forms of reward systems that could be used to reward for employee involvement. In fact, skill-based pay that is linked to profit and gainsharing has been a very effective way to increase employee involvement in organizations.

Involving employees in their work also requires that management share power across the organization; otherwise employees would be unable to make decisions that affect their work. Parallel organizational structures, where special teams or meetings are formed which are separate from the normal procedures of the organization, are one way that employees can become involved. Activities such as quality circles (and other participation groups), **QWL (quality of work life)** groups, and employee surveys are some of the parallel structures used to transfer power down the organization. Other methods utilized in companies include job enrichment and self-managing teams. Because more and more organizations are beginning to use self-managing teams, we will cover them in more detail later in the chapter. Suggestion programs are another way organizations try to transfer power down the organization. However, as for information sharing and training, power sharing across the organization is rare. When it is implemented, power-sharing indicates a new attitude toward employees in the organization.

Lawler, Mohrman, and Ledford's findings (1992) suggest that most companies they surveyed used these techniques selectively rather than across the organization. Companies tended to adopt a variety of practices for information-sharing, knowledge-transfer, reward, and power-sharing, and even those techniques were adopted only for parts of the organization. Of course, this selective adoption then limited the true levels of employee involvement in the organizations surveyed.

If a large firm adopts EI as a way of improving business results, the more likely it is to share information with employees about operations, competitors, and financial results. Larger firms are more likely to use a variety of reward mechanisms, combining individual and group rewards to great effect as AT&T does. They are more likely to share power through use of teams, surveys, job designs, and employee participation methods. They generally have the resources to conduct training in both quantitative and qualitative business processes. The combination of all these factors enables larger organizations to use a variety of EI efforts and to find the ones that fit their organization the best. Small firms may utilize a variety of EI methods, but not as formally as the large ones.

AT&T Universal Card Services, a winner of the Baldrige award, developed several measures to evaluate the performance of their telephone associates such as abandon rate—the percentage of incoming calls abandoned before being answered by a telephone associate. Each quarter they measured the number of days the associates met 95 percent of the targets. Based on this information, associates and their managers received bonuses. For example, in the fourth quarter of 1990, the associates had 76.1 percent quality days, for which they received a bonus of 6.4 percent of salary.

◆ EMPLOYEE INVOLVEMENT: PROGRAM ELEMENTS

Companies implement the employee involvement programs listed previously in a variety of ways. As we saw in Chapter 11 on implementation, EI is difficult to install in organizations. Implementing EI is easier when there is a corporate philosophy or policy on EI, for it indicates management support for EI practice. Whether or not a policy statement exists, senior management's active support of EI as a way to manage is critical. This support requires management at all levels to look beyond any pressures for short-term performance to focus on the longer time frame required for true employee involvement to take effect. Just like any organizational change, employee involvement programs take time and require extensive commitment from all organizational levels. This commitment takes time to achieve.

Organizations can use certain human resource practices to guide employee involvement programs. People usually rely on these as indicators of management's commitment to the new ways organizations need to operate in order to implement EI. Providing employment security is perhaps the most effective way to encourage employee involvement; employees can feel "safe" making suggestions and process changes because their jobs are not in jeopardy. However, employment security is rare in most organizations today. Giving employees a say in hiring new workplace members provides a strong link to EI practices. Flex-time and job previews are other HR practices that can be linked to EI. Finally, as more and more organizations move toward self-managing teams, cross-training and training to work across organizational boundaries becomes a critical part of EI.

◆ EMPLOYEE INVOLVEMENT AND TOTAL QUALITY MANAGEMENT

Lawler, Mohrman, and Ledford's 1992 survey of Fortune 1000 companies revealed that more than 75 percent of those surveyed had implemented some type of Total Quality program for most of their employees. Just as in general employee involvement programs, various aspects of TQM programs are implemented in part of the organization and do not represent a total organizational commitment to TQM. They found that most organizations use direct employee exposure to customers, self-inspection, work simplification, Cost-of-Quality monitoring, and collaboration with suppliers as part of their TQM efforts. Usually, these efforts are concentrated on those employees in the manufacturing side of the business.

General Motors' Cadillac Division, another winner of the Baldrige award, provides a good example of a company involving the employees by exposing them to the customer. Salaried and hourly employees meet customers either by direct phone calls or at the auto shows. Cadillac also invites customers to evaluate the fiberglass models of future car designs. Employees are often at these clinics to listen to the customer. In addition, they visit auto dealers and hear from them suggestions made by customers.

Although TQM involves some of the same elements as the employee involvement programs described earlier, there are some differences between EI programs and TQM. TQM programs may establish teams to create involvement and share power, or utilize the problem-solving tools discussed in Chapters 6 through 8 as a way of developing knowledge and skill. Self-inspection and teams can be used to move decision making further down the organizational hierarchy. Finally, employees' use of TQM methods to examine and change organizational processes, from the first customer contact to ultimate product delivery, is clearly involvement with their work.

TQM does not concern itself, however, with job design in the motivational sense. The work simplification process may alter the motivational aspects of certain jobs, which would limit the level of employee involvement. The other major difference between TQM and EI programs cited by Lawler (1992) is one of rewards and appraisals. TQM tends to look at performance by the system, and not by the individual. EI programs, on the other hand, use individual and group results to measure and reward performance. In addition, Lawler's survey found that most TQM efforts have not utilized team-based rewards in a way that the direct link between work process management and team management is made clear. Finally, Lawler cites a major philosophical difference between TQM and EI programs in that TQM programs tend to be more top-down than EI programs. He also suggests (1992) that rigid use of the problem-solving tools may reduce (intentionally or not) employee control and involvement. On the other hand, Ishikawa (1985) and others argue that providing problem-solving tools to employees is necessary to get them involved. The tools serve to enable employees to improve their job performance, giving them more control over their environment.

Despite these philosophical and implementation differences, Lawler and his group found that organizations with a commitment to employee involvement also had a commitment to Total Quality. They concluded that EI programs set the context necessary for the Total Quality process. There is a commitment to doing whatever is necessary to involve employees and to satisfy customers; both EI and TQM enable companies to work to achieve those goals. In fact, the companies that ran a coordinated effort between existing EI programs and TQM programs were more successful in achieving desired performance results and adapting to changing business conditions.

Lawler (1994) maintains that TQM, with its emphasis on quality improvement, management control, process improvement, work simplification, and recognition rewards, may work particularly well in high-volume, production situations. TQM processes generally are applicable where large numbers of workers are required to produce a product or service a customer. Straight EI programs, with their emphasis on self-managed employee discretion, self-management, feedback, work teams, and overall organizational effectiveness, have been used effectively in continuous, process production situations that are capital intensive and require complex coordination, and where the organization is in a very rapidly changing environment. These organizations need breakthroughs and innovations to respond to competitive conditions; thus, giving individuals with these capabilities the autonomy to deliver these breakthroughs is critical. In fact, the major changes that so many companies experience as they work to respond to changing competitive conditions may require involvement rather than TQM because it entails more radical change (Kotter and Heskett, 1992).

From our perspective, these EI researchers have chosen a narrow view of TQM. As discussed in Chapter 2, TQM has evolved to include good management practices. Historically, total participation has always been part of TQM. When Xerox embarked on its TQM journey in 1983, it explicitly stated that one of the two key enablers was employee involvement. Today TQM believes in using whatever techniques are available to effectively involve all employees.

Delivering the programs in an integrated fashion strongly communicates that a high-involvement culture is critical to organizational success, limits the resistance to participatory management, sharing decision making, and management de-layering, and makes broad organizational change possible. In fact, the relative effectiveness of each program is contingent on the technology, values, and strategy of each organization. Therefore, the particular program each organization should implement depends on the organization's condition, strategic orientation, kind of work required, and where it operates. The best management approach, according to Lawler (1994), is one that uses either EI or TQM in its "pure" form, or modifies each to take advantage of certain elements. Since most organizations are looking for ways to improve productivity and competitiveness, a combination of these approaches which fit the specifics of an organization's situation seems to be the most pragmatic approach.

One organization that has developed an effective system for the vertical deployment of EI or TQM practices is Hewlett-Packard. Its approach is based on the Japanese technique known as Hoshin-kanri. This business planning process links the corporate with 14 groups, each consisting of several divisions. The process would start with the CEO John Young stating a goal such as "a tenfold improvement in quality." This along with roughly stated financial goals were transmitted to the groups and divisions.

At the group level, a 10-step process was used to create a strategic plan. These steps addressed the following elements:

1. Statement of purpose
2. Five-year objectives
3. Customer needs
4. Competitors
5. Product requirements
6. New products
7. Financial analysis
8. Potential problems
9. Intergroup dependencies and external relationships
10. The one-year plan

Hoshin planning was used to construct the detailed one-year plan. Each element of the division was required to specify its objectives. Of these one was to be a breakthrough objective. For example, in order to support the overall goal of tenfold improvement in quality, a division may choose to focus on improving its on-time delivery from 90 percent to 99 percent. (The percentage of late deliveries would have decreased by a factor of ten.) As they set these objectives, "business fundamentals" also had to be specified. These were factors that had to be maintained or improved to sustain the current level of excellence. An example might be the defect rate.

This approach required managers and their subordinates to specify a cascade of goals. For example, the division head may commit to a target for developing 10 new products in the coming year. In discussions with the director of R&D, she may conclude that the means to achieve this objective is to increase the productivity of the Engineering Department (as opposed to simply adding more engineers). The director of R&D, realizing he had developed only five new products last year, states his goal as increasing productivity by 100 percent. By analyzing the product development process, he realizes testing is a major bottleneck. So, together with the testing manager he establishes that the means for increasing R&D productivity is to improve testing productivity. In conjunction, they establish a goal for improving testing throughput by 100 percent. The testing manager then analyzes the reason for low throughput and establishes that the way to achieve this result is to buy a new piece of test equipment. By setting goals and defining means at each level in this fashion, the integrity of the policy is maintained through all levels of employees.

◆ HR POLICIES AND TQM

Although the tools and strategies outlined in this book are critical pieces of the organizational TQM puzzle, the human resource policies that link them together are the glue. In fact, executives ranked methods related to human resource management as most effective in improving quality (Bowen and Lawler, 1992). These items included employee motivation, corporate culture change, and employee education. Demings' 14 points (see Chapter 2) include several HR-related directives: to institute training on the job, to break down barriers between departments to build teamwork, to drive fear out of the workplace, to eliminate quotas, to create conditions that allow employees to have pride of workmanship, and to institute programs of self-improvement and education.

HR managers can support organizational leaders who wish to begin quality initiatives in their organizations. They can serve as *strategic business partners,* designing HR policies that fit with the overall strategy of the organization (Tichy, Devanna, and Formbrum, 1984). There is a natural fit between TQM and effective human resource practice, and critical elements of the HR function today are required for effective TQM programs. For example, in 1992 the Quality champion at Paul Revere Insurance was Robert Lea, the vice president for human resources and quality. When Bob Galvin as chairman of Motorola initiated TQM, he worked intensely with Joe Miraglia, the vice president of human resources, to create the infrastructure needed to support his vision.

◆ A MODEL FOR ORGANIZATIONAL DESIGN

Jay Galbraith describes a model of organizational design that we will use to describe the requisite components for TQM organizations (1994). His STAR model promotes the idea that business strategies enable organizational leaders to determine which tasks are important, and therefore require an organization to be capable (or effective in execution) in these areas. Once these areas of required capability are determined, the company must put into place organizational structures, management processes, rewards and incentives, and the people (or human resource practices) that support performance of the task. All the elements of the model support and depend on each other, and serve to drive the task and thus the strategy of the organization. We will examine these different elements in terms of the Total Quality model.

Organizational Structures

Determining appropriate organizational structures is a constant challenge for managers (see Schlesinger and Schlesinger, 1993, for a good summary of organizational design techniques). Traditionally, organizations were designed by function, so that specialists of each type would work together to complete tasks. Hierarchies developed so that each employee's work could be evaluated on the basis of his or her specialty, and to ensure that tasks were performed appropriately. Although these structures are often appropriate for organizations that face relatively mild competitive situations, with little product change or technological shifts, as things changed functional organizations had difficulties responding. Problems arose as functional organizations tried to adapt to environments that were rapidly changing. Organizations with differentiated (i.e., functional) units were unable to integrate (i.e., coordinate) with each other (Lawrence and Lorsch, 1967). To be effective, organizations had to be designed with a balance between their need for different functional specialties and the requirements for coordination.

As they became more effective, organizations adapted many ways to increase integration and coordination across functions (Schlesinger et al, 1991). For example, formal groups, such as product teams, were formed to ease communication across organizational boundaries. Formal integrating roles, such as product or project managers, were put into place. Other methods for increasing integration include **physical co-location** (locating several functions in the same facility, sometimes even in the same room), **interdepartmental rotation** (assigning individuals jobs so they could gain experience in several departments), and use of information technology. However, reporting relationships in these organizations became quite complex, as formal authority was often spread out across functions and therefore confused the evaluation process. Informally, other techniques for increasing integration occurred as well. Interdepartmental events that enabled people of different specialties to "mix" and talk to each other increased coordination.

Despite all the methods organizational designers have adopted to increase coordination across departments and functions, walls (both real and imagined) have continued to detract from organizational capability. Bureaucracy crept into even the most adaptable organization. In fact, it was during the 1970s and 1980s that organizations that focused on satisfying customer demands with speed survived. Speed of response, not size, was the source of competitive advantage to these organizations. As they attempted to become more responsive to customer needs, these organizations downsized and de-layered. The challenge was to intensify the breadth and depth of integration, while eliminating bureaucracy (Tichy and Devanna, 1990). Control systems, hierarchy, integrating roles, and structures (notably, matrix organizations) needed to give way to an organization designed around information flows, with loose, flexible structures, networks of employees who were knowledgeable and creative, and able to serve the customers' needs.

According to Tichy and Devanna (1990), these **"boundaryless" organizations** are able to bridge real differences in terms of cultural orientation, functional, and organizational goals, in order to create shared goals and to find common ground that enables cooperative behavior. This spirit of cooperation involves a formal elimination of unnecessary work, as well as development of a culture of trust and empowerment. For example, General Electric Company's WORKOUT program first eliminated unnecessary, repetitive work so that more productive time could be spent eliminating organizational roadblocks to productivity. Ameritech's Breakthrough program is beginning to break down the barriers endemic to a bureaucracy with the vestiges of a monopoly! Other organizations, such as Tenneco and Allied Signal, are beginning to do the same things.

For example, a business unit in a large multinational corporation designed and manufactured large electrical boards and systems. For years, it had met customer demands with a product design cycle of three years. However, this unit's key competitor was able to cut the same cycle down to two years, and as a result, sales for this business unit were down. Senior managers in the unit recognized that a key to moving with speed to face the competitive onslaught would be to put together a cross-functional team that would be able to design and produce a product faster than the competition. The company culture had always been an authoritarian one where control mechanisms were king, where employees took the path of least resistance, and where many **stovepipes** (walls) existed among functions. The product design process had typically been termed "over the wall," where one function (e.g., R&D) worked on a product and then threw it over the wall to the next function in line (such as Manufacturing). Any errors uncovered were simply thrown back for rework. Time, money, and energy were wasted on the repetitive processes.

The team, with representatives from sales, marketing, product engineering, process engineering, manufacturing, and information systems, met off site for the first time. In the course of their conversations, as they discussed the existing product design process, they realized the duplication of effort and the frustration each "stovepipe" experienced. Before they began to discuss the new product, they began to reexamine the *way* the product was designed. In Demings' words, they began to "break down the barriers between departments" by discussing the areas of difference, areas in need of coordination, defining when in the design process functions were required to talk and which functions were involved. After three intense days of discussion, a very preliminary process was put together for the team to use. Ultimately, the team designed and built a product in 18 months, and further process analysis enabled future products to be built in even less time. Clearly, the organization benefited from the effort. Chapter 13 provides other examples for instituting such cross-functional strategies in order to shorten the design cycle.

This example illustrates the importance of having the ability to work across **functional boundaries** which limit effective action. Boundaries will still exist, but essentially, the boundaries that matter in the new organizations of the twenty-first century (Hirschhorn and Gilmore, 1992) include an **authority boundary** (who is in charge of what), a **task boundary** (who does what), a **political boundary** (what is in it for our group), and an **identity boundary** (who is, and isn't, our organization). The organization that is flexible enough to develop these boundaries and decrease others that block productivity can compete in the future.

Organizations can use the concepts of boundarylessness in their TQM processes. Boundaryless organizations keep people close to internal and external customers, so that they hear, see, and feel customer requirements. Practices that impede process improvement and promote wasted effort are decreased. Any process or action is viewed in terms of "adding value" to the company as a whole, not to the unit or function of which it is part.

Focusing on the internal and external customer enables business processes to be developed which change both the nature of the work that is performed and the way it is performed. A "chain" of customers can be created so that each employee recognizes his place in the delivery of the product or service to the customer. Ultimately, understanding how one's work contributes to customer satisfaction is intrinsically quite motivating for employees.

Organizations with a quality focus often use teams to carry out and, if necessary, improve, particular organizational processes. These firms are organized not by structure or function, but by process. For example, a team for the billing process might include representatives from many functions such as purchasing, distribution, sales, credit, information systems, and field service. By bringing everyone with responsibility for the process together, practices that compromise quality can be identified and eliminated. In addition, if the entire team is brought together on the analysis of the process, resistance to process changes are reduced (see Chapter 11 for more detail on resistance to change). Use of teams also enables organizations to reduce the levels of hierarchy and control, as teams become "*empowered*" to make decisions that affect their work. While reduction of hierarchy often results in job loss and downsizing, hopefully those middle managers who had served a controlling function in the old organization can be productive, serving other clients or customers to support the organizational strategy.

AT&T starts by identifying the key business processes that are critical for achieving customer satisfaction. Then they map the key business processes against the functional organizations. For example, the repair process would be mapped to Billing, Maintenance, Repair, Distribution, Manufacturing, Product Design, and Product Management. This is done by the Quality Council. Then a major stakeholder of the process who is committed to its improvement is assigned as process owner. This person puts together a cross-functional team consisting of middle managers from each of the functional organizations.

◆ MANAGEMENT PROCESSES

Selection Techniques

According to Bowen and Lawler (1992), organizations that adopt a TQM approach require employees who solve problems and who can maneuver their way through the various problem-solving methods presented elsewhere in this book. Then, selection devices within companies need to be able to determine whether each candidate has the ability to learn and apply these methods. HR departments can document the way each job fits together to meet customer expectations and can design jobs that fit these needs. Selection measures that give a realistic preview of job activities and set clear expectations about job performance enable the employee to choose to apply. Some prospective employees may not want to work when a high level of commitment is required, so they will withdraw. In addition, companies must learn to select people who can work on various levels of teams. In some companies (Taco Bell, for example), front-line service employees hire any new employee. Selecting for these qualities helps companies focus on a quality-oriented culture. In fact, some writers in service quality suggest that developing discretion in hiring to focus on initiative, teamwork, and motivation will advance service quality in organizations in the long run (Fromm and Schlesinger, 1994).

Development and Training

Training and development are key components of all TQM programs. Training typically covers problem-solving technologies, problem analysis, statistical process control, quality measurement, and organizational diagnosis. Because so much problem analysis and discussion occur in groups, usually employees receive training in group process and decision making as well. Training is important because as decisions about working for customer satisfaction move across and down the organization, it is critical that employees need job skills as well as team and decision-making skills. Employees should also be *cross-trained,* so that indirect as well as direct tasks can be learned (Schonberger, 1992).

In addition, TQM training should be directed at all levels of the organization. Senior managers who understand the TQM process are not only able to break down barriers within their own organizations, but they can also serve as role models for others who may resist the change. Self-study methods can be used for those managers who are "too busy" to attend classes. Skills must be taught which participants can use on their jobs. Finally, managers can include training and development of employees as part of the measurement/assessment criteria (Brown, 1989).

◆ REWARDS AND INCENTIVES

Performance Management

Most organizations utilize *performance measurements* that focus on individual performance. These measures determine the level and nature of rewards, aid career development, and facilitate the understanding of job responsibilities and duties. However, these methods are still based largely on individual performance, and not on team or group performance, which are so important for system and process improvement. Individual behavior is still paramount and may lead to a continuation of the kinds of behavior found in organizations marked by strong functional boundaries. It is an old organizational axiom that what gets measured gets done. An employee from marketing may think to him or herself: "Why should I have to cooperate with someone from process engineering on product design; I'm not being measured on that!" Individual measures foster individually based performance, often to the detriment of the organization. For example, the traffic manager at a plant was measured on the transportation cost incurred. To reduce these costs, the manager would hold up shipping to customers in a specific geographical area until a full truckload was ready. The result was that the company did not meet the promised delivery dates. To solve the problem, they increased the leadtime quoted to customers, which only made them less competitive.

Another example involves a warehouse manager for a supermarket measured by the percentage of stockouts per order. As a result, she orders more of each unit to keep on hand just in case there is an unusually large demand for an item. The high-inventory level can lead to excessive spoilage in addition to unnecessarily tying up working capital in inventory.

Although it may be impossible to expect companies to abandon completely the idea of individual rewards, it is possible that systems can be more closely aligned with the principle of shared responsibility for quality (Bowen and Lawler, 1992). Performance management based on developing the skills and abilities necessary to perform well in teams or boundaryless organizations can be measured. Peers can be involved in the appraisal process, and individuals can be evaluated on how much they contribute to team performance. The increasing popularity of **360 degree performance reviews,** where information is gathered from bosses, employees, and peers, illustrates the potential for changes in performance management (as well as the need for human resource managers to begin to diagnose and solve the problems of conflicting measurements).

Pay Systems and Rewards

There is a strong link between measurement and reward systems. Therefore, just as measurement systems are linked to individual performance, so are rewards. Merit pay increases which are so common to organizations today generally reflect how well an individual has performed on the job. Because of TQM's emphasis on *collective responsibility, cross-functional relationships,* and *organizational learning,* there is a direct conflict between these activities and existing reward systems. For example, **job-based pay systems** usually reward an employee for moving up the hierarchy, not across it, as required by TQM. The flexibility in job performance required of TQM is negated in a reward system where individual performance alone is rewarded. While little has been written on new approaches to pay which have been adopted in TQM organizations (Bowen and Lawler, 1992), some organizations are substituting skill-based pay for job-based pay. Skills that are rewarded can include cross-utilization skills, or the ability to work a variety of functions as required in the work process.

As we have seen, however, some attempts have been made to change pay systems as part of employee involvement programs. Gainsharing, profit-sharing, and stock ownership plans may be the key to creating a financial incentive for employees to make process and performance improvements. Hewitt Associates reports that nearly two-thirds of mid- to large-size companies have some form of incentive pay for nonexecutives. The fibers division of DuPont Company made 6 percent of the salary for each of its 20,000 employees dependent on the division's profits. American Express Company established an incentive pay plan for the 10,000 employees in its consumer-card and consumer-lending groups. The payout is based on three measures—customer satisfaction, employee productivity, and shareholder wealth creation. Black Box Corporation markets computer network and other communication devices. Under their compensation plan, a worker can double her salary by acquiring additional skills. For example, an order entry clerk can improve her salary from the $17,000 to $20,000 range to $25,000 to $28,000 by improving her knowledge of the product. If a worker learns a foreign language to handle international sales, his salary can increase to $35,000

Informal rewards also are important. Recognition for outstanding customer service and support, for being on a team that delivers continual process improvement, and for initiating new activities within organizations are all important rewards in any organization. General Electric Corporation recognized its first WORKOUT group's achievements by publicizing them in the business unit newsletter.

◆ SUMMARY: HR SYSTEMS

Let's see how these pay, performance, and structural components interact. A mid-level manager's job had just changed to include process analysis of existing billing practices. This manager had made rapid career advances, based on his ability to meet his individual functional responsibilities. His new job required a great deal of interpersonal skill to perform effectively. When he was required to lead a process team and to work cross-functionally, he had to learn new behaviors. He received training in process analysis, as well as one-on-one coaching in interpersonal style and group process. However, it was difficult for him to make the transition from individual contributor to team leader: (1) the measurement system assessed his abilities to meet functional goals and (2) it was easier for him to behave individually. He found his work frustrating and felt that his hard work was not being rewarded. Eventually, the evaluation system was revised to include achievement of group goals and assessments from peers, bosses, and employees. While he still showed tendencies to act individually, he actually learned how to work better with others. He attributes this learning to the new reward system. "What gets measured gets done," he confided. This changed behavior was recognized and rewarded, and the manager was promoted. His new job was not in his "old" area, which had been downsized considerably, but an integrative role that required increased abilities to work in teams.

Until the evaluation and reward system was changed, this manager felt no real need to change his behavior, despite his understanding of, and agreement with, the principles of empowerment and risk taking espoused by the company. His behavior didn't really change until the new HR systems for job design, performance measurement, and rewards were put into place.

◆ PEOPLE POLICIES IN TQM: TEAMS AND TEAMWORK

Teams are a major part of any Total Quality Management effort because teamwork enables various parts of the organization to work together to meet customer needs in ways that can't be done through individual job performance alone. This section of the chapter outlines the ways teams are used in TQM, and addresses the requirements necessary to incorporate effective teamwork into organizations.

Teams in TQM

TQM utilizes three major types of teams: **steering committees, problem-solving teams,** and **self-managed teams** (Dean and Evans, 1994). Steering committees are usually those responsible for establishing TQM-related policy and for guiding its implementation. Steering committees usually make key decisions about the program, its structure, measurement, programs, training, and so forth. Membership on TQM steering committees usually includes the senior management of the organization and, if there is one, the manager responsible for quality within the organization or business unit.

Problem-solving teams are probably most common. They usually identify, analyze, and develop solutions for organizational quality problems. These teams are usually temporary, existing as long as the problem lasts. Membership usually includes those people directly involved with or affected by the particular problem itself. These teams can contain members from a single department or from a variety of cross-functional departments. Departmental problem-solving teams generally use standard problem-solving methodology to solve a problem within their own unit. For example, a team of purchasing managers can work together to consolidate a list of suppliers for key organizational parts.

Quality circles are a type of team used in some organizations. Usually, these QC teams are formed when a small group of volunteer workers get together to discuss how their tasks can be done effectively and efficiently. Suggestions are made, ideas presented, and plans created. Usually, these circles then go back to management to present their ideas. Managers can respond either positively or negatively to the suggestions, but obviously employees are more willing to participate in QC activities if they believe that their suggestions will be heard and accepted. Many companies in the Fortune 1000 adopted quality circles as a way of increasing employee involvement and participation in TQM. However, Lawler et al. (1992) discovered that today QC is seen as a less successful method of increasing employee participation, probably because they became such a fad and were perhaps not implemented or utilized to best advantage.

Cross-functional teams are common in organizations today, and not just for TQM. They usually are put together to examine organizational processes that require change. For example, the admissions department at the University of Michigan Medical Center was receiving many complaints. A cross-functional team consisting of housekeepers, nurses, transporters, and admission clerks was put together under the leadership of the director of admissions. Using the tools described in Chapter 6, the team made several recommendations, including assigning pagers to housekeepers, changing the priority of work on evening and night shifts, and assigning responsibility for specific tasks to certain individuals. The mean number of complaints in 1990 to 1991, which had been 37.3 per month, dropped to 1.5 complaints per month in the 1991 to 1992 period.

Self-managed teams (also called autonomous work groups or self-directed teams) have been in place for many years in some organizations. Over the years organizations have become flatter and less hierarchical (Tichy and Devanna, 1990) as these self-managed teams have become more common. As more and more organizations downsize and rid themselves of expensive middle management layers, more of the work performed by those mid-managers, such as budgeting, scheduling, and personnel administration, is now being performed by the self-managing teams. These teams can exist with or without a supervisor, and they usually handle all aspects of work organization for that particular unit.

Each type of team has its advantages and its disadvantages, and works best in a particular organizational setting (Parker, 1994):

1. Problem-solving intradepartmental teams work well in traditional organizations, in stable, slow-growth industries with predictable markets. Manufacturers of beer, for example, can use these types of teams effectively.
2. Cross-functional (interdepartmental) teams can be effective in companies with fast-changing markets, where the need to move speedily to meet customer requirements is paramount.
3. Self-directed teams can be used in lieu of problem-solving or cross-functional teams as part of an extended employee involvement strategy.

On the other hand, use of teams may not always be the best way to deal with organizational problems. Using a team to accomplish particular tasks depends on the type of work involved and the individuals themselves. For example, where tasks are clear, there is little new technology, and employees are not dependent on each other to accomplish their work, teams don't make sense. In addition, those employees who aren't motivated to grow in their jobs or who aren't interested in working with others probably shouldn't be in a team. Teams make sense to use when there is a climate of cooperation, high interdependency between jobs, a great deal of flexibility in how the job can be performed, and employees who care about growth and building social relationships. They also need relevant information about the particular organization, and training in decision making and problem solving. If those elements are not present, teams probably aren't appropriate.

Building Teams

Although many organizations talk about teams and teamwork, few organizations have "real" teams in place. According to Katzenback and Smith (1993), real teamwork represents a set of values that encourage listening and responding constructively to views expressed by others, giving others the benefit of the doubt, providing support, and recognizing and acknowledging the achievements and interests of others. Teamwork is different from simply working in groups because teamwork implies collective responsibility. Work groups usually focus on individual accountabilities and actions. The group's purpose is the same as the mission of the organization, and they usually have strong, focused leadership.

Teams, on the other hand, require both individual and mutual accountability. It is here where the link between people, task design, and performance measurement and rewards becomes paramount. Teams use shared leadership and a process for discussion, debate, decision making, and sharing to produce discrete work products through the joint contributions of their members. They are "a small number of people with complementary skills who are committed to a common purpose, set of performance goals, and approach for which they hold themselves mutually accountable" (Katzenback and Smith, 1993, 112).

Effective teams have a common commitment to a purpose. The purpose can be anything from "designing a curriculum which prepares managers for the future" to removing boundaries from the new product development process. This sense of direction can come from within, or without, the team itself. In fact, most successful teams receive a charter from management which provides a performance challenge *but* leaves enough room for the team to develop its own guidelines for goals (the core mission/performance objectives of the team), roles (the allocation of work and requirements), processes (ways to work together for decision making, conflict management, problem solving, and communication), and interpersonal relationships (trust, openness, sensitivity to the needs of others, and participation).

Establishing the **GRPI rules** (goals, roles, processes, and interpersonal relationships), and periodically reviewing them, gives the team a way of assessing their progress over time.

Effective teams redefine their goals into specific performance objectives. In the case of the CT team described in Chapter 11, their goal was to get 80 percent of the patients through the CT area on time. Both well-defined group goals and expectations enable strong team commitment to the goals and lead to improved team performance. Setting specific goals is important for several reasons (Katzenback and Smith, 1993). Setting goals defines work products. Being responsible for specific targets requires the team to work together to accomplish the task in a particular way. A team that is charged with developing new structure and work processes for a media relations organization so that they can target mass media can divide tasks more easily if they know that something specific can happen from their recommendations. Holding meetings to discuss media relations, on the other hand, does little for group performance over time.

The team with specific goals focuses on attaining results. A team designed to examine new uses for an old, established product could measure its sales progress against objective measurements. This comparison not only increases team commitment, but also lets them evaluate their incremental progress toward the goals. The media relations team developed a work plan and had various goals to meet along the way. Each time they met a goal, they became more and more convinced that their task was not impossible, and this in turn increased their commitment to the team. Groups must be sure that each member is clear on the ultimate products of the team; clear expectations about content and format can eliminate problems later on. Because groups cannot complete whole tasks together, tasks must be delegated. Unless specific expectations about products and processes are clear, someone will not conform, and the group will feel let down. Most of you have probably been in groups where people were expected to "come prepared" to meetings. Problems usually arose when definitions of "preparation" differed among members; some would come with all their research done and copied for each member, and others would come with a brief, hand-written note card of results. Setting clear goals and checking them periodically usually decrease the likelihood of such problems developing.

When assembling a team, size and membership must be considered. It is hard for 50 people to be a team; logistics problems alone would be insurmountable. Most productive teams have between 7 and 10 members, but of course this number is not a hard and fast rule. The smaller the number of people on the team, the easier it is to work through the interpersonal and organizational (if the team is cross-functional) differences involved and to set the clear goals so important for success.

Obviously, the team should be composed of members with appropriate skills. Ideally, a team would have people with functional/technical expertise, with problem-solving skills, and with interpersonal skills. For example, it is foolish for a team looking at new product cycle times and not have a member with knowledge of the market. Although all these skills may not be present in each individual, a minimum level of each of these skills should be evident. As teams go about their work, it is possible for them to expand their repertoire of skills. For example, the team charged with studying the media relations function in a large organization did not have a member from the media function, because the managers who gave the team its charge wanted to "*break the box*" and eliminate bias. However, because of their considerable research and benchmark efforts, the team became well-versed in the customer requirements of a media organization.

Most organizations have difficulties with team expertise in the area of interpersonal skills. Often, organizations that make a commitment to using teams put the team members through a variety of training activities to heighten their awareness of, and ability to deal with, interpersonal issues that can arise. These group "process" skills are important as teams go through the various stages of their development. Stages of group development include membership, subgroups, confrontation, individual differentiation, and collaboration (Cohen and Bradford, 1984; Obert, 1979), and careful attention to the ways in which the group works at each stage is just as important as paying attention to the tasks the team is performing.

The **membership stage** is where members individually decide how committed they want to be to the group. Members spend a lot of time trying to figure each other out and often jockey for leadership or status. Interaction between members is usually polite and formal; getting to know people on a preliminary level is important.

During the **subgrouping stage,** members have identified particular allies and tend to speak from partnerships. For example, two people on a task group from a similar background, or who had worked with each other before, are likely to form partnerships. Although disagreement between members, or between subgroups, is present, it is still relatively quiescent. Group norms become established, and opinions about the skills and abilities of members become firm.

Stage three, the **conflict stage,** is the turning point, the place that can turn a work group into a team. Conflict usually arises as groups begin to deal with important issues. Such disagreements are not only inevitable but also desirable. Groups need to be able to face these disagreements head on, deal with them, and move toward a climate where conflict is seen as purposeful and helpful, not as dysfunctional. When well-handled, conflict enables a group to air all views and evaluate different aspects and points of view. If conflict is avoided, the team can never progress to one that is truly collaborative. Conflict can lead the group to a search for integrative solutions to problems.

As members successfully deal with conflict and its resolution, they are able to move to the next phase, that of **individual differentiation.** Members feel comfortable in being themselves, and each member accepts the others, warts and all. They have developed appropriate norms, procedures for operation are clear, trust is high, and individual skills can be effectively utilized.

Finally, the team moves to the final phase, that of **collaboration,** where the team works collectively to solve problems and support each other. The whole really becomes greater than the sum of its parts. People tend to push themselves hard to achieve group goals, members compensate for each other, and solutions tend to be creative and new. The hard work required to get to stage 5 is still required, but the commitment to the team makes it more satisfactory.

During the membership stage, teams work to establish their parameters for performance. It is important to be clear on each member's roles and responsibilities, and on ways the team will work together. Teams by their nature parcel out the work that has to be done to complete their tasks; the team that uses its human resources most effectively has a greater likelihood of success. Usually, in business situations, each team member has a multitude of job responsibilities to which they have to attend. The team must have discussions about the nature of time involvement and commitment, and about the best ways to divide tasks to accomplish goals. If the team pays special attention to these roles and responsibilities as time goes on, each member's contributions usually equals out over time. In addition, as each member accomplishes his particular portion of the task, trust in each member's abilities usually increases (as long as they meet their commitments). As the team moves through the various stages of development, they should continually meet to check and verify the team's goals, roles, processes, and interpersonal relationships.

Establishing these GRPI rules and checking them periodically enable the team to develop a *social compact* among members, which relates to their purpose and guides them in the way they can work together. In fact, maintaining GRPI can mean the difference between becoming a team and simply being a work group. Teams that are able to combine attention to task accomplishment and personal relationships are generally more satisfying to be on, and more productive, than those who get together merely to accomplish a task. This social compact also enables the team to hold itself accountable to each other as a team. The media relations team described earlier felt a strong sense of purpose; no one wanted to "let the team down." Mutual accountability grows as a team shares a common purpose and approach.

It is important, however, that the team members give each other feedback (both positive and negative) about their performance. For real teams, those who have a commitment and a responsibility toward each other, giving and receiving feedback is a natural process, part of the diagnosis of the progress toward goal attainment. For teams at the beginning of their work, or for a group that avoids conflict and confrontation, this can be a difficult task. However, because progress toward goal accomplishment is critical to development of group commitment, it is necessary that feedback about performance as a team member be given. As more and more organizations move toward 360° evaluations, giving and receiving feedback can become more acceptable. Some teams use elaborate rank-ordering procedures, whereas others may decide simply to discuss what each member can stop, start, and continue doing. The technique of giving feedback is not as important as the fact that feedback is given.

To summarize, the approaches used by successful teams include (Katzenback and Smith, 1993):

1. Establishing urgency, demanding performance standards and direction
2. Selecting members for skills and skill potential, not personality
3. Paying particular attention to first meetings and actions
4. Setting some clear rules and expectations for behavior
5. Setting and seizing on several immediate performance-oriented goals and tasks
6. Challenging the group regularly, with fresh information
7. Spending time together on work and nonwork activities
8. Exploiting the power of positive feedback, recognition, and rewards

◆ LEADERSHIP ROLES IN TEAMS

As we have seen, teams are viewed as ways for organizations to increase the speed, flexibility, and methods with which they make key work decisions. Teams are used to build commitment to the organization and to transform the workplace from one of low commitment to high involvement. However, before we move to discuss employee commitment and involvement, we need to address the leadership issues associated with utilization of teams across organizations.

While teams become mutually accountable and committed to each other and to the organization, often an internal team leader is needed to coordinate the team's activities, to keep records and notes, to coordinate training, or to report to more senior management. This leadership role can rotate through the team's members over time.

In some cases, however, the team gets support from people outside the team. In order to make teams work well within the organization, the role of the middle manager who used to be responsible for results now delegated to the team must be clearly defined and outlined (Schlesinger, 1980). These people can serve as administrators, coaches, or advisers to the team. The administrator role exists because most teams, no matter how autonomous, are still part of a larger organization and live in a hierarchy of sorts. The administrator makes sure that the teams have adequate resources, people, materials, and equipment to fulfill their task needs. They can serve to communicate business issues and the results of the work of other teams, to coordinate resource needs, to review team goals, to recognize individual training needs, or to recognize team performance results.

Coaches serve to help facilitate team development and attention to group process. As the team develops over time, the role of the facilitator/coach becomes moot. They generally help the group pay attention to the issues of GRPI and to move through the confrontation stage of group development. They support the team's goal-setting process, monitor member participation, intervene to guide the resolution of interpersonal problems, and ensure that conflicts are confronted and resolved.

Finally, advisers provide technical support to the team. They share their skills with members on an as-needed basis. Frequently, advisers serve several teams, and often they give skill training to team members. One company had a team of people to map and rework the order fulfillment to delivery process. This team had many advisers to help them understand the technical procedures involved. Without the support of the advisers, the team would not have had the expertise to accomplish the task.

◆ SELF-MANAGING WORK TEAMS

More and more organizations today see teams as a way to better utilize their human resources to solve organizational problems. Self-managing teams are becoming a popular extension of the problem-solving, cross-functional teams in place in organizations. Self-managing teams are usually small groups of co-workers who share tasks and responsibilities for a well-defined segment of work. They usually have a **whole work component,** planning, executing, and measuring entire operations. Their work has clearly defined requirements, goals, and objectives, and clearly defined customers (internal or external). They perform multiple roles, and they have clearly defined performance measures. In some organizations, self-managing teams also can hire, evaluate, and reward their members.

Moving toward self-managing work teams has some implications for organizations in terms of their traditional views of roles and authority. Where teams are responsible for whole job performance, the manager's role shifts from one of supervisor/delegator to one of coach/facilitator, responsible for getting the team the resources and help it needs to complete its work. The nature of self-managing teams implies a cultural shift for many organizations. Barriers to implementation of self-managing teams include insufficient training, incompatible organizational systems, resistance of su-pervisors, and lack of management (and possibly union) support.

Despite these difficulties, self-managing teams are seen as ways for organiza-tions to move creatively, flexibly, and quickly to solve problems. For example, Chrysler in 1989 converted its workforce into four horizontally structured, cross-functional product teams. An additional team was put into place for "special pro-jects." This team ultimately developed the Viper (Baskerville, 1993). Team Viper pulled 80 volunteers from all engineering, marketing, and manufacturing func-tions together. They had a set strategy, objectives, and goals, and they worked over time to negotiate objectives and review team progress. In three years, they developed a new automobile from concept car to showroom, within budget. Despite the fact that this is a specialty car, the teams results were viewed within Chrysler as a demonstration of the benefits of the team concept.

Kolodny and Stjernberg (1993) outline seven design principles for self-manag-ing teams:

1. Each team should have a focus on performance, where team activities are task and results oriented.
2. Tasks and roles should be whole and designed by the team (again, the GRPI model is useful here), with careful attention given to gaining the requisite information to complete the task.
3. Identifiable boundaries for team time, tasks, and reporting relationships are critical.
4. Autonomy is also important, as the work team should have control over its own administrative functions, such as self-selection, evaluation, and regulations.
5. There should be minimal critical specifications, and team members should be able to shift jobs to balance the workload as needed.
6. The necessary skills for task accomplishment should be understandable and achievable by all, and facilitation, advising, and coaching should be avail-able as needed. Rewards should be based on the multiple skills of team members and on team results.
7. Teams should be able to change and redesign themselves as the need arises.

◆ UNIONS AND TOTAL QUALITY MANAGEMENT

The traditionally adversarial labor-management relationships in the United States are the antithesis of the kinds of shared responsibility, involved employee, em-powering programs presented in this chapter. In the mid-twentieth century, be-fore U.S. industry was really touched by foreign competition, an authoritarian cli-mate and methods of management were "permissible" because hardly anyone was losing sales or jobs to the Germans, the Japanese, or the Koreans. However, by the mid-1970s, productivity, product quality, and profitability fell. Some econ-omists attribute that fall to the failure of corporate managers to utilize human resources effectively. For example, if a union/management agreement is based on large bureaucratic contracts, with carefully specified jobs and responsibilities, and elaborate grievance procedures, then in all likelihood there is limited possibility for participation, problem solving, and employee initiative espoused by TQM and employee involvement programs. Neither the interest of management nor the commitment of employees is being harvested.

It is possible, however, for unions and management to work together to develop relationships that are compatible with TQM goals. When regarded as a partner in the process of accomplishing organizational goals, unions can take responsibility for quality and help create a climate for employee participation. However, if the union and its leadership are not committed to supporting employee involvement or TQM efforts, then those efforts probably won't succeed.

The organizations that epitomize the ideas discussed in this chapter usually make their employees feel they are part of the "family," encourage open communication about business failures and successes, stress quality and pride in the production of a product or service, and culturally reduce distinctions between manager and worker. In such companies, there is little room for adversarial relationships; the adversary is the competitor. Bluestone and Bluestone (1992) state that virtually all organizations that had kept their competitive edge had implemented substantial labor-management innovations around employee involvement and empowerment such as those described in this chapter. When organized jointly by the union and management, in a mix of cooperation and adversarial relationships, these efforts in unionized organizations seem to be most effective. They cite three conditions that are "absolutely indispensable" for success: full commitment to employee involvement throughout all levels of the organization; mutual trust and respect between union and management; and a real opportunity for broad employee involvement in decision making.

Still other surveys indicate that support is strong for most changes that have to occur to develop the organizational environment espoused in this chapter. Premeaux and his group (1989) found strong philosophical support for these ideas, but did find that management and recently hired employees supported a team approach that would eliminate work rules and job classifications more than union representatives and workers with long seniority. Worker participation especially on the assembly line was supported by a majority of HR managers, workers (old and new), and union representatives. Whether it be increasing union influence, willingness to make a real contribution, or a desire to have a say in their future status, worker involvement seems to be inevitable. There was a split between union representatives and workers with seniority, and managers and recently hired workers around bonuses. The more senior workers and the union representatives opposed team bonus plans. Premeaux surmised that this may have been because some workers may earn more even though they had not contributed as much as others to the team. The same split was found with regard to introducing teams and changing job classifications. Broader job classifications would clearly impact with seniority. The philosophical support for employee involvement, however, is encouraging for organizations wishing to implement such programs. Clearly, recognizing that the union has a stake in how work is organized and managed, and including them as active participants in the process, will give real meaning to the phrase "employee involvement."

A real example of joint union–management cooperation is the experiment at Saturn Corporation. In this case, the union (the United Auto Workers—UAW) was intimately involved, from the generation of the idea in 1982 to facility construction to the assembly of the car in 1990. According to the Bluestones (1992), joint union–management committees combined forces to design the plan, choose the technologies, devise marketing and advertising strategies, and develop the recruitment and education programs needed to select and train the workforce. The union contract was based on joint decision making, involving everyone from the president to the employee on the shop floor. For example, assembly methods were changed from the traditional assembly line to one where moving platforms with employees on them worked the line. The platforms were raised or lowered to gain easy access to the vehicle, and the employees controlled the speed of movement so that quality could be monitored by employees.

The strategy of employee involvement appears to have paid off in terms of productivity and customer satisfaction. In 1992 Saturn was named the 'best buy" of any passenger car selling for under $10,000. In addition, customer satisfaction ratings were very high. The project has several lessons for managers and for union members, interested in achieving workplace cooperation. Through workforce training and sincere management/union efforts at cooperation, increases in satisfaction and productivity are possible. Both unions and managers must broaden their views of each other, by trying experiments in involvement and working together realistically to cooperate.

◆ EMPOWERING ORGANIZATIONAL MEMBERS

In one graphics design software company, a self-managing team conceived, designed, and delivered a new graphic design product. The team was so successful that the company decided to incorporate self-managing teams throughout its organization. In one large chain of fast-food restaurants, unit managers can be responsible for 50 or more stores because each restaurant is run by an employee team responsible for all restaurant operations. This enables the unit managers to focus on market-related problem solving and to dispense with worry about day-to-day store operations.

Giving employees so much control over their work and decision making is difficult in a large or a small organization if it is hierarchically structured. Many management theorists and business leaders believe that today's employees want and need to exercise initiative and imagination. These managers firmly believe that driving decision-making power lower into the organization accomplishes several things at once: customers are better served, and employees are more satisfied and are therefore more productive. The increases in productivity, in turn, can allow the organization to do more with less (human resources, cost, rework, redesign, layers of management). Employees become more aware of, and committed to, organizational goals, and the organizational climate becomes internally aligned.

Empowerment and its concurrent messages are exciting ideas to managers seeking to be excellent and to drive quality initiatives. Some important ingredients for the empowered organization cannot be ignored, however. In some ways, empowerment embodies the idea of TQM, where people take real responsibility for their work and their actions. In others, it is a managerial "fad" that undermines sincere participative efforts because neither the organization's culture nor operating systems supports it. Vaill (1993, 27) describes empowerment as "the feeling experienced by all employees when they feel that they are expected to exercise initiative in good faith on behalf of the organizational mission, even if it goes outside the bounds of their normal responsibilities. If, for some reason, taking that initiative leads to a mistake, then they trust that they will not be arbitrarily penalized for having taken that initiative."

First, in order to be empowered to make decisions regarding their work, employees, regardless of organizational level, must understand and know information relevant to the performance of their business. For example, in the General Electric Company, at the beginning of each of its well-publicized WORKOUT efforts, the general manager of each business unit met with employees to outline the strategy and performance of the business. Employees involved in WORKOUT could then solve problems that would have a definite impact on the performance of the business. While preliminary efforts focused on eliminating reports, meetings, and bureaucracy which detracted from productivity, later WORKOUTS examined such significant issues as cycle time, manufacturing processes, and cross-functional, or even cross-business, issues.

Employees should also be rewarded based on the organization's performance. Au Bon Pain, a chain of French bakery cafes, decided to reward its store managers' entrepreneurial behavior by giving them a percentage of the profits by which the store exceeded the plan. Encouraged by this system to develop ways to cut cost, improve service, and focus on food quality, these "partner managers" helped Au Bon Pain deliver service to the customer in new and creative ways.

Employees who are "empowered" should also have the knowledge that enables them to understand and contribute to the organization's performance, and the power to make decisions that influence that performance. One of the hallmarks of Ameritech Corporation's Breakthrough program is that employees are encouraged to make decisions about their work that directly influence customer satisfaction. This goal can be accomplished in any of the ways to develop teams across organizations which this chapter has presented so far. At General Electric Corporation, empowered employees redesigned a manufacturing process to reduce cycle time and increase productivity. Service workers in department stores are increasing customer loyalty by taking actions that better serve them—for example, a furniture salesman who through his own initiatives, calls people who have been "just looking" to come in when the particular item they have been "looking" at goes on sale (Fromm and Schlesinger, 1994).

Developing programs and policies that truly provide opportunities for employees to influence the work they do, the ways they do their work, their commitment to meeting customer needs, through the methods described in this chapter, can enable companies to have the employee involvement necessary to be productive in the complex competitive environment of the twenty-first century. Organizations such as Ameritech, General Electric, Allied-Signal, and many others large and small have begun such transformations.

◆   Summary

In examining human resource management issues in TQM organizations, this chapter begins with a look at the intricacies of employee involvement, including technique adoption and program elements and their relationship to the TQM process. The chapter also covers the nature of organizational structures and boundary setting; the measurement and reward of teams in TQM; and employee involvement teams and their characteristics.

◆   Key Terms

Suggestion-oriented practices	Stovepipes	Problem-solving teams
Gainsharing	Functional boundary	Self-managed teams
QWL (quality of work life)	Task boundary	Quality circles
Physical co-location	Authority boundary	GRPI rules
Interdepartmental rotation	Political boundary	Membership stage
"Boundaryless" organization	Identity boundary	Subgrouping stage
	360 degree performance review	Conflict stage
	Job-based pay systems	Individual differentiation
	Steering committees	Collaboration
		Whole work component

◆   Assignments

1. In your work or study group, observe the work processes/job design in a variety of service organizations. Is a concern for quality and customer satisfaction evident in their conduct? If so, to what do you attribute that concern? If not, why not?

2. Think of a team you have been on recently. It could be a team from work or school. Would you describe the team as effective? What can you do to improve the workings of any team that you are on? If you are currently a member of a work team, what process observations can you make that can help the team be even more effective? How can TQM methods help your team?

3. Teams are very popular in organizations today. Most organizations struggle to develop rewards that are appropriate for people on teams. What do you think are the appropriate ways to give feedback and rewards to team members? Be sure to use relevant managerial literature to bolster your argument.

◆   Developing Performance Measurements and Deploying Tasks Assignment

The following process develops performance measures for a specific task—making breakfast for the family. Then it shows how to define the tasks required to make breakfast and achieve those performance measures. A similar process can be used for developing measures for other tasks in your business. This process is suitable for tasks conducted on an ongoing basis; it is not intended for one-time tasks such as projects. The exercise is best done in a small group.

Your family consists of you, a spouse, and two children (a 6-year-old boy and an 8-year-old girl). The kids go to school each day, and the spouse and you go to work. So the weekday breakfast is simple, usually consisting of a bowl of cereal and coffee, milk, or juice. But on weekends, you like to arrange a leisurely breakfast for the whole family. The purpose of this exercise is to develop measures for these weekend breakfasts.

The measure development process consists of three steps:
1. Define measures for the outcome.
2. Develop approaches and subtasks to achieve the task.
3. Assign responsibility for measuring the results and performing the subtasks.

Note: We find it convenient to do the brainstorming by putting the ideas down on Post-It notes. Then overlapping ideas can be merged to form a single metric, or subtask, and entered on the appropriate chart.

Define Measures for the Outcome.

On the attached sheet (Exhibit 12.1):

- Write task to be accomplished. Next write the key characteristic (quality, flexibility, timeliness, and efficiency). You will want to select the characteristic that is most likely to ensure customer satisfaction. In this case, the customer would be the rest of the family.
- Brainstorm possible metrics for each of the characteristics (quality, flexibility, timeliness, and efficiency), but special attention should be given to developing measures for the key characteristic. In practice, you may choose several metrics, but, for this exercise, develop at least two for the key characteristic and at least one for each of the others. Examples of metrics may be:

  Number of requests for second helpings.
  Number of options available for each course. For example, can eggs only be had scrambled or are they available as scrambled, fried, or boiled?
  Maximum time a person had to wait to be served.
  Time taken to put the meal together.

- For the rest of this exercise focus only on the key characteristic. In practice, you would include at least one metric for each of the other characteristics as well. Evaluate each metric with respect to validity.[1] A high degree of validity indicates that this metric is a direct measure of the characteristic. For example, when measuring the quality of repair work at a garage, the cleanliness of the station would be less valid than the number of repeat calls for the same problem. Time taken to put the meal together could be considered having a high degree of validity as a measure of efficiency.
- Evaluate each metric with respect to feasibility of performing the measurement (use the same scoring system as earlier). Feasibility means it can be objectively recorded, in an accurate and precise and timely manner. Time taken to put the meal together could probably be measured accurately, precisely, and objectively if there were a clock in the kitchen on which you could record the start time.
- Note in the important column, the one or two results metrics for the critical characteristics that have the highest combined validity and feasibility; that is, simply add the numeric equivalents indicating the strength of the connection. Validity should be weighted slightly more than feasibility. Number these sequentially in the number column.
- Set targets for these metrics. These should be specific. For example, a target for the metric "the number of requests for second helpings" could be two requests per breakfast; a target for the metric "time taken to put a meal together" could be 15 minutes.

[1]High strength should be recorded as a double circle (9 points), medium strength as a single circle (3 points), and a weak connection as a triangle (1 point).

Exhibit
12.1

Defined Outcome Measures

Task:								
Key Desired Characteristic								
Characteristic	Measure	Validity	Feasibility	Importance	No.	Target	Monitor
Monitoring period:								

491

◆ Develop Approaches and Subtasks to Achieve the Task

Once the result metrics have been established, we can develop approaches for achieving the task. This involves generating a list of several means, rationalizing these to form viable approaches, and then evaluating the approaches for impact and feasibility. On the attached sheet (Exhibit 12.2):

- Write task to be accomplished. For this exercise, the task is to prepare breakfast for the family on the weekend.
- Brainstorm ways and means of accomplishing the task. Examples may be:

  Ask family members what they would like for breakfast the day before.
  Construct a menu.
  Shop for food.

Some of these may overlap with each other, but do not worry about that during the brainstorming stage.

- From the list of brainstormed subtasks, select approaches for accomplishing the task. At this stage remove any overlap between activities that may have resulted from the previous step.
- Evaluate each activity (or subtask) for its impact on the task. Use the same scoring system as for the previous step. If this activity is performed, how well does it accomplish the desired results? You are evaluating the activity based on the impact it has on the metrics you had selected in the previous exhibit. Note the measures it impacts.
- Evaluate each approach for feasibility of implementation. Issues to consider include expenses, the other people who must be involved, and their capabilities.
- Number the approaches that have the highest impact and feasibility. In the event of a tie, give more weight to impact. Make sure you have approaches that will impact each of the measures. These are the approaches that are best to implement.

Assign Responsibility for Measuring the Results and Performing the Subtasks.

The final stage of the planning involves identifying the person who will be responsible for implementing each of the subtasks and the person responsible for monitoring the metrics. This may be the same person. You also need to define the monitoring period. That is the length of time before you will review the results. For example, you may have defined one of the subtasks as setting the table. The responsibility for this may be assigned to the 8-year-old child. The metric may be the number of additional pieces she is asked to bring to the table after people sit down for breakfast. The person monitoring it may be yourself. If you choose to review the results at the end of the month, the monitoring period will be one month.

Exhibit
12.2

Task Approaches

Task:

Means of accomplishing task	Impact	Meas. No.	Feasibility	No.	Responsibility

C a s e   S t u d y

Upper Valley Health Clinic

"I know we can do it, Will!" said Charlene DiCicco, as she reached for another low-fat doughnut. "We have to figure out a way to simplify these procedures for our policy-holders. It's silly and wasteful to have so many different pieces of information going in and out at once. Besides, Upper Valley Health (UVH) is supposed to be a Health Maintenance Organization (HMO) of the future. . . . let's not live in the past!"

Charlene DiCicco was the patient services manager for Upper Valley Health Clinic (UVHC), a Health Maintenance Organization serving 8000 patients. UVHC was located in Hampshire, New York, nestled in the Adirondack Mountains, in the Ottawaskett River Valley. Hampshire and the surrounding valley was a four-season tourist area, but also had some small manufacturing plants and a well-known liberal arts college. Patients in the Upper Valley were accustomed to high-quality health care, and although they had embraced HMOs, they were concerned about rising health-care costs and payments. The Upper Ottawaskett Valley was served by a major hospital complex associated with the medical school at the college; the UVHC was just one HMO using this hospital. Most clinicians at UVHC were on staff at the hospital; in fact, most were adjunct faculty at the medical school and worked with medical students, interns, and residents.

Aside from the medical staff, as coordinator of patient services, Charlene and her organization were the UVHC's major contact with patients after they became members. Most patients were part of employee groups, but some were private members. All complaints and compliments came to her and her organization. She then dealt with appropriate administrative staff units either to solve the patients' problems or to pass on the praise. UVHC's administrative staff was functionally organized; most units managed their own areas but had little to do with each other (see organization chart, Exhibit 12.3). The Medical Staff usually wanted as little to do with the administrative side of health care as possible. Ongoing battles between quality of care and cost of care occurred, although neither side wanted either to reduce the quality of patient care or to spend money frivolously. Her group was perceived as the complaint department. However, she and her staff of five felt that because of their closeness to the patient they could gather information that could help the HMO deal with its cost and quality of care choices. The group had only been in existence for a year; people on staff still had to see it as something other than "the source for complaints" which ended up in staff reviews. The medical staff perceived her group as the place for "nudgy patients" to go to complain.

Charlene was 35 years old, married, with two children. Her husband was a sociology professor at the college. Charlene had an undergraduate degree in management from Babson College and had a master's in public health administration from the University of New York. She had worked for five years in the financial services industry in New York City, and there had come to understand the importance of customer service and client satisfaction. Charlene understood that there would be many opportunities in health care for good managers with a solid customer service attitude. She had come to UVHC five years before, after receiving her master's de-

Upper Valley Health Clinic (Continued)

Exhibit
12.3

Upper Valley Health Clinic Organization Chart

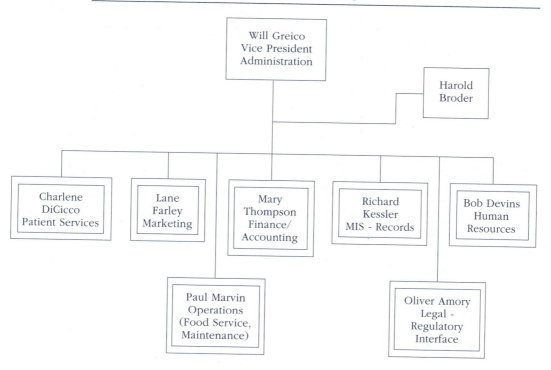

gree. She enjoyed her work. Because of the size of the community, her outgoing personality, her husband's involvement with the college, and her children's involvement in school and extracurricular activities, she knew many people in Hampshire. She wanted to do what she could to improve health care in her community, and felt that her role in patient services gave her a unique opportunity to do so. She had been trained as a quality facilitator; she often became frustrated, however, that quality was emphasized in name only.

UVHC had started a Total Quality effort in 1990. Most of the administrative staff had at-

tended quality training. Bulletin Boards and notices exhorted people to pay attention to quality in all their actions; people in meetings used quality principles for agenda setting and followthrough. Quality teams existed at each level of every function; however, few cross-functional quality teams existed. No "Quality Czar" existed at UVHC; each department head was supposed to exemplify quality in his work and be a role model for his or her employees. Several teams had worked to improve processes and procedures within each function. For example, one team had worked to streamline the ways jobs were posted and filled. Another had worked to

Upper Valley Health Clinic (Continued)

simplify the way patient records were kept and sent to billing and records. Still another had looked at improving food services so that the food wouldn't taste like "hospital" food. One team had tried to work cross-functionally to improve the ways records were sent to patients. However, while the team had worked hard to smooth the process to gather patient information internally, they neglected to talk to the patient services area to see what they could add to the process. Charlene felt that she was in a critical role to reenergize TQM efforts; her focus on the patients and her understanding of the UVHC procedures made her a natural linking pin.

Charlene and her five staff members were the link between the administration, the hospital, and the patients. Patients usually came to them with problems, concerns, questions about bills and charges, or requests for information in general. She had worked hard to build a team of people who worked together to address patient concerns. Several times they had developed programs and procedures for patients before any issues even surfaced. The staff ranged in age from 28 to 45. Education levels varied. James Gardner (28) had a bachelor's degree in sociology from the college, whereas Stephanie Rotherwood (40) had a degree in art history and until recently had run her own antique shop in town. Each staff member had been selected because of his or her interpersonal and problem-solving skills. The staff needed to know how to relate to patients as well as administrators and physicians. Her staff had particular "cohorts" of patients, based on region, with whom they worked, and each had a particular administrative area that they specialized in. For example, James's cohort group lived in the northwest valley, and he specialized in problems in medical records.

Stephanie's group lived in the southern valley, and her specialization was in admissions and emergency care. (See Exhibit 12.4 for a more complete list of patient service staff.)

Charlene and her group had received many comments about the "new" patient information process and about the number of mailings patients were sent at yearly renewal/record update time. Patients were confused about the reports they received. They often had no idea about the treatment they had received, the amount covered, or charged, and what was expected of them. Furthermore, so many forms and requests for data and histories had to be returned to the UVHC records office that patients often lost or misplaced them. When the forms weren't completely returned, the HMO didn't consider the patient a member. These problems and concerns all ended up on Charlene's desk. As the single point of contact between the administrative services and the patient, Charlene and her five staff members were responsible for making sure these problems were solved, or, better yet, didn't occur in the first place. They had to work hard both to gain credibility and to solve the problems they knew existed.

Charlene and her team decided to run a series of "focus groups" on the customer relations problems at UVHC. She and her team talked to a wide range of members, policyholders, nonmembers, and administrative and medical staffers. Although most patients were pleased with UV and the quality of care provided, several issues had repeatedly been mentioned. First, the admitting staff was perceived as inflexible and insensitive. They were perceived as being more concerned with paperwork than with making sure that the patients received appropriate attention, and that families of patients undergoing

Upper Valley Health Clinic (Continued)

Exhibit 12.4

UVHC Patient Services Staff

Charlene DiCicco
Manager Patient Services
35 years old
BS in Management, Babson College
MPH from University of New York

James Gardner
Patient Services Staff
28 years old
BA in Sociology, Upper Valley College
Admissions Specialist

Sam Holtzmonn
Patient Services Staff
35 years old
BA in American History, New York University
MA in Psychology, Upper Valley College
Finance Specialist

Jana Franklin
Patient Services Staff
36 years old
BA in Management, Western University
Marketing Specialist

Samara Smith
Patient Services Staff
45 years old
BA in Social Psychology, Vermont University
MBA, specializing in Service Management,
University of New York
General Patient Services
Coordinator of Special Programs

Stephanie Rotherwood
Patient Services Staff
40 years old
BA in Art History, Upper Valley College
Admissions, Emergency Care Specialist

Upper Valley Health Clinic (Continued)

emergency procedures were informed about conditions and events. Evelyn Miller, the head of admitting services, was a friend of Charlene's. Charlene knew that Evelyn cared deeply about patients, but also was obligated by law and medical practice to be strict about medical histories and consent forms. Evelyn often complained to Charlene over coffee that the paperwork required by all the monitoring agencies was overwhelming, and she wished that there was a way to get most of it in order, and easily accessible, before patients arrived on the scene. Her staff hated to be perceived as ghoulish, choosing procedure over patients.

Patients also complained about waiting time for appointments. This was particularly true for those specialists who were full-time faculty at the Medical School and who consulted with UVHC only occasionally. For example, one patient had to wait eight weeks to see a hand surgeon about a painful ganglionic cyst on one of her joints; then, he canceled the appointment, and she had to wait another six weeks before it was attended to. Another area HMO was spending considerable advertising time on the short waiting time it had for appointments. While most of the UVHC staff chuckled that the competition's time schedule was equivalent to short lines at a bad restaurant, Charlene knew the appointment scheduling was something that UVHC could fix relatively easily. She didn't know Harold Broder, the liaison to the Medical School, very well. He had a formidable reputation and was known as someone who protected "his" doctors from being bothered by what they felt was administrative trivia.

Finally, patients complained about the endless round of mailings they received. Mailings were sent to each patient, not each family, and often families would receive several flyers per day describing services, seminars, new doctors who had joined the HMO, and so forth. Although most patients were pleased with this patient outreach, they believed that they didn't have to receive ALL the mailings about every service offered. Charlene's neighbors, Mr. and Mrs. Evans, were in their sixties. Mrs. Evans wondered why she kept receiving information about pregnancy and well-baby care when all she really wanted was information about senior citizen health issues. Forms and health histories, while on file at UVHC, had to be periodically updated, and demographic information completed. Charlene knew that patients didn't mind doing this and that they just wanted to do it once a year. She had been in touch with Richard Kessler, the chief information systems officer of the UVHC, but he had been more concerned with computerizing the patient record systems at that time and didn't want to devote time to this issue. He did promise to put one of his staff people, Michael McCall, on a project to simplify the records input. Charlene worked well with Mike and knew that he would do his best to compile an appropriate information system.

Employees at UVHC earned slightly less than the average wage for the Upper Valley area. While each manager could give bonuses to reward people for work "above and beyond that expected," few bonuses had been awarded for the past two years. When Charlene asked why most bonuses were not distributed, most managers pointed out that cost and budget concerns were an issue. Charlene wanted to pay the people in her department based on specific performance criteria, such as anticipation of problems, problem-solving, satisfactory achievement of results, and responsiveness. The staff was working together to determine key compe-

Upper Valley Health Clinic (Continued)

tencies and job requirements. However, she knew that as yet she did not have a compelling case for utilizing a different reward/incentive structure than the rest of UVHC.

Charlene knew that emphasizing the TQM focus required at UVHC could work to increase morale, create new efficiencies, and get departments working together to handle organizational and customer problems. She recognized that both medical and administrative staff had to work together to solve the particular problems she had discovered. She wanted to get a cross-functional team, with members from each of the administrative areas, and some key medical staff, together to work on these problems. She believed that they could both solve the difficulties and reenergize the TQM focus of UVHC. She had asked Will Greico, the administrative vice president of the hospital, for his backing in her plan. He had approved the idea in princi-

ple, but wanted to see her design for the organization of the task force, its charge, ways she would reward people, and the timeline for work and results. She knew she could make a case for full-time resources, but she wanted to work out some other options. The stakes were high, both for Charlene and for UVHC.

CASE QUESTIONS

1. Given the information in the case, what organization would you propose Charlene use to solve the problems she faces at UVHC?
2. How should she reward the task force members?
3. What changes, if any, would you propose for UVHC organization as a whole?
4. How can she spread TQM and the results of the task force across the organization?

◆ Bibliography

Baskerville, Dawn M. "Why Business Loves Work Teams." *Quality Digest,* October 1993.

Bluestone, Barry, and Irving Bluestone. "Workers (and Managers) of the World, Unite." *Technology Review,* (November–December 1992).

Bowen, David E., and Edward E. Lawler III. "Total Quality-Oriented Human Resources Management." *Organizational Dynamics* (Spring 1992).

Brown, Mark G. "Commitment: It's Not the Whether, It's the 'How To'." *Journal for Quality and Participation* (December 1989).

Cohen, Allan R., and David Bradford. *Managing for Excellence.* New York: John Wiley and Sons, 1984.

Dean, James W., Jr., and James R Evans. *Total Quality: Management, Organization, and Strategy.* Minneapolis: West Publishing, 1994.

Douglas K. *The Discipline of Teams.* Boston: Harvard Business School Press, 1993.

Fromm, Bill, and Leonard Schlesinger. *The Real Heroes of Business: and Not a CEO Among Them.* New York, 1994.

Galbraith, Jay R. *Competing with Flexible Lateral Organizations,* Reading, Mass.: Addison-Wesley Publishing Co., 1994.

Hirschhorn, Larry, and Thomas Gilmore. "The New Boundaries of the 'Boundaryless' Company." *Harvard Business Review (May–June 1992)*.

Ishikawa, K. *What Is Total Quality Control? The Japanese Way*. Translated by David Lu. London: Prentice-Hall International, 1985.

Juran, Daryl. "Achieving Sustained Quantifiable Results in an Interdepartmental Quality Improvement Project." *Journal of Quality Improvement* (March 1994).

Katzenback, Jon R., and Douglas K. Smith. "The Discipline of Teams." *Harvard Business Review* (March–April 1993).

Kolodny, Harvey, and Tjorbjorn Stjernberg. "Self-Managing Teams: The New Organization of Work." In Allan R. Cohen, ed. *The Portable MBA in Management*. New York: John Wiley and Sons, 1993.

Kotter, John P. "What Leaders Really Do." *Harvard Business Review* (1990).

Kotter, John P., and James L. Heskett. *Corporate Culture and Performance*. New York: Free Press, 1992.

Lawler, Edward E. III. "Total Quality Management and Employee Involvement: Are They Compatible?" *Academy of Management Executive*. 8, No. 1 (1994).

Lawler, Edward, G. E. Ledford, Jr., and S. A. Mohrman. *Employee Involvement in America: A Study of Contemporary Practice*. Houston: American Productivity and Quality Center, 1989.

Lawler, Edward, S. A. Mohrman, and G. E. Ledford, Jr. *Employee Involvement and Total Quality Management: Practices and Results in Fortune 1000 Companies*. San Francisco: Jossey-Bass, 1992.

Lawrence, Paul F., and Jay Lorsch. *Organization and Environment*. Homewood, Ill. Richard D. Irwin, 1967.

Obert, Steve. "The Development of Organizational Task Groups." Ph.D. diss. Case Western Reserve University, 1979.

Parker, Glenn M. *Cross-Functional Teams*. San Francisco: Jossey-Bass, 1994.

Premeaux, Shane R., R. Wayne Mondy, Art L. Bethke, and Ray Comish. "Managing Tomorrow's Unionized Workers." *Personnel,* (July 1989).

Schlesinger, Leonard. *Quality of Work Life and the Supervisor*. New York: Praeger Publishers, 1980.

Schlesinger, Phyllis F., and Leonard A. Schlesinger. "Designing Effective Organizations." In Allan H. Cohen, ed. *The Portable MBA in Management*. New York: John Wiley and Sons, 1993.

Schlesinger, Phyllis F., Vijay Sathe, Leonard Schlesinger, and John P. Kotter. *Organization: Text, Cases, and Readings in the Management of Organizational Design and Change*. Homewood, Ill.: Richard D. Irwin, 1991.

Schonberger, Richard. "Total Quality Management Cuts a Broad Swath—Through Manufacturing and Beyond." *Organizational Dynamics* (Spring 1992).

Tichy, Noel, and Mary Anne Devanna. "Creating the Competitive Organization of the 21st Century: The Boundaryless Company." *Human Resource Management* (Winter 1990).

Tichy, Noel, Mary Anne Devanna, and Charles Formbrun, eds. *Strategic Human Resource Management*. New York: John Wiley and Sons, 1984.

Vaill, Peter. "Visionary Leadership." in Allan R. Cohen, *The Portable MBA in Management*. New York: John Wiley and Sons, 1993.

Chapter 13

TQM and the Product Development Process

◆ ◆ ◆

In 1992 Packard Bell Electronics Inc. with sales of about $1 billion was considered to be a small player in the personal computer market. During the first two quarters of 1995, it became the number one seller of personal computers in the United States with projected revenues of $5.5 billion for the year. A key to its success has been its ability to introduce new technology before the competition. Packard Bell introduced preloaded software, was the first to use the Intel Pentium chip, and the first to include surround-sound technology and dual CD-ROM drives. Alan Bush, president of Tandy Corporation's Computer City chain, has been quoted as saying, "Packard Bell is successful because they build a quality product and bring it to market fast."

◆ INTRODUCTION

What practices enable winning companies to develop high-quality products faster than their competitors? In previous chapters, the various dimensions of quality have been defined, and a wide variety of tools and initiatives to improve quality have been presented. The objective of this chapter is to focus on how the quality of products and services can be assured by the effective management of the development process. As discussed earlier in this book, leading-edge thinking about quality has shifted from "inspecting the quality in" to "building the quality in" and, finally, to "designing the quality in" to the product. This chapter focuses on the techniques and managerial approaches that will help design quality into new products and services.

The critical potential impact of the development process on the quality of the outcome cannot be overemphasized. It is widely acknowledged that the quality of conformance for manufactured products is greatly influenced by steps taken *during* the development process to ensure the so-called manufacturability of the product. Manufacturability strongly impacts the long-run production cost of a product. Studies have shown that the bulk of the steady-state production costs of new products is determined by design decisions made and implemented prior to the release of the new design to the shop floor. It goes without saying that the quality of any new design, measured in terms of how well the functionality of the design delights the customer, is a direct function of how well the design process is structured and managed.

As in any other process, the outcome of the product development process cannot be measured only in terms of the quality attributes (i.e., manufacturability and functionality) of the resulting product. In the context of new product development, at least two other critical performance dimensions need to be considered in addition to quality attributes: development time and development cost. Development time measures the elapsed time from the start of a new product development project through launch or even a later point in the new product's life cycle. Development cost reflects the cost of all the resources, in particular human resources, expended to bring a new concept into reality. Intense competitive forces have in recent years focused much attention on these two factors, in particular on fast-cycle development. However, practitioners are increasingly coming to the realization that the achievement of quality, time, and cost objectives in product development goes hand in hand and does involve tradeoffs. In other words, the same managerial practices that result in fast-cycle development are also associated with high-quality products and low development costs. This chapter reviews some of these practices.

◆ STRUCTURING THE DEVELOPMENT PROCESS

Product development is a process. It is a set of activities that conceives, designs, and delivers a product in response to a perceived market need or opportunity. These activities are clustered into phases, between which there may be "**gates**" or formal points of review. Ideally, each project is positioned within an aggregate project plan, which organizes and tracks all of the development activities and resources of a firm. The organization and management of the resources for a particular project should be matched to the task and should facilitate integrated problem-solving across functions.

Structuring the Work

There are several ways of grouping product development activities into phases. Most companies and researchers use four to six phases, and a wide variety of terms to describe them. We will use five phases which we will describe as

- Product definition
- High-level design
- Detail product/process design
- Prototype-test-and-refine
- Ramp-up to volume manufacturing

Phases of Design and Development

During the product definition (or concept development) phase, customer needs are identified and converted into target specifications for the product. Ideally, a wide range of concepts are proposed, screened relative to customer requirements and priorities, evaluated for their technical and financial feasibility as well as market potential, and one is chosen for further development. This phase terminates successfully in concept approval.

During high-level design (or product planning), the overall architecture of the product, its subsystems, and major components are defined, producing a layout of the product and functional specifications for the subsystems. The overall process architecture is designed, producing a final assembly sequence for the product and a preliminary outline of the production process. The core team is formed, suppliers are identified and verified, and key customers are selected with whom to work.

Design is an iterative process in which the design of product and process are specified and subsequently refined through building and testing a series of prototypes, or preproduction models of the product. These iterative cycles of interdependent product and process design can be roughly grouped into two subphases which, for convenience, we will call detail design and prototyping. However, the product details are finalized in the second subphase, and prototyping for design verification begins in the first subphase.

Detail design specifies each component's geometry, materials, and tolerances. Its drawings and specifications are the basis for the tooling that fabricates the parts. Early prototypes are built and tested for functionality: Is the concept sound? Does the design itself work? Early prototypes verify the product and tooling designs. Whereas the parts for early tests are machined, the parts for later prototypes are built from production tooling. They test not only the reliability and performance of the design, but also the fabrication process. Feedback from tests is used to refine product, tooling, and process, and to verify the production process.

Final testing is conducted using the intended production process during the "ramp-up" to full production. During this period, the workforce is trained, and the actual production process is tested and "debugged." The ramp-up to full-scale production is gradual, though the speed of the ramp-up varies.

Gates and Reviews

Companies that have formalized their development processes have placed major review points, often called "gates," between their phases. Each phase has a package of deliverables that are to be completed before the next gate review. At each gate, a cross-functional group of senior managers evaluates these deliverables vis-à-vis project targets. If the exit criteria have been met and the project is passed onto the next phase, resources for the next phase are usually approved.

The review process is more than a way of making sure that projects are on track. It is a mechanism for making explicit and conscious, albeit on a project-by-project basis, the development activities in which the company is engaged, and for periodically reassessing the continuing viability of projects. Too often, projects are not canceled when they should be; by periodically bringing the spotlight onto them, management has the opportunity to say no when it needs to. On the other hand, projects that should have high priority may not be getting the resources they need, particularly if conditions have changed since the project was launched. The review process is not always followed rigorously, however, particularly since time to market pressures have pushed companies to overlap their development activities. The priority of reducing critical path time may supersede completing the deliverables of one phase before moving into the next phase (Rosenthal, 1992).

The go/no-go point (sometimes called **Gate Zero**) is an especially critical gate, for it gives approval to the concept. Prior to concept approval, several things have been done to assess the validity of the idea: Is it economically and technically feasible? What are the technical risks? Is there a potential market? Are the resources and capabilities available? What are competitors doing, and how are they likely to respond? Marketing and product development plans have been developed, development costs assessed, and a business case has been drawn up to justify the investment. Rosenthal (1992) notes that, "Companies that conduct rigorous Gate 0 reviews seem to agree that this is the most strategic point for managerial intervention." Indeed, the labeling of this gate signifies its importance; companies that began their executive review with Gate 1 discovered that they were entering too late into discussions of critical formative issues of the market and performance for the new product. They subsequently added Gate 0 to the front end of the preexisting set of gate reviews.

The gating process serves not only to control the development process, but also to discipline senior management's involvement in the process. Senior management's ability to influence the project is maximal prior to Gate 0. In practice, however, many senior managers fail to show much interest in new products until they are in the prototype phase; their intervention there can be quite disruptive and may greatly delay the project. A gating process can serve as a mechanism through which an empowered team pushes back on management to solicit its input at the outset but limit their disruptive involvement late in the process.

Behind most high-performing, empowered development teams are senior managers who challenge and scrutinize rigorously at the front end, who champion the project and clear away obstacles, but do not intervene thereafter unless it appears that targets will not be met. At Honda, for example, senior managers review how the project team proposes to meet the guidelines (e.g., vehicle size and performance, price range, capital needs, and launch date). Once they approve the final concept, the program direction is rarely changed. What makes this hands-off style feasible is that concept approval is preceded by intense and thorough discussion of differences and alternatives. It is said that the project team for the 1984 Civic took their concepts for four different models to top management 17 times before it was approved.

Aggregate Project Plan

A company typically has a portfolio of ongoing development projects. The position of a specific project in the development strategy and the development portfolio of the company should be clearly understood, but very often it is not, because very often these strategic management tools are not in place. A development strategy integrates product-market and technology strategies into guidance for a coherent set of development goals, which in turn become the basis for an aggregate project plan. Such a plan links the development strategy and goals with specific projects and resources. It is the outcome of conscious decisions to activate (or cancel) projects, and it defines their scope, their start and completion dates, and their resource allotments. The aggregate plan reflects thinking about what the entire set of projects ought to be. It thereby locates a particular project in time/scope relation to the entire portfolio (Wheelwright and Clark, 1992).

An **aggregate project plan** documents the mix, timing, and sequence of projects for a given planning period. In addition to advanced research projects that may be undertaken in basic research facilities, the major types of development projects making up the mix are: breakthrough projects whose core concepts and technologies may create an entire new product family for the organization; next-generation products whose architecture will serve as a platform for various derivatives; derivative projects, including new models and enhancements of existing platforms; and partnered projects that also draw on the resources of the organization. It is not uncommon to find a concentration of activity on derivative projects and to recognize that the mix needs to be redirected.

When resource commitments to these projects are matched against overall resources, it is not uncommon to find gross overcommitment of resources because the firm has too many active projects. Not only are people in general overcommitted, but, as Wheelwright and Clark (1992) note, overcommitment "tends to mean that a handful of key individuals show up repeatedly and concurrently on different projects." The justification offered for such concurrent assignments is that, because such individuals are a scarce resource, it is important that they not have any idle time. When an engineer focused on a single project is given a second one, utilization often rises because the engineer no longer has to wait for the activities of others involved in that single project. However, if a third, fourth, or even fifth project is added, the percentage of time spent on value-adding tasks drops rapidly, as an increasing fraction of valuable time is spent on nonvalued-added tasks—coordinating, remembering, or tracking down information, for example. In addition, the engineer becomes the bottleneck on all of the projects to which he or she is assigned" (Wheelwright and Clark, 1992).

Organizing the Resources

Human and financial resources must be organized in an optimal way to address the project objectives. For most companies, this has meant a significant shift from a predominantly functional or vertically organized approach to a team-based, horizontal approach. Different kinds of skills are needed from both managers and working members in order to become effective in horizontal, cross-functional work.

The primary objectives of organizing people in cross-functional teams are two: to improve the quality of design solutions, and to get to market much more quickly. The quality of design has two aspects: the quality of the product solution in relation to customer requirements, and the quality of the process through which these solutions are achieved. Both depend on the quality of interaction, communication, and problem solving among team members.

Effective teams bring in all the relevant players early in the process and maintain continuity of personnel throughout. Manufacturing, suppliers, purchasing, industrial design, and other groups that have traditionally been contacted late are now active partners from the outset. Their style of communication and of collaborating around problem solving are critical and are discussed later in this chapter.

Project Organization

To carry out day-to-day, ongoing operations, most firms have become vertically organized by function (manufacturing, marketing, engineering, industrial design, etc.). These often become "silos" or "chimneys" that do not communicate across boundaries and that have to escalate conflicts to upper levels of management, sometimes the vice presidential level, for resolution. Rapid and effective development of new products, on the other hand, requires daily interaction, cooperation, and communication at every level but especially the working level.

To work more effectively horizontally, firms have taken three approaches that we will call "coordinated," "empowered," and "skunkworks." In the first case, a number of people from key functions are designated as members of a project team, but they still reside with their function, and they report to, and are evaluated by, their functional managers. Each function is represented on the core team by a liaison, and a project manager coordinates functional activities. The manager is relatively junior (or "lightweight"), having limited influence in the organization and being unable to reassign people or resources (Clark and Fujimoto, 1991; Wheelwright and Clark, 1992). His or her major role is to see that critical path items are on track. This pattern of organization may be appropriate for derivative projects.

For a major platform project and sometimes for breakthrough projects, a highly empowered team with strong leadership is optimal. The core group is dedicated to the project, and some or all of its members may be co-located during the life of the project; that is, their deskspace is physically contiguous. The importance of being physically adjacent has been underwritten by studies showing that people within 30 feet of each other continually interact and talk informally with each other. After 30 feet, communication drops off so sharply that it hardly matters whether people are in the same building or across the street or in another country (Allen, 1977). Empowered teams have substantial decision-making authority over program operations and decisions.

Empowered teams are headed by senior managers who have robust project management authority and clout in the organization. Sometimes called **heavyweight project managers (HWPM),** they have direct responsibility and budget authority for all aspects of the program's content for the entire period from concept to market. They have direct contact with customers, act as concept champions and translators, and make sure that the product concept is accurately translated into the technical details of the vehicle. HWPMs have direct and frequent contact with designers and engineers at the working level and are rarely in their offices (Fujimoto, 1989).

The effectiveness of this second style of management is suggested by research on the auto industry. Programs that have a HWPM were completed nine months sooner than those headed by a lightweight project manager (LWPM). The latter, in turn, had an 8.5-month advantage over projects managed through functional organizations. The HWPM programs not only had an 18-month advantage over functional programs, but managed to do so with far fewer engineers and technical people (Clark and Fujimoto, 1991). These differences in project organization are related to the competitive advantage of the Japanese. At the time of the Clark and Fujimoto study (1991), Americans still organized their programs within a functional structure or used an LWPM to coordinate across functions, whereas all the Japanese were using some form of project management and were the only ones to have HWPMs.

The **skunkworks** pattern has similarities to the empowered team but goes even further. The team is virtually autonomous and operates outside their functions. Very often, the entire group is co-located at a site that is removed from their former base. This form of organization is particularly geared to breakthrough projects in which there are virtually no rules. Although very effective for rapid development, it is often difficult to integrate the process improvements achieved by the skunkworks into the mainstream of the organization.

◆ DEFINING THE PRODUCT

Companies have given more attention to improving their development activities once a product concept has been approved than they have to the "front end." By development, we refer to the product/process design, testing, prototyping, and ramp-up. The front end is everything that happens before this. It is the work that is done prior to concept approval, budget commitment, and assignment of a formal development team. Only after these decisions have been taken do most companies officially "start the clock" on the project—that is, at Gate 0. The front end is thus also referred to as "pre-project" activities. Phase 0 ends when the project clock begins, but when Phase 0 begins is unclear. It may occur when someone has an idea for a product or someone identifies a need that the company should be investigating.

The best practice companies are recognizing that there is enormous payoff to learning how to approach the front end systematically and to manage it well.

The "Fuzzy Front End"

The front end of development is often referred to as being "fuzzy." It is the weak-est, least structured, least understood, most anemically resourced part of the *new product development* process. Yet it is in many ways the most critical. Time lost here means that, as Preston Smith and Donald Reinertsen put it, "the project clock will lag behind the market clock"(1991). A recent report estimates that 60 to 80 percent of total product life cycle costs are determined by the end of the design engineering phase (Woodruff et al., 1990.) And it is through the front-end process, however it is structured, that the Voice of the Customer is heard (or not heard), and is translated into a concept and requirements whose realization ultimately de-light them or fails to do so.

Consequences of Poor Definition and Management

Most American managers have grossly underestimated the effects of a slow start. Yet because the front end uses few resources, managers often think that nothing is being lost because so little money is being spent. On the contrary, Smith and Reinertsen (1991) find that when they calculate the cost of front-end delays, the true costs are 500 to 5000 times higher than the apparent costs of the few people assigned to the project.

These true costs come from lost market opportunities. Getting to market first is far more important for profitability and sustainable advantage than is staying within development budget. If Company A is late by 18 months, competitor B, having been there all that time, can now cut its prices and still make money or, worse yet, bring out its second product and render Company A's obsolete. This is what happened to Apple Computer after it spent four years designing a portable computer. Weighing in at 17 pounds, the Mac Portable was immediately made ob-solete by the introduction of a 7-pound Compaq just weeks later. Even so, six months of "front-end" work went by before a laptop project and design concept were approved, another two months before all the product engineers were on board, and another nine months—after first prototype builds—before the project got the resource infusion to streamline the box to a quality level on which Apple people are willing to see their names. The result was the Powerbook.

The sources of front-end delays are numerous. Often no one has clear re-sponsibility at this phase or has so many other competing demands that this project slips. There is rarely any system or structure of control to prevent the slip-page. Ideas may have to feed into an annual planning process that does not look at new product ideas until a certain month of the year, and then funds it, if at all, for the next quarter, or, more likely, the next year.

Product Definition

The overall front-end process may be designated as product definition (or as con-cept development). Some of the major activities in this process are identifying cus-tomer requirements, establishing target specifications, generating product concepts, selecting a concept, refining specifications, building a business case, and planning the (full-scale) development project. As part of or prior to this process, ideas and experimental designs may be tested for market acceptance and evaluation, competitive products analyzed, and assessments made of technical and resource feasibility and capabilities. In addition, off-line activities in advanced engineering may have technologies ready to be commercialized, and exploratory studies from industrial design may be available to feed and inspire the concept creation process. At the end of this period (Gate 0), the concept is approved or not approved, and thus there is a go/no go decision about whether to go ahead into "full development."

Identifying Customer Requirements

Listening for the Voice of the Customer is now widely understood to be the true starting point for effective product development. We must not only listen deeply to current needs as described by articulate customers, but also anticipate and tap the latent, future needs that few customers even recognize, let alone are able to articulate. This evolution in customer focus is expressed in many ways, one of them in the continuously evolving meaning of quality described in Chapter 2. Conformance, or fitness to standard, means that the product meets its specifications, something that can be assessed through statistical process control. Fitness of use means that the product does what the customer wants it to, something that can be assessed through market research. Fitness to cost means delivering higher quality at lower cost, something that is achieved through tools of continuous process improvement. Fitness to latent requirements means developing products that meet current and future needs that people may not know they have. Ulrich and Eppinger (1995) describe a systematic approach to identifying these requirements. The methodology, called concept engineering, has five major phases: customer environment, customer requirements, operationalizing learning, concept generation, and concept selection.

However the Voice of the Customer is tapped, what is heard must be translated into customer needs or requirements. These requirements must be identified independently of any particular concept or product but within an envelope that limits the scope of the effort. Customer requirements explored and defined in relation to a mission statement focused around a key customer benefit help narrow down assumptions and target market options, business goals, and stakeholders. Data are gathered through interviews, focus groups, and observation of customers using existing products. Such needs are best interpreted in terms of "what the product has to do, not in terms of how it might do it," and are expressed as specifically as the raw data (Ulrich and Eppinger, 1995). These can be arranged in a logical hierarchy, and customers can be surveyed to establish the relative importance of these needs.

Setting Target Specifications

Whereas needs are expressed in the language of the customer, specifications translate these needs into clear, quantified statements about what the product has to do.

These specifications may be revised later in the process as more information about costs, constraints, and other factors, including concept choice, become known.

The process of turning requirements into specifications can be facilitated by the use of tools such as the QFD approach discussed in Chapter 10 (Hauser and Clausing, 1988). Such methodologies first identify critical customer requirements and often weight them for importance. The team then identifies the design factors that affect these requirements. The cells of the matrix are filled in through estimates of the direction and strength of the relationship between each requirement and each design factor. In some cases, this can be specified quite precisely, and in others, it will be a qualitative estimate. These relationships can then be benchmarked against competitive offerings. From this process, two target values may be set: an ideal target and one that makes the product marginally acceptable.

The translation of customer needs into product specifications is critical to achieving not merely a cluster of desired features, but rather a holistic experience of the product. Thus, some would advocate that the creation of a concept should precede, or be concurrent with, the definition of its target specifications. In this way, the overall concept acts as a guide to a set of specifications intended to achieve both internal and external product integrity. Alternatively, the same key people need to be involved in assessing needs and converting them to product specifications.

Creating Concepts

A product concept has been described as "an approximate description of the technology, working principles, and form of the product" (Ulrich and Eppinger, 1995). Another statement is that a product concept is "a product description that embodies the experiences the product will deliver to the customer." A product concept specifies how basic functions, structures, or messages associated with the total vehicle will attract and satisfy customers. When products are judged on the basis of a few, well-defined, objective criteria, a product concept may be defined by a general product category and a set of specifications: "Product X, our next-generation widget, will be a 500-horsepower machine with half the fuel consumption." When the product is complex and customers subjectively evaluate the total product experience, the product concept must project how the customer will experience the product as a whole; it must encompass the product's character, personality, and image (Clark and Fujimoto, 1991).

When there is a good match between customer expectations and what a product delivers, the product is said to have **external integrity.** A powerful, holistic product concept is essential in translating the desired experience into the design of the product. Not only does it facilitate the external match, but it also serves as the holistic point of reference against which tradeoffs and design details are assessed, and through which **internal integrity** or design coherence is achieved. This is why a strong manager who continually champions the concept and translates it into multiple languages is so important to the success of complex products (Clark and Fujimoto, 1991). It is because of the increasing importance of these subjective and holistic aspects of the product through which firms compete on product integrity that the core of the concept is increasingly likely to take the form of metaphor, or a story, a three-dimensional model or a sketch.

Rarely can an excellent product emerge from a poor concept, although good concepts can be poorly implemented. Because the holistic and subtle aspects of the concept are difficult or impossible to say in words, the ideal situation is one in which the same team of people that was active in identifying customer needs is also involved in setting target specifications and creating concepts. These three processes may overlap as well.

Concept creation is an iterative process that benefits from taking a systematic approach. Input to the process includes needs and specifications, and a wide scan of the external environment. External environment scanning is geared to finding what solutions already exist for the general problem-space, as well as for critical subproblems that the team has identified as central to its definition of the problem. External scanning may include patent searches, published literature, competitive benchmarking, and lead users. **Lead users** are people whose felt needs are substantially ahead of the market and who would benefit significantly from innovation in a given product area (von Hippel, 1988). In some cases, they have already created their own solutions. A number of approaches have been developed to facilitate the generation of concepts, and systematically classify and refine solutions to its subproblems.

Selecting and Refining a Concept

The selection of a final concept is a process of evaluating and narrowing the candidates with respect to several criteria. Some of the major criteria against which competing concepts should be assessed are: addressing major customer needs and priorities; matching or exceeding competitive offerings; reducing time to market; and meeting the process capabilities of the firm and its suppliers.

When specifications are later refined, they often face difficult tradeoffs. Such tradeoffs frequently occur between performance metrics, and between performance metrics and cost. Some of the methods recommended for resolving tradeoffs include the use of cost models and technical models, both analytical and physical.

◆ DESIGNING AND DEVELOPING THE PRODUCT

Product design and development encompasses three big chunks of activity: high-level design, detail product/process design, and prototype-test-refine. In this section, we discuss three key processes that must begin during the first stage: establishing the architecture, designing for manufacturability (DFM), and designing for usability. Because of the iterative nature of design-and-test, our discussion of the second two chunks is compressed into a single discussion. In the next section, we consider the overall organization of all of these design and development activities, particularly with regard to issues of time and the interdependence of tasks and information.

Architecture and Modularity

The architecture of the product is the physical structure of the product. How is it divided into chunks (i.e., physical clusters of components)? How do those chunks interact with each other physically and with the functionality of the product? Architecture then is the structure constituted by the relationships between function and chunking, and between chunks.

There are two overall approaches to architecture, modular and integral. A **modular approach** puts a limited number of functions in each chunk, and "the interactions between chunks are well defined and are generally fundamental to the primary functions of the product" (Ulrich and Eppinger, 1995). An **integral approach** incorporates one function into several chunks, while a single chunk incorporates several functions. The interactions between chunks are ill-defined and have little to do with the functions.

Advantages of Modularity

Best practice firms have shifted to a more modular approach for several reasons. Modularity makes it easier to change a product without having to redo much or all of the product. The product can be upgraded through a replacement module or added to (e.g., adding memory to a computer). Parts that wear out more quickly can be easily replaced. The product platform, such as a camera, can use interchangeable lenses.

Modular designs also have internal advantages. They mediate the desires of customers and marketing for product variety with the desire of manufacturing and retailers for simplicity; by incorporating variety into a limited number of modules. In this way, designers reduce manufacturing costs and inventory. Standard modules, particularly those that are part of the "works" not seen by the customer, provide similar benefits. Risky technologies can be concentrated in one or a few modules.

Conscious Architecture

The system architecture, especially for modular designs, needs to be thought through carefully at the outset of the project by the cross-functional team. Their architectural decisions establish a product platform that may become the basis of an entire family of products. Successive innovations to each model may each be concentrated in one or another module, thereby facilitating a continuing stream of product innovation at low incremental development and manufacturing cost. Interfaces must be robust (and where possible, standard) and defined early so that the detail design of modules can be developed within those parameters.

Frequently, however, the architecture of products becomes embedded in tacit knowledge rather than being consciously challenged and, when appropriate, re-organized. Rebecca Henderson (1988) has found that, when industries are characterized by a dominant design, architectural knowledge is stable and tends to become embedded in practices and procedures. Firms that fail to reexamine their architectures are vulnerable to two kinds of innovation, architectural and radical. Henderson defines **architectural innovation** as "innovations that change the way in which the components of a product are linked together, while leaving the core design concepts (and thus the basic knowledge underlying the components) untouched." **Radical innovation,** by contrast, "establishes a new dominant design and, hence, a new set of core design concepts embodied in components that are linked together in a new architecture."

Design for Manufacturability

Best practice design is conducted with reference to various targets that establish an envelope within which the team makes tradeoffs in its search for an optimal design solution. In some organizations, many of these target criteria may fall under the umbrella concept of "quality" and include: design for conformance, reliability, serviceability, and durability as well as environmental impact, and manufacturability (Garvin, 1987). In other cases, the umbrella concept is also referred to as **design for manufacturability (DFM).** We will use DFM here in this broad sense to encompass all of the target criteria and to illustrate what it means to design within certain parameters.

DFM must be an integral part of the high-level design process. It is an integrative methodology that requires the participation of cross-functional team members who bring their sketches, models, preliminary specifications, knowledge of costs, and knowledge of production and assembly processes and capabilities.

DFM has both physical and cost aspects. DFM means that designers conduct their work within various boundaries that take account of the capabilities of manufacturing processes, the ease with which a product can be assembled, and the properties of various materials. DFM also means that designers work with knowledge of relative costs of components and of assembly, and the impact of these on overhead, and attempt to minimize the overall cost of manufacturing the product. Physical and cost considerations interact because many choices that facilitate the manufacturing process may also reduce costs.

Designers, aided by their team members and on-line design rules, must be familiar enough with manufacturing alternatives, capabilities, and limitations so that they do not unknowingly make choices that are difficult, impossible, costly, and time-consuming to manufacture. They may design a surface or a radius that, although not essential to the functionality or integrity of the design, requires very expensive machining operations. Body panel stampings, for example, cannot fit high-speed presses unless their contour is shallow, and they do not have to be turned over during stamping. Engineers may design parts whose tolerances are too tight for manufacturing to achieve or that do not take account of the way that tolerances of several components "stack up" when fabricated parts are brought together.

Over the past decade, a number of design strategies or rules have been worked out that facilitate ease of manufacture. Some process choices reduce the number of process steps; near-net shape casting, for example, reduces the amount of subsequent machining. Many parts may be combined into one; this works especially well with molded or stamped parts. The IBM Proprinter, for example, integrated 14 parts into one plastic part, thereby requiring only one complex mold and eliminating the need for all of these parts to be assembled.

While in the first instance DFM connotes designing within existing manufacturing capabilities, over the long term, as designers and manufacturing people build their relationships, it means expanding the capabilities of manufacturing. The complex parts of the Proprinter, for example, pushed the envelope of then-current plastics technology. Getting the tools made and without extending the lead time was the result of many factors: early choice of tooling vendors, early freeze of the design, and incredibly close, face-to-face, relationships among tooling engineers, purchasing, and suppliers (March, 1991). In similar situations in which complex molds are required, the lead time could become so extended as to cancel the benefits of part simplification. Thus, the value of lead time must be factored into DFM decisions, and when it is, the tradeoffs can change. By using a cost model to project the lifetime cost of alternative designs for fasteners in a high-volume product, Karl Ulrich et al. (1991) found that the snap-fit DFM option looked very good compared to the screw option until time was factored in. Because the mold for complex parts was on the critical path, the additional lead time of waiting for the molds overwhelmingly canceled out the strictly manufacturing considerations.

Design for Assembly

In its narrowest sense, "manufacturability" refers to the fabrication of components, and at its broadest, to the entire set of criteria that should guide design. Because of the ambiguity of usage and referent, some experts feel it is important to use a term, such as **design for assembly,** that explicitly denotes the integrated level of manufacturing. Two groups of practitioner/researchers have pioneered methodologies focusing on the assembly of products: Geoffrey Boothroyd and Peter Dewhurst of the University of Rhode Island, and Daniel Whitney and James Nevins from MIT. Design for assembly considers not only fabrication, but also the assembly process, including equipment, people, and their interaction. It asks questions such as: How do we design this to go together easily and quickly? How do we make it easy for the operator?

Some of the broad guidelines suggested by Boothroyd and Dewhurst (1989,1994) include: z-axis assembly, in which parts are assembled by adding them from the top, and the product never has to be turned over; parts that are self-aligning, require no tools, are secured immediately upon insertion, and do not need to be oriented. Whether for automated or hand assembly, fasteners (screws, pulleys, springs, cotter-pins, etc.) are avoided as much as possible. Nevins and Whitney (1989) advocate not only designing around final assembly, but also designing sub-assemblies as modules having testable functions. In that way, design, quality control, and assembly are integrated. Some of the issues that come into play here are access to fasteners and lubrication points, access to certain points or surfaces for testing, location points by which to hold components or subassemblies accurately, common subassemblies for multiple models, and reducing the number of times the part or subassembly must be turned over during assembly.

Design to Cost

The cost of manufacturing products is a combination of the costs of components, assembly, and overhead. **Design to cost (DTC)** must consider all of these because simply focusing on reducing the cost of certain components could shift the costs into assembly or the transactions that support the production process. The cost of components and of assembly may be reduced through some of the same strategies and rules that facilitate ease of fabrication and assembly. Overhead, which is the primary cause of spiraling manufacturing costs, is driven by transactions (such as ordering) and complexity. It is constituted by such things as the number of setups, setup hours, and materials-handling movements. Effective DTC requires the use of activity-based costing in order to have an accurate picture of the overhead generated by producing each product.

Design for Usability

High-level design requires paying attention not only to architecture, DFM, and DTC, but also to the usability of the product. **Design for usability,** or user-centered design, is an approach to design that puts user needs high—if not at the top—on the list of design priorities. Usability focuses on how the user will relate to the product physically and on making it easy, even fun, to interact with the product, no matter how complex.

The focus on usability comes from two sources: industrial designers, who have long taken usability as their primary charter, and TQM advocates, whose focus on the customer leads to a broad range of quality issues that can be grouped under usability. Industrial design's involvement, and especially its early involvement at the concept development stage, is especially important for products whose interaction with the user is important. Some of these considerations are the following: How important is ease of use? Ease of maintenance? How many user interactions does the product require? How novel are some of these interactions? Are their important safety issues?

Quality expert Joseph Juran was an early proponent of the idea that quality means "fitness for use" (1974, 1980). This concept of usability has many dimensions, including reliability, maintainability, availability, and producibility, as well as the product's functional performance. Juran designed comprehensive programs to help designers adopt this approach. His reliability program includes setting reliability goals, stress analysis, identification of critical parts, setting tolerances for interacting dimensions, failure mode and effect analysis, design reviews, vendor selection, control of reliability during manufacturing, and reliability testing.

Industrial designers come to usability from a different perspective (Wiklund, 1994). Although many managers still believe that industrial design (ID) is concerned primarily with the aesthetics of a product (how it looks, feels, sounds), designers themselves take a broader view. Their focus is not only on aesthetics, but also on the user's physical interaction with the product, and on making it as easy, intuitive, simple, and comfortable as possible. They incorporate knowledge from traditional quantified ergonomics (spacing, angles, positions, placements of product elements in relation to each other and to the user), as well as more sophisticated, qualitative understandings of the cognitive and emotional aspects of the user's interactions with the product. That is, will a person feel confident or frustrated when using this product? Their design skills are employed in the service both of making the product easy to use and of communicating intuitively what the user should do to maintain, repair, or use the product. Through their human factors expertise and design skills, usability professionals and industrial designers are addressing some of the holistic aspects of the product that cannot be put in words, but are integral to the customer's experience of the whole product (March, 1994).

Prototype-Test-and-Refine

Prototypes are analytical or physical models of some or all aspects of a product that are used to test or verify aspects of the product or process design. Models also allow people to "fail forward," by learning what they still don't know, or what they assumed when they should not have (Leonard-Barton, 1991). Comprehensive physical prototypes reveal interferences among components and whether everything works when connected. Prototypes range from quick foam models to explore the form of the product to fully functioning models made from parts fabricated by the production tooling.

Japanese firms generally rely on detail design and prototypes to a far greater extent than do U.S. firms. One consequence of this difference is that the U.S. designers have to go through more design iterations. This is because there are more engineering changes, and that, in turn, points back to the poor quality of design information (Blackburn, 1991). One of the major strategies for improving the quality and speed of information, and thus the quality and speed of development, is overlapping the phases of development and using concurrent engineering.

It is not uncommon that an overseas firm can develop a prototype in half the time at half the cost. Part of the American problem in developing new products is linked to weaknesses in American manufacturing, specifically of the tool and die, injection molding and other equipment suppliers. Die shops are organized like a job shop—that is, around a particular process. A die moves around hap-

hazardly, depending on its processing requirements rather than on the customer for whom it is intended. Each work center completes a series of tasks before transporting it to the next work center. Yet die-making is a critical path item in any new development project.

Clark and Fujimoto (1991) conceive of development as cycles of problem solving, "problems" being the gaps between current designs and customer requirements. Each of these cycles consists of three phases. "*Design*" frames the problem and generates several design alternatives to close the gap and explore ways in which to do so. For example, a problem with noise in a film rewind system could be framed in terms of reducing noise below a certain level, or of being able to create the right kind of sound; the design parameters affecting noise could be many, including the type of material, tooth profile, or gear width. During the "*build*" phase, several working models are built and subsequently "*tested*" (Wheelwright and Clark, 1992). The information connecting design and customer requirements become the basis for a new cycle.

◆ CONCURRENT ENGINEERING

One of the most effective strategies designed to shorten product development cycle times and to end up with more robust and manufacturable designs is to overlap the various phases of the design and development process. Called **concurrent engineering,** this strategy can be very powerful. Implementing it is far from trivial, however.

In traditional sequential or phased development, the work of one phase is completed before the next phase begins. **Sequential development,** which has been normative in the United States until the past few years, is marked by a series of handoffs in which work, information, and responsibility are transferred, usually all at once, in a process often referred to as "throwing it over the wall." In this sequential model, downstream groups such as manufacturing generally have limited information about how and why upstream groups such as engineering made the choices resulting in the drawings and specifications they have received and are expected to live with; their job has often simply been to make it work.

Concurrent or overlapping development means that downstream work is begun before the prior phase of work has been completed, and the engineering of interrelated tasks is marked by frequent communication. For example, product engineering begins before designs are complete, dies are cut before engineering drawings are final, and significant commitments are made to tooling and equipment before the product is completely defined. Overlapping is sometimes used interchangeably with concurrent engineering or simultaneous engineering.

Best practice firms have shifted toward concurrent development for two major reasons. First, they absolutely must compress the overall development cycle, and there is no choice but to overlap internal phases and tasks. Second, they recognize that they need to get input from all the relevant groups much earlier in the development process. Design problems, including excessive iterations, are rarely due to sloppy, poor work, but rather are often due to work done in isolation, with incomplete information, and to misunderstanding among people.

Design Iterations

As we have seen, design is an inherently iterative process that leads to revisions because new information is created by other tasks. Iteration leads to improved quality because it better meets customer and manufacturing requirements. But the quality of the design process itself can be measured by the amount of rework and redesign it requires—that is, the number of design cycles. Improving the quality of the design process means reducing the number of cycles and their overall length of time.

The difficulty in reducing development cycles is that many tasks are dependent or interdependent. The design of tooling dies and molds is dependent on the design of the part that it will fabricate; the input for die design is the output of part drawings. Traditionally, therefore, drawings were not released to tooling until the detail part design was final. Yet it normally takes many months before tools and dies are available. When tooling waits for final design drawings, the overall cycle is long. Interdependent tasks are exemplified by the design of an electromechanical instrument cluster: the casing design, optical layout, and wiring plan. The input for any of these tasks depends on output from the others. Such interdependent or coupled design tasks lead to multiple design iterations—that is, cycles of design-prototype build-test-and-refine.

Thus, to reduce the overall product development cycle, engineering concurrency is needed for both types of tasks. Dependent tasks—especially those long lead-time critical path activities such as tooling—must begin well before the output from the upstream task is final—that is, the tasks must overlap in time. This makes the upstream and downstream work more interdependent, and it requires far more communication than in sequential development. For interdependent tasks, ways must be found to improve the quality of the design process (i.e., reduce the number of design cycle iterations), which in turn reduces development time and improves the quality of the final design. The key to improving design quality is the real-time sharing of information through concurrent engineering.

Design Structure Matrix

Small projects of five to ten people can easily find their task and informational interdependencies, and are often very successful working together concurrently. Projects that have hundreds or even thousands of engineers have a more difficult time. They must be decomposed into many small projects and organized as a network of teams. Steven Eppinger and Dan Whitney (1993), working with MIT's Leaders for Manufacturing Program and with outside colleagues, have developed a process that allows large, complex projects to organize themselves so as to achieve the benefits of small teams.

They use a "design structure matrix" to find the informational and technical interdependencies among all the tasks. The most straightforward use of the matrix is to establish the small projects of people whose work, being tightly interdependent, ought to be concurrent and perhaps co-located. Other interventions in the sequencing and decoupling of tasks can reduce iterations and time.

Implementing Concurrent Engineering

To be successful, concurrency requires that information as well as activities be overlapped. When sharing information effectively, the upstream group gradually releases preliminary information that provides the downstream groups with clues about how their thinking and the product are evolving rather than dumping their drawings at the end. If overlapping is also combined with cross-functional teams, early manufacturing involvement, or a design for manufacturability approach, then information flows upstream and across as well downstream.

As powerful as concurrent engineering may be in reducing the development cycle time and creating more desirable products, its successful implementation is far from trivial. As Smith and Reinertsen (1991) indicate, concurrent engineering often requires the creation of new skills and attitudes in the organization, such as the ability to process partial information, the ability and willingness to communicate frequently, and a willingness to trust and respect members of the other functional areas engaged in the development effort. These skills and attitudes need to be developed and nurtured consciously in most organizations.

◆ Summary

The quality of new products and services needs to be "designed in," as opposed to later being "built in" during the manufacturing or delivery stages. The chapter reviews several development practices that have enabled leading-edge companies not only to create high-quality products but also to do so much faster and with fewer resources than competitors. Effective management of the development process is imperative because the bulk of a new product's life-cycle costs is usually frozen very early in the design process.

Effective management of the development process begins by recognizing that a typical development process consists of a fairly predictable set of stages that can be successfully managed by instituting a series of gates and reviews. Staffing overloads, a frequent cause of project delays and quality compromises, can be avoided by keeping track of all ongoing development projects in what is called an aggregate project plan. A variety of team-based organizational structures (coordinated, empowered, and skunkworks) are available to remedy the lack of cross-functional integration common in functionally structured companies. The appropriate choice of team-based structures depends on the nature of the product being developed.

Accurately sensing true customer requirements and faithfully translating them into product specifications are critical in developing products that are fit for use. Again, several stages are involved in this effort: product definition, concept creation, concept selection, specification development, and refinement. The actual design of the product is greatly facilitated by the creation of modular product architectures that allow the design of subsystems to proceed more or less simultaneously. Moreover, observing the rules of design for manufacturability early in the design cycle and extensive use of model building and prototyping ensure a good fit between manufacturing capabilities and design specifications of the product. Concurrent engineering is another effective tactic for shortening the development cycle and promoting cross-functional integration, although its effective implementation requires the creation of several new skills and attitudes in the organization.

◆   Key Terms

Gates	Lead users	Design to cost (DTC)
Gate Zero	Modular approach	Design for usability
Aggregate project plan	Integral approach	Concurrent engineering
Heavyweight project	Architectural innovation	Sequential development
manager (HWPM)	Radical innovation	
Skunkworks	Design for manufactura-	
External integrity	bility	
Internal integrity	Design for assembly	

◆   Assignments

1. What are the key measures of performance in new product development? To what extent do you need to trade these performance dimensions off against one another?

2. List a few initiatives or tactics that the manager of a new product development project could undertake to simultaneously improve the quality of the new product and reduce the development cycle time.

3. What are the critical phases of a new product development project? When should critical reviews be held?

4. What is an aggregate project plan? Why is it important for an organization to develop one?

5. What forces cause an organization to overcommit itself to too many new product development initiatives? What are the consequences of such over-commitment?

6. What factors contribute to the generally loose or "fuzzy" conditions during the early stages of new product development efforts? What can be done to tighten up the front end? What are the risks in tightening up too far?

7. Describe the circumstances under which the use of a "heavyweight" project manager is most appropriate.

8. The potential of concurrent engineering in reducing the development cycle time is fairly evident. What are the key reasons why concurrent engineering may also enhance the quality of the final product?

9. Despite its great potential, concurrent engineering is difficult to implement. What are some of the key organizational impediments to the successful implementation of concurrent engineering?

10. Describe the type of hamburger you would make if you were at home and the process you would use. What is the cost of making the hamburger? Suggest changes that could reduce costs. Compare this to the hamburger produced by McDonalds or Burger King. How do their product specifications differ? Do these changes make the product easier to manufacture?

Case Study

Plus Development Corporation (A)—Condensed

The Hardcard®, a miniaturized 10-megabyte hard disk drive that plugged into a slot of an IBM PC, promised to be unlike any other product currently on the market. Getting to market on schedule, however, without compromising the quality or design of the product, presented a growing challenge to the engineering teams of Plus Development and its manufacturing counterpart, Japan Electro-Mechanical Corporation (JEMCO). By late September 1984, with product development underway for nearly six months, the schedule was gradually slipping as the teams adjusted to each other's work style and design philosophies. Something would have to change to meet Hardcard's June 1985 target date.

Background

The inspiration for Hardcard came from customer conversations about what the ultimate low-cost disk drive subsystem would look like: a single unit integrating the disk drive, the disk electronics, and the controller (currently separate components) directly attached to a computer motherboard. See Exhibit 13.1 for a brief description of hard disc drives. James Patterson, president of Quantum Corporation, a maker of hard disks for the minicomputer and workstation markets, was intrigued by the concept but wary of its technical and marketing challenges. The various components and electronics were currently too large to create a single unit to fit inside a

| Exhibit 13.1 | How Disk Drives Work |

A mass storage system, commonly called a disk drive, is comprised of three major elements: the disk drive, the electronic controller, and the disk, also referred to as the "media," where data are stored through the use of magnetics. Small-capacity systems use either hard disk drives with fixed or rigid media—a metal platter with magnetic-sensitive coating—or "floppy" drives made of a plastic or mylar platter. The disk drive has several subcomponents, including a magnetic head, an actuator, an optical encoder, and a servo arm. An electrical current running through the electromagnetic head, positioned over the spinning disk, orients or reads the magnetic direction of the particles on the media to "write" or to "read" data onto or from the media. The actuator controls the speed at which the head can read or write, and the servo arm positions the head over the disk. The optical encoder converts the digital signals received from the computer through the electronic controller into analog signals that direct the servo arm and head. The electronic controller, mounted on a printed circuit board, functions as an intelligent interface between the head disk assembly and the computer, interpreting signals, responding to "seek" commands, and transmitting data between the disk drive and the computer.

Plus Development Corporation (A)—Condensed (Continued)

PC, and there were no clear standards or direction from the market indicating what degree of size reduction would be right. Those concerns diminished in the early 1980s as the market success of the IBM PC created de facto industry standards and drove volume demand for standardized components whose technology was rapidly advancing. While examining the guts of an IBM PC in late 1983, Joel Harrison, Quantum's manager of new product development, suddenly recognized the feasibility of having the controller and the drive on a single plug-in card.

In November 1983, Harrison and three other Quantum executives, Dave Brown, Dale Hiatt, and Stephen Berkley, started Plus Development Corporation, 80 percent owned by Quantum, to develop Hardcard, the most promising design option for an integrated hard-disk-on-a-card. The product would reduce hard disk installation time from hours to minutes and would enable any PC to be easily converted to PC XT capability. Although the largest customers for hard

disk drives in late 1983 were microcomputer manufacturers (Original Equipment Manufacturers, or OEMs) such as IBM, Apple, and Hewlett-Packard, the retail market for add-on hard drives was beginning to develop. Plus hoped to target this retail channel through stores such as Computerland and Businessland and to reach the large number of potential customers eager to expand the memory storage capacity of their personal computers. See Exhibit 13.2 for the installed base of IBM PCs and rigid disks.

Manufacturing Challenges

Believing that the maturing computer industry would be susceptible to domination by Japanese manufacturers, as had watches and calculators in the 1970s, the four Plus managers traveled to Japan to source components and to get a better understanding of the current state of the industry. They found conditions that both encouraged and concerned them. Fearing saturation in the

Exhibit 13.2

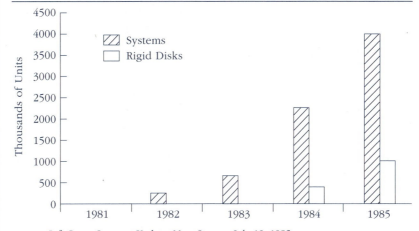

IBM PCs and Compatible Systems and Rigid Disks Installed in the U.S.

SOURCE: InfoCorp, *Segment Update: Mass Storage,* July 12, 1985

Plus Development Corporation (A)—Condensed (Continued)

video market, especially with the advent of large Korean competitors, Japanese electronics companies, such as Sony and JVC, were eager to pursue opportunities in computers. With money to invest and employment to sustain, they were all "damned interested to talk to us." The Plus managers also discovered, however, that electronics components manufacturers, such as NEC and Toshiba, were seeking to forward integrate into computer products, an assault into new territory that threatened to significantly change the competitive landscape for companies like Plus. The tour convinced the Plus team that competing directly against Japanese manufacturing prowess would be extremely difficult.

The Plus managers concluded that an alliance with a Japanese company would be the best way to achieve the high quality and the rapid ramp-up to volume production (5,000–10,000 units per month) that the Hardcard, as a retail product, would require. The logic of a partnership overcame worries about being unpatriotic to American manufacturers and concerns about the resources necessary to manage the venture and deal with pressures related to cultural differences. Toward the end of the tour, the Plus team met with the senior management of JEMCO, the manufacturing arm of the Japan Trading Corporation and the company considered to be the premier electromechanical manufacturer in Japan. A tour of a JEMCO facility, where video machines rolled off the line every few seconds, left the Americans in awe: "You feel insignificant. Their manufacturing expertise is beyond imagination." In addition to the benefits of gaining access to that expertise, Plus managers also felt confident about their ability to work with JEMCO,

whose teamwork and communication style aligned well with Plus values. For JEMCO the partnership would broaden both its sources and range of products. Shortly after returning to the United States and reviewing its options and concerns, Plus made the decision to proceed with the alliance; Plus would supply design and marketing, and JEMCO would provide the manufacturing expertise.

Product Design Philosophy and Technical Choices

With Joel Harrison as the project manager, development of the Hardcard began in earnest in January 1984 and proceeded throughout the time that Harrison and the other three Plus managers were in Japan. The Hardcard was Harrison's fifth hard disk drive development project, and he well understood the design adjustments and challenges involved in miniaturizing a drive to 3.5 inches. He also understood the implications of producing a product for the retail market within a strict time schedule. Plus wanted to introduce the Hardcard for Christmas 1985 to take advantage of holiday consumer sales and year-end corporate purchases, as well as to contribute to Quantum's calendar-year performance. See Exhibit 13.3 for the initial engineering schedule. In contrast to the iterative process of working with OEM customers to incorporate feedback on problems, fix initial bugs, and finalize products, Plus needed to have the Hardcard defect-free for the retail market, which would be unforgiving of a product that failed to meet expectations. Thus, the focus was kept simple: "Convert a PC into an XT on a single board"—a clear target against which to judge design options and proposals.

In addition to the simple focus, the Hardcard project was to involve only proven

Plus Development Corporation (A)—Condensed (Continued)

Exhibit 13.3	Plus Engineering Schedule—April 1984
5/30/84:	Select key technologies
6/30/84:	Breadboard of product operational
9/30/84:	3-board prototypes operational
12/30/84:	Design verification testing (DVT) complete
2/28/85:	Single-board VLSI prototype operational
3/ /85:	Design transferred to factory for production
4/30/85:	Design maturity testing complete
6/ /85:	Production begins

technologies and processes, with a limit of five new items. This approach, dubbed "focused innovation" by Harrison, allowed technological challenge but avoided chaos. The Hardcard was to have the maximum five items: (1) thin motor; (2) new integrated VLSI circuits; (3) controller function on the drive; (4) integrated microprocessors; and (5) new encoding/decoding scheme. Work on the prototypes evolved *from* January's first "show-and-tell" mockup—a block of aluminum with a disk that didn't spin—*to* metal mechanicals and electronics and then *to* working parts and custom-designed chips. The development team selected metal oxide over thin film technology for the media in order to minimize the risks in using a promising but unproven technology.

Manufacturability and Process Philosophy

With a market introduction date of June 1985, JEMCO engineers began work at Plus in April 1984, joining the 20 engineers who were already on the project. The development team typically put in 12-hour days, to which the Japanese added three hours of English classes every night. None of the Plus engineers spoke Japanese, and a translator was present virtually every day. In addition to the JEMCO team at Plus, a Japan-based JEMCO group, with phone veto power, supported the development effort. JEMCO was especially influential regarding the manufacturability of the mechanical HDA subassembly; they had less experience in digital design and thus less say over the digital/electronic controller board subassembly.

The Plus engineers and their Japanese counterparts approached their tasks with very different styles. JEMCO engineers preferred working with prototypes rather than discussing manufacturability issues in abstract terms. The Plus engineers, though initially inclined more to talk through issues, increased their use of prototypes when they saw how quickly the JEMCO team could turn them around and how well the use of prototypes facilitated communication. Details and design problems could be shown and seen rather than just described. The Plus engineers also had problems understanding and adapting to JEMCO's approach to achieving a target production yield goal of 99 percent through up-front attention to specification details. The JEMCO engineers wanted to have specifications for everything—exactly how high, thick, and wide a piece would be. To JEMCO "less than 10mm" was not an acceptable specification. Before starting production, they wanted

Plus Development Corporation (A)—Condensed (Continued)

to know for sure that the product could be made easily. The Plus engineers were used to the typical U.S. approach: do a design, make some mistakes and learn for the next time. They initially viewed the first three months of nearly nonstop design meetings as a waste of time but gradually began to respect the JEMCO approach.

Frequently, JEMCO engineers called for design changes to enhance manufacturability in order to gain even minute production cost savings, even at the risk of lengthening the design process. The repositioning of an actuator latch saved one penny per unit. The encoder underwent a three-month redesign to increase the LED gap from 2/1000 to 10/1000 of an inch in order to reduce the strict tolerance required for volume production. Engineers spent two months reconfiguring a metal plate guard to eliminate the use of screws or glue.

Believing that the design of product parts and the design of the production equipment were inextricable, JEMCO designed the Hardcard production process while Plus designed the product. Plus engineers assumed that JEMCO would automate Hardcard production and therefore would require simple parts, but JEMCO did not equate automation with simplicity. Automation was not to improve quality but to increase volume. What mattered was not the simplicity of the part but its capacity to be made simply and to meet specification, even if a complicated tool were required. JEMCO's philosophy also called for testing at every step of the production process to identify problems early so that "quality and the yield on the line is the quality in the field." Typical U.S. operations performed testing after a number of components had been assembled. Bill Moon summed up the essence of JEMCO's manufacturing excellence: "One: prove the dimensions and toler-

ances up-front. Two: create elaborate assembly tools. Three: check at every step of the process." The implications of this approach were important not only for product development but also for vendor relations.

Vendor Management and the Single-Source Philosophy

Plus managers were committed to the ideal of Plus as a small, entrepreneurial company that added value in its own areas of expertise-design and marketing and relied on strategic relationships with vendors for expertise in other areas. U.S. suppliers were selected by a Plus team according to the following criteria: (1) trust, (2) quality/monitoring, (3) process philosophy, (4) delivery, (5) aggressive pricing, and (6) use of technology. The team visited and evaluated U.S. suppliers of both critical and noncritical components but relied on JEMCO's recommendations and existing relationships for Japanese suppliers. Plus wanted stable companies with mature processes using proven technologies. Although it was averse to *sole* sourcing exclusive technologies, Plus did prefer to select a *single* source for all critical components and then to develop a strong partnership that recognized the vendor's business needs and processes. Managers tried to learn those processes inside and out in order to help devise mutually acceptable improvements.

Plus started by giving all potential vendors a budget that specified a target price that was 20 to 30 percent below street price. They promised to single source the component and to work with the vendor on process modifications or component redesign, with the ultimate goals of hitting budget prices while ensuring vendor profitability. To help achieve these objectives, Plus designed Hardcard to take a "wide distribution" of components, ef-

Plus Development Corporation (A)—Condensed (Continued)

fectively increasing a vendor's yield and thus enabling lower prices. For the Hardcard, Plus "visited vendors of vendors, three levels down" and conducted up-front feasibility tests of all potential "show stoppers."

Market Introduction: Push Ahead or Reschedule?

By September 1984 Hardcard development was progressing slowly; some milestones had been missed (see Exhibit 13.4 for extracts of engineering status reports), and there was much to be done to meet the June 1985 target introduction date. At a meeting of key managers, Harrison identified two options: schedule a later date or push ahead and do a mop-up job once the product was in the market. "We're

falling behind. Making June is getting if-ier by the day, but if we cut some corners maybe we could still do it. I've looked at every way to re-sequence, regroup, and double up—even sounding out JEMCO on steps they might compress—and it's just not possible without skipping some things and cutting a few corners."

"Yeah, well you know why we're behind, Joel," Bill Moon responded. "My guys have been in constant meetings with the JEMCO folks, and I don't need to tell you how many redesigns we've done for them. The amount of detail they want is driving us crazy."

"Isn't some of that detail important to getting this thing manufactured right?" Dale Hiatt countered. "That's why we signed them up, isn't it?"

Exhibit 13.4	Plus Engineering Status Reports

Schedule Status
— The Hardcard Project is on schedule for June '85 production.
— The following milestones are behind schedule or have been rescheduled:
  1. Mechanical Engineering Architecture based upon JEMCO input (was 7/13, now due 7/20). This is on the critical path for mechanical engineering of Hardcard. The 7/20 date just keeps the prototypes on schedule.
  2. Start Test Development has been rescheduled awaiting the hiring of our first test engineer (was 7/16 now 8/15).
  3. The Hardcard Specification requirements are not well defined. This issue must be resolved before the specification can be finished.
  Source: 7/16/84 Plus Report

Recruiting/Staffing
— Recruiting needs focus!
— New Employees: new Mechanical Engineer and Digital Engineer start 8/20 and 8/1.
— Seven Present Openings: Digital Engineer, Mechanical Engineer, Diagnostic Programmer, Computer Scientist, Engineering Technicians (2) and Test Engineer

Plus Development Corporation (A)—Condensed (Continued)

Exhibit 13.4	Plus Engineering Status Reports

Schedule Status
— The Hardcard Project is on schedule for June '85 production. *VLSI and Firmware/software are the present critical paths.*
— The following milestones are behind schedule or have been rescheduled based upon the Engineering/Manufacturing Master Schedule:
  1. Start Test Development (was 7/16 now due 8/1). The first test equipment meeting with JEMCO will be held 8/1.
  2. The Hardcard Specification requirements are not well defined. This issue must be resolved before the specification can be finished.
  3. Software testing plans have not begun. Action will begin when our Quality/Reliability engineer starts.
  Source: 7/30/84 Plus Report

Recruiting/Staffing
— New Manager of Software Development began this week.
— Present Openings: Nine openings with one offer extended for Analog Technician and one other candidate. Offer made for Digital Engineer was turned down; priority of this position is reduced, however. Positions open are: Software Technician, Mechanical Engineer, Diagnostic Programmer, Test Engineers (3), Engineering Technicians (2), Digital Engineer.

Schedule Status
— The DVT Plan is behind schedule. Recovery status by Friday.
— Mechanical Engineering parts for 100 prototype units may be late due to un-planned design iterations. Exact ME parts status will be available by Friday.
— Product Design specifications are late.
— There are technical problems with Start Stop Testing; the testing conditions are not under control; the media had problems which may be due to the lubricant thickness.
  Source: 8/29/84 Plus Report

Discussion continued with strong arguments on both sides, focusing on the value of hitting the Christmas market, the importance of maintaining an image of quality and reliability, the number of staffing vacancies, and JEMCO's requirements. "Okay, what's it going to be?" Dave Brown, Plus president, asked after everyone had had their say.

CASE QUESTIONS

1. What are the key differences between how Plus and JEMCO approach product and process development? Which development approach is likely to result in higher quality products? Why?

Plus Development Corporation (A)—Condensed (Continued)

2. How far behind schedule do you believe the Hardcard development project really is? What are the reasons for the apparent schedule slippage?
3. What options does Plus have regarding the introduction of Hardcard? Which one would you recommend? Why?

This case was adapted by Sam Perkins, under the direction of Professor Farshad Rafii, from the HBS case "Plus Development Corporation (A)," written by Dr. Nan S. Langowitz, under the supervision of Professor Steven C. Wheelwright. The case is intended as the basis for class discussion rather than to illustrate either effective or ineffective handling of an administrative situation. Some of the names and numbers provided herein have been disguised.

◆ Bibliography

Allen, T. *Managing the Flow of Technology*. Cambridge, Mass.: MIT Press, 1977.

Blackburn, J. "New Product Development: The New Time Wars." *Time-Based Competition*. Homewood, Ill.: Richard D. Irwin, 1991.

Boothroyd, G., and P. Dewhurst. *Product Design for Assembly*. Wakefield, R.I.: Boothroyd Dewhurst, 1989.

Boothroyd, G., P. Dewhurst, and W. Knight. *Product Design for Manufacturing*. New York: Marcel Dekker, 1994.

Clark, K. C., and T. Fujimoto. *Product Development Performance: Strategy, Organization, and Management in the World Auto Industry,* Boston: Harvard Business School Press, 1991.

Eppinger, S. D., D. E. Whitney, R. P. Smith, and D. A. Gebala. "A Model-based Method for Organizing Tasks in Product Development." MIT Working Paper 3569-93-MS, Rev. November 1993.

Fujimoto, T. "Organizations for Effective Product Development—the Case of the Global Automobile Industry." D.B.A. diss., Harvard Business School, 1989.

Garvin, D. "Competing on Eight Dimensions of Quality." *Harvard Business Review* (November–December 1987): 101–110.

Hauser, J., and D. Clausing. "The House of Quality." *Harvard Business Review*. 66, No. 3 (1988): 63–73.

Henderson, R. M. "The Failure of Established Firms in the Face of Technical Change: A Study of Photolithographic Alignment Equipment." Ph.D. diss., Harvard University, 1988.

Juran, J. *Quality Control Handbook*. New York: McGraw-Hill, 1974.

Juran, J., and F. Gryna, Jr. *Quality Planning and Analysis*. New York: McGraw-Hill, 1980.

Leonard-Barton, D. "Inanimate Integrators: A Block of Wood Speaks." *Design Management Journal* 2, No. 3 (Summer 1991): 61–67.

March, A. "Meeting Time and Cost Targets: The IBM Proprinter." *Target* 7, No. 3, (1991): 18–24.

March, A. "Usability: The New Dimension in Product Design." *Harvard Business Review* (September–October 1994): 144–152.

Nevins, J., and D. Whitney. *Concurrent Design of Products and Processes.* New York: McGraw-Hill, 1989.

Rosenthal, S. R. *Effective Product Design.* Homewood, Ill., Richard Irwin, 1992.

Smith, Preston G., and Donald G. Reinertsen. *Developing Products in Half the Time.* New York: Van Nostrand Reinhold, 1991.

Ulrich, K. T., and S. D. Eppinger. *Product Design and Development.* New York: McGraw-Hill, 1995.

Ulrich, K., et al. "A Framework for Including the Value of Time in Design-for-Manufacturing Decision Making." MIT Working Paper #3243-9-MSA, February 1991.

von Hippel, Eric. *The Sources of Innovation.* New York: Oxford University Press, 1988.

Wheelwright, S. C., and K. C. Clark. *Revolutionizing Product Development.* New York: Free Press, 1992.

Wiklund, M. *Usability in Practice.* Cambridge, Mass: Academic Press, 1994.

Woodruff, David, et al. "A Smarter Way to Manufacture." *Business Week,* April 30, 1990.

Reengineering and TQM: The Role of Information Technology

❖ ❖ ❖

*M*utual Benefit Life Insurance is the eighteenth largest life insurer in the United States. In 1988 it commonly delivered life insurance policies weeks, and sometimes months, after the order was placed. Three years later, life insurance policies were frequently in the mail a few hours after the order arrived. At the same time volume was up 20 percent, and the staff required to perform the work had declined from 225 to 100.

*A*nalog Devices Inc. is a manufacturer of integrated circuits and systems for collecting physical data and converting it to digital data. Its customers are makers of disc drives, aircraft sensors, medical instruments, and consumer electronics. In 1987 the company introduced a Corporate Scorecard that gave financial results as well as results of the Quality Improvement Process. The results were compared to the performance targets and used in annual performance reviews.

*W*hat these two companies have in common is a heavy reliance on information technology (IT). Mutual Benefit used IT to change its processing practices. It achieved dramatic results by redesigning an antiquated process and by drawing on the strengths of existing technology to support the new design. Analog used IT to collect data and display the data to executives as operational measures that they could act to improve and that they knew supported the corporation's goals. These are two ways IT is supporting TQM. The Mutual Benefit approach is popularly known as reengineering. Analog used IT to create an information structure that supported its vertical deployment of TQM. These two examples illustrate that IT can be used effectively to initiate TQM in improving external processes as well as internal infrastructures.

◆ IT AND PROCESS IMPROVEMENT

In 1990 Michael Hammer wrote a seminal article in the *Harvard Business Review* defining the concept of reengineering as "[using] the power of modern information technology to radically redesign our business processes in order to achieve dramatic improvements in their performance."

As the concept of reengineering caught on, two points of confusion surfaced:

1. TQM also advocated continual process improvement as a fundamental precept. In what way was reengineering different?
2. For years companies have invested heavily in IT; why was investing in reengineering considered something new?

Differences Between TQM and Reengineering

Reengineering and TQM differ only in the way some companies have chosen to interpret TQM. When TQM experts talk of continual improvement, they mean incremental improvement and breakthrough improvements (see Chapter 2). However, in practice, companies tend to focus on the incremental improvement. There are some significant differences between reengineering and incremental improvement:

- Reengineering seeks to change a broader span of the process. When a company decides to improve its warehouse operations, the incrementalists' approach is to involve the employees and to generate suggestions for improving elements such as the layout, the picking process, and the loading of trucks. Reengineering would question why the warehouse operation is needed by examining the entire order-filling process.
- Reengineering assumes that the process being reviewed is poorly designed, if indeed it had ever been designed. Incrementalists assume that the process is basically sound and can be improved by relying on employee suggestions.
- Reengineering tends to be riskier. By wiping out the old process and replacing it with a new one, the company's fortunes can ride on the success of the new system. Greyhound (Tomsho, 1994) tried to reengineer its ticket processing system. The new system never worked effectively reducing ridership and operating revenues by more than 12 percent, which caused stock prices to plummet from $22.75 to almost $2 per share in just five months.
- With reengineering the role of IT is fundamental; with TQM, it is secondary. Hammer (1990) argued that many of the processes existing in companies today were created before the appearance of information technology. When IT was used, companies used it to automate existing processes, thus "paving the cow-paths." This approach did not make full use of IT's capabilities. In order to achieve quantum improvements of performance, the old process design should be thrown away and a new one designed that exploits IT. TQM also pushes for quantum improvements but does not require the process change

to be IT-based. An example is when a company focuses on reducing manufacturing throughput time. Just-In-Time systems have been very effective in achieving dramatic improvements, but IT is not a necessary ingredient.

• Reengineering is performed infrequently. Hammer does not encourage companies to wipe out the old process and replace it with something quite different on an ongoing basis. Reengineering efforts would be best characterized as one-time, whereas incremental improvement is ongoing. Exhibit 14.1 shows the greater benefits to be gained by doing both in contrast to concentrating only on reengineering or incremental improvements.

The Impact of IT on the Bottom Line

Reengineering is also quite different from the traditional applications of IT. These investments and the poor returns they have generated have resulted in many people questioning the value of IT. Davenport (1993), in a summary of these studies, notes that most of the studies rely on government-published measures of productivity in the service sector. These measures have been severely criticized, and by themselves the studies would not be given much credibility. For example, the Bureau of Labor Statistics provides no productivity figures for the insurance industry. However, other studies have also indicated the lack of a strong relationship between IT and productivity. Leading economists such as Lester Thurow (1991) have found the arguments sufficiently compelling, and he has written: "but when it comes to the bottom line there is no clear evidence that these new technologies have raised productivity (the ultimate determinant of our standard of living) or profitability."

Exhibit 14.1

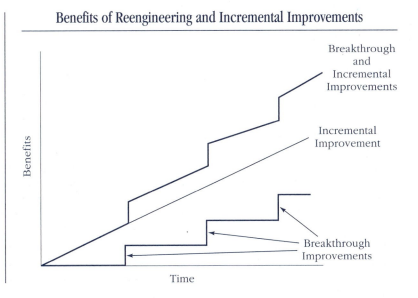

Benefits of Reengineering and Incremental Improvements

Breakthrough and Incremental Improvements

Incremental Improvement

Breakthrough Improvements

Benefits

Time

As reengineering experts argue, however, these dismal results reflect the way the new technologies are deployed. The most common use for computers is word processing; another common use is the creation of spreadsheets. Neither would be expected to significantly impact the bottom line. In fact, implementations of technology are aimed at simply automating routine tasks, and only very few projects are aimed at innovating.

If the investment in computers were to affect productivity, it would have to result in a change in the process and a restructuring of the job. A major investment might even cause a change in the corporate culture. None of the studies described above has confirmed that the introduction of technology resulted in any kind of change to the business processes. Davenport does mention one study of insurance agents that supports this theory. The preliminary analysis indicated that agents with new technology had no improvement in productivity. A more thorough analysis revealed that those agents who had altered their work processes to take advantage of the technology did have higher sales revenues.

Making an Impact with IT

IT by itself may not make a significant impact and so has to be accompanied with other enablers of change. As the business process changes, the other parts of the system also have to change. Hammer and Champy (1993) list four elements of a business system:

- Business processes which is the way the work gets done.
- The jobs and their structures and also whether they are specialized or integrated. Specialized jobs require narrow specialists, while integrated jobs are best done as teams.
- The management and measurement system.
- The values and beliefs of the organization.

These elements are closely linked. Specifically, the business processes determine the ways the jobs are structured and the degree of specialization required; to provide the people doing these jobs with incentives requires a management and a measurement system; and since this system affects behavior, it helps to shape the organization's values. If each of these elements has been properly designed, this set of values should support the business process.

As an example, look at the reengineering project implemented by Blue Cross and Blue Shield (BCBS) of Massachusetts (Donohue-Rolfe, Kanter, and Kelley, 1993) in the small business marketing group. This group sold health insurance to companies with 5 to 24 members. At the beginning of 1990, there were 140 salespeople supported by 300 staff, two incompatible mainframe computers, and two incompatible minicomputers. Because of the incompatibility, it was difficult to answer questions regarding claims, membership, and enrollment or rates. Partly as a result, small accounts were shrinking at the rate of 14 percent per year.

The old process was based on the need for relationship selling, which meant that BCBS had to maintain a direct sales force. Marketing conducted a study of customer needs which found that customers wanted accurate and timely policy information more than anything else. Customers did not need to contact a salesperson if the information was readily available. The market had changed. Customers were satisfied if the policy information was available on the telephone. This suggested BCBS should change its business process.

Management moved to implement the change on three fronts: $2 million was allocated for the technology (business process change), 20 people were assigned as telemarketers to the Small Business Marketing Office (change to jobs and structures), and the marketing organization was restructured (changed the management system). The change in employee values and beliefs was facilitated by an extensive training program that continued even after implementation.

The systems change involved modern IT (a local area network and a client/server architecture), which enabled the 20 people to share information as well as to access information from the other computers. With this system, no caller waited longer than 45 seconds and 90 percent of inquiries were handled by one call. By the end of 1990, the group had enrolled 1001 new members. A year later sales had increased 24 percent and revenues increased by $22 million. At the same time, the costs compared to the old system dropped 62 percent.

◆ A REENGINEERING METHODOLOGY

Each of the major authors in the field (Blair and Loftin, 1994; Davenport, 1993; Harrington, 1991; Manganelli and Klein, 1994) offers methodologies that differ in details but are similar in the overall approach:

Stage 1: Establish the business goals and the constraints.
Stage 2: Select the process to be improved.
Stage 3: Create a new process that effectively uses IT.
Stage 4: Develop the necessary systems and organization structures.
Stage 5: Educate workers to effect the cultural change and introduce the system.

Stage 1: Business Goals and Constraints

There are three issues to consider when establishing the business goals and the constraints:

- The business goals should be closely related to the customer's requirements and should be a "stretch."
- Project parameters should define the schedule, the availability of resources, and the acceptable levels of risk.
- Identify the team and the key players.

Establishing Business Goals

In order to develop an understanding of customer needs, a commonly used approach is to survey the customer as described in the Blue Cross example. In some cases, the customer may not be the buyer of the company's products. Hammer and Champy (1993) describe the reengineering of Ford's Accounts Payable function. Because this process was not broad enough to benefit from reengineering, the process to be redesigned was defined as procurement for which the "customer" was the supplier. Ford was able to identify two major benefits that would accrue to the supplier if the procurement process was properly designed: (1) the opportunity to work closely with Ford and (2) the opportunity to be Ford's primary source.

The business goals most often articulated by companies are:

- Time reduction, that is, to reduce the response time to a customer request as in the Blue Cross case, or to reduce the time to market in the design process as discussed in Chapter 13. Time reductions in the design cycle are often achieved by overlapping several steps. These techniques are more commonly known as **simultaneous engineering** or **concurrent engineering.** When steps overlap, there is a greater need to share information, and this can be enabled by IT.
- Quality of output can be improved in a service industry, especially if the service has an informational component. USAA uses sophisticated imaging systems to respond to questions about claims. IT also helps manufacturing by tracking process information so that the equipment can machine to closer tolerances and thereby ensure conformance and in some cases improve product performance.
- **Mass customization** requires designing an operation that can produce a large variety of products, in small lots and in a short time frame. Such systems rely on information that would describe the product to be made, the tools to be used, and the sequence of activities.
- Cost reduction is usually a secondary goal unless it relates directly to satisfying the customer. Even as a secondary goal, sometimes it is explicitly stated. If it is positioned as the primary goal, then other competitive factors, such as quality, may deteriorate. The Greyhound project described earlier focused on lower costs. But along with the lower costs came a significant deterioration in performance that brought the company to its knees.
- Empowerment and enablement are related to the quality of service. The goal may be to enable the person in contact with the customer to take quick action. American Express, for example, used IT to reengineer the credit authorization process. Now, when a customer calls, the computer checks the customer's record and lets the credit authorizer know the limits. When special cases arise, the authorizer can make a judgment based on a review of similar cases.

A key characteristic of the goals for a reengineering project is that they "stretch" the organization. When Hallmark decided to reengineer its greeting card process, it set a goal for reducing the time from concept to market for a greeting card from three years to one year. Bell Atlantic used to take 15 days to provide carrier access service. It set a goal of zero cycle time. Mutual Benefit demanded a 60 percent improvement in productivity. Although it is difficult to know what can be achieved at this stage of the project, it is a good idea to be as specific about it as possible. One method for reducing the uncertainty is to benchmark processes at world-class companies (see Chapter 15). The benchmarks indicate what has been achieved by others. When Ford began to look at its Accounts Payable process which at the time was staffed by 500 people, it set a goal for a 20 percent reduction in workforce. Then they benchmarked Mazda. Mazda had five people.

Setting the Project Parameters

This issue typically involves understanding acceptable levels of risk, setting time schedules, and identifying resource constraints. For reengineering projects it is also necessary to specify the level of risk that management is willing to undertake. In establishing the level of risk that is acceptable, management has to consider the urgency of the project. Taco Bell realized it was losing market share. If it was to regain market share, it would have to provide better value to its customers, and it did not have much time. The CEO indicated that he would be willing to accept the reengineering team's recommendations even if it mean that the organization had to be completely restructured and all of the jobs redefined.

Most experts recommend that the time frame for the project be within 6 to 18 months. This does not mean that the stretch goal would be achieved in that time, but only that tangible results will be evident. In practice, most reengineering projects are expected to fund themselves after a year. But in setting the project parameters, the team needs to know the available budget and the spending rate until self-funding becomes feasible.

Identifying the Team

The third key element at this stage is to identify the team and the roles they should assume. Team members should represent their constituencies, but they should also be aligned to the goals of the organization. During the team discussions, they contribute through the knowledge of their functional specialty. After the team discussions, they should be able to convey the team's conclusions with strength and conviction to their functional colleagues. The project manager will in some cases also be the project champion. The manager and the champion have to be people of considerable stature in the organization. Thus, when they make recommendations or request resources, they are likely to be heard. Another key participant is a facilitator whose role is to bring a fresh perspective. The facilitator should also be knowledgeable about reengineering methodologies and trains the team when the situation calls for it. Often the facilitator is an outside consultant. One study showed that 54 percent of companies used outside resources for their reengineering project. Of those that did not, 70 percent indicated it was because they had the resources in-house.

Stage 2: Selecting a Process for Improvement

Two processes are suggested for selecting the process to be improved:

- The **high-impact approach**
- The **exhaustive approach**

The High-Impact Approach

Davenport and Short (1990) advocate this approach, maintaining that the exhaustive approach can be too time consuming. People in the company usually know which processes are "broken." Thus, to find the processes requiring work, it is necessary simply to survey the employees. For example, IBM surveyed its salesforce to determine which customer support process was broken. The generation of special bids got the highest priority and was the first to be redesigned.

Since most companies can only focus on improving a few processes, and it is relatively easier to identify the broken ones, the high-impact approach may be quicker. The exhaustive approach, however, will identify the process likely to have the greatest impact on the business and the customer.

The Exhaustive Approach

This approach starts by identifying all of the key business processes. This begins at the broadest possible view. For example, if the entire organization is to be reengineered, top management should define these processes. If customer support is to be redesigned, then the executives responsible for it do the broad process definition.

One approach to defining the key processes is to have each member of the team identify key processes in their view of the organization. Then, the team gets together and arrives at a group consensus. At this level the kinds of macro-processes identified would include

- Product/service design and development
- Product or service delivery
- Sales and after-sales activities
- Marketing
- Capital formation
- Regulatory compliance
- Human resource development

The next step is to create a matrix that shows the relationship of each function to each process. The purpose is to ensure that all of the key processes have been identified. The matrix indicates which areas would be the most affected by reengineering the process as well as which areas would have the most to contribute. Another matrix is created to show the impact each process has on the key business goals defined in Stage 1. Davenport (1993) indicates that the number of processes at this stage should be between 10 and 20. This would result in sufficiently broad processes that they would have to be reengineered (rather than incrementally improved), and there would be little cross-process overlap. Reducing the overlap is important, especially when several processes are reengineered simultaneously. When there is extensive overlap, changes to one process may affect other processes. This makes the task of coordinating the activities on each project very difficult. After the most significant macro-processes are identified, they are broken down into subprocesses. The subprocesses are ranked on the basis of four criteria:

- What is the value to the customer?
- How much can the process be improved?
- What is the impact on the business?
- What resources are available?

The highest ranking processes are then chosen for improvement. As Harrington (1991) observes, Martin Marietta used this approach to identify 200 different processes. Over the next year they implemented changes in 125 of the processes. Generally, Harrington recommends that no more than 20 processes should be improved upon simultaneously.

Selection of the process to be changed is an area of disagreement between the experts. Hammer and Champy's (1993) approach is to focus on one of the major processes and change it. This has been called the **big bang approach.** Some companies adopt this approach when they are faced with a crisis and the need for change is urgent. Most companies, however, take the softer **one step at a time approach** advocated by the other consultants. They recommend reengineering a subprocess before plunging into a major change. An example is Entertainment UK which distributes CDs, videotapes, and electronic games to chain stores. First they reengineered their customer claims process and then they moved on to reengineering the whole of customer service.

When a process is selected as a candidate for reengineering, a "process owner" needs to be identified. The process owner should control or be able to influence the entire span of the process. This person also has responsibility for the performance of the process. When the entire process lies within a specific department, the process owner is identified as the department manager. But in most cases the processes being considered have a span that extends outside any one department. Sometimes the only person that has all parts of the process reporting to him is the CEO. In that case, the experts recommend that the CEO designate a senior person as owner and give him full authority to make changes. The person identified as owner should be capable and willing to change the existing system.

Stage 3: Creating the New IT-Based Process

The process redesign usually follows a sequence of four steps:

- Process specification
- Process rationalization
- Error prevention
- Innovation

Process specification typically involves flowcharting the "as-is" process. This step is also a beginning step for process benchmarking, which is described in Chapter 15. (Chapter 15 also provides an explanation of flowcharting.) The flowchart that is created should document the following characteristics:

- The beginning point
- The end-point
- Interfaces where hand-offs occur
- The functions involved
- Where the process customer is involved
- The strategic relevance of the process

Process rationalization means that unnecessary steps are removed. An unnecessary step is defined as one that duplicates another or one that has a low value-added activity. Some typical nonvalue-added activities are reviewing documents, storing materials, reworking, and setting up to perform a task. Then changes are made, keeping in mind that IT can support (1) a common database of information that could be used by several people simultaneously and (2) parallel processing, which would help to cut down the overall throughput time by easing the flow of communication.

The **error prevention step** is aimed at reducing the likelihood of customers experiencing errors. At this step and the next step of *innovation,* the team needs to become familiar with some of the capabilities of modern IT. This is where a facilitator can help if the in-house expertise does not exist. The nine items described below are some common tactics used when a process is reengineered:

- Automation is the typical use of IT where the manual work is removed from existing processes. In manufacturing the enabling technology often consists of robots, flexible machining systems, and so on. When paper flow is involved as in service companies or the "hidden factory" parts of manufacturing, improvements can be made using imaging systems and computer-aided design.
- Information can be captured and stored on databases for subsequent analysis. The Blue Cross Blue Shield example described earlier was an example

of IT storing vast quantities of data and making it possible to rapidly access the information to answer questions from the customer.

- Parallel processing has been particularly helpful in reducing design development time. One approach is to share the database. Phoenix Mutual changed its sequential underwriting process into a mix of sequential and parallel processes, enabling them to issue 70 percent of their policies overnight.
- The tracking of packages or vehicles allows better control and less loss. Railways and trucks use satellites for systems to track the movement of freight cars and trucks. Federal Express has developed a very sophisticated tracking system that enables them to locate a package precisely within minutes.
- Analytical systems can support decision-making capabilities. American Express uses the Authorizer's Assistant to authorize credit card purchases. Digital uses XCON to configure orders for computer equipment correctly.
- Communicating over large distances can be enabled using electronic mail and teleconferencing. Digital developed its Ultrix operating system using software engineers in Massachusetts and California. United Parcel Service uses networks to provide information so that shipments can be cleared before they arrive.
- Several activities can be integrated and assigned to one person. At Mutual Benefit each application used to be checked by 19 people, including the underwriter for credit data, medical records, and so on. The entire process was redesigned, and one case worker was given responsibility for everything. Since underwriting is a sophisticated process, analytical systems were provided to support the case worker.
- Employees' knowledge and skills can be made available for others. Hewlett-Packard provides a database to support its hotline all over the world. When a customer in Georgia calls with a problem, the person who responds may be from Australia. But that person can access the corporate database and answer questions as well as any other hotline responder.
- **Disintermediating** involves removing humans who pass information between sequential process steps. There is great pressure on the Stock Exchanges to establish automated trading, thereby reducing the role of the stockbroker. This tactic would try to involve the customer in doing some of the work. Federal Express enables the customer to track his package without having to contact a customer service representative.

Stage 4: Developing the Systems and the Organization Structures

This stage involves obtaining the hardware and developing the software, as well as creating a plan for the human side of the system.

The Systems Issues

The process for developing the hardware and software has been written of extensively in most information systems textbooks. With reengineering projects two tactics are particularly recommended:

- Modularizing
- Prototyping

Modularizing means dividing the system into subsystems, each of which could be deployed independent of the others. But to get a significant impact in the first deployment, a group of modules could be selected for implementation. After these modules are implemented, the next group of modules would be implemented and so on. With the modules defined, it is possible to formulate a timeline specifying the modules, when they would be completed, and the expected benefits of each.

Prototyping of a new system should be done early. The purpose of prototyping is to put together a model of the entire system so as to identify

- The technical resources and technologies needed.
- The best way to acquire these resources.
- A clear definition of all the information needed by the new process.
- The points at which the process interacts with people.

One approach to prototyping is to use computer simulations. Many software packages are available to simulate a process. These can be used to determine whether the improvements expected would happen and to predict the robustness of the proposed system. Robustness would indicate how sensitive the system's performance would be if elements did not function as expected. Other approaches to prototyping may be a test of the process on paper or design of a functional system that uses a personal computer and a small database, or a larger scale system with the appropriate screens and access to the actual databases. The computer-based prototypes can be developed using very high-level languages such as object-oriented languages or code-generating CASE tools.

The People Issues

The earlier steps concentrated on system issues. If the model of a business system as articulated by Hammer and Champy (1993) is used, the processes will influence the job definition, organization structure, management, and measurement systems. Now that the new process has been defined, the team's attention turns to these critical people-related issues. These elements have to be defined over two time frames: the post-implementation and system development periods.

When creating the post-implementation system, the following questions need to be considered:

- What will the new job descriptions be? And what training will be required?
- How many people will be required to meet the demand?
- What will the new organization structure look like?
- What career paths are open to people in this organization?

The changes created by reengineering the jobs can be profound, and many employees will be concerned if they are not told their position in the new organization. Frequently, jobs are redesigned to be broader in scope. The broader jobs may be handled by teams of people. Those in direct contact with the customer are often empowered to act. Thus, for each process the reengineering team needs to define the tasks to be performed, specify the knowledge and skills required to do the job, and identify the tools that will be available. When all the tasks are identified, the reengineering team can assess whether these tasks could be performed by a single case worker as in the case of Mutual Benefit Life or whether a team of people is required.

The next step is to estimate the number of case workers or teams that will be required. Since the demand is usually not steady but instead has peaks and valleys, an approach for meeting peak demands has to be worked out. Among the approaches used are ways of modifying the demand so that some of the peak demand is moved to the valleys. This can be done by offering customers incentives to order off-peak. The Massachusetts Motor Vehicle Registry offers people a discount for sending their registration renewals by mail, reducing the demand from people coming to the window on the last day of the month. Cross-training enables people to fill in for absentees. Many retail stores make use of part-timers. The store hires and trains several people, promising them only part-time work. When the demand increases, they assign the part-timers more hours. **Staff sharing** is done between companies that experience peaks at different times. For example, some communities share their fire companies when a fire occurs in one community.

The new jobs typically cross existing organizational boundaries; therefore, a new management structure has to be created. Ideally, all of the process would be allocated to one organization, as Blue Cross Blue Shield did in the case described earlier. This is not always possible, but the aim should be to assign it to the smallest number of departments. A manager of one of these departments would be assigned as process owner and would be held accountable for the process performance. The restructuring often reduces the need for managers because the newly empowered employees will be managing many aspects of the job themselves, cutting down on the managers' tasks. Taco Bell had 350 area supervisors for 1800 restaurants. After reengineering it was able to reduce this ratio to 100 market managers for 2300 restaurants. The new organizational hierarchy can be structured with fewer levels of management.

Employees also want to know the career path that is open to them in the new organization. Designing these new career paths requires that the new jobs be compared, a task that is more difficult to do since each of the new jobs covers a broader scope. One rule that has been useful when evaluating two jobs A and B is to determine in which direction the movement is more difficult. Does the person have to learn more skills when moving from A to B or when moving from B to A? If the A to B move is more difficult, then B follows A as the next job in the career path. The most difficult jobs would be the last position on the career path in the new organization. Equivalent jobs in other parts of the company have to be identified to complete the definition of the career path.

These are the jobs as they would appear after the reengineering project has been completed. During the transition, there would be changes in job structures and the organization. These changes would usually take place at milestones when one group of modules has been implemented and work has started on the next. Some effort has to be made to design the jobs in this transition stage.

Stage 5: Effecting the Cultural Change and Implementing the System

Changing the Culture

Chapter 11 describes what needs to be done to effect the cultural change. For reengineering projects the following items are crucial:

- Management's vision
- Identification of benefits for the worker
- Definition of measures
- Data collection and feedback mechanisms

Management needs to clearly articulate its unhappiness and dissatisfaction with the existing process and also needs to put forth a vision. Although the vision may describe the lofty goals of the organization, it should also provide workers with some tangible benefits.

Herzberg's two-factor theory (1966) of motivation provides some guidelines for identifying benefits that may be directly meaningful to workers. Herzberg maintained that workers are motivated by two groups of variables: job context and job content. **Job context** consists of pay, benefits, office space, equipment, and information. **Job content** includes the challenge and variety of work, the autonomy experienced by the worker, the opportunity provided for learning and for recognition and the sense of completion. The reengineered job would directly affect the job context elements of equipment and information. Almost every element in job content could be positively impacted.

During this stage the measurements to be used initially and the corresponding targets should be specified. Data used for measurement can be classified as attribute or variable. One way of distinguishing between the two types of data is to think of attribute data as counted and variable data as measured (Chapter 7 discusses this distinction in more detail.)

The measures can be classified as effectiveness measures or efficiency measures:

- **Effectiveness measures** are directly related to customer needs. In Chapter 2 we described the five dimensions of service quality—reliability, empathy, responsiveness, assurance, and tangibles. The effectiveness measures should be defined in terms of these dimensions.
- **Efficiency measures** reflect the consumption of resources to complete a task. Typical efficiency measures would include cost, or labor hours expended, or machine hours used.

Along with measurement definition, data collection and feedback mechanisms have to be designed. Ideally, the empowered operators would collect the data themselves. Because of the type of equipment required or because of time constraints, it may not be possible for the operator to be the data collector. In this case, the data collector should be objective (automated procedures are better than human inspectors), and the summarized statistics should be fed back to the operator as quickly as possible. New England Business Services provides a mail-order service. An effectiveness measure it devised for its customer service area is the time an incoming call has to wait before it is answered. The data are collected automatically. In the room where the customer service staff is located, an illuminated sign lets all of the staff know the number of callers on the line and how long they have been waiting.

System Implementation

System implementation has been discussed in detail in many IT textbooks. In general, implementation of reengineered systems is not significantly different. The specifics of the implementation approach have to be planned. Project management tools should be used to schedule activities, collect information about project progress, and reschedule tasks when necessary. What distinguishes reengineering from most IT projects is the degree of risk involved. So, attention has to be paid to reducing the possibility of defects in the implemented system. Practices that are recommended include:

- Using standard packages and high-level languages
- Enhancing the developer's capability for self-testing
- Being prepared with contingency plans when the system goes "live"
- Reassigning of people to jobs in the new system

Standard packages or high-level languages can be used for the initial design. These packages enable parts of the system to be built and tested quickly. The result is shorter delivery times for each module. By building a little and testing it quickly, errors can be detected and fixed before the entire system is implemented.

Most testing of systems involves two approaches—standards and independent review. Standards are set in consultation with the client. They are communicated to the system developers so that they know the expectations. Independent review is done by testers who are required to formally inspect every part of the job, or by clients who may be involved in "alpha" and "beta" testing and in demonstrations. When testing, testers design programs that can conduct a series of standard tests that would take much longer to perform manually. When these are created, they can be given to the developer to self-test their systems before passing it on to the tester for an independent review.

Contingency plans should be ready just in case there is a problem during implementation. This is especially true if the system is being implemented "**cold**

turkey." In other words, the old system is cut off and the new system is started. Manganelli and Klein (1994) tell of an electrical parts distributor who reengineered an order fulfillment system. The new system was to go in operation on Monday. That Friday the distributor fired 75 percent of the order processors. On Monday, the new system failed to work. It took almost a month to fix the problem. Meanwhile, the remaining order processors could not keep up with the flow of orders. It was a mistake from which the company took months to recover.

The new jobs in a reengineered system differ markedly from jobs in the old system. Since the human element is critical to ensuring that a system will work, a great deal of attention needs to be paid to assigning the appropriate people to these jobs. Each person available for assignment should be evaluated on four dimensions:

- Skills
- Willingness to be trained
- Aptitude for the new system
- Buying-in to the change

◆ POST-REENGINEERING

Once the reengineering has been completed, organizations adopt several different approaches:

- If the reengineering had focused on a subprocess, move toward reengineering the entire process. This is what Entertainment UK did, as described earlier.
- Stabilize the effects of the reengineering effort and focus on incremental improvement. This is the approach used by Blue Cross Blue Shield of Massachusetts.
- Spread the reengineered system to other locations. Woolworths reengineered a set of merchandising activities. Then it proposed to replicate the system across other locations to ensure consistency. British Petroleum created a "reserves appraisal" process and plans to replicate this in each of the areas where it is operating.
- Broaden the process, extending it to the systems of suppliers and customers. The idea is to cross the organizational boundaries extending to other parts of the value chain.
- Continue reengineering and flattening the organization. Fidelity's Retail Operations Division claims to be 40 percent of the way there. The aim is to have only a few managers handling several operational process teams and supported by a few centers of excellence. The entire company would be directed by an executive board.

Reengineering is a difficult project to conceive and implement. There have been many failures such as Greyhound, but there have also been some spectacular successes. This indicates that IT can facilitate substantial improvements that can have a lasting impact on the business. In addition, a properly reengineered process is difficult for the competition to match. In part, this is because of the investments involved. But an equally significant reason is the difficulty in replicating the culture and values surrounding the reengineered organization. One of the first reengineering projects was American Airlines' construction of the SABER reservation system. For years this gave American an edge over the competition. General Electric's Answer Center provides advice to GE customers 24 hours a day and has given GE an edge over other suppliers of appliances and electrical equipment. Since the concept of breakthrough improvements is a critical element of TQM, reengineering is likely to continue to be part of the TQM tool kit for many years to come.

◆ QUALITY INFORMATION SYSTEMS

In addition to supporting an organization's drive to provide better quality for their customers, IT can support TQM by strengthening the infrastructure. When TQM is initiated, information needs to flow in several directions:

- Communication of QI teams' activities
- Process-related information to the QI teams
- Operational information to support the corporate goals

Communication of QI Team Activities

For an organization just beginning on the quality path, it is important to promote TQM by spreading success stories around the organization. When a company has deployed these practices extensively, it may be useful for ideas that worked in one part of the company to be copied by others. The diffusion of successes can be accomplished through celebratory activities such as Quality Days. But these kinds of events are periodic. The flow of information can be greatly accelerated by using IT. For example, Digital Equipment Corporation provides a bulletin board for news about quality-related activities. Any interested party within the company can access the bulletin board and see what is being done in other parts of the company.

When sharing information between teams, it is important to recall that the purpose of the QI activity is twofold: to solve a problem and to enable the team members to learn problem-solving skills. By simply adopting the recommendations of another team, the team members miss an opportunity to learn how the problem-solving techniques can be applied. This is crucial to building a learning organization. The team also fails to have the satisfaction and camaraderie that results from successfully solving a problem. So using IT to share information about QI stories may be more useful for the mature TQM organization where most of the team members are already familiar with the problem-solving tools.

If the QI activity results in a change in procedure, then IT can provide a rapid means of disseminating it through the organization. Duracell, the maker of batteries for flashlights and other products, maintains existing company policies on a computer. When a change is suggested and approved, the new policy is entered on the central database. Then, the current policy can be quickly accessed at networked personal computers.

When these changes in procedure are part of a massive process change such as a reengineering project, communication with all affected parties is critical for maintaining morale and marginalizing rumors. Babson College provided an anonymous account that could be used to ask questions from any terminal on campus. The questions would be reviewed daily, and the reengineering project's leader would answer all of the questions.

A more controversial use of IT is to enable management to track and control the progress of the QI teams. Most companies encourage the voluntary participation of employees in these teams. Some of these companies feel that reporting on the activities of the team introduces a coercive dimension. Other companies have made QI teams a compulsory practice. They want all employees to be coached in the QI tools and to be active practitioners. Some of these companies require that the QI teams log their progress so that management can monitor it. Paul Revere Insurance Company monitors the progress of each QI team. Each team enters the description and the starting date for a QI activity. When the idea is submitted to a certifying group, its disposition (scrapped, implemented, or certified) is recorded.

Johnson (1992) suggests using IT and the accounting system to track improvements. He argues that when teams first begin to make improvements, the results may not show directly in the accounting numbers. This is because, at the beginning the process improvement creates redundancies or excess capacity. Until this excess has been removed, by selling excess equipment, or redeploying excess space, or reassigning people to alternative tasks, the accounting numbers will not show any improvement. Some companies have put together a process improvement account. As improvements occur, the anticipated dollar savings are placed in this improvement account. The size of this account is an indication of the slack in the system. Management's task would be to reduce the slack, and the size of the account would be a measure of management's ability to realize the benefits of the improvements.

Process-Related Information for QI Teams

Work teams need to collect and analyze data and to ensure that the process is under control. These process control data have to be collected regularly and frequently. Teams also need data when engaged in a QI activity. It is difficult to predict the kind of data that will be requested by a QI team, for most such requests are made on an ad-hoc basis.

Gathering process data, performing the analyses, and presenting the reports can be a chore. It may also call for skills that the team may not possess. One al-

ternative is to call upon resources outside the department, such as industrial engineers, for help with flowcharting and quality control for help with interpreting control charts. Another alternative is to provide this capability as a set of IT tools. Today several companies provide sophisticated statistical packages. At a minimum they offer the following functions:

- Simple statistics such as means and tables
- Analysis of production data
- Management reporting
- Compliance reporting
- Automated data collection and data entry

Some of these providers have bundled their software with sophisticated IT hardware, but in some cases the hardware has to be acquired independent of the software. Companies targeting the market for quality control in operations provide devices to automate data collection and entry, specifically:

- Workstations and software to analyze the data in real time and provide feedback so that action can be taken in timely fashion.
- Local area networks to facilitate the collection of data and their report to workers and managers who may not be located next to each other.
- Integration of data to corporate databases that would also facilitate providing information to executives.

The data can be displayed on workstations as run charts or control charts. In a TQM environment, the teams are encouraged to display their performance results. As management tries to make the team more aware of their contribution to the company performance, financial data also become important. IT in most companies has easy access to the accounting database. So, the team can have access to both operational and financial data. Johnson (1992) describes a Japanese company where each department compiled control information into 12 graphs. Eleven of these graphs described operational measures such as average setup time per job, number of defects, number of line stops per day, and inventory levels. One showed the cost information as a percentage change each month in total costs. The aim was to reduce the total costs. The operational measures indicated what had to be done to reduce the total costs.

When a QI team is formed, it is likely to require information that has not previously been requested. IT's task is to make these data available on a timely basis. This can be done by making the corporate databases accessible through **query programs.** These programs allow the team to access the data and to format them as a report without much training in the software. At the same time as the data are made more accessible, the IT function has to consider ways to capture more data. One tactic is to enable the person generating the data to record them so that others can retrieve it. At Kodak, the benchmarking coordinator records all of the benchmarking activities in the company. If a team wants to find benchmarks, it can look at this database and see if another team has already established them. In addition, when the team wants to benchmark another company, a look at the database tells if that company had benchmarked Kodak and so would be more likely to provide access.

At the same time as these islands of information are being constructed, IT has to figure out ways to connect them. One approach is to link everyone to a network and provide a shared directory. When Department A wants information from Department B, the information can be placed in the shared directory by B. Another approach is to use groupware. This has the virtue of automatically categorizing information, making access easier.

Making information broadly available is critical if the aim is to achieve total participation where any employee would be encouraged to provide suggestions. Johnson (1992) describes the experience of process improvement teams at Connor Formed Metal Products, a small-job shop making custom metal springs in Los Angeles. The company made available to all employees information about every job in the plant: the customer, the price and margin, and special notes and instructions from engineering and the customer. The availability of information encouraged people to come up with ideas.

Two employees in customer service knew that they spent most of their time reacting to change orders. After querying the system to find the source of the change orders, they found that 20 percent of the changes had occurred because of errors when the orders were first entered. Then they created a purchase order checklist to eliminate those errors.

Operational Information to Support Corporate Goals

Perhaps the most significant contribution of IT in support of the quality infrastructure is to provide management with control information that enables them to set plans and make decisions. The traditional approach has been to provide management with accounting-based financial information. Management would then have to reconcile what had happened in their function with the accounting records. Often they would find that these differences could be explained by differences in the cutoff date for the data acquired from each department. But as management focused on the bookkeeping task of reconciling the data, they reduced their focus on the operations.

IT was collecting and providing all of these accounting data, but the data did not provide information to run the business. It seemed logical to approach accountants to come up with a way of converting these data into useful information. The accountants developed a methodology called **activity-based costing** (ABC).

The original concept appears to have been developed at General Electric in 1963. When GE realized that indirect costs amounted to 52 percent of every dollar of sales, they decided to make people aware of the costs they were generating. They identified the activities that controlled these costs. Then they added the cost of these activity drivers to the cost of each activity. Johnson (1992) provides an example with the cost of new drawings. If an engineer causes a new drawing to be drafted, the cost of the drafting activity is charged to the new drawing. So, if the cost of the drafting was determined to be $95, that number would be added to the new drawings cost. In addition, there would be inspection costs, data processing costs, new tooling costs, and so on. All of these would be added to the cost of the new drawing. The result would be to make the engineer aware that the new drawing resulted in a cost of $275, whereas modifying an old drawing would only cost $60.

In 1981 Arthur Andersen & Co. (now Andersen Consulting) licensed the technique from GE and promoted it as Activity-Based Costing. It proposed an approach for continuous improvement based on this cost analysis. First, each major business activity was defined, and the cost of each activity in each department was determined using traditional methods such as work measurement techniques. Then the generator for each of these activities was identified. All of the costs would then be added and assigned to the generator. The continual improvement step was then to examine these generators to see if there was some way of reducing them.

ABC systems advocated continual improvement in terms of reducing costs. In an example provided by Arthur Andersen, a generator of many of the costs in an organization is sales orders. So, the suggestion is to reduce the number of sales orders. This would be done by increasing the order size per sale or otherwise eliminating any order deemed unprofitable. This approach does not fit with the TQM philosophy for three reasons:

- There is little emphasis on customer needs.
- The system is often too complex for the average worker to understand, making it difficult to be used as a basis for QI teams.
- There is no emphasis on process improvement or reengineering.

Today the focus is on creating and reporting operational measures. With more capacity in IT to collect and report data, the financial measures have been relegated to what they always were—a way of keeping score. It seems axiomatic that, if the right operational measures are selected and if they trend in the right direction, the financial measures should improve. If the financial measures do not improve, it indicates that the operational measures need to be reviewed. This puts management in closer touch with the operational measures and learning what is important in managing the business better.

These newer systems have been called **quality information systems** (Schlange, 1991). In broad terms, these systems

- Collect external data such as the customer's requirements, the design standards, and the results in terms of customer satisfaction.

- Collect internal data required to control the process such as early warning information (are machines being properly maintained?), process control information (levels of in-process inventory, time spent setting up machines), and output quality (percentage defective).
- Facilitate analyzing the operational and financial information to support planning and coordination of the several parts of the enterprise.

Such systems have also been called executive information systems and executive support systems. There is a fine distinction between the two types of systems which is beyond the scope of this book. For our purposes, the two systems can be considered as types of Quality Information Systems. Implementing these systems has much in common with IS implementation. But there are some differences that the following discussion will highlight by focusing on the experiences of three companies:

- Lockheed-Georgia produces cargo aircraft such as the C-5B for the U.S. Air Force and the Hercules which is shipped worldwide. The president of Lockheed-Georgia felt that the information provided was unsatisfactory because (1) it was difficult to locate information when a particular problem had to be addressed, and (2) the reports were not current, which meant managers could not make decisions on the same data. Over the next few years, they created a management information and decision support system (MIDS), which provides information about cash flow, production levels, as well as employee contributions to company-sponsored charities and labor grievances.
- Xerox Corporation competes in the business products and systems and financial services. When Xerox initiated its drive for Total Quality, it quickly became evident to senior management that critical information was not being provided in a timely manner. A Corporate Information Management group was formed with the charge of (1) identifying the key items management should monitor and, (2) creating a system to deliver that information in timely fashion. The system was the basis for reporting operating performance, management decisions, and communicating with managers worldwide.
- Analog Devices was described at the beginning of this chapter. When Analog began its TQM program, it found that the information systems were aimed at providing financial information for reports to stockholders and government agencies. But the TQM program asked Analog to focus on issues of product quality, on-time delivery, lead time, and so on. The company developed a "corporate scorecard" that showed financial performance along with operating performance. The information was available to all managers. If the manager noticed that an indicator was out of control, he could "drill down" to lower levels to uncover what might have caused the problem.

All of these systems followed a similar implementation procedure. Key aspects, discussed below, were:

- Justification of the project
- Determination of user requirements
- Obstacles to implementation

Project Justification

At the outset, each system had strong backing from the top of the organization. Each CEO knew the information system was inadequate, and each recognized changes had to be made. They suspected that the technology existed to radically improve the existing reporting systems. It was becoming easier to access information, and the graphical user interfaces reduced the fear of interacting with computers for most managers. In addition, communication capabilities were being greatly improved through networks. But the system was not providing the information these managers would identify as critical to operating the business.

Since management knew it needed a better system, justification was informal. Relying on the accounting system was like driving forward while looking in the rearview mirror. Typically, development of the system was authorized by stages. As each stage was completed, new enhancements would be added in response to the user's requests. For example, MIDS was first created with only 31 screen displays. A terminal was placed in each manager's office, and the usage of each screen display was monitored. If a screen was not useful, it would be deleted. Over the years more screens were added. After eight years, MIDS offered 700 screen displays.

Determination of User Requirements

Wetherbe (1991) describes some typical approaches that have not been successful:

- The managers define their requirements. Ideally, the system designers will get management to sign a document agreeing to what the system should deliver. The problem is that when managers see the systems reports they typically want more information. If these were not designed into the system earlier, the cost of introducing them later could be very expensive.
- The manager is shown a variety of reports before the system is designed. These reports could be constructed to simulate the final product, or they could be a compilation of reports from several "off-the-shelf" packages. The problem is that the manager tends to ask for all of the reports—just in case. The result can be a system designed to deliver far more reports than will ever be used.

As a way of resolving this problem, Wetherbe proposes the use of indirect questions and prototyping. The indirect questions he recommends are derived from IBM's Business Systems Planning, Rockart's Critical Success Factors, and his Ends/Means analysis:

1. a. What are the major problems encountered in accomplishing the purposes of the organizational unit you manage?
   b. What are good solutions to those problems?
   c. How can information play a role in any of those solutions?
2. a. What are the major decisions associated with your management responsibilities?
   b. What improvements in information could result in better decisions?
3. a. What are the critical success factors of the unit you manage?
   b. What information is needed to ensure that the critical success factors are under control?
4. a. What is the end or good or service provided by the business process?
   b. What makes these goods or services effective to recipients or customers?
   c. What information is needed to evaluate that effectiveness?
5. a. What are the key means or processes used to generate or provide goods or services?
   b. What constitutes efficiency in the providing of these goods or services?
   c. What information is needed to evaluate that efficiency?

Based on the information requirements derived from these questions, the system designer should now construct a prototype. Using some of the software available today, one can create prototypes in as little as a day. By allowing managers to use the system, a better definition of the requirements can be obtained.

Lockheed used several approaches to determine the systems requirements. They interviewed the managers and their secretaries. They also reviewed the usage of current reports. Xerox and Analog started with a definition of the critical success factors. At Xerox the CEO listed 15 key strategic issues. Then line managers were asked to identify a Direct Action List that linked their tasks to the key issues. Analog defined their business objectives as market leadership and revenue growth. The senior management team then identified the external and internal levers, which would help them reach these objectives. External levers were products, defect levels, on-time delivery, and lead time. Internal levers were time to market, process parts per million defect rate, manufacturing cycle time, and yield.

In developing the system, it is best to do it in stages. The first version of MIDS was developed in six months and provided 31 displays. It was used mostly by the CEO. Later versions spread it through the ranks. Over an eight-year period, it provided 700 displays to 30 top executives and 40 operating managers. Xerox used a similar approach. The first application changed procedures for creating briefing materials, recommendations, and management decisions as they were shown to the top executives. Next, they created a database that could be used to provide operating information to all of the senior managers and the specific responsibilities for tasks. At Analog, those at the executive level were the first to see the scorecard. Over time more levels were provided, so it would be possible to search for causes of problems that appeared at higher levels.

Obstacles to Implementation

Whenever a new system is introduced, obstacles arise, some of which are technical and others are people-related. The people-related problems have to be solved by technical means or through negotiations between different layers of management.

Among the obstacles reported with these systems are:

1. Rekeying the data. The financial data are quickly available in existing systems, and some of the other data may also be available on computer systems. However, these systems are often not set up for easy interfaces. So, the data have to be rekeyed. Xerox created a new database called COM. Information for it was derived from some internal sources and in some cases was rekeyed. The same was true of the database for the Analog Devices scorecard. Until the islands of data are automatically connected, this human interface can be a major weakness.
2. When all divisions have to use the same data, the structure of the data has to be identical. Some divisions are reluctant to give up control over the data definitions.
3. The way these systems are used can differ by management style. Some will examine all of the screens in a particular sequence. Others will stop part way through, use another part of the system (e-mail for example), and then return to their examination of the screens. The systems need to be designed to accommodate the various approaches.
4. Lower level managers are not happy with the idea of senior management being able to "drill down" to their operating data. Xerox solved this issue by assuring managers that the system would only enable their superiors to look three levels below.
5. Since the system restructured the reporting relationships, some of the staff viewed it as a threat. Xerox addressed this issue by having the president assure the staff that the system would foster closer ties with line management. This would allow the staff to be more responsive to their needs.

Several of the managers using these systems have extolled their benefits:

1. The system allows people to share more information in less time. When information is entered into the database, it is immediately available to all users.
2. It provides an overview of the business with a few keystrokes. Previously, people would have to search through several pages.
3. The user friendly features allow people to examine the information the way it is most comfortable. If they want to examine an issue in greater detail, they can. Alternatively, they can continue to examine the rest of the data. In other words, they can look at the data the way they want to and not rely on it being packaged properly for them.

4. All of the users see the information in the same format and based on data from the same time frame. This makes it easier to communicate.

5. The Quality Information System will typically have electronic mail capabilities as well. When questions arise, messages can be sent immediately.

6. The system can be constructed in modular fashion. So, when Xerox wants to add a new capability to the system, it constructs the new module and adds an icon to the user's screen when it is available for use. MIDS uses it in a proactive form. Once a manager has seen information in a specific format, the person is prompted for additional information that may be useful and alternative formats.

7. New technology can be tested on the system. For example, when Lockheed wanted to evaluate the mouse technology, it first tested it on MIDS. When Analog wanted to test Lotus Notes, it tried it on their ESS.

8. The benefits of the system for management decision making are hard to evaluate. Xerox points to time savings resulting from eliminating briefing books. But otherwise hard savings are difficult to quantify. Analog managers pointed out that this system provided them with key information, while the accounting system information was neither timely nor relevant.

◆ Summary

IT plays a significant role in supporting TQM as a competitive strategy and as a resource for vertical and horizontal deployment of the corporate goals. Some companies have chosen to focus their improvement efforts primarily on using TQM tools. For many of these companies this approach has led over time to a mentality of incremental improvement. This is probably acceptable if the company is not facing a serious competitive threat. But it indicates that the company has not completely accepted the TQM philosophy. As Chapter 2 indicates, the TQM philosophy would suggest that companies also target breakthrough projects. When Bob Galvin at Motorola initiated the six-sigma program, he was pushing for an improvement in performance of several orders of magnitude. When John Young at Hewlett-Packard pushed for a 10X reduction in defects, he was pushing for breakthroughs. In order to achieve such massive changes, the entire approach to performing a specific task has to be redesigned. Major redesigns can be facilitated by using state-of-the-art technology. And the technology experiencing the most change in recent years is IT. When companies marry the push for breakthroughs with the use of IT, they are reengineering processes. This chapter discusses the failings of traditional information systems projects and highlights practices that can increase the chances of success for reengineering projects.

When top management wants to deploy their quality goals through the organization or when they want to encourage the spread of quality objectives across the organization, they have to increase the flow of information. This means more information needs to be collected, stored, and made accessible. It is not sufficient to have "islands of information" that can be used by only one function. IT plays a significant role by building the bridges to facilitate cross-functional access to data. Companies that have constructed such Quality Information Systems such as those described in this chapter find they are critical for planning and control.

◆ Key Terms

Simultaneous engineering	Process rationalization	Effectiveness measures
Concurrent engineering	Error prevention step	Efficiency measures
Mass customization	Disintermediating	System implementation
High-impact approach	Modularizing	"Cold turkey"
Exhaustive approach	Prototyping	Query programs
Big bang approach	Staff sharing	Activity-based costing (ABC)
One step at a time approach	Herzberg's two-factor theory	Quality Information Systems
Process specification	Job context	
	Job content	

◆ Assignments

1. Do the following functions add any value for the customer?
   a. Taking an order for take-out food
   b. Checking the airline ticket
   c. Filling out a health questionnaire when visiting the doctor
   d. Answering market survey questions

2. A toaster has a heating element in the middle and two flaps on either side. When a slice of bread is placed on one of the flaps and the flap is closed, one side gets toasted. To toast the other side, the flap has to be opened, the slice of bread turned around, and the flap closed again. Toasting each side takes one minute. So, making one slice of toast will take two minutes (assuming the time required for opening the flap, turning around the toast, and closing the flap is negligible). Making two slices of toast will also take two minutes since then both flaps will be used simultaneously. One way of making three slices is to make two first and then make the third toast. This would take a total of four minutes. Suggest a change in the process to reduce the time to toast to three minutes.

C a s e   S t u d y

Morewood Enterprises

John Chang reviewed the notes for his presentation with satisfaction. The reengineering project he had been responsible for had been implemented last week. It had taken 12 months to complete, and the results had been as spectacular as promised. He felt ready to take on his next reengineering project.

Morewood Enterprises had grown to $600 million sales in just 15 years. Morewood sold business software to professionals such as dentists, lawyers, and doctors. The software was used to issue bills, track payments, and manage transactions such as insurance reimbursements. The software was easy to use. In addition, Morewood had maintained its functionality at the state-of-the-art. When networks became widely accessible, Morewood added software to enable users to access databases over Internet.

Meanwhile, Morewood's corporate staff had grown. Benchmark data obtained by Al Atwood, the director of Corporate Planning, indicated that some functions had as much as 40 percent more people than needed. As long as rapid growth was sustained, Morewood could tolerate the extra people. But the last two years had seen a leveling of sales. And as competition had increased, the profit margins had shrunk. As a result, the president of Morewood, Silvia Olivetti, realized that the staff had to be trimmed. However, she was reluctant to arbitrarily reduce headcount without making sure the work would continue to be performed. She realized that the processes had grown without being given much thought. Surely they could be redesigned and made more efficient.

John Chang had recently joined the company in the Accounts Receivable Department. Silvia had been impressed by John's verbal ability and organization skills. And since Accounts Receivable was an area that Al Atwood's benchmark data had shown as being overstaffed, she appointed John as reengineering project leader. His charter was to redesign the accounts receivable process, including the issuing of invoices, checking credit, and collecting the money. The goal was to reduce headcount by 60 percent and to complete the project in 12 months.

Now, one year later, John was going to report the "stretch" goals Silvia had said had been met. A new computer system costing almost $1 million had been installed. The system had been brought into operation in stages. As each stage was completed, some functions were eliminated. The people doing those tasks had either been reassigned to other areas in the company or had been let go.

One of the first had been the manager of the Accounts Receivable Department, Harry Dutton. Harry was an affable person who was looked up to by all his subordinates. He had joined the company when he was forty. He had headed the Accounts Receivable area for the last five years. When John Chang joined the company, Harry had taken him under his wing. He had helped John on more than one occasion. When he was let go, John felt a twinge of sadness. He knew many of the others in the department shared his feelings. To make matters worse, he knew that Harry had not found a job yet. He had now been without a job for eight months!! He also knew some in the department blamed him for Harry's situation.

Morewood Enterprises (Continued)

Subsequently, many others had been let go. There had been 80 people in the functions that were reengineered; today there were 25. Fifteen had been reassigned and 40 had left the company. Some of them had been offered other jobs in the company. But rather than take a job that paid less, they had opted to leave. The job market in the area had been weak, and John knew many of them had not yet found another job.

John recognized that the layoffs had affected morale. But he was confident that as the dust settled and the staff came to appreciate their increased effectiveness, the morale would improve.

CASE QUESTIONS

1. What are some of the human costs associated with a reengineering project? What can be done to reduce these costs?
2. Would an incremental improvement approach have been more appropriate? Would it have resulted in less human suffering?

◆ Bibliography

Blair, J. M. and R. D. Loftin. *"Boxes and Lines": A Manual for Enterprise Engineering,* Carefree, Ariz.: Blair/Loftin Intergalactic Press, 1994.

Davenport, T. H. *Process Innovation: Reengineering Work through Information Technology.* Cambridge, Mass.: Harvard Business School Press, 1993.

Davenport, T. H. and J. E. Short, "The New Industrial Engineering: Information Technology and Business Process Redesign." *Sloan Management Review* (Summer 1990).

Donohue-Rolfe, F., J. Kanter, and M. C. Kelley. "Implementing Business Process Reengineering: A Case Study." *Information Management,* Auerbach Publications, 1993.

Hammer, M. "Reengineering Work: Don't Automate, Obliterate." *Harvard Business Review* (July–August 1990).

Hammer, M., and J. Champy. *Reengineering the Corporation.* New York: Harper Business, 1993.

Harrington, H. J. *Business Process Improvement,* New York: McGraw-Hill, 1991.

Houdeshel, G., and H. J. Watson. "The Management of Information and Decision Support (MIDS) System at Lockheed-Georgia." *MIS Quarterly* (March 1987): 127–140.

Herzberg, F. *Work and the Nature of Man.* Cleveland, Ohio: World Publishing, 1966.

Johnson, H. T. *Relevance Regained.* New York: Free Press, 1992.

Keen, P.G.W. *Shaping the Future: Business Design Through Information Technology.* Cambridge, Mass.: Harvard Business School Press, 1991.

Manganelli, R. L. and M. M. Klein. *The Reengineering Handbook.* New York: American Management Association, 1994.

Osborn, C. S. and L. M. Applegate "Xerox Corporation: Executive Support Systems." Intercollegiate Case Clearinghouse, 9-189-134, Cambridge, Mass., 1990.

The Role of IS in Business Process Reengineering. Center for Management Research, Surrey, England, 1993.

Schlange, T. G. "Quality Information Systems." *The 1991 Juran Impro Conference,* Atlanta, pp. 9B-35 to 9B-49.

Schneiderman, A. "Performance Measurements." *Proceedings of the 1989 Academic-Practitioner Liaison Workshop,* American Production and Inventory Control Society, Falls Church, Va., 1989.

Thurow, L. C. "Foreword." In *The Corporation of the 1990's: Information Technology and Organizational Transformation.* New York: Oxford University Press, 1991.

Tomsho, R. "How Greyhound Lines Reengineered Itself Right into a Deep Hole." *The Wall Street Journal,* October 20, 1994.

Wetherbe, J. C. "Executive Information Requirements: Getting it Right." *MIS Quarterly* (March 1991): 51–65.

Benchmarking

◆ ◆ ◆

In 1983 David Kearns, chairman of Xerox Corporation, called a meeting of the top 25 executives who would be responsible for rolling out the quality strategy he envisioned. The Leadership Through Quality program was to rely on two key tools: employee involvement and benchmarking. Successful benchmarking projects included:

- *The Information Products Division benchmarked IBM when they wanted to enter the electronic typing business. Xerox entered the market in late 1981, and by 1983 it was the market leader with a 20 percent market share.*
- *The Reprographics Business Group established standards for cost, quality, and reliability performance for a new line of copiers. The result was the 10 series copiers which were the most successful Xerox introduced.*

◆ INTRODUCTION

The **benchmarking** process as it is known today was formally developed by Xerox in 1979. Initial benchmarking efforts were for the purpose of comparing unit manufacturing costs. Over the years it has become a study of processes and a significant strategic tool. The word is derived from the benchmark used by surveyors to indicate "A mark in stone or metal, or other durable material firmly fixed in the ground, from which differences of level are measured as in surveys or tidal observations."

Businesses began the practice of establishing benchmarks early. It was standard practice for many to compare their wage rates and prices to those of the competition. The wage rate comparisons formed the basis for negotiations with unions, and the price comparisons were used for establishing their own prices. In the early 1980s, as companies increasingly felt the effects of global competition, management tried to identify the cause. Several studies, some of which were described in Chapter 1, indicated that the competition was simply more efficient. But this was not evident by simply comparing wage rates and prices. It became clear that a different set of metrics should be used. For example, in 1984, GTE measured defect rates and found that its Japanese competitors had defect rates a hundred times less. This benchmark motivated them to devise plans to improve their processes and close the gap.

Businesses have also visited other companies to pick up new ideas for improving their processes. A recent example is the development of the **Just-In-Time (JIT)** production management system. This system aims to eliminate waste in a production process by reducing inventory. The idea came to Taiichi Ohno of Toyota Manufacturing after he saw how inventory was managed in an American supermarket. Such improvements to process happened in a "hit-or-miss" fashion.

Xerox was the first to define a formal process for establishing benchmarks. Benchmarking at Xerox evolved as a sophisticated methodology for process improvement. Several American companies picked up the methodology and used it to compare themselves against the competition.

The Strategic Planning Institute Council on Benchmarking defines benchmarking as "A systematic and ongoing process for measuring products, services and practices against external partners to achieve improved performance." An example of benchmarking on a personal level is controlling your weight. Assume you went to the doctor's office for a physical checkup. The doctor takes your weight and with a frown on his face pulls out a chart to show you what the appropriate weight should be for your height and age. The doctor has just shown you a benchmark. However, you have no idea how to reach the target. The doctor tells you to diet and exercise. But you decide to talk to some friends who have had similar weight problems and see what they did. If you do this in a systematic fashion, then you are benchmarking. When you adopt what has been learned in this process and change your behavior, the benchmarking project can be called successful.

Xerox views benchmarking as a structured approach for looking outside the organization. They consider it to be a learning experience that can help set realistic performance goals and identify the practices to put in place in order to achieve them. Milliken has remarked approvingly that benchmarking is "stealing shamelessly." Xerox also views benchmarking as part of a discovery process that enables it to learn ways to work better. In this sense it supports Deming's call for managers to develop "profound knowledge" (see Chapter 2).

Companies that have been benchmarking have recognized the significant advantages that result:

- Convince employees that challenging goals can be achieved by setting targets on the basis of hard data, not intuition. Bogan and English (1994) remark that benchmarking complements reengineering efforts, increasing improvements of 5 to 10 percent to a more spectacular 50 to 75 percent.
- Facilitate the implementation of process improvements. The benefits of benchmarking include reduced cycle time and reduced costs for implementing the process improvement. Bogan (1994) noted that the development time for one company was six weeks and costs were slightly more than $5000, while the company it borrowed from had taken four years to develop the system at a cost of more than $500,000.

- Increase awareness of the benefits to be derived from using new technology. Bar coding is a technology that was used by food chains five years before other manufacturing industries began to adopt it. If these companies had been using benchmarking, the implementation of the new technology could have been much more rapid.

The next two sections describe the evolution of benchmarking. They clarify the distinctions between different types of benchmarking—competitive benchmarking, process benchmarking, and strategic benchmarking. This chapter provides several examples of the different types of benchmarking. Finally, it addresses some of the critical issues that have to be handled for a benchmarking project to be effective.

◆ TRADITIONAL APPROACHES TO GATHERING INFORMATION

Even before Xerox developed the formal methodology known today as benchmarking, companies would traditionally compare themselves to each other. Among the better known methods they used are:

- Site visits
- Reverse engineering
- Competitive analysis

Site visits, also known as **industrial tours,** were general information-gathering trips. One company would visit another that had been touted as having a "good" or innovative practice. The purpose would be to see what was being done and possibly to collect new ideas that could be adapted. Typically, the results expected were only vaguely defined, and no significant prework was done by the visiting team.

Reverse engineering involved comparing products. The company would buy the products of several competitors. The marketing and engineering people would study these for functionality. Performance characteristics and new features would be noted and evaluated to improve the product line. The product would then be taken apart by the engineers, who would study it to see what parts and materials were used and how it was put together.

Competitive analysis examined the strategies and tactics employed by the competition. By using printed material, information from suppliers, and market intelligence, it would be possible to determine some of these. For example, by looking at a company's annual report, it is possible to tell if the company is investing heavily in plant and equipment. This could signal a change in strategy, possibly an effort to improve the process, or a desire to increase capacity for a particular product line or an effort to gain a foothold in a new market area. While the competitor's behavior might influence a company's decisions, it would not necessarily result in a better decision or an improvement to a process.

◆ THE EVOLUTION OF BENCHMARKING

Benchmarking focuses on improving existing products and processes. Over the years it has broadened in scope to include improving business strategies and competitive tactics. We can understand these differences better by reviewing the evolution of benchmarking.

In 1979 as Xerox faced increasing competition from Japanese copiers, it initiated its first benchmarking activity. The object was to determine the competitor's costs. Fuji Xerox performed the study and found that the Japanese copiers such as Canon, Minolta, and Ricoh were being priced at Xerox's cost of production. The costs of the Japanese copiers, 50 percent lower than Xerox costs, were established as the benchmarks. The study went beyond merely establishing the product costs; it also looked at the components being used and studied the processes. The approach used was similar to reverse engineering. Xerox would buy the competitor's products and tear it down to its components. As it did so, it would note the materials and parts being used and how the product was put together.

In 1981 Xerox decided to expand the scope of benchmarking to nonmanufacturing operations. Creating the benchmarks to compare the performance of their processes to others was conceptually similar to practices it had created when benchmarking products. But while products could be torn down and reverse-engineered, this could not be done for business processes. Xerox developed a methodology for studying business processes.

The initial process benchmarking studies continued to focus on the competition. These **competitive benchmarking** efforts enabled the process to become as good as the competition. Xerox next set its goal as becoming superior to the competition. To do this, the team would look at companies outside the industry which performed the same function. This is sometimes called **functional benchmarking** to distinguish it from benchmarking only competitors. Taiichi Ohno's study of supermarket inventory management practices and their adaptation for manufacturing is an example of process benchmarking. A classic example of process functional benchmarking is the Xerox study of L.L. Bean's process.

When Xerox decided to improve its logistics operations, it compared its performance against businesses with similar characteristics. The three primary characteristics Xerox identified were:

- Products had to be warehoused and shipped.
- Products had a variety of sizes, shapes, and weights.
- The operation had to be manual but could be directed by a computer system.

Several companies were considered, including Sears Roebuck, American Hospital Supply, and Westinghouse. But L.L. Bean stood out as an excellent performer. Although L.L. Bean handled camping and outdoor goods, the product it shipped had similar characteristics to the product mix shipped by Xerox. Products warehoused and shipped included large items such as canoes and small items such as packages of fishing hooks. Products came in a variety of shapes and sizes since L.L. Bean shipped hiking boots, camping gear, and clothing. And their performance was significantly better—shipment accuracy was 99.85 percent, while orders shipped per man-day was 69 compared to Xerox's 27.

During the benchmarking exercise, the project leader kept the functional managers involved. These managers were involved in creating the questionnaire, going on site visits, and contributing to the trip reports and the final report. The reports were circulated widely through the logistics and supporting functions. Finally, there were reviews for upper management in which functional management participated. Upper management also made it clear that managers should integrate the best practices in their business plans.

The benchmarking exercise resulted in several changes to Xerox's warehouse operations, some of which were:

- Using computer support for order processing
- Bar coding
- Locating material based on "velocity"
- Directing picking activities to minimize travel distance
- Checking item-weights to assure accurate shipments

Benchmarking continued to evolve as businesses realized that the same process could be used to improve business strategies:

- Helene-Curtis studied ways companies structured their organizations to have a wider global impact.
- AT&T's Universal Card Service company studied Walt Disney to find ways to focus a large workforce on a customer-focused approach.
- Bath Ironworks studied the Royal Schelde and other shipyards in Holland to devise a business strategy when it realized the Navy would not be needing as many combat ships after the cold war ended.
- DuPont conducted a study to improve the leadership development process.
- General Motors Service Parts Division developed a strategy to turn the diversity of its workforce into a competitive advantage.

Over the years, the scope of benchmarking has broadened from products to processes to strategy. Companies have recognized the advantage of looking at what others do when improving their own processes. They have also realized that greater benefits could be obtained by examining similar processes outside the industry. At the same time, companies found they could learn from companies in other countries. As a result, the practice of benchmarking has been spreading, and Total Quality organizations consider it an essential tool. All Baldrige award winners perform benchmarking studies. By one estimate, more than 50 percent of the Baldrige points are linked to benchmarking activities.

◆ COMPETITIVE BENCHMARKING

Competitive benchmarking attempts to determine what the competition is doing with respect to product design and to establish the competition's costs.

Benchmarking Product Characteristics

When benchmarking focused on products, the comparisons were most obviously made against the competition. As a result, electronic companies faced with competition from Japan compared yield rates against competitors. Automobile companies compared the prices of their products against those of Japanese cars. But many of these efforts concentrated on determining benchmarks. Competitive benchmarking was an effort to determine product characteristics that provided a competitive edge.

- Ford's development of the Taurus and Sable is an example of competitive benchmarking. The mission for the Ford team was to design a car with features that were the **"best in class"** in several important categories. Best-in-class meant they would be superior to cars that competed with the Taurus and Sable. The first step was to identify the features and the important categories. The Taurus team was organized to obtain input from many different functions. In addition to engineering, it included marketing, manufacturing, service, and public relations. The team developed a list of important features based on input from market research, focus groups, insurance companies, and car repair shops. The team required that the features would attract customers when they first saw the car and also add to their enjoyment of the car as they continued to own the car. Over a period of two years they came up with a list of 400 items. Next, they had to determine the "best-in-class." They purchased 50 cars including European cars that were not sold in the United States. Juries determined which cars performed the best on each of the 400 items. Ford used these specifications in designing a new car to meet the customer's requirements. The success of the Taurus and the Sable convinced Ford of the importance of competitive product analysis.
- Sunbeam, faced with a declining market share of its steam and dry irons, set a goal to reverse the trend and increase its share to 30 percent. It established that the critical success factor was cost. Sunbeam bought several competing products, tore them apart, and studied several parameters. The study showed that these products had 74 to 147 parts, 16 to 30 fasteners, and 9 to 15 fastener types. The benchmarking study determined that the factors with the greatest influence on costs were the number of configurations, parts, fasteners, and fastener types. Sunbeam designed a new product line with just 51 parts, 3 fasteners, and only 2 configurations. The result was a product costing substantially less than that of the competition.

Benchmarking Product Costs

Benchmarking costs is one of the more difficult tasks. Legal authorities know that the risks of sharing cost information with competitors could make the company vulnerable to antitrust suits. But costs can be estimated based on knowledge the company's purchasing function already has on its files.

Another approach to comparing costs is to ask industry groups for information that can be used to generate an accounting statement for an average company. The problem with this approach is that companies define cost items differently. For example, a cost statement for one fast-food restaurant may include waste in the cost of materials, whereas another may classify it as direct variable overhead. One may have franchise fees as part of the overhead. The utility costs for one may be included in the rent. This makes it difficult to compare numbers with any feeling of confidence.

A more robust approach is to derive costs after identifying the **cost drivers.** These drivers should be the same for all the companies being studied. They should also have universally understood definitions, and collectively the drivers should capture most of the costs. Some typical elements and their drivers are:

- Raw materials—usually only those contributing the most to product cost. Typical drivers might include
  - Supplies
  - Freight costs
  - Duties
  - Yield
- Direct labor—usually driven by the wage rate, benefits rate, the headcount, and average hours worked per week. To find the direct labor cost per unit, production volume should also be known. The wage rate and the benefits can usually be approximated as the local rate. It may have to be adjusted for the skill and education level of the workers. The headcount may be more difficult to determine since part-time labor may be included.
- Indirect labor, which includes inspectors, maintenance people, and supervisory staff. Drivers might include the number of managers to direct labor, salary level and benefits, and age and experience.
- Sales costs, which are driven by the compensation plan, quotas, cost of literature and samples, efficiency of the sales staff, and the organization of the sales force (national, regional, or by industry).
- R&D, Marketing and Administration costs, which are driven by the headcount, productivity, wages, and age/experience level.
- Fixed and Working Capital costs drivers, which include depreciation rates, lease costs, cost of capital, typical terms for payables and receivables, and days of inventory on-hand.

Examples of Cost Benchmarking

Example 1

Kaiser Associates (1988) describes a study for a small bank which faced competition from three large national banks. The national banks had moved into the territory served by the small bank after deregulation made it possible.

Step 1 Describe the company's **cost chain.** For this bank the total cost chain consisted of five elements: cost of funds, sales and delivery of funds, marketing, operations, and overhead.

Step 2 Identify the key drivers of these elements and the percentage each contributes to the total cost.

Cost of funds was 75.4 percent of the total cost.

Sales and delivery of funds consisting of the number of branches, ATMs, accounts and so on was 8.5 percent of the total cost.

Marketing, operations and overhead, which were driven by head-count, salaries, rents, and so on, was 15.1 percent of the total.

Since cost of funds was the largest, the study focused on this element.

Step 3 Gather internal data for the key drivers of this element. The funds consisted of noninterest bearing demand deposits, interest (8 percent) bearing deposits, short-term borrowings from other institutions (8.7 percent interest), and long-term borrowings (11 percent interest).

Step 4 Gather competitive data. The bank looked at the performance for three other banks—a midsize regional bank, a large regional bank, and a national bank. This showed that the best performer was the large regional bank with a cost of funds of 5.69 percent, more than 100 points lower than the small bank's costs of 6.83 percent.

Step 5 Determine changes in strategy that would enable the bank to reduce its costs. One change was to manage the short- and long-term fund borrowings more aggressively, in order to reduce the corresponding interest rates. An attempt was made to encourage new accounts to invest in the noninterest bearing accounts.

Example 2

Fuld and Company performed a cost benchmarking study for Cleveland Adhesives (1994), the makers of Elephant Glue. Until 1986, Cleveland Adhesives held a major share (almost 40 percent) of the market. In 1985 Ozark Glue Works started production of Mule Glue in Missouri. They sold it for 10 percent below Cleveland Adhesives' price. As quality improved, *Consumer Reports* rated Mule Glue a "Best Buy," and by 1990 its market share was 20 percent, mostly at the expense of Elephant Glue.

Efforts to determine what gave Ozark a competitive edge failed. The CEO of Cleveland Adhesives planned to buy the company. But a tour of the Ozark plant failed to indicate the reasons for a cost advantage. R&D tried reverse engineering Ozark's product but could not find any significant differences. It seemed likely that Ozark was operating with a low profit margin or saving costs by buying in bulk or reducing waste removal costs by hiring an unlicensed hauler.

In 1990 Ozark decided on a major plant expansion. That decision seemed to indicate that the company was, in fact, making substantial profits. Cleveland's CEO put together a benchmarking team to establish reasons for Ozark's cost advantage. The benchmarking team interviewed industry experts to determine the critical factors. They gathered data from Cleveland Adhesives and then began to compile data related to Ozark Glue. These data were obtained from the filing office, UCC documents and interviews with suppliers and industry experts. The "gap" data (Exhibit 15.1) showed that although Cleveland had lower material and packaging costs, Ozark's costs in all other areas were significantly less.

The study also showed the reasons for the lower costs. Ozark had modified its machines, and as a result its yields were higher and its machine downtime was less. This resulted in greater productivity, leading to lower per unit costs for labor and fixed overhead allocations. The modified machines had also resulted in lower energy needs and less waste to be disposed.

Exhibit 15.1

Elephant Glue vs. Mule Glue: The Gaps Per Unit

COST IMPACT PER POUND	ELEPHANT GLUE	MULE GLUE	ACTUAL GAPS
Cost of materials (per lb.)	$4.197	$4.304	$0.108
Cost of downtime	$0.096	$0.010	($0.086)
Cost of labor (not including Downtime)	$0.548	$0.269	($0.279)
Packaging materials	$4.117	$4.272	$0.156
Waste disposal	$0.048	$0.004	($0.043)
Energy	$0.048	$0.004	($0.044)
Administrative costs (including depreciation)	$1.993	$1.211	($0.783)
Corporate charges	$0.251	$0.000	($0.251)

SOURCE: MULEPRS, Fuld & Co. Inc., Cambridge, Mass. Copyright © 1993.

Exhibit
15.2

Benchmarking Template

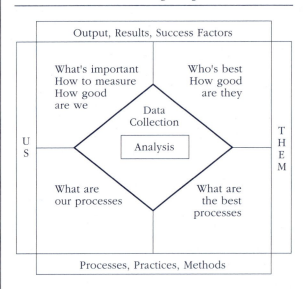

SOURCE: Benchmarking Seminar: Boeing, Digital, Motorola, Xerox.

In this case, Cleveland needed to hire special expertise to support the benchmarking study. The consultants knew where the data might be available. In fact, when studying critical aspects of a competitors operation, it is common practice to use consultants.

◆ PROCESS BENCHMARKING

Exhibit 15.2 presents the version of the benchmarking process developed jointly by Boeing, Digital, Motorola, and Xerox. The left portion of the chart shows the activities to be performed within the company. Determining what is important requires an understanding of the output of a process, the critical success factors, and the desired results. benchmarking partners that are selected should have similar outputs and critical success factors. Ideally, they would also use the same measures. When this is not so, the measures have to be adjusted. The measures are compared to establish the performance gaps. These gaps can be shown graphically as a **Z-plot** or on a **spider plot** (see Exhibit 15.3). The advantage of a spider plot is that several dimensions can be viewed simultaneously. Companies that perform significantly better would be potential benchmarking partners.

Although efforts are being made to find who is best, the team needs to establish its own process. Many companies find they are not in touch with their processes. One company found hazardous waste was getting mixed with other

Exhibit
15.3

(a) Z-Plot and (b) Spider Plot

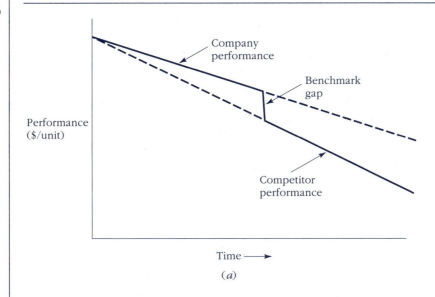

(a)

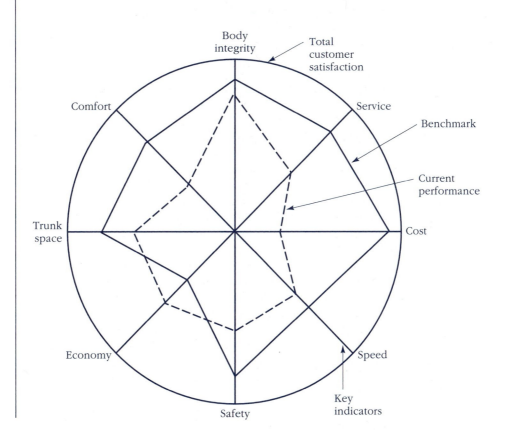

(b)

waste, thereby significantly increasing the costs of waste removal. When it started to map the process, the problem suddenly disappeared. It appears that the process mapping activity had made the workers aware of the necessity to deposit the hazardous waste in the appropriate container.

Once benchmarking partners have been identified, their processes also have to be mapped. Although one might expect an operation that runs better would be aware of its process, it may not always have a map of the process.

When both processes can be studied, the differences can be identified. Then recommendations for improvements can be made.

Central to a benchmarking project is data collection and analysis. The team needs to know how processes are mapped, where to obtain data, and how to analyze the data.

An Example of Process Benchmarking

The CDI Corporation (1993) initiated a benchmarking project before reengineering its billing and payroll process. CDI consists of three divisions:

- CDI Engineering Group with 14,500 employees and 150 offices across the country is the nation's leading provider of temporary technical employees and services.
- Todays Temporary places clerical employees and has 10,500 employees in 80 offices.
- Management Recruiters International finds permanent placements for middle managers and has 400 employees.

The billing and payroll process was a key activity for CDI Engineering. Along with expense reimbursements and cash applications/collections, it formed the largest portion of the accounting costs. CDI realized that improvements to the process would reduce costs as well as enable them to reallocate resources to functions that could provide more value.

The team organized for this effort was chaired by the division president and the controller. Working members included people from accounting, operations, information systems, and a consultant from the Hackett Group.

In order to identify the existing practices and systems, the team visited eight field offices and four paycenters. They asked each location to respond to a standard questionnaire (provided by the consultant), flowcharted the processes, documented special handling, and asked for improvement opportunities.

The team identified several weaknesses, including duplication of work, time-consuming manual processes, and rework. For example, the field offices were connected to the corporate paycenter by FAX. As a result, all of the information related to the employee—name, address, billing instructions, and wage rates—had to be reentered.

The Hackett Group was able to provide CDI with benchmarks so that they could identify the gaps:

Gap 1: The percentage of financial resources allocated to transaction processes. CDI allocated 86 percent compared to the benchmark average of 65 percent.

Gap 2: The percentage of financial resources allocated to decision support. CDI was a mere 2 percent compared to the benchmark average of 12 percent.

Gap 3: Number of data centers. CDI had more than others of similar size.

CDI then had the Hackett Group arrange visits to the best practice companies. To study the payroll operation, it visited Digital Equipment. Digital had centralized the payroll process for all U.S. facilities; 88 percent of their people had their checks deposited directly. Employee work time was entered directly from remote locations. In fact, Digital viewed a phone call as a breakdown of the system. To study the billing process, CDI visited Bearings Inc. Among the significant process improvements observed were on-line data entry and validation, centralized invoicing, and automatic generation of invoices.

CDI also wanted to examine a competitor's process. For this exchange, the scope was clearly defined as MIS/Accounting issues; the questions were developed in advance and sent to the competitor. They were also cleared through the legal department.

Even when the team is not visiting a competitor, there is a risk of legal liability. To avoid such situations, the Strategic Planning Institute Council on Benchmarking created a Benchmarking Code of Conduct (Exhibit 15.4).

As a result of the study, CDI realized that a centralized Accounting Center could be cost effective. It located the center in Philadelphia outside corporate headquarters. Data could be entered using Electronic Data Interchange (EDI) from the customer directly to the paycenter. When this was not possible, the employee would use scannable time cards. Employees were also encouraged to increase their participation in the direct deposit program.

Process Flow Mapping

Certain key tools are part of the benchmarker's kit. One of the more significant tools in the kit for process benchmarking is **process flow mapping.** Industrial engineers use this tool to map the set of steps and activities that convert materials to product or respond to a customer's request for service.

Flowcharting a process has several advantages:

- It gives an overview of the process.
- It identifies relationships and interfaces.
- It facilitates comparison with other processes.
- It can facilitate troubleshooting.
- It serves as a tool for designing a process.
- It provides a common language for people to discuss a process.

Exhibit

15.4

The Benchmarking Code of Conduct

Benchmarking—the process of identifying and learning from best practices anywhere in the world—is a powerful tool in the quest for continuous improvement.

Keep It Legal
Be Willing to Give What You Get
Respect Confidentiality
Keep Information Internal
Use Benchmarking Contacts
Don't Refer Without Permission
Be Prepared at Initial Contact

To contribute to efficient, effective and ethical benchmarking, individuals agree for themselves and their organization to abide by the following principles for benchmarking with other organizations:

1. *Principle of legality.* Avoid discussions or actions that might lead to or imply an interest in restraint of trade: market or customer allocation schemes, price fixing, dealing arrangements, bid rigging, bribery, or misappropriation. Do not discuss costs with competitors if costs are an element of pricing.
2. *Principle of exchange.* Be willing to provide the same level of information that you request, in any benchmarking exchange.
3. *Principle of confidentiality.* Treat benchmarking interchange as something confidential to the individuals and organizations involved. Information obtained must not be communicated outside the partnering organizations without prior consent of participating benchmarking partners. An organization's participation in a study should not be communicated externally without their permission.
4. *Principle of use.* Use information obtained through benchmarking partnering only for the purpose of improvement of operations within the partnering companies themselves. External use or communication of a benchmarking partner's name with their data or observed practices requires permission of that partner. Do not, as a consultant or client, extend one company's benchmarking study findings to another without the first company's permission.
5. *Principle of first party contact.* Initiate contacts, whenever possible, through a benchmarking contact designated by the partner company. Obtain mutual agreement with the contact on any hand off of communication or responsibility to other parties.
6. *Principle of third party contact.* Obtain an individual's permission before providing their name in response to a contact request.
7. *Principle of preparation.* Demonstrate commitment to the efficiency and effectiveness of the benchmarking process with adequate preparation at each process step, particularly, at initial partnering contact.

Exhibit
15.4

The Benchmarking Code of Conduct *(continued)*

Etiquette and Ethics

In actions between benchmarking partners, the emphasis is on openness and trust. The following guidelines apply to both partners in a benchmarking encounter:

- In benchmarking with competitors, establish specific ground rules up front, e.g., "We don't want to talk about those things that will give either of us a competitive advantage, rather, we want to see where we both can mutually improve or gain benefit."
- Do not ask competitors for sensitive data or cause the benchmarking partner to feel that sensitive data must be provided to keep the process going.
- Use an ethical third party to assemble and blind competitive data, with inputs from legal counsel, for direct competitor comparisons.
- Consult with legal counsel if any information gathering procedure is in doubt, e.g., before contacting a direct competitor.
- Any information obtained from a benchmarking partner should be treated as internal, privileged information.
- Do not:

Disparage a competitor's business or operations to a third party.

Attempt to limit competition or gain business through the benchmarking relationship.

Misrepresent oneself as working for another employer.

Benchmarking Exchange Protocol

As the benchmarking process proceeds to the exchange of information, benchmarkers are expected to:

- ✓ Know and abide by the Benchmarking Code of Conduct.
- ✓ Have basic knowledge of benchmarking and follow a benchmarking process.
- ✓ Have determined what to benchmark, identified by key performance variables, recognized superior performing companies, and completed a rigorous self-assessment.
- ✓ Have developed a questionnaire and interview guide, and will share these in advance if requested.
- ✓ Have the authority to share information.
- ✓ Work through a specified host and mutually agree on scheduling and meeting arrangements.
- ✓ Follow these guidelines in face-to-face site visits:

Exhibit

15.4

The Benchmarking Code of Conduct *(continued)*

- Provide meeting agenda in advance.
- Be professional, honest, courteous and prompt.
- Introduce all attendees and explain why they are present.
- Adhere to the agenda: maintain focus on benchmarking issues.
- Use language that is universal, not one's own jargon.
- Do not share proprietary information without prior approval, from the proper authority, of both parties.
- Share information about your process, if asked, and consider sharing study results.
- Offer to set up a reciprocal visit.
- Conclude meetings and visits on schedule.
- Thank the benchmarking partner for the time and for the sharing.

The Council on Benchmarking of the Strategic Planning Institute and the International Benchmarking Clearinghouse, a service of the American Productivity and Quality Center, have adopted this common Code of Conduct. We encourage all organizations and individuals involved in benchmarking to abide by this Code. 3/1/92

SOURCE: SPI Council on Benchmarking, Cambridge, Mass.

Exhibit 15.5 shows some of the typical symbols used to create a flowchart, and Exhibit 15.6 uses these symbols to describe a process for baking cookies.

Flowcharting the Flow of Material

The process starts, and the first step is to mix the cookie batter. The batter in-cludes pieces (chocolate chips, butterscotch, raisins) that had to be added to the cookie. Then the batter is spooned onto the cookie sheet. The cookie sheet is placed in the oven and the timer is set. Periodically, the timer is checked. When time is up, the pans are removed from the oven, and the cookie sheet is placed on a table to cool. If the cookies are burnt, they are checked to see if only the edges need to be trimmed. Badly burnt cookies are scrapped. Undercooked cook-ies are returned to the oven. Good cookies are held in the cookie jar.

Flowcharting Service Delivery

Exhibit 15.7 shows the flowchart for a service. Unlike a product, with a service it is important to highlight when the customer is being served. Points of interaction between the customer and the organization are called **"moments of truth."** Each of these points represents opportunities for the company to convince customers that they are getting good service. Alternatively, if the service provided at any of these points is not satisfactory, the customer is likely to be unhappy. Transactions

Exhibit	Flowchart Symbols
15.5	

Flowcharts use standard symbols.

Start or stop

Decision point

Action step

Meeting

Document

Input

Process

Rework

at these points occur across the **line of visibility.** Activities beneath the line of invisibility are not evident to the consumer. However, some of these may be critical for providing satisfaction at a moment of truth.

Once the process is documented, certain elements should be clear:

- What is the output?
- How is the output measured?
- Who is the customer?
- How does each task in the process help satisfy the customer's requirements?
- What is the input?
- Who are the suppliers?
- What are the boundaries?
- Who owns the process?
- Who ensures the effectiveness?
- How is effectiveness measured?

◆ STRATEGIC BENCHMARKING

The process used for conducting a **strategic benchmarking** study is similar to process benchmarking. However, in this case instead of changing a process, the purpose is to create and implement a new strategy. The key is to cause a shift in

Exhibit
15.6

Baking Cookies

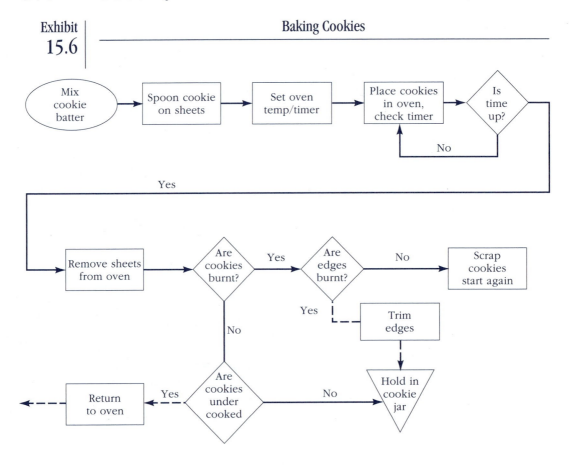

strategy or the adoption of a new business practice, which management expects to result in a competitive advantage.

An Example: Benchmarking Diversity

Although General Motors Service Parts Operations (GMSPO) had been allocating resources to diversity since 1986, there were few bottom-line measures of effectiveness and efficiency. As a result, in 1993 GMSPO launched a benchmarking study called managing diversity which determined that managing diversity really meant managing culture. So, effective management of diversity would require a culture to change and to acknowledge that diversity could be an asset and the norms should change to accept people. The division felt it was strategically important for GM to change the traditional thinking that diversity was a liability and that the only route to success was whether people conformed to the cultural norms.

Exhibit
15.7

Flowchart for a Service Help Desk

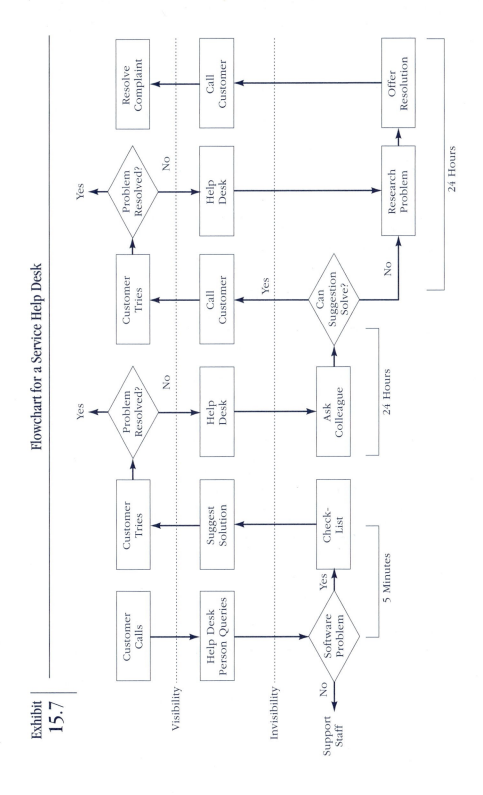

As a first step, the team wrestled with the meaning of the phrase "managing diversity" and the kinds of measurement and evaluation tools that could be effectively used. These discussions resulted in a set of criteria the team could use to choose appropriate benchmarking partners:

- The promotion of diversity should be linked to the reward system.
- Courses in diversity should be offered.
- Diversity should be linked to the business plan.
- Effectiveness measures should be defined
- The responsibility for promoting diversity was assigned with a structure put in place.
- Key measures were defined to include:
  - Turnover by diversity
  - Years of service by diversity
  - Organizational makeup by diversity

The team visited five companies. The companies were not necessarily the best-in-class, but they did meet the selection criteria and were considered to be "significantly better." The partner's profile was large company (sales $10B to $38B), number of employees from 48,000 to 110,000, percentage of union workers ranging from 10 to 59 percent, and promotion of diversity for 10 to 15 years.

The team found the best practices to effectively manage diversity were as follows.

- *Top leadership commitment*—This was shown by their personal involvement and allocation of time and money to employees, as well as customers, suppliers, and the community. Leadership clearly understood the link between managing diversity and the business.
- *Structure*—Line management was given primary responsibility for promoting diversity. The managers had been educated to understand that diversity extended beyond race and gender. Support structures such as networks and resource groups were provided for employees as well as customers, suppliers, and community.
- *A business focus*—The benchmarked companies recognized the impact of managing diversity on the bottom line. Diversity was integrated in the business plan. Companies linked diversity to market segmentation and used it for relationship marketing.
- *Link to rewards*—Appropriate behavior was defined and expected of managers. Input was gathered from across the organization to evaluate the managers effectiveness in promoting diversity and used to adjust earnings.
- *Communication*—Messages were communicated from top management through the organization and through visual diversity messages.

The team was also able to identify significant benefits as increased market share, more productive teams, greater retention, increased workforce flexibility, and improved relations with employees, customers, suppliers, and the community.

◆   KEY ISSUES IN BENCHMARKING

Key issues for benchmarkers are:

- What should be benchmarked?
- Who should be on the benchmarking team?
- Who should be selected as benchmarking partners?
- What are the legal issues involved in benchmarking a competitor?
- What are some common pitfalls?

What Should Be Benchmarked?

The benchmarking project should focus on a task that is important for the organization. The first step is to identify the customer. Then **critical success factors** (CSFs) need to be defined. These factors impact customer satisfaction and are vital practices that must be done well for the organization to succeed. These CSFs should be prioritized. Criteria for choosing among them should include practices that influence customer satisfaction, and those most in need of improvement. The project should be well defined with an estimated time to completion of less than a year. If the project tackles a significant task, management will be willing to allocate the time and the resources necessary. When the team is inexperienced, a more modest project can be selected. The purpose is to build organizational experience and have a successful first project. While this project may not be critical, it should be significant enough that the results would still be of interest. The estimated time for completing this first project should be around six months.

Another way to build benchmarking expertise is to select a competitive benchmarking study aimed at improving a product. This approach follows the evolutionary path of benchmarking studies as described earlier. Camp (1989) notes that in 1981 100 percent of the benchmarking projects at Xerox focused on products. By 1992 only 10 to 20 percent were focused on product, while 80 to 90 percent were focused on practice. If a company initiating the benchmarking activity started with a competitive benchmarking project, it could then evolve naturally to process benchmarking and finally strategic benchmarking.

Once a benchmarking project is selected, an explicit mission statement needs to be crafted. This should document the purpose and the deliverables expected from the study. This document should be communicated to others in the organization to preclude duplicating efforts.

Who Should Be on the Team?

The quality of the people on the team should reflect the importance of the project. But, in addition, certain specific skills and resources are necessary:

- A person who has knowledge of benchmarking—ideally, a person with experience who has facilitated a benchmarking team.
- Someone with "hands-on" knowledge of the process being benchmarked.
- Someone who understands the requirements of the customer of the process.
- People empowered to implement the recommendations.

Team sizes can range from two to eight. But it is important to make sure that all key stakeholders are represented. When the scope of the project is so large that the numbers may be larger, temporary members can be assigned. They would be kept informed of progress and be responsible for providing input.

Who Should Be Selected as Benchmarking Partners?

While it may be tempting to benchmark only world-class processes or the "best of breed," it may not be fruitful. As discussed in Chapter 2, this approach seems to be beneficial only for companies that are already performing well. That study recommended organizations performing slightly better would provide more useful models to benchmark. The approach to selecting a partner starts with a clear definition of what is being benchmarked. Then a set of criteria needs to be constructed. Typical criteria might include type of business, employee characteristics, product and process, distribution channels, and financial performance. The costs of gathering data also need to be considered. One company restricted the choice of partners to within a 50-mile radius. Another chose to rely on questionnaires and phone calls with no site visits. The partners chosen may be internal, competitors, or generic.

Internal partners are in the same company but in different divisions. Watson (1993) describes a study performed by Hewlett-Packard to improve the time-to-market performance for its R&D projects. The San Diego Division studied the performance of 12 in-house projects to identify best practices.

Competitors may provide ideas for improvement but sometimes will not want to cooperate. When Ford's Taurus team benchmarked their product, they did not need the competition's cooperation. They simply went and bought the cars and proceeded to take them apart. However, when CDI wanted to study a competitor's billing and payroll process, it had to be careful about the legal implications. When competitors are not cooperative, information can be obtained from public sources as described in the Cleveland Adhesives example earlier. These sources include published literature, public seminars, company publications, information from industry groups, and taking apart the product the competitor sells.

A **generic partner** is a company outside the industry that shares some of the same issues. Xerox found that L.L. Bean faced similar problems in its warehouse and distribution systems. CDI's study of the billing and payroll process extended beyond other temporary technical placement firms to include Digital Equipment and Bearings Inc. Other examples of generic partners are:

- Florida Power and Light wants to distribute power reliably. It looked for other industries for whom breakdowns in distribution lines could be critical.

The petroleum industry which has to ensure the uninterrupted flow of oil from wellhead to tankcars was one, so Philips Petroleum was selected as a benchmarking partner.

- Remington, the manufacturer of guns and ammunition, found that customers wanted smooth and shiny shells. They searched for other industries where smooth and shiny casings were made, and they selected Avon as a benchmarking partner.

What Legal Issues Are Involved?

The concern is that antitrust or other legal issues may rule out potential benchmarking partners. As of the end of 1993, no case had been brought to court accusing companies of antitrust collusion. Still this has been an issue of concern to benchmarkers, especially when they are partnering someone in their own industry. Snead (1993) outlined 10 risk evaluation factors to consider:

1. Concentration of the industry and if it has been the target of an antitrust inquiry.
2. Stability of prices or costs or levels of output, raising the concern that collusion may be occurring.
3. Public availability of information; if the information being requested is publicly available, it should be collected from those sources rather than from a competitor.
4. The nature of the information to be exchanged. Information involving price, output levels, market definitions, or cost data would constitute collusion. However, information that can be classified as generally useful to society would be low-risk. The rule is to avoid the appearance of agreeing with the partner to perform a task or implement a technology.
5. Whether the exchange is direct or through an intermediary. Going through an intermediary greatly reduces the risk of a jury concluding that an agreement was made.
6. Whether the information is past, present, or future. Past information is low-risk, while exchange of present or future information may imply collaboration.
7. Identity of parties to be masked. This can be done by aggregating or averaging the data.
8. Added analysis, commentary, or recommendations, which may cause a jury to infer that one company is suggesting what the other should do.
9. Frequency and regularity of exchange. Infrequent exchanges would indicate collusion is less likely.
10. Whether the information is made public. If it is, the risks are generally less. But in many cases benchmarking information must be confidential. If the partner is a competitor, then the risk is greater.

What Are Some Common Pitfalls?

Pitfall 1: Pressure from the benchmarking project's client to obtain the result before the study can be properly performed.

Pitfall 2: Establishing the metrics. Care must be taken to ensure that the metrics can be compared directly to metrics the partner uses. If not, an adjustment method to make the metrics comparable must be devised.

Pitfall 3: Too broad a topic. The topic should be so chosen that the team can implement the recommendations.

Pitfall 4: Questionnaires that ask unnecessary questions but do not ask the important ones; that is, questions that provide information necessary to change the process. All questionnaires should be piloted.

Pitfall 5: Unclear questions. (Sometimes that is because they contain company jargon the partner may not understand.) When piloting the questionnaire, it is best to have someone from another company answer it.

Pitfall 6: Failure to take full advantage of the site visit. The site visit is the best opportunity to obtain the information. So full advantage should be taken otherwise; a significant opportunity could be lost. In preparation, it is worthwhile to conduct a dry run. While on the site visit, watch body language and listen to what is said informally at the watercooler or at lunch. Sometimes this can lead to information not expected from the prepared questions.

Pitfall 7: Use of separate teams. The benchmarking team makes recommendations, and another group forms the implementation team. When the teams are separate, the process improvement is least successful. Separate teams are usually formed because the two teams together are too large. It is still worthwhile to merge the two so that the benchmarking and implementation teams are the same.

◆ THE PARTNER'S PERSPECTIVE

As the focus of benchmarking practice has shifted from product to process to strategic level, the benchmarkee has become more involved. Furthermore, as a company's reputation for excellence spreads, the number of incoming requests can increase dramatically. For the benchmarkee to participate in all of the proposed studies would require a commitment of enormous resources and management time. The average number of companies screened in one year was reported as 123 in one survey, with one company screening as many as 2000 (Langowitz and Rao, 1995).

This makes sense only if the benchmarkee can also gain sufficient value from the exchange. Many of these would not be characterized as serious requests. For example, one visitor said he wanted to visit "because he was visiting another company in the area." The average annual acceptance rate for "serious" requests was reported as 58 percent. In short, there is plenty of competition for access to some prospective host companies, and many of the benchmarking experts screening requests are inundated with work.

Handling Benchmarking Requests

Exhibit 15.8 shows a generic process flow that many companies use for handling benchmarking requests. It consists of five major steps, the first three of which are frequently iterative. Requests are initially screened by a benchmarking expert with an eye toward the potential benefit for the benchmarkee. A second phase of this screening is to involve appropriate line managers who might ultimately sponsor the project. These managers must be persuaded of a potential payoff as well as the availability of resources to undertake the benchmarking partnership. If a project is agreed to, a third step occurs toward proper advance structuring of the benchmarking exchange. The predominant format for accepted benchmarking requests was an on-site exchange, which was nearly evenly split between half- and full-day visits. (Teleconferencing was another popular exchange format.) After the exchange takes place, appropriate followup is implemented by the majority of companies.

Exhibit 15.8 Generic "Benchmarkee" Process Flow

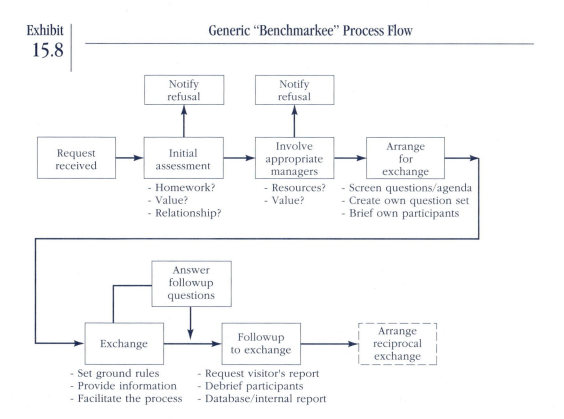

Benefits of Being a Host

Experienced benchmarkees are value driven. Project acceptance and realized learning depend on delivering value to the host organization. Benchmarkees conceive of this value in terms of both the ends and the means. In terms of the end-point value, companies with experience as hosts agree that multiple potential benefits accrue from serving as a benchmarkee:

- *Improved relationships*—where benchmarking partners are key customers, suppliers, or business allies, strengthening relationships through goodwill.
- *Process audit*—enabling the host company to validate the excellence of its process or to identify details for incremental improvement.
- *Opportunity for reciprocity*—gaining entree to the benchmarker's organization and studying processes where they are best-in-class.
- *Internal promotion of benchmarking*—providing an opportunity for people in the host organization to observe the value the benchmarker can receive from the project.
- *Morale booster*—from other companies recognizing the world-class caliber of the host's processes.

Exploiting one of these potential benefits is a proactive approach to delivering value to the host. But they also have concerns about the means for achieving a potential end-point benefit. Given the required investment of organizational time and talent combined with the inevitable disruption of ongoing business activity, benchmarkees don't want their limited resources wasted. Companies who want to successfully gain access and information from a benchmarkee must do so through careful preparation for and execution of the benchmarking exchange.

Criteria for Screening Requests

By far the most important criteria for screening are **level of advance preparation** and **perceived value** to our company.

Level of Advance Preparation

This criterion tests how well resources will be used. There is a strong expectation that the benchmarker has done its homework in advance. That is, the benchmarkee expects the benchmarker to be able to articulate why their organization was identified and what business or function in the organization the requester wants to benchmark. Simply saying, "Well, you're a Baldrige winner" is not enough. Also, asking a company such as AT&T to benchmark customer service is not enough. AT&T will want to know exactly what kind of customer service and in which business area the benchmarker is interested, for example, long-distance service, cabling service, or Universal card service. A second aspect of advance preparation is an assessment of the benchmarker's readiness or sophistication with benchmarking. The benchmarker must be seen as understanding its own process well, having a commitment to the spirit of interchange in benchmarking, and having a clear focus on process improvement. Prospective benchmarkers should have documented their own process and be able to provide a question set to the benchmarkee concerning what they hope to learn. The bottom line on the advance preparation criteria is that doing your homework counts.

Perceived Value

Delineating the potential value of the proposed benchmarking partnership is another important aspect in gaining access to a prospective host company. Demonstrating the seriousness of the effort through up-front homework may serve to convince the host that a project would provide valuable process audit information or be a strong benchmarking promotional experience. Access can also be obtained by highlighting the status of a business relationship as either customer or supplier. Many companies are hard-pressed to turn down a request from a major business partner and may even go out of their way to coach the prospective benchmarker on appropriate project structure, should advance preparation prove inadequate (hence the iterative nature of the screening steps). A third way to provide value to the benchmarkee is for the benchmarker to offer a reciprocal exchange in an area of the company that is already world-class.

Maximizing the Benefit from an Information Exchange

After agreement to host a benchmarking project is obtained, an important issue for the benchmarker is to use the opportunity for maximum benefit both to themselves and the benchmarkee. The concerns of most significance to the host are availability of resources and confidentiality. Careful execution is critical in assuring that the means to the benchmarking partnership is as valuable as the ends. Experienced host companies review the benchmarker's question set in advance of the benchmarking exchange. Many will ask the benchmarker to complete the question set for its own organization and send it in advance to the benchmarkee. This allows the benchmarkee to understand more about the benchmarker's needs and, in particular, to understand the level of detail required for answering each question. Often, this technique helps to overcome problems with semantics as well. In addition to clarifying what content is to be covered during a benchmarking exchange, it is also important to establish appropriate conduct for the exchange. This means that participants should be carefully trained, a practice extensively used by experienced host companies, especially with a view toward dispelling hosts' concerns with regard to confidentiality and appropriate exchange of information. To be as effective as possible, the benchmarker team should include well-prepared managers who are process experts and have been trained in benchmarking practice.

Upon completion of the exchange, followup is essential to reaping the rewards of benchmarking. At a minimum a written report should be made documenting the entire exchange, data collected, and major points of learning. This report is essential not only for the benchmarker but for the benchmarkee as well. Most host companies request a copy of the benchmarker's final report on the project.

Some additional tips for companies hosting a benchmarking project are:

- Prepare your own question set for the exchange.
- Document the exchange after the visit has taken place to record what was learned.
- Debrief the host managers involved in the exchange.
- Based on learning during the exchange, specify an action plan for implementing.
- Enter a description of the exchange in the company database, so that others will know of the opportunity for exchange.

◆ Summary

Benchmarking is an important tool for supporting the continual improvement effort. It has evolved from competitive benchmarking to process benchmarking and, today, to strategic benchmarking. It has proven effective for incremental as well as breakthrough improvements. One caveat was based on the International Quality Study which observed that it was of most benefit to high-performing companies. The study concluded that if the company was a poor performer it would benefit from benchmarking companies that performed somewhat better, though not necessarily at world-class level. There is also some evidence to suggest that a benchmarking study goes far in ensuring the benefits of a breakthrough reengineering project. Finally, participating in a benchmarking study has certain benefits for the host company. However, the host company has to formalize the support structure to derive the maximum benefit from a benchmarker's visit.

◆ Key Terms

Benchmarking	Functional benchmarking	Line of visibility
Just-in-time	"Best in class"	Strategic benchmarking
Site visits or industrial tours	Cost drivers	Critical success factors
Reverse engineering	Cost chain	Internal partners
Competitive analysis	Z-plot	Generic partner
Competitive benchmark-ing	Spider plot	Level of advanced preparation
	Process flow mapping	Perceived value
	"Moments of truth"	

◆ Assignments

1. Go to a local fast-food restaurant and plot the flow of service starting with the time you enter the door to the time you leave the establishment.

2. The process to be benchmarked is the bill-paying activity. Exhibit 15.9 shows the existing process flow.
   a. Who is the customer for this process?
   b. Define at least two suitable metrics.
   c. Perform a gap analysis by comparing your performance on these metrics to that of four of your classmates.
   d. Compare the process in Exhibit 15.9 to the best processes of your classmates and suggest changes to the existing process.

3. Assume you are conducting a benchmarking study for the library services of the college. The mission for the library is: Support faculty and student research by providing access to existing articles and books in a timely and cost effective way.
   a. What are some of the critical success factors for library services?
   b. Assume the critical success factors were determined to be:
      • Customer satisfaction
      • Timely delivery of materials
      • Ease of use and maintenance
      • The library staff's primary support
      • Obtaining of material from external sources
   c. The next step is to determine who is best at providing these services. List criteria for selecting the benchmarking partner.
   d. Assume the criteria chosen were:
      • A supplier of information
      • An innovative organization
      • Use of outside electronic data sources
      • Use of electronic means to locate material
      • Information requests covering many disciplines
      • Users not paying for information
   Name some of the places you would go to find potential benchmarking partners.
   e. While the search for potential partners proceeds, the college's process is mapped. The team has also decided to send a survey to the benchmarking partners and not to go on any site visits. The survey would inquire about demographics, the partner's mission, the ways they use computers and networks, and the methods for communicating with the customer. Describe how you would go about getting a response from potential benchmarking partners.
   f. Some of the best practices resulting from this study include:

Exhibit
15.9

Paying Bills Each Month

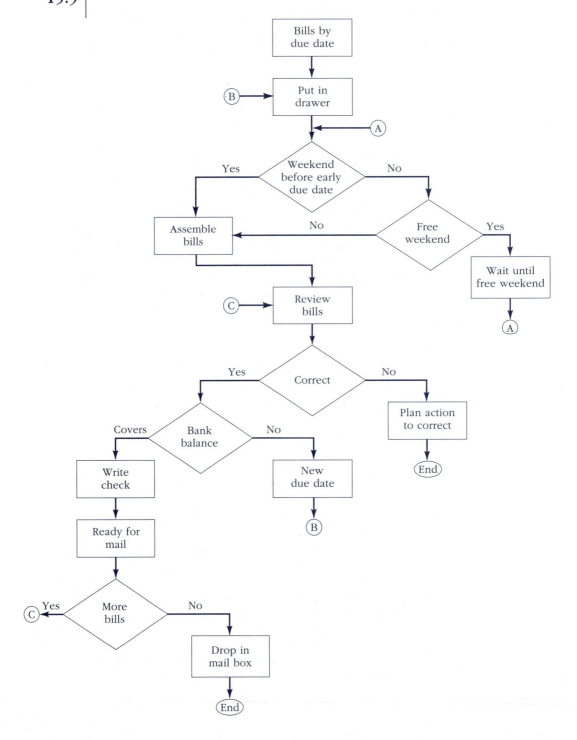

- Desktop library service
- Regular customer surveys to measure satisfaction
- Use of electronic mail for delivery
- A proactive approach to making customers aware of the mission of library services.

Explain how you would decide which of these processes should be implemented.

4. A commonly used metric to assess efficiency is to compute dollar revenues per employee.
   a. Rank the following companies using this metric:
      - Wal-Mart
      - Compaq
      - Apple
      - Exxon
   b. Is this metric appropriate for measuring the efficiency of these companies?
   c. For each company identify a metric that is more appropriate for measuring efficiency.

C a s e   S t u d y

Simon Alphin—The Benchmarking Study

Simon Alphin was a disappointed man today. He had spent a year and several thousands of the company's (Teklite Inc) dollars locating and identifying best practices in new product development. All along, management had supported him. Last month he had presented them with the final report. Immediately after the presentation, his superior, Andrew Botolph, complimented him. "I've been talking with the vice president of R&D and the president about your findings. They are eager to begin implementing them. God knows, this company could really improve their product development process. Now thanks to your study, it is clear to the president. And Helen Bridges (the vice president of Research and Development) is eager to implement your suggestions. Your presentation today just confirmed what I had been telling them." But so far no significant changes had been

made in the new product development process. For all purposes it seemed that the study had been put on the shelf.

Simon reviewed the project in his mind. Where had it gone wrong? He remembered the day Andy Botolph had asked him to do the study. As the vice president of finance, Andy was also responsible for Corporate Planning. He had data that indicated others in the industry were bringing new products to market in less than a year. Projects at Teklite typically expected to take two years from concept to market. And then many of them were late. Andy had presented his data to the president and the vice president of R&D. Both had agreed this would be a worthwhile project to benchmark.

As Simon put the benchmarking team together, he included Jerry Newton, the director in R&D who was responsible for new

Simon Alphin—The Benchmarking Study (Continued)

product development. Jerry had complained of the lack of time, but when Helen told him of the importance, he agreed to take part.

Simon had found companies that were known for their new product development process and were willing to share their knowledge. The six companies he identified were not direct competitors of Teklite but had products with similar technical, production, and distribution characteristics. All the members of the benchmarking team had visited each company—all, that is, except for Jerry Newton. It seemed that always at the last minute an emergency situation occurred, and Jerry would have to stay behind to handle it.

But, Simon reflected, upon returning from the trip he always updated Jerry. If he could not meet with him, he made sure Jerry received the trip report. He had also sent the final report for Jerry to review. It had come back the next day. Scrawled across the cover page was Jerry's handwriting "This is an excellent report. Simon, you and your team have done an excellent job. This is really going to help."

Simon had just talked with Jerry. He'd asked him which of the many recommendations made in the report had been implemented. "We haven't got around to it yet, Simon. As you know we've been really busy here. Your recommendations were great. But I need some time to figure out how to integrate it with our existing practices. And, after I do that I have to talk it over with Helen. And as you know she has been really busy lately. I haven't even seen her the last two weeks." That did not sound like a person who was going to implement the recommendations anytime soon.

CASE QUESTIONS

1. When should Simon have realized that the benchmarking project was in trouble?
2. What could have been done to improve the chances of success for this project?

C a s e   S t u d y

Shawmut Industrials—Marta's Visit

Alan Jaworski, vice president of finance for Shawmut Industrials, was bemused while answering the telephone call. The person at the other end of the line was Jill Furman, the chief financial officer for Marta Corporation. She wanted to benchmark Shawmut's order acknowledgment system.

Jill had met him at a recent conference on benchmarking. Alan had gone to the conference since he had recently been given the responsibility for introducing benchmarking to the company. At the conference he had heard that hosting a benchmarking project could help promote benchmarking within the host organization. He wondered whether this was a good opportunity.

Jill was saying she had heard Shawmut's system was excellent in talking with some of the vendors Shawmut and Marta had in common. Alan had not thought Shawmut's process was anything special, and he knew Ed Jacobs (the head of the Order Acknowledgment process) had been working at improving it. He made a mental note to find out what Ed had done. To Jill he said, "I'm glad to hear that. I know Ed has been

Shawmut Industrials—Marta's Visit (Continued)

working to improve the process. I'm glad his efforts have borne fruit already."

Jill continued, "We have been planning to improve our process for some years. Finally, we have put together a team to benchmark it. The team consists of the Head of Accounts Payable, the Shipping Supervisor, a person from Quality Control, a person from Information Systems. We have put together a questionnaire. We'd like to send you the questionnaire. Then we would like to arrange a one-day meeting with you within the next month."

Alan responded carefully, "Shawmut would be happy to be of help to you especially since you are such a valued customer. I'll have to contact my people to see if we could put aside a day next month. Meanwhile, send me the questionnaire." The conversation finished on a pleasant note, with Alan promising Jill he would call her back to make arrangements.

As he hung up the phone, Alan was already dialing for Ed Jacobs. Ed, too, was amazed that someone had labeled his Order Acknowledgment system as world-class. "We've made some changes," he mumbled, "but, I still think we have a long way to go.

We have been talking to the information systems people to enhance our system. And you know how they are. It'll be months before they get around to doing for us what needs to be done."

Alan said, "Marta is a good customer of ours. We should probably do this just to improve our relations. I've asked for a list of questions they plan to ask. They want to come for a day-long visit. See if you can get a group together to meet with them."

Two days later Jacobs called Alan; "Did you read this questionnaire? They are looking for information we don't have. They want a process flow. We have it for pieces of our system but not for all of it. They ask for specific measures such as time to respond to vendor requests. We don't collect such data. If you want me to put this together, it will take us several days of work. What do you want me to do?"

CASE QUESTIONS

1. What are the benefits to Shawmut from hosting Marta Inc.'s benchmarking team?
2. What should Alan do?

◆ Bibliography

Bogan, C. "Where Is Benchmarking Going for Senior Executives?" Presented at the SPI Council on Benchmarking, 1994.

Bogan, C. E. and M. J. English. *Benchmarking for Best Practices: Winning Through Innovative Adaptation.* New York: McGraw-Hill, 1994.

Camp, R. C. *Benchmarking: The Search for Industry Best Practices That Lead to Superior Performance.* Milwaukee, Wis.: ASQC Quality Press, 1989.

Cannello, A., and R. Gage. "Diversity as a Competitive Advantage." Presented at the SPI Council on Benchmarking, 1994.

Fuld, L. "When Best-in-Class Is the Competitor: What Is the Mule Doing?" Presented at the SPI Council on Benchmarking, 1994.

Kaiser Associates. *Beating the Competition: A Practical Guide to Benchmarking*. Vienna, Va.: Kaiser Associates, 1988.

Langowitz, N., A. Rao. "Effective benchmarking, learning from the host's viewpoint." *Benchmarking for Quality Management and Technology,* 1995.

Ransley, D. R. "The Do's and Don'ts of Benchmarking." Research-Technology Management, 1994.

Snead, W. G. "Evaluation Factors for Benchmarking Proposals." *Corporate Counseling Report* 7, no. 2, Spring 1993.

Strayer, J., H. Hurdle, E. Landis, and J. Kinsey. "Case Study: Reengineering of the Billing/Payroll Process." Presented at the SPI Council on Benchmarking, 1993.

Watson, G. H. *Strategic Benchmarking*. New York: John Wiley and Sons, 1993.

Xerox. *Competitive Benchmarking: The Path to a Leadership Position*. Stamford, Conn.: Xerox Corp., 1988.

Landmarks on the TQM Road

◆ ◆ ◆

In 1989 John F. McDonnell, chairman and CEO of McDonnell Douglas Aircraft Company, was facing a major crisis. Customers of the Douglas Aircraft Division were defecting to the European Airbus Consortium. It was clear to McDonnell that a major structural change had to be made in the organization. Specifically, there were too many managers, and he wanted to reduce the nine levels of management to five. He also wanted to cut down the number of top management positions by two-thirds. The empowerment aspects of TQM appealed to him. He reasoned that these managers could be removed by empowering teams of employees. First, 8000 employees were sent to Long Beach, California, for two-week training seminars, and following that, they had several weeks of training for TQM on the job. Meanwhile, managers were given a two-hour evaluation. If they were not evaluated as being effective, their employment was terminated. The management structure was changed, and new work procedures were implemented. In spite of these changes and a huge backlog of orders for commercial planes, the company lost $224 million in the first half of 1989. About two-thirds of this was attributed to the TQM program.

This vignette provides an example of a failed attempt at initiating TQM. This chapter will provide additional examples of companies that have failed. The good news, in the authors' experiences, is that when TQM fails, it "fails soft." That is, failure is rarely a disaster. Some companies that failed have been known to successfully resurrect the effort in later years. This chapter describes the initiation of TQM at Xerox as an example of success. But, it is important to recognize that TQM is not a program that can be implemented and completed. TQM is an ongoing effort. Deming when he says, ". . . Push the above thirteen points everyday," and Crosby when he says, "Do it all over again . . .," are very clear on this point (see Chapter 2). When companies continue to practice the TQM philosophy, they progress to a level of maturity that sets them apart. The last section provides specific landmarks indicating if a company has reached that level.

◆ OTHERS THAT FAILED

Company A is a high-tech company and a market leader. In 1980 the CEO became interested in TQM after reading Crosby's philosophy, an interest that was further reinforced when he attended a seminar taught by Deming. By 1984, the company had started to develop a quality program. Quality training was delegated to a line manager as part of his responsibilities. This person chose Juran's material as the basis of the program for the company. Participants were involved with the program for a year during which time they identified a project, diagnosed the cause of the problem, and implemented remedies. While the projects were successful, it was not enough to save the company from a severe downsizing in 1985. The program became moribund. In 1988 a new president was named, who appointed the vice president of Human Resources as the Director of Quality, and a second attempt was initiated. In 1989, when a major customer, Motorola, won the Baldrige award, the vice president decided to adapt the Motorola six-sigma process to the company. But by 1991, of the 14 teams that were started only 5 had made it through all of the problem-solving steps. The others had either abandoned the effort or were bogged down. Once again the director of Quality reviewed the training program. Meanwhile, sales and profits were deteriorating. It was difficult to get volunteers for projects when people knew more layoffs were imminent.

Organization B is an Army installation. In 1987 the Department of Defense signed on to the TQM bandwagon. The Secretary of Defense issued a memorandum directing all organizations to create teams of line managers at all levels to remove organizational and procedural impediments to production and quality. The Army supported this effort with a Total Army Quality (TAQ) program. It was early 1990 that Organization B received orders to establish a TQM program. But they could not find a regulation outlining the Army program or any directives to guide them. Management selected a supervisor to run the program. This person located the minimal training requirements specified by the Army but could not find any trainers. Under pressure from her superiors for results, she organized a one-day seminar for the entire installation. Then she organized an Executive Steering Committee (ESC) that included the commander and his deputies. They started to implement Deming's 14 points. When that turned out to be too difficult, they brought in a consultant who took over as leader of the ESC. Management wanted people trained quickly and did so by assembling large classes of 90 people. The consultant guided them to selecting a project: Improve the local procurement process. The team got as far as trying to identify relevant measures to provide a baseline. The Army had a regulation that told them how long they had to process a request. So, they had trouble trying to identify measures that might be suitable to a customer. As this effort ground to a halt, management made some organizational changes, and the second-in-command took over as leader of the ESC. It was now established that the goal for each directorate in their installation should emphasize customer focus, and each would also form its own steering committee and be responsible for implementing TQM. A team of trainers was formed that trained all of the midlevel managers over a one-year period. Evidence of diffusion of TQM practices began to appear. Affinity diagrams appeared on walls, and many directorates had periodic TQM meetings to monitor progress. But there was significant resistance at the senior management levels. Neither the Installation commander or any of the directors visibly supported TQM. Some directorates openly said that they did not see the need to emphasize customer focus since they already did. Several people indicated that they were too busy. Still the quality director pushed on with training the workforce. But with little enthusiasm at the upper levels of management, the midlevel managers had begun to lose interest.

These and other examples of TQM failures indicate that the philosophy is not easy to deploy through the organization. Harari (1993) estimates that at most one-third of the TQM programs initiated in the United States achieve significant or tangible improvements. Arthur D. Little's survey of 500 companies showed that only 36 percent found TQM had significant impact. Critics add other examples: Florida Power & Light for one, was awarded the Deming Prize in 1988, but later the company ran into some serious problems and the CEO was forced to resign. When the new CEO took over, he slashed the TQM program. The Wallace Company won the Baldrige Award in 1989. Later it went into Chapter XI. What happened at both companies is discussed later in this chapter.

◆ SOME WHO ARE SUCCEEDING

The literature is replete with success stories dealing with the initiation of TQM. The results have been impressive and dramatic. Below is a sampling consisting of a manufacturing company, two service companies, and a small manufacturer:

1. AT&T Transmission Systems won the Baldrige in 1992. Its approach focused on teams. In the late 1970's and through the 1980s it was only seeing small improvements. Management identified a key missing element as the setting of strategic priorities and driving these through the business. As the TQM program began to take hold, the results were dramatic. Over the six years through 1994, product quality improved tenfold. Time to market was slashed by 50 percent, from 39 months to 19.5 months. Customer satisfaction increased by 25 percent, the number of customers increased by a factor of ten, and sales outside the United States doubled to $600 million.

2. The Ritz-Carlton Company, though only created in the early 1980s, has always had a reputation for quality. In 1986 and 1987 it won several awards from consumer organizations and travel agent groups. Horst Schulze, the president and CEO, felt they did not really know if they were good because they had never benchmarked outside the industry. They visited Milliken, Motorola, and Xerox, and then they used the Baldrige Criteria as a roadmap and realized they had not paid sufficient attention to the Voice of the Customer. When they did, they found that the customer wanted one key

product, "the caring customer interface." They defined processes to meet 18 key customer demands. Training was initiated so that all employees understood the goals of the corporation, obtained necessary skills, and learned ways to make the customer feel good. Training materials were sent out from corporate, and every day all 14,000 employees were taught the same thing. Tangible results included a drop in employee turnover from 90 percent to under 30 percent, whereas customer satisfaction climbed from 91 percent to 97 percent. The new goals are to reduce the number of defects per million transactions for the 18 key processes to six-sigma levels. Customer satisfaction has a goal of 99.7 percent, and the cycle time of the 18 processes is targeted to shrink by 50 percent.

3. Marlow Industries makes such devices as thermoelectronic coolers, infrared detectors, and semiconductor lasers. Traditionally, 60 percent of their sales is to the military aerospace industry. In 1994 they employed 160 people and had sales of about $14 million. In about 1987 they started a TQM program. Everybody was made familiar with Crosby's 14 steps. They then took the Baldrige Criteria and combined them with their TQM program to create their own unique approach to TQM. They focused on management by fact. All employees were educated on the basics such as reading control charts, and measurement systems were devised. Benchmarking was used to establish goals and to devise ways to achieve them. They developed visual systems and plotted key indicators such as engineering change notices, order entry errors, and yields. They developed a strategic planning process that relies heavily on customer input drawn from different customer segments. The TQM council, which is led by the chief operations officer, defines major projects to support the quality plan. A team with a champion for each project and a mentor on the TQM council then creates a detailed implementation plan.

4. The University of Michigan Medical Center (UMMC) initiated its TQM efforts in 1987 with a focus on meeting customer requirements and improving the quality of work life. A Total Quality Task Force was organized to drive the process. The group selected Admission/Discharge as a pilot project to verify that TQM tools could be of value. In 1989 the process began to gather steam. Physicians were made aware of the benefits of TQM, and plans were developed to deal with several major issues:

   - Acceptance of TQM by physicians
   - Identification of customer requirements and measures
   - Communication at all levels
   - Reward and recognition
   - Training and education
   - Increased sensitivity to needs of a diverse workforce

These plans were implemented in 1990 and by 1991 a total of 19 teams had completed a quality improvement process. UMMC conducted a study to establish the cost/benefit of these projects. The savings and revenue increases, 17.7 million, were obtained at a cost of $2.5 million plus training costs of $1.5 million. Convinced of the value of TQM, a plan was developed and implemented for improving clinical quality. At the same time, a gainsharing program was instituted to align employee incentives with the organization's goals for cost effectiveness.

◆ THE WALLACE COMPANY

The Wallace Company was founded in 1942. By 1981 it had sales of $100 million and employed 450 people. Its main products were piping products for engineering and construction (E&C) projects and replacement equipment for maintenance and repair operations (MRO). Eighty percent of the sales were to the E&C market. By 1985, the Wallace Company was struggling to survive. E&C projects had slowed down, and two of its competitors had filed for bankruptcy. At the same time, the MRO market was also shrinking. That was when the Celanese Corporation, a major customer, informed Wallace that it would be shrinking its supplier base to those companies that demonstrated a commitment to quality. Wallace Company decided to initiate Total Quality Management.

They formed a Quality Management Steering Committee consisting of all the senior management. They found out about the philosophies of the TQM gurus such as Deming and Crosby, taking the ideas they felt would work for them. They also formed quality circles. But these changes did not seem to be effective.

In 1987 they hired Sanders and Associates, a training firm. As a first step Sanders surveyed the employees to assess their needs. In addition to training, Sanders discovered a large fear factor. Wallace knew from their understanding of TQM that this was unacceptable. In order to change it, they increased the communication level between managers and employees. During training sessions, members of senior management were always present. Offsite retreats were held to encourage employees to speak out.

By 1989 Wallace felt they had come a long way on the TQM journey. The Baldrige Award had just been created, and a small company—Globe Metallurgical—was among the winners. Wallace had leadership commitment, statistical process control had been implemented, and over the past few years more than $700,000 had been invested in training. They felt they should be in a good position to win the Baldrige Award. As a first step, they used the Baldrige Criteria to perform a self-assessment. Out of 1000 points they felt they earned only 210!! They developed a one-year plan to improve.

The plan called for developing a clear set of objectives. Using the Baldrige Criteria, they created 16 Quality Strategic Objectives. All improvement projects had to be related to one of these objectives. Nine objectives were related to people issues. Several associates gathered at a retreat to improve the human resource processes and defined issues including performance evaluation, career development, and employee relations.

One result was the Performance Enhancement Program. During training an associate is expected to acquire 50 specific quality skills. Before an evaluation meeting, both the associate and the supervisor rate the importance of the skill to the job and to the associate's performance, and then the two get together to discuss strengths, weaknesses, and gaps.

Another area for improvement was the information system. Wallace examined all the data to ensure its adequacy for supporting its Quality initiative. All data had to meet either the internal customer's needs (sales reports, inventory records) or the external customers' needs (on-time delivery, defect rates) or help improve leadership practices (turnover, training, or promotion). In addition to maintaining all the control chart data from the shop floor, Wallace also monitored service performance in such areas as on-time deliveries and invoicing errors. The data were made available to all associates and audited frequently to ensure accuracy. The data were used to facilitate improvements in such areas as sales performance, inventory, and accounts receivable. The information system was also used to provide new services to the customer. For example, Wallace provided customers with a Material Test Report. If a customer wanted test results for a pipe sold six months earlier, the data could be retrieved and faxed.

In 1990 Wallace applied for the Baldrige. The TQM initiative had already paid off in terms of increased sales (up 69 percent from 1987) and market share (up eight points from 1987). They guaranteed 98 percent on-time delivery to customers. Wallace provides a Total Customer Response Network which handles customer complaints in 60 minutes or less. Customers appreciated Wallace's dedication to Quality. Monsanto gave them their highest supplier rating whereas Brown and Root Inc. and Bechtel chose them as their first distribution supply partner. Every employee attended a Quality Alert "Safety First, Family First" program. As a result, they were reinstated by their insurance carrier. Winning the Baldrige Award was just icing on the cake.

But in 1992 Wallace filed for Chapter XI. It has been frequently cited in the literature as an example of the failure of TQM. What happened??

It turns out that Wallace had lost money—$691,000 on sales of $88 million. The problem with credit only compounded a serious cash flow problem. In an effort to improve on-time deliveries, the company had added $2 million to overhead. But this had been a necessary expense. The company had managed to reduce its debt from $30 million in the early 1980s to $5 million by 1992. But all banks in Texas were losing money, and the company's bank was no exception. It was forced to cut off credit. Other banks, too, were not in a position to loan Wallace money. As word of Wallace's cash position became known, some Wallace suppliers would only deliver C.O.D.

John Wallace, the CEO, assigned some of the blame to chasing the Baldrige Award: "We were so busy doing presentations [a requirement for Baldrige winners] that we weren't following up and getting the sales." On the other hand, he noted that the Baldrige Award was a significant factor later in Wilson Industries' desire to acquire the Wallace Company. John Wallace became a vice president of Wilson Industries and is assembling a quality program for the whole organization.

While winning the Baldrige is a badge of having traveled far on the TQM journey, this example illustrates that good practices do not replace the need for a good strategy. Clearly, Wallace should have realized how weak a cash position it had and adopted a different strategy. For all that has been written about it, none of the critics has suggested a viable strategy that would have kept Wallace solvent.

◆ FLORIDA POWER & LIGHT

Another classic example quoted by critics of TQM practices is Florida Power & Light. The company won the Deming Prize in 1989 and is the only non-Japanese company to have won it. It also is an example of good practices not compensating completely for bad strategy.

In 1977 FP&L was in crisis. There was an oil shortage that had caused energy prices to skyrocket. Customers were expressing dissatisfaction with the service received, and FP&L needed to invest more money to satisfy the demand for energy. With the pressure on to keep prices down. FP&L's return on investment was falling.

This was the first time FP&L had experimented with quality principles. The St. Lucie II nuclear power plant was being constructed, and the company could not afford project cost overruns and delays. The results were eye-opening. The plant was completed in 6 years instead of the industry average of 9 to 12, it cost $1.4 billion compared to the average of $4 billion, and "energy availability" was 90 percent compared to the industry average of 60 percent.

McDonald, the chairman of FP&L, announced in 1981 that the company would establish a TQM program. Crosby's book, *Quality Is Free,* was distributed to the top 30 executives. This was followed by trips to Japan, and seminars and consultation with Deming, Juran, and several Japanese Quality counselors. He established a Quality Improvement Department whose mission was to support the process.

FP&L started by introducing Quality Improvement Teams. Beginning with 10 teams in 1981, by 1986 there were 1400 teams. Each team followed the standard seven-step method, which is similar to the problem-solving process described in Chapter 6. When teams finished, their work would be written up as a Quality Improvement story using a standard format. This would be critiqued by managers so that the team could improve their problem-solving skills. Teams were recognized and rewarded with gifts such as baseball caps and sometimes a trip to Japan.

The results were quite encouraging. By 1987 customer approval had risen to 71.2 percent, customer complaints had dropped 61 percent, and the reliability of customer meters improved 30 percent.

This had been going on with middle managers only superficially supporting TQM. FP&L realized that the middle managers were needed to make the program more effective. For example, by 1984, only 25 percent of the workforce had volunteered for a QIT. So, extensive training was provided to this managerial level.

Policy Deployment, introduced in 1984, is similar to the process described for Hewlett-Packard in Chapter 11. This planning process started with a problem diagnosis that took into account key stakeholders such as consumers, senior management, and employees. Solutions to the problems were devised and short- and medium-term plans were formalized.

Then in 1986, FP&L started the Quality in Daily Work program. Policy Deployment was aimed at aligning each department's goals with company strategy. The new program hoped to institutionalize QI problem-solving techniques. The message they intended to convey was that employees were no longer expected to do quality improvement tasks in addition to their work, rather, they were to make quality improvement part of their daily work.

The growing success of FP&L's TQM program prompted the chairman, John Hudiburg, to seek the Deming Prize. He invited Japanese examiners to review the company's progress. When problems arose, such as the Nuclear Regulatory Commission's complaints about the Turkey Point nuclear plant, he simply hid it from the Japanese consultants. In 1989 FP&L won the Deming Prize with an application that exceeded 1000 pages.

At the same time, FP&L had been buying into other industries: mail-order insurance, cable television, real estate services, citrus groves, and credit reporting. These acquisitions proved to be a big drain on the company. In 1990 the company lost $464 million. The board of directors accepted McDonald's resignation in 1989. Instead of promoting Hudiburg to that spot, they selected James Broadhead from outside the industry. Broadhead started to dismantle the TQM program, reducing the formal structure supporting TQM to a department of only six people.

The TQM practices were already well embedded in the organization, however. Away from the spotlight, FP&L has continued its efforts to intensify the quality efforts. In 1994 FP&L invited the Deming examiners back to assess their progress in TQM. The examiners commended FP&L on their progress. Cost per KWH is a key indicator of competitiveness, and it has been trending downward. The Turkey Point nuclear plant rated one of the worst by the Regulatory Commission and a factor in the Board's releasing McDonald and Hudiburg, was one of the best in 1993. In 1993 FP&L met or exceeded its performance targets in 19 of 23 corporate indicators.

◆ THE XEROX STORY

The story of Xerox's journey as it initiated TQM starts in 1980 as David Kearns, the CEO of Xerox, became aware of the problems Xerox was having in the marketplace, and the story ends in 1990. But, TQM has continued at Xerox as it has at many other companies. As evidenced by the experiences of the Baldrige winners described in Chapter 1, a commitment to supporting TQM through ups and downs does pay off. While the formal structure supporting TQM may change, many companies continue to intensify their efforts.

In 1959 the Haloid Corporation (renamed Xerox in 1961) introduced the first officer copier based on xerography technology. The product was an instant success. By 1966 employment rose to 24,000 from 700 just seven years earlier. For many years, Xerox enjoyed a virtual monopoly as it owned most of the necessary patents. Gradually, others began to enter the market. In the early 1970s IBM and Kodak entered the market, and by the late 1970s, the Japanese, in particular Ricoh and Canon, were entering the market. Xerox's overall market share had dropped from 100 percent in the 1960s to less than 50 percent by 1980.

In 1962 Xerox established a partnership with Fuji Photo. This firm, Fuji Xerox, supplied copiers to the Far East. Rank Xerox was the operation that supplied copiers to Europe and Africa. By 1976 Fuji Xerox was having trouble holding its own in the Japanese market. In part, this was because it relied on the designs supplied by Xerox and Rank Xerox that were not designed for the Japanese market. Fuji Xerox decided to initiate a TQM program and called it the "New Xerox Movement." As its first goals, it aimed to design and build a copier in half the time and at half the cost of previous machines.

In 1977 David Kearns was made president of Xerox. By the late 1970s, Kearns began to realize the problems facing Xerox. Xerox leased many of its machines, but the lease base was shrinking rapidly. Margins had dropped from 70 percent to 10 percent. The Japanese had taken over the low-end of the market, and in 1981 Canon began to attack the middle-volume portion of the market. As Kearns later came to know, the Japanese had targeted Xerox and intended to claim the copier market as they had the videocassette recorder and motorcycle markets.

But Xerox could not understand how the Japanese were able to price their products so low. Comparing themselves to other American corporations, Xerox had annual productivity improvements of 7 to 8 percent, whereas typical American corporations had only 2 to 3 percent. Kearns dispatched a team to Japan and found:

- Japanese inventory levels were six to eight times less.
- Incoming parts were at 99.5 percent quality, where Xerox was at 95 percent.
- Japanese overhead was half that at Xerox.
- Unit manufacturing cost was two-thirds the cost for Xerox.

So, in 1980 Kearns came up with the concept of improving business effectiveness based on two tools: benchmarking and employee involvement. In previous years, Xerox would compare its machines to each other. Then it would set goals as being 10 percent better than last year's. The study of the Japanese affirmed that they had to look at the products built by competitors. The practice started in 1979 and spread to all divisions by 1980. Also, in the late 1970s, Xerox had initiated a quality circle activity. This formed the basis of the employee involvement thrust.

Building Union Support for TQM

How Xerox went about gaining employee and union support while they were reducing the workforce is particularly interesting. In order for Xerox to encourage
employee involvement, it had to rely on the participation of the union.
Manufacturing was done primarily in four plants at Webster, New York. Workers
here belong to the Amalgamated Clothing and Textile Workers Union. In 1980 the
union and Xerox agreed to develop problem-solving teams focused on shop floor
activities. Over the next two and a half years, over 150 groups successfully solved
problems related to eliminating chemical fumes, machine upgrading, organizing
tool storage, and reducing machine downtime.

There were problems, however. A major problem was the high turnover in the
groups. One cause for the turnover was the bumping and bidding rights guaranteed the workers by the contract. In addition, during 1981 and 1982 almost 5000
people in the Rochester area were laid off, 1200 of whom were union employees.
Employees were also dissatisfied with the time required to solve problems and
subsequently to implement the solutions.

There were other problems as well. Late in 1981, the company announced a
plan to subcontract the assembly of wire harnesses, and it was thought that the
entire assembly department of 180 people would be laid off. The union stepped
in and persuaded management to suspend the outsourcing plans. A study team
was organized to find ways to become more competitive. The team, consisting of
managers and hourly employees, was trained in problem-solving and communication techniques. They studied the problem for six months, finally presenting
recommendations that would exceed the team's targeted savings of $3.2 million.
The recommendations that could be implemented without violating the labor contract were immediately implemented. The remainder were placed on the bar-
gaining table for the 1983 negotiations.

The 1983 negotiations resulted in a no-layoff guarantee for the three-year period of the contract. Joint decision making was encouraged. In return, changes
were made in seniority rights, and personal allowances were reduced. Additional
teams were formed, usually as a result of crises, and resulted in substantial improvements in productivity in other areas.

The 1983 negotiations resulted in several controversial concessions:

- No wage increase for the first year
- Changes in health benefits to include co-payment
- An absenteeism control program

The immediate result was an increase in the number of grievances as well as a
significant decline in the number of quality circle groups. Some informal changes
were made to the absentee control program, which was the most controversial
provision. These were later approved in the 1986 negotiations, but the decline in
the number of groups continued.

About this time, David Kearns introduced the Leadership Through Quality (LTQ) program. When training of manufacturing plant managers started, the union leaders were immediately suspicious. They were not being included in the training, some of which was very similar to the training for QWL teams. They thought that management was trying to create an alternative to QWL and step away from the concept of joint governance. Today, all managers and union officials get three days of LTQ training.

Top management was keenly interested in encouraging employee involvement. So, they conducted investigations by interviewing groups and administering an attitude survey. They found that the employees liked the notion of participative management but did not feel quality circles was a satisfactory approach. The survey also provided some clues as to how to improve the system.

By 1985 Business Area Work Groups (BAWG) were formed in the Components Manufacturing Operations. This was a flexible approach that consisted of individual contributors, quality circles, or autonomous work groups, as appropriate. Similar groups were used in other plants. For example, in the New Build Organization the groups were called "work families." Initially, supervisors were designated as leaders of these groups; over time it was decided the groups could elect their own leaders.

Buoyed by the added emphasis given employee involvement through the company's TQM plans, these groups flourished. Autonomous work groups formed voluntarily. They addressed activities such as monitoring inventory, maintaining absentee's records, and participating in work redesign. In the 1986 agreement, leaders of these informal groups were given an additional pay premium and time to work on administrative tasks.

Workers began to be included in strategic level decision groups as well. For example, when a new Toner plant was to be constructed, initial studies showed that a location in the South would be preferable. But a planning team with a majority of hourly members recommended changes in the work organization, reduction in supervisory levels, and new computer-based inventory control procedures. As a result, the new plant was constructed in Webster. Hourly workers are also involved in the introduction of new products. They help resolve manufacturability issues even in the early stages of product development.

Although management offered union leaders the opportunity to participate on the management operations committee for manufacturing, the union declined, feeling it would tie them too closely to managerial decisions that they may have to oppose at a later date.

The history of this collaboration shows the importance of a flexible approach and a willingness to attempt new organizational arrangements. No one form such as quality circles, autonomous work groups, or other type of team effort is a universal panacea. Both union and management had to be willing to redesign organizational structures when issues arose in the workplace. It was also helpful that the union was independent of the international union, so innovations did not raise issues in other areas.

Building Management Support for TQM

In 1982 David Kearns became CEO of Xerox, and the quality movement started in earnest. By now Xerox's share of the American copier market had declined to 13 percent, and the Japanese had begun to flood the market. In addition to Canon and Ricoh, Sharp, Minolta, Konishiroku, Toshiba, Mita, and even the Tokyo Aircraft Corporation entered the market. Kearns visited Fuji Xerox in 1982 and returned visibly impressed by its commitment to Total Quality Control. Fuji Xerox had won the Deming Prize and managed a remarkable turnaround in its business, with increases in market share, revenues, and profits. Bill Glavin, a close friend of Kearns and one of the senior managers, attended a TQM seminar at the Crosby College. He became an early instigator of TQM. Kearns saw this as the next step in the business effectiveness program.

First, he realized he would need a constituency of support among the people in power. The current champions of the business effectiveness program and the employee involvement program (Norm Rickard and Hal Tragash) were keen to spearhead this effort. They met with the six most senior managers and found that the interest was lukewarm. Then they met with the eight managers at the next level and found seven of them were supporters. This group of managers identified 11 people for Rickard and Tragash, who could help get the quality program going. This group studied quality and tried to create a model for Xerox. Tony Kobayashi, the head of Fuji Xerox, met with them regularly on his visits to the United States and provided valuable input. They did not understand at the time that TQM was a new way of managing. Accordingly, the Commitment to Excellence approved by the Corporate Management Committee focused solely on quality.

Kearns next hired David Nadler, an expert in organizational behavior, who interviewed many of the senior managers and concluded that three major issues faced Kearns:

1. Although everybody wanted to do quality, quality itself was poorly defined.
2. Kearns had very little constituency of support.
3. There was no transition plan on how to achieve quality.

A plan developed to invite the top 25 people in the company to a conference in February 1983 at Leesburg, Virginia, to kick off the effort. Before the meeting, Nadler, Rickard, or Tragash visited each of the 25 and explained their vision of quality. Many of them were skeptics. To convince them, Rickard circulated books showing what people were doing, highlighting the important passages to make reading easier. The team also arranged for some key people to visit IBM and Westinghouse and to take a trip to Japan. They also met with the quality gurus, Crosby, Deming, and Juran. By the time the February meeting took place, Kearns had a Blue Book that stated the mission of Xerox, what Xerox would look like once it had quality, and a road map proposing what had to be done. Key items were as follows:

- Quality improvement was a key to long-term success.
- Quality was determined by the customer who could be internal or external.
- Quality improvement was a result of doing the right things well.
- Quality was to be achieved by introducing problem solving and quality training throughout the company; senior managers becoming role models for the new type of behavior; and a reward system to recognize people who used the quality tools.

The material was sent in advance to the meeting participants, along with 34 questions they planned to discuss during the meeting. Questions were action-oriented:

- What should Xerox's quality strategy be called?
- How should units develop the Cost of Quality?
- Is there agreement to train all employees?

The purpose was to develop a Quality policy for the company and a process to achieve it. What came out of the meeting were a name—Leadership Through Quality—and specific processes such as a six-step problem-solving process. Kearns concluded the meeting with a list of six key elements that all participants agreed were necessary for TQM: reward and recognition, training, standards and measures, communications, a transition team, and appropriate senior management behavior.

Kearns also composed a 30-second speech that explained the concept when he met people by chance. Another approach to convincing senior management was to have them listen to customer calls. Each day of the month, one of the senior managers would be assigned to take customer calls. Complaints ranged from lost shipments and burning machines to simple problems that employees should have fixed. In a short period, management was sensitized to the customer's concerns.

Meanwhile, the stockholders were expressing their dissatisfaction with Xerox. The market had come to realize what Kearns had noted years earlier—that market share and profit margins were declining. Several reports were being published in the media. Kearns estimated that only half of these were true. Kearns hired a public relations firm to help explain to Wall Street the steps Xerox was taking to fix these problems. Many new products were introduced and advertised heavily. When these products got good reviews, the public relations firm made sure the analysts heard. Gradually, the stock recovered. By the time of the stock market crash, the stock was selling at $85, up from $27 when Kearns had taken over as CEO.

Kearns had asked other managers to be role models, and he decided he should provide one as well. One way was to have his own performance reviewed. Once a year, he would meet with Nadler and conduct a personal performance review. Benchmarking against others was also high on his agenda. He provided a role model by organizing meetings with other chief executives who were trying to induce their organizations to change. These meeting included CEOs at Corning, Alcoa, and AT&T.

After the Leesburg meeting, Kearns began to organize the Quality Implementation Team. As the leader, he picked Fred Henderson. Kearns added people from corporate. Others were nominated by the operating units. Some of the people nominated by the units were sent there for the wrong reasons. They were not real change agents. The group first met in April and spent a month studying TQM principles. They visited IBM, Hewlett-Packard, and Westinghouse, and they went to Japan. Nadler taught them about change management.

As the work progressed, it became evident that some of the people were not very effective, and so Henderson gradually got rid of them. By August 1983 the team had put together the Green Book, which outlined in great detail the transition timetable. The goal was to have all 100,000 employees trained by 1986 and to be seeing tangible results from the efforts by 1987. They also set annual targets for Return on Assets, market share, and customer satisfaction.

One of the tactics delineated in the Green Book was a novel training approach, "learn-use-teach-inspect" (LUTI). At each level, managers would learn from the management level immediately above it, and then they would use it. Their use of the tools would be inspected by the managers who had done the training; then they, in turn, would train the next level of employees and inspect their use of the tools. Training consisted of half-a-day of quality awareness and five and a half days devoted to quality and problem solving. The training was started in January of 1984. Many of these methods are discussed in this book. In addition, at Xerox they added material on handling meetings.

But as 1985 began, it was clear that the quality effort was not going right. Xerox had introduced a desktop laser printer, and it was a disaster in the marketplace. Only a little more than 50 percent were classified as satisfactorily installed, and clearly it was not meeting customer expectations. Yet the quality officers were saying things were going well. People were getting upset at David Kearns's performance. Anonymous letters were sent to Peter McColough, the chairman of Xerox, representing views contrary to those of Kearns. They suggested Kearns was losing control and asked McColough to take charge of the business again. The year 1986 saw the Xerox copier group making overly optimistic revenue projections. They created 10 new office products but were not able to bring them out on schedule. Also, the salesmen were not trained properly to sell those that did come out on schedule. The year also witnessed poor performance. Kearns found that he could not keep up with the day-to-day work of TQM as well as the longer range strategies of the company. So, he appointed Paul Allaire president and chief operating officer; in addition, Fred Henderson was replaced by Norm Rickard as chief quality officer.

In early 1987 an employee survey was done to determine the state of quality progress in the company. The results were mixed. Although everybody supported the quality strategy, it had not been integrated into the company's daily work life. The pressure was still there to achieve financial results. And where there was a conflict with quality, the desire for better profit numbers usually won. Some units had absorbed the message better than others, but in some units when sales were slow, the survey found that the quality training had been stopped. In these cases, organizational changes were made, and quality officers were replaced by more aggressive individuals.

One aspect of the training that had not been working well was the inspection portion of the training. An additional workshop was designed to train managers to give continual feedback to teams and not wait until the project was complete. Another failing was the reward system. It appeared that some of those being promoted were not believers in the quality process. Thus, management reconfigured the promotion criteria. Another mistake that became evident to Kearns was that at the inception of the program he had placed equal emphasis on three objectives: return on assets, increasing market share, and better customer satisfaction. Until then the focus at Xerox had been on return on assets. Given this cultural background, many managers interpreted the focus on three objectives to imply that ROA was still the most important. In 1987 Kearns decided to focus on just one: bettering customer satisfaction. Allaire and Kearns also started to place much more emphasis on the Leadership Through Quality program at the monthly review meetings with the business units.

By the end of 1988, all Xerox employees had been exposed to quality training; work groups were springing up voluntarily in response to problems and issues; and Teamwork Days used to communicate results and reward performance were getting more popular. In May 1988 the 50 series of copiers was introduced. It had more features and better quality than anything else Xerox had produced. Even the instruction manuals showed improvements as they were made more readable. In 1989 Xerox applied for and won the Baldrige Award.

By 1990 sales from the office equipment business had risen to $13.6 billion, with profits of $599 million. Return on assets had grown to 14.6 percent, seven percentage points of market share had been taken back from the Japanese, and customer satisfaction had increased by 38 percent in four years.

Xerox after Winning the Baldrige

But the effort continues at Xerox. Allaire and Nadler have recognized that TQM is a management style. Their continuing efforts are aimed at intensifying the attitudes they wish to foster:

- A customer defines the business.
- Success depends on the involvement and empowerment of trained and highly motivated people.
- Line management must lead quality improvement.

- Management develops, articulates, and deploys clear direction and objectives.
- Quality challenges are met and satisfied.
- The business is managed and improved by using facts.

Even after winning the Baldrige, the TQM journey continues. In 1990 Allaire embarked on a program called 2X designed to double the rate of change. Xerox introduced a new planning process to intensify the deployment of corporate quality strategy. For example, the Americas Operations created a detailed action plan by country. The plan followed the by now familiar Plan-Do-Check-Act cycle. Each quarter the results would be checked, root causes for unfavorable variances identified, and modifications to the plans made. The vision for the Americas Operations was 100 percent satisfied customers. This was supported by specific goals in three major areas:

- Customer satisfaction as measured by customer surveys, complaints, internal quality measures, and the inspection process
- Identification of key processes affecting the customer and reduction of errors by a factor of 10
- Workforce preparedness, which included training in customer orientation, empowerment, and recognition and reward

Specific targets were based on benchmarking studies. Argentina, for example, identified four key processes such as complaint management and administrative support. The corresponding measures were percentage of complaints solved beyond five days (target set at 4 percent) and percentage of invoice errors during the first run (target set at 0.75 percent).

Xerox has also emphasized innovation. In 1993 Xerox brought out products for a new market segment, the home office. In 1992 it worked with Sun Microsystems Inc. to create a new high-speed printer, and in 1994 it created LiveBoard that supports real-time group collaboration over a network. Another product was VerdeFilm, a nonsilver, nonpolluting digital film for the graphic arts industry. The genesis of this strategy was a strategic exercise in 1990–1991 that called for shortening the time to market. They established a Technology Decision-Making Board consisting of the presidents of the nine divisions of Xerox. Then they changed to a "quick development" process that involved Xerox engineers and researchers working with the customer. A Market and Technology Development group was charged with evaluating orphan technologies—that is, technologies that have no alignment with a specific division. This unit helped bring LiveBoard and VerdeFilm to market quicker.

Xerox continues to thrive. A recent Fortune survey ranked it in the top 100 most admired corporations in America. Their share of the copier market continues to increase. In spite of having divested themselves of the financial markets, revenues continue to increase. In 1994 they were estimated to reach almost $16 billion, with profits of $725 million.

◆   LANDMARKS ON THE TQM ROAD

When assessing a company's progress, it is easy for the layperson to be taken in by a series of success stories. A more sophisticated student of TQM may apply the Baldrige framework. But a naive assessment using these criteria may indicate more progress than exists. This section provides some guidelines that can help distinguish between three landmarks: Awareness, Understanding, and Maturity. In general, companies that have won the Baldrige would be classified as Understanding. Companies that have persisted and grown beyond Baldrige would be classified as Mature. When evaluating an organization, it is typical to find peaks of excellence. So, a company may be well along on Leadership but may be only at the Awareness level in Information and Analysis. Such a company would be classified as having reached Awareness. In order to reach the succeeding landmarks, performance in all categories has to be at the level of the landmark.

The First Landmark: Awareness

LEADERSHIP
- The CEO has attended some speeches describing the advantages of TQM.
- The CEO has accepted the need to introduce quality in response to the demands of major customers.
- Senior managers have attended a basic seminar dealing with TQM.
- Senior management has at least one "heroic" act they can describe to illustrate their commitment to TQM. An example is delaying the launch of a new product until the product achieves acceptable quality levels.
- Senior management has yet to have disappointments in their TQM efforts.
- Reports received about the progress of TQM or the satisfaction of customers are only through other departments rather than through direct contact.

INFORMATION AND ANALYSIS
- The company has collected some competitive information.
- The company has benchmarked some of their processes against one or two companies that are known to be excellent.
- Benchmarking projects have not been tied to a clear business need.
- There is a process for requesting financial information that is available for all people in the company.

STRATEGIC QUALITY PLANNING
- The responsibility for implementing TQM has been assigned to an individual.
- The approach is to achieve a baseline goal such as getting registered ISO 9000.

- Management has hired a consultant or selected a consultant's approach to TQM as opposed to tailoring one to fit the company's needs.
- There has been an assessment of the existing corporate culture. Often this is done using the Baldrige guidelines or the ISO 9000 framework.
- The strategic priorities of the organization have been explicitly stated and related to the TQM initiation plans.

HUMAN RESOURCE DEVELOPMENT AND MANAGEMENT

- Banners are placed around the plant proclaiming a dedication to quality, and employees are encouraged to do quality work.
- Employees are given training in topics such as quality awareness, managing meetings, and brainstorming. There is little, if any, emphasis on training in data-driven problem-solving techniques such as described in Chapter 6.
- A rudimentary recognition system is in place. Evaluation of suggestions is cursory, with little understanding of the linkage of the suggestion to the strategic goals of the organization.
- Each person in the organization is aware of the emphasis on quality.

MANAGEMENT OF PROCESS QUALITY

- Process control charts are being constructed. The charts are typically constructed using process control software acquired from an outside vendor.
- All process control charts are in the production area or in the operations area of a service. There are few charts in support areas such as finance or legal departments.
- Process quality is measured based on the output-using measures such as defect rates and number of customer complaints.
- Several processes have been flowcharted. For some of them, key measures have been listed, but the processes have not been identified as key processes for the organization.
- A few processes in support areas have not been mapped and flowcharted.
- Suppliers are encouraged to initiate their own quality programs.

QUALITY AND OPERATIONAL RESULTS

- Charts showing quality results are visible at several operational sites.
- There are several examples of dramatic improvements.
- The time taken to complete certain activities such as new product development has improved slightly.

CUSTOMER FOCUS AND SATISFACTION

- Customer satisfaction measures are collected. But it is collected by the people responsible for delivering the service.
- Performance "gaps" have been identified for several products.
- Customers are interviewed but not in a formal, statistically sound manner.

The Second Landmark: Understanding

LEADERSHIP

- All senior managers devote more than 10 percent of their time to quality-related activities such as speeches (both inside and outside), training, meeting customers, and recognizing quality improvements.
- Senior managers have communicated the key aspects of TQM, including customer focus, continual improvement, management by fact, and employee involvement. The version of TQM being promoted is specific to the company, and is not the generic prescription of one of the gurus or a consultant.
- These managers recognize that TQM is an ongoing process. They expect the organization to be continually striving to achieve higher goals.
- Senior managers have also been involved in their own quality projects.
- The results are evident in a focus on customer satisfaction. Each employee would be aware of the significance of his or her work in satisfying the external customer either directly or through a chain of internal customers.
- A steering committee would be set up at the corporate as well as division and department levels to manage the quality improvement teams.
- Although a formal organization structure has been put in place to support TQM, the organization is not a bureaucracy. That is, the number of people in the TQM organization is small, usually less than 10.

INFORMATION AND ANALYSIS

- Information systems are at an advanced technological level.
- These systems track and measure key quality measures for the organization.
- Data, especially financial and accounting data, are easily accessible by all employees.
- The data are clearly used for making decisions.
- An effort is made to compile external data to establish benchmarks and assess performance relative to the competition.

STRATEGIC QUALITY PLANNING

- A quality plan has been written that may be included in the business plan. The process of developing such a plan has involved customer suppliers and employees.
- The production area has set specific quality goals. In other areas, employees have quality goals as well.
- Quality goals include "stretch" goals such as six-sigma goals. Although these may be long-range goals, intermediate goals should also be set.
- The quality plan includes strategies that are designed to meet these quality goals.
- There is a clear link between employee compensation and achievement of the quality goals.

HUMAN RESOURCE DEVELOPMENT AND MANAGEMENT

- A large number of teams are focused on quality improvement projects especially of critical business operations. As a result, many success stories have been recorded.
- Many employees submit suggestions. And, the suggestion system is formalized with a required response time.
- All employees receive basic quality training. Training is extensive, with expenditures amounting to 3 to 5 percent of the annual budget.
- Safety and health-related issues are a primary concern.
- Employee surveys are used to assess employee morale.
- Employees have a passion for making the product or providing the service.
- Employee recognition programs offer rewards for various types of improvements, not solely quality.
- In older organizations there is a significant reduction in the number of levels of bureaucracy; that is, the organization has become "flatter."
- Traditional measures such as turnover, absenteeism, and injuries are measured and show an improvement trend in addition to being better than the industry averages.

MANAGEMENT OF PROCESS QUALITY

- The new product services introduction process has been greatly improved. The process includes a customer focus, cross-functional teams, and data-driven approaches to enhance the offerings such as Taguchi methods.
- Manufacturing companies have identified the critical processes, and these are under control using SPC. The processes are capable. Service companies have also identified their critical processes and have created measures that are monitored and show some stability. In addition, the measures that have been selected are known to impact the customer.
- At least one process improvement has been implemented with dramatic results. Examples are Just-In-Time production and employee involvement.
- A continuing effort is made to change the processes in order to improve performance. The employees involved with it are not satisfied merely by documenting the process and determining that it is capable.
- The measures are not static but are continually being ratcheted upward. So, the organization recognizes that improvement is ongoing and does not come to a halt when a goal has been achieved.
- Processes are improved by quality improvement teams. These process improvements are not restricted to only one area of the organization, but also exist in support departments such as information services and human resources.
- All teams use the basic methodologies. Sometimes, these teams use sophisticated methods such as Taguchi.

- An audit function exists to assess the production processes.
- There are extensive programs with suppliers, which include audits of the supplier's systems, training for the supplier, joint quality improvement teams, and supplier recognition programs.
- Relationships with suppliers are cooperative and not adversarial. Practices such as pitting one supplier against another for the purpose of getting lower prices or better terms are not condoned.

QUALITY AND OPERATIONAL RESULTS
- These companies can demonstrate their products, and services exhibit higher quality than the competition.
- Key measures are linked to improvements in performance, such as higher customer satisfaction.
- In key areas of the operation, they can show sustained and strong improvement trends. Other areas also show improvement, though the trends may be weaker.
- Quality results from key suppliers also show improved and sustained trends.

CUSTOMER FOCUS AND SATISFACTION
- The customer is frequently surveyed to assess customer needs and satisfaction. Sometimes, this is also done through focus groups.
- There is a trend to providing customers easy access to services and quick response to their needs.
- There are clear standards for customer service, such as time to answer the telephone and time to respond to complaints. These measures are tracked.
- Customer service representatives are given extensive motivational training in addition to product training.
- There is a formal approach to resolving complaints. Management is also made aware of the types of complaints. When this is done through providing warranties, these should be stronger than those of competitors and easy to administer.
- Customer service representatives are empowered to satisfy the customer. The extent of empowerment is increasing.
- Customer satisfaction levels are higher than those for similar U.S. companies. Customer satisfaction trends are improving and sustained. Market share trends are also favorable.

The Third Landmark: Maturity

LEADERSHIP
- Senior managers are aware of the direct quality measures on a periodic basis.
- They apply TQM-based data-driven approaches to their own processes and do not rely solely on financial measure and experience.

- They understand the role of all levels of the organization in the promotion and execution of TQM.
- The focus is more on the process used to achieve the results. This implies that they have a thorough understanding of the key processes.
- They would use basic TQM analysis techniques to identify the reasons for key types of customer complaints and be aware of the trends.
- Senior management has a stronger understanding of the customer's perception of the service.

INFORMATION AND ANALYSIS

- The data available for continual improvement include operational measures. They not only are financially oriented, but also display additional measures such as those described in the balanced scorecard in Chapter 14.
- The competitive comparisons in the database extend beyond the immediate competition. Benchmarking is extended to looking at companies in other industries.
- Benchmarking extends beyond merely looking at products and processes and also is used as a way of restructuring the organization and developing new strategies.
- The systems are flexible enough to support change. When process improvements are made or processes are changed to accommodate customer expectations, the information systems are considered to be supportive of the change.

STRATEGIC QUALITY PLANNING

- The quality planning process should be well developed, with plans based on analysis of meaningful data from customers, operations, employees, and the business environment.
- The plans document the steps required for successful implementation, and the measures to ensure the implementation process are properly executed.
- The link between the overall plans of the company and the individual's goals is clearly set.
- All employees in the organization know the priority to be placed on the various goals they have to achieve.

HUMAN RESOURCE DEVELOPMENT AND MANAGEMENT

- Most teams are using the basic problem-solving tools outlined in Chapter 6. They are not relying solely on informal brainstorming.
- The effectiveness of the training is measured especially with respect to the degree of integration to the employee's work.
- The relationship between the employee recognition and the quality goals of the company is clear. Rewards are given for creating and executing good processes, and not simply for results that may often be outside the employee's span of control
- Training in company practices and policies is also given to employees who are in functions that support the production process.

- Empowerment is coupled with enablement so that employees who are given certain authority feel comfortable in applying it.

MANAGEMENT OF PROCESS QUALITY
- The new product development process is well defined and tries to anticipate customer demands. There is an emphasis on defining the Voice of the Customer and identifying latent customer needs as described in Chapter 10. Service companies also have such a process.
- Processes outside the production area are also well defined. Flowcharts describing processes should exist in areas such as human resource, marketing, and finance.
- In addition to measuring the results of processes, the inputs to the processes are also monitored.
- An effort is made to control processes on more direct measures, as opposed to relying heavily on customer feedback data.
- The quality improvement teams extend to include cross-functional teams and teams including managerial and technical staff.
- Quality improvement efforts are frequently written up in a standard format following the problem-solving methodology. These stories are then disseminated through the organization.
- There is a periodic audit of the quality systems. Frequently, these are initiated by senior management.

QUALITY AND OPERATIONAL RESULTS
- Management tracks measures such as process capabilities and does not rely solely on measures of defect rates and customer complaints.
- Data are collected to measure trends, and managers are aware of adverse trends. In addition, they have developed plans to change those trends.

CUSTOMER FOCUS AND SATISFACTION
- People conducting these surveys have a sound understanding of the technical aspects of surveys such as bias, variability, and accuracy.
- There is a clear link between the customer data that are collected and the input to the new product/service development process.
- Surveys only access the existing customers. No effort is made to obtain information from lost customers or from competitors' customers.
- Customer service standards are well defined. Training is intended for improving customer service in addition to simply being motivational.
- All complaints are tracked. A system is in place for collecting informal or minor complaints. Furthermore, these complaints are used to drive improvements in service and product offerings.
- The customers are stratified by attributes that are important to the customer. Instead of simply segmenting the market by account size or geographical location, an effort is made to define market segments by common customer characteristics using the methods described in Chapter 8.

◆   Summary

All the examples of TQM failures at the beginning of the chapter could have been predicted to fail based on the understanding of TQM you have obtained by reading this book. The "failures" at the Wallace Company and Florida Power & Light were more difficult to predict. In both cases, incorrectly conceived strategies led the company astray. In the case of Florida Power & Light, the advantages to be obtained from using TQM practices were so compelling that the organization continued to use them.

Since recognizing progress is difficult for even the most practiced eye, the last section of the chapter provides specific signs that indicate progress on the TQM road. The signs have been categorized using the Baldrige framework described in Chapter 3. The initiation and intensification of the TQM process at Xerox were described in detail. To many, Xerox is considered one of the prime examples of TQM success. As a final exercise, you should assess the progress Xerox has made along the TQM road.

In conclusion, it should be clear that TQM has a lot to offer as a set of management tools and practices. Success stories in this chapter and those described throughout the book illustrate time and again the benefits that can be gained. By subscribing to the TQM philosophy, you would expect these tools and practices to evolve over time. This has happened. Chapter 2 reviewed the evolution of TQM in Japan. As more U.S. companies have adopted the continuous improvement philosophy articulated by Tom Peters as, "If it ain't broke, FIX IT," new practices continue to be developed. Considerable work is being done on developing better, more effective ways to manage change. Partially in response to failures such as Wallace, the Center for Quality Management and the Massachusetts Institute of Technology are developing new approaches to creating strategy. Hammer and Champy spearheaded reengineering, and Analog Devices pioneered the Balanced Scorecard (both discussed in Chapter 14). Today it is a necessity to adapt the basic techniques described in this book to your organization.

◆   Assignments

1. If you were to visit the Xerox Corporation and wished to assess its progress on the TQM journey, what questions would you ask? Use the points listed under "Landmarks on the TQM Road" to arrive at three questions at least for each of the Baldrige Criteria.

2. Read a recently published book describing the successful turnaround of a corporation. An example is the book describing the Xerox story by Kearns and Nadler, 1992.
   a. Summarize the practices employed by the company using the Baldrige framework.
   b. Assess the progress the company has made along the TQM road.
   c. What questions would you ask this company if you visited it?

◆ Bibliography

Benson, T. E. "Quality: If at First You Don't Succeed." *Industry Week,* July 1993.

Brennan, N. "Lessons Taught by Baldrige Winner's" The Conference Board, Report Number 1061-94-CH, 1994.

Brown, M. G. "The Baldrige Award: How Do You Win?" *Automation,* October 1991.

Cutcher-Gershenfeld, J. "Tracing a Transformation in Industrial Relations." Report to the U.S. Department of Labor, 1988.

Easton, G. S. "The 1993 State of US Total Quality Management: A Baldrige Examiner's Perspective." *California Management Review* (Spring 1993).

Gaucher, E. J. and R. J. Coffey. *Total Quality in Health Care.* Jossey-Bass, 1993.

Garvin, D. A. "How the Baldrige Award Really Works." *Harvard Business Review,* (November–December 1991).

Harari, O. "Ten Reasons Why TQM Doesn't Work." *Management Review,* (January 1993).

Hill, R.C. "When the Going Gets Rough: A Baldrige Award Winner on the Line." *Academy of Management Executive,* 1993.

Johnson, A. B, and L. A. MacIsaac. "Xerox Corporation: Leadership Through Quality (A)." Harvard Business School Case, #490-008, 1989.

Kearns, D. T., and D. A. Nadler. *Prophets in the Dark: How Xerox ReInvented Itself and Beat Back the Japanese,* New York: Harper Collins, 1992.

Sheridan, J. H. "A CEOs Perspective on Innovation." *Industry Week,* December 19, 1994.

Smart, T. "Can Xerox Duplicate Its Glory Days?" *Business Week,* October 4, 1993.

Smith, J., and M. Oliver, "The Baldrige Boondoggle." *Machine Design,* August 6, 1992.

Author Index

◆ ◆ ◆

Subject Index

◆ ◆ ◆